Finding the Truth
with Criminal Investigation

Finding the Truth with Criminal Investigation

Suspect, Subject, Defendant

Daniel A. Reilly

ROWMAN & LITTLEFIELD
Lanham • Boulder • New York • London

Published by Rowman & Littlefield
A wholly owned subsidary of The Rowman & Littlefield Publishing Group, Inc.
4501 Forbes Boulevard, Suite 200, Lanham, Maryland 20706
www.rowman.com

6 Tinworth Street, London SE11 5AL, United Kingdom

British Library Cataloguing in Publication Information Available

Library of Congress Cataloging-in-Publication Data

Names: Reilly, Daniel A., author.
Title: Finding the truth with criminal investigation : suspect, subject,
    defendant / Daniel A. Reilly.
Description: Lanham, MD : Rowman & Littlefield, [2019] | Includes
    bibliographical references and index.
Identifiers: LCCN 2018060842 (print) | LCCN 2019000912 (ebook) | ISBN
    9781538113868 (Electronic) | ISBN 9781538113844 (cloth : alk. paper) |
    ISBN 9781538113851 (pbk. : alk. paper)
Subjects: LCSH: Criminal investigation. | Forensic sciences.
Classification: LCC HV8073 (ebook) | LCC HV8073 .R4975 2019 (print) | DDC
    363.25—dc23
LC record available at https://lccn.loc.gov/2018060842

♾™ The paper used in this publication meets the minimum requirements of
American National Standard for Information Sciences—Permanence of Paper
for Printed Library Materials, ANSI/NISO Z39.48-1992.

Contents

Acknowledgments   vii

Preface   xi

1   Criminal Investigation Defined   1

2   Criminal Code   23

3   Constitutional Rights   61

4   Teamwork   97

5   Prioritizing Investigations   121

6   Victims and Witnesses   139

7   Crime Scene Analysis   159

8   Investigative Plan   183

9   Goals and Steps for an Investigation   209

10   Physical Evidence   231

11   Administrative Procedures   257

12   Bringing the Case to Court   271

13   Interviews and Interrogations   291

14   Confidential Informants   307

15   Investigative Intelligence   325

16   Tactical Considerations   333

17   Covert Investigations   345

Contents

Epilogue	375
Glossary	377
References	385
Index	391

Acknowledgments

This is my second book. In both projects, I was given extraordinary support from my family. My wife, Kay; son, Dan; and daughter-in-law, Becky, have supported me without pause or concern. They have been my rock and have given me the strength and confidence to say the things I have said and to have the temerity to believe it is worth reading. So I also have to thank any of you who are reading this book and finding it worthwhile. My two grandsons, Gunner and Tucker, have helped by just inspiring me to leave them a legacy of who I am.

My brother, Mike; and my sisters, Pat, Clo, Mary Ellen, Toni, Julie, and Mary, have always encouraged me to share my ability to write, which I got from my father and mother, with the rest of the world. My wife's family has been equally supportive, especially my sister-in-law Susie Coleman, who edited my first book, and my sister-in-law Nancy Oppermann, who read drafts of my work and provided encouragement.

For this project, I have to say a special thanks to my sister-in-law Beverly Oppermann, who read every word I wrote and did her best to make it right, so I call her my copy "righter" for all of her extraordinary work. My wife's brother, Hank, who is married to Bev, had to put up with all the extra work I gave Bev, so I want to acknowledge his wholehearted support. So, in effect, this book is a "family affair." I even had my nieces, Angelique Dudoussatt and Mary C. Dantzler, read the chapters and give me a younger audience's point of view.

I worked for a number of years with a group of some of the world's finest criminal investigators, cops, detectives, marshals, special agents, inspectors, and on and on. I learned everything I know from these men and women. The single most important accolade one criminal investigator can give to another happens when the criminal investigator himself has been victimized and wants a particular criminal investigator coming up his driveway to help get to the bottom of the case. I knew at least fifty men and women whom I thought of in that way. SA Mike Hartman, SSA Al Witzgall, Dep. US Marshal Karen Fechter, Det. Angelo Parisi, Det. Norma Horne, SAC Vince Lisi, Det. Steve Kirshner, and ASAC Phil Rendin are just a few of the skilled dedicated and determined professionals who impressed me, taught me, and made me happy that I had them at my back.

When I started this project, I asked some of my closest colleagues and friends to help. I was intent on providing the students with a road map on how to conduct investigations. I wanted the road map to be real and comprehensible. I tried to keep the rigors of academic research out of this book. I simply wanted to let the readers know what I believed *worked*. After all, I and my colleagues were very successful "making" cases. A lot of crooks are still in jail, and they are where they belong. Ultimately, that is one part of the equation: putting away the bad guys. One other part is more human and rewarding. Sometimes we made the case with persons who were "less guilty," caught up in a pattern of criminal conduct that they couldn't escape. Sgt. Don Lyddane, Det. Angelo Parisi, Det. Steve Kirshner, I, and others identified these potential cooperating witnesses and helped turn their lives around. In one case in 1991, we investigated and supported the prosecution of twenty-four bad guys, known as the R Street Crew, in Washington, DC. More than sixty other persons were involved in various ways in their crimes, and all of those sixty had to testify in the two main trials. We were able to protect them before, during, and after their testimony even though the Crew was intent on killing any insider witnesses. At the successful conclusion of that case, where all twenty-four were convicted, one of the most positive statistics from my career is that all sixty of those "insider" witnesses left the criminal life, and as of my final days in the FBI in 2002, none had been arrested or charged with any other crimes. So part of what we do is try to fix a wrong, show the way out, and make decisions that support a better way. Ultimately, the other piece of the puzzle is to be there for the victims and families of victims who can't be a part of the process. As a criminal investigator, my concern was with Alveta Hopkins, Evelyn Carter, Yolanda Burley, Jamal Ali, Paula Adams Taylor, and so many others who no longer have a voice because evil men decided that even though they were innocent, they somehow didn't deserve to live. I was concerned about victims who had been ripped off and victims who had suffered awful pain and torture. I was concerned about witnesses who were courageous enough to step up and testify, and I was concerned that they and their families survived the ordeal. The sensitivities of the criminals and their own sense of "victimhood" did not move me. I wanted them out of the lives of the community so the community could be free of their ilk.

Retired Sgt. Don Lyddane, retired SA John Bevington, and retired SSA Ray Smith were drafted by me to read what I wrote and offer suggestions and changes. They happily handled this task for me, which gave me the confidence in many of the methods I discuss in this project. Each of these colleagues knows me well and understands my approach in investigation. But they are extraordinary professionals in their own right, and their advice is more than support; it is expertise and creative insight. Without their help, I would not have been able to complete this work.

Part of my effort in this book was to make it relevant to future investigations. Clearly, my approach is more or less "old school." I took some steps to update and explain what kind of obstacles criminal investigators will face in the twenty-first century. One of the most important parts of that future work is computer technology. The internet's digital infrastructure expands the availability of information, which should be a gold mine for criminal investigators. The advances in smartphone graphics and data storage are problems that need to be solved. Maintaining security and protecting digital resources are essential problems facing the criminal investigator. In 1981, a colleague from the FBI Lab, retired SA Tom Murray, joined me at the FBI Washington Field Office. Tom introduced me to the world of computer technology. He taught me how it worked and how I could use it in my investigations. In the beginning, it was just word processing, but eventually it expanded to data mining, collection, and manipulation. With the passage of time, Tom became an office-wide resource in the area, and eventually, he was joined by an academically trained computer engineer, retired SSA Robert Osgood. Bob is a full-time faculty member and professor of computer forensics at George Mason University in Fairfax, Virginia. Bob knowingly and, in some cases, informally offered his advice to me in this book. I hope that what I learned from Bob and Tom over the years has ensured that the instruction is explained correctly in the relevant chapters.

I would also like to add a new colleague whom I met during my research for this book, Darryl G. Huff, a captain with the Mobile Alabama Police Department, who is also a retired FBI agent. Capt. Huff provided some insight and investigative strategies used by his department to conduct research and ensure security of digital data for his intelligence unit, which is representative of many midsized police departments.

Because throughout my career I spent time trying to stay up to date with the fast-moving advances in forensic science, I hope that the relevant information in this book is instructive and forward thinking. My colleagues from the lab who provided most of the information I write about were acknowledged in my first book, and again, I would like to mention their names. They are the scientists who helped me in my career and with my background in the area of forensic science: Joseph Dizinno, retired assistant director of the FBI and current professor at George Mason University; Jack Quill, Hal Deadman, Barry L. Mones, and James Cadigan Jr., retired supervisory special agents; and Messrs. Carlo Rosatti, Terry Green, and Jackie Bell, forensic experts retired from the FBI.

This book is a compilation of my life's professional work. Every aspect is drawn from personal experience and has a basis in an actual case, event, or circumstance in my career. I have included from time to time special personal experiences that I hope will highlight an important concern in the context of the subject matter being discussed. In my career as a college instructor, I attempted to keep my war stories out of the classroom, but my students don't seem to want that. They appreciate it when I make a point with a relevant story from my career. I hope you, the reader, will feel that way too.

Preface

Students in the criminal justice field who wish to become criminal investigators should be exposed to the tools and processes needed to conduct investigations, but they also need to consider the real-life consequences of working to support other people at their worst, most vulnerable time. Anger, frustration, hatred, defiance, and revenge darken the hearts of otherwise kind and caring people. The impact of taking a person's loved one away or sexually denigrating another person is so disturbing that it causes these reactions and so many more. Those of us who have been "ripped off" or assaulted are not willing to give up on a search for justice, and if just one person will join us in the fight to recover, we are grateful. If one person comes to our aid and says, "I know what you are going through and I am here to help," we are grateful. The truth is we won't ever be "satisfied" even if we can take the criminal and roast her on a barbecue spit, but if another human being sees our pain and takes a little of that on, we can see the light at the end of the tunnel and be happy we live in a society that has such people ready and able to do the job. It may be that they act distant and "professional" or they may be warm and friendly, but their concern and effort will be directed toward getting the person who wronged us and making that person pay for the transgression. That is all we can ask from a friend in our time of need.

I spent more than forty years in federal law enforcement. I ended up specializing in task force investigations. That meant I was responsible for investigating local crimes until I could combine them together in some manner that fit the mold required for a federal prosecution. Many of my investigations began as street crimes, burglaries, armed robberies, rapes, and murders, and my hope was to take those cases and somehow incorporate them together into major federal cases. It didn't always work, and sometimes I found myself in local court with my local police colleagues demanding justice for the victims. The work was long and hard, but it was also rewarding and entertaining.

Being a criminal investigator was "my thing." I was thanked and patted on the back by families of murder victims. I was thanked for caring and thanked for "giving a crap." Most of all, I would see not only people's continuing pain, but also a satisfactory glance that acknowledged I had done what I could to turn the ripped and shredded page on the victim's life. The work I did was not about those acknowledgments.

It was about serving the community. Students I now teach are trying to decide what they will do with their lives, and I am simply offering a career choice where the employers are the taxpayers and the job is making sure the taxpayers are provided with the work they need done. As an FBI agent, I was paid well enough, but the dedicated police officers and detectives I worked with were paid "not so much." We all had something in common: get the bad guy. Make the bad guy pay, and stop him before he hurt somebody else.

The laws we sought to uphold were very straightforward: consider the law, apply the law, prove the violation, and take the bad guy into custody; but it was never that simple. The other parts of the system had to weigh in. Some laws had to be less stringently adhered to. Some laws required immediate attention. Some laws provided too many gaps that couldn't be filled. It was often left up to us to show we could work the facts (the square pegs) into the right interpretation (the round holes). The case becomes a puzzle that needs to be solved. Make sure you follow the rules of the game. Don't do bad to make the good happen. Oh, Mr. Investigator, you are on your own until you have to endlessly explain yourself to a judge, a jury, a defense attorney, and a prosecutor. It is a hard job with a price to pay intellectually and emotionally. It is also extraordinarily satisfying when you make the case, prove the bad guy is guilty, and *find the truth*.

Chapter One

Criminal Investigation Defined

Defining what a criminal investigation means; discussing reactive and proactive crime investigations, the two major categories of criminal investigations.

This book is intended to be a guide for students in the criminal justice field. It is intended to provide the step-by-step process for gathering facts, information, data, and evidence, which, collectively, answer all the questions raised when a violent crime occurs. It also gives the student a set of tools and a process to follow in answering the questions who, what, where, when, why, and how that crime was committed.

Before we begin to discuss what criminal investigation means, it is appropriate to provide a little historical perspective so we can understand the primary motivation laid out in the title of this book: "finding the truth." Criminal investigations, as they are conducted in twenty-first century, are less than 100 years old. Modern criminal investigation began as men and women tasked with maintaining and supporting the rule of law in our society began the practice of analyzing criminal conduct with the goal in mind of finding out what happened, why it happened, and who did it. Prior to the American Revolution, the thirteen colonies and the counties established therein followed the rules they learned and carried with them from England and elsewhere. The social contract of doing good and avoiding evil, following the Golden Rule, and abiding by the Judeo-Christian moral code provided the structure for the early sheriffs and magistrates in Colonial America to protect the citizens and punish the criminals who broke the code. This was all done in the name of the King of England and with the power and authority of the Crown. What the early colonists came to believe was that the king was not present, and the decisions to honor and support the social contract, or the rule of law, derived from the community that the early criminal justice system served. The authority of the king was primarily manifest in the British army. Local communities in Colonial America were tasked with ensuring the general welfare and lawful interactions among the populace.

After the Revolution, the focal point of power and authority shifted from the king to the people. This was stated in the preamble to the US Constitution, which was a summary of the beliefs and philosophy of the colonists, who wanted to be self-governing.

In the preamble, the framers said "We the People of the United States, in order to form a more perfect union, establish justice and insure domestic tranquility," thereby stating that the people were now the ultimate authority and justice and domestic tranquility were high on the list of goals to be achieved by the government. The preamble goes on to prioritize the goals of providing a common defense, the general welfare, and blessings of liberty, but establishing justice and ensuring domestic tranquility get to the heart of what the framers believed was an essential justification for any government. The revolutionary idea that the power and authority of the people was now a fact and would not be challenged carries on today, as shown by most criminal cases in courts across the United States bearing case titles such as *The People of the United States versus the Defendant or The People of the State of Maryland (The commonwealth of Virginia) versus the Defendant.*

Source: iStock 645154792

Just as the US Constitution established the executive, judicial, and legislative branches, each US state or commonwealth followed suit. The legislative branch, which contains duly elected representatives of the people, is tasked with passing laws and establishing or defining conduct that is criminal. The executive branch in the federal system and in most local jurisdictions is tasked with executing or implementing those laws. The judicial branch is then tasked with ensuring that the laws are fair and the administration of executive authority is proper and just in its execution. Criminal procedure, or due process of law, acts as the framework for the execution of the laws passed by the legislative branch.

So, for the most part, law enforcement officers, such as sheriffs, police officers, agents, marshals, constables, district attorneys, and prosecutors, are the men and women who are responsible for conducting investigations of criminal activity and crimes against the people. Since law enforcement is serving the people and has to answer for its actions to the community, it is essential that law enforcement follow the path in all investigations to a finding of the truth. In some cases, the criminal justice

Source:iStock 157593232

system will short-circuit this search for the truth in favor of fair and proper procedure. The rules of evidence state that the rights of a defendant must not be violated and are an impenetrable wall at which investigative findings may have to be limited. It is still the responsibility of the law enforcement authorities to complete the task of getting at the truth and working in the system so violations of proper procedure and due process do not occur. Sometimes this issue will lead to frustration and even distrust of the system. Law enforcement officers need to overcome these negative elements and focus on the task at hand. Investigations in which law enforcement professionals believe they have answered all the questions and found the truth but still end up with unsatisfactory outcomes should not deter them. Results are important, but protecting the system of justice is vital to the rule of law. There are elements of the criminal justice system, such as decisions made by judges, juries, or even fellow officers, which will lead to unsatisfactory results. These decisions are part of the fabric and texture of a system that is making the effort to implement the will of the people. Sometimes, the will of the people is not necessarily in line with what a law enforcement official believes is right, but it may be just or fair. The people have determined that the power of the state is enormous and that it sometimes needs to be carefully and thoughtfully curtailed. These limitations or binders to criminal investigators are meant to level the playing field and create an environment where the people accused can believe they are receiving just due process and a fair shake. The most prominent example of a limitation and perhaps its most important facet is the fact that the accused has a right to a trial and that during that trial, the state or the government has to prove the case beyond a reasonable doubt. This is a high standard, and it ensures that the criminal investigator has to reach the goal of finding the truth. The truth uncovered needs to be so compelling that judges and jurors are convinced that the defendant is in fact guilty.

To begin our discussion about the process of criminal investigation, it is necessary to provide a realistic definition. Criminal investigation is a multifaceted effort that involves the study of facts presented by a criminal act or pattern of criminal conduct. These facts are then used to identify, locate, and prove the guilt or innocence of a person or persons. Criminal investigation is usually carried out by a law enforcement agency using all the resources available to the government, local, state, or federal, to discover, locate, or establish evidence proving and verifying the relevant facts for presentation to a court or other judicial authority.

The facts discovered can become evidence and may involve statements from witnesses; documentary or photographic evidence; physical evidence, which are fruits of a crime; instrumentalities of a crime; incidental evidence; and logs, data, and details of analysis that show access to crime scenes. It is characteristic of any criminal investigation that aspects of the crime may manifest in a variety of ways. Therefore, many criminal investigations rely heavily on a logical, organized process, but there are also aspects of crimes that derive from chaos and sheer luck of happenstance. This serendipitous development requires that criminal investigators be both flexible and purposeful in their approach.

Crimes occur in a human context, meaning there is usually a perpetrator and a victim. Sometimes there are a number of perpetrators, and sometimes there are a number of victims. In fact, a crime has not occurred unless and until human actions, as defined by law, are criminal. In other words, a crime has to be defined by legal authority as having certain elements, and those elements have to represent human actions that take something from someone, injure someone, create an atmosphere of danger, or actually cause significant harm to a person or persons and the society in general. In this country, most crime definitions are rooted in our history and tradition of common law. Much of the legal basis for common law derives from ancient legal precepts from the Judeo-Christian tradition, such as the Decalogue (Ten Commandments). Almost all crimes defined in the United States have their origin in English common law. Every state and the federal legislature have more precisely defined criminal conduct in criminal codes or written statutes that take the definitions provided in common law and either expand or narrow the proof required. This is done to make the crimes more applicable to the advances of our society. Common law crimes that required significant and harsh penalties have been modified to include lesser crimes that don't demand penalties that are too harsh for the conduct that is proven. Varying degrees of crimes have been codified to make it more realistic to prove an offense based on actions, without having to prove the full nature and extent of the criminal intent. Burglary, for instance, has been codified in all state codes, which have varied certain elements that fit into more present-day versions of actions that in the past were consistent with the capital crime (a crime demanding a punishment of death) of common law burglary. So the breaking and entering of a commercial establishment with the intent to commit a felony is a kind of burglary, but it doesn't have the element "of the dwelling house of another." In ancient times, if any element of a crime defined in common law was not proved or did not happen, there was no crime. So, in the case of burglary, if the location was not the dwelling house of another, there was no crime; even though there might have been the breaking and entering of a commercial shop with intent to steal goods, there was no crime of burglary. The common law crime of larceny may have occurred, but the actual fact that the crime event was not the breaking and entering of a dwelling house of another meant there was no burglary. Legislatures in England and the United States determined to fix these kinds of loopholes by codifying or more precisely defining a variety of similar crimes. The legislatures developed a variety of headings so more criminal activity could be precisely defined and penalties for these acts could be detailed for the courts and magistrates. Statutory definitions of crimes expanded to make the job of government prosecutors more precise and allowed justices to carefully consider all the actions of the defendant.

This "redefining" of crimes became a break from the common law, which permitted states and other appropriate jurisdictions to allow the punishment to fit the crime. In the eighteenth and nineteenth centuries, criminal justice reforms led to the use of penitentiaries, jails, and other detention facilities to punish criminal conduct. Under the old common law requirements, many of the serious offenses required a penalty of death, beatings, and even torture. Judeo-Christian values and humanism allowed for the reevaluation of criminal conduct in the context of the belief that all people had some good in their heart and as a society we needed to seek a way to rehabilitate and restore criminals to law-abiding members of society. The first step in the reform process was determined to be time confinement for the criminals to contemplate their conduct and ask for forgiveness from God and society. So prisons were meant to be the places where criminals would evaluate their conduct, fix the moral compass they had inside, and spend the time needed to eventually return to society after a sufficient time of punishment. These lofty goals were met with little success, so recidivism became a serious problem for most government-sponsored incarceration. As criminal justice reform continued in the twentieth and twenty-first centuries, new efforts were made in rehabilitation but with only limited success. Convicted criminals should be taught or trained to make better decisions, but again the early efforts at rehabilitation were not successful. The majority of our society continue to demand punishment, which is a major part of the solution, but rehabilitation and reform also continue to offer some hope to get criminals to turn their lives around. Students of criminology and criminal justice may wish to further study the evolution of rehabilitation and reform, but for purposes of this book, recidivism, or career criminal conduct, should be part of the investigators' analysis when a suspect is developed. Criminals' past conduct may indicate current or future behavior. So this book will consider only the effects of incarceration and recidivists' behavior and not the efficacy of prison reform. Further discussion of how an investigator should consider previously incarcerated suspects will be explored in chapter 8 of this book, "Investigative Plan."

American society has advanced from being too severe in its level of punishment (stealing a horse in nineteenth-century America was an offense for which the perpetrator could face hanging) to the point where our punishment fits the crime. Concerning ourselves too much with the mens rea, or evil intent of a criminal, allows us to codify offenses with more precision, proving actions instead of delving into the minds of criminals to verify their motives for the conduct. In considering how students of criminal investigations should proceed, it is essential for future law enforcement professionals to understand and master the elements of each crime they are tasked with investigating. Once students become investigators, they must carefully analyze the criminal statutes they are required to apply to their jurisdiction and the community in which they work. Each statute needs to be broken down into the elements that are required to be proved in each case. In chapter 8 of this book, I will provide a spreadsheet that provides examples of how this can be accomplished. Suffice it to say that, at this point, every crime has more than one basic element. The law, statute, or code is passed by the appropriate legislature and specifically lays out the human conduct that makes human actions a crime. That is why every investigation is an analysis of human conduct and is required to be considered in a human context. The federal or state government or the local community may also assert victimization, so investigators have to concern themselves with the effects on the community at large when conducting an investigation. Given this human context, a crime, such as assault, rape, or even robbery, may have a victim who refuses for some reason to consider himself a victim or to openly admit he was victimized, but since the state or community as whole has an interest in controlling or responding to acts of violence, the alternate victim is that same community. A violent predator who would harm one person is potentially willing to harm any other member of the community. Personal victimization may be difficult to prove in court without a cooperating victim or witness, but that does not lessen the responsibility of the law enforcement officer to investigate and solve the case. Again, the criminal investigator should be seeking the truth in spite of the reluctance on the part of a victim in a serious crime. The investigations in this book will be concerned with violence and disturbing human behavior. Law enforcement professionals have to be ready to confront real life examples of brutality as is depicted in this image to be able to find the truth behind the despicable behavior.

Source: iStock 507032227

There are, of course, less serious crimes for which the community displays indifference or even tolerance, like the perpetrators and the victims in a barroom brawl or an angry confrontation at a sporting event, but the nature of the injuries and the catalyst that initiated the melee may be the best indicators as to the need for a serious criminal investigation. Most states lessen criminal responsibility if there is an indication that the victim is in some way responsible for what happened. On the other hand, any serious injury to an innocent victim should initiate an intense investigation even if the victim refuses to cooperate.

Case is a designation that is universally accepted for the matter under investigation. A detective, investigator, or agent needs to establish an administrative record of the progress of an investigation, which is the case file. Private investigators, private citizens, defense attorneys, and all other nonsworn investigators create a similar investigative file or administrative depository for the investigation. This administrative designation is very simply a convenient way to distinguish each investigation undertaken by the investigative entity. It is also the best way to compile all the reports, data, interviews, and minutiae that are discovered along the way. In chapter 11 of this book, I will discuss the compilation of a case file and how best to create it.

TYPES OF MUNICIPAL AND COUNTY CRIMINAL INVESTIGATORS

Now that we have discussed the definition of criminal investigations and how the origins of our criminal justice system affect the process, it is necessary to identify those persons in our society who are tasked with handling the investigations. Obviously, the first and most important group of persons who investigate crimes are police officers, deputy sheriffs, and detectives working for local communities. At this time, these men and women start out as job applicants for local agencies and are then hired by the communities in which they serve to be the first level of response to any criminal conduct. Generally, they are expected to serve and protect the community in which they work. A local police agency, whether it is an urban police department or a county sheriff's office, typically has two prongs: a patrol function and an investigative function.

Uniform Patrol

In most departments, uniformed officers handle the patrol responsibilities. Nonuniformed officers and detectives handle the investigative responsibilities. Just because uniformed officers have primarily been tasked with patrol responsibility does not mean that they are not expected to conduct a large number of preliminary investigations. In some cases, very fast-moving, serious investigations that happen in the presence of the officers who respond to a call for service and actually personally observe the criminal conduct in whole or in part constitute the bulk of a criminal investigation. Patrol officers are in most cases the first responders to serious crimes, which may require serious, long-term investigations by their cohorts in the investigative branch of their departments. Because of these realities, the patrol officers very often become astute students of human behavior, advocates for victims and witnesses, and serious experts in the analysis of crime scenes. Young, newly minted police officers will usually find themselves on patrol duty in the beginning of their careers; this work is an excellent postgraduate study program for career detectives. Future patrol officers should consider all the aspects relating to criminal investigations in this book and be prepared to follow the investigative process as it develops until the case is taken over by the appropriate investigative unit. It is likely that the first steps made at a crime scene and the treatment of victims and witnesses by these professional officers will have long-term ramifications on the successful progress of any criminal investigation. Responding immediately to fast-moving leads, such as identifying suspects, suspects' vehicles, and additional witnesses who may not be immediately available, and gathering the intelligence information the uniformed patrol officers may have about the neighborhood, which may be part of their regular patrol service area, are vital to the successful progress of any investigation.

A substantial number of patrol officers have little or no interest in becoming full-time detectives. Their career paths usually involve crime prevention and the normal patrol efforts to keep the community safe by guarding the community against unsafe drivers and dangerous neighborhood environments and developing and maintaining safe zones for the weakest and most vulnerable in our society. They also wish to act as first responders to help injured persons, sick children, and the elderly. All of these acts of community service should receive the same or, in some cases, higher priority by the police administration. Patrol officers in many jurisdictions are able to see a clear path for promotion because most police departments consider patrol work their primary responsibility. Crime prevention is the hallmark of any successful department, so the patrol officers have a direct path to police administration. Investigators, in many cases, are required to develop the facts presented in a criminal case that is intensive and focused. Their cases are time-consuming and often don't have results that are acknowledged by the community as a whole. Their work can become an even higher priority than crime prevention when the result of investigation may allow for the removal of a serious criminal element that is taking advantage of the fact that all crime cannot be thwarted by uniformed patrol. Sophisticated criminals who take the time to hide their activities from normal police scrutiny or violent criminals who cause harm to their victims and take the extra time to create fear and intimidation in the community can be dealt with only by effective criminal investigation. This is the reason that almost every police department and most sheriffs' offices divide their departments into patrol divisions and investigative divisions. So the central figure in criminal investigations in the United States in the twenty-first century is the police detective.

Detectives

It is not likely that brand-new police officers who were trained to handle uniformed patrol duties will be suddenly turned into detectives. Detectives in large urban police departments and small-town departments are usually experienced officers who have been successful in their ability to work on patrol duty. They usually have passed competitive tests to be considered for the elevation to detective and are often required to pass an interview panel, which tests and evaluates their fitness for the work. For most departments, becoming a detective is a promotion and may carry with it a rank higher than the officers who work routine patrol. In some large departments, there is an investigator rank and a patrol rank. Criminal investigators who have not acquired the rank of detective are an interim investigative level between patrol and detectives. Detectives sometimes carry the rank or equivalent rank of sergeant in the quasi-military structure of a police department. They also may carry the equivalent rank of corporal. Most of the varieties of rank are generally irrelevant. Detectives receive their assignments from their branch or unit commanders, and they are expected to consider the case, examine the crime scene, develop an investigative strategy, follow all the leads, and determine who is responsible for the crime.

The assignments may be distributed using some kind of rotational logic, or they may be provided based on the perceived expertise, experience, or level of training demonstrated by the detective. In large, well-funded departments, detectives will be divided up into general-assignment branches, robbery branches, sex crime branches, white collar branches, and homicide branches. Occasionally, these branches are combined, such as in a robbery–homicide branch or a major crimes branch. In some very large urban police departments, each district police division will have detectives assigned who will work a general rotation of assignments that occur inside the geographic parameters of the police district. In large cities, such as New York, Chicago, and Los Angeles, there will be headquarters investigative branches and district detective branches. The distribution of assignments can vary in these departments based on the needs of the investigative effort required. A headquarters investigative branch will usually have more time and resources to bear on a difficult and wide-ranging investigation; therefore, it may be necessary to assign a high-profile or difficult case to that higher-level investigative unit. The expertise, effectiveness, and resourcefulness of the detectives at all levels is not a given based on their assignment as a district detective or a headquarters detective; it may also not even be a given between a general-assignment detective and a priority crime investigative branch. Detectives in each of these units or branches can have all the tools, investigative passion, and experience that provide the community with an equal level of proficiency and ultimate success in seeking the truth. Being assigned to a sought-after position as a detective in a big city headquarters homicide unit does preclude the fact that a detective in a district-level or general-assignment unit is just as capable as an investigator. Experienced veteran detectives whose case work is shown to be successful and productive are competent professionals and should be sought after as mentors for young law enforcement professionals who wish to advance in their careers to become high-caliber detectives. These same effective detectives need to be willing to share their knowledge and experience with the constant flow of new detectives who advance to the position.

If there is a general profile of police detectives nationwide, it is usually a police officer with five to eight years of patrol experience who has shown an ability to conduct investigations to his chain of command and has taken written and oral examinations that have demonstrated an ability to be promoted to detective. A college degree is generally not required, but as the modern era of law enforcement continues to evolve, a college degree is more likely to be a requirement. It is necessary for a detective to understand the statutory requirements of criminal law and to be well versed in an understanding of the constitutional rights of the accused. It is further necessary that a detective have a working knowledge of forensic sciences, especially fingerprinting (crime scene recovery of latent fingerprints and identification techniques), ballistics (firearms and tool mark identification), serology (bodily fluids, including advances in DNA science), trace evidence (hairs, fibers, and materials analysis), and pattern evidence recovery and examination (shoe prints, tire treads, and other physical materials that can lead to class characteristics identification). Another equally important area of competence for a detective is an ability to communicate in conversation and testimony and with the written word. Finally, a detective needs to be curious and have a finely tuned memory. When working detectives reach a point in their investigations when the case appears to be at a dead end, it takes a burning curiosity to find the truth to push the case beyond these points of frustration. Detectives also have to constantly evaluate the information, evidence, and fact patterns they have and recall how all the information fits together. Small details at the beginning of an investigation may become essential facts corroborating proof elements in a crime. Most cases will have serious lag time between the time the crime happened and when the case is set for trial. A competent detective needs to be able to recall the facts and information uncovered during the investigation and the ability to present that information to a jury one to two years after the information was obtained. In the modern era, detectives should also have significant education or academic study in psychology and sociology. Understanding criminal behavior, and especially aberrant patterns of behavior, along with a view of group dynamics and how these human patterns of behavior affect social interaction, can provide the detective with the insight necessary to properly understand motive-triggering mechanisms that may help solve a case.

For the purpose of this book, there are other important assets detectives need to have as part of their profile, but because they are not always relevant to investigative responsibilities, I will mention them only as needed qualities, even though they may have very little to do with the effectiveness of a criminal investigation. Tactical expertise is a necessary asset for a police detective. This quality includes proficiency with firearms and hand-to-hand combat training and the ability to formulate safe and effective plans to execute arrests and search and seizure raids. An appropriate level of courage and tenacity when it comes to confronting and removing violent offenders from the community in the furtherance of completing or wrapping up a successful criminal investigation is also a necessary aspect in the detective's profile. It is the responsibility of a criminal investigator to ensure the safety of witnesses and surviving victims and their families who may be at risk from a violent predatory criminal offender. In the real world of law enforcement, it is often necessary to protect the community by placing professional law enforcement investigators in harm's way, to confront a criminal underworld that uses violence as a tool of survival. Intelligence and sophistication by criminals make up only one aspect of their effort to avoid being caught and to continue their criminal conduct. When those nonviolent strategies don't work or are considered ineffective, criminals, especially killers, rapists, robbers, and thieves, will use violence against witnesses and law enforcement officers whom they consider to be threats. Detectives and all criminal investigators need to be able to effectively protect themselves and the persons they are sworn to defend.

STATE POLICE DETECTIVES

At this point, we have spent a great deal of time discussing police detectives, also known as officers, inspectors, and investigators; that discussion was necessary because there are literally thousands of local police investigators in this country whose profiles and personal characteristics are similar. Many of the assets mentioned above for detectives are universal in their application to other criminal investigators. State police investigators and federal special agents usually need the same background and training that local police detectives have. There are criminal investigators at a number of levels in government whose job it is to conduct internal investigations to detect crimes such as embezzlement, accounting fraud, or corrupt contracting practices. These specialized investigators are generally not involved in crimes against persons or violent criminal conduct; therefore, they won't be discussed in this book. The expertise of these investigators and, therefore, their required backgrounds usually involve computer forensics, auditing, and accounting education along with white collar crime experience and fraud detection. The next category of criminal investigators for consideration in this book are state criminal investigators.

Most of the state police agencies in the United States are primarily concerned with highway patrol. The enormous work of patrolling millions of miles of highways, including the federal interstate highway system, comes under the jurisdictional responsibility of the state police. The origin of many of these agencies developed as the American automobile became the main element of transportation during the early twentieth century. As state police agencies were established, state police criminal investigation bureaus were also determined to be necessary divisions in these agencies. Some states, such as California, Kansas, Indiana, and South Carolina, opted to establish separate criminal investigative agencies. Usually, these separate agencies were established to prioritize the investigative work of the state agencies. Additionally, most states used their state police agencies to create state-run forensic laboratories, which can conduct sophisticated criminal forensic science examinations for the state police and all of the local police and sheriff departments in the jurisdiction. There are some large urban jurisdictions in the United States that have their own forensic science laboratories, but for the most part, the state labs conduct most of the forensic work associated with local and state police criminal investigation bureaus. (The Federal Bureau of Investigation [FBI] laboratory in Quantico, Virginia, has always provided forensic science examinations to state and local jurisdictions at no cost, but with the nationwide proliferation of state forensic laboratories, the number of examinations needed by states has been reduced.)

The detectives who are state police officers are in many cases recruited or derived from state highway patrol officers, who have received extensive police training and experience as highway patrol officers. In most cases, the state police investigative bureaus mandate high school diplomas or equivalency; extensive background investigation; the passing of written examinations; and intense, competitive oral interviews. Applicants with college degrees are required by some states; any educational experience, including college courses, is usually evaluated for the purpose of determining competitiveness among the recruit pool. So state police detectives generally follow the same route as their colleagues in city, town, and county police agencies. They are, therefore, going to have the same kind of profile as the local police detectives mentioned above. Becoming a state police investigator is a sought-after position in most state police agencies, but it is not the only career path for state police officers. Staying in patrol and moving up the ranks as a uniformed supervisor of state police is just as highly prized for officers in those agencies.

FEDERAL AGENCY CRIMINAL INVESTIGATORS

There are a number of differences between federal investigators and state and local detectives, but in general, the day-to-day work is the same or similar. As far as qualifications for the career, most federal agencies require a bachelor's degree or higher from all their applicants. They all have to pass rigorous written and oral examinations and evaluations by managers and peer evaluators; rigorous physical examinations; and rigorous background investigations, which generally lead to high-level security clearances.

Sixteen or more federal agencies have special agent investigators who have arrest power and are sanctioned to carry weapons. These investigators are classified in federal parlance as 1811 series employees. Their responsibility to investigate criminal activity varies with the agency that employs them. They are usually very limited in their jurisdiction and often are responsible for investigations of fraud, corruption, and embezzlement inside the specific agency in which they are employed. The Department of Housing and Urban Development, the Department of Education, and the Department of Veterans Affairs are examples of agencies that have 1811 series investigators working in this capacity. It is likely that these agents are recruited from inside the particular agency because it is extremely helpful for these investigators to be familiar with the bureaucratic processes, rules, and regulations of the agency. It is rare that these investigators widen their inquiries to include outside civilians who are not directly tied to the agency in which they are employed. These investigators rarely concern themselves with any crimes that are not in the realm of such white collar crimes as contract fraud, embezzlement, and bribery. These investigators also rely heavily on the assistance of the FBI, the US Marshals Service, and local and state criminal investigators if their investigations widen to include persons outside of the agencies.

For purposes of this book, federal agents who find themselves involved in the kind of criminal activity that will be discussed herein are detailed below. Violent crime, larceny, car theft, burglary, and other serious crimes can become investigative priorities for the following federal agencies.

US Marshals Service

The oldest federal law enforcement agency is the US Marshals Service. Deputies and marshals are the investigators. Their primary responsibility is similar to that of a county sheriff. Marshals have federal court duties, which include serving civil process; executing arrest orders; and acting as court security, such as bailiffs in US district and magistrate courts throughout the country. Deputy marshals must have a college degree, be a US citizen, be twenty-one years of age or older, qualify for rigorous physical activity, meet criteria in a competitive oral interview, have a valid driver's license, and pass the training academy at Glencoe, Georgia, which is a multiagency federal law enforcement training facility. Most of marshals' investigative responsibility is to locate and arrest interstate fugitives from justice, who can be murderers, thieves, rapists, and robbers with local outstanding arrest warrants that the marshals can develop into interstate fugitive arrest warrants. This investigative responsibility is the evolution of marshals' criminal work dating back to the nineteenth century, when they were the only law enforcement agents of any kind in vast swaths of territory in the United States, especially in the wide-open Western territory. As a result of their work federal marshals became legendary peace officers who tried to ensure justice was delivered to a large number of hardened criminals. Marshals continue to work these fugitive cases, but they are very likely to be coordinated with the FBI and state and local police agencies to combine resources and expertise to capture and prosecute violent criminals. US marshals' investigations are thereby limited to search for criminals once their participation in the crime has been established. Marshals also carry out investigations of threats and violent attacks on the federal judiciary. They may also involve investigations of major organized crime groups and even terrorist groups who seek to undermine the administration of justice in this country. Finally, the marshals play a significant role in seeking the arrests of suspects investigated by other federal agencies.

US Secret Service

The Secret Service is the second-oldest federal law enforcement agency. It is a part of the US Treasury Department. It was established as a security force to protect the president and vice president of the United States and their families. Secret Service agents are drawn from an applicant pool with minimum standards similar to all federal law enforcement: college degree, US citizen, driver's license, and successfully passing a series of written and oral examinations. They are chosen from among other highly competitive persons whose education, life experience, and law enforcement background can be judged to be extraordinary. Local and state agencies and even the US Marshals Service attract excellent applicants, but as you move into the agencies such as the Secret Service; FBI; Drug and Enforcement Administration (DEA); Immigration and Customs Enforcement (ICE); US Postal Service (USPS); and Bureau of Alcohol, Tobacco, Firearms and Explosives (ATF), you start to see applicants who have higher levels of education, significant military and/or law enforcement experience, and in many cases, some kind of specialty background or experience that separates them from the quality applicants in local law enforcement. These high-quality applicants have to be competitive against each other, which bolsters the applicant pool beyond the average of other law enforcement. This of course does not mean that federal agents at this level are superior investigators; it just means that their backgrounds, experience, and education are generally superior. Investigative prowess is usually a function of training; on-the-job experience; and a few intangibles, such as investigative passion, communication skills, and curiosity, which are hard to measure in any new applicant. The Secret Service's investigative responsibility is limited to counterfeiting investigations, bank and credit card fraud cases, and related white collar crime matters. Their criminal investigations are usually suspended when they are needed for matters relating to presidential protection. Their investigative areas will not be covered in this text.

FBI

The FBI began its work in 1908; for the first few decades, it was limited to investigations of counterespionage, and it targeted radical extremists and anarchists who wanted to do away with government of all kinds. In the 1920s during the so-called gangster era, the FBI added criminal investigations of interstate criminals who sought to avoid arrest and prosecution from local authorities by "hopscotching" across various states to avoid detection. The federal criminal statute against the interstate transportation of stolen motor vehicles gave the FBI useful jurisdiction over those violent criminals who were gun-toting gangsters committing crimes in various states. The FBI was eventually given full authority to carry weapons and exercise discretion over the investigations of violent interstate offenders, such as Baby Face Nelson, John Dillinger, the Barker-Karpis Gang, and Machine Gun Kelly. Federal criminal statutes against additional interstate criminal conduct progressively provided FBI special agents with the authority to pursue these violent gangsters for a number of violations that support and close jurisdictional loopholes in various state criminal statutes.

The FBI also established the first interstate data collection of arrest records and fingerprints, the first nationwide forensic laboratory, and other records management that assisted the FBI and other law enforcement. The FBI then began to expand its jurisdiction to include more than 200 federal crimes. The interstate nature of crimes expanded to include crimes that affected interstate commerce. In the 1950s and 1960s, the FBI expanded its investigative responsibility in the area of nationally recognized organized crime. In the mid-1980s, the FBI again expanded its jurisdiction to include all manner of illegal drug crimes. (It joined in a coordinated effort to cripple international and national illegal drug trafficking conspiracies.) Finally, the FBI has also established primary jurisdiction for all crimes related to national and international terrorism. With all of this evolution, the FBI has become the primary federal law enforcement agency.

The FBI has developed the National Crime Information Center (NCIC), Combined DNA Index System (CODIS), National Integrated Ballistic Information Network (NIBIN), and Integrated Automated Fingerprint Identification System (IAFIS), all of which maintain identification data and scientific information on many violent crimes committed across the United States. With all of these developments and the training and significant background of special agents, the FBI's investigative responsibility is very similar to that of local or state detectives. FBI special agents have become the go-to federal agency for responding to all sorts of criminal conduct. FBI special agents in large divisions or field offices may be limited to a single jurisdictional area, but investigations and routine transfers will expand the involvement of individual FBI special agents—just like local police detectives—to a wide variety of investigative areas. Because of these circumstances, FBI special agents need to improve their exposure to all manner of effective investigative skills to develop successful approaches to solving criminal cases in an ever-broadening range of crime. In spite of the fact that the FBI is one of the largest investigative agencies in the federal government (approximately 14,000 agents and another 20,000 professional, nonsworn law enforcement employees), special agent applicants are drawn from an equally large pool of highly qualified persons. Lawyers, accountants, engineers, and scientists with impressive educational backgrounds usually beyond master's level along with experienced law enforcement officers and military veterans with substantial and successful careers are very often the base line of qualified candidates to become FBI special agents. This impressive pool of candidates does not ensure that these persons will be successful criminal investigators, but it does set a standard of high-quality people who can advance to that goal. The FBI has a fine reputation and a well-earned status of success, so the applicants hope to become a part of that reputation and success.

DEA Special Agents

DEA criminal investigators are also federal special agents assigned to conduct criminal investigations. Like their colleagues in ATF and the Internal Revenue Service (IRS) and inspectors for the USPS, they share administrative oversight responsibilities in controlling the legal distribution of the material for which their agency was designed. The DEA is responsible for the administrative control of legal drugs used for medical purposes. It oversees licensing policies for doctors who prescribe drugs and monitors the manufacture and distribution of pharmaceuticals, which can be abused and used to create a serious black market involving the illegal distribution network of painkillers and other highly addictive legal medicines.

DEA criminal investigators work in the United States and in a variety of countries worldwide on major cases in which illegal drugs, heroin, cocaine, marijuana, methamphetamine, large quantities of illegally manufactured opioids, and designer drugs, such as ecstasy, are distributed by criminal conspiracies, gangs, cartels, organized crime entities, and terrorist organizations. DEA special agents are focused on crimes relating to drug dealing and money laundering and the violence related to these crimes. In this capacity, they may become intricately involved in investigating the violent crimes addressed in this text, but more often, DEA special agents rely on investigative support and coordination with state and local authorities on these matters.

DEA special agents have to meet significant educational requirements, and in many cases, they need to have significant language ability in Spanish, Portuguese, Farsi, and other Middle Eastern languages along with Chinese and Japanese. DEA applicants also have a highly competitive hiring process in which special skills and background experience (such as prior law enforcement experience and training) are required to be chosen for the position.

ATF Special Agents

ATF special agents' criminal cases are focused on the illegal sale and distribution of firearms, explosives, alcohol, and tobacco products. During the 1920s, bootlegging illegal alcohol was investigated under the purview of Treasury agents, or T-men, who made every effort to enforce the Eighteenth Amendment to the US Constitution and its accompanying statute, the Volstead Act. This group of federal agents was the beginning of the ATF. Currently, though they keep their taxation and administrative responsibilities over alcohol, tobacco, and firearms, ATF special agents are reassigned from the Treasury Department to the Department of Justice. ATF special agents investigate gun running, arson cases, and the use of explosives in cases not related to terrorism. They continue to have responsibility for tracing ownership records of firearms and the investigation of rural and urban "moonshine," or "untaxed" liquor, which continues to be a persistent health problem nationwide.

Again, as is the case with their other federal colleagues, applicants for the position of special agent are well educated (bachelor's degree or higher) with significant experience in law enforcement or related careers. ATF agents also draw from arson experts with experience with local fire departments along with scientists who have expertise in explosive materials. ATF special agents are occasionally involved in violent crime investigation, but just like their colleagues in the DEA, they are usually supported by state and local police authorities in these matters.

USPS Inspectors, IRS Special Agents, and ICE Special Agents

Special agents from the USPS, IRS, and ICE are involved in significant criminal investigations directly related to their agency's responsibilities. But for the most part, they don't usually become concerned with violent crime investigations unless there are specific statutes that give them jurisdiction, for example, armed robbery of a postal employee or station. These professionals are highly skilled federal agents with impressive educational backgrounds and experience who have met very competitive standards to be chosen by these agencies for the criminal investigator position.

Department of Defense (DOD) Special Agents

DOD special agents are found in the US Army Criminal Investigation Command, Naval Criminal Investigative Service, US Air Force Office of Special Investigations, US Coast Guard Investigative Service, and Department of Homeland Security. They are assigned to work on criminal investigations directly related to their military branches. They become involved in a variety of violent crime investigations, such as murder, rape, robbery, larceny, and burglary, on military bases and facilities. Their investigative priorities and requirements are very similar to those of state and local detectives.

Generally, they are civilian 1811 series investigators, but they can be on-duty military personnel in their respective branches. Because of their unique position in the various military branches, they will usually have significant experience with that branch before they are deemed qualified for the career. These special agent positions are also staffed by well-qualified applicants with significant experience and training from other federal, state, and local law enforcement agencies.

In a profile similar to FBI special agents, DOD special agents will have significant counterintelligence and counterespionage responsibilities along with their criminal investigative responsibilities. Again, these special agents most closely align with state and local police detectives, but their jurisdiction is much more controlled given their relationship with the military branch to which they are assigned.

Source: FBI.gov, 1998 Nairobi Embassy Bombing

DEFENSE/PRIVATE INVESTIGATORS

Nonsworn investigators who work for the defendants in criminal cases or for private persons or entities with an interest in proving the innocence of a particular defendant or determining facts and discovering evidence in a crime event are nongovernmental criminal investigators. They can consider many of the factors presented in this text, but they are usually relegated to reviewing reports and reading statements provided by witnesses before they can actually develop significant insight into a particular case. These investigators can be well-qualified former law enforcement officers or well-educated but inexperienced interns, support staff, and newly minted attorneys working for experience in a law firm and assigned to defend a criminal suspect. Once they have established a legitimate reason for their inquiry, they will be given access to information in the hands of the government so they can follow their own line of inquiry in the case. All too often, defense investigators spend most of their time looking for errors by government investigators. It is usually easier to find flaws in a case than make the effort to determine if the government's investigation is accurate and has reached the proper conclusion. From the perspective of a defense attorney uncovering a fatal flaw by the government's investigators is the most direct method of winning in a trial and securing the release of the client. Proving guilt or innocence is a much more difficult process with a number of difficulties that may frustrate these private investigators. This text is about trying to explain the process of solving a crime, uncovering the truth, and making sure the right person is charged with the criminal conduct alleged. Looking for errors in procedure is not an essential part of the process.

SCOPE OF THIS BOOK

In this book, I will limit my discussion to violent crimes or offenses when a victim has suffered injury or death as the result of the actions of another. I will consider burglary and some larcenous crimes in my discussion. Violence or injury by the perpetrator on a particular victim will be considered for study in this text. Burglary and larceny act as gateway crimes for violent criminals, and as such, it is essential that any study of the criminal conduct of violent offenders should be viewed in the proper context. Does a rapist who attacks women in their homes learn techniques of breaking and entering when he begins his "career" as a rapist, or does he break into and steal from houses as a way to practice what he is ultimately preparing himself to do? Just as drug use is a predicate criminal pattern for a number of violent crimes, car theft, residential burglary, and larceny by stealth are the practice field for violent criminals. Residential burglaries can develop into sophisticated art theft, and snatch-and-grab pocketbook thieves can turn into armed robbers. Any evolution of criminal conduct can include an inherent desire to become rich without working, but in many cases, a warped sense of values and violent or abusive upbringing can create monsters who learn their methods and then apply those methods to their real calling in life. Serial offenders, like most people, advance and evolve to meet their own goals and satisfy their own needs. Sometimes their needs involve money, power, and psychosexual gratification.

Successful criminal investigators need to understand the evolution of criminal activity to put immediate observations in the proper context. They need to see a career criminal in the same way they look at noncriminal citizens who learn and advance in their careers. People evolve with certain goals in mind. Professional baseball players can usually benefit from time in high school and college playing varsity baseball; then they will also learn from minor league experiences to the point when they are ready for the big leagues. Career criminals develop along these same lines. As criminal investigators, we also learn from our experiences and the investigation of less serious crimes to the point that we become highly skilled investigators who begin to be able to anticipate behavior, understand motive, and develop successful investigative strategies that allow us to remove the career criminal from our community.

White collar crime, fraud, and computer crime, which can be devastating to large numbers of victims and devastating to a community as a whole, should be discussed in a broader, more expansive context. Examining the broad range of statutory definitions, details about internal security, control of computerized data, and the difficulties in establishing how the loss and "larceny after trust" occur would be the subject of an extensive text on white collar crime. Explaining how victims sometimes act as perpetrators and determining how the evidence can be discovered in the context of very sophisticated human relationships in which these cases occur are also too wide ranging for this text.

TYPES OF INVESTIGATIONS

Reactive Investigations

In very general terms criminal investigations focused on crimes against persons or violent crimes are broken down into two categories. *Reactive* investigations are police or law enforcement's response to a criminal incident. Examples of reactive cases are homicides, robberies, rapes, burglaries, thefts, assaults, etc. These crimes are reported directly to the police or other appropriate jurisdiction by a citizen, a victim, another police officer, or other interested parties as events that require immediate investigation. Following are some specific examples of reactive crimes:

- A person arrives home and discovers her house has been broken into and property has been stolen.
- A person discovers his car has been stolen from its normal parking location.
- A person is attacked by a known or unknown assailant and is sexually assaulted; the victim then calls for law enforcement to come to her aid.
- A person discovers an unconscious body of a person on the street, in a house, or in a commercial establishment.

First Responders

First responders are, in most cases, patrol officers who, as a result of their proximity and immediate availability, are the first officers on the scene. I will refer to them and their responsibilities several times in this text when it is logical to explain how the criminal investigative process occurs. These officers are well trained in police academies to handle their duties, and they receive further training in this important function from their training officer and chain of command. So, in reactive crime investigations, first responders will begin the investigative process. When the call goes out for these cases, law enforcement will respond with the appropriate resources to investigate the crime that has occurred. The response and initial investigative plan will be driven by the reporting person. Usually, the first officer on the scene then acts as the "gatekeeper," or security, for the crime scene until investigators and crime scene specialists arrive to take over the scene. First responders' responsibility is to render aid to any injured persons and notify and ensure that emergency medical personnel are called to the scene if needed. First responders then have the responsibility to protect the physical evidence on the scene and identify witnesses and separate and hold them for investigators, who will interview them and release them to return to their normal activities. First responders will obtain preliminary statements from witnesses, to be able to brief investigative personnel when they arrive. In emergency situations when evidence is in danger of being lost, destroyed, or otherwise altered by conditions, first responders will secure and protect that evidence. Because of this responsibility, first responders may also need to be prepared to photograph and otherwise record the scene, again, if there is a danger of losing or contaminating evidence.

Finally, first responders may also be called upon to initiate legal action to establish control of the scene. When a crime occurs in a location that is legally under the control of a third party, such as a third party's home, car, or property, it may be necessary to obtain a court-ordered search warrant so law enforcement will have exclusive control of the scene. If law enforcement was called to the scene of a crime by a responsible party who is legally present at a crime scene, first responders can establish dominion and control of the scene, but to conduct an effective examination of the crime scene, they may need to obtain permission of the owner of the property or obtain an emergency court-approved warrant to have all the legal access needed. If there are exigent circumstances and law enforcement is legally present on the scene, a warrant may not be immediately necessary, but any subsequent actions and especially seizure of evidence is subject to judicial review and may become tainted. So it is best to immediately move forward to obtain a warrant. (Exigent circumstances and how they affect this stage of an investigation will be discussed further in chapter 9.) Obviously, if the third-person owner is the victim or the family of the victim, she can certainly authorize law enforcement to conduct all the appropriate examinations needed.

If the crime event happens on public space, sidewalks, streets, or open fields owned by the jurisdiction, the police can proceed with the examination without any further legal authorization. As long as the first officer on the scene and subsequent responsible law enforcement officials are acting reasonably and have an articulable basis for believing they are conducting the crime scene with proper authority, the recovery of physical evidence should not be challenged. In this manner the actions of the first officer on the scene are an integral part of the investigation and should be adopted by the assigned investigator as a part of her case.

It should also be remembered that any third persons who claim that law enforcement acted improperly will have to demonstrate that they were in some way injured by the actions and that they have some interest in the outcome of the investigation. The evidence recovered can be suppressed only by a legal action brought by the defendant in the case. In other words, the third persons have to have "standing" (to have a legal interest in the disclosure of the evidence) to have the evidence suppressed or withheld from a trial. The key distinction is law enforcement needs to act properly with good intentions and not disregard the constitutional rights of a suspect or potential suspect.

Jurisdictional control of the crime scene is the first potential stumbling block to an effective reactive crime investigation.

Proactive Investigations

The second major type of criminal investigation is a *proactive* investigation. Instead of a particular act of criminal conduct the law enforcement agency may conduct an investigation of a person or group of persons whom the agency has reason to believe are involved in an ongoing criminal pattern. Some of the examples of this kind of investigation would be the targeting of career criminals who are serial offenders, targeting of a violent street gang, targeting of an armed robbery gang whose offenses are characterized by extreme violence or very high financial losses to the victim(s). The essential distinction is the fact that the perpetrators are targeted before the offense is actually committed or the targets' lives and daily routine are scrutinized in an attempt to discover facts and evidence proving their involvement in past crimes.

In many ways, proactive investigations are attempts by law enforcement to detect patterns of criminal activity, anticipate behavior, and develop evidence leading to the successful prosecution of a community's most proficient criminals. Proactive investigations rely heavily on intelligence and covert investigative steps, such as surveillance and undercover operations or the use of deception to trick the targets into revealing their methods and practices.

Proactive crime examples are patterns of all of the known crimes listed above with the addition of organized criminal enterprises, drug enterprises, terrorist cells, and any significant major conspiracies. The main distinction is proactive investigations target the criminals, not one event. (Conspiracies are crimes defined as an agreement among two or more persons to commit a criminal act or a number of criminal acts with at least one act in the furtherance of the conspiracy.) Conspiracy and patterns of criminal conduct are usually based or predicated on the commission of one or more of the crimes under discussion in this text.

As a result, information leading to the initiation of a proactive investigation requires solid law enforcement intelligence demonstrating the need for the investigators to protect the community against the targets of the case or the pattern of criminal conduct. This text will spend time explaining how proactive investigations use standard investigative procedures and coordinate all of the investigative resources available to determine if the targets are in fact involved in the criminal conduct alleged. In a proactive investigation, the following list of investigative steps are applied:

1. Understanding how particular crimes and their elements are proven
2. Constitutional considerations
3. Crime scene analysis
4. Forensic science support for an investigation
5. Establishing an investigative plan
6. Interviews and interrogations
7. The use of confidential sources
8. Tactical considerations
9. Intelligence support and digital data mining
10. Covert investigative operations

These steps are the same as those followed for reactive crime investigations, but there is a requirement to sort out the information from multiple crimes and find out if there are direct connections or uniformity in the method of operations or other factors that provide another layer of proof that the crimes were all associated with the targets. In these proactive investigations, investigators may not have a firsthand relationship with each crime under consideration, so they need to rely on written reports and notes from a variety of other investigators. Therefore, it is in the interest of investigators to develop a positive relationship with all previous investigators so there is a firsthand connection with each crime that is connected by the intelligence that was the predicate basis for targeting the suspect or suspects.

A successful proactive investigation should result in the closure or solution to a number of related offenses, thereby streamlining the use of investigative resources and closing or solving the unsolved. Conducting proactive investigations can become a next step for a reactive crime that has hit a brick wall and seems to elude the possibility of finding the truth. Finally, proactive investigations are most helpful in serial investigations (serial killers, armed robbery rings, burglary rings, and sex trafficking gangs that use violence to intimidate the victims), street gang violence investigations, and conspiracy investigations (traditional and nontraditional organized crime operations) involving the use of violence.

Chapter Two

Criminal Code

Criminal statutes, the outline of what needs to be proved.

There are several very important aspects of criminal investigations that all students should realize: (1) The great majority of crimes reported to the police are solved, and the right person is charged with the crime within the first day the crime is reported. (2) Since the right person is charged with the offense, it is also true that the offender is very likely to be a repeat, or serial, offender who has committed a large number of the same kinds of crimes. (3) Career criminals, who are serial offenders, who are caught and charged will often enter the criminal justice system and take a plea to lesser charges to forgo being charged with any or all of their previously uncharged crimes. (4) During the first few years of investigative careers, if investigators are assigned to routine assignments, such as burglary, low-level street robberies, or car theft, it is possible that all their arrestees will plead guilty and save the state a lot of money for needless trials. (5) The fact is that most of the people arrested for crimes are guilty, and solutions are rarely that difficult until the cases get more complicated and involve criminals who take their time and carefully follow a plan to avoid being caught.

This chapter is devoted to providing an understanding of crimes or criminal violations that investigators will be tasked to solve. Each state and federal government has a legislature whose function it is to prepare and upgrade a criminal code or series of statutes with a definition of the crime. The definition is usually two or more elements meant to explain what *needs to be proved* for the police or law enforcement to solve the crime. Solving the crime means the investigator identifies the person responsible for committing the violation and charges that person according to the requirements of the jurisdiction. Generally, charging the person can be accomplished by arresting the suspect (with a court-approved warrant or based on the existence of probable cause and thereby using a statement of facts laying out the probable cause) or providing evidence to a grand jury, which then indicts, or charges, the person with the crime as defined by the legislature. In either case, the investigator is saying that there are sufficient facts discovered in the investigation that *prove* the suspect is responsible for the crime. This *proof* usually consists of evidence, witness testimony, or physical evidence. Since this is the first time I have used the term *evidence*, it is appropriate to use *Black's Law Dictionary* to define it:

> Any species of proof or probative matter legally presented at the trial of an issue through the medium of witnesses, records, documents, exhibits, or concrete objects for the purpose of inducing belief in the minds of the court or jury as to their (the government or the defendant in a criminal trial) contention. Testimony, writings, or material objects offered in proof of an alleged factor proposition. That probative material legally received by which the tribunal may be lawfully persuaded of the truth or falsity of a fact in issue.

It is evidence that convinces a reasonable person that the elements of the crime as defined by the statute will be supported and verified in a trial. The next step in the investigation is to raise that *standard of proof* to beyond a reasonable doubt. The definition of *probable cause* and *proof beyond a reasonable doubt* will be discussed further in chapter 9 of this text. For the purpose of this chapter, students should begin to comprehend the crimes they will be called upon to investigate and consider the ways that the individual elements of these crimes can be proven. In other words, the criminal investigator is not expected to understand what needs to be proven until the investigator has a chance to break down the elements in a logical and expository fashion. By looking at each crime you will investigate, you will begin to understand what investigative strategy you should use to solve the case. If you know the elements that need to be proven, you can create a logical approach to every case and succeed in establishing the evidence to fit the elements. An example of this approach is to ask "What is the best way to prove an important element of homicide, that element being proving a person was killed as the result of the actions of another?" Your answer will probably be to have a medical examiner conduct an autopsy on the body and provide his expert opinion as to what the cause of death was and to further provide an official ruling that the person died as the result of homicide. That may sound elementary (and it is). Sometimes the proof is as simple as that.

Taking the next step to prove who is responsible is the tricky part of the work. Therefore, from here on, we will look at the various crimes that we will discuss in detail in this text and make an effort to break them down into their elements. At this point, we can start to have a glimmer of understanding as to the facts of the crime. I will use a number of generic definitions of the crimes because there are fifty state criminal codes; the District of Columbia and Puerto Rico have their own criminal codes; and the US government has its own set of criminal codes that provide crime definitions. Many of the definitions are the same from state to state, but there are too many subtle differences to account for, and there are sets of legal precedence in each state and judicial jurisdiction that make it impractical to compile all the variations in a single chapter. Each state legislature has, for reasons relating to particularly heinous crimes that have occurred in its jurisdiction, decided to improve on the normal or routine view of crimes defined in each state's and commonwealth's codes. Some states have added the adjective "aggravated" to their crimes or made some specific crimes capital offenses, meaning the crime carries the death penalty. Ultimately, these kinds of additions to first, second, and third degrees of crime may carry additional elements that need to be proved for those adjectives to have some useful meaning. Generally, serious crimes, such as murder, rape, and robbery, have three degrees of definitions, which present slightly different elements among the three degrees. Aggravated rape or homicide may indicate the victim was particularly vulnerable. Capital murder may indicate the victim was a law enforcement officer or a child or an instance where there was more than one victim. I will try to cover some of these types of distinctions, but in general, the proof is usually a verification that the victim fit into a category. There are other occasions when the tools of the violence used to commit the crime were so exaggerated that it showed a reckless disregard for innocent bystanders, such as in a bomb or arson case.

It should be understood that proving the elements of a crime always involves finding a way to put that proof in human context. Using scientific evidence, for example, requires that the investigator consider the capability of the scientific expert to present the evidence as testimony that is compelling and believable. Forensic science evidence has to be presented in court by a person whose education, training, and experience provide the person with the extraordinary capability to understand, examine, and report on the results. The scientific basis for reaching the conclusion has to be believable and relevant to any legal proceeding like a trial or other preliminary or post-trial review. There will be further discussion of this issue in chapter 10, but it is necessary to make the point here that the presentation of any evidence in a criminal case is the proof needed, and there is a very clear way to present that proof in a human context. In continuing with this concern, the eyewitnesses to the crime, the character of the co-conspirators in a crime, and the effectiveness of all witnesses need to be considered as proof in some kind of objective way. So an investigator has to be able to evaluate the proof used to verify the elements of a crime and show how those elements can be blamed on the suspect.

The analysis of the criminal statutes and discussions of proof will be broken down into categories of crime. These categories are umbrella designations that incorporate several criminal statutes. Before we proceed with that discussion, we will consider how a criminal suspect is identified. The term *positive identification* refers to a process required to prove probable cause and proof beyond a reasonable doubt. It is a term that is regularly used in arrest warrants, grand jury indictments, and trials and other preliminary hearings. The term very simply states that the person who committed the crime is the person named in the charging document, indictment, or the title of the court case.

POSITIVE IDENTIFICATION

Aside from the statutory elements of a crime, one important element that is universal in all criminal inquiries is *positive identification of the suspect*. Positive identification can be proven in a few ways using witnesses. A person who commits a crime discusses the crime and its details with a friend, family member, or associate; then the person who received the information passes the details on to the investigator. In most cases, this person becomes an essential witness in the case. Since the person is very familiar with the suspect, this will involve a simple process of showing an officially recognized photograph, mug shot from a previous arrest, a driver's license photo-graph, or a passport photo from the files of the Department of State. The investigator has to ensure that the person identified by the witness is the same person the investiga-tor plans on making the prime suspect in the case.

Many criminal acts, such as murder, will occur in a particular crime scene or venue where the violence is carried out. In these cases, physical evidence of the crime will be left at the scene. A murder or any physical assault where the victim and suspect come into close physical contact will also facilitate an exchange of trace evidence, in-cluding hair follicles, textile fibers, bodily fluids, skin epithelium, fingerprints (latent and patent), and other potentially identifiable sources of evidence, such as ballistic evidence and all manner of documentary or photographic evidence that can be used to identify the suspect. The recovery and examination of this kind of evidence will be discussed at length in chapter 10, but here, for purposes of understanding proof needed for a positive identification, there will be a short discussion of how this physi-cal evidence can be used to provide this positive identification. The first and foremost example of this kind of evidence is *fingerprints*. When fingerprints are found at the scene of the crime, it is prima facie (true or valid at first impression) evidence that the person whose fingerprints are identified was at the scene. If that person's presence at the scene is unexplained, the person will then become a prime suspect in crime. An explained justification for the prints to be at the scene may be that the person lives or works where the crime occurred. The value of the evidence proving the person is responsible for the crime is reduced. Then it is essential to evaluate the exact location of the prints to determine if the prints were left in a suspicious location. Fingerprints alone can provide the necessary positive identification needed in an investigation if a known standard of the person's fingerprints is on file in an official database and used for the identification by the fingerprint expert, who then becomes an essential witness in the case. If the suspect's prints are not in an official file collection database, the known fingerprints of the person who will become the suspect have to be obtained with permission or with a court order or grand jury subpoena. Again, the identification will be accomplished as the result of an examination by an expert.

Other physical evidence that can be used to provide positive identification is *se-rological material* or *skin epithelium* recovered at the crime scene. If this evidence contains the DNA of the suspect and is extracted using appropriate scientific expertise and a DNA profile is obtained, that profile can be compared to known DNA profiles that exist in a database, such as the FBI's CODIS, which compiles known profiles of violent career criminals. All of these matters will be discussed at length in chapter 10. If the suspect's profile does not exist in the database, a known sample of the DNA has to be obtained from the suspect, who can either voluntarily provide the sample or be the subject of a court order to do so. Using a positive identification of the suspect's DNA is sufficient to prove that person was present at the scene, and if the evidence was found on the body of the victim or in some kind of suspicious position in the crime scene, that person will become a prime suspect. If, on the other hand, the DNA can be easily explained as being present because the suspect lives or works in the location where the crime occurred, the investigator has reduced the possibility of ensuring a positive identification of the suspect. Other physical evidence, such as pattern evidence that goes beyond a general identification of a brand of shoe or type of tire tread, can result in a positive identification of the suspect. In this kind of case, the evidence is examined by a shoe print or tire tread expert, and the pattern is identified. But the expert has to go further and locate specific unique characteristics that positively connect the shoes or the tires owned by or in the possession of the suspect. In effect, the expert will testify that the shoes or tires obtained from the suspect are the same shoes or tires that made the impressions at the crime scene. Ballistic evidence is likewise a source of positive identification if the suspect can be directly linked to the weapon that was used in firing a bullet or that ejected a shell casing left at the crime scene. As you can tell, these forms of positive identification are interdependent on solid investigative work. Linking a suspect to generic physical evidence has to be more than general characteristics in common. It has to be the result of positive scientific analysis and direct association with that evidence to be of help in positively identifying a suspect. So even a hair fiber and textile association with a crime scene has to support the investigative findings to be used to positively identify the perpetrator. It is necessary for the investigator to show or prove the logical link between the crime and the physical evidence relied upon to verify that the suspect is connected to the evidence. This kind of logical conclusion has to be articulated to the trier of fact, the judge, the magistrate, or the jury.

The last way to identify a suspect for proof of involvement is the most often used method and also the most controversial. The average crime takes seconds to be completed. There may have been some lead-up time to the actual crime or more exposure to the suspect in a few crimes, but for the most part, *eyewitnesses* will have very limited exposure to the suspect with a limited chance to study the suspect enough to make a positive identification. The ability of eyewitnesses to remember the kind of detail necessary to make an identification varies from person to person. Interracial identifications can be difficult, and the trauma of watching a violent crime, such as a murder or armed robbery, may limit the ability of a witness to look over mug shots or a stand-up lineup to positively identify the suspect. It is true, however, that these kinds of identifications are routine and, in many cases, very effective. If a judge hears from a single witness that the suspect was positively identified in a lineup or a photo spread, he will find probable cause for an arrest. The identification will then be subject to more intense scrutiny during the trial, and if the witness sticks by the identification and is convincing to the jury, the matter of positive identification is proven. When the investigator sets up a lineup or a photo array using mug shots (Mug shot photographs are official record photographs taken simultaneously with an arrest by a law enforcement agency. Police departments and all other investigative agencies are usually required to take head and shoulder pictures of every person they arrest. They are also required to take a ten-print fingerprint card as an objective verification that the person whose name appears on the official arrest record is the person photographed and fingerprinted.) or driver's license or passport photos, the investigator has to be careful to make the lineup "nonsuggestive." All members of any lineup or array need to match the suspect in race, hair color, facial hair, eyewear, and any unusual marks or facial variations, especially if they were noted by the witness in her original statement. As long as the investigator sticks to objective fairness of the lineup and makes no unusual prompts to the witness, the lineup should stand as solid proof. Statements made by the witness such as "it's him," "that's the person I saw," or "number 4" (in an eight-person lineup with number cards) are acceptable for a positive identification. Statements such as "it looks like her," or "I believe that is her," or "maybe that's her" can be helpful to the investigator to know she is on the right track; they just don't rise to the level of surety necessary for a positive identification.

In the US criminal justice system, a positive identification of the suspect in open court is a much-sought-after procedure. Therefore, many prosecutors will demand the identification procedure if there are eyewitnesses to the crime. Even if the investigator is convinced the effort will be a waste of time and the positive identification of the suspect is proved in another manner, the prosecutor may still demand a try with a lineup. It is essential that the procedure be carried out fairly with no regard for the outcome. Any positive identification will be icing on the cake and therefore should never be corrupted by a wrong identification, which can have deleterious effects on the case.

Personal Experience

Early in my career, I was assigned to work the largest armed robbery in the history of Washington, DC, at that time. The Neiman Marcus department store, a very high-end jewelry and clothing store, was robbed by four men who got away with more than $1 million of merchandise. The loot included Rolex and Patek Philippe wristwatches and some high-priced 18-carat gold jewelry. When I responded to the scene, the crime scene examination and witness interviews had already been completed, so I had to wait for the reports and support the investigation in any way I could. In the short term, the case was the responsibility of the DC police. I did receive the list of the property that had been stolen, and all the wristwatches had unique serial numbers, which I immediately entered into the NCIC stolen article database. Over the next couple of months, the police showed a huge number of photo arrays to the witnesses who had provided very detailed descriptions and artists' renderings of the robbers. Not a single identification was made. About two months after the robbery, a Los Angeles, California, detective called me and said he had recovered several of the wristwatches stolen in the case. He kept regular tabs on a jewelry fence (a dealer in stolen property) in his jurisdiction. After recovering the items, he contacted a confidential source who knew the fence and people the fence dealt with and supplied me with the names of the four men who had carried out the robbery. We took the case from there and proceeded to prove every aspect of the information provided by the source. The source had a pending minor drug charge and was willing to testify against the robbers and the fence in exchange for consideration about her charges. Armed with her information, we were able to put together all the proof needed for charging the five suspects, including the fence, with armed robbery and interstate transportation of stolen property. We were also able to close other similar armed robberies in Montgomery County, Maryland; Aurora, Colorado; and Fort Lauderdale, Florida. By the time we had all the suspects in DC in custody, months had passed since the robbery at the store. The eyewitnesses had been, in my opinion, tainted by all the previous photo spreads. There was reason to believe that based on the abilities of the witnesses, who were all jewelers and had an eye for detail, that another lineup might work. I arranged for the lineup and got all four of the robbers positively identified by two of the eyewitnesses. Both of the eyewitnesses told me that I finally showed them the persons they had seen in the store that day and that they matched the descriptions they had given to the police. Since that case, I have never been reluctant to try a photo array or a lineup because, with the right witness, it works.

CATEGORIES OF VIOLENT CRIME HOMICIDE

Black's Law Dictionary defines *murder* as follows:

> The crime committed where a person of sound mind and discretion (that is, of sufficient age to form and execute a criminal design and not legally "insane") kills any human creature in being (excluding quick but unborn children) and in the peace of the state or nation (including all persons except the military forces of the public enemy in time of war or battle) without any warrant, justification, or excuse in law with malice aforethought, express or implied, that is, with a deliberate purpose or a design or determination distinctly formed in the mind before the commission of the act, provided that death results from the injury inflicted within one year and a day after its infliction.

Murder is the top crime in the category of homicide when an investigation is usually warranted. Each state and the federal government have codified or more particularly defined this crime, but murder and aggravated murder, murder in the first degree, and even felony murder carry the most serious penalties allowed in the United States, with the possible exception being treason, in the federal criminal statutes. *Black's Law Dictionary* states that murder can only be committed by a person who knows what they're doing. It implies that a murder might be the direct result of cognitive actions. So a person who kills another person with criminal design can have reckless disregard for the lives of others, can be committing a felony crime where a person intended to commit that crime and death resulted from that crime, or can fully intend to kill his victim and purposely plan and carry out the killing. The element of *malice aforethought* is a legal construct that indicates some plan or positive knowledge where the crime was considered before it was carried out. That planning can be any period of time prior to the deed itself. In other words, it can be planned for days, weeks, months, or years beforehand, and it can be planned in the moments leading up to the crime.

Murder has the following four main elements: (1) sound mind, (2) killing of a human being, (3) malice aforethought, and (4) deliberate purpose. Each element has variations of proof. *Sound mind* is usually not under consideration by the investigator until the case is solved or close to a solution. The ability of a murderer to have sufficient mental ability to formulate a plan and carry out that plan to kill another person, and in the mind of the killer, the murder is done with criminal design or intent are the basics. Some of the proof needed for this element can be a psychiatric or psychological profile of the killer. Therefore, proof would be provided by a mental health professional who has evaluated the killer and determined that the killer has the requisite mindset to commit the crime. There are also a number of other proofs that can show how the killer was thinking. Steps taken by the killer prior to the crime that show the intent to avoid detection and steps by the killer to avoid detection after the crime has occurred may be uncovered during the investigation and are evidence that needs to be presented as truth. Examples of these kinds of proofs are as follows: purchasing or procuring an untraceable weapon using a false or misleading identity, conducting covert surveillance on the victim prior to the crime to choose the best time for committing the act, making covert efforts to leave the jurisdiction where the killing takes place, and setting up a bogus alibi. These are examples of elaborate plotting that can be uncovered during an investigation. Uncovering these facts and procuring witnesses who will present these facts in court not only help to prove the guilt of the killer but also can be used to show the cognitive ability the killer applied to the crime, which proves the killer acted with a "sound" mind.

The second element, *killing of a human being*, seems simple to prove. Usually the best proof is an examination of the remains, known as an autopsy, by a medical professional—the coroner or medical examiner in the jurisdiction. Proof can also be enhanced if the victim's remains are present at the crime scene, and photographs depicting wounds can be taken. There is also a need in most homicide trials for the family of the victim to testify that the victim lived and interacted with others. The only tricky part of this proof process is if the medical examiner can't make a determination as to the cause of death, especially if the remains have been left in a wooded area or dumped in a body of water where environmental or animal deterioration is so acute that the cause of death cannot be scientifically determined. The key word in this element therefore becomes "killing." The obvious counterpoint is the victim died of natural causes and it just so happened to have occurred outdoors where the remains were altered. In the event that this kind of hurdle develops in a murder case, the investigator has to rely on developing witnesses who know what caused the death of the victim. It could include testimony by co-conspirators or other witnesses who heard or saw the killer carry out the crime, or testimony that the killer discussed dumping or getting rid of the body to avoid detection—any testimony and proof that the killer acted in accordance with a plan or followed a pattern of removal of the remains of this victim and other victims can be proof of the second element.

Without a clear and convincing statement from the medical examiner or coroner scientifically verifying the dead person died as the result of homicide at the hands of another, it becomes a very difficult case to prove. Even if the other elements are proved, juries are reluctant to find guilt unless there is a reasonable and compelling level of proof that the defendant killed the victim.

The third element is *malice aforethought*. This element can be proved in a variety of ways. Developing evidence for a motive that explains a logical and, for the killer, compelling reason to commit the crime is one step in this process. Again, witnesses who are familiar with both the victim and the killer will be sources of this kind of information. A search of the residence of the killer may provide analog and digital notes or diary or journal entries that detail the anger, frustration, or disappointment the killer has for the victim. It may also yield verification of the motive, which further verifies the logic that compelled the killer. Proof that the killer obtained a weapon in advance of the crime is another way to show malice before the act. Any actions taken by the killer to avoid detection can also be used to prove this element in a similar fashion to proving the killer is of sound mind. Covert actions by the killer to choose the best time and place for the crime is also solid evidence of malice aforethought. Evaluating malice is an attempt to get inside the mind of the killer. A person can form malice aforethought in an instant. Evaluating the circumstances and actions taken by the killer to avoid detection after the crime has occurred may be the only way to prove this element of the crime. If a killer uses a weapon of opportunity or kills in a last-minute rage, it is difficult to prove malice aforethought, but the careful examination of the relationship between the killer and the victim may provide insight that helps to prove this aspect of the crime. The killer who slowly poisons the victim over time is the prime example of malice aforethought. A person who has a long-standing grudge against another person and has discussed killing the other person with musings to friends and family members and then kills using a kitchen knife or heavy blunt-force object that just happened to be handy can be proven to have committed murder as long as the proof supports the conclusion. Malice aforethought is an intentional desire that just so happens to coincide with an opportunity to kill and is not always the intentional desire and a well-considered plan.

The investigator does, however, need to be able to prove that a series of actions taken by the killer were the result of a plan to eliminate the victim, not just a general dislike or even hatred for the victim. The best way to prove this is to develop physical and testimonial evidence showing that the killer followed a process that would not only eliminate the victim, but would also ensure that the killer took steps to avoid detection for the crime. Again, the mind is in many ways impossible to penetrate, but the actions before and after the crime may provide insight into how the killer planned to proceed and did in fact proceed to achieve these goals.

In a sense, many of the proofs discussed are interdependent. Proof of malice, deliberate design, and even sound mind may depend on similar evidence, but fully explaining each aspect of these facts will provide the road map to the investigator on how to show to a jury of reasonable people that this particular homicide carries the extra elements that are defined as murder. It is really the responsibility of the prosecuting attorney to present this evidence to the jury and make it clear that the evidence proves the elements. A certain amount of forensic argument has to be applied to the testimony or scientific evidence, which provides the basis for the proof. What is very important in this effort is that the investigator needs to be aware of the elements and how each element is instructive to the triers of fact. The final element is *deliberate design or purpose*. This element is closely aligned with malice aforethought but goes further than prior motive. The murderer has to be shown by actions and evidence thereof to have put into action a plan to carry out the murder. The investigator has to put into effect an *investigative plan* that will allow the investigator to meet the goal as described in the elements. An investigative plan is *a well-ordered logical scheme on how to proceed in an investigation*. In the case of a murder, the plan starts with the immediate on-the-scene witnesses and the medical examiner's analysis and ruling. The plan then moves on to the secondary witnesses; the victimology, or facts learned about the victim that may help to explain motive; and the temperament or anger driving the killer. Once the suspect has been identified, the next step in the plan should be an analysis of the killer and an important effort to discern the mindset, motivations, and any other driving force that caused or led to murder. This step also includes any alibis or potential witnesses who are known to have information about the suspect's whereabouts before, during, and after the murder. An overall timeline arranged according to the accuracy of the time of death offered by the medical examiner should be applied to the witnesses and the victim's and suspect's timelines. Based on the usual process, the final step of realizing the importance and relevance of any physical evidence gives the investigator the opportunity to shore up the facts developed so that the presentation in court will be detailed, specific, and most of all accurate.

The above process can be viewed as an example of an appropriate investigative plan, with a few alterations, that can be followed for a number of violent crime investigations. The key to a successful investigative plan is thoroughness. Is every lead covered? Are all suspects considered and eliminated before moving forward with official charges? Will the investigative analysis stand up to the withering criticism that occurs in a trial?

Manslaughter is a homicide in which the element of malice aforethought is missing or unprovable. As an investigator proceeds with all of the steps mentioned above for murder, there will be a point when it is clear that the killing happened as the result of a heated argument, an egregious example of infidelity, or merely a happenstance related to facts and circumstances when a person is killed, but there does not appear to be any deliberate design or planned effort to kill the victim. In some cases of manslaughter, reckless disregard for human life can be a driving factor. In those cases, the manslaughter may be the highest degree of manslaughter not rising to the level of murder. The classic example is firing a weapon into a moving train or infecting a person with a deadly virus. Murder could be charged if there were some underlying corrupt or criminal purpose for such an act. But if it is proved to be an action without discernible cause or reason, it is likely in most states that it will be charged as first-degree manslaughter. Most of the cases like this lead to significant penalties and long prison sentences, so even though it may seem like the killer is getting away with something, it is up to the investigator to prove the highest degree of the crime possible. The investigator should make the effort to ensure that the proper punishment is available based on the facts uncovered and the elements that are proven. Manslaughter will also be charged if the proof discovered by the investigator reveals an unnecessary effort at self-defense—killing a person because the circumstances presented to the killer indicate that the victim is trying to harm him. In these cases, the killer may have misinterpreted the actions of the victim or overreached in her response to actions of the victim, for example, a person is involved in an argument with a neighbor, and it turns heated. The killer sees the neighbor pick up a rake to continue gardening, but the killer sees the action as an attempt to assault the killer. His response is to pull out a gun and shoot the neighbor. This may be a case of manslaughter. A perceived threat or an overreaction to another's actions can be the basis for manslaughter if the evidence clearly shows the lack of malice on the part of the killer.

Most states have demarcations between forms of manslaughter. Those forms, or categories, are voluntary manslaughter and involuntary manslaughter. Under *volun-*

tary manslaughter, the killer has no prior plan to kill another person but has to kill the person to protect her own life because there is no other way out. It is also presented as a killing in the heat of the moment. For example, if a victim has to release himself from a rapist and accomplishes that by killing the assailant, that can be in some states a voluntary manslaughter. In most cases, such actions may not be considered criminal conduct and may be viewed as simple self-defense, but the voluntary nature of the action puts the act in the manslaughter category. *Involuntary manslaughter*, on the other hand, results as an involuntary action that again had no prior planning but just happened. This may be a result of a scuffle or argument that began as a peaceful social interaction. The killer involuntarily kills another person to protect herself. The intention of killing, a factor in voluntary manslaughter, is not present in involuntary manslaughter. In a manslaughter, the killer comes with no plans to kill and usually makes no effort to evade an arrest. The killing is something that just happens, perhaps due to a heavy hit to the victim's body.

Vehicular homicide may be one of the largest categories of investigation under the heading of homicide. Some recent statistics indicate that vehicular deaths and gun homicides are close in numbers. Vehicular homicide is a criminal violation in most states and carries similar penalties as manslaughter. Most of the vehicular homicide deaths are not carried out by career criminals and, as such, are not being fully explored in this text. Criminal investigators will, however, act as part of a team to investigate these cases to help determine the facts. Some of the proofs required are the same as any homicide case and therefore should be considered. Proof of the victim dying as the result of blunt-force trauma is usually provided by the medical examiner or other trained trauma surgeons. In most cases, there has to be an analysis of the vehicle's equipment and a reconstruction of the incident by a trained and experienced *accident reconstruction* technician or expert. Many states and large urban police departments have these experts on hand and may even have a separate unit or branch that investigates vehicular homicide. The proof a criminal investigator must uncover is determining if the death resulted from corrupt intent, distracted actions, or drug or alcohol abuse, and he must explore the possibility of malice aforethought, which could raise the crime to the level of murder. The criminal investigator, who may be a trained accident reconstruction officer, has to determine the state of mind of the driver at the time. If this event occurs in the normal course of the day or night, there may be an immediate response by law enforcement. The investigator will discuss the actions and demeanor of the driver with experienced traffic patrol officers who can attest to how the driver acted in the immediate aftermath of the incident. If there is no immediate investigation because the incident occurs when no one is around and the driver has left the scene, suspicion exists that some kind of corrupt action on the part of the driver occurred. In that case, the examination of the scene is the only evidence for the investigator to rely on to begin the investigation. At this point, creating a timeline and finding out the exact time of death becomes important to locate potential witnesses who may have been driving by the scene at the time of the homicide. Again, the investigator is relying on the scientific analysis provided by the medical examiner. In these days of traffic cams, speed control cameras, ATM cameras, and security cameras, the investigator may be able to determine if any digital imagery exists, if the time and route of the driver can be determined or guessed. There are a number of reasons a driver might choose to leave the scene of a vehicular homicide—the driver was under the influence, believed she had hit an animal instead of a human being, or intended to kill the victim and was intent on escaping investigation.

States will take these categories of homicide and apply degrees of seriousness to them and attempt to make the punishment fit the crime. The actual facts of each case are then used to apply the statutory penalties and level of criminal culpability. It is up to the investigator to ensure that the facts are known to the prosecutor so an appropriate charge can be applied. In each case, the investigator will have to prove the elements that can be proved and provide an analysis to the prosecutor if there is a missing element and how that missing element affects the seriousness of the actions of the suspect/defendant.

Assault with Intent to Kill

The crime of *assault* is actually a category of crimes that include a spectrum of criminal acts when one person threatens violence and, in some cases, carries out that threat against another person. *Black's Law Dictionary* defines *assault* as follows: "An unlawful attempt or offer on the part of one man, with force or violence, to inflict a bodily hurt upon another." To commit the crime of assault, it is not necessary to actually physically harm the victim. Carrying out the violence against the victim adds the second crime, which can be described as *battery* to the threat, attempt, or offer. As the crime becomes complex in this manner, the elements can be inextricably linked to proving two crimes. The term *simple assault* has two elements: the first is the attempt or offer to do bodily harm, which then becomes a crime of communication that can be proved by testimony of the victim as verified by at least one other person. The threat can also be proved by a written communication, letter, note, digital posting, or even a video or audio communication. The second is that the threat has to be proven to be a promise, statement, or proposal that the doer will commit a violent act. An act of bodily harm is relatively easy to define. A threat to hit, shoot, or inflict some kind of trauma and even a threat to kill are likely threats that constitute the violence required by the statute. A threat to disrupt the mental health of a victim and some other effort to carry out some kind of psychological disruption directed at the victim may also be considered. *Stalking crimes* where the victim is overwhelmed by a feeling of dread or uneasiness can be a type of harm that is considered. Stalking crimes are serious assaults that are legislated as separate crimes because they involve criminal behavior by the assailant that may not directly fit into the typical provable features of an assault. The victims in these cases are overwhelmed with a constant threat of communication meant to engender fear loathing and a disruption of a victim's day-to-day life. The actual threats are not always direct, but the effort by the assailant to impose himself into the life of a victim whom he may not even know or may have had a casual relationship with becomes serious when the assailant implies serious consequences if the victim does not comply with the desires expressed by the assailant.

These kinds of crimes have been constantly growing in modern culture with the advent of social media and instant communication via cell phones and computers. Legislatures around the country have fine-tuned the crimes of assault to fit into these categories of sexual violence or implied threats of bodily harm. Usually, stalking crimes will have their own statutory authority. Proving the elements requires testimony from the victim, verification by a witness, and verification by recovery of the method used by the perpetrator to communicate the threat. Forensic computer analysis provides proof and may also provide the source of the communication. The written communication, letter, note, digital posting, or even a video or audio communication, has to be recovered and considered evidence of the crime. Threats of this nature when they are communicated over the internet or by telephone or mail may also prove a federal crime if the communication is part of the interstate communication networks. The federal crime of *extortion* can be part of this spectrum of threats to do harm to a victim. Occasionally, these threats are delivered using coded language, or openly harmless text, but should be considered serious threats based on who sends the message and if a determination can be made suggesting violence because of the relationship between the perpetrator and the victim. A Christmas card sent from the boss of a violent criminal organization to a person who is set to testify against the same criminal organization may be a way the boss shows he knows where the victim is living, thus communicating the threat. Proof for the crime of assault can be extremely difficult in these cases but should be a priority in the underlying investigation. In most jurisdictions, the element of threatening bodily harm has to be obvious and not subject to interpretation. During the course of an investigation, the law enforcement professional will recognize that actions of some perpetrators are in fact threats to do bodily harm and should be addressed the same way actual and obvious threats are.

Battery

Battery is defined by *Black's Law Dictionary* as follows: "Any unlawful beating, or other wrongful physical violence or constraint, inflicted on a human being without his consent." Battery is very often an adjunct to an assault investigation. The additional element of verifying or proving bodily harm through the use of violence or even constraint can be proved by obtaining the opinion of a medical professional. The second element of determining that the bodily harm was inflicted without the consent of the victim can be proven from the testimony of the victim unless the victim is unable to communicate as a result of the injuries. A person who perpetrates an assault with *circumstances* of *aggravation* or of a heinous character or with intent to commit another crime can be guilty of aggravated assault and battery. In the state of Pennsylvania, for example, "if any person shall unlawfully and maliciously inflict upon another person, either with or without any weapon or instrument, any grievous bodily harm, or unlawfully cut, stab, or wound any other person, he shall be guilty of Aggravated Assault and Battery" (*Pittsburgh Legal Journal*, vol. 54, January 2007). Generally speaking, the two crimes of assault and battery are inextricably linked if the violence threatened is actually carried out. The level of punishment faced by the assailant is dictated by the serious nature of the crime or the relative status of the victim. The victim's vulnerability will in many cases dictate the level of punishment. Assault and battery of a child or an elderly or infirm person will be viewed as aggravated in most states and in most instances. The extent of the injuries will also factor into the proposed punishment. Finally, the amount of effort expended to carry out the assault and the use of a knife or firearm may raise the crime to the related offense of *assault with intent to kill*. Many of the elements of these crimes have to be proved in the same way murder and manslaughter are proved. The assailant's intent needs to be determined and proved. The assailant's state of mind needs to be considered. If the assailant doesn't have the requisite malice aforethought, it is difficult to prove assault with intent to kill. As with murder, prior malice and deliberate design are factors that can be proved by witness testimony and the actions of the assailant at the crime scene. Did the assailant bring the weapon used to commit the crime? Did the assailant stalk or surveil the victim prior to the crime? Did the assailant reveal his plan to assault the victim to another person? Since assault also requires the element of a threat, did the assailant communicate his threat to the victim? Testimony from the victim, who is hopefully available and lucid enough to provide testimony, goes a long way in providing proof in this case. Finally, testimony and medical expertise about the nature and extent of the injuries must scientifically prove that the injuries were caused by the actions of another. Evidence of blunt trauma, stabbing, shooting, or a physical beating have to be explained and provided for proof.

All manner of serious assaults can be considered using these elements. The level of proof when you have a living victim witness is lessened because the victim is able to explain to the judge and jury what happened. There are, of course, cases of serious gun and weapon assaults that leave the victims unable to speak for themselves. This puts the burden on the investigator to provide the necessary proof in the same way the investigator has to provide the proof in homicide.

Examples of these kinds of crimes are drive-by shootings, witness assaults for the purpose of discouraging cooperation, and extraordinary violence for the purpose of causing serious bodily harm up to and including physical incapacity. Political or retaliatory acts of terror and any serious assaults on children, the elderly, or the infirm will come under this category. The seriousness of these cases provides the incentive to the investigator to determine the mindset of the assailant and proves that she acted with the intent to inflict the serious harm to the victim and the likelihood that the assailant may have wished to go even further. In the modern era, *serious gun assaults* are routine crimes in many urban jurisdictions. It is difficult for criminal investigators to get a handle on these cases because of the sheer numbers, but since many of these cases are homicides without the result desired by the assailant, it is incumbent on law enforcement to continue to combat the proliferation of these serious cases. Investigative units need to keep coordinated intelligence information about these cases and commit to associating cases by forensic evidence, method of operation, and victimology. The solution of one serious assault with intent to kill may be the catalyst for solving a series of similar crimes.

Rape and Other Sexual Violence

Rape as defined by *Black's Law Dictionary* is "the unlawful carnal knowledge of a woman by a man forcibly and against her will." It is a relatively simple definition that will be expanded to include a series of very serious crimes inside the category of sexual assault crimes. In the first place, we are long past the idea that the crime has to be a man as the assailant and a woman as the victim. Any forced sexual encounter between two persons is probably a more appropriate definition. The variations exist when you begin to define the sexual encounter and the force used. When a man forces sexual intercourse on a woman at gunpoint or knifepoint, that is a more classic example of rape. But in some statutory definitions, there has to be proof of penetration by the assailant, so forcible sodomy or forced oral sex is defined as a different crime. Each state legislature will define various sexual assault crimes to fit specific actions by the assailant to ensure that these violent assaults are dealt with equally no matter the nature of the actions by the criminal. The most important feature for the investigator to determine is the nature of the violence used or threatened by the assailant. In this manner the crime is no longer viewed as a sexually motivated crime; it is a crime involving the exercise of power over the victim. The investigator should be less concerned about any so-called provocation by the victim pushing the rapist to the assault. The investigator will find that the social and psychological impact of the rape or forced sexual conduct will be dramatic on the victim and, because of this, the investigator needs to become an advocate for the victim in a more committed way than in almost any other criminal case. In most modern interpretations of the criminal conduct in a sexual assault, the concept of "provocation" is a reaction a defense attorney may choose to use as a defense. It is unnecessary and counterproductive for a criminal investigator to consider provocation as anything but an irrational excuse offered by a guilty assailant.

Rapes and crimes involving sexual violence are the most serious crimes that go unreported or fall into a category of crimes where the victim is less than cooperative. In cases of sexual battery, it is best for a victim who survives to report the crime immediately afterward and allow for a full medical examination, to determine the extent of any bodily harm inflicted and to recover any trace evidence, including biological material. Unfortunately, this is not usually the case. Victims, female and male, are sometimes so traumatized by the event that they want to forget it ever happened and avoid any further discussion about the crime so they can somehow place the event into a bad memory box that never has to be thought of again. There are a number of reasons this is a bad idea: (1) the assailant will strike again; (2) the victim will relive this traumatic event as a nightmare over and over, and it will never be fully forgotten; (3) without the medical examination, the evidence needed to prove the case will be lost forever, and any medical treatment needed for the victim will go unaddressed, which can have long-term health effects on the victim; (4) the victim will find it hard to overcome the loss of empowerment and may lose the opportunity to fully recover a past meaningful life—the victim can experience a loss of intimacy with loved ones and distrust and avoidance of the opposite sex if the crime was a cross-gender assault; (5) rape and sexual assault are serial crimes, and even if the victim knows or doesn't know the assailant, it is likely the perpetrator will commit a series of similar crimes; and (6) unfortunately, especially if the assailant was careful about leaving any identifying evidence, the only way law enforcement will ever solve the attacks is by comparing and developing investigative leads from various cases.

Victim Witness Relationship

In every criminal investigation, the law enforcement professional needs to develop a positive relationship with victims and witnesses to a crime. A more detailed study of these relationships will be presented in chapter 6. In considering this relationship in a sexual assault investigation, there are several components and strategies that are more intense and focused for the investigator in advocating for the victim. The emotional connection between the victim and the investigator has to include empathy and sympathy. The connection for the two has to develop into a journey for the victim to regain her power and develop an appropriate level of anger that is so frustrating and callous that disregard for her truth will not be acceptable. Initially, finding a way for the victim to trust the relationship is essential. The victim in many cases will have trouble sharing intimate but necessary details of her attack, especially with a male investigator she just meets for the first time in the aftermath of such a trauma. Female investigators may also have similar responses from the victim because of cultural or sociological taboos, which frustrate or confound the victim. Victims can and do feel they are somehow responsible for the attack. Their dress, mannerisms, and even vulnerability made them victims, not the despicable character of their assailants. Victims need to be continually shown that the investigator is their advocate and the advocate of other people who are living through the same horror. When a person (especially a person who has suffered a sexual assault) feels alone, that person begins to overemphasize those negative thoughts and stereotypes that permeate the victim's mind in the aftermath of such a horrible experience. It is up to the investigator to find solutions for this self-loathing blame game or malaise. Sometimes adding team members to the investigation formally or informally is the solution. A medical professional, or a psychologist with experience with rape victims, or a well-trained and experienced civilian counselor who can provide support and opportunities for therapy can help the victim overcome feelings of helplessness and blame. Most investigators will have contacts in these areas who can help support a victim going through the investigative process and who will understand that the process may last one to two years if the investigation is successful and the case goes to trial. Empowerment of the victim is the goal to be achieved, not just locking up the perpetrator.

From an investigative standpoint, the benefit of this positive relationship is the important ability to prove the elements in the case. The element *force* is best proved from the perspective of the victim. How will her testimony stand up to criticism that it was role-playing and not real force? The victim's negative response to the demands of the assailant is an issue in some cases unless there is medical evidence of significant bodily harm. The victim is the best and, in many cases, the only witness who will be able to say and testify to the force that was used to get her to comply. I have been using the female pronoun in this discussion, but it should be noted here that male victims are going to be subjected to the same crucible of detailing the proof of force. Male victims in many cases will have even deeper emotional reactions to overcome, especially if they are subjected to same-sex abuse and are in fact heterosexual in their personal preference. There are simply no easy solutions to the range of negative responses a victim may internalize. The investigator must be able to continually point to the suspect, or defendant, as the person to blame and not the personal internal reaction of the victim to cultural, sociological, or moral standards that are struck moot by this crime. The use of force is best proved by the testimony of the victim along with the expert testimony of the medical professional who examined the victim.

Carnal knowledge, sexual intercourse, sexual penetration, sodomy, forced oral sex, and any other degree of unlawful forced sex are best proved by the victim's testimony, but in some cases, the victim may block out the details of the attack as a psychological coping mechanism or may have been rendered unconscious by the assailant in the attack. It will be necessary to prove this element with a competent medical professional who not only gathers any important physical trace, biological evidence, and other forensic material but can also offer an expert opinion about the nature and extent of the forced sexual actions by the assailant. A nurse practitioner with significant experience in the area of sexual assault and a physician who has significant experience with sexual assault victims are usually on staff at most urban trauma centers. Less experienced professional nurses or doctors can offer similar opinions with the assistance of a sexual assault expert, who can consult during or immediately following the examination. It is up to the investigator to ensure that the right expert conducts or participates in the examination or oversees the steps taken to properly protect the evidence, makes a record of injuries, and records physical indications of the forced sexual conduct. In any case, the medical examination needs to be done by an aware, caring, and professional practitioner. The investigator needs to provide personal support to the victim during this critical time so that a bond of trust is properly developed.

When proving the element of sexual assault, the combination of victim testimony and the expert testimony of a medical professional is necessary. There will be cases when victims for a number of the reasons discussed here refuse to be medically examined. Then, days, weeks, months, or even years later, the victim has a change of heart and decides to go forward with a claim of sexual assault. In these cases, the testimony of the victim is the only proof available. If there is some type of connection that can be made between two or more separate cases of sexual assault that place the assailant in the position of committing the crime in a manner like the older, unreported crime, proof can be sustained by showing that similarity and stating whether the similarity is sufficiently unique. Characteristics of the modus operandi (method of operation, or MO) and signature (unique feature observable at the crime scene) act as a common denominator. Common characteristics of separate crimes have to come together to show the investigator the existence of a pattern of criminal behavior that is indicative of the same person being responsible so that the jury can't ignore the links. Obviously, this kind of proof is much less effective than the sought-after combination of a solid victim/witness statement backed up or corroborated by scientific medical science supporting the testimony. It is incumbent on the investigator to produce results with whatever proof is available.

Sexual assault is not ordinarily an isolated event. Rapists are repeat offenders. It is up to the investigator to thoroughly examine the background of a rape suspect to determine if there are other victims or crimes that can be proved. This behavior is not ordinarily the action of a mentally stable person. Violent predators who desire power and the ability to intimidate commit sexual assault. There are usually aspects of their own sexual evolution that supply or inform their inclination to do sexual violence. If these perpetrators are anonymous or unknown to the victim, their identification and removal from the community are imperative. Predators who are known to the victim may appear normal and innocent. It is up to the investigator to ensure that the person a victim says committed a sexual assault is thoroughly and properly investigated to prove or disprove the allegations made by the victim. In chapter 6, we will discuss how to decipher the veracity of the victim witness.

There have been some false claims of rape and sexual assault by victims, but the numbers are not substantial. A careful and thorough investigation and a complete and thoughtful evaluation of the victim-witness by experienced investigators should be done. The investigator can assess the normal or consistent reactions of a victim and determine if there are indicators of a false report. Some victim witnesses will be enraged, and some will be subdued and even fearful. The range of emotions and how a victim acts or reacts will be the kind of clues a professional experienced criminal investigator will rely on for evaluating the veracity of the victim. There are no easy answers, but if the investigator is seeing behavior from the victim that is unusual and the investigation is turning up inconsistencies and even lies, the investigator can make the decision to confront the victim. However, until that happens, the victim should be believed and leads followed to make the case. Victims who are normally stable, law-abiding citizens do not submit themselves to a sexual assault investigation without understanding how personal and pervasive the investigation may become. That is why the investigator needs to develop that special relationship highlighted in this discussion.

Sexual Assault of Children and Mentally Disabled Adults

There is nothing more abhorrent than an adult sexual predator who victimizes children. In trying to prove a case of child sexual assault, the investigator needs to realize that the use of force element is slightly different. Neither a child nor a mentally disabled adult can legally give consent. Merely proving that the child or disabled adult had a sexual encounter with a person who is legally responsible is enough to prove the elements. A medical examination and a scientific opinion may be enough evidence to sustain a prosecution in a case of sexual assault.

The definitions of a person who can legally consent vary slightly from state to state, and it is necessary for investigators to make sure they know the rules governing consent in their jurisdiction. Some states recognize some younger ages of consent, especially if the perpetrator is of similar age. Child sexual assault is not normally prosecuted when the victim is sixteen and the perpetrator is eighteen and there is reasonable proof of consent between the parties.

There will also be borderline incidents, and if the investigator can prove that the victim was tricked or lured with lies and grand plans to participate, there may be enough evidence to sustain a prosecution. A pattern of fraud or lying to an unwitting, vulnerable teenager may be enough to prove use of force in a sexual assault case. The main issue is the victim will assert that the action was consensual because of the embarrassment from being tricked. It is similar to the victim in a fraud larceny-after-trust case. In these cases, the investigator needs to advocate for the victim in spite of the victim's protestations. Finally, a child predator who victimizes very young children can operate in two ways: aggressive and forceful assaultive behavior, which usually ends in death for the child, or the slow, careful seductive behavior where the predators explain to the child that their relationship should be kept secret and concealed from parents, teachers, and friends. The first type of behavior is fundamentally investigated following a plan used in homicide investigations and other stranger-suspect cases. The suspects will be socially challenged background players with access to the child. The second type of behavior will be close friends or relatives, teachers, coaches, and other adult authority figures who usually have a go-to venue for their sexual assaults. They will often reuse the same venue or crime scene and rely on their glib and persuasive personality to keep their actions hidden from detection. Investigations of these predators is a primary concern to law enforcement. All law enforcement is sworn to protect and defend the community. These most vulnerable victims—children and mentally regressed adults—require the highest level of protection law enforcement can produce.

Kidnapping/Abduction

The set of crimes called kidnapping, abduction, and imprisonment are all related to the offense of *taking a person by force or strong persuasion by another person*. In many states, abduction usually involves some type of domestic dispute; therefore, the definition is refined to the person being taken as "wife, husband, child, or 'other person.'"

A state definition for abduction, as per *Black's Law Dictionary*, is "the taking by force or strong persuasion of a wife, husband, child or another person." Once the person has been taken, that crime is over, and therefore, the two elements—"taking the person" and "by force or strong persuasion"—need to be proved. In this case, the most compelling way to prove an abduction is with a comprehensive statement from the victim and any witnesses that may have observed that actual abduction in progress. Taking a person in a private location can limit the proof to just the victim unless there happens to be security camera footage or other surveillance recording of the act in progress. The most likely second part of an abduction, which is a separate crime, is imprisonment.

According to *Black's Law Dictionary*, *imprisonment* is "the act of putting or confining a man in prison; the restraint of a man's personal liberty; coercion exercised upon a person to prevent the free exercise of his powers of locomotion." It is not a necessary part of the definition that the confinement should be in a place usually appropriated to that purpose. It may be in a locality used only for the specific occasion, or it may take place without the actual application of any physical agencies of restraint (such as locks or bars) but by verbal compulsion and the display of available force. The "prison" can be a room, house, apartment, warehouse, a temporary coffin and grave, a vehicle, an outdoor space that is confining to the victim due to remoteness, or some other restraining environmental conditions. The prison's utility will be based on the motive for the abduction. If the most likely result of the abduction is the death of the victim, the prison conditions can be harsh and psychologically destructive. If the motive behind the abduction is torture or to instill fear in the victim and others, the prison will have to be the type of location where chances of interferences are lessened or eliminated.

If the motive behind the abduction is sexual sadism, rape, sodomy, or other sexual assault, the prison will have to be set up for that purpose. Proving imprisonment is again reliant on the statement of the victim, but proof can also be obtained and bolstered by a careful crime scene examination when and if the prison is discovered.

There is a great deal of similarity between working with the victim of an abduction and many of the concerns discussed above for victims of sexual assault. The victim in an abduction who is not sexually assaulted will have experienced that same overwhelming loss of self-control. The most helpful way back to a somewhat normal state is finding a way to empower the victim by using the anger at the perpetrator as a catalyst for making that extra effort to remember and report all the details of the abduction and imprisonment. If there is reluctance on the victim's part, it is usually related to horrific mistreatment by the captor. In the most basic instances of this crime, the abduction is usually motivated by a need to take control of the victim, abuse the victim, or frighten the victim and the victim's family to encourage some kind of action or lack of action to be completed by the victim or the victim's family. In the end, if the victim is somehow kept unaware of who the suspect is, there is a chance for survival. Unfortunately, in most cases of abduction where there is no financial motive driving the crime, it is hard to believe that the victim will survive. This crime and its likely combinations are so heinous the perpetrator would be facing decades of jail time if not life in prison.

That brings us to the second and more complicated crime under this category, *kidnapping*. Kidnapping adds the extra element of taking and holding the victim for ransom. Ransom in most cases is money or something of value for the kidnapper. This kind of abduction and imprisonment is usually a crime of conspiracy. A lone criminal may have difficulty taking the victim and then imprisoning the victim for a relatively long period of time until arrangements for a ransom can be set and paid. In many instances, there is more than one kidnapper. A conspiracy adds additional proof that needs to reflect that all persons in the group are responsible, but mere participation in one overt act by any other person in the group proves the conspiracy and thereby allows for the prosecution of all participants. In that way, if each member of the group handles different tasks in the furtherance of the crime, the whole group can be charged in an overarching "conspiracy to kidnap" case. Proof of the elements of the crime and the individual crimes, abduction, assault, imprisonment, and extortion (demanding ransom) proves the conspiracy even if participants take part in only one aspect of the criminal conduct. In this manner, the criminal investigator can create a matrix or schematic of all the acts in the furtherance of the crime and lay out the proof for each participant. Even persons who act corruptly without a full understanding of the whole crime can be proved to be a part of the conspiracy by showing that person's involvement in just one of the aspects of the crime.

The big question at that point is, *Will the victim be released?* Kidnappers may hold the victim for a period of time to allow the victim's family to verify proof of life, but once that is done, the victim will be expendable and may not survive the crime. The elements of this crime include *abduction by force, imprisonment by force,* that is, against the will of the victim, and the *demand for a ransom.* In the case of the federal crime of kidnapping, there also has to be an *interstate aspect* to the crime. In most cases, the interstate aspect can be inferred if the victim has been held for more than 24 hours. Prosecution of the kidnappers or the co-conspirators will be handled at the level where these important elements are proven. In many cases of kidnapping, the police or the FBI will monitor negotiations for the ransom, thus providing positive proof of the demand for ransom and, in some cases, the interstate aspect of the crime. The victim will have to be the most important source of proof about the abduction and imprisonment if law enforcement is able to rescue the victim from the place of imprisonment. This can provide additional evidence of the force used and the verification of the imprisonment by physical evidence. The demand for a ransom usually is provided by the person contacted to pay the ransom or arrange for the payment of the ransom. The methods of communication for the ransom demand can be a document, a digital communication, a face-to-face meeting, or a telephonic conversation. All of these methods will provide the opportunity for the criminal investigator to recover a copy of or to record the demand so that proof of the demand can be obtained. The statement provided by the witness to whom the demand was made is the most significant proof of this element of the crime. The proof that more than one person committed the crime or conspired to further the crime (by acting as captors, ransom procurers, or lookouts during the exchange) is best proved by surveillance, victim testimony, and proximity to the venues where the criminal activity was carried out. Therefore, if a person is present in a location where a victim is being held against his will or if a person is observed where a ransom drop occurs, proof of that person's involvement in the crime is supported.

Kidnapping, like many of the crimes discussed in this chapter, have elements that need to be proven in a fashion that satisfies the parameters of the criminal code or statutes for each jurisdiction. Taking these cases further with conspiracy charges usually requires the additional support of proving the participation of the conspirators. Conspiracy can be charged in every crime discussed in this chapter, but due to the range of actions needed to commit a kidnapping and/or abduction, the complexities of each action taken in the furtherance of the crime and the actual commission of several crimes making up the overall conduct in a conspiracy case are likely. We will examine conspiracy in more detail in this chapter, but for purposes of explaining kidnapping in the most comprehensive manner possible, this examination was necessary.

Armed Robbery

In the category of *armed robbery*, there are again several crimes that can be committed that have similar elements of proof that verify the crime took place. *Black's Law Dictionary* defines *robbery* as "the felonious taking of personal property in the possession of another, from his person or immediate presence, and against his will, accomplished by means of force or fear." The definition of *armed robbery* is "where the person carrying out the crime of robbery is armed by having a lethal weapon and threatens his victims with bodily harm." In many states, there are distinctions made that grade the seriousness of the crime by levels of value, including determining if the crime has a commercial establishment as the victim or if any harm was done to the victim or victims in the course of the robbery. States will designate robbery and armed robbery by numerical descriptions based on seriousness and, in some cases, will add the adjective "aggravated" to the crime category. The crime of robbery always includes the threat of violence and is therefore a serious felony perpetrated by potentially violent offenders who have every intention of violence if their demands are not met. Commercial armed robberies where a large amount of cash, jewelry, or other valuable property is taken can be prioritized not only because of the value of stolen property but also because these robberies usually involve informal gangs of repeat career criminals who often use real violence in carrying out their crime. One-on-one street robberies, or muggings, often fall into the category of lower priority because these kinds of crimes may have less violence, fewer victims, and less amounts of valuable property stolen. Reconciling this lack of investigative priority to a person who was mugged and had the proceeds from her paycheck stolen makes the law enforcement response sound less than helpful. So as a matter of course, all armed robberies should be handled as serious events where a real threat to do bodily harm was coupled with a significant loss of personal property.

To prove the elements, the investigator must rely on the victim/witness to provide the actual demands made by the robber. In the case of bank robbery, for instance, the victim/teller is the essential witness who will express the impression that the robber induced a "force or fear" to ensure compliance. In any commercial robbery, that same kind of inducement needs to be expressed by the witnesses to prove the element. As far as the inducement being expressed by the use of a weapon, the witnesses have to conclude that the robber intended to use the weapon to carry out his demand if the victims didn't comply. As such, the crime of armed robbery has aspects of assault and, in some cases, battery built into the crime. Use of force, fear, and intimidating presence can be the kind of expressions from the robber that sustain the proof necessary. The taking of the property has to be proved by the victim's supplying an inventory of the property taken, by the victim's providing a witness statement under oath as to what was taken, and some independent evaluation of property so it can be shown to be of value. The evaluation can be an expert's opinion if the property is artwork, jewelry, or intellectual property. This kind of evaluation provides the proof needed to prove the level of harm done and the verification that the crime of armed robbery is charged and meets the level asserted by the government in assessing the seriousness of the crime. Along with that, some level of proof verifying that the robber did in fact take the property is inherent in the proof. The simple statement by the victim or other witness testifying that the robber left with the property will cover this element.

Armed robbery involves the use of a weapon to strike fear and intimidation and ensure the cooperation of the victim in a robbery. Proof of this element can be derived from witness statements, surveillance video, and the discharge or use of the weapon at the scene. Bank robbers and other commercial robbers have been known to intimidate and gain attention for their crime by shooting bullets into the ceilings or walls of the places they intend to rob. The recovery of these expended bullets and photographic proof that the shooting happened are a significant level of proof that supports the statements of the witnesses and provides physical evidence of the use of a weapon in the crime. The use by the robber of a replica or toy weapon may tend to lessen the seriousness of the crime, but the most important aspect of this proof is whether the victim believed that the weapon was real and a real threat. The victim has to feel intimidated or fearful. Bank robberies where the robber passes a note to the teller that she has a gun, knife, or bomb may not rise to the level of seriousness of the same robbery where the gun is discharged and obvious to the victim, but the intimidation and fear *can* be the same and is therefore proof of an armed robbery even if the weapon was not visible. It will be up to the criminal investigator to verify the use of an actual weapon if that is possible.

In this discussion, robbery and especially armed robbery involve serious assault and the crime of larceny. There can also be elements of the crime of extortion, and in the case of major commercial armed robberies, there are conspiracies that include the person or persons who "cased" the target to determine the best manner to carry out the crime; the person or persons who carried out the actual robbery and theft; and the person or persons who fenced (converted stolen property), laundered the large sum of cash stolen, or converted the property to useful cash or resources for the robbers. So major criminal conspiracies can be uncovered during successful armed robbery investigations, and in every case, there has to be the main elements of armed robbery proved along with proof that the actions of others not necessarily involved in the crime carried out criminal actions in the furtherance of the robbers' central crime or pattern of crimes. Remember, armed robbers are very often found to be career criminals who are serial offenders and therefore repetitive in their actions, modus operandi, and support structure. Knowledge of these characteristics provides the criminal investigator with a number of avenues to support proof of the individual elements of the crime or crimes committed.

INSIDER WITNESSES

This opens the door for obtaining proof of the crime from insiders, or co-conspirators. In obtaining the cooperation of insiders, the criminal investigators will have an extraordinary perspective on how the criminal conduct was facilitated. The investigator needs to be skeptical about the information and to review every detail to determine two significant questions: (1) Can the details provided by the insider be verified or supported by other, more reliable facts and scientific evidence? and (2) Is the insider diminishing or lessening his own part in the criminal scheme in hopes of facing a reduced penalty for participating? Defense attorneys will always intimate that the criminal insider who testifies in a trial is lying to have the government reduce or suspend altogether any prosecution and subsequent punishment. There is really no way to avoid that allegation. If the insider provides truthful testimony and fully admits his participation the government can verify or corroborate the details provided by him. Testimony from reliable witnesses and/or scientific opinion testimony that verifies the details, lets the investigator find that important level of proof for the criminal elements along with the compelling "insider" testimony laying out the whole pattern or scheme of conduct. There are other ways to verify the reliability of insider witnesses, which will be discussed at length in chapter 6.

COMPLEX CATEGORIES OF CRIMINAL CONDUCT

Multidimensional crimes, such as professional commercial robberies and kidnappings for ransom, are prime examples of criminal investigations that invite sophisticated conspiratorial conduct. In the final section of this chapter, we will turn our discussion to *conspiracy* as the central crime and show the elements that need to be proven. It is necessary to introduce the concept of criminal conspiracy here and with the section on kidnapping because of the complicated nature of these categories of crimes. Murder, rape, and even assault are most often one-on-one crimes, with a victim and a suspect. They can occur inside of a major conspiracy, but in routine criminal investigations, these crimes appear to be a kind of single event crime with a limited number of persons. Even if there is a strong suspicion that the offender/suspect is a serial offender, it is likely that a conspiracy will be limited. Career criminals who are responsible for serial murder or rape are very often lone wolf operators who keep their participation in such crimes as well-kept secrets.

Arson

The best definition for the common law version for *arson* is "the act of unlawfully and maliciously burning the house of another man" (*Black's Law Dictionary*). Obviously, that definition is arcane, but the fact is the elements are simple. Fire is an age-old way of destroying or damaging houses, buildings, and any edifice that is no longer useful or needed. Fire can be started from simply lighting a match and putting it in contact with flammable material inside or adjacent to a building in hopes that the fire will grow larger and spread to inundate the whole structure. In the case of criminal arson, destroying a structure to exact revenge, causing financial and personal damage to an adversary, or burning a structure to carry out some sexual fantasy are crimes that can result in damage to the intended target, but a serious fire can jump from the originally intended target to other structures that may have innocent victims trapped inside and have devastating consequences for other persons in the community.

Arson is a serious crime with these two elements in almost all state statutes: (1) the structure, edifice, or real property is set on fire for criminal or corrupt purposes, and (2) the act was malicious or intended to cause destruction. Commercial arson is the burning of a business or store. Residential arson is the burning of a dwelling house. Some commercial arsons are insurance fraud schemes where the actual owner arranges to burn and destroy the business in hopes of getting a significant payout from the fire insurance carrier. Cases of this nature need to be proven by detailing the personal and business expenses of the owner and making an evaluation to determine if such an act will relieve some kind of financial burden. Proof can be derived from an audit by an accounting professional.

Arson Investigative Expert

The less investigative aspect of the proof in this case, but an essential proof in all arsons, is a ruling by an expert in arson investigations that the fire was intentional. This ruling is sustained in a thorough scientific examination of the burned structure and an evaluation of the scientific evidence from the crime scene that leads an expert in arson investigations to conclude that the fire was intentional and shows some kind of scientific proof of human casualty. Accidental fires can occur and get out of control when a person accidentally discards a lit cigarette or match. Accidental fires can be caused by bad electrical wiring, faulty gas lines, and mistakes in cooking or preparing meals using open flames.

The crime of arson is an intentional act using the application of flame or spark to provide an intense point of origin. Then, in some cases, the further application of a fire accelerant, such as gasoline, lighter fluid, or any of myriads of flammable chemicals, can create an unstoppable inferno, which can quickly and effectively destroy the structure completely. It is a fact that many homes and commercial structures have fire-stops built in, and a random accidental fire that is not enhanced by an accelerant can stop burning or the property damage can be reduced. A serendipitous end to a fire is not an optimal outcome for a criminal arsonist, so besides that age-old method of starting a fire with a match, spark, or other singular source, criminal arsonists will ensure the destruction of their targets by adding the accelerant to enhance the destructive power of fire. Obviously, the presence of an accelerant at the crime scene allows the expert to conclude the fire was in fact arson.

Along with the detection of the use of accelerants and scientific concepts of physics and chemistry, structural engineering adds additional scientific certainty to the expert's evaluation. The way the fire advances through a structure and the pattern of burn destruction along with any determinations that can be made about the heat temperature of the fire and how that would affect the structure of the building are taken into account. The beginning of the examination for the arson expert is the point of origin for the fire, which is followed by a reconstruction of the exit pattern by the arsonist if that can be determined. Method of operation and signature aspects of the crime can be significant in limiting the pool of suspects. Aside from the expert analysis, arson is usually proved with crime scene photographic evidence showing the charred remains of the building.

Arson investigation experts are most often specialists in fire departments who have jurisdiction in these fires. Once it becomes certain that the fire is criminal arson, the fire department will usually join forces with the police or federal agency to identify the suspect. These firefighter experts are specially trained and experienced in the scientific analysis of fire-related crime scenes. Many have received special academic training in the sciences related to their field of expertise, and some attend the US Fire Academy, a training school under the US Fire Administration, in Emmitsburg, Maryland. The training academy and the USFA are agencies under the US Department of Homeland Security, and the training is federally funded and available to arson investigators from all over the United States. Local jurisdictions will also offer their own training for their arson investigators.

In summary, the best method to prove the two main elements of an arson case is to start by recording or photographing the damage when a fire destroys or damages a structure. Scientific analysis of the evidence will then be done by an expert arson investigator, who will provide a ruling based on scientific opinion that the fire was the result of human action. Like many crimes discussed in this text, arson is often carried out by first-time amateurs who are sloppy and leave lots of evidence. Arsonists are also career criminals whose methods and techniques can create a profile for detection. Career criminals who commit arson generally have financial goals in mind, but they may also have psychosexual motivations, which elevates the serial arsonist to becoming an extreme danger to the community. Persons who can't help themselves and are not motivated by economic gain will most likely commit more and more horrific fires to satisfy their deranged needs.

Bombings

Bombings are crimes with many of the same characteristics as arson. A bomb is "an explosive device that can instantly cause massive destruction to a building, an automobile or people" (*Black's Law Dictionary*). Bombs can be sophisticated devices with military-grade explosives and timing mechanisms or, at the other end of the spectrum, pipe bombs filled with black powder and metal fragments meant to send high-velocity projectiles in all directions to cause destruction and/or death, which can be initiated by a simple fuse or blasting cap. There are a number of criminal statutes covering the crime of bombing. Homicide, assault, and destruction of property are usually directly related offenses committed by a bomber. The indiscriminate use of an explosive device shows a general lack of concern for the safety of people in the location where the explosion takes place. Malice aforethought is usually a given in these cases. As in arson, proving the destruction usually requires just photographic evidence from the crime scene documenting the destructive power of the device. Just like in arson, scientific experts are tasked with proving that a bomb device was used in spite of the fact that explosions are viewed as so destructive that there is nothing left to examine.

Bombs leave plenty of evidence, from minute pieces of metal used in a timing device to chemicals and chemical compounds, which when analyzed, provide the expert with exactly what explosive material was used. Bomb experts are highly educated scientists who travel from crime scene to crime scene overseeing the search and recovery of evidence and then conducting forensic analysis of the evidence to support their findings. Bomb techs, specialists in bomb evidence recovery, and postblast technicians are teams formed in many jurisdictions in the United States who are tasked as first responders in these cases, and they will coordinate the recovery of the evidence with the experts from the FBI and the Bureau of Alcohol, Tobacco, Firearms and Explosives (ATF). Some explosions can happen as a result of faulty natural gas lines or other accidental factors, but for the most part, a careful examination of the crime scene will prove some kind of human agency caused the explosions. This is slightly different from arson, for which accidental fires are not a rarity, so the science and recovery of physical evidence is essential and usually instructive.

As a result of the increase in political terrorism, there are some jurisdictional factors that have to be considered in bombing cases. If it is preliminarily ruled to be the actions of a terrorist (homegrown or international), the FBI will have primary jurisdiction and conduct the investigation with the support and participation of the local police authority. If, on the other hand, the bombing is motivated by economic greed or revenge, the local authority will carry out the investigation, with ATF as a support agency providing bomb or explosive expertise. The FBI may reenter the picture of jurisdiction if the bombing is determined to be related to organized crime. (In the 1970s and 1980s, a number of sophisticated car bombs were used in ongoing feuds between two La Cosa Nostra/Mafia groups in the state of Ohio.) Jurisdictional considerations don't change the basic elements since motivation and association with gangs, political groups, violent jihadists, and even bombings extorting money or compliance will add layers of proof to a given crime.

Weapons of Mass Destruction

The federal government and most state legislatures have added statutory violations referred to as crimes involving the use of *weapons of mass destruction* (WMDs). These statutes are meant to cover crimes such as terrorist bombings but also include the use of chemical and biological weapons, which can be just as devastating as bombs and, in some cases, more so. These crimes will require expertise at a level above most local jurisdictions. Federal agencies, such as the FBI and Department of Homeland Security, will generally support and participate in investigations of these matters and provide the needed scientific expertise to prove the nature and effectiveness of the WMD device used. Chemical and biological weapons are very sophisticated and usually are the result of some type of state-sponsored research and development. Delivery systems for the weapons need to be thoroughly examined, and the chemical or biological makeup of the material needs to be qualitatively and quantitatively profiled to provide information about the origin of the material. Biological weapons, for example, will usually have a DNA profile, which can be compared to material in the hands of cooperating governments or research laboratories. These kinds of examinations are not usually available to local law enforcement. Federal investigative resources are usually needed for WMD crimes.

Bombings and all crimes using WMDs very quickly elevate an investigation beyond the reach of local jurisdictions, so criminal investigators in these cases need to be flexible and sufficiently trained to participate effectively in an investigation of this nature. Federal investigators need to recognize the contributions of the local criminal investigators, who are familiar with the venue and potential suspects where the crime occurred. The local investigators need to recognize the contributions of their federal counterparts for resources and expertise, including data searches for interstate or international pools of suspects.

Burglary

Burglary is defined by common law as "the breaking and entering the house of another in the night time, with intent to commit a felony therein, whether the felony be actually committed or not" (*Black's Law Dictionary*). Because this definition is almost too restrictive, states have established a number of crimes under the heading of burglary. Any breaking and entering of a building with intent to commit a felony is burglary or, in some local parlance, a B&E. The building can be a home or a commercial establishment. The felony can be the crimes of *murder, rape, assault, larceny*, and even *destruction of property*. The burglar can be *armed* or *unarmed*. The seriousness of the crime will be evaluated by those characteristics. In spite of all these variations, the elements of burglary consist of (1) the breaking and entering, which can be proved by a thorough crime scene examination of such factors as consisting of broken windows, pried open doors, or the compromising of garage doors or locks with sophisticated electronic devices or even the more sophisticated use of lock picks and other locksmith equipment—photographic evidence depicting the method or likely method of entry provides the proof needed to show there was a breaking and entering; (2) establishing the ownership of the house or business by another, proven by the testimonial statement of the victim or the victim's representative; (3) proving the time of day of the crime, which again is best accomplished by the victim's testi-mony—there are nighttime and daytime burglaries, and it is expected that a nighttime burglary of a residence puts the victim and the victim's family at risk; (4) addressing "with intent to commit a felony," which is another one of those elements that requires the investigator to get inside the head of the criminal unless the burglar actually does commit the felony.

The commission of a felony will be best proved by the victim. The victim can provide an inventory of the property stolen, the evidence of rape or a serious assault, and even a statement about any destruction that occurred. Obviously, a deceased person in the residence or business is strong proof the intent of the burglary was to commit a homicide. In this manner, proof of the felonious intent can be verified. On the other hand, if there is no proof or verification that a felony occurred, it is up to the investigator to prove intent by whatever evidence is available. Proof may be from the confession by the suspect, statement by a co-conspirator, and a reconstruction of the events that indicates the burglar was interrupted in the middle of the crime and fled to avoid detection.

In most cases, one of the important ways to prove a burglar's involvement in a particular crime is if the investigator recovers stolen property or other fruits of the crime in the possession of the suspect within a short time of the crime. The related crime of possession of stolen property or any of the federal crimes, such as interstate transportation of stolen property, requires mere possession of the contraband to allow for a prosecution, but proving the next level, verifying the suspect did in fact commit the burglary, is going to require physical evidence linking the burglar to the specific crime. In some cases of burglary, there may be eyewitnesses or even surveillance video evidence of sufficient quality to prove the suspect was on the scene.

Burglars who are career criminals are serial offenders. Based on my own experience in investigating burglaries and related federal offenses, I never knew a burglar who committed just one or even two burglaries. Burglary is a gateway crime and is often the first criminal activity of a person embarking on a career as a criminal. Juvenile offenders often start with minor breaking and entering offenses, such as thefts from garages or garden equipment stolen from work sheds. Eventually, these offenders move up the crime chain to the commission of residential burglaries. Usually, burglars are motivated by the need for money to finance a drug habit or other corrupt demands. Just six months of this kind of criminal conduct can lead to the suspect doing as many as five burglaries per day. As long as burglars have a readily available fence for converting the stolen property, they usually continue their crime spree until they get caught. Their method of operation and an incessant return to the same neighborhoods where they successfully committed crimes, which yielded high takes, allow criminal investigators to locate and identify the burglar and prove the elements of the crimes by showing patterns and recurring aspects of a series of crimes. As burglars progress with their profession and become more sophisticated, apprehension becomes more difficult, but the reality is they will continue to rely on certain patterns of MO along with a reliance on a willing stolen property fence. In this fashion, burglars become predictable and subject to treachery by their criminal associates.

As a result of the criminal evolution that takes place for the burglar, it is in the interest of law enforcement and new criminal investigators to work burglary cases with significant effort. There is no better training about how to evaluate crime scenes than the examination of hundreds of burglary break-ins during the beginning of a career as an investigator. Techniques developed by burglars and used over and over are eventually applied to more serious crimes, such as murder, rape, and significant commercial robberies. Evaluating the logical and, in some cases, the creative manner that burglars use to gain access to a venue where a crime is committed allows the investigator to develop expertise in how physical evidence at a crime scene can best be evaluated.

Larceny

Black's Law Dictionary defines *larceny* as "the wrongful and fraudulent taking and carrying away by one person of the mere personal goods of another from any place with a felonious intent to convert them to his (the taker's) use and make them his property without the consent of the owner." Taking the property illegally and converting the property to the use of the thief are the two main elements of this crime, and a number of statutes laying out the variations that are included in theft can require other, more specific details of proof. Theft by embezzlement usually requires that the thief have some kind of legitimate access to the property. Stealing then is a crime of convenience, or opportunity, or a pattern of lying that allows the criminal to gain control of another's property without consent and *without any force or violence* associated with the conversion. Sneakily stealing property, setting up an elaborate scam or con to have the victim willingly turn over personal property, and then using the property or in some other way converting the property for use by the thief are the hallmarks of the crime. Since there is no force or violence used in this category of crimes, their seriousness and priority are reduced. Value then becomes a tipping point for how these crimes are prioritized. Generally, in most jurisdictions, $100 to $250 worth of personal property stolen are felony values. Values exceeding $50,000 will usually place a theft case into the higher categories of criminal priorities. If other crimes are related to the theft, such as burglary or a multitiered con scheme, the case will also be prioritized, but thefts, such as embezzlements of cash from retail stores or businesses, are often handled by private security, who conduct internal audits and investigations to identify the thief. Situations in which large commercial establishments, such as banks and other financial institutions, have a serious embezzlement problem or a computer hacking scheme identified as targeting the company for theft evolve into major white collar crime investigations. The concern for these kinds of value-related priorities is the possibility that the theft will have a more community-wide impact. Banks have funds from hundreds or even thousands of victims in the community. Banks and other financial institutions are in many cases protected, or insured, against theft by the government, which means that taxpayer funds will be used to reimburse any losses. The impact may be small on individual taxpayers, but the theft is still a crime against the whole community.

For purposes of this text, larceny investigations will be considered as adjunct investigations that connect with crimes of violence or are shown to be relevant to a more substantial criminal conspiracy.

TRADITIONAL ORGANIZED CRIME

Organized crime is a pattern of criminal conduct that supports or bolsters one or more business enterprises to enrich the members of a specific group of co-conspirators and has as one of its main elements long-term success and survival. In the United States, many of these organized crime groups have certain ethnic or geographic aspects to membership. Membership in an organized crime group is usually the result of a person's successful career as a criminal, who then joins or begins an association with the criminal enterprise to take advantage of the financial, corrupt judicial, or corrupt political support provided by the group. These groups use violence and intimidation to ensure loyalty and approval of the ruling leadership. Soldiers or individual criminal members or associates are required to produce financial resources or to carry out violent crimes to further the goals of the group.

A number of criminal statutes have been established by state legislatures and the US Congress to effectively investigate and prosecute these groups. RICO (the Racketeer Influenced and Corrupt Organizations Act) is a primary federal statute, which is now the model for state laws dealing with the problem. In actuality, the requirements for a RICO case are simple. There must be proof of a criminal enterprise (money-making business) that is involved in a pattern of criminal conduct. The statute identifies the following two types of *enterprises*: (1) any legal business (e.g., dry-cleaning stores, restaurants, social clubs, insurance companies, stock brokerage companies, entertainment businesses, strip clubs, and bars) that acts as a conduit for illegal funds to be laundered so the funds will appear to be legally obtained funds and (2) an illegal business, such as drug dealing, gun running, and gambling. Proof that one of these two types of business enterprises is used by the organized crime group to produce profits, hide activities of the group, and further the goals of the organization requires the investigator to conduct a forensic audit of the funds used by the group or develop inside witnesses who can testify effectively about the flow of funds going in and out of the group, in other words, proof that a business is being conducted that is supported by criminal activity or is in fact criminal activity.

The pattern of criminal conduct is usually three or more serious felony crimes done by members of the group to further the goals of the organization. The crimes will vary with each statute, but in the federal RICO statute, it is a combination of local and federal crimes that qualify as predicate acts for proving the pattern. These crimes include murder, assault, illegal drug distribution, illegal gambling, prostitution, wire fraud, mail fraud, interstate transportation of stolen property, witness intimidation, and a number of other enumerated violations that are intended to cover the wide spectrum of criminal activity committed by members and leaders of these groups.

The primary justification for these statutes is the widely held belief among law enforcement that these criminal groups can be defeated only by an effective use of cross-jurisdiction and task force operations to bring all the state and federal resources needed to investigate and prosecute the management level and most violent offenders in these groups. Like many bureaucratic groups and organizations, *survival of the group* is the number one goal of an organized crime conspiracy. Criminal organizations will commit any crime to make sure they survive. Crimes of violence, bribery of public officials, and the criminal replenishment of financial resources will be immediate actions in response to an effective criminal investigation. Law enforcement needs to be able to effectively respond to these counterattacks to be successful. Too often, a lack of investigative resources and prosecutorial resources will allow an efficient organized crime group to frustrate, delay, or even derail a prosecution.

GANG CRIME

Over the past thirty years, urban violence has been attributed to the proliferation of street gangs. These gangs are, in many cases, neighborhood criminal conspiracies with profiles of membership, such as race, immigrant status, or ethnocentric factors. African American street gangs, such as the Bloods, the Crips, and the Black Gangster Disciples, have formed into national umbrella groups that adhere to principles established by the founders in large US cities such as Los Angeles, Chicago, and New York. Sets or cliques founded to conform with these principles have been established in African American communities across the country. Latino street gangs, such as the Almighty Latin Kings, MS-13, and the Norteños and Sureños factions in California, have formed into similar national and, in some cases, international umbrella groups, that encourage the founding and proliferation of productive and flexible cliques or neighborhood street gangs. Irish American gangs, skinheads, outlaw motorcycle gangs, and white supremacist gangs have also formed to commit violence as a structural component to ensure the gangs' survival. Numerous other immigrant groups have formed violent street gangs in the Asian and Pacific Rim communities throughout the United States. These gangs are often financed by an illegal enterprise or business, such as illegal drug distribution, gun running, or human trafficking. Some of the gangs have close ties to traditional organized crime groups, such as the Chinese Tong or Japanese Yakuza. In the early part of the twentieth century, Irish street gangs were mainstream organized crime entities with major financial support coming from bootlegging, gambling, and prostitution. These Irish gangs are now using their dominance in Irish immigrant neighborhoods in Boston, New York, and Chicago to maintain their existence. African American and Latino street gangs have risen in power and influence while dominating the sale and distribution of heroin, crack/cocaine, marijuana, fentanyl, and other street drugs. These drug distribution operations are huge money-making operations. Consequently, the gangs are becoming wealthier and sustained.

Every state in the United States has established gang statutes designed to target, disrupt, and dismantle these gangs. Unfortunately, the definition of what a gang is frustrates some of the cases from moving forward because the definition as per the state code needs to be proven in order to charge an offender with any of the underlying gang crimes. The simpler approach mentioned above in the organized crime discussion can be applied here. If the state statute is clear and applicable, the gang statutes are very similar to the RICO statute in the federal system. Proving the gang's business model and predicate criminal acts to charge gang crimes is the process for applying the statute. Gang crime predicate acts are generally the same as the RICO predicates for local crimes. Examples are murder, assault, rape, armed robbery, and drug distribution. State gang crime statutes also include more prevalent youth gang criminal violations, such as destruction of property (tagging gang territories) or violent or sex-related initiations to include jumping in gang members by beatings or sexual assaults. (These crimes are usually done with the consent of the victims, but charging violent gang behavior allows for more wide-ranging investigative proof.) From an investigative viewpoint, the focus should be on applying the local statutes and using the federal statutes if necessary. These cases are best worked in federal and local task force operations to take advantage of resources from both jurisdictions.

Some gang crimes on the surface may be considered minor offenses: thefts, marijuana dealing, physical assaults without the use of weapons, and minor retaliations against nongang members and opposing gang members. When these minor offenses occur in middle school or high school environments and indicate a substantial recruiting effort at the school, local police will prioritize these crimes and apply maximum resources at the problem. In most cases, federal resources will not be available for these investigations, but investigative units must work cases that the community prioritizes, and any threat to a safe school environment should not be tolerated.

CONSPIRACY TO COMMIT VIOLENCE

Our final discussion of statutory proof is *conspiracy to commit violence*. In the discussions of kidnapping, gangs, organized crime, and other of the above sections, there have been explanations of conspiracy in the context of particular criminal behavior. Conspiracy statutes exist in a general manner as an all-inclusive conspiracy to commit any criminal violation. In the federal system, 18 USC Section 371 says:

> If two or more persons conspire either to commit any offense against the United States, or to defraud the United States, or any agency thereof in any manner or for any purpose, and one or more of such persons do any act to effect the object of the conspiracy, each shall be fined under this title or imprisoned not more than five years, or both.
>
> If, however, the offense, the commission of which is the object of the conspiracy, is a misdemeanor only, the punishment for such conspiracy shall not exceed the maximum punishment provided for such misdemeanor.

Proof of the conspiracy includes showing with convincing testimony or documentary evidence that two or more persons agreed to commit a crime. This kind of proof can be difficult to obtain since most conspiracies occur during private conversations while the parties of the conspiracy work hard to avoid detection. If the crime is carried out and the parties of the conspiracy are proven by physical evidence and testimonial evidence to have combined to commit the crime, the evidence proving the conspiracy relies on the proof of the criminal act. In this fashion, criminal conspiracy can be charged in most cases where two or more persons commit the crime. There are also ongoing or continuing conspiracies where insiders are expected to be a part of the criminal conduct. In the case of a gang or organized crime entity, the conspiracy is part of acceptance of responsibility that the individual members are associates who know the nature of the group. Insider testimony can be sufficient proof to support a conspiracy in organized crime and gang activities if the insider can be shown to be reliable and truthful by independent corroboration with testimonial and physical evidence.

In the definitions used in most conspiracy statutes, the second and final element that needs to be proved is an act in the furtherance of the conspiracy. To use a simple example, two persons agree to murder a third person, and one of the two conspirators buys a weapon to be used in the murder. At this point, both parties are guilty of conspiracy. One further example would be if one person joins a drug gang that sells heroin and that person buys a quantity of cutting agent, such as mannitol, that person is then guilty of conspiracy with the drug gang (even though the purchase of mannitol is not a criminal act). In these two examples, the agreement and the act in the furtherance of the conspiracy constitute the crime.

Finally, individual crimes in both the state and federal systems recognize the seriousness of certain crimes and make an adjunct crime of conspiracy to those particular crimes. This recognizes that the criminal investigator and the police may thwart certain crimes from being committed but the conspiratorial act is so heinous that the punishment for conspiring should carry a punishment more in line with the punishment for the crime if it had been carried out.

SUMMARY

Developing an investigative plan or scheme usually begins with a comprehensive understanding of what needs to be proved. The elements of a criminal statute usually provide the best instruction for this purpose. It should be noted at this point that proving a case relies heavily on the input of witnesses and victims. In my experience in teaching criminal investigation, students often believe that forensic evidence and scientific results are the most important and reliable factors needed to prove a suspect is guilty. This is just not the case. A criminal investigator has to spend most of the time and energy solving a case by putting the whole event into a *human context*, relying on human witnesses and checking and verifying the strengths and weaknesses of witnesses and victims. The chart below provides a matrix detailing the obvious need for having witnesses and victims, which puts the crime in a human context, just as the persons who wrote the criminal statutes intended. The availability of scientific results that are both relevant and inculpatory is never a sure thing. Therefore, most cases will be solved by skillful communication with the victim and the witnesses in every case. The ability of the criminal investigator to communicate with a variety or a whole spectrum of society makes all the difference in how successful the investigator will be.

Table 2.1. Types of Crimes and Proof Chart

Crime	Types of Proof
Murder	
Causing the death of another person	Medical examiner expert analysis (scientific proof that death was the result of human action).
Knowingly, recklessly, or negligently	Shooting the person with a gun; stabbing the victim with a knife; driving a car into another person; disregarding the safety of others by perpetrating a life-threatening action without due consideration of the consequence. Witnesses, forensic proof, prior statement of the suspect.
Malice of forethought	Proving the suspect's desire to end the life of another. This requisite mindset can be decided with due consideration or may be the result of an immediate mental process. Witnesses, documents, analysis of actions, admission by the subject, provable facts and circumstances supporting motive.
Rape	
Forcible sexual intercourse	Victim and witness statements, medical examination, forensic evidence found at the crime scene (e.g., serological trace evidence of sexual contact, physical material at the scene that supports the fact that an *assault* occurred).
Against the victim's will	Victim and witness statements, medical examination, any physical evidence of *violence* or *coercion*.
Forced sodomy	Victim and witness statements.
Forced sexual assault	Victim and witness statements.

Crime	Types of Proof
Statutory rape	Producing an underage victim or victim with reduced mental capacity. The victim's state of mind is less important than the status of the victim, which would have to be proved. Witness statements.
Child molestation	Victim and witness statements, *expert opinion* by a recognized psychologist or a psychiatrist with significant experience in dealing with child trauma.
Assault with intent to kill	
An unlawful *attempt* or *offer* on the part of one person, with force or violence, to inflict a bodily hurt upon another	Victim and witness statements, forensic evidence from the crime scene, video surveillance, co-conspirator statements.
Battery: Any unlawful beating or other wrongful physical violence or constraint inflicted on a human being without that person's consent; includes gun and knife attacks.	Victim and witness statements; results of medical examination; photographs of the victim depicting wounds and physical harm; crime scene evidence, such as expended bullets or shell casings and blood spatter.
Intent to kill	Victim and witness statements, admission by the subject, provable facts and circumstances supporting motive.
Robbery	
The taking and carrying away of the property of another (usually felony value)	Evidence of taking money, jewelry, securities, any personal items of value usually valued higher than $250 in most jurisdictions. Victim and witness statements, inventories, evaluation by experts, security camera recordings.
By use of force	Weapons displayed; threats of force verified by witnesses; actual threats carried out, such as the pistol whipping of victims or the firing of weapons to emphasize the threat. Proof by victim and witness statements, security camera recordings, forensic evidence left at the scene (i.e., shell casings, blood, wounds on the victim).

Crime	Types of Proof
For personal use	Evidence that the robber kept or converted the proceeds. Admission by the subject, provable facts and circumstances supporting motive.
Larceny	
The taking and carrying away of the property of another	Proof that something of value belonged to the victim (payroll voucher, annuity voucher, indicia of wealth), witness testimony or statements, bank records, photographs of valuables in the possession of the victim.
Convert for personal use	Stolen property discovered in the possession of the suspect, conversion proof with postincident spending without proof of legitimate income, admission by the subject, provable facts and circumstances supporting motive.
Arson	
The burning of the dwelling house of another	Victim statements, crime scene analysis, forensic analysis provided by an expert arson investigator trained at the National Fire Academy or other certified academy.
Commercial arson	Insurance policy, financial data verifying the benefit of the property being destroyed.

The above chart gives six of the categories of crimes with the elements of these crimes detailed in the column on the left. The column on the right provides the most likely source of facts and evidence that will be used to prove each element. When a criminal investigator becomes part of a unit, squad, or division that is assigned to investigate crimes, the investigator should take the time to prepare a similar chart that she can use to break down the elements of the particular statutes she will be investigating. This is the first step in developing an investigative strategy or plan. Eventually, each element of every crime you investigate and then take to trial will need to be proved. When you anticipate the breakdown of the elements and begin to understand how each element is proven, you will begin to understand how investigations work.

Along with establishing your investigative plan, this kind of chart will provide insight into how to prioritize your investigative effort. You will recognize that witness and victims are the essential priority in making a case. Scientific evidence may provide significant incontrovertible facts, but as you work on more and more investigations, you will come to the conclusion that no case can be made without witnesses and victims to put the criminal activity in a human context. Cases can be solved without helpful scientific evidence that yields positive results, but they can't be solved without proving important elements of the crime in a human context.

Chapter Three

Constitutional Rights

Appropriate criminal investigative procedure and jurisdictional concerns are examined to explain due process *and* reasonable *procedures to follow to protect the rights of the accused.*

The US Constitution's first ten amendments are referred to as the Bill of Rights. These rights, or protections from unreasonable actions by the federal government, were developed as an extension of human rights considered essential to a free society and a society where the rule of law would be respected. The founding fathers, or authors, of the Constitution (circa 1787) believed that the government's (especially the federal government's) power should be restricted. So George Mason, James Madison, and members of the Virginia delegation to the Constitutional Convention considered these rights as necessary controls of a government that could at some point become as despotic as the English monarchy.

In the beginning, Virginia and other states applied these same restrictions to their own state constitutions. By this method, every US citizen would be protected by these

Source: Mark Rasmussen / Alamy Stock Photo C2C4GY

rights in their dealings with the state and federal governments. Generally, this was considered the appropriate method to ensure the rights of US citizens in our country. The states, for their part, were to be primarily concerned with curbing criminal conduct, controlling police actions, and ensuring the rights of the accused. In the words of the Constitution, the police powers resided with the states, not the federal government. But delegates to the Constitutional Convention wanted to ensure that these protections against unreasonable government actions were codified in the federal Constitution because of the mistrust many of the delegates had for the power they were getting ready to bestow on the US government. The Bill of Rights was the effective compromise between advocates of states' rights versus the federalist movement.

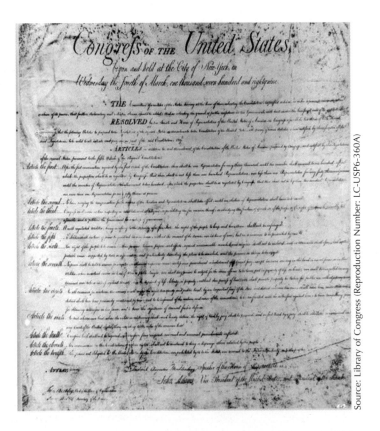

Source: Library of Congress (Reproduction Number: LC-USP6-360A)

With the passage of history and especially following the Civil War, the power of the federal government and its legal authority became more dominant. While the role of the federal government expanded, there were significant occasions when human rights were sacrificed in favor of states' rights. Concepts such as "separate but equal" government and commercial facilities became the norm throughout the country. As the Industrial Revolution took hold in the United States, the federal government began to be concerned about social issues, issues that affected the quality of life for the citizens. The federal courts evolved to become concerned that these "civil rights" of citizens were not being protected by the states. In the post–Civil War era, states in the

South endeavored to limit the voting rights of newly freed slaves. Congress and the states' constitutional conventions added the Fourteenth Amendment to the Constitution, the amendment that extended the Bill of Rights to all US citizens. The concept of *due process of law* was defined to include the rights of all citizens to be protected from unreasonable actions by states. Due process included the rights of the accused, the right to be free of "unreasonable searches," and the right to be protected against forced confessions. It also included the right to be protected from "giving testimony against yourself," the right to trials with a "jury of your peers," the demand for grand jury procedures, the right to have an attorney, and protections from "cruel and unusual punishment."

In spite of this extension of due process, it took extraordinary examples of injustice to get the courts to act to preserve these rights. In the 1932 cases of a series of Scottsboro, Alabama, trials of a group of young black defendants in a rape case, the facts were deemed to be a disturbing and grave injustice that the Supreme Court ruled in *Powell v. Alabama* that the defendants were denied their Sixth Amendment right to have an attorney. It was many years after this case that states began the process of finding a way to ensure that indigent defendants were routinely provided with this right, and it wasn't until *Gideon v. Wainwright* in the 1960s that this fundamental right was extended to all indigent defendants on a routine basis. Persons with the financial resources would have to hire their own attorneys, but defendants who could show the judge they didn't have the financial resources to pay could have competent legal counsel assigned by the court.

It actually took 100 years after the passage of the Fourteenth Amendment for most of these rights to be fully extended to all citizens. Following the Supreme Court decision in *Brown v. the Board of Education of Topeka, Kansas*, and the dismantlement of the concept of *separate but equal*, the Supreme Court became the arbiter of last resort to ensure that the rights of persons charged with a crime would have these rights secured. The rights enumerated in the Bill of Rights would become the framework for due process. Ultimately, what was missing was a rule that ensured that states and law enforcement in general would be penalized if a person's rights were not protected. The *exclusionary rule* was the extraordinary mandate that was used to ensure that the states abided by the rights and ensured the protections for all criminal defendants. Consider the fact that our rule of law provides that all persons are innocent until proven guilty. Evidence such as confessions, physical evidence from improper searches, and any "fruit" or direct result of improper actions by the state and law enforcement would be thrown out of court, thereby gutting a case. Investigations that relied on improperly obtained evidence or evidence that secondarily resulted from improperly obtained evidence were equally banished from use by the state. An investigation that did not follow the tenets of due process would be dismantled even if the evidence against the defendant was overwhelming. The guilt or innocence of the defendant would not be relevant if law enforcement acted improperly to uncover the evidence proving guilt.

The immediate and, in many ways, continuing reaction to this sea change in the application of the rights of the accused by law enforcement is that cases that fail to meet the constitutional requirements are considered lost for mere administrative reasons, or due to a technicality. The failure to follow the process established by the Constitution is not a technicality; it is a failure of a law enforcement officer to abide by his oath of office. It is also a violation of the well-established belief that these rights represent fundamental fairness in our system of justice. The only troubling area in this controversy is the fact that some judges who are sometimes swayed by public outrage, previous corrupt conduct, or an imbalance in their own perspective call actions that properly and objectively follow the constitutional requirements improper. Be that as it may, the trial judge, and/or his immediate appeal judge or panel, is adhering to the system of justice by which criminal investigators' actions are judged for fairness and reasonableness. Accepting that the rulings are a necessary part of our system may be considered a disappointing but necessary fact of life. The criminal investigator should very simply disregard the technicality argument and remember that if the investigator follows the Constitution, her case will be more just, fair, and solid. Taking the time to compose a proper search warrant affidavit allows the investigator to organize and detail the facts of an investigation for review by an uninvolved third party, who will then be able to provide valuable criticism of the case. Taking the proper steps to conduct an interview or interrogation of a criminal suspect and following proper steps to prove the defendant waived his right to have an attorney present allow the investigator to use the information from the interrogation freely and without reservation. There should never be a need to threaten, torture, coerce, or otherwise force a confession or admission from a defendant in a free society.

Following the constitutional requirements to protect the integrity of confessions or admissions by a defendant is another example of how the investigation will be stronger and stand up to judicial review. Other constitutional requirements, such as trial by a jury of a defendant's peers, a grand jury indictment, protection against double jeopardy, and the right to counsel are in the hands of the judicial branch of government and do not directly relate to the responsibilities of the criminal investigator, but as interested parties, professional law enforcement officers need to make sure they do nothing that interferes with those rights. In general, it is in the interest of the professional law enforcement officers to make sure the right to due process for a criminal defendant is not abridged. The protection and enforcement of the rights of the accused are not only proper and fair; they are, as I stated above, the responsibility of a professional law enforcement officer because the oath of office usually includes a sworn statement that she will uphold the Constitution.

As a result of a series of landmark Supreme Court cases, law enforcement had to evolve to become more professional and educated about the rights of the accused. Investigators have to be able to follow the leads in an investigation and make sure that the rights of the accused are not compromised. Below is a summary of the specific amendments in the Bill of Rights that relate to criminal procedure and how they apply to the rights of the accused.

THE RIGHTS OF THE ACCUSED

Fourth Amendment

"The right of the people to be secure in their persons, houses, papers, and effects, against *unreasonable searches and seizures*, shall not be violated, *and no Warrants shall issue, but upon probable cause, supported by Oath or affirmation*, and particularly describing the place to be searched and the persons or things to be seized."

Fifth Amendment

"No person shall be held to answer for a capital, or otherwise infamous crime, unless on a *presentment or indictment of a grand jury*, except in cases arising in the land or naval forces, or in the militia, when in actual service in time of war or public danger; nor shall any person be subject for the same offence to *be twice put in jeopardy of life or limb*; nor shall be compelled in any criminal case to be *a witness against himself*; nor be deprived of life, liberty, or property, without *due process of law*; nor shall private property be taken for public use without just compensation."

Sixth Amendment

"In all criminal prosecutions, the accused shall enjoy the right to a *speedy and public trial* by an impartial jury of the state and district wherein the crime shall have been committed, which district shall have been previously ascertained by law, and to be informed of the nature and cause of the accusation. The accused shall also have the right to be confronted with the witnesses against him, to have compulsory process for obtaining witnesses in his favor, and to have the *assistance of counsel* for his defense."

Eighth Amendment

"Excessive bail shall not be required, nor excessive fines imposed, nor cruel and unusual punishments inflicted."

Fourteenth Amendment

This amendment was passed in 1868 and applied to the states in the mid-twentieth century. As we begin our study of how the US Constitution, the Bill of Rights, and the constitutional construct known as due process affect how we conduct criminal investigations, it is helpful to explain why it is in place and why it affects how we carry out our criminal justice system. For the most part, the foundations of our democracy and our republican form of government are a direct reaction to martial law imposed by the British Crown. We the people wanted more and we detailed in our founding documents what that "more" was and is.

Section 1

"All persons born or naturalized in the United States, and subject to the jurisdiction thereof, are citizens of the United States and of the State wherein they reside. *No State shall make or enforce any law which shall abridge the privileges or immunities of citizens of the United States; nor shall any State deprive any person of life, liberty, or property, without due process of law; nor deny to any person within its jurisdiction the equal protection of the laws.*"

Section 2

"Representatives shall be apportioned among the several States according to their respective numbers, counting the whole number of persons in each State, excluding Indians not taxed. But when the right to vote at any election for the choice of electors for President and Vice President of the United States, Representatives in Congress, the Executive and Judicial officers of a State, or the members of the Legislature thereof, is denied to any of the male inhabitants of such State, being twenty-one years of age, and citizens of the United States, or in any way abridged, except for participation in rebellion, or other crime, the basis of representation therein shall be reduced in the proportion which the number of such male citizens shall bear to the whole number of male citizens twenty-one years of age in such State."

Section 3

"No person shall be a Senator or Representative in Congress, or elector of President and Vice President, or hold any office, civil or military, under the United States, or under any State, who, having previously taken an oath, as a member of Congress, or as an officer of the United States, or as a member of any State legislature, or as an executive or judicial officer of any State, to support the Constitution of the United States, shall have engaged in insurrection or rebellion against the same, or given aid or comfort to the enemies thereof. But Congress may, by a vote of two-thirds of each House, remove such disability."

Section 4

"The validity of the public debt of the United States, authorized by law, including debts incurred for payment of pensions and bounties for services in suppressing insurrection or rebellion, shall not be questioned. But neither the United States nor any State shall assume or pay any debt or obligation incurred in aid of insurrection or rebellion against the United States, or any claim for the loss or emancipation of any slave; but all such debts, obligations and claims shall be held illegal and void."

Section 5

"The Congress shall have power to enforce, by appropriate legislation, the provisions of this article."

LANDMARK SUPREME COURT CASES

These case reviews are not meant to be flawless legal interpretations of the most important cases but rather are meant to provide instruction to criminal investigation students about the signifance of these cases and their impact on law enforcement today. Comprehensive legal briefs on these cases are available from a number of law libraries, and there are scholarly examinations of these cases available for the serious student conducting research. These summaries are meant to explain how the day-to-day actions of law enforcement professionals should be adjusted to meet the standards inherent in these landmark rulings. Key elements of concern are laid out so it is easy for the student to meet the standards and follow the procedures suggested by these cases.

Right to Counsel (Sixth Amendment)

As a practical matter, the right to counsel is not a constitutional requirement for which the law enforcement officer has any direct responsibility. Investigators have to directly *remind* criminal defendants that they have the right to stay silent and the right to an attorney, who will be appointed if they can't afford one, but it is not the responsibility of the investigator to go beyond that admonition. It is not the responsibility of the criminal investigator to provide that attorney. It is also improper for a criminal investigator to make recommendations about defense counsel or to let defense counsel know anything about a particular investigation. All government communication with a defense attorney should be handled by the prosecutor's office. The prosecutor (a district or US attorney or other governmental prosecutor) is responsible for these contacts. The prosecutor may ask the criminal investigator to provide access to evidence and investigative reports, but for the most part, the criminal investigator should keep the relationship with defense attorneys at arm's length and very professional.

Our system of criminal justice is an adversarial system in which government investigators are responsible to the people of their jurisdiction and not the interests of a single citizen who is charged with a crime. This does not mean that criminal investigators should be myopic, disconnected, or unfair in their actions. It is ultimately the responsibility of the criminal investigators to seek and find the truth. If members of defense counsel offer an alibi for their client or provide an investigative lead that they think will help exonerate their client, it is the job of the criminal investigator to thoroughly investigate that information and adjust the analysis of the criminal case if needed. More often than not, defense attorneys don't trust the objectivity of law enforcement to conduct this kind of follow-through investigation, but a successful criminal investigator will want to take these steps to ensure that the truth is discovered.

So, as stated, making sure the defendant has the assistance of a lawyer is not under the control of the criminal investigator, but it is a part of due process that places the burden on the criminal investigator to inform and remind a criminal defendant of his rights. It is a matter of fundamental fairness that a defendant, especially a defendant who has never faced criminal charges, be in a position to ask for an attorney and have an attorney protect his interests throughout the process. This concept of fundamental fairness for criminal defendants began in 1932 and progressed through 1963 when the law regarding the state and federal governments' responsibilities for the right to counsel was settled.

Court-Appointed Counsel

Currently, if a person is charged with a felony offense in local, state, or federal court (a criminal violation that carries a penalty of one year or more) and she does not have the financial resources to pay for an attorney, the person can ask for a court-appointed lawyer. A criminal defendant has the right to refuse the assistance of an attorney and can act to defend herself, but in these kinds of cases, the presiding judge will very likely suggest that the defendant change her mind and accept the help of an attorney. This waiver of the right to counsel has to be a knowing waiver. If the defendant is determined to be mentally incompetent by the judge, the waiver will not be allowed. States, counties, and federal jurisdictions derive court-appointed attorneys from a variety of lawyer pools. There are state and federal public defender agencies, local Bar Association rosters where criminal defense attorneys are assigned on a rotating basis, and major legal partnerships that provide pro bono services (free services) to indigent defendants to meet their responsibilities to the Bar Association and to their company's financial charitable contributions.

Public defenders' agencies are law firms established and paid for with taxpayer funding. They are government employees whose main goal is to defend indigent clients from the particular jurisdiction. Since these agencies are usually overworked and underpaid, they have to carefully consider what cases they can take on and what cases may get them involved in some kind of conflict of interest. For example, if multiple defendants are charged in a single criminal conspiracy, the public defender's office may take on only one of the members of the conspiracy. This limitation and other serious conflicts will lead to the public defender services needing the assistance of outside private attorneys to handle all the clients in large urban jurisdictions. As a result, court-appointed attorneys will be assigned by judges from various pools of criminal defense attorneys. Many of the court-appointed attorneys are paid from public funds at a rate that is usually less than their normal fees, but occasionally, these fees can be more reliable than waiting for payments from private parties. Public defenders face the same financial challenges as most government employees; therefore, it is hard to claim financial hardship to the taxpayers when police and prosecutors are in the same difficulty.

All of these variations tend to have an impact on the quality of the legal services, but again, they should have no effect on how a criminal investigator conducts the case. In the real world, experienced, high-quality attorneys from Bar Association pools and legal partnerships acting pro bono can be found in public defender services. They can also be going against newly minted, less experienced attorneys who work for the local prosecutors' offices. It is impossible to determine in many jurisdictions if court-appointed counsel is somehow inferior to well-paid private counsel. Again, this should have no effect on the quality of the investigation. A review of the Supreme Court cases that affect the issues relating to the right to an attorney follow.

Powell v. Alabama, 287 US 45 (1932)

In March 1931, nine black men—Charles Weems, Ozie Powell, Clarence Norris, Olen Montgomery, Willie Roberson, Haywood Patterson, Andrew (Andy) Wright, Leroy (Roy) Wright, and Eugene Williams—were accused of raping two young white women, Ruby Bates and Victoria Price, on a train in rural Alabama near Scottsboro. The group of young black men were traveling on a freight train with seven white men and two women. A fight broke out, and all but one of the white men were thrown from the train. The women accused the black men of rape, although one woman later retracted her claim.

All of the defendants, except for thirteen-year-old Leroy Wright, were sentenced to death in a series of three one-day trials. The defendants, who were under military guard to protect them from any mob violence, were not told they could hire lawyers or even contact their families. They had no access to a lawyer until shortly before trial, leaving little or no time to plan the defense. They appealed their convictions on the grounds that the group was not provided adequate legal counsel. The Alabama Supreme Court ruled 7–2 that the trial was fair. Chief Justice Anderson wrote a strongly worded dissenting opinion. The defendants appealed the Alabama Supreme Court's ruling to the US Supreme Court.

The Supreme Court reversed and remanded, holding that due process had been violated. Writing for himself and six other justices, Justice George Sutherland explained the Court's ruling as follows:

> In the light of the . . . ignorance and illiteracy of the defendants, their youth, the circumstances of public hostility, the imprisonment and the close surveillance of the defendants by the military forces, the fact that their friends and families were all in other states and communication with them necessarily difficult, and above all that they stood in deadly peril of their lives—we think the failure of the trial court to give them reasonable time and opportunity to secure counsel was a clear denial of due process. But passing that, and assuming their inability, even if opportunity had been given, to employ counsel, . . . under the circumstances just stated, the necessity of counsel was so vital and imperative that the failure of the trial court to make an effective appointment of counsel was likewise a denial of due process within the meaning of the Fourteenth Amendment.

The Supreme Court limited its ruling in this case to include capital cases (death penalty cases) and also limited its ruling to state that the defendants had to be incapable of mounting their own defenses due to feeblemindedness, or lack of intelligence, but the case opened Pandora's box in defining what due process could mean and thereby extending the wording of the Fourteenth Amendment to cover state actions that were deemed unconstitutional.

In its ruling, the Supreme Court found that the defendants were treated fundamentally unfair and, as a result, it was the state's responsibility to not only provide counsel but that counsel had to be at least adequate and capable of providing a reasonable defense. In this case, an attorney assigned to one of the defendants was a real estate lawyer with no experience in criminal law.

Eventually there was a second and third trial in this case, which involved still another due process concern. This time there was a lack of African American jurors on the jury, and the case devolved into a significant case of racial injustice. Ultimately, five of the defendants were found guilty and sent to prison. Two escaped, and the oldest defendant lived long enough to be pardoned by the governor of Alabama. All of the five convicted defendants were released from custody or had escaped by 1946.

Johnson v. Zerbst, 304 US 458 (1938)

In 1937, defendants Johnson and Birdwell were convicted in federal court in Charleston, South Carolina, of felony charges relating to the possession of counterfeit US currency. Johnson and Birdwell provided their own defense in the trial, and according to the record, their efforts were marginal at best. Neither man had much education or any legal training. The Supreme Court, following the lead from *Powell v. Alabama*, extended the protections of the Sixth Amendment to all felony trials in federal court. The justices determined that absent a knowing waiver of the right to have an attorney, indigent defendants could ask for court-appointed counsel. Eventually, this ruling became the basis for Rule 44 of the Federal Rules of Procedure and allowed for the establishment of court-appointed counsel and the federal public defender's services. In his ruling, the Supreme Court Justice Hugo Black provided the following concerns: "The Court has looked to the gravity of the crime, the age and education of the defendant, the conduct of the court and the prosecuting officials, and the complicated nature of the offense charged and possible defenses thereto."

Johnson v. Zerbst did not apply to the state court system, which stated in *Betts v. Brady*, 316 US 455 (1942), that the due process clause was less rigid and more fluid when applied to state courts. Justice Owen Roberts said in his ruling that the Sixth Amendment doesn't demand that a defendant have an attorney in all cases and fundamental fairness does not require that a defendant needs defense counsel. In his ruling, he further suggested *legislative action* to establish policy for state criminal courts in felony matters.

Gideon v. Wainwright, 372 US 335 (1963)

In June 1961, Clarence Gideon was charged and ultimately convicted of a commercial burglary and petty larceny from a pool hall in Panama City, Florida. He was sentenced to five years in prison. Prior to trial, he asked for and was refused an appointed attorney to represent him because he was indigent. Subsequently, while in prison, he filed a handwritten appeal to the Supreme Court stating that he had been denied his Sixth Amendment right to counsel.

The Supreme Court provided counsel to Gideon, and by a unanimous opinion written in 1963 by Justice Hugo Black, the appeal was ruled in favor of Gideon. This case therefore extended the right to counsel to indigent defendants charged with felony offenses (generally, charges where the defendant faces more than one year in jail) in state courts who requested attorney assistance. This case reached that extraordinary level of bringing about a fundamental change in the way the criminal justice system works in this country. Again, this change has very little effect on how criminal investigations should proceed, but it does ensure that any person charged in a case will ultimately be able to review the facts with the help of a professional defense attorney. The defense attorney needs to make sure his cases are carefully well-ordered, fair, and ultimately truthful based on the evidence and supporting material uncovered in an investigation. As far as criminal investigators are concerned, the selection and proficiency of defense counsel is and should be of little concern. Investigators should work carefully and with great objectivity to find the truth and ensure the right person or persons are charged with the crime. When the defendant is facing a court or a trial procedure, it is only fair that she has effective defense counsel. Although the criminal investigator is usually in an adversarial relationship with the defense attorney, there should be no animosity or unprofessional conduct between the two. The one important concern that a criminal investigator should be concerned about is that any discovery prior to trial is properly handled by the prosecutor so the case is not negatively affected by investigative reports that are not properly distributed to the defense counsel. This aspect of discovery is not the responsibility of the investigator, but a failure to follow proper procedure can put the case in jeopardy. I will discuss *Brady and Giglio* material in the context of landmark rulings later in this chapter, but the key aspect of discovery is that the rules have to be followed or a judge can rule a violation of the Constitution and dismiss the case.

Finally, there will be occasions when a criminal investigator needs to conduct a subject interview or interrogation in the presence of an attorney. The defense attorney in this case will attempt to control the information the defendant shares with the investigator. This is a legally accepted practice, but the investigator should make it clear in his report that the legal counsel affected the information provided by the suspect. The investigator will also need to sharply focus the inquiry to keep the defendant from answering questions so broadly that the answers have little weight as evidence, keep the interrogation on track, and aggressively cover the points that need to be covered.

When a defendant has an attorney present during an interview, it is clear that his rights are being protected, so any and all areas of an inquiry should be thoroughly covered to include relationships with the victim, timeline questions, motive questions, and alibi questions. Other important information, such as the defendant's criminal history, work history, and background talents and resources should be detailed in the interview report. Nothing should be off limits in this kind of interview. In a standard interrogation, the investigator may want to avoid sensitive areas of discussion to make sure the defendant continues to talk in the interview. If an attorney is present and the interrogator has sensitive questions to ask, let the defense attorney protect her client.

We move on with a discussion about search warrants and the Supreme Court cases that govern an investigator's responsibility in this area of the law.

SIGNIFICANT SUPREME COURT
CASES AFFECTING FOURTH AMENDMENT RIGHTS

The paragraphs below provide a brief description of the process of obtaining a search warrant, with case briefs and summaries of many of the most significant landmark cases that affect search and seizure of evidence and directly apply to criminal investigations.

Search Warrant Affidavits

A search warrant is a judicial order signed by a judge or magistrate who is authorized by law to issue such an order, meaning the judicial officer has the right to demand that appropriate law enforcement officials go to a specific location to discover and find evidence of a crime. This judicial officer is therefore acting in accordance with the limitations placed on him by the Fourth Amendment of the US Constitution, legal precedence, and statutory authority. The constitutional prohibition is against unreasonable searches. The judge or magistrate must have a finding of probable cause based on a legally sufficient affidavit supporting the issuance of the warrant. This finding of probable cause makes the search reasonable. This circumstance then becomes part of the due process of law, meeting the standards set in the Bill of Rights for civil protection against unbridled government intrusion into the home of a citizen.

The best response to all of the potential uncertainty in gathering evidence in an investigation is for the law enforcement officer to be prepared to write a sufficient affidavit detailing facts that a magistrate or judge can read and be able to find probable cause. The investigator needs to recognize that his work is part of the due process of law and his actions should always be subject to review.

Any affidavit submitted for a search warrant should be written in plain English as a narrative. It is appropriate to use a third-person or first-person narrative and refer to the author as the "affiant." (An affiant is identified by statute as a person with appropriate legal authority to execute a search warrant.) The document is a presentation of the relevant facts to the judge or magistrate.

The affidavit should contain an introductory paragraph providing the experience and training of the affiant. It should contain positive statements from witnesses—descriptions known firsthand by the affiant or police officers or agents who are reporting facts to the affiant and considerations supported by significant law enforcement experience or information provided in training and provided to law enforcement officers. The affidavit should contain a complete and accurate description of the property to be searched. It should contain a summary of the evidence the affiant expects to find in the search. It must not be construed to provide the affiant with a general search for evidence or in any way to allow what can be construed to be a fishing expedition search.

It should be noted that very few cases reach the Supreme Court challenging the finding by any magistrate that probable cause exists supporting the issuance of a search warrant. In fact, for a defense attorney to challenge a finding of probable cause is extremely rare. This is why criminal investigators should be careful in their preparation and crafting of an affidavit to ensure that the affidavit provides the judge or magistrate with the proper jurisdictional identification of the affiant. The judge or magistrate is told in a general way that the affiant is trained and experienced, which allows the judge or magistrate to rely on the affiant. The property to be searched is correctly described. The items to be seized are specific, as required by search and seizure precedence, or fit in a category of evidence discovered in plain view. The facts constituting probable cause are articulated in plain English and fully supported by the affiant's investigation, whether the evidence is direct, observable, circumstantial, hearsay, or otherwise legally probative for probable cause. The following landmark cases are the basis for most of the rules or procedures that should be followed to recover physical evidence through the process of any investigation.

Mapp v. Ohio, *367 US 643 (1961)*

Dollree Mapp was convicted of possessing obscene materials after an admittedly illegal police search of her home for a fugitive. She appealed her conviction on the basis of freedom of expression.

In May 1957, Mapp, upon advice from her attorney, refused to allow Cleveland, Ohio, police officers entry into her home. The officers did not have a search warrant, and therefore, she was within her rights to deny them entry. The police had an anonymous tip that a suspect in a bombing was hiding in her home and that she was involved in illegal gambling. They did place the house under surveillance. A half day later, the police returned with a paper indicating they had a warrant, and they began their search. They secured the premises, handcuffed Mapp, and located their bombing suspect. They also recovered betting slips, gambling paraphernalia, a pistol, and a cache of pornographic pictures and books. No warrant had actually been obtained, and the state of Ohio refused to acknowledge the ruse paper presented as a warrant. Mapp was arrested and charged with possession of the gambling evidence, but that case was dismissed. She subsequently refused to cooperate with the state's investigation of the organized gambling ring with which she allegedly was involved and which had attempted to extort and threaten a rival gambling operation's leader.

Mapp was arrested again and charged with knowingly possessing the pornographic materials. She was convicted and sentenced to one to seven years in prison. Mapp's appeal was her belief that the police did not have probable cause to search her house for pornographic materials, and since the police didn't have a warrant, her appeal was the denial of her Fourth Amendment right against an unreasonable search and seizure.

Mapp's attorneys offered two theories for overturning the case. The confiscated pornographic material was protected by the First Amendment, and the search without a warrant was a clear violation of the Fourth Amendment.

The court disregarded the First Amendment issue and declared that "all evidence obtained by searches and seizures in violation of the Constitution is, hereby [the Fourth Amendment], inadmissible in a state court." Mapp had been convicted on the basis of illegally obtained evidence. This was a historic and controversial decision. It placed the requirement of excluding illegally obtained evidence from court at all levels of the government. The exclusion of evidence obtained in an illegal search and seizure was in this case ruled inadmissible and subject to the court's previously established *exclusionary rule*. (The exclusionary rule was used in *Weeks v. United States*, 232 US 383 [1914], against the federal government marshals who obtained documents and records of using the US mail to facilitate a gambling enterprise.) Since *Mapp v. Ohio*, this rule has been the court's only reasonable method to ensure that illegally obtained evidence was not used in state and local trials.

The exclusionary rule continued to be controversial in a 1963 Supreme Court case having to do with drug trafficking, *Wong Sun v. United States*, 371 US 471 (1963). Admissions and physical evidence were recovered by federal agents who entered a laundry business without a warrant, and their presence pressured the defendant (Sun) and another trafficker (Jonny) to admit drug dealing when drugs were found in their possession. Wong Sun's attorney argued that the evidence was obtained as the result of an illegal search in violation of the Fourth Amendment. The court ruled that the admissions and other evidence were "fruits of a poisonous tree," a legal metaphor first stated in a federal case in the 1930s that banned "derivative" evidence from being used in a case where the initial evidence was tainted or obtained illegally. It was at this point that federal and state restrictions on the use of illegally obtained evidence were conflated and law enforcement in federal and state jurisdictions were limited in the same manner from using constitutionally banned evidence.

In *Brewer v. Williams*, 430 US 387 (1977), and *Nix v. Williams*, 467 US 431 (1984), the Supreme Court reviewed the case of a defendant who kidnapped and killed a ten-year-old child, Pamela Powers. Williams requested at the time of his arrest that he not be interrogated until he was removed back to the jurisdiction from which he had been charged with the crime. During his transport back to the jurisdiction, one of his law enforcement escorts appealed to his humanity about the child, whose remains were about to be covered by a pending snowfall. Williams agreed and provided information to the investigator as to where the child's remains could be found. Williams's admissions and the information about the location of the child were used to convict him. In a previous case, *Brewer v. Williams* (1977), the Court ruled that Williams's right to counsel had been violated, thus tainting the evidence relating to the discovery of the child's body and the evidence on the body. The Supreme Court justice noted in his opinion that it was likely that the police would inevitably discover the body and, because of this, the body and the evidence on the body might be an exception to the *fruits of the poisonous tree doctrine* and thereby the exclusionary rule exception.

The Supreme Court avoided painting evidence obtained in the normal course of investigation and evidence recovered as the result of well-meaning intentions with too broad a brush. Well-meaning actions by police that were not meant to be coercive should be evaluated to determine if the actions were meant to be violations of the defendant's rights. The likelihood that evidence of importance should not be immediately dismissed (if there is sufficient belief that it would have been discovered anyway) can and should be reviewed to determine if its use is acceptable. Evidence that may be tainted by the corrupt intentions of law enforcement officers, if its exclusion would have a deleterious effect on the administration of justice, has to be carefully reviewed and analyzed to make sure it is not dismissed for a cause that is frivolous or unjustified. These are areas of legal analysis that lead to further narrowing of the exclusionary rule, but for the criminal investigator, it is essential that actions that can be viewed as corrupt should be scrupulously avoided and that the criminal investigator should maintain a higher standard than the rule set to protect the integrity of the investigation. If investigative steps taken are subject to broad interpretation that includes corrupt practice, the professional criminal investigator should make every effort to exclude the behavior or find a way to clarify that the investigative steps were proper and legal.

The *Nix* case was supported by seven of the nine justices, thereby giving the exclusionary rule exception a strong basis for evaluating how much damage is done to constitutionally questionable evidence. Evaluating the actions by law enforcement to determine if evidence is properly obtained can occur, but a skilled professional law enforcement officer will take steps to ensure that there is scant chance for the evidence to be excluded. Follow the rules, and view the Constitution as a guiding spirit in your investigations. That way you will protect the rights of the accused to make your case credible, productive, and reliable.

Personal Experience

During my career as a criminal investigator in the early 1980s, I had an occasion to conduct an investigation of a stolen car ring in which high-dollar luxury cars were stolen and delivered to a warehouse in northeast Washington, DC. A very reliable confidential informant told me on a particular night that four cars were going to be delivered to the warehouse but he didn't know the exact address, only that it was in a neighborhood where several other similar warehouses were located. I was able to get the assistance of nine other agents and police officers to surveil the neighborhood. We missed the delivery of the vehicles, but the source was able to provide firsthand proof as to where the cars were delivered and told us the car thieves had dropped off the cars at the warehouse and would return the next day at 10:00 a.m. to get paid. We went to the address, and it matched the description provided by the source. We established a security perimeter around the building and discovered it was locked up tight and no persons were inside. I had probable cause for a search warrant, but it was 11:00 p.m. Late-night search warrants in a city the size of Washington, DC, could be obtained through night-duty judges and prosecutors.

The normal procedure was for the investigator to write an affidavit and provide the affidavit to the prosecutor for approval, and then the prosecutor would notify the night-duty judge that a criminal investigator would be bringing a search warrant to him to have the search warrant signed and approved. I wrote the affidavit at the location so we wouldn't lose control of the scene. I was able to transmit the affidavit to the night-duty prosecutor, who approved the affidavit but refused to contact the night-duty judge until the morning. It was difficult for me to believe that this reluctance was nothing more than an opportunity for the prosecutor to exercise his power and control over me and my fellow investigators. I pointed out to him that all of us had been working all day on this case and the sooner we were able to get inside the warehouse, find out who owned it, and recovered the stolen cars, the sooner we would be able to go home to our families. Otherwise, he was making us wait to hold security on the evidence all night long. He still refused to bother the judge. I pointed out to him that this was just the kind of obstruction cops felt happened often enough to avoid getting warrants even when they had plenty of time. I said search warrants should not be hard to obtain if the investigation has been sufficiently conducted. This was especially true if there was a system that was set up to handle emergency or off-hours warrants. The prosecutor's response to me was that my case was "just a stolen car case." It didn't warrant any emergency. I told him that wasting the time of ten criminal investigators properly involved in a criminal investigation of multiple felonies made the matter an emergency. He refused to relent. I called the management of my agency, who thereupon called the boss of the prosecutor, and within a few hours, we had our search warrant, which we executed, allowing us to recover four $80,000 automobiles and identify the leader of the car theft ring.

The Importance of Search Warrants

The reason cases such as *Mapp v. Ohio* became the law of the land is because search warrants were not viewed by old-school police as steps in the investigative process that should be routine for criminal investigators. Search warrants were considered unnecessary disruptions. I made it my own practice to be ready to get search warrants as often as possible. The evidence recovered is always protected from dismissal and is usually very relevant in proving the facts in any investigation. It is not only good practice in a criminal investigation to obtain search warrants, but it is also the best way to apply real legal pressure on a target in an investigation while maintaining the appropriate control and legal authority in a case. Anytime you exercise your authority within the proper constitutional context, you are making the suspect aware that you are making your case properly and with integrity. A career criminal should begin to believe that your work will inevitably lead to the proof needed to win a conviction.

In chapter 9 of this book, I will discuss probable cause and what it means, but at this point, it is important for the student to consider that search warrants and other steps required by the Constitution may seem "limiting." The ability of the criminal investigator to abide by due process in this instance and in others, is just the opposite. "Taking a breath" in an investigation to review the facts and detailing those facts in an affidavit allows the investigator to take stock of the facts he knows and how those facts can move the case forward. Organization of an investigation should always include evaluation and review.

In fictional accounts of criminal investigators, there is often some reference to a "gut feeling," an extrasensory perception. Gut feelings in criminal investigations often derive from experience and a déjà vu a veteran criminal investigator has when the case is proceeding. Judges will in many cases rely on these gut feelings if they are properly articulated as elements of the professional law enforcement officer's experience and training. When properly detailed in an affidavit, these kinds of police judgments may offer the small but significant piece that provides enough probable cause in a case. When a search warrant is properly obtained and the results of the search are not successful, the fact that the investigator obtained a search warrant indemnifies him and his investigation from frivolous accusations of improper conduct. It also allows him to continue the investigation uninterrupted. He will have time to determine if his judgment or timing was wrong. When a search warrant is not obtained and the officer's actions are deemed improper and a violation of the Constitution, myriads of bad results can happen, including a total dismantling of an important investigation. This simple binary summary should be enough to encourage all persons who wish to become professional law enforcement officers to "take that breath" and have their cases evaluated and reviewed whenever possible. Get the search warrant, and take that important step forward in your investigation.

Warrantless Searches

In the previous section of this text, a lot of time and thought was spent suggesting that a competent professional law enforcement officer should always take the step of procuring a search warrant, even when the progress of an investigation may seem to be impaired. Keeping that in mind, there are occasions in criminal investigations when searches without a warrant are appropriate. These warrantless searches account for a large number of Supreme Court cases meant to provide clarity to officers about when it is acceptable to forgo obtaining a search warrant. If I were a Supreme Court justice, I might tell you in almost all cases to get a warrant, but there are confrontations, scenarios, and encounters for which it is impossible or impractical to do so. Think of the range from impossible to impractical as scale from 1–10. Ten is impossible, and 1 is impractical. Any scenario lower than 1 requires a warrant. Generally, there are two standards for forgoing a search warrant. One is that you have probable cause, but a delay on your part to get a warrant will result in the loss of the evidence (critical evidence) in your investigation. The other standard is that you are suspicious of the actions and the activity of a suspect, so you ask permission of that suspect to "let you look" (search) at personal property or in a location for evidence, and the suspect gives you permission. Is your request too coercive? Is the environment or your demeanor so coercive that the suspect believes she has no choice?

So having probable cause but also an honest belief that evidence will be lost in the time it takes to get a warrant is one basis for a warrantless search. Being suspicious and simply asking for permission to search—with the understanding that the suspect has the right to deny permission, and having the understanding that law enforcement actions and demeanor should not be so oppressive as to make the suspect believe he has no choice but to comply—is the second reasonable basis for conducting a warrantless search.

Carroll v. the United States, *267 US 132 (1925)*

In 1925, federal prohibition agents conducted a traffic stop on George Carroll, near Detroit, Michigan. The agents were aware that Carroll and his compatriot were bootleggers of illegal alcohol, which was in violation of the Volstead Act. The federal agents searched the vehicle and found the contraband alcohol. Carroll and his partner were arrested and eventually convicted of the federal violation of the liquor possession. Carroll asked for the Supreme Court to review the case to determine if there was a violation of the Fourth Amendment and consider whether the federal agents should have obtained a search warrant for the vehicle. The Court ruled in establishing the *Carroll Doctrine*, which states that because a vehicle is mobile and could be easily transported elsewhere, vehicles are not subject to the same protection as homes and offices, where a suspect enjoys the Fourth Amendment protections. In the wording of their decision, they stated that practical law enforcement should obtain a warrant. In practice, if law enforcement agents have probable cause, they can search a vehicle they encounter for evidence of the crime for which they have probable cause. In other words, it is not carte blanche and open season for warrantless searches of vehicles. There has to be a finding of probable cause for the evidence obtained to be admissible. The professional law enforcement officer (criminal investigator) has to be able to *articulate* the probable cause to a judge for the evidence to be available and admissible.

In the Supreme Court case *Arkansas v. Sanders*, 442 US 753 (1979), the court ruled that closed and locked containers in a vehicle are outside of the authority granted by Carroll. In *United States v. Ross*, 456 US 798 (1982), the Supreme Court ruled that containers, such as bags or zippered valises, are subject to warrantless searches if the police have probable cause. The rules governing Carroll Doctrine searches of automobiles are not fully settled. On the one hand, the Carroll Doctrine is controlling, but it is in the interest of a criminal investigator with probable cause to consider the fact that the vehicle is in the custody of the police and therefore is not going anywhere. In warrantless searches of automobiles, the criminal investigator should be careful not to be dismissive of obtaining a search warrant as a result of inconvenience. If there is time and the resources are available, a search warrant should be obtained.

Warrantless searches of automobiles should directly follow the guidelines established by the Carroll Doctrine. The mobility of the vehicle, in other words, the likelihood that it will move out of the control of law enforcement, should and needs to be justification for the search. If, for example, you arrest a person operating a vehicle and you want to follow up the arrest with a search of the vehicle, there are limitations that a scrupulous investigator should consider prior to going forward. A search incident to arrest is an acceptable search but should be limited to the "wingspan" of the person arrested. If the vehicle will be left unattended following the arrest and needs to be impounded for safekeeping, it may not be necessary to conduct a warrantless search. In the case of a vehicle that is impounded, there is no need to rush headlong into a search. An inventory of personal property in the vehicle in conjunction with a seizure is a procedure followed by law enforcement.

When a vehicle is impounded for safekeeping, the controlling agency needs to create a list of all the personal property in the vehicle. It is essential that the investigator follow the normal administrative procedures followed by her agency. If in plain sight, the investigator finds contraband, such as drugs, stolen property, weapons, or other obvious evidence, which should be seized in furtherance of his investigation, it is right to seize that material and legal to do so. In this kind of case, the investigator is acting reasonably and within his law enforcement duties. If an investigator or any law enforcement officer is legally performing his duties and is legally present in a constitutionally protected area, he can seize evidence he sees and recognize the material as evidence or contraband.

In the Supreme Court case, *Texas v. Brown* 75 L.Ed.2d 502, 103 S.Ct. 1535 (1983), the Court explained and helped define the *plain view doctrine*. In June 1979, Tom Maples, an officer of the Fort Worth police force, assisted in setting up a routine driver's license checkpoint on East Allen Street in that city. Maples stopped Clifford Brown for a license check. Brown was alone in the vehicle, and Officer Maples was standing alongside the vehicle. Maples looked into the car with his flashlight. While he waited for Brown to produce his license, he observed Brown carefully manipulate a balloon next to his pocket. As Brown withdrew his right hand from his right pants pocket, Maples clearly saw the green party balloon with a knotted tie at the top. Brown let the balloon fall to the seat beside his leg and then reached across the passenger seat and opened the glove compartment for his license and registration. Maples was an experienced officer, and he had seen similar balloons used as containers for illegal drugs in Fort Worth. Maples was then able to shift his position slightly, and he noticed other small plastic vials containing loose white powder. He also noticed an open bag of party balloons. Brown rummaged briefly through the glove compartment and eventually told Maples he had no driver's license. Maples removed Brown from the car and immediately recovered the green party balloon. He could tell that there was a powdery substance inside the tied-off balloon. Maples showed the balloon to his fellow officers, who immediately understood that the balloon contained drug contraband. Their experience mirrored Maples's, so they immediately arrested Brown. The officers conducted an on-the-scene inventory of the vehicle, which was being impounded. Among the personal items inventoried, they discovered marijuana and cutting material for use in heroin distribution. Subsequently, a toxicity examination was conducted on the powder in the balloon, and it was discovered that the material in the balloon and other similar balloons found in the car was heroin.

The trial court convicted Brown, but a review by the court of appeals overturned the conviction. The case was carried further for review by the Supreme Court. Justice William Rehnquist, in his ruling supported by a majority of the Court, decided that Maples, the police officer, acted reasonably in taking actions based on his legal observations and experience as an officer. So he met the two standards of legally seeing evidence in plain view and believing the material was in fact evidence of heroin distribution. These two standards have to be the basis for the seizure of evidence in plain view. The plain view doctrine in this case was more fully explained. In the wording of his ruling, he also verified the Supreme Court's view of warrantless searches and accepted searches incident to arrest and vehicle searches following the Carroll ruling: warrantless searches incident to arrest (*United States v. Robinson*, 414 US 218 [1973], and *New York v. Belton*, 453 US 454 [1981]).

Notwithstanding all this settled law, a search of a vehicle that has been legally seized and held by the police for impoundment procedures should be searched using a lawful warrant. It is not likely that there will be time constraints on the investigators, and it is also not likely that if a valid arrest precipitated the vehicle's impoundment, the officers would have probable cause to search the vehicle using a warrant. Again, I am advocating the use of a search warrant whenever possible to preclude any loss of evidence. Also, it should be noted that if an inventory of an impounded vehicle uncovers evidence, contraband, and the like, it is good investigative policy to use that discovery as an element of probable cause and get a search warrant. Officers conducting traffic stops for which they don't have eventual control of the vehicle or its contents may have to act expeditiously to avoid losing evidence, but in the regular pace of a criminal investigation the investigator, should act more carefully. If the suspect has a friend or family member to whom the officers conducting the arrest can turn over the vehicle, they should do so under the authority granted in the Carroll Doctrine. The key element is the officers or investigators need to have articulable facts supporting probable cause.

Terry v. Ohio, *392 US 1 (1968)*

Stop and Frisk: The Controversy of Racial Profiling A Cleveland, Ohio, detective, Martin McFadden, was patrolling a downtown beat with which he was very familiar. McFadden observed two strangers (John Terry and Richard Chilton) on a street corner. He saw them act in a manner consistent with actions in preparation for committing the crime of breaking and entering or armed robbery. They were then joined by a third man (Carl Katz), who had conferences with the two. In total, the two men approached a business, looked in the window, withdrew a total of twelve times, and then joined up with the third man (Katz) for a discussion. Katz left the area, but McFadden continued to surveil Terry and Chilton. McFadden was a veteran police officer who had distinguished himself in apprehending pickpockets in the downtown area where he patrolled. Based on his experience, McFadden suspected the two men of "casing a job for a stickup." McFadden followed them and saw them rejoin Katz a couple of blocks away from the front of a store. McFadden and other supporting officers approached the three, identified themselves as policemen, and asked their names. The men "mumbled something," acting in an uncooperative manner. McFadden spun Terry around, patted down his outside clothing, and felt the outline of a pistol in his overcoat pocket. He was unable to remove a pistol. McFadden ordered the three men into a store out of the cold weather. He removed Terry's overcoat, took out the revolver, and ordered the three to face the wall with their hands raised. He patted down the outer clothing of Chilton and Katz and seized a second revolver from Chilton's outside overcoat pocket. He did not put his hands under the outer garments of Katz (since he discovered nothing in his pat-down that might have been a weapon) or under Terry's or Chilton's outer garments until he felt the guns. The three were taken to the police station. Terry and Chilton were charged with carrying concealed weapons. The defense moved to suppress the weapons.

Though the trial court rejected the prosecution's theory that the guns had been seized during a search incident to a lawful arrest, the court denied the motion to suppress and admitted the weapons into evidence on the ground that the officer had cause to believe that petitioner and Chilton were acting suspiciously; that their interrogation was warranted; and that the officer, for his own protection, had the right to pat down their outer clothing, having reasonable cause to believe that they might be armed. The court distinguished between an *investigatory stop* and an *arrest* and between a *frisk* of the outer clothing for weapons and a full-blown search for evidence of crime. Terry and Chilton were found guilty, an intermediate appellate court affirmed, and the state supreme court dismissed the appeal on the ground that "no substantial constitutional question" was involved.

The Supreme Court in the opinion of Chief Justice Earl Warren determined that Det. McFadden acted properly (absent a search warrant) in that he curtailed his actions to what was needed to respond to the suspicious actions he observed, which were based on his experience as a "prudent" police officer acting in a manner consistent with self-protection and a reasonable exercise of his authority. The chief justice recognized the right of Terry to have his personal right against an unreasonable search and seizure, which was his Fourth Amendment right and not some protection of his house or other property. He said in his opinion that "the Fourth Amendment right against unreasonable searches and seizures, made applicable to the states by the Fourteenth Amendment, protects people, not places." The right to be protected against unreasonable actions of police had to be balanced against the right of the police to act reasonably, which in this case, they did. So the concept of *reasonable suspicion* by police was established.

Going further, Chief Justice Warren said that "the Fourth Amendment applies to stop and frisk procedures such as the following: (1) Whenever a police officer accosts an individual and restrains his freedom to walk away, he has 'seized' that person within the meaning of the Fourth Amendment. (2) A careful exploration of the outer surfaces of a person's clothing in an attempt to find weapons is a 'search' under that Amendment." The question then becomes whether the search is unreasonable.

He went on further to note the challenge of applying the exclusionary rule in this case: "The exclusionary rule cannot properly be invoked to exclude the products of legitimate and restrained police investigative techniques, and this Court's approval of such techniques should not discourage remedies other than the exclusionary rule to curtail police abuses for which that is not an effective sanction." So, in other words, there may be restraints to police conduct like this, but it must be shown to be outside of normal and reasonable "restrained" investigative procedure. Finally, Chief Justice Warren rightly observed that "the officer here was performing a legitimate function of investigating suspicious conduct when he decided to approach the petitioner and his companions. An officer justified in believing that an individual whose suspicious behavior he is investigating at close range is armed, may, to neutralize the threat of physical harm, take necessary measures to determine whether that person is carrying a weapon."

The police have to be able to articulate their suspicions in support of their actions. So to compare a Terry stop to controversial racial profiling, the police need to be able to defend their actions with articulable facts that support their reasonable belief a confrontation with a citizen is supported by suspicious behavior and not the race (or other nonrelevant facts) of the person confronted. If an officer cannot defend her conduct effectively, she will breach her oath of office in protecting and defending the Constitution.

The impact of *Terry v. Ohio* is felt significantly today. Investigators who become suspicious of a person based on their observations, articulable facts, and circumstances, such as the suspect's presence in high-crime neighborhoods during the time of day consistent with criminal activity, have the right to conduct a cursory examination interview and a pat-down of a suspect if deemed necessary to protect the officer from harm. This action by police should be carried out only when the circumstances warrant this exercise of authority. There have been examples when police officers have discovered contraband, such as bags of drugs and stolen property, as the result of a Terry stop. These types of cases put the authority to conduct Terry stops at risk in the same fashion that racial profiling can lead to diminished judicial support for this investigative technique. Investigators should make sure they act reasonably with appropriate facts supporting the investigative stop. If an investigator goes too far in a pat-down or fails to be able to carefully state why he was suspicious, he should avoid using this technique. In the same way, when an investigator is following up on evidence recovered in a Terry stop, the technique should be objectively reviewed to make sure that the evidence will not be dismissed because it failed to meet the standard articulated by the Supreme Court. Det. McFadden set a high bar in his work in the Terry case. All professional criminal investigators should recognize that standard and make sure their "blueprints" follow this standard.

Consent to Search

There are many occasions when an investigator will need to ask for permission to search a constitutionally protected area or person. The standard that has to be met for consent to search to be upheld is a knowing waiver of the right to object to the search. The investigator needs to assess if the person providing consent is intellectually competent and has the authority to allow the police to search. The owner of a house who rents a room to a suspect does not have the right to allow the search of the rented space. That same owner may have access to the rental space and be able to provide a witness statement, which can be an element of probable cause for a search warrant, but the owner does not have the right to authorize a search in an area rented by another person. Parents have the right to authorize the police to search the rooms of their children as long as they are not accepting rent from their child. Intellectual impairment, a person under the influence of drugs or alcohol, or a person who is coerced or intimidated by police authority does have the right to provide a knowing waiver or consent to search. Co-occupiers of constitutionally protected space or vehicles can provide consent as long as no other co-occupier objects to the search.

Aside from those exemptions, consent to search is a broad allowance that gives the investigator authority to search and seize items or evidence deemed by the investigator to be appropriate. In that sense, it is a broader authority than that provided by a search warrant, which has to be limited to any evidence in plain view and specifically designated evidence described in the warrant. On the other hand, the consent can be limited by the authorizing person and withdrawn without notice at any time during the search. There are Supreme Court cases that control what is and is not allowed when following the steps for a consent to search. Most important, the consent has to be authorized with a signed document. That document can and should be a verification that the consent was given freely without reservation. The following cases explore some of the many variations that investigators may confront and what an investigator should do when confronted by similar circumstances.

Schneckloth v. Bustamonte, *412 US 218 (1973)*   This is a Supreme Court case in which six persons were stopped in a vehicle, but only one person was identified as having legitimate authority over the vehicle. That person gave consent to search to the police without knowing he had the right to refuse permission. Evidence was discovered that was used in a felony check-passing scheme. The Supreme Court ruled that the consent was reasonable and the person giving the consent did not have to be specifically aware of his right to refuse consent. Unlike *Miranda rights*, investigators conducting a consent search are not required to warn people of their right to withhold consent for that consent to be valid.

The Supreme Court ruled that the police are not required to conduct a search in a way that gives the individual an opportunity to revoke consent, as determined in *United States v. Rich*, 992 F.2d 502 (May 1993). The Supreme Court also established the *objectively reasonable* standard to control what officers or investigators can surmise from a knowing consent. In the *Rich* case, the officer simply asked if he could look in the defendant's vehicle. Rich gave consent after much consideration. He did not limit the officer's understanding as to what that consent meant. It is then left to the officer to act reasonably. In this case, the officer opened the back door, looked in an unlocked suitcase, and found drug contraband wrapped in scented material meant to thwart detection of the pungent odor emanating from the suitcase filled with marijuana.

Once consent is provided by the controlling party, there are no special procedures that *have* to be followed by the investigators; however, if the officers act unreasonably, the evidence seized can be excluded. Unreasonable actions (such as forcibly opening locked containers, damaging or destroying interior walls, or dismantling and damaging home furnishings or the normal vehicle appointments [i.e, dismantling car seats or leather- or carpet-covered dampening walls]) are going beyond the standard of acting with *objectively reasonable* demeanor. These kinds of actions may be reasonable in the case of the execution of a search warrant, but in consent to search, law enforcement has to act in a manner expected by the person who is giving consent. That person can impose restrictions on a consensual search, but in lieu of that, consent cannot be considered a carte blanche for the investigator to act in a manner beyond expected normal behavior.

The search has to be viewed from the perspective of an average person, not from the perspective of an average law enforcement officer. Latitude that allows the forcing open of locked or sealed containers can happen when an experienced investigator is executing a search warrant and searching for stolen property, drugs, and other evidence if the experience and elements of probable cause known to the investigator inform him that the locations where such evidence can be secreted need to be aggressively examined. The same latitude is not available to an investigator who is searching under the authority of an average citizen especially if there is no probable cause or prior evidence indicating that evidence may be in a secret location.

The person conducting the consent search does not necessarily have to be identified as a law enforcement officer, and the person granting consent need not be the person police suspect or ultimately charge in the investigation. In *Lee v. United States*, *Lopez v. United States*, and *Hoffa v. United States*, the courts ruled that evidence found by undercover police officers in searches based on consent obtained from confidential informers or even unwitting associates who provide consent is legally obtained in spite of the informal nature of the police actions. These cases have the requisite standard of reasonableness, and the consent was granted by a person who has the necessary authority over the area that was searched. A party other than the defendant can, in some limited cases, grant consent. The consenting party needs to actually possess or is believed by the searching officer to possess "common authority over or other sufficient relationship to the premises or effects sought to be inspected." For example, the Supreme Court in *United States v. Matlock*, 415 US 164 (1974) held that a co-occupant of a house had actual authority to consent to a search of the house.

In *Illinois v. Rodriguez*, 497 US 177 (1990), the Supreme Court held that a search was valid if the police reasonably believed that the party giving consent had actual authority over the premises but were incorrect in their belief. When two co-occupants are present and one consents to a search but the other expressly objects, the Supreme Court has found that the police cannot validly search the premises.

Georgia v. Randolph, *547 US 103 (2006)* When police arrived at the home of Scott and Janet Randolph in July 2001, she complained that he was a cocaine user, and he said she was a drug and alcohol abuser. When police asked if they could go inside to search the house, he unequivocally refused, but she agreed and took the police upstairs, where one of the policemen saw a powdery substance that looked like cocaine and a straw, which the policeman put in an evidence bag and took to the police station. Randolph was subsequently indicted on drug charges, but the Georgia Supreme Court ruled that the evidence against him had been taken in an illegal search and could not be used at trial.

The US Supreme Court agreed by a 5–3 vote. Writing for the five-justice majority, Justice David Souter said that police cannot search a house without a warrant based on the consent of one occupant when the other objects. He acknowledged that under previous Supreme Court rulings, if Randolph had not been present, the police could have searched with the wife's consent alone, but Scott Randolph was there. There was no indication of any exigent circumstances or any threat or danger to Mrs. Randolph, and if police were worried about the possible destruction of evidence, said Justice Souter, they could have secured the premises while going to get a warrant.

However, if the objecting party is subsequently lawfully arrested and removed from the premises, the Court has held in *Fernandez v. California*, 134 S. Ct. 1126 (2014), in 2014 that the police may search with the consent of the co-occupant remaining on the premises.

As a result of all this case law, which is current as of 2016, the criminal investigator should consider the rules governing consent to search to be unsettled. An investigator should make sure to apply the standard of *objective reasonableness* and avoid any indication of coercive behavior when considering the use of a consent "warrantless" search.

As the investigator, you should also remember that, as the search proceeds, if you get to the point where probable cause for a search warrant is established, you can consider freezing the situation and continue the search with an approved search warrant, thereby avoiding an unnecessary reversal or exclusion of evidence. In this case, you are acting reasonably and ensuring the court can review and support your actions. You are meeting your responsibility to the Constitution and avoiding the appearance of denying the investigative suspect's rights. Don't let the extra burden of obtaining a search warrant be a consideration.

There will be many cases for which stopping to get a search warrant will be difficult or impossible. As an investigation proceeds, there are going to be meetings and confrontations with suspects and their friends and family. During these meetings, the investigator may be convinced that the friend or family member is completely unaware of the suspect's involvement in a crime and is more than willing to cooperate with law enforcement. These situations present themselves enough in investigations. The investigator needs to consider asking for permission for a "look around" search or otherwise to examine constitutionally protected areas associated with the suspect. It may be that the person contacted is anxious to clear up any misunderstanding about her friend's or family member's connection to criminal activity. If this is the case and the person contacted has authority over the space, whether it is in a house, apartment, business, or vehicle, the investigator can always ask for permission to search, or look around. The criminal investigator should be relying on his ability to make the request without pressuring or using any coercive behavior. The investigator should be professional and solicitous of the contact who has the authority and make sure that a consent to search form or document is signed. The document should say unequivocally that no pressure or coercion was used and that the permission was granted freely. The document should also contain verification that the person granting permission has controlling authority over the space. The administrative mechanics of a consent search will vary from department to department and agency to agency, but the general outline will be the same. It helps if the investigator's department or agency has a well-used and approved form for this purpose so that it contains all the information needed. Often, in the course of an investigation, the opportunity to conduct a consent search pops up, and the investigator may have only her notebook. In that case, informal handwritten consent to search can be prepared. The investigator should be familiar with the wording of a formal consent to search form and follow the text provided in the formal consent to search document so the handwritten consent to search follows her department's or agency's standards.

The investigator has the responsibility to be honest and trustworthy with the person granting permission so that, as the case progresses, the person doesn't start considering the investigator an enemy who tricked him into giving consent. It is always a very positive step in a case if persons close to a suspect see the investigator as an honorable law enforcement officer who is doing the job without creating unnecessary problems. Executing a court-ordered search warrant at the residence of a viable suspect in a criminal investigation can lead to harsh feelings by family members and cut off any chance of cooperation. So even if you obtain a search warrant, you can always approach family members in a considerate and compassionate way and ask permission to search in order to maintain or establish a working relationship with innocent members of the family of a prime suspect.

Personal Experience   In a proactive investigation I conducted in 1994, I targeted a violent offender in the District of Columbia who was eventually charged with several murders. Immediately following his incarceration on an armed robbery and assault with intent to kill case (a matter for which he was found not guilty and released), he was identified by a shooting victim as the person who killed the witness's friend and shot and seriously wounded the victim. The suspect was supposed to be living at his sister's house, so when we obtained a search warrant for his sister's house and arrested him, we were trying to determine if he had been staying anywhere else.

In the investigation leading up to this time, I had been in touch with the suspect's girlfriend, who lived in the "close in" Maryland suburbs. I had no way of knowing if he had been staying with her and had no probable cause for a search warrant of her residence. I and another officer went to her house to interview her, and during the interview, we discovered that the suspect had in fact stayed with her overnight on a few occasions since his release from jail. During the interview, I told her that the suspect had been arrested for murder and he was currently in jail. She became very upset and said she was willing to cooperate in any way she could but she didn't know anything about that side of his life. I asked her if she knew if he had left any belongings at her house, and she mentioned he had left some clothes and other personal items in her bedroom. I got from her a consent to search to look at the items and elsewhere in her bedroom. I kept my demeanor very cordial and concerned about her feelings. When I was looking around the room, I noticed that a screw was loose on an air-conditioning vent. I *asked her if I could* look inside the vent in her presence. She allowed me to do that, and when I reached into the vent, I found a .45 caliber ammunition that matched the ammunition used in the murder. The ammunition was of an unusual color and type that made that evidence more significant than just finding ammunition of the same caliber. I also found an extended .45 caliber magazine and other interesting firearms and related evidence. The suspect's fingerprints were found on the evidence when it was examined by the forensic laboratory. When I carefully brought the evidence down from the vent, the girlfriend began to cry and became even more upset that her boyfriend had brought this material into her home. I was careful to let her know that we would not consider her in some way culpable, because it was clear to me that she had little knowledge of her boyfriend's activity.

Here is the rub about this story. Eventually, we found out that she was pregnant by the suspect and she would continue to stick by him throughout the grand jury and trial phase of the case. She was a nineteen-year-old single mother who was very petite and unsophisticated. I was a forty-five-year-old six-foot, two-inch tall FBI agent with many years of experience. We expected that she might claim at some point that I had intimidated her in obtaining permission to search her bedroom. It was a big concern that we may lose important physical evidence in the case. The way the scenario played out was that we had no choice but to hope that she would be honest on the stand. When the day finally came for her to testify, she did in fact tell the truth and explained to the jury exactly how I had treated her and never once accused me of pressuring her in any way, even though the defense attorney who represented her boyfriend tried to make it sound like that had happened. This is an example of how consent to search can create a problem. Luckily, in this case, it was not a problem.

Criminal investigators have to conduct their investigations as if every step will be scrutinized from different perspectives and make every effort to avoid constitutional violations. In this case, the evidence was recovered well within the legal framework of a consent to search, and when I decided I needed to act outside of the objective reasonableness standard, I was able to point out the problem with the vent and get additional permission to continue the search. The authorizing person allowed me to continue my search to include the venting in the ceiling of the residence.

Standing to Object

Finally, in this discussion of warrantless searches, the criminal investigator should know that any objection to law enforcement actions has to be raised by a person who has standing to object to evidence recovered in violation of constitutional rights. In the case described above, the girlfriend and other members of her family had the right to object to anything I found in my search that could potentially be used against them. The suspect, who was merely an overnight visitor, may not have had standing to object to the evidence and thereby have that evidence excluded. This is a routine way to defeat the exclusion of evidence recovered at the residence, office, or store, or in the vehicle of a third party who is not charged in the case. Obviously, the inherent problem with this approach is you still have to ensure that the evidence is logically connected to the suspect/defendant in the investigation. Standing is an important legal evaluation that the criminal investigator has to understand in cases where warrantless searches have been used. It may be the only way important evidence seized as the result of a warrantless search can be rehabilitated if a court rules that the investigator may not have followed proper procedures and adhered to constitutional standards.

WIRETAPS, ELECTRONIC
SURVEILLANCE, AND THE FOURTH AMENDMENT

In the early part of the twentieth century, the telephone became a vital utility for communication. Additionally, as the century progressed, technology expanded to wireless radio communication and eventually television, motion picture photography, and videography. As you know, technology has continued to evolve, as digital technology the size of a US quarter and smaller has been developed and networks, such as the internet and cell phone networks, have become commonplace methods carrying conversation, emails, text messages, and a number of other types of encrypted and open messaging. Communication among the criminal elements has evolved right alongside this growing number of ways people communicate.

As long as communication in all these ways is happening, law enforcement has an interest in trying to establish methods to intercept this communication to obtain evidence that is relevant to criminal conduct. In the early days of establishing a legal framework for interception, it was decided that eavesdropping was an age-old method of overhearing and gathering evidence of criminal conduct. If the criminals were foolish enough to talk or write or in some other way memorialize their criminal conspiracy, it was fair for the police to make an effort to gather this kind of evidence. In the following cases, you will see how that less-than-restrictive attitude changed.

Olmstead v. United States, 277 US 438 (1928)

Roy Olmstead and his co-conspirators were convicted of possession and transporting and selling illegally manufactured alcohol in Seattle, Washington. Olmstead's conviction was obtained by the presentation of evidence, specifically conversations between Olmstead and others during calls he made on his telephone. Extensive handwritten notes were taken by the federal agents who were able to tap the phones without entering Olmstead's residence. Wires from his phones were located in a telephone switching array, and the agents were able to overhear the personal conversations of Olmstead and his codefendants. Justice William Howard Taft wrote in a close decision that the government's recovery and use of the evidence did not violate the Fourth Amendment since the residence of Olmstead was not breached. He also posited that this kind of eavesdropping on private conversations was a tried-and-true method of obtaining evidence from the utterances of the criminal suspects. Since the vote was so close on the issue, Taft further stated that the legislature could (if it chose to) extend protections against this kind of intrusion by passing a law that would limit or eliminate the use of the conversations.

Katz v. United States, 389 US 347 (1967)

Charles Katz used a public phone booth to make and receive phone calls for his interstate gambling business. The FBI attached a listening device to the outside of the phone booth, recorded all the conversations, and used those recordings to convict Katz of an interstate gambling business. Two previous cases, *Osborn v. United States*, 385

US 323 and *Berger v. United States*, 388 US 41, indicated that a move by the government to ask for specific court orders to conduct these kinds of overhears of private conversations sufficiently protected the rights of the accused against unreasonable searches. The fair and reasonable standard was anywhere a man is and he should be free of unreasonable search and seizure of private material, including his conversations. Electronic surveillance must be limited and supported by facts presented detailing the type of constitutionally protected conversations that will be seized. The court stated further that it turns on what conversation carries a "reasonable expectation of privacy." Justice Thurgood Marshall wrote the opinion that was supported 7–1 by the Supreme Court. He established a new concept in constitutional law that explained when a person had a reasonable expectation of privacy. She should expect to be free from government intrusion on her private conversation. Justice Marshall wanted government agents to obtain "antecedent" justification for this kind of intrusion, which he deemed was a search for evidence in the same way a residence or a business is searched for documentary or physical evidence. Justice Marshall viewed this kind of seizure of private conversations as more disturbing than an illegal search. He wanted a procedure for the government to follow that would make such unauthorized electronic eavesdropping be a part of processing a legally authorized procedure. It would also include protocol in which the government would have to show a judge that such evidence was probably going to be overheard, that specific persons would be overheard, and how specific evidence relating to specific crimes would be obtained:

> Only last Term we (The Supreme Court) sustained the validity of such an authorization, holding that, under sufficiently "precise and discriminate circumstances," a federal court may empower government agents to employ a concealed electronic device "for the narrow and particularized purpose of ascertaining the truth of the . . . allegations" of a "detailed factual affidavit alleging the commission of a specific criminal offense. . . . [T]he order authorizing the use of the electronic device" in *Osborn* "afforded similar protections to those . . . of conventional warrants authorizing the seizure of tangible evidence." Through those protections, "no greater invasion of privacy was permitted than was necessary under the circumstances."

The Omnibus Crime Control Act of 1968

As a result of the *Katz* case, the US Congress passed and President Lyndon Johnson signed the Omnibus Crime Control Act in June 1968, which established specific procedures federal agents had to follow to obtain a court-ordered wiretap or electronic overhear. Based on the title of the section of the legislation where the details of the requirements are laid out, Title III Court Orders is the nickname for the court orders envisioned by Justice Marshall. These orders require a number of elements to be met by the investigating agency, and the orders lay out the technical procedures to be followed by the agency to establish the overhear and a very detailed listing of *probable cause* supporting the affidavit. These orders are well beyond a simple search warrant affidavit, but the level of proof is very similar. The timeliness of the probable cause is an element that can be hard to maintain because these orders have to go through a lengthy approval process, including approval by the US Department of Justice. About forty of the fifty states have similar legislation that allows law enforcement to obtain electronic overhear orders.

Miranda v. Arizona, 401 P.2d 721 (Arizona 1965)

In *Miranda v. Arizona*, the Supreme Court held that both incriminating statements and statements of innocence made in response to an in-custody interrogation or interview of a suspect/defendant would be admissible at trial *only* if the state or government prosecutor could show that the defendant was informed of the right to consult with an attorney before and during questioning and of the right against self-incrimination before police questioning and that the defendant not only understood these rights but also voluntarily waived them.

As mentioned above, the assignment of defense counsel is not the responsibility of the criminal investigator, but since 1966, the criminal investigator and any police or law enforcement officer involved have been required to ensure that suspects/defendants who are in custody or in a "custodial" circumstance are notified of their constitutional protection against self-incrimination and that they have an absolute right to counsel before being interviewed or interrogated about the crime for which they are suspects. These rights have to be read to the suspects using specific language and ensuring that the suspects understand the rights. When suspects are willing to talk or be interviewed or interrogated, they have to then sign a knowing waiver to allow law enforcement to use whatever statements they make in court at a later date. This requirement is referred to as the suspects' *Miranda* rights. It is the result of the following circumstances with an Arizona rape investigation.

In March 1963, a petty criminal named Ernesto Miranda, whose knowledge of the criminal justice system was very limited, was arrested and charged with rape in Phoenix, Arizona. Miranda's arrest was based on circumstantial evidence presented in an arrest warrant affidavit, which generated an arrest warrant by a local judge. (Circumstantial evidence is in many cases significant evidence, but it is not direct testimony or physical evidence that is directly related to the defendant.) Following his arrest, Miranda was interrogated for two hours and provided the police with a handwritten confession to the crime. In his handwritten confession, he seemingly approved a paragraph inserted by the police verifying that he had been advised of his right to counsel and that he provided the confession voluntarily without any coercion.

In spite of that statement, Miranda was *not* advised by the police of his constitutional right to legal counsel. He also was not advised that anything he said to the police could be used against him in court. At trial, Miranda's defense attorney argued that the confession was not "truly voluntary." His defense attorney's objection was overruled, and Miranda was convicted of rape/kidnapping and sentenced to twenty to thirty years of imprisonment. The Arizona Supreme Court affirmed the conviction and pointed to the fact that Miranda had never asked for an attorney. In its affirmation, the court emphasized the fact that Miranda had not specifically requested an attorney.

Chief Justice Earl Warren wrote the majority opinion, and in his view, the interrogation or interview by the police was "inherently" coercive, so it was essential that all suspects and defendants be made aware of their rights. He further stated that as soon as a suspect asks for an attorney, the interrogation is over until an attorney can be made available to the defendant, also based on the case law that if the suspect is indigent, an attorney will be appointed for him. Continuing in his ruling, Chief Justice Warren said that the right to remain silent during an interview or interrogation is also absolute. So if the suspect says that he does not wish to talk, the interview should cease. Chief Justice Warren pointed out that a variety of police manuals and the routine followed by the FBI with regard to these rights suggest that the police and law enforcement have already introduced these protections to suspects in their investigations. The US Supreme Court took this broad approach to protect the right to legal counsel and the right to remain silent as a response to a number of coercive interrogations that had taken place throughout the country. Twelve- and 14-hour interrogations, physically abusive interrogations, and the use of coercive threats and demands involving law enforcement actions targeting the family of the suspect are examples of police overreach that the Supreme Court was hoping to end. By using the *Miranda* case as the standard, the Supreme Court chose the most inoffensive example of a coercive confession to remind law enforcement that these rights were to be respected.

This case had a significant impact on law enforcement in the United States by making what became known as a *Miranda* warning and waiver part of routine police procedure to ensure that suspects are informed of their rights. The Supreme Court decided *Miranda* with three other consolidated cases: *Westover v. United States*, *Vignera v. New York*, and *California v. Stewart*.

Impact of Miranda *Decision on Criminal Investigations*

The importance of the *Miranda* decision on criminal investigations can't be overstated. One of the most significant parts of all criminal investigations is interviews with the persons who are witnesses, suspects, and victims for evidence to be used in court. There are a number of occasions where a witness or even a victim may become a suspect in the middle of an interview. How the investigator handles that circumstance is an ongoing puzzle. Interviewing suspects following a lawful arrest or indictment is also an important high point in any investigation. The investigator needs to ensure that when important statements are made, those statements can be reliably presented in court. Confessions, inculpatory statements, and exculpatory statements are so significant in every investigation that they need to be accepted in court as legal representations of the carefully considered statements by the defendant. Lies provided by suspects who claim alibis that are proven to be false are also examples of important statements that need to be preserved and presented in court. Information about a suspect's motive or lack of motive needs to be preserved and presented in court. Every interview and interrogation needs to be preserved for future presentation in court.

The investigator has to follow the carefully drawn guidelines inherent in the *Miranda* warning so interviews are not tainted by constitutional violations. Prior to the *Miranda* decision, interviews of suspects were important features of every investigation. Time and resources were spent to give the criminal investigator special rooms for interrogation with harsh lighting and easily controlled environments meant to intimidate suspects. These techniques have not varied much, but the investigator has to be a little more aware of the effects of the intimidation. The investigator does not want to create such a coercive environment that easily intimidated suspects with low mental acuity or incapacity will confess to anything to end the interview. The investigator needs to evaluate the interviewees to make sure they can stand up to intensive interrogation and not succumb simply to avoid being put in such an awkward situation. Following the rules established by *Miranda* helps law enforcement avoid false or phony confessions and further allows that consciousness of guilt can flow from guilty suspects who just want to tell the truth and take responsibility for their actions. Going forward with this discussion, examples of situations where the *Miranda* warning is required will be considered to help students understand how best to proceed.

As an investigation proceeds, there will be times when the investigator is confronted with information in an interview that tends to indicate the person being interviewed may be guilty of the crime under investigation. As the interview proceeds, there are two possibilities: (1) advise interviewees of their *Miranda* rights and ask for a waiver before continuing with the interview or (2) continue the interview as before but realize that the suspects cannot be arrested as a result of the information they are providing. The only way the interview can continue uninterrupted is if the interview is not custodial in nature, meaning that as soon as you develop probable cause, you have to decide that the suspect has to continue to be free to leave the interview at any time after you know you have probable cause to arrest. In a case where you are investigating a person who committed a violent crime, such as murder, rape, or armed robbery, it may not be tolerated by the community to allow that person to leave the interview. Any person who poses a threat of violence to the community should be arrested as soon as you are sure that probable cause exists. Further violence perpetrated by the suspect while the suspect is free becomes the responsibility of the investigator. In some cases, the mere threat of violence is enough to make the investigator take law enforcement action.

Finishing the interview and immediately going to a judge or magistrate with an affidavit using the information obtained in the interview can put the use of the interview without a proper *Miranda* warning in a legally acceptable light. You will have the time to explain in the affidavit or personally to the judge that you did not have any intention of conducting an interrogation of a suspect and the information that was provided by the suspect was volunteered outside of a custodial environment. The investigator who takes this approach will probably be seen as obtaining the confession or incriminating statement in a constitutional manner but can expect to be grilled as having approached the suspect with corrupt intent. If you get a confession and/or an incriminating statement from a suspect, whom you then stop and give a *Miranda* warning and who then provides a knowing and signed waiver, the statement will be viewed negatively in court; but again, you should be able to use it in court. There is just no simple solution to this problem. Following the requirements in *Miranda* is a hard and fast standard. As Chief Justice Warren's opinion stated, police interrogation is intimidating in and of itself, which puts even the most scrupulous investigator in a difficult position. Any method that the investigator can use to show his intent was appropriate is the approach required to keep the statements made by a suspect acceptable.

The Fifth Amendment says, among other rights, that a defendant shall not be compelled to be a witness against herself. The Sixth Amendment says, among other rights, that a defendant has the right to be represented by counsel in a criminal prosecution. These two aspects of the Bill of Rights are the underlying authority for the *Miranda* warning. It is very difficult to gauge how much impact the *Miranda* warning has on a successful criminal investigation. All investigations should proceed toward the goal of proof without relying on the confession or admissions of a suspect/defendant. When the case reaches this level of proof, any admission or confession should be considered icing on a cake. If the interrogation of the primary suspect is one of the last steps in the process of the investigation, the use of the *Miranda* warning to begin an interview or interrogation can have significant impact on the person to be charged with the crime.

In many cases, and in my experience, most cases, people sign the *Miranda* waiver in order to hear from the investigator the specific details about the evidence that has been gathered against them. Even career criminals are curious about what the evidence is so they can be prepared to attack the case with the help of their defense attorneys, or in some cases, they are interested in identifying witnesses against them for the purpose of threatening, intimidating, or committing acts of violence against the witnesses. If defendants choose not to talk or allow an interview, they will not be able to learn anything about the case against them. Choosing to remain silent and not allowing an interview tends to frustrate the suspects/defendants in their attempt to defeat the prosecution. Because of this dialogue between the investigator and defendants, it is rare when defendants decide to remain silent in the face of criminal investigation. It is also an important element for the investigator to consider when preparing for a suspect interview/interrogation.

The investigator should be prepared to protect the identities of witnesses and ensure the safety of any surviving victims. Even sensitive sources of evidence should be scrupulously kept secure until it is appropriate for defendants to be provided information in the discovery process. During any interview with suspects, there will have to be some kind of give-and-take dialogue, especially if the investigator is making an effort to obtain a confession or an incriminating statement. In my experience, it is the best approach in an interview to allow defendants to talk as long as they want. The only way investigative leads can be used from such an interview is if the defendants have been properly advised of their *Miranda* rights and they have provided an approved waiver. Once the rights have been provided and the waiver obtained, the investigator is free to interview or interrogate for as long as necessary. Reasonableness is the controlling factor. Hours or even days of interview/interrogation can be reasonable if defendants are properly fed, allowed to rest, and provided routine bathroom breaks. Don't judge reasonableness on some kind of law enforcement standard. Judge reasonableness based on an objective standard in the community. Suspects can end the interview or withdraw the waiver at any time, so it is best to ensure that the interview lasts long enough to satisfy the needs of the investigation.

It should also be understood that during the interview, threats, coercion, and improper promises are still not allowed or acceptable. Even a hard-edged interrogation, which may be laced with appropriate anger and disdain from the investigator, can be tolerated if the actions of the investigator don't cross the line into abuse, assault, or threatening claims or actions. Obviously, physical torture of any kind is prohibited. Even so-called advanced interview/interrogation techniques, such as physical or psychological deprivation and breathtaking or frightening techniques that don't rise to the level of physical torture, are also prohibited. In other words, in a legally acceptable interview/interrogation, law enforcement officers have to be careful not to cross acceptable lines of behavior. The only somewhat controversial technique that can be acceptable is lying to defendants/interviewees. Making suspects believe something that is not true, such as a criminal associate is cooperating in an investigation or a witness has made a positive identification, can be a useful technique that forwards the goals of an investigation without compromising the legality of the interview. Making the decision to be deceptive in the interview can interfere with any chance for future trust building between the investigator and the defendant.

Today's defendants may be tomorrow's cooperating witnesses, especially when the investigation involves ongoing patterns of violence, conspiratorial behavior, or some kind of organized criminal enterprise. Deception in an interview should be used sparingly and only when it is necessary to plant uncertainty in the mind of the suspect. Again, if your whole investigation depends on a confession or admissions by your main suspect, it is not appropriate to use deception unless the investigator sees no other option.

The single most troubling aspect of this kind of adherence to appropriate behavior by law enforcement is when a person's life is in immediate danger. Threats and serious intimidation may be and, in some cases, have been used to save the life of a person in danger. The obvious result is that any evidence found in conjunction with saving that person's life or any admission made by a defendant who might have been intimidated into admitting knowledge about the crime in such a scenario will not be available for use in the trial of the suspect. The investigator has to realize that the protection of the rule of law, the constitutional rights of the accused, and the potential for the accused turning around and filing a complaint are what is at stake in taking these actions.

Finally, to fully appreciate the *Miranda* warning, there are certain elements of the warning that need further explanation. In the first place, the warning has to be given when the interviewee is in a custodial situation. *Custodial circumstance* means the interviewee is not free to leave at any time. An arrest or even a police station interview, where the freedom to come and go is restricted, is custodial. A Terry stop, when the police restrict the freedom of an interviewee, can be considered custodial. An interview at the home of an interviewee whom law enforcement does not intend to arrest immediately is noncustodial and therefore does not require a *Miranda* warning. But any action similar to that which can be misconstrued as being a corrupt avoidance of the *Miranda* warning is likely to be viewed as a violation of the rights of the accused. If there is any fact that indicates the police were acting in a fashion to make it appear noncustodial when it was a ruse set up so that the defendant could be arrested in a close time proximity to the interview.

A knowing waiver of the rights is all that is necessary. That waiver does not have to be formally signed. It is the absolute right of the defendant to refuse to sign anything when arrested, and in some cases, defendants will refuse to sign a waiver but are still willing to be questioned and provide a statement. These kinds of interviews will be viewed as questionable because most judges adhere to the belief that law enforcement officers are intimidating and therefore see a suspect's refusal to sign the waiver as enough evidence to suspect that the officer acted improperly. The FBI, which has a time-tested process for the advice of rights that predates *Miranda*, has as part of its manual of operations that a refusal to sign the waiver is equivalent to a demand for an attorney, which abruptly ends any interview.

The last aspect of the *Miranda* warning that should be discussed is the form of the warning. Most police departments use a small printed card that has checkmarks representing each right laid out in the warning, including the constitutional right to avoid self-incrimination and the right to have an attorney. Additionally, the additional aspects of the "rights" card or "rights" warning are the right to remain silent, the right to have an attorney present during any interview, and the right to have an attorney appointed for you if you cannot afford one—the right guaranteed by *Gideon v. Wainwright*. The guarantees inherent in the Fifth and Sixth Amendments are covered. The FBI and other federal investigative agencies use a rights form and waiver on a sheet of letter-size bond paper. In truth, as long as the rights are properly detailed, the *Miranda* warning is properly provided. Unfortunately, when the whole process is either in part or as a whole done orally, there is a tendency on the part of judges to rule that the rights were not properly delivered. As a result of this tendency, criminal investigators should always make the effort to have the rights card and waiver signed by the interviewee so there is no hint of improper conduct.

Defense attorneys will claim that even when the *Miranda* rights were properly given, law enforcement used intimidation and coercion to obtain incriminating statements. They will also claim that tricks, threats, and even an overbearing presence are evidence of the violation. Pretrial court hearings are used to resolve these issues, so the criminal investigator should anticipate the kinds of questions that will be covered in a hearing where the suspect/defendant makes a confession or an incriminating statement. In the past twenty years, these confrontations have involved the increased use of videotaped or digitally recorded statements. The judges in these hearings can make their decision about the coercion or pressure used against a defendant by observing the statement and evaluating the demeanor of the defendant and the investigator. There is no surefire solution for these controversies. It is up to the criminal investigator to provide the *Miranda* warning, follow the standards for proper interviews, prepare a detailed reconstruction of the statement, follow the spirit of the constitutional rights, and endeavor to secure the rights of the accused while conducting a thorough and comprehensive interview or interrogation.

Personal Experience

My last felony arrest occurred in Washington, DC, in 2002. The suspect was observed by task force officers purchasing a small packet of marijuana. As soon as we moved in to make the arrest, the suspect fled on foot through an alley and discarded the marijuana, but as we caught up to him, we also observed him discard a handgun, which at the time was a felony violation in Washington, DC. We were able to catch up to the suspect and recover the weapon when he was observed throwing it; we charged him with felony possession of a gun. When we transported him to the office for booking, I read him his rights (the *Miranda* warning) and asked him if he wanted to be interviewed. He said that he understood his rights and did not wish to answer questions but wanted to make a statement. He never asked for an attorney, which would have ended our effort to talk to him. I then told him that I was willing to listen to anything he had to say. I further requested that he sign the *Miranda* form, which he refused to do. I also asked if he would be willing to sign a written and prepared document that included just his statement. Again, he said no. He was not going to sign anything. In the presence of a second investigator, I asked him to just tell me what he wanted to say. He admitted that "the gun was his and that it was not loaded and he carried it for self-defense when he was on the streets of DC because it was a dangerous place." At that point, we continued to process him for the arrest, and we did not question him or demand any further information. Following the arrest, I wrote a report (FD 302) for testimonial purposes, which detailed the incriminating statement and eventually told the prosecutor in detail how the statement was obtained.

At the trial almost two years later, the defense counsel argued that the statement should be disallowed because the defendant did not sign the waiver and the only verification that the statement was voluntary was my report, which was also signed by my partner in the investigation. The judge had a midtrial hearing about this matter, and my partner was called to the stand. She repeated the circumstances exactly as stated above. The defense attorney tried to get her to admit that I was an intimidating figure because of my age and size. She said the whole incident was very cordial and not in the least intimidating for the defendant. I was also called to the stand. Again, the defense attorney asked if I had intimidated the defendant, and I said that I really didn't have any time or inclination to pressure him because the whole "interview," if you wanted to call it that, lasted less than a couple of minutes. The judge ruled that the defendant was properly advised of his rights and accepted our testimony that he provided the statement freely without any coercion. When I testified in the trial before the jury about the statement, the defense attorney again tried to characterize our conduct as intimidating, but in this case, the jury didn't accept that characterization and found the defendant guilty.

SUMMARY

Any law enforcement actions will always be viewed from the perspective of two lenses: the defense's and the prosecution's. It is the essence of our adversarial court system of justice. As criminal investigators, we have to act appropriately and then leave it to the judge to determine if our actions are objectively proper. There are so many occasions when most of our actions are not really tested in court. When we arrest and charge the person who committed the crime in the US system of justice, it is the rare instance when the case goes all the way to a trial. However, we need to act as if it is likely that our work will always be reviewed by the two perspectives. The primary reason for this is that, in most cases, the person charged with the crime is actually guilty. The strict adherence to the constitutional rights of the accused is in place to protect the innocent from government overreach and unfair treatment. These rights are also used by the guilty to avoid prosecution. As criminal investigators, we have to prove our case in court and make sure we follow the rule of law. *Miranda* warnings;

the use of search warrants, Terry stops, and consent searches; and any of the issues regarding the rights of the accused are complicated and require real consideration throughout the arc of a criminal investigation. But as long as the criminal investigator acts in a manner that is considered fair and reasonable, it is likely the investigation will be viewed as fair and reasonable.

There are other US Supreme Court rulings that affect the investigative process, but the responsibilities for following these rules lie with the prosecutor. They should be considered by the investigator at the time leading up to a trial, but they should not affect the actions of the investigator during the investigative process. If exculpatory information is uncovered during an investigation, for example, the investigator should become satisfied that the information does not affect the truth of the investigations, but the investigator needs to be able to defend the investigation against any inconsistency. Therefore, consider the following cases and the rules of evidence that are affected by them in consultation with the prosecuting attorney to ensure that due process is followed, but do not delete, alter, or diminish the information for the purpose of hiding this kind of information.

Court standards set in *Brady v. Maryland* (1963) and *Giglio v. United States* (1972) and a host of other rulings have led to policies and procedures governing the rules of evidence and the discovery process, which requires disclosure of evidence gathered by the government. These rules were put into place to ensure that the constitutional concept of *due process* is adhered to in all criminal cases. These standards are the responsibility of the prosecutor and the defense attorney, but the investigator needs to make sure that all aspects (reports, interview notes, and confidential source documents) of an investigation are known to the prosecutor so no violations of due process occur.

Chapter Four

Teamwork

Organizational structures of investigative units and evaluation of investigative resources.

Source: Matthew Richardson / Alamy Stock Photo DJ0NMD

Police departments, sheriff's offices, state police agencies, and federal investigative agencies distribute investigative resources in a fashion similar to each other. The similarity is usually a "squad" section or bureau with investigative responsibilities with enough resources to meet the needs of whatever community it is charged with protecting. These squad-level groups provide the individual investigators with training in legal and tactical computer access, administrative resources, and data analyses along with open source evaluations, which give the investigators insight into facts and, in some cases, evidence that may affect their investigations. More important, the squad-level group will usually contain a team of investigators with a variety of skill levels, expertise, and cultural experience, which allow for the development of a team of professionals who can apply much-needed *perspective* to every investigation. The following graphic represents the hierarchy of most police departments that is deployed for most investigations.

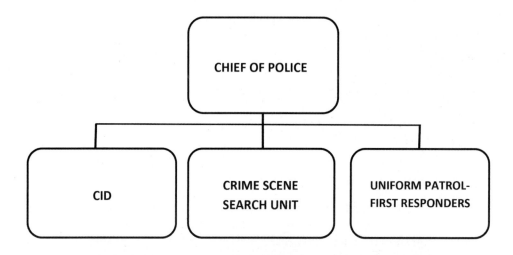

REACTIVE CRIMINAL INVESTIGATIONS

CID is the shorthand term for the criminal investigation division. The crime scene search unit is the forensic team tasked with gathering physical evidence at the scene of a crime. The uniform patrol officers are most often the first responders to any crime scene reported through routine or emergency contacts with the police department. The top of the chart represents the police chief. This person is the highest administrative and investigative person in the chain of command. This person (with slight variations in the names of the units and the top person in charge) will simply be the head of the local FBI, DEA, ATF, state police, sheriff's office, or any other investigative entity. Nonuniform investigative agencies will not have first responders in uniform, but the first responding agents will in most cases act as custodians and security for the crime scene until a management decision is made as to which investigator and/or investigative squad will handle the case. The chart depicted above represents the first-tier team involved in any reactive criminal investigation. This team must act effectively to round up and sequester the witnesses at the scene, set the parameters of the scene, and determine what venues inside the scene are most likely to yield physical evidence. The first responder must make an initial judgment as to legal control of the scene and make a preliminary finding as to what happened.

The following graphic provides a list of crimes that most often require a crime scene examination and therefore are likely to be the types of crimes that begin a *reactive criminal investigation.* As stated earlier in chapter 1, reactive crime means a criminal investigation begins at the crime scene where the criminal act or incident occurred. These cases are then reported to the police or the appropriate law enforce-

CRIMES FOR WHICH A CRIME
SCENE EXAMINATION IS APPROPRIATE

- Homicide
- Rape (sex crimes)
- Assault
- Robbery
- Burglary
- Arson and explosions
- Larceny and car theft
- Drug investigations and organized crime matters
- Serial offenders

ment jurisdiction. Immediate response to the scene follows, and every effort is made to "freeze" the scene and maintain control of any persons present who may be victims or witnesses. This initial response is a critical time period due to the fact that witnesses can leave the area, never to be heard from again. Physical evidence can be removed, destroyed, or damaged. Environmental conditions, such as bad weather, can cause deterioration of the scene and remove or alter physical evidence. As discussed in chapter 1, it is the responsibility of the first responder to protect and preserve life. If one or more live victims are at the scene, the first responder needs to ensure that emergency medical treatment is called for and every step possible is taken to preserve the health of the victims. If the crime was particularly traumatic, it may also be necessary to provide additional medical care for witnesses.

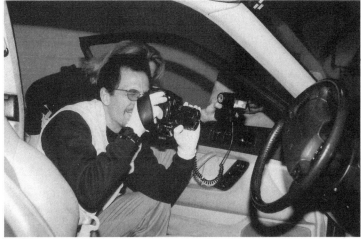

Source: D.Reilly

The crimes listed in the graphic are reported. The team of criminal investigators responds as per an appropriate "call out" protocol. Usually, the patrol or first responder is, as the designation suggests, first on the scene. When the first responder arrives, the first concern is to ensure the health and safety of all persons present and to determine what crime has occurred and call out the appropriate investigative unit.

The first responder will then call out a crime scene team if needed. Some crimes that have lower priority, such as car theft, may not require a crime scene team. Crime scene units may have limitations on their response depending on the crime. Some large urban areas in the United States don't call out crime scene units for street robberies (muggings) or residential burglaries. Other towns and cities have a single crime scene officer to respond to all manner of crimes, such as those listed in the preceding graphic. Burglaries and car thefts are prioritized in smaller jurisdictions primarily because more serious crimes, such as homicide, rape, and armed robbery, are rare events.

THE SQUAD

The next step for the first responder is to call out the investigative unit assigned to handle matters based on what is believed to have occurred. Local police departments will have squads broken down by the seriousness of the crimes under the CID banner. Homicide squads, robbery squads, and sex crime squads are examples of these kinds of units. General-assignment detective squads have immediate responsibility for all crimes in a small geographic area of a city. Specialized squads, such as *major case* squads and *robbery–homicide* squads, are also the type of units that may have the initial investigative responsibilities in a reactive crime investigation. In the case of federal investigations, similar squad breakdowns in the agency's organizational structure become the units that respond to a particular crime. FBI and local police in large urban centers have squads or units responsible for investigating jurisdictional crossovers or case investigations of a similar nature. The city's robbery squad will be in regular contact with the FBI's bank robbery squad. These same units or squads will have responsibility for a variety of reactive crimes. Kidnapping and extortion at both the local and federal levels are often the responsibility of the units with similar crimes requiring investigation. The FBI has bank robbery squads, theft of government property squads, kidnapping squads, and terrorist squads or task force units that combine FBI resources with local police and other federal agencies. The ATF, DEA, and Secret Service will have squads similar to the FBI's that are designated for reactive response to cases in their jurisdiction or with cases where they have joint jurisdiction with other agencies.

Almost all investigative units, local or federal, use a rotating assignment protocol for each case. Assignment of cases to particular investigators may be somewhat of a random choice for particular units. It is necessary in some cases to alter assignments based on the attributes of investigators when the possibility is obvious that some level of experience or expertise would be more appropriate for a particular case. Adjustments in these assignments may be made following the initial distribution when an analysis of the case is complete and the case is determined to be complicated and requires some particular level of expertise or experience.

The reality is that criminal investigators have usually gone through an extensive evaluation process before being assigned, and the agency is usually satisfied with the quality and competence of all of its squad members. These investigative units are usually made up of a cross section of investigators—male, female, young, old, and racially or ethnically diverse. It may be that once the picture of the investigation is clearer, the investigator assigned needs to be reconsidered to meet some important criteria or perspective. Since the diversity in many police agencies is limited, there are times when this readjustment of assignment is counterproductive. Senior experienced detectives may end up taking on the more complex or socially sensitive investigations by virtue of their experience. However, the management of investigative assignments usually falls on the squad or unit supervisor or a sergeant, lieutenant, or supervisory agent whose knowledge of the unit's capabilities should be the best guide in determining who should take lead in a case. Since this is a possibility in some cases when the investigative team responds to the crime scene, the case should be worked as a real team effort and organized based on the chain of command in the unit. Senior investigators should take on the role of coordinating the distribution of manpower and resources and should prioritize the leads as they are developed. Leads are *proposed investigative steps* that require specific action. For example, a witness says another person knows the location of a security surveillance video of the crime scene, but the witness is not sure if the video is properly secured. This kind of information needs to be acted on immediately and requires the lead investigator at the scene to assign an investigator to follow that lead as soon as possible. Another example is when an injured victim has been transported to a hospital and this victim witness needs to be interviewed but the priority is getting the victim medical treatment.

As the facts about the crime become clearer, the choice as to who should be ultimately responsible for the investigation should also become clearer. Normally, adhering to the routine assignment protocol will be the most likely approach. Solid investigative standards and the reliance on a good team of criminal investigators should

Source: iStock 472949780

provide the best chance to find the truth and solve the case. The characteristic of most solid investigative units is cooperative effort. Investigators who work similar investigations in a known jurisdictional work environment will begin to rely on the strengths of their teammates and make up for any weaknesses. Jealousy, impetuousness, and a competitive intrigue have no place in a good criminal investigative unit. Competition can be a solid source of creative enthusiasm, but it should not be the cause of unnecessary rancor or lack of cooperation among the team. The weakest member of a good investigative team should be bolstered by the strongest members; then, more cases will be solved. Unit cohesion and positive interaction among the unit's members will provide the kind of intelligent speculative analysis needed to consider scenarios and possibilities not obvious in the gathered evidence and facts. *What works? What is possible? And what is likely?* are the options in many criminal investigations. The best and most reliable opinions are going to come from colleagues who are in the same trenches as the lead investigator.

Developing a system of communication or collegial discussion is a positive way for the squad to see and hear all the facts, understand what leads need to be followed, and distribute the work among the squad members. After the initial crime scene investigation and after the witnesses and victims have been interviewed, this system will be less about distributing the work and more about analysis, evaluation, and setting priorities. Everyone on the squad should be familiar with the general facts of every investigation being handled by the squad. The squad members will then be able to openly offer advice and suggestions for moving all the squad's cases along.

After the initial investigative work, the day-to-day leads will be covered by the lead investigator assigned to the case. The lead investigator will be the person responsible for establishing an *investigative plan*. This plan can be a well-ordered, logical approach to the investigation developed by the lead investigator as the method to find a solution to the crime. The plan needs to be fluid enough to adjust to facts and evidence that change the trajectory of the investigation. Usually, for safety purposes, the lead investigator will have a partner who is also handling her own leads and acts as backup for handling interviews, confrontations, and other dangerous circumstances that come up in criminal investigations. This partnership will be discussed later in this chapter.

The squad then becomes the sounding board for theories about the crime. This way, the talents of all the criminal investigators on a squad will inform the investigation going forward. The lead investigator can float theories, no matter how outrageous, to a group of seasoned professionals who can provide reasoned and informative criticism. The squad members can suggest alternate theories and help develop the best investigative plan with the highest chance of success. Ultimately, those case investigations that are not immediately focused on a suspect, or cases that don't have any logical leads remaining, can be discussed and argued about in an effort to help pry open the closed door toward finding a solution. Finding the truth on all the squad's cases then becomes a team goal with the best talent pool available. Any investigative squad with years of experience and a solid intelligence base will have investigative approaches that can form a usable plan or strategy to move the case forward.

The *intelligence base* is another resource that an investigative squad can rely on. This base is made up of human intelligence (confidential sources), investigative case files that have similar factors presented by previous cases under investigation, and digital databases containing criminal histories of those persons who come in contact with the squad. There will also be digital databases that are focused on crimes under the squad's jurisdiction. Finally, the squad's intelligence base is grounded by the veteran detectives who have seen similar crimes and broken cases with previously successful investigative plans and failed to break cases with investigative plans that were not so successful. Primary among these elements of the intelligence base are confidential sources. These sources are part of the criminal ecosystem in the community. They are often career criminals who are so familiar with active criminal activity in the community that they can find out, speculate, or in some cases, immediately *know* the identities of the persons responsible for a particular crime. For example, major armed robberies with large scores (takes or proceeds) are the kinds of crimes openly discussed and speculated about among knowledgeable criminals. These criminal ecosystems have gossips and insiders who hear about a crime and can't wait to tell their criminal associates. High-level confidential sources hear these stories and pass them along to their law enforcement handlers to continue to support the relationship they have with law enforcement. (Chapter 13 has a more complete discussion of confidential sources.) Skilled criminal investigators should have at least two confidential sources operating for them at any given time. On an average squad of ten to fifteen investigators, that means twenty to thirty confidential sources will be providing intelligence to the squad on a routine basis. This, of course, does not mean that all the sources will be providing a continuous stream of high-quality and current intelligence, but it does mean that on any given case, some kind of reliable human intelligence should be factored into the investigative plan.

The next most important staple of the squad's intelligence base is the experience of veteran investigators who have conducted successful investigations for years. Their experience provides best practices, methods, and creative solutions to roadblocks in a criminal investigation. It is this core of knowledge that moves a case from a dead start to a discovery of probable cause and to a solid belief that a suspect is in fact the perpetrator, thus providing a path to success for a squad. A solid investigative squad will have a mix of veterans with a positive group of younger investigators who are willing to learn from their older colleagues. Law enforcement skills, such as interview techniques, courtroom demeanor, effective testimony, tactical awareness, and tactical planning for the safety of the investigators, are taught and reinforced by a cadre of seasoned investigators. In this way, the squad provides the best first-tier training for its team. Some legal and tactical training will be provided by agency-wide instructors, but internal experience in conjunction with the daily exposure to the types of cases a squad investigates provides the best approach for young investigators to learn. It takes those needed skills and customizes them for immediate use. Young investigators will see immediate results from their exposure to law enforcement professionals who are facing the same problems they are confronting. The key is the comradery among the squad. Consistent performance is usually the result of a successful relationship among the squad members.

On the other side of the ledger, the experienced investigators should learn from their younger colleagues. They need to be open to new ideas, technology, and perspectives.

Criminal investigations are reflective of social trends and cultural variations. Younger investigators may have a more nuanced familiarization with these new trends and perspectives. A solid, successful squad will take advantage of all its resources to build its intelligence base into a well-tuned and efficient unit. Younger investigators will also enhance the tactical capability of the squad. Investigating violent criminals and being responsible for arrests and search warrant raids along with potentially violent confrontations require the squad in a violent crimes investigation unit to immediately respond to dangerous criminal behavior. It is a fact of life that violent criminals are very often young career criminals aged from the late teens to the early thirties. Arresting and controlling these offenders poses a need to be able to respond swiftly and effectively to their assaultive behavior. Younger, well-trained law enforcement professionals will help balance the scales physically. Older law enforcement professionals may have experience, but just like athletes, it doesn't hurt to have youth on the side of the "righteous."

PARTNERS

As we step back from our criminal investigation squad and evaluate its effectiveness, we want to see that balance of persons who will provide the unit with all the resources it needs to make cases, solve the puzzles, and find the truth. But going forward with our discussion of teamwork, we must consider the basic investigative unit, a *partnership*. Most criminal investigative units have individual detectives, special agents, or inspectors whose job it is to take the assignments covered by the jurisdictional distribution of cases for the agencies. These individual case detectives are responsible for conducting the investigation and following the steps that will lead to finding out how, why, and who committed the crime. From an administrative perspective, the agency can immediately determine who is handling what matters under the CID's jurisdiction. In actual practice, the lone-wolf aspect of one case handled by one investigator in a criminal investigation is *not* the best method to produce positive results. As stated above, the normal process of conducting a criminal investigation will place the criminal investigator in some dangerous situations, and the benefit of having two well-trained law enforcement professionals cannot be overstated. In most criminal investigations, there is also a need to have more than one perspective. Because of these two compelling reasons, most investigations benefit significantly from having at least two investigators following the leads, conducting interviews, developing solid relationships with witnesses, and responding to surprise conditions that evolve in a case.

The best partnerships are made up of two investigators who complement one another. Since human emotions, interaction, and context are a part of every case, complementary human emotional response can be very helpful in a partnership. Fictional depictions of police using the "good cop–bad cop" technique in interrogations is scoffed at as too predictable and elementary, but in actual practice, elements of an offsetting response to difficult interviews or interrogations can be very helpful. It is not necessary to strictly abide by the good cop–bad cop approach, but to have one partner displaying empathy and sympathy while the other partner expresses disbelief and consternation is very effective in putting the witness or suspect off guard and thereby eliciting a range of responses that eventually include the truth. The average career criminal will try to satisfy both interrogators; in this respect, key variations with the truth can be gleaned from the interrogations. Partners who work well together can adapt their personalities to variations of this approach and even switch roles if needed to effectively conduct difficult interviews. Personality characteristics such as empathy, trustworthiness, harshness, and even cold or calculated professionalism can come in handy if the partners have these characteristics in their toolboxes. Toughness balanced by genuine human sympathy provides the kind of mix that is easier when presented by two members of a partnership. These personality characteristics are the kinds of complementary factors that a creative criminal investigative team can display in response to difficult interviews. It should be noted here that routine questioning interrogations, and "difficult interviews" don't always involve a suspect.

Witnesses who don't wish to be involved in an ongoing criminal investigation can present many problems and require the team to press hard and work to glean from the witness the information needed to make the case. Difficult interviews happen organically in an investigation. Many witnesses will gladly cooperate without a second thought. As long as there are no glaring falsehoods or evasive answers, the interviews can be done by any competent police officer. It is the witnesses who sometimes have a hidden agenda and a desire to be uninvolved or something to hide about why they were present at the scene of a crime. It is important that the partnership knows instinctively that the interview is not going to be easy and can immediately use its interview talents and tandem approach to work the witness successfully.

During suspect interrogations, the partners will also have easy interviews when the suspect will give it up immediately. Fine-tuning the facts and making sure there are no glaring inconsistencies in these interviews are the goals for an easy interrogation. On the other hand, when a suspect is being difficult but is allowing the interrogation to proceed in other words, he signed his waiver of rights form, the partners have to know if the suspect is trying to find out what kind of case the police have against him,

Source: Marmaduke St. John / Alamy Stock Photo BXG604

and who is cooperating with the police, or is trying to supplant a false narrative about the investigation to make the investigators question their work. Suspects lie for any number of reasons, and their lies should be expected. Neither part of the team should show any particular animus to the suspect when he lies, but it is okay for the team to express its disbelief and even its outrage over the crime. A good partnership will carefully steer the interrogation and avoid giving up anything but the basics to the suspect. Eventually, the suspect will be allowed to see the government's case during trial discovery, but until that time, there is no reason to prove anything to the suspect. In chapter 13, we will have more discussion about interviews and interrogations, but for purposes of this discussion on teamwork and what makes an effective partnership, you must know that the most important aspect of a good partnership is how well the two investigators complement each other during interviews and interrogations.

The next area to cover in a good partnership is special talents or resources. A solid partnership may be made up of one partner having experience, knowledge, and expertise in crime scene analysis, forensic science analysis and procedure, computer training, or forensic medical training or experience. For a criminal investigation of violent crimes to be successful, the investigators need to have a thorough working knowledge of how the physical evidence recovered in a case can be used and how relevant that evidence should be viewed. For example, if the partnership is working a homicide case in which the initial suspect is a spouse, the presence of the spouse's DNA and fingerprints around the scene of the crime becomes less important and of little value. But if it turns out that another person becomes a suspect, that same evidence needs to be exploited and evaluated effectively. In chapter 10 there will be a more detailed discussion of physical evidence and forensic scientific examination.

In a successful partnership, striking a balance between some experience or special training in forensics with expertise in computer technology is another example of specialized talents enhancing the team. In fact, any hard science, clinical experience in psychology or psychiatry, or extraordinary experience in history can be the kind of resource that makes a good balance between partners. The obvious benefit of specialized knowledge that can be shared among the team and especially between partners makes the partnership more effective and will enhance the ability of the partners to find the truth and close cases. This specialized capability extends to unique knowledge of social trends, popular music, and all manner of popular culture to include art, music, books, movies, and literature. No investigative resource should be disregarded when determining the best partnerships. It is very important to have complementary skills.

Finally, age and experience, male and female, and cross-racial partnerships can have very positive outcomes for criminal investigations. In most partnerships in investigations, law enforcement agencies will try to team an experienced investigator with a new and younger investigator. This combination can be very beneficial if the senior investigator takes on the role of mentor and teacher. This kind of partnership in which the senior investigator uses the younger colleague as a "gofer" and "lackey" is inappropriate and disrespectful. It is very rare that such persons successfully advance in their careers in law enforcement to a point where they are placed in an investigative unit without having significant ability and potential. Young and old partners should see that benefits can be obtained from both partners to make the partnership effective. As mentioned above, tactical ability may be enhanced by the addition of a younger, more athletic partner in dangerous situations. Perspective and experience are important elements that improve the possibility of a successful partnership between a senior and junior investigator.

When a male investigator is teamed with a female investigator, there needs to be a strong element of mutual respect and appreciation for the different perspectives, and both sides of the partnership should embrace the positive aspects of such a partnership. In the male–female dynamic, a female detective may be more effective interviewing female witnesses, victims, and suspects, *or not*. The balance of a male and female partnership can have a lot of benefits even if the age and experience levels are significant. Flaws in these partnerships can develop if the junior partner thinks he is being used or one of the partners feels disrespected. These kinds of built-in cultural flaws, which may be reflective of the society as a whole, have no place in law enforcement. There are too many times when just the right perspective, talent, ambition, and passion combined with experience, dedication, and a demand for perfection provides the partnership with resources needed to solve the most difficult case. These complementary age, sex, and racial variants should be an important part of perfecting an effective professional squad or team.

It is a fact that, currently, law enforcement agencies throughout the United States do not accurately reflect that 20 to 25 percent of the population is nonwhite (racially) or that 50 percent of the population is female. Police agencies are heavily populated by white males. This makes any effort to more accurately reflect the diversity of the community a goal to be achieved. Remember that it also is not fair to say that a woman will be a more effective criminal investigator when the witness, victim, or suspect is a woman. It is also not fair to say that an African American criminal investigator will be more effective investigating a case in an African American neighborhood. The combination of special investigative skills, the ability of the investigators to exhibit appropriate human emotional characteristics, and cultural and human diversity will encourage the broad range of perspective, understanding, and scientific objectivity required to be an effective investigative team. Gender and race can have a positive effect on how the partners are perceived by the community, but that is not the only reason for meeting that abovementioned goal. Complementary partnerships and squads with a variety of special skills will always be the preferred objective for an investigative collaboration. Teamwork begins at this level and will become fine-tuned as an investigation proceeds through to the criminal justice system.

COURT TEAM

As will be discussed several times throughout this text, most cases that are investigated will not proceed through the criminal justice system to the point where a trial will occur. Most investigations will end when a solid suspect is developed and charged with an offense that approximates the actions that led to the investigation in the first place. In most cases, suspects who are arrested and charged with a crime will discover it is in

Source: iStock 108348460

their best interest to avoid a trial and take a plea to a charge that the community prosecutor believes represents a level of justice for the victim or victims and an appropriate level of justice for the community. Remember, as stated in chapter 1, the criminal
cases in the system are reflected in the title of the case, which includes the designated
jurisdiction (state or US government represented by the *People*) versus the Defendant.
Criminal investigations have interested parties, such as the victims, witnesses, communities, and suspects–defendants. The *prosecutor* is the legal representative for the
victim, witness, and entire community. The *defense attorney* is the legal representative
for the defendant and is charged with providing a vigorous defense case.

   Government prosecutors must consider the expense of a trial, the seriousness of
the crime and the disruption of the lives of the witnesses and victims along with any
legal constraints, evidence rulings, and possible weaknesses in the case, and then they
decide what the defendant should be charged with going forward for the trial. Defendants and their attorneys need to take into account whether the government's case can
be effectively defeated or obscured and also, just as important, whether the defendants
are actually guilty of the charge and feel they have to take responsibility for the act.
These factors take the main responsibility for the investigation from the control of the
lead criminal investigator and establish the prosecuting attorney as the case manager.

   In federal jurisdictions and many state and local jurisdictions, the *lead investigator*
continues to work the case and follow leads that may develop in the run-up to the trial.
Victims and witnesses must be educated about the rules of evidence and how their testimony will need to be presented. In the normal course of social interaction, a person
may explain an event to friends and associates with statements from other persons,
descriptions of the event with factors filled in by logical conclusions, and personal
impressions of the people involved in the event. None of those normal descriptive
comments can be used by a person who is describing an event in a trial. Testimony is
made up of facts and circumstances seen, heard, or felt by the witness, in other words,
firsthand knowledge. Some hearsay (overheard conversation or discussion) can be
excluded, and some hearsay can be allowed. The witness must be schooled in how

to provide relevant and legally authorized testimony. For example, if a witness sees a person commit a crime and knows (from living in the community) that the person is regularly in trouble with the police, that witness cannot provide testimony about the character or reputation of the defendant. She can only say what she saw about the incident. The rules of evidence and the approach of the witness to relaying the story of the crime must stay inside the lines of what is acceptable evidence in a trial.

In preparing witnesses and ensuring that all the physical evidence in an investigation is ready for presentation at a trial, the lead criminal investigator will usually be responsible for continuing to work on the case, but at this time, the lead investigator will be acting on behalf of the prosecutor and no longer independently deciding what needs to be done. He will also be responsible for any new leads, such as vetting alibi witnesses, put forward by the defendant and his counsel. Any other leads that develop regarding other physical evidence and some potentially important data or digital information will also have to be examined and made available to the prosecutor. The lead criminal investigator must continue to conduct the investigation and make sure that his findings are consistent with any new facts developed in this phase of the investigation. As this process occurs, the new court team is put in place to replace the squad and potentially the investigator's partner. Many local jurisdictions have criminal investigators who work for the prosecuting attorney's office. These employees of the prosecutor's office are usually well-trained criminal investigators with prior law enforcement training and experience. They then become a member of the investigative team and usually try to work well with the lead police investigator.

The next members of a court team are *forensic scientists*, who will be testifying about their scientific findings. When a prosecution requires the proof supplied by the results of scientific tests and examinations, these expert witnesses will become important members of the court team. From the lead criminal investigator's point of view, these persons are witnesses whose importance is directly related to their expertise and *ability* to successfully offer their opinions about the results of the scientific examinations. Most of the time, these experts are employees of a government forensic laboratory, and as such, they are part of the court team. Careful consideration needs to be given to the fact that they need to maintain objectivity in their suggestions and advice. They are nonetheless part of the court team. Their expertise and guidance are essential in informing how the defendant's countervailing scientific experts should be evaluated. For example, a county medical examiner's opinion derived from his autopsy should be critically compared with autopsy results of an outside medical examiner expert hired by the defendant. A government firearms expert should be able to evaluate the findings of a defense expert in the same field. In trials, there are occasions when scientific evidence is examined and experts disagree about the results. This makes the government's case weak; the best counterbalance is to be ready to explain the discrepancy in the opinions. Expert testimony is a significant area of conflict in trials, and that is especially true in new or rarely used areas of forensic science.

The final important part of the court team is the *crime scene examiner* who handled the gathering of physical evidence at a crime scene. In most cases, these persons are police agency employees who may be sworn officers or forensically trained civilians. Their job can involve the recovery of physical evidence and the forwarding of that evidence to the appropriate forensic expert. State or federal laboratories, outside contract labs, or other approved, independent forensic experts who are expected to conduct appropriate scientific examinations on the evidence are the appropriate experts with whom the Crime Scene technician works with. These entities then issue formal reports, which are not necessarily relevant for the trial. It is only when the report is relevant and offers scientific proof of a significant fact to be proposed and argued at trial that the information is significant. The crime scene examiner will generally be responsible for explaining the chain of custody of evidence and how the evidence was obtained at the scene. She will also provide the court team with the reports, both relevant and not relevant, so all the physical evidence is accounted for and any examinations done are documented.

The crime scene examiner is usually a significant colleague of the lead investigator since they collaborate on the best methods to handle the physical evidence throughout the bulk of the investigation. These examiners also try to maintain a level of objectivity to avoid the appearance of any corrupt actions, such as evidence tampering. Even though the crime scene examiner is a police agency employee, it is essential that the judge and jury view her actions as distinct from the criminal investigator's. The caveat to this sought-after relationship is inherent in small, local police agencies and remote investigative agencies where the crime scene work is done by the criminal investigator. Even well-funded federal agencies, such as the FBI, will have crime scene examinations conducted by the criminal investigator because of the remoteness of some crime scenes. In fact, it wasn't until the 1990s that the FBI established crime scene examination teams, known as evidence response teams. Prior to that time, the FBI relied on local police crime scene teams and agent investigators to conduct their own crime scene examinations.

CRIMINAL INVESTIGATION TEAM

- Detective/Investigator
- Crime Scene Specialist
- Prosecutor
- State or Commonwealth Attorney's Investigator
- Forensic Expert

The court team for criminal cases is described below.

A criminal investigation that progresses to court must include the development of effective teamwork among all these components to ensure success. Teamwork does not always reflect this kind of linear progression. Solutions to reactive crimes will, in many cases, go through this process. First responders, investigative units or squads, prosecutors, and an appropriate cadre of experts are viewed as the main investigative components, but most cases don't flow directly from crime to solution. Investigations are not always this simple. There is usually a need for specialized components, which are significant support units in local police, state police, and federal agencies. These specialized components are essential to the solution of many criminal cases.

SPECIALIZED UNITS

Most police agencies create units whose functions are not only investigative but are also tasked with crime prevention. As discussed in chapter 1, uniform patrol officers have limited criminal investigative responsibilities. Their main mission is crime prevention. The management of the department will review the crime data in their jurisdiction and deploy patrol resources to high-crime neighborhoods or to important commercial areas where businesses may be victimized by criminal elements. In this manner, the police are distributing police resources to the geographic locations where they are most needed. This will reduce response time and, in some cases, act as a deterrent by the mere fact that police units are highly visible symbols causing criminals to avoid detection and arrest. In some jurisdictions, these uniform patrols will not only reduce crime but also confront suspects and report on their activities. This can be of significant help to some criminal investigations in the same neighborhood. These uniform patrols don't necessarily constitute specialized units, but it is essential that criminal investigators develop solid communication with the officers in the patrol

Source: iStock 479495677

Source: iStock 531174819

service area of their criminal investigations to take advantage of the patrol officers as part of their team.

There are specialized units, such as vice units, tactical squads, surveillance squads, bicycle patrol units, gang units, and organized crime units that are established to prevent crime, identify ongoing criminal conspiracies, and conduct short-term or, in some cases, long-term investigations focused on significant criminal conspiracies or significant crime problems. There are also computer tech squads, which have two important missions when it comes to criminal investigations. These two missions may mean the squad members have two different levels of training and experience. The first mission is data recovery, open source mining, and accessing the variety of law enforcement websites that contain suspect data lawfully obtained from multiple law enforcement units. Technicians in these units are trained to know how to search out available information from the internet that provides reliable and some questionable information about a suspect or group of suspects. The second mission is forensic examination of personal devices legally recovered in search warrants, searches incident to arrests, and any evidence that has been encrypted using sophisticated software. Criminal investigators need to develop relationships with members of these units to broaden the resources available to an investigative partnership or squad so that all the police resources are tapped to ensure the case or cases are solved. Specialized units become part of the team relied on by the lead investigators.

Vice Units

Vice units work cases involving crimes against the morals of the community. Prostitution, gambling, and drug use are the criminal patterns they are responsible for deterring and disrupting. In most jurisdictions in the United States, it is impossible to stop these crimes. These crimes are considered victimless crimes in that the participants on both sides of the transactions want to commit the crime. This analysis is very faulty when consideration is given to the fact that street prostitutes are victims of human trafficking, child rape, and sexual exploitation. They also become involved in addictive behavior, such as drug abuse and alcoholism. Gambling takes a horrific toll on the financial resources of the gamblers and their families. Gambling also generates income for organized crime enterprises with little risk of prosecution.

Drug use has the dire consequence of drug addiction, which leads to other criminal behavior, such as burglary, theft, murder, and gun assaults. Violence erupts over the control of lucrative drug markets. The compromise and corruption of police and court systems by bribery and quid pro quo transactions that disrupt the whole criminal justice system are perpetrated because of the enormous profits from the enterprise. Drug distribution is also a profitable enterprise that fuels organized criminal activity. These units can be called by many names, such as drug units, special investigative units, and strike force units. They usually have the following two missions: (1) *immediate response* to complaints from citizens about open-air neighborhood drug dealing and (2) *short- and long-term* investigations of drug dealers and their suppliers. The units try to meet these two missions by surveillance and undercover transactions with the drug dealers. They will also make controlled purchases from residences to develop probable cause for a search warrant. This allows the unit to recover drug contraband and develop usable intelligence against the drug distribution enterprises operating in their jurisdiction. They meet the first mission by aggressive policing of the drug operations to frustrate or disrupt the sales in a particular neighborhood and move the drug operation from the affected neighborhood. They meet the second mission by carefully arresting suspects, executing search warrants, and conducting physical surveillance of the drug distribution, which yields valuable intelligence about how the operations work. Arrest reports, search warrant reports and inventories, and surveillance reports become a treasure trove of high-level intelligence for use by criminal investigators who are trying to make connections to other criminal conduct. The drug enterprises often act as a central structure in the community's criminal ecosystem. Burglars sell stolen property to drug dealers. Armed robbers decompress after a big score by buying and using drugs along with taking advantage of local prostitutes. Murderers and rapists also use drugs to cope with their criminal mindset. Murderers also are employed by major drug suppliers who are interested in paying back a criminal enemy. In other words, the intelligence developed by a vice unit can be essential to solving a number of crimes in a community. The reason vice units are effective is that their cases are, in many instances, based on mere possession of the contraband drugs. If the drugs involved are dangerous drugs, such as heroin, fentanyl, cocaine, crack, PCP, and methamphetamine, and the amount is felony weight, the charge can be extremely serious without much investigative effort. Finally, these vice units develop confidential sources as their lifeblood. These informants are usually persons who are arrested by the unit and have significant charges hanging over their heads, so it is in their interest to provide accurate and quality information to the police for consideration.

A criminal investigator must make sure she has an intelligence pipeline to the vice unit for any criminal case because the vice unit's responsibilities will inform other criminal investigations.

Tactical Squads

Tactical squads (Tact squads) are crime response and crime prevention units that are tasked with a variety of criminal offenses apart from vice units. These units go by a variety of titles but the mission is the same. *Tact* is the short form of *tactical*, meaning these squads have a focused mission whereby they are expected to use every legal means available to respond to a crime problem. Officers assigned to these units are expected to be tactically sound in their immediate response because these teams make arrests, execute warrants, and conduct instantaneous surveillance and interviews on the fly in fast-moving, short-term investigations. Car thefts, car burglaries, residential burglaries, and commercial burglaries that proliferate in a particular neighborhood or a distinct geographic area will be targeted by a tact squad. Their job is to locate and arrest the person or persons responsible for the spike in a certain criminal activity. Obviously, these units will also generate important intelligence about larcenous activity in a particular neighborhood. They will have contact with suspicious persons who frequent the neighborhood and will know or hear about criminal associates. They will develop confidential sources who may provide the right information about a specific crime under investigation by an investigative partnership or squad.

A criminal investigator who is working crime events that are part of a tact team's assignment needs to make the tact team part of his investigative team. This is especially important in burglary cases in which the suspect is likely to be a career criminal. Burglars, like several other categories of criminals, are serial offenders, and as such, any successful intervention or arrests by the tact team will provide informative intelligence in helping to close the case. The tact team's work can also be essential in determining that the singular investigation needs to be turned into a proactive investigation involving the combining of similar cases into one investigative cooperative effort.

Tact teams in some departments and agencies are also assigned to more significant cases, such as commercial armed robberies or commercial burglaries in a dense commercial neighborhood. These teams will employ surveillance, both static and mobile, to make a significant effort to deter gangs of robbers who frequently attack businesses in the area. Detectives or investigators who have individual armed robbery cases will need to make sure they have a solid relationship with the tact squad so that all the intelligence developed by the team is analyzed for pertinence.

It should be noted at this point that vice units and tact units are usually made up of younger, aggressive officers who come to these units as stepping-stones to promotions in a department. As such, some of the more capable officers will eventually become detectives or inspectors. Senior criminal investigators should be considering these officers for future assignment and spending the time to mentor them and support their ambition while respectfully taking advantage of their work.

Vice units and tact squads can be referred to by several names: narcotics investigation squads, morals units, crime prevention squads, strike force teams, and target squads.

Surveillance Squads

Surveillance squads are specialized units whose main function is static and mobile surveillance of *important targets* of proactive investigations. These squads will be employed only for significant criminal investigations. They will have a variety of technical and vehicular resources. Photographic and videographic training and resources are tools that squads can employ. They will also be trained in tactical driving and be able to immediately blend into suspicious neighborhoods. These units will also have specialized tactical training for armed confrontations. These kinds of units are occasionally part of vice units or organized crime squads. The average criminal investigator may have access to these units only if the case warrants their use. Obviously, the hope is that the surveillance squad will observe direct criminal conduct or a meeting with conspirators, contraband suppliers, and the like. These units should be employed only when solid intelligence is developed that indicates major criminal conduct or conspiratorial behavior is anticipated. Day-to-day surveillance conducted to establish a pattern of behavior by a target should be requested only if the surveillance squad is able to spend the time for this routine work.

Bicycle Patrol Units

Bicycle patrol units are specialized units utilized in high-crime neighborhoods where more effective response can be expected by uniform officers. These are intense units with physically demanding requirements. Their investigative support function is the same as the patrol service area or beat patrol officers. These units employ aggressive, young, physically fit officers whose activity is usually focused on a very distinct neighborhood. It is likely they will be very familiar with career criminals in their patrol area and may have firsthand experience with criminal targets. (Depending on the financial resources and the location of the department or agency, these units may be on small, low-powered motorcycles or even horses.) These units have been developed to ensure a more one-on-one relationship between the police officers and the people in a high-crime community and to enhance police and community relations in neighborhoods where the citizenry believes that police officers have lost touch with the community because they are unapproachable when they are patrolling in their police cruisers. The bicycle allows the citizens a more reasonable chance for positive interactions. These units, in many jurisdictions, are the evolution of the beat cop, who walks around a neighborhood in hopes of preventing crime and responding to the variety of calls for service by modern police officers. Based on this up close and personal form of policing, these officers can be essential sources of reliable information about a particular neighborhood.

Gang and Organized Crime Units

Gang and organized crime units are specialized squads whose mission is intelligence gathering and conducting long-term conspiracy investigations. Investigations conducted by these high-priority squads can subsume criminal investigations conducted by general-assignment squads and detectives. This can be a source of conflict in some departments and agencies, but it is also likely that after information about the criminal investigation is shared, the lead criminal investigator can work out an accommodation with the supervisor or lead investigator of the gang or organized crime squad. Control of sensitive evidence, access to confidential sources, and exposure of significant investigative techniques, such as electronic surveillance, undercover operations, and sophisticated computer technologies, are the kinds of information resources that cannot be compromised by a general investigation. Using and protecting these sources of information while finding a way to close an armed robbery, rape, serious gun assault, or murder case can usually enhance and support a major criminal enterprise investigation that requires underlying or predicate offenses as part of the overall prosecutorial plan of attack for that major investigation.

Computer Squads

Computer squads are important units in every law enforcement agency in the United States. For the most part these units have evolved from crime data analyses units, which were part of the intelligence services in these agencies. The members of these squads are computer technicians and IT specialists who can provide up-to-date information about crime patterns in a community as well as access law enforcement and open source data from a variety of legally available digital file caches of information. Criminal investigators will need law enforcement database searches for witnesses, victims, and suspects in every investigation. The law enforcement databases include information from the FBI's National Crime Information Center (NCIC), which maintains computerized rap sheets on most persons arrested anywhere in the United States for a crime. NCIC also contains information about gang affiliation, terrorist connections, and significant information designed to ensure officer safety when a person identified via an inquiry on the database has an outstanding warrant or designation of danger, such as *armed and dangerous*. NCIC also maintains a list of stolen vehicles and property if the item has a nonrecurring serial number. NCIC is a growing and evolving database, which has been a bulwark of US and international law enforcement since it began in 1967. The underlying data in the system are derived from fingerprint arrest cards submitted by every law enforcement agency in the country and by theft reports submitted by those same law enforcement agencies.

The information necessary to derive a hit (a positive response) from NCIC is the name with the date of birth or other nonrecurring identification number, such as a police department identification number. Stolen item hits are derived from inputting the nonrecurring serial number, tag number, or vehicle identification number of the item stolen or recovered. NCIC is therefore limited to law enforcement use only (with the exception of firearms sales). NCIC is also used to check for any previous criminal history of persons who wish to purchase a firearm (usually a handgun). A background check may preclude them from making the purchase and is limited to checks where the search can't be completed with the specific date of birth, identification number, serial number, or vehicle identification number. NCIC is therefore a very important database for criminal investigators, but to use it, the investigator needs to know the nonrecurring numbers. As a result of these limitations, a criminal investigator needs to have access to local and regional DMV and law enforcement databases for which just a name, address, or other information can provide a positive return of data. In the Washington, DC, region WALES, MILES, and VCIN are state-sponsored databases in which names can be searched without a date of birth or other identification number. Similar local and regional databases exist in every jurisdiction throughout the United States. DMV records need to be maintained by local jurisdictions so that immediate response is available to uniform patrol officers who are making routine traffic stops 24 hours a day, 7 days a week. If these records are then coordinated with local arrest sheets and crime complaint data, the criminal investigator can recover a treasure trove of reliable information about a suspect, witness, or victim. Computer data technicians in these specialized units can provide extensive profiles of all the persons developed as suspects, witnesses, and victims in any investigation. Many of these local databases will even have digital identification photographs of the persons searched from DMV files or criminal databases. These kinds of computer data on persons who come up in criminal investigations provide reliable information and, in some cases, photographs that can usually be relied on in preliminary court proceedings, allowing for the positive identification of suspects by witnesses.

NCIC, local and regional law enforcement, and DMV records are therefore considered the basic individual background records that criminal investigators will need to begin their investigations. These checks then become an early preliminary step in any investigative plan. The capabilities of the computer support squads or units and their vital mission to a criminal investigation team does not end here.

Drug task forces, gang task forces, and organized crime operations throughout the United States have systematically gathered law enforcement and police intelligence from active police investigative efforts and entered that information into a series of national and regional databases. Access to these databases generally requires that the police agency seeking access participate or input data into the system. Once the access to the database is verified, the computer analysts can conduct checks in these more sophisticated databases to provide a more detailed profile of suspects, witnesses, and victims in an investigation. The main control of these data files is that they all contain law enforcement-sensitive information and carry penalties for abuse similar to classified documents in the realm of national security data. Databases such as Gang Net, Case Explorer, and CJIN MDN are searchable databases and computer programs with the capability of case management. In other words, case investigators can use these specialized and tightly controlled databases to administratively manage a long-term investigation. As such, any access granted to a criminal investigator who is working an otherwise unrelated investigation will be identified to the overall case manager.

Computer squads are also capable of conducting relevant searches of open source databases and recovering important intelligence information from any number of internet systems that gather and share information. For example, anyone with a computer can search Facebook and some of the social media platforms and determine if a particular person has an account on the platform. Access to the details on the account can be accessed in two ways. Anyone can send a friend request to join the list of persons who have access. Law enforcement can officially obtain a court order to access the data without notifying the account holder. A covert approach can be made using a name or profile consistent or pleasing to the account holder and thereby receiving access to the account from the account holder.

In these and other ways, the computer squad or IT resource analyst can provide an extraordinary amount of intelligence from public data sources, such as the US Bureau of Prisons Inmate Locater website, county land records, real estate sales databases, and state and county tax records. There are also official records that can be accessed by any criminal investigative agency as open source records. Finally, public databases or platforms (Facebook, Twitter, Tumblr, Myspace, and other social networking sites) with account restrictions can be accessed in various legitimate ways to further inform a criminal investigation. The tech industry is evolving and coming under increased scrutiny. At some point, these platforms may become more restrictive and regulated, but as of 2018, the data on these websites are less controlled.

Personal Experience

After retiring from the FBI, I assisted in the prosecution of a violent drug gang in Flint, Michigan. Members of that gang posted photographs of drug proceeds, illegal weapons, drug contraband, and a number of incriminating statements about violence committed by the gang members on their Myspace social network. These postings were used to help convict all the gang members and to fill in gaps about their ongoing criminal conspiracy. These impetuous examples of bragging and attempts at intimidation are not limited to one group of foolish criminals, but as the criminal ecosystem becomes aware of the use of these kinds of postings in investigations and prosecutions, it is expected that they will become less direct and more sophisticated. Fortunately for law enforcement and criminal investigators, young criminals find it hard not to tout their aggressive criminal conduct and celebrate their successes. Developing a complete social profile of criminal suspects can greatly enhance the criminal investigator's ability to anticipate behavior and catalog leads that may help in determining the suspect's whereabouts and social interaction on the day the crime occurred. These kinds of social network computer exploitations provide a new avenue of reliable intelligence.

Finally, computer squads will have very sophisticated and highly educated forensic experts who are skilled in opening Pandora's box when it comes to encrypted computer software. Digital devices, such as cell phones, tablets, and laptop and desktop computers, are used in any number of criminal behaviors. The criminals have evolved with their tech skills and taken advantage of methods to hide the files they use in openly documenting or describing their criminal conduct. They may have target files of victims; casing, or setup, files containing notes about their crime targets; and financial records exposing their criminal income. Depending on the nature and extent of their criminal behavior, criminals' devices can be used to hide evidence of homicide, rape, child abuse, armed robbery, and every type of financial crime or money-laundering apparatus. Access to this evidence usually requires a court order or search warrant, but the forensic computer expert is an essential member of the investigative team who will be able to reveal the hidden files. Based on the size and resources of the investigative agency, these experts may be available in the department as a computer squad resource or part of a centralized regional or national computer forensic lab similar to the more traditional forensic science experts used to examine physical evidence. Computer squads will in many cases act as a conduit to the most expert practitioners of this kind of sophisticated analysis to speak the language and communicate with the criminal investigators whose sophistication in this area may be woefully inadequate. These squads are also essential if electronic real-time surveillance is authorized by a Title III court order. The computer experts will be able to ensure access to text messages, emails, FaceTime, and Skype communications along with other computerized communications. To capture the criminal conversations or communications, a technical expert is needed to gain proper access while adhering to the restrictions of the Constitution and Omnibus Crime Control Act of 1968 and subsequent statutory and court rulings.

SUMMARY

All of this immediate access to reliable intelligence makes the criminal investigator's investigative planning easier and more productive. On the surface and in many ways, the success or failure of a criminal investigation relies on the work of the lead investigator and his partner, but in fact and in almost all cases, the success of any investigation relies on teamwork as well as solid and productive relationships and avoidance of any jealous or demanding counterproductive rancor or egotism. The lead investigator needs to know that the decision-making process is in her hands, but without the team, there will be no positive conclusion. A primary skill the lead investigator needs to develop is the ability to form the team, consider what resources from his agency will help solve the case, and ensure proper communication among the team members. For the most part, with every iteration of an investigative team, the lead criminal investigator is the manager of the investigation until the case enters the court system, at which point, the investigator will relinquish that role to the prosecutor. A good criminal investigator learns that inspiration and creative results can come from any member of the team. Therefore, expressing appropriate praise and admiration for an important contribution in an investigation is essential. Remembering this very human construct will curtail some of the angst created when the lead investigator and not the rest of the team is praised by management from the agency or department and given credit for solving the case.

Chapter Five

Prioritizing Investigations

Priority based on serious violence, property and financial crimes, vice or morals investigations.

In our discussion of criminal investigations, we have defined what a criminal investigation is and determined that there are at least two major categories of criminal investigations: *reactive* and *proactive*. We have introduced the job titles and descriptions of governmental employees who are responsible for conducting the investigations. We have also discussed the criminal laws or statutes that particularly define a crime and explained methods of proving specific elements of those laws. We then turned our attention to the most important guidelines that must be followed in conducting criminal investigations. Those guidelines are memorialized in the US Constitution and further defined as the "rights of the accused," which are detailed in the first ten amendments to the Constitution known as the Bill of Rights. We have discussed the group, or team, that most often gets the assignment and works to get at the truth and obtain justice for victims and our community. We should note at this point that, in most cases and under most circumstances, the local, state, and federal governments use the "police" power or authority of the government to establish, fund, and support the investigative agencies that do the work required.

Historically, the police power of the government was handled by mediation between parties in a dispute. These were often Roman centurions, or Vigiles, who acted as firemen and community "watchers"; monarch-appointed magistrates; and jurisdictional lawmen, such as sheriffs, or "shire-reeves." It wasn't until the nineteenth century that urban populations became so large and unwieldy that law enforcement became the responsibility of governmental units known as police. The Home Secretary of England in 1840 was tasked with developing the first professional organization given this responsibility. The actions of England and the evolution of Western civilization directly affected the United States. Just as England provided the statutory basis for our criminal code, it also provided us with a model for police departments. Principles for police were fashioned by Sir Robert Peale, whose name was used as the eventual nickname for the London police officers, "bobbies." Bobbies followed nine

important principles as to how police should conduct themselves. These principles are as relevant today as they were almost 200 years ago.

Among the nine principles are concepts of police and community cooperation. In other words, it is impossible to police a society without the will of the people supporting that effort. In the nineteenth century, when so many countries were still ruled by monarchs, the "divine right of kings" was an actual basis for the law. Police and community cooperation establishing control of a civilian population was revolutionary.

The Industrial Revolution took place in the latter half of the nineteenth century. This led to a major shift in our societies from agrarian to industrial urban population centers whose teeming populations with endemic anonymity created a new wave of criminal conduct that required professional policing and a cooperative effort from the community. Try though they might, monarchies were unable to establish real control of population centers such as Paris, Lisbon, Rome, Barcelona, Berlin, and London without the "consent of the governed." In the United States, cities such as New York, Philadelphia, Chicago, and New Orleans had the same problem, but at least in this country, there was no need to blame a king for inadequate police response.

In the United States, police power derived from the community, and the will of the people determined how effective policing would be. As a result of this evolution, there arose a need to set priorities for policing by the people. A bank robbery in a small town in nineteenth-century America was a devastating financial calamity for that community. Able-bodied men from the whole town would immediately call together a posse and aggressively pursue the robbers (who were usually outsiders from other towns). This is an example of the level of importance given to such a crime. In the same way, stealing a horse or cattle that provided essential transportation and a living to a rural family was a particularly heinous crime calling for significant police actions. The penalty for such a theft could in many cases be death. This showed the priority of such a crime.

Any crime that threatened the livelihood or life of a victim was a high-priority crime. A crime or group of crimes that threatened these same needs for more members of the community demanded significant law enforcement action. Throughout the country, taxes were levied, police agencies were established, and the people made a compact with their police practitioners to forgo certain freedoms to create a safer atmosphere for themselves and their families. In other words, the people granted the police the authority to do the job within the confines of criminal statutes and the Constitution's guaranteed rights of persons accused of crimes.

In larger cities and towns, the criminals were able to blend in and disappear into anonymity. Towns such as Chicago, San Francisco, and New York began experimenting with criminal investigation units whose priorities would be the same kinds of crimes. They would spend the time and resources needed to identify the suspect and prosecute the offender. Crimes against the life or livelihood of the victims resulted in a high-priority investigation when more people were affected. Rape, child molesting, and spousal or child abuse were considered serious offenses, but the documented history of these crimes was not as clearly detailed. Subjects who were determined to be responsible for these kinds of offenses were severely punished, but it is likely the citizen complaints about these types of crimes were suppressed because of the sexual nature of the offenses in a puritanical or culturally conservative consciousness. The society was not willing to openly confront these types of aberrant behavior as being anything but unusual anomalies. Police and local communities may have taken extralegal actions to punish these offenders to try to cut out this malignant, abnormal conduct from the community. How effective that strategy was is not well documented by historians.

In today's modern law enforcement, crimes against persons, in the form of murder, serious and aggravated assault with dangerous weapons, rape and other sexual assaults, armed robbery, and any major or significant larcenous actions where high-value property or funds are stolen, are considered high-priority investigations. The concept of prioritizing crime hasn't changed that much, so any criminal action that indicates a complete disregard for the life, well-being, or livelihood of the community is necessarily a priority for criminal investigation units.

PRIORITY BASED ON SERIOUS VIOLENCE

To determine which investigations should be considered a priority by an investigative unit, it is necessary to consider (1) the impact on the community, (2) the investigative or law enforcement resources necessary to solve the case, and (3) the prosecutorial resources needed to complete the investigation. Criminal investigators can identify the level of violence perpetrated on the victim and gauge how that violence disturbs the sense of security in the community. Indiscriminate and unrestrained violence will shake the community and instill fear. A series of burglaries where the residences are empty and property is stolen will disturb the community *if* the number of incidents is high. Individually, these burglaries will have a considerable effect on the individual victim but should be prioritized only if the jurisdiction's numbers are very high.

There are some cases (homicide, rape, gun assaults, bombings, and arson) that just by their very nature and level of violence will generate fear in the community.

That fear may be lessened if the victim and the perpetrator know each other and the conflict that led to the violence is determined to be personal and not a more universal danger. Unsolved examples of these very violent offenses committed by strangers for some unknown motive will stoke the embers of fear and can disturb that sense of safety communities demand from their police agencies. Additionally, if these cases exhibit extraordinary levels of violence or disturbing calculation, such as in the cases of terrorism or gang violence, the community will express a desire to have the law enforcement community expend resources and place these cases in an even higher priority. Terrorism, gang violence, serial homicide, serial rape, serial arson, and any use of weapons of mass destruction will put extraordinary pressure on law enforcement to solve the case and capture, kill, disrupt, or dismantle the persons responsible for the fear.

Prioritizing violent crime justifies the establishment of a homicide bureau, unit, or squad. In the same way, a *special victim's unit* or *sex crimes unit* whose primary responsibility is sexual violence will also be established, staffed, and funded separately by a police agency. Gang squads and counterterrorism squads will be established in communities where criminal violence is carried out on a regular basis by gangs or cells of homegrown or international terrorists. (For purposes of this discussion, *gangs* are criminal enterprises by groups of persons who conduct a pattern of criminal activity, including violence to control and intimidate a community. *Terrorism* is defined as indiscriminate violence carried out to support or embolden some radical political cause.)

Almost every major urban community in the United States has two or more of these kinds of units or squads in its criminal investigation division (CID). In most cases, local police departments will establish these units if they have a significant number of these kinds of crimes to justify the continued focus of veteran investigators. The investigators assigned to these units are usually handpicked, skilled investigators who have proven their ability to handle these kinds of cases. Extremely large communities, such as New York, Chicago, Los Angeles, and San Francisco, will also have violent crime investigators who conduct homicide and rape investigations at a district or precinct level. This level of law enforcement then adds another layer of investigative resources if the violent crime problem is so extensive as to overwhelm a centralized homicide or sex crimes unit or squad.

In smaller, local communities, suburban or exurban police agencies will be established only if a community is convinced that the number of violent crime incidents justifies the need for a specialized unit. *Robbery–homicide units* or *homicide–sex crimes units* and similar hybrid squads may be established and staffed to allow for veteran, experienced investigators to handle these serious assignments. Rural county police and small-town police will usually maintain a single investigative unit with veteran police detectives who investigate whatever violent crimes occur in their jurisdiction.

In all these police agencies, violent crimes will always have high priority, and the agency will devote significant investigative resources to solve the cases. It should be noted that criminal investigators in major urban communities and small towns may have very similar backgrounds and experience. Just because the investigators work in general-assignment CID units in small jurisdictions or have a significant team of well-trained colleagues in specialized homicide squads in large urban jurisdictions, their abilities and success rate may be very similar. Criminal investigators with dogged determination, good communication skills, excellent memory, and familiarity with the criminal ecosystem in which they operate will be successful in their case work.

State and federal investigative agencies also prioritize violent crime investigations. Obviously, most state police agencies will operate using the same criminal statutes investigated by local police, but they will establish guidelines and circumstances by consulting with the local police and the state prosecutor's office where they assume primary responsibility for major violent crimes. A murder or rape in a rural community without investigative resources will become the responsibility of the state police. Violent crimes that have some kind of political or statewide controversy (for example, a police-involved crime, racially or ethnically motivated crime, and violence to or by a celebrity whose notoriety may affect the significant pressure on a local jurisdiction) may become the responsibility of the state police. Any multijurisdictional crime spree or serial violent crime may also become the responsibility of the state police so that the investigation can be more focused and well directed. The priority is the fact that the crime is violent and demands significant attention, and the state police may have more significant resources to handle the case to ensure that aspects of jurisdiction and eventual prosecution are not compromised.

The prioritization of violent crimes by federal law enforcement usually involves investigations for which statutory federal authority and jurisdiction is clear and the extra financial and investigative resources of the FBI, Bureau of Alcohol, Tobacco, Firearms and Explosives (ATF), Drug Enforcement Administration (DEA), and other federal criminal investigative agencies may be more effective in finding the truth and solving the case. The most typical example of how federal agencies enter violent crime investigations is *organized crime* cases. It is a fact that local police agencies won't have the time and resources to spend months and years targeting a criminal organization in their community that is responsible for significant violence. It may immediately be well understood that a criminal organization is responsible for a murder, serious assault, or even violent rape. However, the anonymity of violent predators inside a criminal organization may require significant time and carefully targeted one-off investigations to develop an inside source of reliable intelligence to identify the person or team that carries out violence for the organization. These slowly developing investigations will require manpower and an exorbitant amount of time and financial resources to break through to this inside source of information.

In the world of federal law enforcement, *organized crime investigations* are considered high priority primarily because they are centered on groups of criminals who are violent, intimidating, and make every effort to deter community cooperation to law enforcement. The effort to deter community cooperation adds the extra dimension of corrupting the local criminal justice system, adding to the high-priority nature of these criminal investigations. Nationwide and especially in large urban centers where organized crime groups have established their corrupt foothold, the federal agency will establish multijurisdictional task forces to investigate the group and successfully prosecute, dismantle, and disrupt the organization or enterprise. These same kinds of federal high-priority investigations will also be used to establish street gang task forces and significant drug trafficking task forces. These violent criminal organizations are targeted with an all-encompassing investigative approach. Electronic surveillance and myriads of other sophisticated surveillance techniques (which will be discussed in detail in chapter 17) are used. The need for extraordinary devotion of manpower to these cases makes them local, state, and federal priority investigations. In general, these cases will also develop a nationwide or international network of criminal conspiracy, which can be properly investigated only by an investigative agency with federal authority.

A second, very public display of federal investigators prioritizing violent crime is *kidnapping cases*. When a criminal or group of criminals abducts a victim and holds that victim for ransom, the FBI is usually brought in to oversee the investigation since it is likely to involve interstate commerce. Ransoms demanded are usually huge amounts of money to be paid by the families of wealthy victims. Unfortunately, kidnapping for ransom is not the only motive for these crimes. Child and many adult abductions may require federal investigative resources. The average police department can't sustain the kind of long-term diversion of investigative manpower that the FBI can. Child abduction investigations are also a part of the FBI's intense investigative interest in trying to thwart child predators who sexually assault children for personal gratification and even profit.

There are generally two archetypes of sexual predators: socially sophisticated sociopaths and socially awkward, violent-prone offenders. *Socially sophisticated sociopaths* use their manipulation skills to avoid detection by law enforcement. These predators don't often abduct children. They commit their crimes by using their charisma, charm, and openness to allow children any behavior that leads them to submit to seduction. These offenders rely on children's fear of retribution and embarrassment about their conduct avoid being detected. *Socially awkward, violent-prone offenders* will abduct a child to gratify their desire and then destroy the child and any evidence tying them to the crime. Since any child predation is viewed by the community as evil and despicable, these criminal investigations will receive as much investigative support as is possible in most communities. Since these cases may be investigated by local, state, and federal entities, there is usually a case-centered task force established to follow leads, conduct interviews, and perform other required investigative steps. Ongoing multijurisdictional task forces may also play a part in providing the kind of prioritization of resources an investigative strategy needs to address this problem.

Prioritizing violent crime investigations ensures that the cases are supported by necessary manpower, budgetary resources, and management review. This support allows the community to believe that these crimes will be worked on and solved to ensure that the number one law enforcement priority of keeping the community safe is met. The community needs to see that law enforcement is using its authority to remove violent criminals and make every effort to ensure justice for the crime victims and their families. By making violent crime a number one priority, the criminal investigators are delivering on a promise and protecting the most vulnerable in our society.

PROPERTY AND FINANCIAL CRIMES

The second level of priority for investigative resources is crimes where property or money is stolen. There is a crossover with violent crime because armed robbery is both a violent crime and a financial crime. Residential burglary is a property crime, but the personal impact on the victim can have significant effects on a person's sense of security. Because burglary is a significant invasion of a victim's personal space, victims have experienced real traumatic psychological effects. The nature and extent of the financial loss is usually the gauge that governs the number of investigative resources that will be used to work cases and prioritize the resources available. For example, DNA examinations of physical evidence from a burglary crime scene are not usually conducted due to the cost of those exams. Much has been mentioned in the media about rape kits not being examined to determine a DNA profile of the suspect until an individual suspect is actually identified by other investigative means. This shortfall in budgetary support for rape kits shows that even in more high-priority violent crime investigations, there are budgetary restraints on expensive scientific examinations.

Burglary investigations are usually handled by general-assignment detectives who work all manner of larcenies and automobile thefts. Conducting DNA profiles on hundreds of burglaries per year in a given state is just too much for most local police departments. The individual investigators may be overwhelmed with 50 to 100 investigations per year, and their closure numbers (cases ending in arrest) may reach only 50 percent per year. But by sheer numbers, twenty-five to fifty arrests per year would be high numbers and indicate a successful investigative response by a local detective.

Which detectives work armed robberies is usually broken down by the facts relating to the incident. High-dollar commercial armed robberies, such as bank robberies and supermarket robberies, are usually worked by a robbery squad with veteran detectives who work low numbers of cases. In most jurisdictions in the United States, a typical robbery squad detective may handle no more than twenty-five to thirty-five cases per year. Street robberies, also known as muggings, are one-on-one incidents in which small amounts of cash are stolen with credit cards and the like. These cases are lower priority and usually worked by general-assignment detectives. It should be noted that how these cases and the investigative responsibility break down depends on the jurisdiction.

An average or large-sized city may experience hundreds of armed robberies per year and require a well-trained robbery squad. Suburban jurisdictions with scattered commercial areas whose main areas are residential neighborhoods may experience hundreds of burglaries and car thefts per year. These jurisdictions may have only minimal numbers of serious armed robberies and homicides per year, so the bulk of investigative manpower will be used to handle burglaries and car thefts. Rural jurisdictions will experience less crime in general, and therefore, veteran investigators may work all types of criminal investigations and prioritize violent crimes over property crimes, and hybrid crimes (such as armed robberies) over burglaries and larcenies. The number of property crimes and existence of patterns, or recurring activity, by the same criminals will cause the cases to be prioritized along with the availability of manpower. Usually, the will of the people will be expressed by the agents of political governance who oversee the departments and local police agencies. These agents can be mayors, councilmen, and other elected officials who take their oversight authority seriously. Police managers will respond to these influencers who are acting for the people because their budget is managed by these representatives of the community.

Personal Experience

During my career, I assisted a detective sergeant from a small, rural county in Virginia who was working a double homicide. The suspects in the case were low-level Washington, DC, crack cocaine dealers. They brutally killed two local buyers of their product who failed to pay the money they owed. The detective sergeant was told by his department that he should work the case until it was solved. When I began working with him, he had been on the case for more than a year and a half without an arrest. His police department had limited manpower, but for more than two years, he was removed from any other investigative assignments due to the priority nature of the murders. These two murders were the only two murders in the region for more than five years, so they had to be solved no matter what investigative resources had to be sacrificed. Because of his hard work and resolve, we were able to execute search warrants of the residences of the drug dealers and consequently provide enough evidence to prove the two were involved in a drug enterprise. That evidence together with the physical evidence from the crime scene and witness statements from all the drug users in his jurisdiction provided the proof he needed to convict the two dealers of the murders in the furtherance of the drug enterprise. The case ended in a successful prosecution in the regional US-Federal district court for murder in the furtherance of racketeering enterprise.

The local prosecutor refused to prosecute the case on the physical evidence and testimony from the local witnesses because the detective did not have a confession. The detective had no choice but to try to build a federal case against the suspects.

Jurisdictional priorities and the crime problem become significant factors in how property crimes and financial crime investigations are viewed. All too often, it is very simply a value game. A $20,000 commercial theft is more important than a $10,000 commercial theft. A $10,000 loss in a residential burglary may have a higher priority than a $500 loss of property. The variation that changes this dynamic is when the crime becomes repetitive. As discussed in chapter 2, armed robbery and burglary are *serial crimes*. The offenders who commit these crimes are career criminals who determine the best way to avoid detection, establish a single fence for stolen property or a person to launder the cash proceeds of their robberies, and then commit multiple offenses. In this way, the individual crimes become less important, but the pattern of criminal conduct pushes these cases into the forefront. In many cases, the connections between cases may not manifest immediately, and the numeric value of each case will determine its relative importance. (There will be further discussion about modus operandi [MO] and serial offenders in chapter 8.) For now, the priority of a case that is a property crime or financial crime will depend on the amount or value of the property stolen unless a pattern of crimes raises the importance of the investigation for the community.

A similar dynamic occurs in the distribution of resources in federal agencies. Federal investigators from the FBI, Secret Service, and ATF and inspectors from the US Postal Service (USPS) along with agents from the Naval Criminal Investigative Service (NCIS), US Army Criminal Investigation Command (CID), and others conduct investigations of property crimes and financial crimes. The FBI prioritizes high-value robberies, burglaries, and thefts, but the agency pays particular attention to fraud against the government, bank fraud and embezzlement, and white collar crime investigations (which are not discussed in this text). The FBI also prioritizes bank robbery investigations because almost all banks in this country are federally insured, which makes each bank robbery a case that will be prosecuted federally. That is the single most important aspect of the FBI's response to property and financial crimes. Will the case be considered serious enough to be prosecuted in a US district court?

The FBI has responsibility for investigating interstate transportation of stolen property (valued higher than $5,000), theft from interstate shipments (value for a felony is $1,000 or higher), and interstate transportation of stolen motor vehicles. US Attorney offices throughout the United States have established very strict guidelines on the prosecution of these crimes. In most jurisdictions, the federal prosecutors won't consider these cases unless they are part of an ongoing pattern of theft or the single value of a case exceeds $50,000. The statutory values of these cases are so small that a field office or division of the FBI can work these cases in conjunction with local police agencies until they meet the criteria set by the local federal prosecutor. Interstate fencing investigations (purchase, resale, and storage of large amounts of stolen property); interstate car theft operations (chop shops, vehicle identification number–tampering operations, and conspiracies to traffic in high-end stolen cars); and FBI divisions whose responsibilities include overwhelming numbers of criminal investigations in other fields of investigations, such as drug trafficking, counterterrorism, and foreign counterintelligence, may exempt themselves from property crimes as a whole genre of investigations to pay attention to the higher-priority investigations. In this way, the agency is setting the priority based on *manpower* and available resources along with *prosecutorial discretion* (when the local federal prosecutor restricts their desire to prosecute property crimes investigations). These kinds of decisions may appear to be shirking the statutory responsibility for the agency, but in reality, because of concurrent jurisdiction with local authorities, this may simply be a more efficient use of law enforcement resources.

The Secret Service has significant jurisdiction for investigation of credit card theft, identity fraud, and related white collar crime investigations. Currently, these cases may be high priority due to the internet's impact on criminal behavior. Major international criminal organizations hack in or steal thousands and even millions of financial profiles to carry out credit card fraud, bank fraud, and wire fraud. Since enormous amounts of money and consumer products are stolen using these sophisticated methods, the investigations are prioritized and may even involve the USPS inspectors and other federal investigators.

The ATF conducts criminal investigations into any large-scale thefts of firearms, explosives, and shipments of tobacco, especially untaxed cigarettes. These property crime investigations are prioritized because of the likelihood that the contraband will be used by criminal or terrorist organizations.

The Department of Defense (DOD) investigative agencies, NCIS, CID, Coast Guard Investigative Service (CGIS), and Air Force Office of Special Investigations (AFOSI) investigate thefts of government property. These investigations are usually joint cases with the FBI and, as such, are prioritized by the value of the property stolen. These DOD agencies can seek prosecution in local or federal courts and in the military's Uniform Code of Military Justice (UCMJ) courts if the suspects are military personnel. When the FBI is participating in these investigations, case priorities are raised by the fact that it is likely cases will be prosecuted effectively.

Finally, the FBI has jurisdiction for *Hobbs Act* cases, which in some instances are significant armed robberies of armored cars. These robberies are not necessarily thefts of federally insured funds, but due to the high value of the loss and the violence involved, the jurisdiction of the FBI is considered based on the impact of the theft of the funds on interstate commerce. Named after Congressman Sam Hobbs (D-AL) and codified at 18 USC § 1951, the Hobbs Act is a US federal law enacted in 1946: "Whoever in any way or degree obstructs, delays, or affects commerce or the movement of any article or commodity in commerce, by robbery or extortion or attempts or conspires to do so, commits, or threatens physical violence to any person or property in furtherance of a plan or purpose to do anything in violation of this section shall be fined under this title or imprisoned not more than twenty years, or both."

Hobbs Act investigations base their federal jurisdiction on the interstate commerce clause of the US Constitution and not on the interstate transportation of stolen property. Hobbs Act violations are high-priority property crimes usually carried out by organized criminal conspirators, gangs, and organized crime families (e.g., La Cosa Nostra, Russian Mob, and Asian organized crime). They are prioritized because of the hybrid use of violence in carrying out the theft and the high probability that the case will be prosecuted at a federal level; therefore, the large volume of FBI investigative resources are necessary for the case. Hobbs Act investigations can also be carried out by the Department of Labor criminal investigators when the suspects are involved in the obstruction of labor union activities.

The priority of the investigations of these kinds of federal criminal statutes is based on the investigative resources available from the federal agency and the opportunity to bring the case to federal court. Congress oversees the actions of these federal law enforcement agencies, and Congress acts for the people to prioritize the work of every federal agency. Historically, the people chose to limit the investigative reach of federal law enforcement and keep local agencies involved in crime control. Congress sets priorities based on the complicated nature of the criminal conduct and the jurisdictional confusion that can occur when the criminals use jurisdictional boundaries to frustrate and avoid local enforcement. Federal law enforcement and criminal investigations change priority and undergo restructuring of their criminal investigative resources based on changes in the federal law that occur with advances in technology.

It is therefore the community (people who set the priorities of criminal investigations through their elected officials) that decides how the taxpayers' money is spent.

This is true for violent crime and property crime investigations. There is one last priority to be discussed: crimes that violate the cultural mores of the community.

VICE, OR MORALS, INVESTIGATIONS

A discussion of criminal investigative priorities would not be complete without understanding the role of criminal investigators in dealing with the criminal conduct that takes advantage of our human instinct to act foolishly. Prostitution, gambling, and illegal drugs have been codified by our legislatures, both federal and state, as crimes. The crimes have historically been identified as victimless crimes since the persons who provide the drugs, prostitutes, and gambling venues are merely acting in accordance with the desires and wishes of the society. These crimes are categorized under the general heading of *vice,* or *morals, crimes.* The legislature views these crimes as denigrating and dangerous to the moral fabric of our society. Participants on both sides of the illegal transactions are viewed as corrupt. Participants can and should be prosecuted for this illegal behavior. The harsh reality is that there are victims to these crimes on both sides of the transactions.

Prostitutes are viewed in the eyes of the community as empowered women and men who provide a service for money. They are accepted for entrepreneurial spirit and effort. The truth is that 90 percent of the persons involved in prostitution are victims of child sexual abuse and human sex trafficking. At some point in their careers as sex workers, they may break from the control of a pimp, madam, or organized criminal syndicate. They may then be independent contractors, but it is rare to find a prostitute who hasn't experienced long-term violence, degradation, and abuse at the hands of career criminals who wish to control their transactional behavior. The response of most prostitutes to their participation in the sex business is to self-medicate with alcohol or illegal drugs, so this vice crime acts as a gateway to other criminal behavior. These participants are also damaged physically and have significant mental health concerns. To consider prostitutes as nonvictims is absurd on the face.

Johns, or customers who are on the other side of the transaction, are in most cases less damaged by the sex trafficking, but they are the reason the business exists. Some johns may act as grateful customers whose actions with the prostitutes are benign and not necessarily destructive, but since the transactions are a pay-for-play scenario and criminal in nature, all manner of disturbed, angry, and violent persons may choose prostitutes as an outlet for their rage. There are endless possibilities for violence and unpredicted behavior.

Throughout the United States, prostitution is practiced in a variety of ways. Outcall services involve customers making an appointment and paying a high price for the service. This is, generally, the high-end part of the criminal conduct. In some of these operations, the sex workers are provided security for the assignations and protected from unwanted contact by being provided with a layer of anonymity. Bordellos, or whorehouses, are also considered high-end operations in which the men and women who provide the sex service are housed and protected against violent behavior by clients. The sex workers are anonymous. Their real identities and home residences are protected from errant johns.

Most of the prostitution in this country occurs on the street using what is commonly referred to as a "track," a well-known street or neighborhood used as a meeting spot for prostitutes and their customers. Often, these tracks are overseen by pimps who make sure their stable of sex workers is protected, but in reality, the pimps are monitoring the transactions to ensure that a proper accounting of the money earned by the workers is made. In the United States, streetwalkers are the bottom rung of the ladder in prostitution. It should be noted that all the enterprises mentioned above have a management layer that is usually a criminal actor or enterprise that controls the sex worker and dominates the industry. These managers, whether pimps, madams, or criminal syndicates, make prostitution anything but a victimless crime. There are independent prostitutes, but in most cases, they have fled or found a way to extract themselves from the management layer and are constantly being pressured to reconnect with a pimp, madam, or syndicate, especially if the sex worker is still considered an attractive and sought-after commodity.

Prostitution exists in every community, large and small and urban, rural, and suburban. Most of the time, investigation of prostitution is a low-priority criminal matter. The concept of "live and let live" is followed. Consensual sex between adults is not a matter of concern to the community at large. But a persistent and disturbing feature of prostitution has emerged in recent times. Sex trafficking by criminal organizations has always been a part of the fabric of prostitution as a business enterprise. Business persons who manage the enterprise need a constant flow of new workers who meet the specifications of their customers. It has become more obvious that the new workers come from abused and discarded underage children. This has always been the case, but it has been only in the past twenty years that this disturbing aspect of prostitution has surfaced and the communities (the people) have demanded action against the criminals behind the business. There are laws against child sexual abuse and overt pimping or maintaining a bawdy house, but a more specific variation targeting sex traffickers, besides the typical organized crime statutes, may be required with a new emphasis on how sex workers are recruited and trained. Like most criminal behavior, this criminal conduct is difficult to detect, and the anonymity of the traffickers is ensured when the new workers are turned over to a madam or pimp (the end user), who may be the only persons who can be charged with prostitution-related offenses (which are notoriously weak in punishment). The sex workers themselves are compromised as witnesses by forced drug addiction and physical abuse to the point of torture. The workers are so fearful of their captors and disoriented by their surroundings that they may not be able to provide the kind of reliable testimony needed against their tormentors. Proving the case against a trafficker with testimony from an unsophisticated and abused child is a daunting task, but the community supports the prioritization of these kinds of criminal investigations.

Gambling is a low-priority criminal matter. Gambling generates enormous profits for bookies (sports-betting entrepreneurs), illegal casino operators, numbers runners (illegal lottery operators), illegal card game operators, and on and on. Gambling's main victim is the addicted gambler who wastes her livelihood and family's wealth trying to score that one big streak or win. This addictive behavior is just like alcoholism and drug addiction. Its effects can be devastating to the addict's loved ones, leaving them homeless and destitute. But gambling is becoming legal in so many ways throughout the nation that criminal investigations are rare. It may be the lowest of priorities for criminal violations still on the books.

Major interstate gambling operations have always been associated with traditional organized crime enterprises. The Mafia, or La Cosa Nostra, and the Asian Tong or Yakuza have major gambling syndicates throughout the United States. Most of them are illegal, but the communities' desire to pursue cases for these operations has lessened. Investigative resources may be used in certain communities for illegal sports betting associated with sports bars and other meeting places where gambling and socializing are attractive. However, interest in pursuing and prosecuting these enterprises for misdemeanor cases is very limited. Successful gambling operations also spawn other illegal enterprises that may be more significant. Gamblers often have a need for an infusion of cash. Loan sharks pursue their prey around gaming places. These career criminals who make enormous amounts of money charging usurious interest on short-term loans use violence and the threats of violence to intimidate those victims who choose not to pay the vigorish on time. Loan sharks are considered violent predators and may be the subject of aggressive criminal investigations.

DRUGS

Illegal drug possession and sale are significant and pervasive law enforcement problems in every community in the United States. Most local and state police agencies establish and maintain a significant unit or branch primarily responsible for investigating, dismantling, and/or disrupting this very lucrative business enterprise. Drug investigations and eventual prosecutions evolve from any number of other criminal investigations. Armed robbers who score large amounts of money may use these proceeds to invest into the business by purchasing at wholesale illegal drugs for retail sale with high profit margins. When a burglar is arrested and his residence is searched, it is likely drugs or drug paraphernalia will be located. Thieves, con men, gang members, and prostitutes use illegal drugs to recreate, relax, and self-medicate. It is almost impossible to work in criminal investigations without determining at some point that the suspects (career criminals) have some connection with illegal drug sales.

The priorities established in our communities about which illegal drugs should be most aggressively investigated are relatively simple. The level of danger inherent in the use of a drug raises its priority. The high danger factor has to do with a concern that if the drug is used, there is a chance that its mere use will cause death. Heroin, fentanyl, cocaine, and methamphetamine in above-normal levels will cause overdose deaths. Other drugs, such as PCP, bath salts, and many of the unregulated designer drugs, may cause dangerous hallucinations that may result in accidental death. Heroin, fentanyl, meth, and cocaine (crack) are highly addictive and will cause debilitating addiction that can destroy a person's ability to make a living, provide for a family, and maintain a normal life. In fact, overdosing on any of the above hard drugs may cause death or serious long-term impairment. The most important reason to consider these illegal drugs dangerous is that they are not regulated as to potency, adulterants, additives, and pharmaceutical safety. When properly manufactured, all these drugs have some kind of medicinal benefit. However, drug cartels, meth lab cooks, cocaine labs, and heroin labs in the jungles or fields of the Middle East or Southeast Asia have no quality control apparatus to ensure that the end product is safe. Synthesized drugs, such as MDMA (Ecstasy or Molly), were manufactured to avoid being placed on the federal government's illegal drug schedule, which is the basis for most criminal statutes investigated by police agencies. The attempt to avoid making a drug that meets the definition of a criminal statute is an ongoing cat-and-mouse game between criminal chemists and the DEA, which monitors and updates the schedule of illegal drugs.

Federal enforcement of illegal drug possession and sales is the chief responsibility of the DEA. The DEA evolved from the early twentieth-century effort to curb recreational drug use by taxing the sale and distribution of drugs. When these federal taxes weren't paid by a drug dealer, he could be charged in federal court with tax evasion, a traditional federal crime providing the government jurisdiction over this public health crisis. The tax collection function morphed into the Bureau of Narcotics and Dangerous Drugs, which eventually became the DEA. The DEA still maintains significant civil and administrative control responsibilities over the sale and distribution of legal pharmaceutical drugs. It also provides approval and monitoring of physicians' licenses to prescribe drugs to patients.

The DEA is a relatively small federal agency with enormous responsibilities. From 1984 to 1985, the FBI was tasked with providing more investigative resources to the DEA for criminal drug trafficking investigations. This change in federal priority was a policy decision in support of the war on drugs. Initially, the jurisdictional blending caused some difficulty and wrangling over cases, targets, and policy, but most of that has been worked out and the DEA and the FBI share investigative responsibility. The DEA in the years prior to this blending of responsibility established DEA drug task force units in many local jurisdictions throughout the country. The DEA's lack of investigative manpower was bolstered by these local police officers, who benefited from the infusion of federal money to carry out long-term criminal investigations.

The investigative priorities shifted from local street sales to a major effort to target major traffickers who run wholesale distribution networks supported by major importation of large quantities of drugs into the United States. The DEA conducted international drug trafficking cases targeting Colombian, Southeast Asian, and Middle East Asian suppliers. Colombia and Peru in South America, Southeast Asia, and the Middle East are agriculturally suited for growing coca plants for cocaine and poppies for opium.

International cartels, crime syndicates, and gangs and organizations supported by corrupt military units became the top rungs of the drug supply ladder. Currently, Mexican drug cartels are the most successful groups supplying the United States. Middle East growers and manufacturers have combined with jihadist terrorist groups to take advantage of the huge profits from the wholesale distribution of heroin and other drugs derived from poppy plants. China has become a major manufacturing source for fentanyl and man-made designer drugs. Methamphetamine is a home-manufactured product, but large-scale manufacturing of meth takes place in Mexico. The effort to quell the importation and manufacture of illegal drugs is close to impossible. Criminal investigations are focused to the extent possible on sophisticated and well-funded criminal enterprises operating in the United States that have established sources of supply from the cartels and international syndicates. Coordination with Mexican, Chinese, and Afghani law enforcement allows for a reasonably secure flow of intelligence information. Success in investigations is extremely difficult. Many of the successful cases are worthy targets, especially those who use violence, witness intimidation, and police and court corruption to thwart arrests, prosecution, and conviction.

Federally sponsored task forces under general headings such as Organized Crime Drug Enforcement Task Force (OCDETF), High Intensity Drug Trafficking Area (HIDTA), and Safe Streets prioritize drug interdiction, drug gang dismantlement, and the targeting of organized crime syndicates to frustrate the career criminals' business models in these cases. Locally assembled vice units and narcotics units focus on local drug entrepreneurs who buy wholesale and sell retail in open-air drug markets and other more covert distribution models.

There is also a continuing black market and drug business model that controls the distribution of less dangerous illegal substances. These substances are primarily marijuana, peyote, and hallucinogenic mushrooms. These naturally growing substances have a significant history of sale and distribution by criminal entities. In the past ten years, marijuana has been legalized for use in medical cases. It has also been legalized for recreational use in many states. Over the past thirty years, possession and sale of small amounts (less than half a pound of the substance) were relegated to misdemeanor criminal cases, and the priority for investigating marijuana cases was eliminated. With the legalized sales happening in various states, there will be more medical and psychological studies to determine if marijuana is in fact beneficial and safer than alcohol or if there are problems that have never surfaced because of the illegal taint. Marijuana continues to be an illegal drug in the federal statutes. This complicates the discussion since even federal law enforcement agencies are reluctant to investigate marijuana cases.

One of the primary reasons that drug investigations receive the attention they do from law enforcement is the enormous profits. In the early and middle part of the twentieth century, organized crime flourished from the sale of illegal alcohol, prostitution, and illegal gambling, three vices that criminals knew would always have a significant customer base. That customer base now includes illegal drug users, addicts, and potential addicts driven by the need to experience the euphoria to meet the physical and emotional demands of addiction. Millions of dollars in an underground economy support criminal enterprises in a manner never before seen. Money is spent to pay off public officials, purchase weapons used to protect the criminal entity, and provide over-the-top lifestyles, including expensive cars, homes, and vacations, for the criminal managers. All of these benefits are financed by the drug business. The community is therefore deeply concerned about criminality that a drug enterprise facilitates. Criminal organizations protect their profits by eliminating threats even if that means killing innocent persons. The priority level of these criminal investigations exhibits a full circle of concern because the priority for criminal investigations is to stop violence. Even though vice cases are lower-priority cases, they tend to shoot up in importance when the criminal organization and conspiratorial conduct are blended with violence and community fear.

The next important aspect is to reduce corruption of the criminal justice system. Drug investigations are relatively simple in their content. All an investigator needs to prove is the suspect had drugs in her possession. Secondarily, the suspect can exhibit the distribution aspect of his operation by having quantities logically deemed too large for personal use. Even so-called dry conspiracy cases, which are made without the actual drugs being found on the person of the suspect or in her control, are less complicated than proof required in other investigations. The primary need is insider testimony and evidence displaying indicia of wealth. A person who lives a lavish lifestyle who can't prove legal employment is a relatively easy target. All that being said, when a wealthy criminal is backed into a corner by witnesses, there is the strong possibility that the suspect will resort to violence and intimidation to avoid prosecution. Evidence and facts may be simple, but carrying the case forward to a conviction at trial will always be difficult.

In summary, illegal drug crimes are prioritized because of the inherent danger of the drug, the violence perpetrated by the dealers to protect the enterprise, and the volume of drugs distributed. These three factors don't carry equal weight. The importance of the factor needs to be viewed in the context of the criminal ecosystem where the drug enterprise is operating. Large urban jurisdictions and small rural jurisdictions will prioritize and aggressively pursue different levels of each of the abovementioned factors and thereby meet the expectation of the community in which they serve and protect. More broadly, vice investigations will meander up and down in priority based on various factors that close the circle of concern. Prostitution cases in which sex trafficking of minor children is discovered will have higher priority than a well-funded outcall service.

Gambling operations that fund violent organized crime syndicates will ascend the priority ladder, whereas neighborhood bookmakers operating in a sports bar will hardly make a ripple in the demand for police action. Money laundering, loan sharking, and any attempt to corrupt legal businesses with funds derived from illegal vice businesses will have more investigative and therefore prosecution interest than the underlying business that generates the profits to begin with. The people in the community don't want to enforce strict moral standards, but they do want to frustrate, limit, and prosecute professional criminals who are violent, corrupt, and too wealthy to be controlled. The challenge for the criminal investigator is to meet the standards the community demands without wasting time and resources on cases that don't concern the community.

SUMMARY

Criminal cases must be placed in a hierarchy of seriousness so that police budgets and resources can be distributed where they are needed. If a jurisdiction has under ten homicides per year and most of those homicides are the results of domestic arguments, the suspect may not be considered a violent career criminal. The fact that the crime is a homicide automatically establishes the event as a matter to be dealt with by all the investigative resources necessary. Small-time larcenies, muggings, street-level drug dealings, and bookmaking will usually be placed in a lower priority. Investigations of those matters won't stop, but the investigative resources will be reduced.

A student in criminal investigation should be aware that, in recent years, quality-of-life crimes, such as destruction of property, tagging, drinking in public, and even disorderly conduct, have been more aggressively policed by patrol and strike force units. This is because, in high-crime neighborhoods, a reduction in these small-time crimes has been shown to have a correlation with a reduction in violent crime. When the criminal ecosystem is disrupted or career criminals believe there is too much police presence in a neighborhood, they are less inclined to shoot, rob, or rape in their preferred surroundings. If the number of crimes can be reduced and police commanders can deploy more officers in troubled neighborhoods, the criminal investigators will have more resources to use to solve cases and a significant body of high-quality intelligence to support investigations.

In recent years, gang and terrorism crimes have become publicized by the media. This extra publicity tends to inform the community to demand more police attention. By adding investigative resources and creating focused task forces with significant investigative resources, these cases will have the push needed to improve investigative success. There are significant programs, from increased patrol presence to improving investigative training and numbers of detectives, that have yielded positive results in reducing the most serious crime problems in a community. Each of the programs and changes in the quantity and quality of criminal investigators must be evaluated in conjunction with the number of crimes committed, the relative sophistication of the criminal ecosystem, and the quality of the support by the community. If every veteran detective was able to limit the number of his cases (for example, fourteen property crimes, five homicide cases, and four rape cases per month) along with developing an effective line of communication with the community, cases would be solved more easily. Providing the financial resources necessary to protect witnesses and budgeting to supply high-end technology and state-of-the-art forensic science laboratory facilities also will help increase success in criminal investigations. In most jurisdictions, all of these enhancements in law enforcement would lead to major success in finding the truth and solving crimes.

Chapter Six

Victims and Witnesses

Developing a relationship with victims and their families; non-law-enforcement witnesses, professional witnesses; developing a profile of the victim, and victimology.

All criminal investigations begin with an interview with a person who tells you that "something" happened. It may be that the person doesn't know what that was, but no doubt the person will have a story to tell. In many of the reactive crime investigations that we have discussed so far, there is a crime scene, a place where the crime happened, or substantial evidence of the presence of a crime.

The criminal investigators may be dispatched to the scene in the normal procedure followed by the agency for whom they work. For the crime of murder, that scene may be someone's home or office. It may be an outdoor location where a body is found. It may be a remote and unusual location that is not frequented by people or a space with regular public access. The scene may not be where the actual crime took place. It may be just a location where the killer decided to dispose of the body.

In an armed robbery, the crime scene may be a commercial business, a bank, a grocery store, a pharmacy, a restaurant, a check cashing storefront, or any place where there is a ready cache of currency.

In the case of any serious assault, the investigators are called to the location where the victim, who is alive but injured, may be found. This would include the victim of a sexual assault. The location may be where the assault happened or where the victim was dropped off or escaped from the scene of the crime.

In the case of a burglary, it will be the home or business that was broken into. This would be the same for an arson, a bombing, and even a car theft. The venue where the crime occurred is the starting point in most cases, but it can also be where the case first becomes the concern of the law enforcement jurisdiction. In most cases, there will be other people present when the criminal investigators arrive. First responders will have done the best they could to "seize" the location and round up all the persons who were present when they arrived at the location. They can then speak to the detectives, inspectors, agents, or investigators responsible for finding out what happened, why it happened, when it happened, how it happened, and who did it. There may be persons at the scene who are very familiar with what happened because they are the victims of

Source: iStock 507952557

the crime. The other people present may have simply seen, heard, or experienced the criminal act in a number of ways that will provide evidence to the investigator. There may also be persons who are traumatized by the crime and are therefore in immediate need of physical or mental help from a doctor or a hospital.

   Anyone who has firsthand personal knowledge of the event is a witness. At this point in an investigation, that may not mean that the person saw the crime or the suspects, but it does mean that he has some information of value. The person may have heard a noise or attempted to render aid to the victim or was present immediately before or after the crime and therefore can help with a timeline that may be of significance. Witnesses are persons who can testify to relevant aspects of the crime in a court and thereby offer testimonial evidence in the trial.

Source: istockphoto 598222530

During the early stages of an investigation, witnesses will be persons who need to be interviewed so that the criminal investigator can start putting the pieces of the puzzle together and begin to understand what happened. Eventually, witnesses will be persons who know facts, data, or information or have a scientific opinion about the crime or some important element related to the crime that will be considered relevant to any court or tribunal examining the crime. As an investigation expands, persons at the scene may become less important while forensic specialists and custodians of records or digital files may become more important. Additionally, the first responding officer and several other police officials, whose responsibility is to protect a crime scene, gather physical evidence, and conduct preliminary interviews, will be professional witnesses to the events before and after the crime.

As the picture of the crime emerges, there is a group of persons who will be part of the case up to and including any trial, which may not occur until months or years after the crime happened. This creates the first predicament for the criminal investigator. The investigator and hopefully her partner must begin to create a relationship between themselves and the people who are witnesses so that the witnesses will be available when needed.

In recent studies and for many students of criminal justice, witnesses are viewed as unreliable because it is thought that they make mistakes in identifying the wrong person as the suspect or they are caught lying to investigators or have some hidden agenda that compromises them as less than reliable as testimonial witnesses. Hard science, with its clean results that are judged as either right or wrong, is given more weight and considered more reliable than weak, venial, and unreliable human beings. The enormous problem with that kind of thinking in the world of criminal investigation is that it is still very rare that a piece of physical evidence with a relevant opinion from a scientific expert will carry the whole weight of proof beyond a reasonable doubt.

As we discussed in chapter 2, witnesses ("flawed human beings") prove many of the factors required by the criminal statutes. Laws were written by human beings with the intent to police the actions of human beings. Every case of a crime needs to be presented to a group of human beings by witnesses, persons whose reliability has been tested and verified by the criminal investigator or another human being. That is the human context in which criminal investigations need to be examined. Even the experts must present their findings not as indisputable scientific facts but as opinion based on scientific examinations. All this must be discussed and argued in front of a panel of nonexperts (the jury), who must be persuaded by the intelligence, experience, education, and personality of the forensic scientist. There is a human context even in the clean science of DNA, qualitative and quantitative chemistry, ballistics, and fingerprints.

In consideration of all the factors that go into a successful criminal investigation, the investigator must be able to work with witnesses, to communicate effectively with them, draw them out, make them feel comfortable, and earn their trust. This chapter will focus on certain categories of witnesses who are part of the case. The evidence provided by witnesses must be protected and sustained throughout the process. The categories to be discussed are as follows: victim witnesses, victims' families, eyewitnesses, fact witnesses, evidence custodians, forensic experts, and professional witnesses.

Source: iStock 482466420

VICTIM WITNESSES

Homicide victims are unable to provide testimonial evidence about what happened to them, but with the help of a medical examiner, forensic science experts, and victims' families, they can supply an extraordinary amount of relevant evidence, which can significantly improve the quality of an investigation. Information such as the exact time the killing happened, the weapon used for the crime, or additional trauma committed on the victim and recovery of ballistic evidence or trace evidence and even the determination as to what the victim's last meal was provide significant facts. These revelations focus the investigation on parameters that are indisputable facts based on a high level of scientific certainty. Most important, the official finding by the medical examiner that states that the victim died as the result of a homicide by another is the first level of proof required to charge the case as a homicide once the suspect has been identified.

Certain scientific examinations can even reveal if the killing happened where the victim's remains were discovered or the victim was killed elsewhere and dumped where the remains were found. A thorough examination of the victim's clothing and personal effects may provide important details about where the victim was immediately prior to his death. Some of this evidence will be immediately understood by the criminal investigator and can inform the case going forward. (In chapter 8, we will discuss how to establish an investigative plan.) The physical evidence discovered on the victim provides important leads that need to be covered to build and populate a timeline for the crime. Other evidence recovered from the victim may be impossible to understand in the beginning of an investigation but become more relevant as a more substantial set of facts are revealed by the investigation. In other words, some evidence will corroborate facts or statements by other witnesses and allow the criminal investigator to gauge the reliability of information and testimony from these other witnesses. For example, the victim's last meal may not be important until the investigator finds a person who claims she met with the victim at a restaurant or residence for the victim's last meal. All these bits and pieces of facts derived from the scientific examination of the victim are details that should never be revealed to witnesses or suspects until all the factors are accounted for. Conflicts between witness statements and these kinds of scientific conclusions should be resolved before promoting the reliability of a witness to a prosecutor. It is true that witnesses, even those not involved in the crime under investigation, will choose to lie about their contact with a victim for personal reasons, and so it is essential that these witnesses should be vetted as to their truthfulness.

It is these scientific examinations, the location of the victim's remains, and the initial timeline that begin to inform the investigation and create a solid starting point for a homicide case. In this way, even a homicide victim is a witness to the truth, but since that witness cannot provide testimony or even speculation about the person who committed the homicide, the investigator must rely on another approach to derive evidence and facts from the victim.

The term *victimology* is the study of the victim. In this context it means that the criminal investigator must develop a detailed sociological, psychological, and personal profile of the victim so that all of the family, close friends, business associates, and enemies of the victim can be identified. The normal routine of the victim must be established if there is one. The manner the victim used to operate in his personal life as well as business life needs to be known and exploited as to why the victim became a victim. The start of this victimology will usually begin with the victim's family. A spouse, a mother, a father, siblings, and children will be able to give the investigator a sketch and, in some cases, a very detailed sketch as to the manner referred to above. There will also be victims who hold back or even eliminate their family members from their real world. Friends and business and social acquaintances will be the next logical source of information. It should be noted here that the effort to study the victim is especially important in homicides where the killer is believed to be a stranger or even a hired assassin. Homicides that present themselves as most likely to be committed by a person who knows or is very familiar with the victim will require that all the close relationships in the victim's life need to be examined before a full profile of the victim is created.

Stranger homicides are obviously the most difficult to solve because there is no discernible evidence linking the homicide to other cases or to a person. How the victim crossed paths with the assailant is much more relevant. In the case of a hired assassin, there must be a motive determined from a person close to the victim. In both kinds of stranger homicides there is not likely to be any personal animosity against the victim present at the scene or on the body.

On the other hand, if a killing displays some kind of anger or passion, the victims are likely to have been killed by persons close to them. There are, of course, other telltale signs in a killing by a person known to the victim, which will be discussed in chapter 7. As is well documented, homicides are in many cases very personal, and there is a high percentage of killings done by spouses or domestic partners.

As an adjunct to stranger homicides, there are also examples of extreme violence and even torture being used to send a message of intimidation to the family or the community at large. Gang violence or violence committed by organized crime syndicates often has characteristics of extreme violence meant to send a message of intimidation. For the most part, the most likely characteristic of gang violence in urban areas today is the killing of a young male criminal in an open-air or neighborhood-gathering place with little or no physical evidence. The killings are carried out in a perfunctory manner, such as in a drive-by shooting or a simple walk-up shooting. The killers purport to be professionals who are just operating in a business fashion, but their motives can, in many cases, be personal if they have had past interactions with the victims and they are acting out of anger and disrespect for the victims. They hold back on their personal animosity and perform the act in a simple, direct fashion. In these cases, victimology and a detailed forensic examination verifying any connection to other gang violence are essential.

VICTIM ADVOCATE

In assessing the importance of the information provided by the deceased victim and determining the value of the victim's family, the criminal investigator needs to understand and embrace one very important responsibility. *Any victim who is no longer capable of speaking for herself must rely on the criminal investigator to be an advocate for the victim.* In many cases, the family will feel this responsibility, but the criminal investigator's responsibility is an essential part of being successful in working the case. There will be many times that the family will not be able to care as much about the need for justice for the victim, but the criminal investigator can never shirk that responsibility. This responsibility can weigh heavily on the mind of the investigator and become a burden if the case is not solved. That burden is necessary so that, when there is a break in the case (weeks, months, and even years later), the case will have the same passion and investigative interest as it did in the beginning of the inquiry.

In the world of criminal investigation, the need to advocate for the victim is required for deceased victims, victims' children, and victims who have been deprived of their ability to speak of the crime. The reason that this responsibility is essential is that, in most cases, the criminal investigator needs to develop an effective working relationship with the family of the victim. There must be a bond of trust and open communication. Profiling the victim for a victimology analysis is just one part of the relationship. It is important to maintain a relationship that will carry forward until a trial because to meet the statutory standard for homicide, it is usually necessary for a family member (spouse, parent, or sibling) to testify that the victim was "a person."

It is also the job of the investigator to explain the twists and turns in an investigation to the family as the case progresses. Briefing the family on court procedures, defense arguments by the suspect's attorney, and court rulings may frustrate the family and limit the state's case. All and all, it is a very personal relationship that develops, and it can last for years. At the same time, a member of the family may be complicit in the homicide or even solely responsible for the crime. It is in this circumstance that the loyalty to the victim by the investigator must supersede the relationship established with the family. The investigator must be professional and judicious in the relationship, but it is usually impossible for the investigator not to develop an emotional connection with the family. It is difficult to find a balance and work the case to a successful conclusion. Since this is an important part of almost every case and an aspect of working with victim witnesses and witnesses in general, the criminal investigator must be able to apply the principle of *finding balance* and *working the case* to every important relationship in a criminal investigation. It just so happens that, in the case of a family who has experienced such a terrible loss, the emotions, the need to proceed logically, and the demand to reach a truthful conclusion all come together. It is expected that the law enforcement professional will handle the full range of experience.

Inevitably, criminal investigators must be comfortable protecting victims and their families and witnesses who provide the most significant evidence in a case. They must also be sure that the intellectual, emotional, and trust relationships built during an investigation are professional and human. Rancor, mistrust, and the beliefs held by the victims and their families and the witnesses will destroy an investigation and be the surest route to failure. As we proceed with this discussion of witnesses, these factors need to be considered and acted on.

VICTIM WITNESSES IN SEXUAL ASSAULT

As discussed in chapter 2, the victims of sexual assault are the most important witnesses in the investigation of a sex crime. These crimes are primary examples of violence, a desire for power, and a despicable form of human degradation of another human being. Even murder is somehow more easily explained in human discourse than sexual violence, which is the denigration of acts that involve human beings sharing love, passion, and trust that are then turned into an acts of anger, rage, and revenge or even savage torture. It is the sexual assault of children who have not even formed any real understanding of sex and using that naiveté to satisfy an unnatural appetite derived from some kind of disconnect with normal human social interaction. The sexual predators who violate children use their sophistication and charisma to obscure their real intentions and create a sense of fear in the hearts of their victims. It is also sexual predators who assault women and men because they want to dominate, control, and satisfy their warped understanding of human sexuality.

Because of these motivations, the victims of sexual assault find it impossible to trust a criminal investigator no matter how much they know intellectually that they should. The victims have been turned away from normal social interaction by the violent predator who abused them. The victims are embarrassed at the idea that they had sex with a vile person and wonder if they somehow brought it upon themselves. Were their actions somehow the reason they were victimized? In cases of sexual violence by an unknown person, was there something in the clothes they wore or the way they walked or talked that somehow invited the predator? Even in a case where their attacker was known to them, did they somehow make themselves easy victims whose actions were misunderstood? All these emotional responses make the concept of trusting another stranger, even though that stranger is a law enforcement officer, extremely difficult. Some victims are sophisticated enough to understand that a rape case will eventually go to trial, the whole experience will be parsed in court, and they will have to answer a series of very uncomfortable questions. They may even believe that telling their story to an investigator will make them relive the worst event in their lives, an event they would love to be able to forget. All of these issues make rape and other sexual assault the most underreported serious crimes.

Just like a homicide victim, the fact that sexual assault involves close contact between the victim and the criminal means a thorough medical examination and the recovery of trace evidence are essential parts of a sexual assault investigation. A victim may not even know who the assailant was. She may not be able to provide a description of the assailant. Since this is true, the medical examination and the recovery of physical evidence may be the best way to positively identify the suspect. Rape and most other sexual assaults occur out of public view. These crimes may have outdoor crime scenes or indoor locations that have been picked by the assailant to ensure privacy. The assailant may also go through extraordinary effort to keep the victim unaware of the location in an effort to frustrate an examination of the crime scene. These crimes also occur in the residence of the victim and, in a few cases, in the residence of the assailant. It is up to the victim to lead the investigator to the right venue. All too often, victims choose to escape the crime scene if they survive, with intentions to never return. Physical evidence of the assault and the possible recovery of trace evidence are other essential aspects of a proper sexual assault investigation.

In view of all these factors, the relationship between the victim and the investigator is likely to be a slowly evolving, long-term series of interviews. The location of the interviews must be where the victim feels safe and comfortable. A police station may offer that kind of location, but the investigator needs to consider all kinds of possibilities. Open-air restaurants, city parks, homes of parents, or business offices where the victim feels safe and in control are examples of places where interviews can take place. It usually results in the victim being more satisfied that the investigator is, in fact, his advocate. The investigator needs to be able to respond logically to the interviews but also to make an emotional connection with the victim. This is the kind of connection that the victim sees as supportive. With some victims, that emotional connection will be a protective response. It assures the victims that the investigator will be with them to protect them against any further violence. Alternatively, the victim may want to feel that the investigator is competent and professional and will get to the bottom of the matter and bring the assailant to justice. Finally, some victims may simply want a friend they can confide in who will lead them to resources to help them cope with the trauma. The investigator should never lie and avoid holding back bad news. Part of a victim's returning to normalcy is taking back control. If an investigator feels a need to lie or hold back, the victim may see that as losing control and not being respected. The victim, after all, has been through a life-changing trauma, so some bad news is not likely to push the victim over an imaginary cliff.

Because criminal investigators are not trained psychologists or psychiatrists, it is very helpful for them to have contacts with experts in rape crisis centers and professionals who can help with the victim's recovery. In a more macro view, mental health professionals are resources that investigators need to have when working with all manner of crime trauma. A child who has lost his parents, a person who has lost a spouse, or any victim of violence may need professional counseling to deal with the trauma, be able to move on, and then be prepared for dealing with the criminal justice system if a case becomes a reality. The good news is there is usually plenty of time for the traumatized witness to recover some equilibrium.

All these concerns place an additional responsibility on a criminal investigator. That is why teamwork, discussed in chapter 4, is so important. Individual investigators, for reasons of personal background or even age, race, or sex, may not be the best persons to make the kind of connection necessary to shepherd the victim through a sexual assault case, which eventually will find itself in trial. Criminal investigators need to recognize their own shortcomings and rely on the strengths of their partners or other squad members. In chapter 8, in our discussion on establishing an investigative plan, there will be a discussion of evaluating the investigative resources so that you can apply the right person to the right task.

At this point, the criminal investigator needs to evaluate the witness and objectively decide how that witness will be best served throughout the investigation. Victim witnesses can evolve from being an emotional wreck to recovering their confidence and reestablishing control. In that case, the investigator must be flexible and see if any changes in providing support for the victim need to be altered. Crime and criminal investigations are the result of human interaction, and there needs to be evaluation and response by the people involved.

VICTIM WITNESS OF SERIOUS VIOLENCE

There is a spectrum of violent criminal behavior that results in victims being subjected to serious bodily harm. Gunshot victims, stabbings, blunt-force trauma, torture, and even beatings with fists and feet can cause lifelong disability and a struggle to survive. The psychological effect to victims may be somewhat lessened if they fully understand the motive behind the criminal behavior, but it is likely that the long-term trauma will have the same or similar effects as sexual assault. These kinds of crimes can range from a dispassionate drive-by shooting by street gang members to violent acts intended to intimidate witnesses. They can also be violent overreaction to a dispute or argument that began as normal social interaction.

These crimes can also be expressions of rage and anger from a mentally deranged person who is acting on stimuli that may never be understood. Serious bodily violence to victims can result in the loss of mobility, limbs, or sight or any of the other senses or cause internal damage to important organs. Psychological trauma accompanies these physical effects and can range from anger to a desire for revenge to posttraumatic stress disorder (PTSD). The criminal investigator must find a way to connect with the witness and develop a positive relationship that will lead to discovering all the facts necessary to inform the investigation. As in sexual assault cases, there may also be a need to determine what physical evidence of the attack can be recovered from the person or victim. The investigator needs to keep in mind that there will be a need in many cases to establish a long-term dialogue and association that may culminate in a trial or other final judicial hearing. The criminal investigator needs to be adaptable to these victim witnesses, who may have a full range of emotions and reactions to the crime. The criminal investigator is the victim's advocate and should make every effort to make the victim part of the team to find the truth and recover some level of justice.

The effects of substantial violence on a victim is compounded by a loss of control and may have a negative effect on the person's sense of worth and confidence. The investigator may not be able to restore these characteristics, but with time and empathy, the investigator can help. It may also be necessary to direct the victim to the appropriate mental health support person or organization. Over the past twenty years, police and federal investigative agencies have established various victim witness programs, which offer a variety of support for victims, including financial help. These programs are just becoming effective and productive, but together with community outreach programs for victims, there are many more resources available to the criminal investigator. Local resources can be limited by local budgets. Federal programs are not fully funded, and there are instances when these programs fall far short of the needs of victims who have suffered catastrophic bodily injury or significant mental health trauma.

OTHER VICTIM WITNESSES

Incidental violence, threatened violence (as in an aggravated armed robbery), or burglary will take a toll on the victim of the crime. Even a bank teller whose personal money is not stolen but who is forced to comply with the wishes of a gunman and turn over funds from her employer will feel a loss of control and anger facing a possibility of violence. Burglary victims, if they were home during the crime, or even those whose residence was broken into while they were away will suffer psychological trauma. Any intrusion into our personal space and the theft of our belongings instills fear and makes us lose the belief that we have a safe place to go at the end of the day. Most crimes have one or more victims, and when there is a criminal investigation, the investigator has to work with the victims to restore a sense of normalcy and hopefully recover the stolen property or that stolen sense of safety. Contact, communication, and support are characteristics that criminal investigators need to rely on during their work so that victims will begin to get their confidence and sense of security returned to them. In most cases, the victim witness who has been threatened or in some way deprived of control or safety will not have the same feelings of violation that sexual assault victims or victims of serious bodily harm do, and so criminal investigators need to be more objective and professional in their communication. It is never okay to disregard the emotions of a victim, but these victim witnesses normally do not expect anything more than professional efficiency and some amount of respectful humanity. It is not the kind of deep empathy that will develop in cases of extreme violence or sexual abuse. It is empathy and compassion that fits the circumstance. Patient concern and appropriate effort to bring the case to a proper conclusion are what is needed in these less violent matters. In most cases, the role of the investigator is less intense, but again, it is critical for the investigator to make sure the victim witness has faith that the case is being given appropriate attention.

EYEWITNESSES AND FACT WITNESSES

It is always possible that a victim witness will also be an eyewitness. In this discussion, we consider an eyewitness a person not necessarily victimized by the crime but someone who was present when a crime happened. This person gets a good look at the suspect and is able to provide an accurate description of the suspect. Recently, in criminology studies, eyewitness testimony has been denigrated and become more suspect. In any case, when a criminal investigator is able to present testimonial evidence to a judge or magistrate that a witness to a crime has positively identified a suspect in a stand-up lineup or a properly presented photo array of mug shots, that identification will be substantial proof supporting *probable cause* to arrest the person identified. (In chapter 2, I established that a positive identification of a suspect is required to make an arrest, and I provided a compelling personal experience with eyewitness testimony that is contradictory to the studies mentioned above.)

Eyewitness testimony that leads to a positive identification should *always* be supported by other significant evidence before a case is truly solved. Witnesses can be influenced by subtle keys from an investigator and pushed toward absolute certainty when they may not be so certain. Solid eyewitnesses are important witnesses in any investigation, but the investigator should invest the time and energy in verifying their identification.

The investigator should also prepare the eyewitness for the kind of withering cross-examination a defense attorney can conduct in determining if the witness and the identification will hold up. The investigator should make sure that no matter what kind of lineup or photo array is used, the witness should not be influenced in any way. The investigator should also make sure that the witness is confident and direct in her identification. Having an eyewitness fall apart on the stand in a trial will almost surely lead to an acquittal. A positive identification of a suspect by an eyewitness should be considered by the investigator to be a positive and important step for probable cause but a long way from proof beyond a reasonable doubt. The exception to this rule is when the positive identification comes from a person who knows the suspect and has had a long-term relationship with the suspect. A positive identification of this type becomes direct evidence and places the eyewitness in the position of being a *fact witness*.

A fact witness is a person who can provide testimonial evidence about a certain fact or group of facts. A fact witness can be a bank security officer who is able to testify about the authenticity of the video surveillance camera in a bank. That witness is the custodian of the bank's video records. A fact witness can be a landlord who can testify that the suspect in an investigation is the tenant in a residence that was searched for evidence in a crime. A fact witness can be a criminal associate who can testify that the gun used to kill a victim was provided to the suspect by the witness. A fact witness's testimony can be asserted as truthful. An eyewitness to a crime who supplies the details needed to prove the statutory offense and/or the proof of identity can also be a fact witness. Any fact witness can be subjected to cross-examination so that truthfulness can be tested.

When a fact witness testifies, the truth of the fact asserted by the witness is to be considered by the judge and the jury. Fact witnesses provide some of the most significant testimonial evidence at a trial. They can also provide context, opportunity, and motive for the crime. The deliberation for the judge and jury tends to be grounded in the facts. Occasionally, emotions, judgment, and the veracity of a witness are jumbled together into the decision-making process in a trial. All of these factors affect how the judge and jury view the evidence. The more facts that are proved and considered as concrete truth and the more the testimonies of the fact witnesses, victims, and police witnesses coalesce as verified, the more likely it is that the standard of proof beyond a reasonable doubt is met or achieved. As you can see, the categories of witnesses can cross over and be intertwined depending on the facts of the case and the investigative discoveries.

Almost all witnesses discussed so far are civilians or citizens from the jurisdiction. Their testimony is presented in all the preliminary investigative steps as truthful until there is some kind of proof that a citizen witness is lying or mistaken. Testimony and statements can be taken as fact and on face value as long as the investigators consider them truthful. If one of these very important witnesses falls apart on the stand in the face of cross-examination, the case can be lost, and the truth may never be known. There are at least three important occasions when these witnesses may be called upon to testify before a trial. A preliminary hearing and/or an evidentiary hearing may require the government to argue that there is probable cause to hold the defendant for a grand jury procedure and trial. The evidentiary hearing may be ordered to consider the relevance or lack thereof of certain facts or evidence to be presented in the trial. These kinds of hearings are usually very limited in testimony, but if the government's attorney decides to put forth a civilian witness, that witness may be cross-examined, and the defense attorney will endeavor to discover as much as possible about the government's case. The use of a civilian witness for these hearings is usually poor strategy, but in some cases, it may be necessary and unavoidable. Usually, in these hearings, the lead detective or investigator is the only witness. As a sworn officer, the investigator can testify to hearsay from other witnesses, other law enforcement officers, and any other witnesses whose testimony is relevant to the matter. This way the testimony of any number of persons can be summarized and presented for the purpose laid out in the hearing.

Citizen witnesses and, in some cases, victim witnesses will occasionally be needed to testify in a grand jury hearing. A grand jury procedure is a probable-cause hearing, and therefore the witness is not subjected to cross-examination. The grand jurors may ask questions and evaluate the truthfulness of a witness. But these hearings are not usually adversarial, and therefore, the witness will be called upon to tell the story in a truthful manner that will be limited or directed by only the prosecutor. The most frightened or skittish witnesses will usually be encountered by friendly or neutral persons in a secure and secret grand jury hearing. The witnesses' testimonies will be under oath, and the grand jury can consider the veracity and demeanor of the witnesses.

The grand jury's job is to render a decision as to probable cause for an indictment and, in that kind of hearing, the jurors are managed by the government prosecutor, who controls the details that are revealed. The lead investigator is very directly involved in these hearings and usually involved in escorting important witnesses to and from the hearing and providing a level of security and support for the witnesses. In the grand jury, the deputy sheriffs or marshals acting in their capacity as court security protect the witness while he appears in court. Throughout this process, the investigator should be closely monitoring the witnesses to make sure the testimonies are consistent and truthful. Mistakes or errors in recollection need to be brought to the attention of the prosecutor so that those mistakes can be accounted for in the trial testimony. Transcripts of testimony will eventually be provided to the defense attorney. Emotional reactions, which can derail cooperation or raise unnecessary concerns, should be dealt with immediately by the investigator. Any time a victim witness relives the crime, it can cause psychological trauma that upsets the witness's equilibrium, and it may become necessary to renew the witness's stability to move forward. Sometimes these hearings can have a very negative effect, something the witness was not prepared for, because things can happen during trial preparation that can't be planned or strategized. Part of the responsibility of the investigator is to support a fragile witness through any rough spot or surprise in the run-up to a trial. The criminal investigator is the advocate for the victim, and as such, continued support and encouragement to confront the assailant and seek justice are the responsibility of that investigator.

WITNESS SECURITY

As a result of the experiences in the State of New York Organized Crime investigations, the FBI and the US Marshals Service developed a formal program for protecting critical witnesses who, in the beginning of the program, were insiders and part of the criminal conspiracies/enterprises. An extensive process of relocating and developing new identities for witnesses provided a way to make the witness disappear only to reemerge when needed for a trial or other important testimony. The US Marshals Service began the serious and formidable Witness Security Program (WITSEC) to ensure the safety and availability of witnesses who were under threat in violent crime investigations, especially violent crimes that further the criminal enterprise of numerous conspirators who are out on the street and may be tasked to kill or intimidate important civilian witnesses. The program devised by the Marshals Service in 1970 was primarily responsive to Mafia, or La Cosa Nostra, organized crime entities who have nationwide and, in some cases, international reach. The hallmark of the program was to change the identity, profession, and, in some cases, physical appearance of the witness and his immediate family. The witness was to cut off all ties to his old life and relocate to a completely different part of the country. New backgrounds and different career paths were part of the relocation formula. Over time, the program has expanded, and protected people have included witnesses against violent street gangs, international drug cartels, and the ever-increasing variety of the alternative organized crime syndicates. The program has been extraordinarily successful. Few or no witnesses have been lost while they were under the protection of the program. Unfortunately, the program has strict rules, and when a rule is broken, the people protected are removed from the program and may be left to fend for themselves, unless the originating investigative agency picks up the witnesses and finds the resources to continue the witnesses' protection. When a witness makes a mistake that compromises the program but the witness is still in imminent danger, it is up to the original investigator to try to accommodate the witness, especially if the witness is still needed to testify.

Some of these witnesses are insiders in a gang crew or mob, so it can be very difficult for them to suddenly turn straight. Even persons who are not insiders but who have strong family or neighborhood ties to their old community find it difficult to completely break off their relationships. These witnesses who need and deserve protection can't thrive in a system such as WITSEC. Local police agencies don't have the budgets to support a relocation to safety that may be needed. Local and even state prosecutors don't have an official budget for these witnesses. Federal agencies, such as the FBI, DEA, and ATF, have funding to protect witnesses for extended periods of time, but they don't have contacts and tried-and-true skills to relocate and reidentify witnesses and develop new careers for them. Any money spent by these agencies will usually require some creative adaptation. There can also be some consideration about the threat; for example, in many local street gang investigations, removing witnesses to another city where they have family and a support structure may be all that is needed. Evaluating the reach of the criminal conspirators who pose a threat can provide a number of less disruptive transformations of the targeted witnesses. Fine-tuning the threat and getting the witnesses off on the right foot can solve the problem, but it takes financial and security support from a police agency where the witnesses end up.

Serious criminals who have testified against nationally connected gangs, mobs, or syndicates need to find a home in WITSEC, but if there is a problem with the witness that is strictly a matter of bad judgment, then the lead investigator has to come up with an alternative. Witnesses who are scared of a local threat, which can be lessened by locking up the violent criminal, need to be supported and provided extra security, such as heightened police patrols, local relocation, and avoidance of old haunts and neighborhoods. There is no single solution to this problem, but the lead investigator has to ensure the safety of witnesses and that they are available for testimony.

Personal Experience

In my career, I investigated and prosecuted a Washington, DC, street gang. For the prosecution, we needed the testimony of sixty civilian witnesses. A few of the witnesses were secured in a local witness security jail because they were serving time for various drug offenses, but most of the witnesses had to be relocated away from Washington, DC. The police department and the US Attorney's Office had a budget for putting up the witnesses in a local hotel before and during their trial testimony. In this case, there were two trials, each lasting six months. In addition, the mother of two of the gang leaders was employed by the US Marshals Service in the administrative part of its WITSEC program. Rather than compromise her loyalty to her children and relocate a number of young uneducated or undereducated men without any work skills, we chose to develop ways to relocate these witnesses ourselves. Luckily, the FBI had sufficient funds for this purpose, and we successfully protected all sixty of our witnesses and ensured their testimony at trial. We convicted all the subjects in the trials, and throughout the rest of my career, these witnesses were able to go on with their lives and thrive in the new circumstances. There are creative approaches to witness security, but the main approach has to be the commitment of the lead investigator.

LAW ENFORCEMENT PROFESSIONALS

There are many times throughout the course of an investigation that professional law enforcement officers and other government officials, such as medical examiners, intelligence analysts, and keepers of official records, are called upon to be witnesses in a criminal matter. Most of the time, sworn police officers are the ones who respond to crime scenes and participate in search warrant raids or arrests. These persons are law enforcement professionals supporting an investigative effort. Once they assist in a case, it may be weeks, months, or years before the law enforcement action they took will need to be presented to a court. Their actions may be observations, overhears, or responses from the suspect that become relevant testimonial evidence. It is likely that whatever they heard, saw, or experienced would have been properly documented or reported by the investigator or independently detailed in an appropriate document, which is made a part of the investigative or case file. For many years, law enforcement professionals from police departments to state or federal agencies have had an orderly and structured method of documenting these important events in an investigation.

It is also the normal procedure for police officers to keep and maintain handwritten notes informally recording the day-to-day actions of the officer. These notes may be kept in spiral notebooks and resemble a diary or a logbook. In the digital age, it is likely that officers will keep these running logs in a digital notebook with supporting digital photographs. Personal or agency-provided smartphones, tablets, or laptop computers have become the new spiral notebooks. The reason for these logbooks or diaries is because working police officers spend a great deal of time going from case to case and incident to incident. Under these circumstances, their recollection of important law enforcement actions that they have taken can be blurred by the sheer volume of incidents. Being able to recall the events of an important investigation weeks, months, or even years later is impossible without the help of written notes, which act as a memory refresher.

Today, fictional criminal investigator protagonists are portrayed as geniuses who have all manner of special abilities. Some are skilled psychologists, masters of observation with photographic memories. In truth and in the real world of law enforcement, a solid, reliable memory is an essential tool for an effective criminal investigator. Students of criminal investigation should practice and train to improve their memory. Law enforcement professionals need to take notes or write reports in a manner that keys their recollection and places them back in time to be able to recall with specificity the actions they took, the observations they made, or the statement they heard so that the jury will be able to rely on their memory.

Personal Experience

Beginning in 1983, there was a series of bombings in Washington, DC, including the bombing of the US Capitol Senate cloakroom. The bombing took place after business hours in the hope that there would not be any casualties. I was working late that night and was the first FBI responder to the bombing. I and a team of agents were to establish a crime scene and begin processing the scene for evidence. It was the beginning of an extraordinary investigation in which I had no role. The investigation was conducted by a squad working homegrown terrorism investigations of the 1960s-era Weather Underground. The suspects were radical extremists from the antiwar movement, which began in the 1960s. These suspects were stridently antigovernment and had become violent based on their frustration with society's response to their movement.

What is important to note is the dates of the bombings, around 1983 and 1984, and the date this case was prosecuted, 1989. Six to seven years after I worked four crime scenes of bombings in Washington, DC, I was asked to be ready to testify about the work we did and material we recovered. I was able to reconstruct and recall the work based on the seriousness of the case, and even though I had taken hundreds of pictures and written detailed reports within months after the bombings, I had no contact with the investigation during those years. A case that lasts this long is not the norm, but it is very possible that the time between important work being done and testimony about that important work being needed will be well beyond the recollection of the average person.

Specific recall and the reliance on notes, photographs, or reports are the functional imperatives necessary for reliable testimony from a law enforcement professional. It is the responsibility of the lead criminal investigator to make sure that copies of notes and reports and an occasional jogging of the memory for law enforcement colleagues are done to ensure the professional witnesses in a case are ready to provide the needed testimony. Professional witnesses provide reliable information and significant testimony that is usually believable and convincing. The fact is that a person who regularly testifies in court and provides testimony with the support of documents, notes, and photographs can allow the jurors and the judge to feel a sense of comfort, especially when that witness appears to have no personal attachment to the investigation.

The objectivity of crime scene officers, first responding officers, and officers or agents who supported the investigative team to make an arrest or seize evidence in a search warrant is an important asset when a trial is the result of an investigation. Communities will have some level of distrust for the police, but in the context of a violent crime, when it is obvious that a person or persons were victimized, most jurors will find the professionalism and careful preparation supplied by career law enforcement officers trustworthy.

EXPERT WITNESSES

As a result of the advances in science and technology, it is not surprising that forensic science has taken an important position in the investigation of crime. The natural sciences, such as biology, chemistry, and physics, have become more useful in criminal investigation. The extraction of human DNA, toxicology, trace evidence examination, and utilization of scanning electron microscopes and mass spectrometry provide incredibly powerful scientific proof that physical evidence recovered at the scene of a crime or from a victim suspect or even a witness in a crime gives the criminal investigator a new source of facts and scientifically supported opinion that argues in favor of the truth. (We will discuss these fields of study in chapter 10.) When you add these advances in natural sciences to the other fields of forensics, such as autopsies, medical examinations, fingerprint analysis, ballistics, handwriting analysis, and pattern identification, the criminal investigator is presented with a whole new category of witnesses.

Experts are highly educated and experienced scientists who examine the bodies of victims, the bits and pieces of minute evidence found at the scene of a crime, shell casings, bullets, smudged prints, and all the evidence that is used to argue facts under dispute at a trial. This evidence is examined and found to contain scientific proof, or "proof to a scientific certainty," that the physical evidence shows that the suspect was *present at the crime scene*, the suspect had *close physical contact* with the victim, or the suspect's *weapon was used* to attack the victim.

These are just some of the conclusions that can be reached in a thorough scientific examination. During the course of an investigation, these conclusions become facts that inform and, in some cases, solve the unanswered questions about the crime. When a person's DNA fingerprints or other biological evidence are found at the crime scene and that person has no reason to have ever been at the scene, the criminal investigator will have good reason to conclude that the person may have committed the crime. Developing information, facts, and other evidence that supports this conclusion can lead to the logical conclusion that the case is solved. All the facts and conclusions are important milestones in an investigation, but until those facts and conclusions are presented in court, the case is still in doubt. A judge and jury need to consider the same facts and conclusions and come to the same understanding as the criminal investigator.

As a result of that final hurdle, the forensic science expert, the medical examiner, and the computer expert need to be able to effectively testify as to their examinations and conclusions and provide the court with their opinion as to the scientific certainty of their opinions. The judge and jury must then give their opinions the same weight as the criminal investigator and the prosecutor. Occasionally, defense attorneys, who work for persons charged with the crime, will challenge the scientific results and put forward their own expert. They may also challenge the expert to get the jury to believe that the government's expert is just wrong or too aggressive in her opinion or too reluctant to offer alternative conclusions. As a result of all those possibilities, the lead investigator and prosecutor need to prepare the expert for her testimony. It is essential that the witness be truthful and competent. Making an expert witness trustworthy and believable may be a matter of preparation.

An incredibly well-educated scientist may have trouble relating to a panel of average citizens. The witness may come off as too enmeshed in the scientific world to be able to explain the results of the exams in plain English. The science used to conduct the examination may be too complicated to explain and be understood. At some point, the lead investigator and the prosecutor will have to find a way to get the truth across to the jury. Expert witnesses, like all witnesses, come from various backgrounds and circumstances. It is necessary for the lead investigator to find common ground, mutual concepts that can be applied by the expert to translate complicated science into understandable and acceptable communication. Finding a way to humanize and develop a social bridge between the expert and the jury can result in the trust and personal connection required to allow the expert to be more believable. Expert witnesses are crucial to many cases, especially violent crimes in which there is close contact. Any physical evidence associating the victim and the assailant becomes critical. Just because a highly skilled criminologist is awkward in explaining the scientific findings, there is no reason to squander the results of the expert testimony.

In the same fashion, local medical examiners can be considered tainted by their close association with the local police. In highly publicized, politically charged cases, their testimony might be compromised. Outside "celebrity" medical examiners may be called upon by a defense attorney to provide alternate theories about the cause of death or even what kind of weapon was used. It is up to the criminal investigator with the help of the local medical examiner to prepare the prosecutor to fulfill his function in cross-examination and balance the opinions of the experts.

SUMMARY

In most cases, witnesses in a criminal case are average persons whose statements of fact or even beliefs are seldom questioned; their lives and actions are rarely scrutinized. Even their personal conduct is rarely considered wrong, selfish, immoral, or scandalous. All of these day-to-day facts of life are turned upside down when the person is placed in a position where a sharp, insightful lawyer plans to "eviscerate" the person on the stand in a highly charged criminal trial. Often, it is impossible for an investigator to properly prepare an important witness for the kind of personal assault that may be used to attack his credibility. Even law enforcement professionals and expert witnesses are vulnerable to unfair innuendo or even lies and misrepresentations that can be used by an aggressive defense attorney. It is how the witness reacts and what the judge and jury perceive that matters in a trial. If a victim witness in a rape case is castigated for past social behavior or a criminal associate to the defendant is called a liar who is out to avoid prison, the reaction of the witness is what is remembered by the jury. That reaction has as much to do with the character and personality of the witness as it has to do with the perception of the jury.

The lead investigator needs to work with the witness to go over the possible attacks and see the response and judge how that response will seem to a jury. It may be that the witness needs to react with heartfelt sincerity or controlled anger or even some kind of counterargument. The investigator should help control the response and encourage the witness who is telling the truth to be humble and show appropriate human reaction to the challenges. The investigator's best approach should be to support the normal reaction of the witness but to curb the anger and frustration with subtle humor or sincerity, whichever is most appropriate. He must also make sure the witness

speaks directly to the jury and not to the source of the attack, the defense attorney. Just that kind of response will automatically tone down any visceral anger.

Individual witnesses will be challenged in all sorts of ways, so it is up to the investigator to advise the witnesses what would be appropriate for them. Witnesses can and do make mistakes. "To err is human." A jury that is reasonable and well prepared will understand the anger, frustration, and very personal nature of most of the attacks on the character of the witness. It is necessary to keep the witness's responses appropriate. It is up to the prosecutor to repair any damage from mistakes in testimony. The most important truth the witness needs to know is that the charges from a defense attorney mean nothing unless a witness is truly lying. Telling the truth on the stand is the only rule to be followed. At the end of the day, the witness will go home, and the defendant will still be facing serious charges and jail time. Witnesses need to know they are not alone and that they are going through the crucible of testimony to help their community right a wrong and maybe even recover some level of justice for themselves. Even if the results of the trial go against the government, it is up to the investigator to let the witness know that she followed the rule of law and endeavored to provide the judge and jury with the truth. If the jurors choose to believe something else, that does not change the facts and the ultimate truth of the matter.

Chapter Seven

Crime Scene Analysis

Crime scene analysis is also the analytical process of interpreting the specific features of a crime to help determine the possible relation to other crimes under investigation.

The first example of analysis by the investigator in a reactive crime investigation is a subjective evaluation of the crime event. The investigator needs to pay attention to what questions are posed by the scene where police response occurs.

The most important ten questions to consider are the following:

- Is this scene *the* crime scene?
- Is it the only crime scene?
- Is it likely that this scene was merely a location where the remains of a homicide victim were dumped?
- Are the obvious parameters of the scene correct or should the scene be expanded?
- Is the scene fresh enough to consider that it is exactly how the perpetrator left it, or is it likely to have been compromised by other persons, environmental factors, or the passage of time?
- Does the crime scene have enough visual proof that allows the investigator to believe there is more than one venue that may yield additional physical evidence and insight into how the crime happened?
- Is the scene instructive?
- Does the scene exhibit chaos?
- Does the scene exhibit order?
- What physical evidence left at the scene provides answers, and does the physical evidence left at the scene simply add to the questions to be answered?

To answer all these questions, the best place to start is to use deductive reasoning, considering the observable facts and material evidence, and determine if conclusions can be reached. The investigator needs to look at the scene and begin to make logical conclusions from the information available or consider his own experience and training to inform conclusions. If you are called to investigate a homicide and there is no body, the conclusion would be that no homicide occurred. In the same way, if the investigator is called to the scene of a homicide and there is a deceased person surrounded by upended furniture, blood, shell casings, and other indications of conflict, then a homicide investigation can begin by radiating out from the body of the victim to reasonable parameters constituting the crime scene. In this manner, certain conclusions can be made from the observable aspects of the scene. Physical evidence, disruption of the surrounding area, and any obvious factors that seem related to the crime should be considered and noted in a logical analysis.

To make sure that the observations and conclusions provided by the observation are detailed for future analysis, the investigator needs to begin by recording the scene. There are generally two productive approaches an investigator can take to record the scene. The first is to immediately take down notes about what observations and conclusions can be made in the initial analysis. The second approach is to photograph or sketch the scene so that this analysis can continue long after the scene has been dismantled or fully examined by the crime scene specialists assigned to the investigation. This second approach in most police agencies is done by the crime scene search team, forensic team, crime scene investigation team, or other named unit responsible for conducting crime scene examinations. In the FBI, for example, this unit is called the evidence response team. In my book, titled *Working the Scene*, I provide detailed instruction on how a crime scene team should conduct the examination. The purpose of this chapter is to augment the information in that book for the criminal investigator.

If an investigator is making observations at the scene of a reactive investigation, the process of documenting or taking notes about the scene should be done to begin the process of developing logical theories about the crime. The investigator may be carrying out this analysis of the scene at the same time the crime scene technicians are doing their work. It is necessary that the work of the crime scene unit take precedence over the observational analysis of the investigator. With modern digital smartphones, an average person is walking around with a high-quality point-and-shoot camera and an instant notepad capable of taking copious notes enhanced by high-resolution digital images.

Investigators are no exception to the average person, but there are a couple of points that need to be made. Going back to the first productive approach, take down notes and begin an initial analysis. Most investigators will consider using their smartphones and even their audio-recording capability to create the informal notes and images of the scene for future use and to inform the investigation. Digital file copies of any images and digital recordings at a crime scene should be immediately turned over to the lead crime scene technician, who is responsible for documenting the scene and maintaining a complete file of the work done at the scene.

In court, weeks, months, or years later, there can't be any extraneous digital files of notes and images being relied on by an investigator that are not maintained as part of the original crime scene file or report. When the notes and photographs relating to the crime scene examination are reviewed in court, they should be considered as part of an entire effort to document the scene. Overall record snapshots and observations from the scene by the investigator may be informal investigative steps, but the court will want to make sure there are no discrepancies or distortions between the notes and images from the investigator and the crime scene team. The most important concern is that there is absolute coherency between the two reviews of the crime scene. The investigator can then keep a copy of the digital file for personal investigative use. The formal crime scene file and report may take a long period of time before they are available to the lead investigator, but the investigation must proceed from the beginning.

The goal of this investigative crime scene review process is for the investigator to begin making notes about details of the crime scene that provide investigative clues. (*Clues* is an "old, worn out word" for logical investigative signals or provocative insights.) The details, measurements, and inventory of physical evidence should be left to the crime scene team. But the general information that can inform the investigation in the beginning of the case is what the investigator should be developing as a running commentary about the crime. The investigator must decide if the crime scene is chaotic or orderly and there is any indication that the criminal activity was localized or spread over several areas of the scene. The investigator should be using deductive reasoning to observe and make conclusions from those observations. What is critical to remember is that these observations and conclusions are the beginnings of a theory of the crime. At some point in the future, the theory will be tested with all the facts and testimony that can support or debunk the original theory of the crime. The reality is that the investigator must start somewhere, and making logical conclusions based on observations is a good way to start. A criminal investigation is an evolutionary process. Theories in the beginning that prove to be wrong are part of the elimination process that narrows the focus of the investigation based on facts and evidence. Theories that prove to be right or consistent with the facts help the investigator move the case forward and provide essential context required to make the case reach a truthful conclusion.

In the field of law enforcement, there are many academic disciplines, such as the study of law and the study of forensic science in fields such as ballistics, serology, microscopic analysis, or fingerprinting, which require serious research in the specific academic fields of study. Even psychology, psychiatry, and medicine have law enforcement–related subareas, such as abnormal psychology, criminal psychosis, and pathology. These disciplines require academic rigor and a scientific method. Analyzing a crime scene is different. The graduate-level course in crime scene analysis is the day-to-day response activity of a police patrol officer. In a given jurisdiction, urban or suburban police department patrol officers might encounter twenty to thirty different crime scenes per week. With this many encounters, a patrol officer could become an expert in evaluating a crime scene within the first couple of years as a patrol officer. Logical conclusions, observational skills, and realistic methods used by criminals who commit burglary, larceny, rape, and murder will become second nature to a patrol officer. It is as if you are judging the proficiency of a professional athlete who spends seven days a week fine-tuning her skill shooting baskets, hitting a baseball, or throwing a football. Some will be more talented than others, but the skill baseline will be very high. The skill baseline for a first-responding patrol officer in crime scene impressions is extraordinary if the officer makes the effort.

Even a professional psychologist, who may see a hint of aberrant behavior in a crime scene, will not be experienced enough in observing and understanding specifically how a residence is entered, how criminals will react to interference, or when criminals feel they have achieved a level of proficiency in their methods of operation. There are certain traits that become obvious to first-responding patrol officers based on the mechanical requirements of committing crimes that are obvious to an *experienced* observer. First responders must be able to make a "quick and dirty" assessment of a crime scene and, with the help of the complainant, to make the right callout for a criminal investigation team. Then, the officer has to turn that information over to the investigator so that the investigation is properly initiated. If patrol officers handle this responsibility hundreds of times per year, it is likely they will end up with a very polished and unique experience level in assessing a crime scene. Veteran criminal investigators depend on this experience from first responders and maintain a close professional relationship with these officers, who may in fact become investigators in the future.

To begin the study of crime scene analysis, it is best to start with certain categories of crimes in much the same way the criminal statutes and priorities were discussed. Sometimes certain crimes provide logical inferences that may carry forward to other, more serious crimes.

Crime report data and law enforcement experience teach that burglary and car theft are two gateway crimes. *Garage surfing* (theft of tools, beer, or other commodities from residential garages) is usually done by first-time juvenile offenders. *Joyriding* (stealing a car to experience the thrill and freedom of driving a valuable and possibly attractive high-dollar car) may be the beginning of criminal conduct that motivates a juvenile offender toward more serious criminal conduct. *Shoplifting* is another juvenile crime that can start a juvenile offender down the wrong path. Usually, when these offenders are caught and their parents conduct appropriate behavioral adjustments, the teens and subteens cease their criminal conduct. Successful burglars, car thieves, and shoplifters fine-tune their skills and become more proficient as their experience level expands.

If behavioral adjustments for juvenile offenders do not work and juveniles accomplish their goals of obtaining easy money or goods that they desire, it might be the beginning of a career as a criminal. This goal of easy money and getting what the nascent criminal wants is often exacerbated by drug use, which costs money. One thrill feeds another thrill. These needs become interdependent, and the young person advances to residential burglary, for which the proceeds are much higher along with the danger. Or the joyrider might discover that stealing valuable car accessories, such as batteries, tires, entertainment centers, or air bags, will produce much-wanted cash. The trainee crook will be well on his way to committing more and more serious crimes. Even shoplifters, who may have once been motivated to steal clothes or electronic devices that they wanted for themselves, may become motivated to steal goods that may be valuable to others who are willing to pay cash to get the goods. This transformation or evolution of criminal activity from a personal goal to a more commercial goal is the beginning of real criminal entrepreneurship and therefore can indicate the beginning of a career choice.

CLASSROOM EXERCISE: A PRELIMINARY CLASSROOM DISCUSSION EXERCISE IN CRIME SCENE ANALYSIS

Consider the following crime scenes:

1. A patrol officer is called to the scene of a residential burglary. The house was entered through the main front entrance by use of a pry bar tool. The suspect left a trail of muddy boot prints and upturned furniture. The kitchen is ransacked, and the refrigerator is left open. The master bedroom is ransacked, and the jewelry box is emptied of gold and silver jewelry and jewelry with precious stones. The family room, with a full entertainment center, has also been ransacked and furniture upended, but the only thing missing is a Sega video game console. The linen closet is disturbed, and it appears one or more pillowcases have been removed. *Provide a logical analysis.*

2. A patrol officer is cruising a warehouse district and comes upon a late-model Honda Prelude with missing tags and obvious evidence of being abandoned. The tires have been removed, and the hood is up. The officer runs the vehicle identification number and determines the car was stolen two days earlier. The officer calls for a tow truck to retrieve the vehicle, but she checks the interior for any evidence. The ignition switch has been destroyed, allowing access to the wires and switch components. The car entertainment/satellite mapping system, the two front air bags, and the battery have been removed, and a variety of fast-food bags and wrappings are left in the passenger seat of the car. *Provide a logical analysis.*

3. A patrol officer is called to a Home Depot store by the manager. Small but valuable items were stolen from various departments all over the store. The items stolen are power tools, batteries, hinges, plumbing valves, boxes of deck screws, paintbrushes, and specialty kits for plumbing repair. The manager reports that a group of "teenagers" with backpacks entered the store during a busy time, spread out throughout the store, and eventually exited the store, making no purchases. *Provide a logical analysis.*

Given your understanding of case priority and investigative resources, suggest the steps needed going forward in these cases.

In our discussion of crime scenes, it is important to begin discussing the crime scene analysis of residential burglaries because techniques learned by career criminals when their careers begin as burglars are returned to if they evolve into becoming high-end professional burglars, assassins, serial killers, or rapists.

Persons whose aberrant behavior turns them into repeat murderers or rapists do not begin their criminal behavior as either of those. They usually start with residential burglary because of the psychosexual thrill that sneaking into someone's house and "having their way" with the property of another person gives them. This thrill satisfies a need. Eventually, that initial thrill goes away, but the techniques learned, the tried-and-true methods of making entry and ensuring that the chances of being detected are kept to a minimum, become part of the criminal's behavior.

A beginning burglar may use brute force to enter a house. A more sophisticated burglar may use sophisticated entry tools, such as lock picks, but a burglar who is concerned about immediate access or speed to avoid detection from outside witnesses may use glass-cutting tools to attack a hidden and vulnerable window. That is why determining the point of entry in a burglary is so important. There has been some general discussion in this text about modus operandi, or MO, but the fact is, the actions the criminal takes to carry out a crime are usually very consistent and can help narrow the pool of suspects when trying to solve any house break-in, from a burglary, to a homicide, to a rape.

Criminals evolve and improve their techniques. If this is apparent in a string of related house break-ins, it can be helpful to informing the investigation. The evolving techniques can help in narrowing the suspect pool. The criminal investigator must be able to account for subtle changes if they become part of the criminal's process. MO is not necessarily unique to any criminal. MO is sometimes shared by criminals when they exchange methods in open training seminars in jail or prison. MO can include enough variations so it can be distinguished in a series of crimes. These techniques will be helpful when the time comes to interview suspects. Additionally, the use of similar techniques is not so widespread as to become irrelevant to a logical evaluation of the MO.

The criminal investigator needs to assess the techniques and create an evaluation based on the set or compilation of the techniques and how the MO is followed. Certain techniques may be used by burglary suspects, but the MO will become more unique as various other factors are observed and if there is a process or plan that is obvious. For example, some professional burglars use lock picks, but then, do they all attack the front door, back door, or side entry door? Some burglars steal jewelry, but how many steal pillowcases to carry their stolen property from the scene? Some professional burglars are careful not to disturb furniture, but do they all steal food or snacks from the kitchen? MO is a general way of operating, but there are factors of timing, approach, and deception that make even the most mundane MO somewhat unique. That is what the investigator is looking for in the evaluation of the crime scene.

Stepping away from the importance of MO in advancing a serial investigation and returning to the reactive investigation of a residential burglary, the lead investigator should walk through the whole scene, note anomalies and aspects of the burglar's MO, and try to determine the points of entry and exit. It is also necessary for the investigator to look at the physical evidence and identify the venue in the house that occupied the time of the burglar. Most burglaries are motivated by the theft of valuable items that can be sold for a substantial profit. If a burglar enters a house and sees a valuable work of art but does not have a fence to whom to sell the item, the valuable artwork is useless to the burglar. If a burglar notices the house has valuable electronic gear, such as HD or 3D flat screen TVs, but he doesn't have a way to transport that kind of bulky gear away from the scene, the burglar will have to stick to stealing what he is prepared to leave with. These realities help the investigator narrow the pool of suspects and can provide information about the likely places where the stolen items can be converted into cash profit for the criminal.

These examples of logical interpretation can also provide insight about the capabilities of the burglar. A career criminal who is a sophisticated burglar is generally more likely to gain access to the house and have an idea as to what should be stolen. The veteran burglar should plan to move in and out of the residence as soon as possible. An art thief will work the venue where the art is displayed or stored and avoid any other venues in the house. An experienced jewel thief will hit the master bedroom and search quickly for a safe or another secure storage place.

These professionals will also have a ready place to sell the stolen goods and a tried-and-true method to remove and conceal the items so as not to walk away from the house with suspicious-looking items in their possession. It is not likely that these kinds of burglars will disrupt the house in any other way. In fact, a serious professional burglar knows that the more disruption, the more likely forensic evidence may be left. Discipline is a hallmark of the veteran professional burglar. Professional burglars who steal large, bulky items, such as numerous flat screen TVs and entertainment centers or high-end appliances and even furniture, will hit homes only where there is a secure way to load the proceeds into an escape vehicle, such as a truck hidden from passersby or neighborhood witnesses.

Preparation, planning, and discipline with a built-in effort to avoid detection are hallmarks of an experienced professional thief. Any indication that the burglar or team of burglars lacks these qualities tends to put the suspect population into the beginner to intermediate criminal category. On the other hand, a beginner who is just developing an MO will usually use force to break into a house. The beginner will ransack and disrupt multiple rooms looking for any material to steal that will yield profit without being certain of where the items can be sold or fenced. The beginner may also ransack and disrupt to show disrespect or disdain for the victim. Burglary is a crime of "intentional subjugation." There is a psychosexual aspect akin to rape, but in most cases, burglars move beyond these unconscious motivations. Eventually, burglars who are not jailed immediately for their crimes advance their expertise. They become better and use more sophisticated methods of entry, their discipline in the house is better, and their focus on valuable, salable property limits the areas in a house where they operate. They also find ways to plan better and build into their plan an appropriate escape route. They may advance to larger items if those items are the most lucrative for them, but they finally begin to realize that there will be more financial benefits if they steal items "to order."

Burglary is a crime of symbiosis in that stealing valuable property is workable only if there is a ready outlet for the property and the burglar is getting something of value for the effort. Because of this concept, when the investigator is observing the crime scene and interviewing the victim, it is important to understand the nature of the property being stolen. The investigator can then make logical conclusions about the burglar's fence based on an ongoing intelligence base developed by the investigator and her colleagues.

In continuing with an overall analysis of residential burglary crime scenes, it is important to repeat and narrow down some of the physical aspects of a crime scene that indicate the level of experience displayed by the crook. Displays of disruption and disorder indicate a beginner. Forced and sloppy entry is indicative of a beginner. Less disruption and more focus on what to steal is characteristic of a more advanced burglar. An intermediate burglar will have developed a subtler method of entry, with attention to being well hidden from outside observation. Carefully considered points of entry and exit indicate a more logical and planned approach with more discipline and therefore more experience.

Lock picks, for example, may not be detected, so the point of entry may never be determined. Lock picks also take a little more time, so a burglar needs an entry door hidden from outside scrutiny. If the timing of the entry needed is short, a glass cutter and a well-hidden lower-floor glass window affords a prime entry point, but the point of entry will be discovered. Lock picks (so entry is not detected by the homeowner) may be the best way if a burglar prone to violence wants to sneak in and hide until the house is occupied. Finally, alarm systems and watchdogs can be effective deterrents for beginners and even some veteran burglars, but two factors should be considered. First, experienced burglars sometimes prefer houses with these kinds of alarm systems because they expect there is something of value in the house if the homeowner can afford a system. Many alarm systems can be disabled by cutting phone lines or cutting internet access wiring, coax cable, or fiber-optic cable. Burglars who take on this challenge are looking for a big score. The burglar will take the time to case the target to learn about the alarm system, time the police response time to a false alarm, or judge the strength of the locks and other security equipment. There may even be an attempt to get insider help from a trusted employee or recalcitrant family member.

Dogs are the second factor and are more difficult for most burglars because well-trained dogs are not easily diverted. Burglars poison dogs using raw meat with poison as bait and will have no trouble disposing of a dog if they think the take is worth it. If a dog is present at the scene and was probably alerted when the intrusion happened, that is another fact that needs to be asked when conducting a neighborhood investigation and in determining a timeline. (Most reactive investigations require a neighborhood investigation, in which the investigator contacts all the neighbors in the surrounding area to determine if any of them noticed any suspicious activity that might be related to the crime.)

Outside factors, such as the choice of targets, are a part of the crime scene analysis the investigator needs to consider. An isolated residence where the victims are routinely absent indicates surveillance or inside information, especially if the score is valuable. A similar scenario where the burglar hits the house at night while it is occupied is indicative of a burglar who is thrill-seeking and not afraid to use violence. This is a dangerous perpetrator who should be prioritized for investigations. Another outside factor that is important is a close suburban neighborhood near a big urban center where most of the homes are empty during several hours in the day, usually due to homeowners' commuting to work. This presents a target-rich environment for anxious, highly motivated, middle range–experienced burglars. These burglars are most likely to have a drug habit that needs constant maintenance. Their crimes will be daily occurrences with little profit. They will be taken advantage of by their fences. The investigator, when called to the scene, should take notice of every aspect of the MO because it is very likely that a repetitive pattern of multiple crimes will manifest in the current neighborhood and other similar neighborhoods in the community. She should also pay special attention to the method of entry. A pry bar, a claw hammer, or a glass cutter will frequently be used. The stolen property will be sold to the same fence, pawn shop, or secondhand dealer. Any guns stolen in these burglaries will be sold to the drug dealers the burglar has as a source for his drug habit.

The following pictures are examples of orderliness and disruption of crime scenes.

Source: D.Reilly

Source: istock 523035163

The following pictures are examples of blunt-force entry and more subtle techniques. Once the point of entry is determined examine the access door for marks consistent with sophisticated lock picks or blunt force weapons.

Source: D Reilly

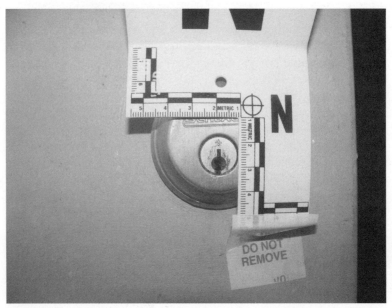

Source: D Reilly

Tool marks can verify what specific pry bar was used to gain access to a residence.

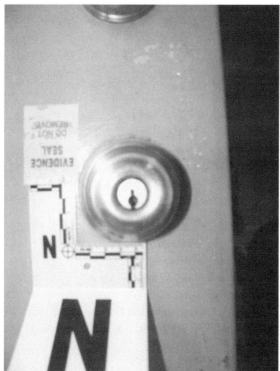

Source: D Reilly

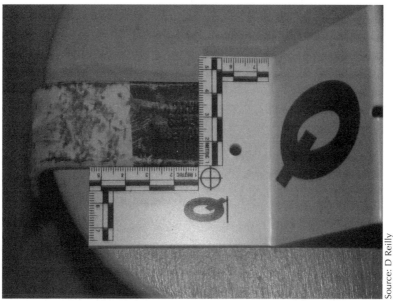

Source: D Reilly

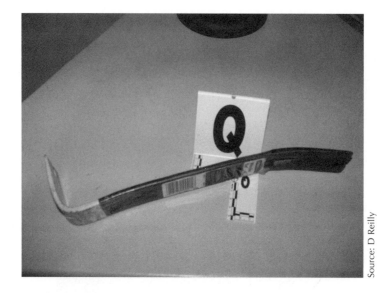

Source: D Reilly

The following pictures are examples of venues in a residential crime scene.

Source: D Reilly

Source: D Reilly

The following pictures are examples of venues in a commercial crime scene.

Source: D Reilly

Source: D Reilly

Source: D Reilly

Source: D Reilly

COMMERCIAL CRIME SCENES

Burglaries, Armed Robberies, and Other Crimes in Business Establishments

Commercial burglaries are, in most cases, the work of experienced criminals. The crime scene analysis will begin with viewing the point of entry. Most commercial buildings housing valuable property, cash, or prescription drugs will have a sophisticated alarm system and doors and windows made of high-grade security materials, such as steel grates and shatterproof materials. Depending on the location of the building, there may also be a short response time from local police or even a private, professional security firm. Given the security precautions, the burglars who target these facilities may have limited options and almost certainly will have to case the crime in advance. Insider information is also a major concern for investigators. Employees or even customers may be able to provide significant details regarding the burglars that will flesh out their plan.

Banks and jewelry stores will also have high-end safes or security vaults that must be breached to get at the valuables. Most criminals who are new to commercial burglaries will confine their crimes to drugstores, clothing stores, and gun stores. The *smash-and-grab* technique is effective in these kinds of thefts. Access to the business can be made using automobiles or heavy-duty wrenches, crowbars, and sledge hammers. These approaches, if they are well-timed and coordinated, will give access to the valuables in the business for short time periods, which allow the crooks to commit the crime and make their escape before the police or private security people have a chance to respond. The perpetrators may even take small safes, ATM machines, and other equipment containing valuables so they can break into them later in a secure area unhampered by time restraints. In these cases, the suspects won't display any special abilities, but if they act efficiently within time parameters and access very valuable material, they should be considered veteran criminals.

In recent times, a European syndicate, known as the Pink Panthers, scored valuable jewelry thefts using the smash-and-grab technique. The jewelry was stolen from high-end stores in resort areas. The targets were trying to attract rich clients who frequently visited the resorts but didn't want to be bothered with the typical security procedures utilized by jewelry stores in more commercial urban areas. The Panthers hit with military precision and were responsible for millions of dollars' worth of stolen jewelry.

During the 1980s, West Coast street gangs used the same techniques for robbing midlevel jewelry stores for hundreds of thousands of dollars' worth of consumer-range jewelry, which would have been easy to fence, but instead, the gangs bartered the stolen jewelry for the wholesale weight of cocaine for street distribution. The gangs acted in a coordinated, planned, and efficient manner and hit the stores during the daylight hours when the businesses were open. The perpetrators were veteran criminals, but they had no specific skill set, just planning and teamwork. In all of their robberies, the gangs were prepared to use violence and acted in an intimidating fashion to deter any interference.

More sophisticated thefts of jewelry and cash require experienced technicians who have the skills needed to defeat alarms and open safes and secure vaults with cracking skills. The population of these kinds of perpetrators will be very limited, although the support staff will be made up of seasoned criminals who are considered reliable. These support persons may be more difficult to identify based on their limited skill set, but there is usually a vetting process and strict guidelines in place for the support subjects. Once a suspect is developed who has the skills to carry out the crime, that person becomes the focal point of the investigation.

Finally, armed robberies of banks, supermarkets, and other cash-rich businesses are carried out by veteran criminals who have a history of violent crime involving the use of weapons and, in some cases, sophisticated body armor. In all these commercial burglaries and robberies, the crooks will leave little forensic evidence unless they discharge their weapons to get the attention of the victim witnesses.

The crime scenes should be organized; there should be an effort to avoid leaving fingerprints or biological material, but even career offenders will make mistakes. All effort to secure forensic evidence should be followed, and the lead investigator should make the effort to identify any venue at the scene where this kind of evidence can be recovered. The MO of these professional stickup artists can inform an investigation going forward.

VIOLENT CRIME SCENES

Homicides, Murders, Manslaughters, Rapes, Mayhem, and Other Crimes of Violence with Serious Bodily Harm

Crime scenes of violence fall into several categories. A crime scene can be where the body or remains of the victim are found. There is evidence of a disturbance around the body, which may include blood, shell casings, a blunt weapon, a knife, or another cutting instrument. Furniture may be upended and in disarray. Shoe prints or tire treads may be present in an outdoor scene. If there is little or no odor or signs of decomposition and the stiffness, or rigor, of the body is not noticeable, there is a likelihood that the person died within hours of the response.

The ambient temperature affects decomposition and *rigor mortis*, which is a stiffening of the muscles that occurs between two to six hours of death in a normal crime scene venue. *Liver mortis* and *algor mortis*, two other scientific methods to determine time of death, are also equally affected by the ambient temperature and the temperature and size of the body. *Liver mortis* is generally an observable phenomenon that indicates how the body was positioned at the time of death. Because blood in the body is no longer affected by a pumping heart, the blood pools in the lowest part of the body, causing a purplish color in that area.

The timing of this gravity-controlled phenomenon can be estimated by the medical examiner to help in determining the time of death, but it can also provide a clue as to whether the body was moved from its initial position postmortem. Any way to fine-tune the time of death is an important factor to learn in the initial stages of the investigation. A pronouncement by a medical examiner is essential, but that scientific pronouncement may take some time. Obvious wounds to the body can provide some indication as to the cause of death, and the positioning of weapons near the body may be significant if the weapon matches the wounds. It is also likely that weapons left near a body were used by the victim in an unsuccessful attempt at self-defense.

A crime scene that shows signs of a struggle indicates the killing may not have been planned. A crime scene that shows signs of a struggle and the presence of the weapon used to kill at the scene is further evidence that the killing was not well planned. The crime scene left in disarray with no effort to eliminate fingerprints and trace or biological evidence is even more evidence that the person who did the killing is a novice or a person who is somehow uninterested in avoiding detection. None of these logical conclusions can be certain, but in most cases of homicide, some preplanning or postplanning is normal. The penalties for homicide are so serious that it is simply logical to assume that the killer would try to avoid prosecution. Even a person who commits a homicide in self-defense will feel justified and may be present at the crime scene to provide his side of the conflict. An orderly and "efficient" crime scene without a murder weapon or obvious sign of a struggle, vacuumed or swept floors, clean physical objects absent, and only a normal number of latent fingerprints may indicate an effort to clean the crime scene and remove any evidence. This kind of effort to clean the scene is indicative of an experienced killer or thoughtful amateur.

A planned murder is likely to have been done with a weapon brought to the scene by the killer. If a gun, knife, or blunt-force weapon that may have been at the crime scene prior to the killing has been removed, the killer may not have been considering the crime prior to the killing. This may be a helpful bit of deductive reasoning to narrow the pool of suspects from a motivated assassin to a close associate who was planning a less deadly effort to encourage compliance from the victim. If the weapon was removed and the crime scene cleaned and restored, there is evidence of an effort to avoid detection. Finally, if the weapon was generic and untraceable as to its origin and the crime scene is clean, there is a likelihood of a well-planned homicide with "malice aforethought."

Even the choice of weapon can be significant, such as a knife that is more a weapon than a tool. A hunting knife versus a chef's knife is indicative of some level of skill and confidence. A nine-millimeter or higher caliber handgun versus a hunting rifle or shotgun also indicates a level of skill that is significant. This kind of variation can indicate a career criminal versus a novice beginner. A heavy metal candlestick with enough heft to cause death versus a baseball bat that may require multiple blows to cause death indicates a level of confidence and physical strength that may be significant in considering the possible suspects. Just the choice of a weapon and how effective the death blow is administered is significant.

Finally, any indication of overkill or extra damage to the victim can be evidence of a personal animus, and it can also be evidence of sending a message to intimidate others in the victim's personal or professional orbit. Multiple stab wounds are indicative of psychosexual anger. Multiple bullet wounds are indicative of a need to make sure the victim is truly dead. This is a kind of anger and displacement resulting from prior rage and even abuse. Ritualistic dismembering or postmortem disfigurement may be the result of a type of mental psychosis. The investigator should remember that unusual violence and even psychotic overkill does not preclude a business or personal dispute. Killers often have several motives for violence. Some of those motives may predate the immediate motive, so even if the victim appears to be the victim of a deranged killer, don't discount some earlier conflict between the killer and the victim.

Stranger homicides are the result of killings that have well-hidden motives. A *murder for hire* is one category. The killing may be well planned and almost perfunctory, with an appropriately lethal weapon done and with proficiency and effectiveness. A paid assassin is not likely to leave much chance for the victim to defend or defeat the assault. A sniper, a bomber, or an up close and personal combatant who is skilled with a handgun or knife and arranges the timing of the crime to catch the victim at a vulnerable time is a hallmark of a murder for hire. Homicides that include indicators of this kind of professional efficiency may indicate a murder-for-hire assassin. At this point, the investigator needs to rely on a deep analysis of the victim's circle of both personal and professional associates. The suspect list will include anyone close to the victim who had a significant motive to want the victim dead and the necessary wealth to pay a professional killer. Indications that the suspect has a rock-solid alibi is a logical inference that the suspect knew how and when the crime was going to happen.

The investigation includes the victimology (study of the victim), discussed in chapters 2 and 8, and is best accomplished with extensive interviews with family, friends, and close business associates. All of them may have a nefarious agenda, but suspicion must be broad in the beginning and focused on who has motive and financial ability. There is, of course, other currency for payment to an assassin and a possibility of a close personal relationship with the killer, but in most cases, the transaction is very straightforward and will involve the transmittal of funds to the person hired. A transaction of this type can usually be in a $5,000 to $10,000 range and handled in a very covert fashion. Proving the transaction happened may be the only way to prove who is behind the murder unless the killer is caught and provides the name of the employer. Even then, proof is very difficult.

The next types of stranger homicide are *serial killers* and *psychosexual killers*. The crime scene evaluation may be significantly different from a murder for hire, but it may exhibit characteristics like killings done by a person known to the victim. In fact, in these cases, the killer has specifically targeted the victim based on some perceived prior and special knowledge. The killer may have a type of targeting mechanism based on the victim's appearance, sex, age, race, hair color, or any one of a series of obvious features known only to the killer. Because of these idiosyncrasies, the crime scene may appear to have been done by someone the victim knew. Unusual MO may be apparent at the scene. The orderliness or chaos of the crime scene may reflect a desire on the part of the killer to let law enforcement know the crime is in fact the work of the killer. Part of the insatiable desire to kill is the desire to be known as the responsible party. This also can be characterized as having dueling agendas. One is to get caught and the other is to avoid detection.

Serial killers want to be known, feared, and celebrated for their acts. Sometimes these acknowledgments can be realized only if the killer is eventually caught and lionized in the media. Most of these killers are not interested in being caught, but they are not necessarily motivated to act out their rage against their victim and carefully clean up the crime scene to avoid leaving clues. In some cases, they present a "tableau" to their law enforcement pursuers. They leave staged crime scenes that have messages they hope will be delivered to all their future victims. They have left a special signature of their "work." The signature is usually an unusual item of evidence that is neither a part of the crime nor in any way instrumental to the crime. It is usually a recurring message identifying the crime as their work. It can be a ribbon, a note, a written message, or even a gratuitous postmortem disfigurement of the victim that may have meaning only to the killer. When confronted with a crime scene that exhibits these kinds of characteristics, the investigator must take extra time to review and evaluate every part of the scene so as not to miss any method, message, or configuration that may lead to a logical investigation.

In addition to exhibiting some of the characteristics of a serial killer, a psychosexual killer is motivated by sexual assault on the victim. Rape, sodomy, and any manner of aberrant sexual contact will be obvious on the victim, and in many cases, the victim will meet certain physical characteristics that in some way match the features of the primary or even "fantasy" victim in the killer's past. Ultimately, the psychosexual killer is trying to re-create a fantasy of dominance over some past model of obsession. Evaluating the crime scene usually starts with the same overall analysis. Is the scene orderly, staged, or chaotic? Is there evidence to be gathered, or was the scene cleaned and scrubbed so no forensic clues were left? If the scene has a signature or symbolic message, can the nature of that message be understood, and is the signature recurring?

Stranger homicides are very difficult investigations. Motive and access to the victim, the choice of the crime scene, and the variety of methods used by the killer may be obvious once you develop a logical suspect, but until that time, every aspect of the investigation is a mystery. A close friend or a spouse can carry out an outwardly appearing stranger homicide with intelligent planning, so there never is a comfortable sense of moving the investigation in the right direction. Serial killers and psychosexual killers are pattern killers, and the best way to know you are heading in the right direction is to have multiple victims whose crime scenes are so unique as to provide a logical connect-the-dots pattern. Unless there are aspects of the MO that are kept secret, you may never know if you are dealing with the same killer in every crime. In the Atlanta Child Murders in 1979 through 1981, several young African American males were killed and associated with the same killer, but there has never been any official closure on the "outlier" cases. The city police and officials relied on the fact that the killings stopped when Wayne Williams, the accused and convicted serial killer, was incarcerated. Williams was convicted of killing two victims, but he is alleged to have killed as many as twenty-three victims.

CRIMINAL ENTERPRISES, CRIME SYNDICATES, GANGS, MOBS, AND CREWS

These criminal groups operate in ongoing or continuing criminal "bureaucracies" whose priority is survival. Their survival often depends on removing enemies, territorial rivals, and persons who may cooperate with law enforcement by cooperating with criminal investigations. These groups have violent killers on their payroll who carry out murders to protect or enhance the position of the group. These killers may be cool professional assassins or psychotic killers. Examining a crime scene and making the connection between the victim and one of these killers is difficult without an understanding of who the victim is and how or why she may have been targeted by a criminal group. There should be some indicators. In the first place, enemies or rival gang members will protect and secure their residences by extraordinary means, so if a target is identified by a gang, it is highly unlikely that the killer would be able to quickly figure out where the target lives. On the other hand, if the target has operational control of an open-air drug market, hangs out at a social club or bar, or has a relationship with a spouse, girlfriend, or paramour, the killer can clock the target (in other words, surveil the victim and pick the best time to commit the crime.) Members of criminal gangs or syndicates rely heavily on the criminal ecosystem for the best information about a potential target. Computerized intelligence, law enforcement databases, and DMV records are available to these groups from corrupt officials with access, but any search might be traced back to the corrupt official, which would provide an important investigative lead. Most criminal groups will try to avoid this kind of scrutiny, so relying on criminal intelligence is the preferred method. The attack on the target will often occur at an outdoor crime scene or some public venue rather than a residence or business. The crime will most likely be done with a firearm with sufficient stopping power, a nine-millimeter or higher caliber. The crime will involve several shots fired with at least one coup de grâce, which is most likely a head shot to ensure the death of the target. Shell casings may be left because the killer plans to discard the weapon immediately after the crime, thus rendering the ballistic evidence found at the crime scene useless. In fact, gang members and syndicate killers may use the same gun multiple times and then pass the gun on to another killer just to flummox law enforcement. The idea of several unrelated shootings involving the same weapon but having no connecting theme is considered an unsolved puzzle to frustrate law enforcement.

Another category of homicides related to crime groups are drive-by shootings. These shootings are random attacks on rival gangs or groups to intimidate and disrupt the activities of the adversarial criminal group. These shootings can involve homicides and, in some cases, involve the wounding or killing of innocent bystanders. The crime scenes of these kinds of shootings will again be open-air neighborhoods. Evidence of shootings may include shell casings and auto glass strewn on the street where the victim or victims were attacked. There may also be evidence of return fire in self-defense, which will not be admitted to by the bystanders and victims.

The personal profiles of killers who operate in the furtherance of criminal groups as suggested above are cold, professional, and calculating assassins, including psychotic chaotic killers. They often have an elevated position in the gang or group and may even be top shot callers. MO and even unique aspects of their crimes may manifest in the same fashion as discussed above with the other stranger killers. Violent gangs or criminal group killers may not fit the exact profile of being a stranger to the victim, but their actions as viewed at the scene will usually have the dispassionate, business-oriented factors of other stranger homicides.

Personal Experience

During the early 1990s, I worked a violent gang investigation in the District of Columbia. The gang's primary method of setting up a target was to use young, attractive female gang members to seduce the target; then, when the target and female arranged a tryst, the target was killed when he was most vulnerable to attack. The homicides usually occurred at low-rent motel rooms. One of the important witnesses in that case refused the advances of the honey-pot female, which saved his life because the gang was never able to locate where the witness lived. The witness's life was saved by his fidelity to his spouse.

RAPE AND SEXUAL ASSAULT

Many of the factors detailed above about analyzing a crime scene apply to crime scenes where a rape or sexual assault has occurred. The main distinction is the living witness and the likelihood that the crime was a close physical struggle between the victim and the suspect. The physical struggle automatically makes the careful and methodical examination of the exact location where the assault occurred essential. It is almost impossible for the suspect to clean or sweep trace evidence from a place where such a struggle took place. Even if the suspect gained and maintained strict control of the victim, the exchange of microscopic evidence is inevitable because of the nature of the crime. This is, of course, why it is so important to get the victim to a hospital for medical and forensic examinations. It is also necessary to recover any clothing worn by the victim so it can be thoroughly examined. Chaotic crime scenes with upturned furniture and evidence of further disruption are likely the work of a newly minted rapist. As mentioned elsewhere in this text, rape and sexual assault are serial crimes.

Aside from a very few examples of date rape or drug or alcohol rage leading to sexual assault, most rapists are repeat offenders. Even the average suspects in a date rape attack have or will have similar experiences more than once in their lives. The obvious fact that a date rapist is known to the victim provides an excellent starting point for a criminal investigation. It is therefore the responsibility of the investigator to prove violence, coercion, or threats in a date rape scenario. The medical examination should include a toxic chemical screen (drug screening) for any of the variety of date rape drugs, but the medical examination and the rape kit screening are part of the investigation unconnected to the evaluation of the crime scene. Any effort on the part of the suspect to hide evidence, clean up the crime scene, or in some other manner avoid detection can be viewed as consciousness of guilt. Date rape can evolve into a finger-pointing argument over what constitutes consent. If the suspect claims mutual consent, then there is no need to avoid detection. Taking the necessary time to examine the scene with the crime scene technician and determining the importance of obvious evidence along with any anomalies will help in future interviews with the suspect to make sure the truth is revealed.

It is unknown whether date rape or stranger rape is more prevalent in our society. The reporting of rape incidents is limited, for all the reasons discussed in chapter 6, but stranger rape is more likely to be reported, especially if the victim shows up at a hospital for medical treatment or calls 911 for emergency assistance. In many cases of stranger rape, the crime scene may have been abandoned by the victim because it is not the victim's residence or it is a semiprivate public space, such as a garage, a parking lot at night, a walkway/sidewalk, or even a park. These places are not the kind of places a victim who has been assaulted will wait for police assistance. It is then necessary for the criminal investigator to determine where the crime occurred and when so that a successful crime scene examination can take place.

Once the scene has been established, the crime scene review and analysis are done in the same way that they are done in the above crimes. Is the scene chaotic with obvious signs of a struggle, or is it cleaned or swept to remove any forensic evidence? If the scene is in an open-air or outdoor area and the assault appears to be a stranger attack, is there a lookout venue used by the rapist to view and target his victims? Is there a location where the rapist was lying in wait to choose the target, or was the crime simply a crime of opportunity? Is there a way to determine from the crime scene if the victim was an intended target, or is there the possibility that the victim was just in the wrong place at the wrong time? For example, if the victim was the intended target, does the crime scene reflect a location where the victim regularly visited or passed by? Is the location similar in any way to other rape crime scenes or lookout spots? Taking in these factors informs the investigation and provides a vital area of inquiry for use throughout the investigation.

Stranger rape at the home of the victim happens at least as often as rape and sexual assault in a semiprivate crime scene, such as parks, garages, and walkways. In these cases, the rapist has used criminal skills to enter the home to hide until the victim is vulnerable and alone. As mentioned in the beginning of this chapter, the skills of the burglar are used by a more advanced and violent criminal who has graduated from burglary to rape and sexual assault. The extra benefit in analyzing the crime scene is some crime scene details can be discussed with the live victim witness so that a better conclusion can be reached about unusual or anomalous factors. It is important to determine points of entry and exit, evaluate the MO, and look for the range of experience and concern about avoiding detection. How much time does the perpetrator spend in the residence, and is there a venue in the crime scene other than the location where the assault occurred that could require extra attention? This rapist may also be motivated by greed and, therefore, would be stealing valuable property belonging to the victim, which may provide additional leads in solving the case.

CHILD RAPE AND SEXUAL ASSAULT

There is no real distinction between the crime scene analysis in a child sexual assault investigation and any other sexual assault case. The one major exception is the crime scene is very likely to have been used for several victims. As discussed in chapters 2 and 6, child assault victims are preyed on by two types of serial offenders. The first kind of perpetrator can ingratiate himself to the victim and, in many cases, the victim's family. The seduction practiced by these sociopathic predators is subtle and intense. The offender is usually a charismatic person who uses bribery and secret gift-giving to make the child feel indebted. He uses his manipulative behavior to control the victim and reinforce the need for the victim to avoid revealing their "special relationship" to other adults. He may even use threats of violence against the victim's parents to ensure the child cooperates. Since this kind of predator keeps his victims quiet, it is their normal practice to use the same location for multiple crimes against multiple child victims.

Serial child predators who don't have these personality skills and the ability to use the seductive behavior are very simply *violent predators*. Their psychosexual behavior is so compelling they are aggressive in their abduction and assault on their child victims. They are more than capable of snatching children in shopping malls and off the street, after school. They use whatever force or tranquilizers necessary to ensure cooperation from the victims. These predators almost never leave their victims alive; therefore, the crime scenes are analyzed in the same fashion as those of psychosexual killers of adults, with the added variation that because these crimes are so heinous and the intelligence level of the predators may be well below average, mistakes are much more likely. The chance that forensic evidence is left behind is significant.

SUMMARY

It should be noted here that the abovementioned scenarios are not meant to provide all of the much broader range of crime scene variants. These scenarios are meant to be used to explain theoretical factors that can be observed and may have significant meaning. It is possible that an experienced criminal will commit a crime without considering some of the factors mentioned above. It is also just as likely that an inexperienced novice will carefully plan and execute a crime with skill and appropriate discipline. Planning and avoidance of detection are not rocket science. The criminal investigator needs to approach every investigation with an open mind and a boatload of suspects and theories, but it is best to narrow the focus and use the information available to begin to form the best and most well-supported theory possible. Adjustments based on facts and evidence will correct and educate the investigator. Starting with the crime scene and applying deductive reasoning until the truth emerges allows the investigator time and motivation to analyze, develop, and research the case until the case comes together. Even using this technique in the reanalysis of crime scenes in a proactive investigation may provide a somewhat different view of the block of cases to invigorate the investigations to the point of finding the solutions.

Chapter Eight

Investigative Plan

'   *Process, plan, or strategy.*

In our discussion of criminal investigations, the preliminary concerns have been addressed. Now it is time to start the process. We considered what an investigation is and how it needs to be initiated. Reactive investigations usually begin with an event that indicates someone has been killed, injured, ripped off, or otherwise diminished. The event appears to be the act of another. That person is likely to have broken the law and should be held accountable for the crime. We defined the laws and the jurisdiction where the investigation should occur. We determined which law enforcement agency is responsible for conducting the investigation. We made sure that the investigative responsibilities are clear and the investigator knows what needs to be proven to reach a conclusion.

We have considered how the investigator's authority is defined in a free society and what the rights are of any person accused of a crime. We understand why those rights provide a landscape and process by which the investigation is to proceed. We then turned our attention to the investigators and decided how a team approach has proven successful in the past and how it should be applied to the process going forward.

We have determined that witnesses are the key sources of evidence. All criminal investigations need to be considered in the human context in which they are defined and subsequently solved. We discussed witnesses' concerns for their own safety and for justice and the adjustment in their responses, which is needed to tell their story appropriately within the criminal justice system of rules and rulings.

We have considered the logic and science of evaluating the scene of the crime event so that the investigator can start to use informed speculation and reasonable analysis to begin an investigation.

This same approach and process is used to take on proactive investigations, which involve a much larger landscape of criminal conduct. Multiple crime scenes or events will be studied, and tactics will be developed. In proactive investigations, we no longer trace the origin back to a single event. We review multiple crimes or even future crimes and focus our suspicions on one or more persons who are believed to be regularly involved in criminal conduct. The investigation's goal is to ensure that law enforcement intelligence or suspicion evolves to the point where crimes are solved and certain patterns of criminal activity are eliminated.

THE PLAN

An investigative plan includes speculative analysis based on experience and logic. The facts and evidence available to the investigator after the initial introductory phase of an investigation are reviewed, and certain determinations about that crime are made. A good working plan begins with answering the following basic questions and establishing the best way to apply the answers to a specific set of facts.

- What criminal statute or statutes were violated?
- Does the investigator and the agency have jurisdiction?
- How large is the population of suspects who could have committed the crime?
- Does the investigator have the authority to effectively resolve all the questions raised by the crime event or series of events under investigation?
- Is there a pool of witnesses who can be helpful in the investigation?
- Is the crime solvable based on reliable witnesses, a reliable intelligence base, or the recovery of physical evidence, which can provide forensic identification of the suspect?

A plan should be a predictable road map leading to a solution of the crime. Cohesive organization with a step-by-step process should provide the best approach, but there are as many variables as there are constants when you consider the nature of proof, the value of evidence, and the determination about how facts are best used to prove or support an argument. The criminal investigator needs to understand that, from one case to another, it is rare that the same process will yield the same results. Investigation is not just science, psychology, or precise planning. It may be all three, but there are times when an investigation presents as chaos that turns into an understandable and orderly process by the criminal. Some violent crimes, for instance, may appear to be random violence with no motive. As the investigation evolves, the criminal's plan becomes apparent and almost predictable. A plan, therefore, must be malleable and adaptable. As soon as the investigator begins to uncover what is going on in the mind of the criminal, a more orderly path to solution will be available.

In an investigation, there are certain factors that hopefully will always be available. Each investigation needs at least one witness who can testify about the crime, the criminal, or even just about circumstances relating to the crime. Each investigation needs at least one victim and one criminal. Aside from these needs, the possibilities are endless. Even so-called victimless crimes may affect the investigative plan. Well-organized and precise plans reflect the criminal investigator's capabilities and the teamwork that is applied to the investigation.

The most important goal of a plan is effectiveness and success. If the facts, evidence, and proof come together and present the truth for a judge or jury and the criminal is made to pay for the action, the case is a success and the plan worked. In our discussion, we will present steps that can be followed that will result in a successful investigation. You will note that the steps are multifaceted and may appear to be a jumble of disparate processes, but this is how criminal cases manifest themselves. The investigator is usually hit with multiple needs all at once, and throughout the steps, the limits of time management and organization are tested until all the leads are covered. Then, there is dead time and space during which the investigator must be creative, patient, and sustained in applying pressure to achieve the goal. Law enforcement work is a process of daily routine and boredom, which is then punctuated by sheer terror and sustained emergency demands. In following certain steps, there are points at which the investigator can adjust, implement decisions, and produce much-needed support to reach the goal.

After the initial investigative step has been completed, the plan usually becomes an exercise that considers one or more theories and determines the answers to who, what, where, how, why, and when the crime was done. Most of the time with reactive crime investigations, the what and where are self-evident. Occasionally, the when is also known. In some cases, such as commercial armed robberies, the crime might have happened in front of several eyewitnesses. The theory or speculation about what happened is not a mystery. In homicide investigations, it is more demanding when investigators are called to the scene of a deceased person. Crimes that occurred without a definitive crime scene are even that much more demanding. The initial information that a crime occurred may be supported by one or more witnesses, but no physical evidence is immediately available. The theory or speculation develops from the details provided by the complaining witness, as in a kidnapping case.

Investigative inquiry is a waste of time and effort if there is no reliable source of information upon which to base a theory or speculation about the crime. The sources of that information are a physical crime scene or dump site, knowledgeable and reliable witnesses, victims, and then any other supporting information that exists and allows progress in an investigation.

The two types of investigations have two separate starting points. A *reactive* case usually begins with the crime scene. If there is no known crime scene, then begin with the complainant who reports the crime to law enforcement. Once the crime scene has been established, proceed as follows:

1. Determine if there are witnesses to and/or victims of the crime present, and conduct initial interviews.
2. Begin the detailing of leads that need to be followed.
3. Coordinate with the crime scene examiners. If there is no crime scene team or unit, begin processing the scene yourself.
4. Go over the actions of the first responders, and make sure they send you any notes, photos, or reports they generate. (In the current state of technology, these items may be digital files, which will eventually find their way into the investigative file.)
5. If appropriate, determine if there is outstanding investigative or tactical activity being carried out by responding patrol units. (This outstanding activity may involve following up on a lookout for a getaway car or a suspect who matches the description of the criminal.)

These five procedures are prominent examples of the investigative actions that need to be taken when responding to a crime. They can be adjusted and applied to every investigation; even proactive investigations will have multiple crime events that have to be reviewed for this same basic information.

In a *proactive* investigation, begin with a thorough background investigation of the suspects identified in the case as being responsible for a pattern of criminal conduct. It is also a starting point to begin with the crime reports, crime scene examinations, witness statements, and any follow-up significant physical evidence recovered. Proactive investigations often have known (or unknown) suspects who are responsible for the pattern of crime. Focus is on the suspected pattern of crimes or the backgrounds of the suspects themselves. Most proactive investigations are initiated by reviewing reports, statements, photographs, and any evidence related to the investigation. The investigator must become thoroughly knowledgeable about all aspects of the suspects or the suspected activity.

Most proactive investigations are initiated by actionable intelligence that is reliable and can be accessed for further information when the case is advanced to the second phase. (Actionable intelligence is information from a reliable source who provides details sufficient to generate investigative action or tactical response.) Both proactive and reactive investigations move into a second phase when the investigator begins the effort to catch up with the suspects. *Catch up* is a term that refers to the fact that, as an investigator, you are behind in a race to the truth. It is your job to recover and move forward to the point where you are not just even but ahead in the race.

The following steps are an effort to customize the various plans to particular violations. These violations are (1) crimes against persons and (2) crimes against property. There are individual criminal acts discussed with each three-step plan of action. Crimes against persons include homicides, sexual assaults, and aggravated assault and battery. Under crimes against property are armed robberies, burglaries, and car theft. Three-step plans discussed in this fashion provide the student with an orderly plan of action, so the three-step approach affords a simple "beginning, middle, and end" to each investigation.

Step 1: Crimes against Persons

When considering a plan or a scheme to follow in any investigation, there are some logical compartments in which to place investigations. One compartment is *crimes against persons*. Any crime that involves violence or assault on a person is considered a crime against persons. The victim is the starting point in the plan. There may be times when the crime scene, or where the violence occurred, may not be known. When the police are called to the venue where the complainant determines there is evidence of a crime, that evidence may simply be the person who was victimized. When the first responders arrive, the body of the homicide victim is present, or the victim of a rape or a serious physical assault where there is significant bodily harm is present. Step 1 in the plan of crimes against persons is to make sure any person who needs medical help gets that care.

Homicide Case

When the lead investigator arrives at a homicide scene, the body of the victim may be removed if the victim was in the process of dying when the complainant called for the police. The lead investigator needs to ensure there will be coordination among the emergency medical responders, the emergency room staff, and the coroner or medical examiner. Each person who came in contact with the remains of the victim needs to be documented, and her work space needs to be examined for evidence. Important evidence can be recovered at each step in the treatment and examination process. Investigators or officers need to trace the process through or accompany the victim until the victim is turned over to the medical examiner. In most jurisdictions, the autopsy of a homicide victim should be observed by the criminal investigator, and any physical evidence recovered in the autopsy should be turned over to the investigator or the police evidence technicians.

In the next example, the body remains at the response location. This happens when medical assistance is not necessary. In these cases, the lead investigator, a representative from the coroner or medical examiner, and the crime scene team work the venue together to make a preliminary finding as to what happened. Witnesses are identified at the location and separated from each other or monitored to avoid witness contamination. Each aspect, from discovering and recovering physical evidence to conducting on-the-scene interviews, is done without missing important facts resulting from these efforts.

It is usually best to start with the complainant who called the police to the scene. This person can be anyone: a close associate of the victim, a suspect, or a witness to the whole incident. This person can also be a total stranger who just happened upon the victim. Any other bystanders, witnesses, and potential suspects need to be interviewed. A review of all the witness statements needs to be done before any witness is released from the scene. This demand for cooperation is an essential part of step 1. Exercising police authority in a matter like this may be unpopular with the civilian witnesses, but it is a necessary inconvenience.

After the witnesses have been interviewed, the lead investigator needs to coordinate the findings from the witnesses with the physical elements determined from the crime scene. If the findings of the crime scene team point to the fact that the death of the victim does not appear to have occurred at this scene, further investigation needs to occur. The lead investigator should attempt to consult with the medical examiner or tech for any scientific indicator that may support the movement of the victim postmortem.

On the other hand, if the crime scene team has recovered significant physical evidence that the crime occurred on or near where the body was recovered, the lead investigator needs to make sure there are no immediate discrepancies between the witness statements and the locations and type of evidence that were discovered. For example, if expended shell casings were recovered that indicate the assailant in a shooting murder was standing in a certain location but witnesses state the shooter was standing elsewhere, every effort should be made to resolve the conflict. That kind of discrepancy can be resolved in one of three ways: (1) The witness is mistaken based on poor observation skill, a false claim, or suspicious behavior; (2) the shell casings were moved, or they represent evidence from a shooting that did not result in the death of the victim (two shooters, and the killer shot the victim with a revolver); (3) a third person, possibly even the shooter, moved the casings.

Any resolution of the discrepancies based on supportable facts and reasonable logic will help the case going forward. A permanent record of the discrepancy should be made. It may be that the discrepancy can't be resolved. In that case, the investigator is aware of the problem and will have to resolve the issue before it becomes a sore point at trial time. The investigation conducted in step 1 will have flaws and gaping holes that need to be filled. However, completing the examination of the crime scene and interviewing all the available witnesses puts the investigation on the right path to success.

In most jurisdictions in the United States, it is the responsibility of the lead investigator or designated police official in homicide cases to notify the family, next of kin, or other appropriate person of a death. This notification process is a requirement that normally takes place during step 1 in an investigation. Obviously, the identity of the victim needs to be determined. It may take days or even weeks for this to be done with a victim whose identification is missing from the remains and is found in an area where no one will come forward and provide a preliminary identification.

Once a name is officially connected with the remains, a formal identification process by the next of kin or close family member must be done in a manner consistent with a protocol for the jurisdiction. This can range from an identification that takes place at the medical examiner's office to a display of photographic images of the remains by the investigator to the next of kin or appropriate family member. Given this requirement, the investigator's first contact with the next of kin may be very traumatic and unsettling, but it must be done. Even though the investigator may be dealing with extreme grief and anger, there can be observations made that will inform the investigation. If the investigator acts with genuine human concern and empathy, it is likely that the next of kin and the family will be willing to help the investigation. Following are a few questions that must be asked during this very traumatic interview:

- Does the victim have anyone who would have wanted him killed?
- Does the victim have enemies?
- Why would the victim be found where the body was found?
- Where does the victim work or frequent?
- What is the general reputation of the victim?

These questions and a few more should be judiciously put to the family to see how they react specifically and try to determine if the family is being open and honest or closed and protective. Some families in this circumstance will be astonished at the thought of someone killing their loved one. Some families will be aware of a dark side to their loved one and won't be overly surprised. Other families may be saddened but, in some ways, relieved. There is no stock reaction to this notification, but the investigator should read the reaction and decide how to proceed. The investigator may make the notification, arrange the positive identification, ask the immediate and preliminary questions, and then arrange an appointment to go over the background of the victim in depth. He may walk away from this notification with leads on the victim's business and social life and begin the important relationship with the victim's family that will be ongoing for the course of the investigation.

Rape or Serious Assault Cases

Step 1 in a rape or serious assault case is very similar to step 1 in a homicide, except that the victim is transported to the hospital for medical treatment. When the victim's health is stabilized, the investigator must initiate an effort to recover any physical evidence from the live victim. This can be done only with the permission of the victim. A victim who is unconscious and unable to consent may require that permission be obtained by proxy from a next of kin or, if the victim is a child, by a parent. In the event there is no one available to give consent, a court order may be needed; however, the physical evidence must be obtained legally.

In a rape case or any sexual assault, the examination for trace evidence is usually very invasive and requires a well-trained, forensically experienced medical professional. This is usually the beginning of the imposing personal and emotional relationship between the lead investigator and the victim, as discussed in chapter 6. If the investigator feels unable to handle this relationship, another investigator on the team needs to work with the victim.

On serious assault cases, the recovery of a bullet is a medical procedure that is usually necessary in a gun assault case. Permission for this procedure is usually given in the *consent to provide medical treatment*. More invasive or even extraneous examinations for trace physical evidence may require the same permission required in a sexual assault case. Victims in these cases may have been beaten, bitten, strangled, or otherwise physically assaulted, leaving the suspect's trace material on the victim. An exchange of physical evidence from a blunt-force weapon or knife is also the kind of trace evidence that can be recovered from the victim. Recovery of this evidence may be essential in proving the crime.

Once that treatment and evidence recovery effort is completed, step 1 in a sexual or serious assault case proceeds the same way the step proceeds in a homicide case. There is usually a complainant or complaining witness. That person may be the victim, but that is not always the case. Interviewing that person and any other bystanders or suspects at the scene where the victim was recovered is the important process that begins the investigation. Also, the exploitation of the scene where the police were called is part of this process. If possible, determine that the crime occurred where the first responders were called, and try to resolve any discrepancies. Interview witnesses on hand, conduct a crime scene examination, and resolve conflicts between witnesses and crime scene variations.

Step 1: Property Crime Investigations

For purposes of this text, property crimes are any criminal investigations that result in the theft of property, currency, or anything of value. This category includes armed robbery, robbery, shoplifting, burglary, embezzlement, and any other kinds of larceny, including auto theft.

Step 1 involves responding to the scene as instructed by the complainant. In cases of this kind, it is not "normal" that anyone at the scene will need medical attention, but in some armed robbery cases, it is possible that a victim who refused to cooperate with the criminals is injured. Emergency medical care and accompanying the victim to the hospital or urgent care facility is priority. Aside from that possibility, these cases involve a process similar to that used for *crimes against persons*. The complainant and any bystanders must be interviewed, and a thorough examination of the crime scene must take place.

This crime scene examination will be disruptive to a commercial establishment, such as a bank, grocery store, restaurant, or drugstore, because these stores must be closed until all areas related to the crime are examined. This usually involves multiple venues in a crime scene. As discussed in chapter 7, venues are separate areas in which suspects carried out parts of their crime. They include points of entry and exit as well as the route used by the suspects to arrive at and leave from the main venue where the crime occurred. In the case of an armed robbery of a bank, for example, the venues may be the *front entrance* of the bank, the *hallway* leading to the *main teller area*, and the *hallway* leading to a *rear exit* from the building, which was used by the suspect or suspects committing the crime. In this case, there are five venues in one crime scene. There can also be auxiliary venues where other aspects of the crime were carried out. Auxiliary venues in a robbery can be vault areas, safe deposit box areas, count rooms, or locations where cash is prepared for final distribution.

In burglary cases, the main venues may be bedrooms where jewelry is stored or electronic equipment is housed. But in burglary cases, the points of entry and exit as well as the routes to and from the main venue should be examined. In residential burglaries, burglars have been known to steal food and drink from kitchen areas. The kitchen may be a venue that is appropriate to examine even though the criminal aspect of the case is not centered there.

The focus of the crime scene examination must be customized to each crime. Each venue needs to be examined and exploited for physical evidence, including fingerprints, trace evidence, pattern evidence, and biological material. Logic and witness information can guide the work that is needed. The other important consideration is the unusual, suspicious, or mysterious variation that is observed during the crime scene examination. During step 1 in any investigative plan, the crime scene examination must be thorough, and all the facts must be known because the investigative team usually has only one chance at the scene.

Once the investigator reaches the point when all the witnesses have been interviewed and all the crime scene venues have been examined and exploited for physical evidence, the scene will be turned over to the property owners for a return to normal use. Only when the deceased victim of violence is killed inside her own home or business can the crime scene be sealed for any extensive period. Crime scenes where commercial robberies or thefts, such as shoplifting, occur are usually places of business, which must be returned to regular use as soon as possible. Crime scenes such as burglaries of residences and businesses also must be returned to regular use as soon as possible. These kinds of decisions are made by the crime scene technician in conjunction with the lead criminal investigator. In unusual cases where the seizure of a crime scene is determined necessary, a court order will usually be required absent the permission of the property owner.

Car Theft

Car theft is one of the most reported grand larceny crimes in the United States. Car theft occurs so often (about one million cars are stolen every year in the United States at an average cost to victims of $6,000) that it is hard for most police agencies to spend the time necessary to investigate the crimes thoroughly. The victimization is also indemnified by the auto insurance industry, which most states mandate, and all auto loan entities require allowing the complainants to receive compensation for their loss within days of the crime. These two things tend to make the priority of these crimes even lower. The community just doesn't demand an immediate investigative response even though the value of the car is usually much more than the average larceny. In a larger sense, the real victims of auto thefts are the insurance companies, which have established the National Auto Theft Bureau to assist the police in the identification and recovery of stolen cars nationwide. Since most of the physical evidence that can be recovered from a stolen car can be recovered only from the car itself, the crime scene may be nothing more than an empty slot in a parking lot or spot on a public street.

All of the information that can inform an investigation of a car theft is most likely going to come from the owner. A detailed interview with the owner is the primary starting point. If the car is recovered, an actual crime scene examination can be done on the car itself. Witnesses can be found around the location where the car was stolen, but very few people will even notice an unknown person getting into a car and driving away. Older model cars with key entry and ignition are stolen using blunt-force methods, which may include crossing ignition wires and overriding the ignition cylinder. Newer-model cars and most high-dollar vehicles, such as BMWs, Mercedes, and Range Rovers, use keyless entry and ignition systems. Honda Accord sedans are among the most stolen models in the world. They also have keyless entry and ignition systems.

All of the high-tech keyless entry vehicles rely on the onboard computer systems, which are vulnerable to computer hacking, thus making the job of the thief simple if the thief has been schooled in this method. Expensive computer programs can be used to disrupt the onboard computer system through the onboard diagnostic port, a digital access connection under the dashboard of most modern cars. These ports are to be used by professional auto mechanics and dealers to discover mechanical problems, but they also allow professional thieves to reprogram the keyless entry and ignition system to respond to their key fobs, thereby allowing them to simply drive away and operate the vehicle as if they had the original key fob. All the thief needs is a laptop, a smartphone, a tablet with the right reprogramming app, a tool to break into the car or smash the window, and a blank key fob. Even if this software is expensive and technically difficult to use, the profit from stealing a $100,000 vehicle or even a $30,000 vehicle makes the investment worthwhile.

As discussed in chapters 3 and 5, car theft is a low-priority investigation unless there is a professional organization stealing cars and then shipping them overseas for resale or chopping them up for their valuable parts, which can be sold on the black market for more than the intact vehicle sells for in brand-new condition. Engines, transmissions, radios (entertainment systems), computer modules, wheels, air bags, and other major parts or systems when sold individually can yield profits that are more than buying the used car for the standard price. In many overseas countries, a stolen high-value car can sell for double the asking price than in the United States or Europe. If there are no repercussions for reselling a stolen car, that MO for a car theft ring is also very lucrative. The other very lucrative approach that professional car thieves can use is to switch the vehicle identification number (VIN) with a number that can pass a police database search to establish a legitimate provenance for the car. The vehicle can then be resold with the new VIN. This kind of operation is complicated but also very lucrative. If the VIN switch is successful, the thieves can resell the stolen car for an amount close to the car's actual value.

When considering all the high-tech requirements of a professional car theft ring, the only way successful investigators can achieve positive results is by conducting a proactive investigation. This type of investigation would involve developing a crime pattern from individual crime reports, determining if certain models are being targeted or certain geographic areas are being targeted, and then combining that analysis with any vehicles that are recovered. Confidential source intelligence and data analysis are investigative priorities for an auto theft investigation that is part of a car theft ring or pattern of theft. A proactive investigation's step 1 is to begin by comparing every new theft with the intelligence and data from the previous thefts. Finally, many of the high-value cars are equipped with GPS, which when activated can immediately locate the vehicle. Professional car thieves have ways to frustrate this system, but any targeted vehicle that generates its location and is recovered may provide a great deal of important information that can inform the investigation and help lead to a successful conclusion. Two important investigative responses to a car theft, whether the investigation is a single investigation or part of a theft ring, are to include in step 1 the activation of the GPS tracking system as soon as possible and to make sure the vehicles are entered into the National Crime Information Center (NCIC) stolen car database as well as into any appropriate local car theft databases.

Car theft investigations are more successful if they are targeting more than one stolen car. Car thieves never steal just one vehicle unless they are amateur beginners. Stolen car rings and chop shops are complicated enterprises. A variety of career criminals generate a lot of physical evidence and, at some point, require interaction with local governmental entities, such as the Department of Motor Vehicles, or must declare the VINs to be able to transport the vehicles to other countries. All these steps, which make the enterprise lucrative, leave open a very public digital trail.

Rush to Judgment

The important fact to know at step 1 in an investigation is that you may have developed a suspect and a full array of outstanding investigative leads that can be followed in taking the case to a logical conclusion. There are also cases when the suspects are prominent and central figures in the crime scenes and their actions make it necessary to arrest them on the spot. So why has the investigation gone from a snail's pace to the sprint of a jaguar? The steps going forward appear to be unnecessary, and all that is needed is to turn the case over to the courts. Consider the following three scenarios, which are based on real cases.

1. The police respond to the scene of a reported homicide. They discover a female victim lying in a pool of blood with multiple gunshot wounds to her torso. A person identified as her husband is seated next to her in a despondent and uncommunicative state with a handgun in his hand. He keeps complaining over and over that she shouldn't have done it. The first responding officer takes control of the handgun and handcuffs the husband to secure the scene. The husband continues to act compliant but disconnected from reality.

2. Police respond to the scene of a bank robbery and discover a person seated in a vehicle in the parking lot of the bank who generally matches the description of the bank robber, who wore a ski mask and gray coveralls and was armed with an AR15 assault weapon. When the police carefully approach him, he is busy trying to get his car started and is angry and frustrated. A police officer observes a ski mask and an AR15 assault rifle on the back seat of the car along with a sack filled with unknown materials. The responding officers immediately detain the person by handcuffing him and putting him in a patrol car.

3. A rural county deputy sheriff responds at the home of a local farmer who just reported a burglary. The farmer's residence is at the end of a long road, which is almost a half mile from the highway. As the deputy drives toward the house, a pickup truck comes toward him driven by a person the deputy knows from having arrested him in the past for burglary. He stops the truck and observes several flat screen TVs, video game consoles, and handguns and rifles in the bed of the truck. He cuffs the driver and asks the radio dispatcher to contact the victim and ask for a summary of what was stolen. Within a short time, the dispatcher advises that the burglar stole rifles, handguns, three flat screen TVs, and other property. The deputy detains the pickup truck driver and places him in the sheriff's cruiser.

In each of these cases, the officers acted on the facts presented to them while responding to a crime. In only one of the scenarios did they have actual verification that a crime had been committed, other than the initial report from an unverified complainant. Are these actions a rush to judgment or the logical response to a crime? First-responding officers, agents, or investigators have a responsibility to act in accordance with the law. If they know a crime has been committed and develop facts and evidence proving that a person is responsible for that crime, they can and should make an arrest. The detention of all three suspects in these cases is the logical and safe response to information presented to these law enforcement officers.

Variations of scenarios like these cases occur more often than expected. Most criminals are not genius masterminds with perfect timing and good luck. A human being who resorts to killing his spouse because he is enraged by some personal slight or act of infidelity may not be able to immediately react to the crime by hiding his actions and turning off the anger that led to violence. A human being who commits an armed robbery may not be able to overcome the fact that her car won't start, because engine malfunction is not always predictable. And finally, a human being who burglarizes a house can't always be certain the police response will be slow and predictable. The inescapable logic of *Occam's razor*, a problem-solving principle devised by a twelfth-century friar, justifies the actions of the police officers. A more recent variation of that principle, the KISS principle, which means *keep it simple, stupid*, supports the same theme.

Is it really a rush to judgment? Any criminal act is going to be subject to flaws, lack of judgment, and poor timing. The reason there are almost one million police officers in the United States is to take advantage of the flaws and have a law enforcement official in the right place at the right time to exploit the error or failure of judgment by the criminal. The truth is that, in each of the above scenarios, significant investigation was needed to make sure the case could move forward in the criminal justice system. From the administrative viewpoint of the police agencies in each of the cases, once the crime was verified, it allowed matters to be closed as felony investigations. The armed robbery of the bank was verified by witnesses and the victim tellers in the bank, so the case was closed. There were additional proofs that were needed for court, but when the police were the primary officials, the investigation was over.

The residential burglary required proof that the house had been entered, the items in the pickup truck were the actual property of the victim, and the value of the property constituted a larceny. These facts sustained the proof that the burglary occurred. Additional proof would be needed to make the case at trial, but the police had closed their investigation.

In the homicide scenario, it turned out that the medical examiner found gunshot residue on the hands of the victim and the wounds to the torso were self-inflicted. Follow-up investigation determined the victim had inoperable cancer, which would cause grave pain and financial distress for her family. Eventually, the husband came out of his grief and explained that it was his gun and that his wife had waited until he had gone to the store for groceries and then killed herself. He returned home to find her and instinctually grabbed the gun from her hand. He sat and cried and could not respond appropriately due to the shock and sadness. A neighbor had heard the gunshots, looked in the window, saw the victim on the floor, and called 911. In this case, the medical examiner ruled the cause of death to be suicide, and the husband was not charged with a crime.

Step 2

Step 2 in the investigative plan will provide information to begin the process of developing theories of truth to anticipate the investigative goal. Investigative choices and decisions will come from leads generated from step 1 and provide the new leads needed to inform the investigation going forward. It should be noted that millions of criminal investigations end each year after early findings reveal a solid suspect and viable theory. In almost eight out of ten of those cases, there are no trials because the eventual suspect pleads guilty to the crime. This is primarily because the suspect is guilty and will receive a lighter penalty by not forcing the government to go to trial. Statistics for plea bargains vary each year and in each jurisdiction. The eight out of ten estimates are just that, estimates, but the reality of criminal investigations that go to trial is a small percentage of investigations that take place and get beyond step 1. Every case needs to be treated like it will go forward to trial. In our study, we need to progress to that next step in the plan.

The second step in homicide investigations is to obtain a commitment from the medical examiner that the ruling will be homicide, arrange interviews with witnesses identified in step 1, and evaluate the case to determine, if possible, whether the killer was known or not known to the victim. That determination will affect the degree of background needed in the study of the victim. The spouse or other family member as well as the business and social life of the victim needs to be fully explored to determine whether the investigation needs to focus on aspects of the victim's life.

During this step, it is also necessary to consider physical evidence that was recovered and submit the evidence for forensic examination. This is a part of the step that needs to be worked in association with the lead crime scene technician, who knows which forensic examinations are needed and which examinations need to be prioritized. Many of these examinations may take weeks or months, and the impact of any positive results will not be known until the examinations are done and the reports are written. Having this process start as soon as possible after the crime is a necessary early part of any investigation.

The next step involves witnesses, the victim (victimology), and physical evidence. There is, however, a new process, which is the exploitation of digital data and the vetting of all witnesses and any suspects by way of conducting background investigations to determine who among the witnesses and victims have a criminal history or something in their backgrounds that may be a problem in the future. With the proliferation of social media platforms, a homicide investigator should also initiate the process of discovering what information is available on these networking platforms. Each law enforcement agency will have computer analyses that may allow deep dives into the social media profile of the victims, suspects, or witnesses. This information, together with criminal record checks and law enforcement–sensitive information, can provide extraordinary amounts of information about each person. Some of that information may be helpful in providing leads and directions for the investigations. It is therefore necessary to begin this data dive process as early in the investigation as possible.

The only problem with this new data is its value as evidence. It is always necessary to evaluate the source of the information that is recovered to determine its reliability. A person's Facebook profile may contain false or misleading information posted on purpose by the person whose profile it is. Reliability and any concerns about whether the information was legally obtained control how the data are used. Some of this social media platform data is considered open source, and some is protected by contractual privacy agreements with the persons who own the accounts. Regardless, much of the data are easily accessible for data mining by knowledgeable computer specialists.

Referring back to our discussion on teamwork in chapter 4, the criminal investigator should enlist the help of the agency's *intelligence* unit or squad. That unit is usually able to perform the kind of data recovery required. Additionally, an active intelligence unit can use creative covert and legal means to gain access to a social network platform. Using a covert friend profile that matches the profiles acceptable to a suspect, or even using an existing confidential source to extend the appropriate invitation to a suspect, can be a successful way into the suspects' social media page.

In Andrew Guthrie's book, *The Rise of Big Data Policing, Race and the Future of Law Enforcement*, Guthrie examines the impact of all of his computer data on the future of law enforcement. What he refers to as "big data" incorporates all the computerized data available to law enforcement, including law enforcement–sensitive data and the manipulation of that data to create target lists of career criminals. This list may be so informed by racial or cultural stereotypes that the data can create misinformation when acted on by law enforcement. During the process of working a case, this information, if reliable and legal, can allow the criminal investigator to anticipate behavior, analyze past behavior, and determine the best way to plan and to target criminal suspects. It is essential that the information be legally obtained so as not to taint an investigation.

As the investigator proceeds in step 2, it is necessary to understand that following first step leads, interviewing witnesses, developing relationships with victim families, coordinating the examination of physical evidence, and conducting computer background checks will take time and burn investigative resources. Whereas step 1 is usually accomplished in the first 24 hours of an investigation, there is no average time for step 2. It takes what it takes.

The end game in step 2 is when there are no outstanding investigative leads. The second characteristic of step 2 is that it is consistent in investigative compartments of other crimes against persons and property. The main distinction is the need for the criminal investigator to develop communication and a relationship with the victim of the crime. A long-term and productive relationship is a necessary part of this step.

Rape victims and victims of serious violence are handled differently than burglary or robbery victims. If the case continues for any length of time as it heads to trial or just takes a long time to get at the truth, investigators need to stay in contact with victims to update them on the progress of the case and anticipate all the frustrations and difficulties they face as victims of a crime. Criminal investigators are *advocates* for

INVESTIGATIVE PLAN: HOMICIDES

Step 1
- Examine body
- Conduct interviews of persons present
- Conduct crime scene examination

Step 2
- Coordinate with medical examiner for ruling on cause and time of death
- Contact family to notify, identify, and begin victimology
- Continue investigative interviews with business and social contacts
- Conduct outstanding interviews with potential witnesses
- Coordinate scientific examination of physical evidence and trace evidence
- Evaluate intelligence

victims and should make it possible for them to regain control and enjoy a return to a safe feeling so that the long-term impact of the crime is diminished.

Step 2: Crimes against Persons

This compartment of step 2 encompasses the following actions:

- Cover all leads by interviewing and evaluating every witness developed.
- Coordinate the scientific examination of physical evidence.
- Gather any physical evidence and medical reports relating to the injuries received and the trace evidence recovered from the appropriate medical professionals.
- Work with the victim to help in their recovery, and be available to counsel the victim about the criminal justice system if and when a suspect is charged.
- Initiate the process of data mining as needed relating to the suspects, victims, and witnesses.

INVESTIGATIVE PLAN: SEXUAL ASSAULT OR VIOLENT ASSAULT WITH SERIOUS BODILY INJURIES

Step 1
- Emergency medical treatment and forensic examination
- Crime scene examination
- Interview witness and victim witness if available

Step 2
- Establish proof of the assault with medical professional
- Develop productive relationship with the victim witness if available; otherwise, conduct a victimology background investigation
- Continue witness examination
- Coordinate scientific examination of physical evidence and trace evidence recovered
- Evaluate appropriate intelligence

Step 2: Crimes against Property

This compartment of step 2 encompasses the following actions:

- Cover all leads developed from interviewing and evaluating every witness.
- Coordinate the scientific examination of physical evidence. (It should be noted here that expensive scientific examinations, such as extracting DNA profiles from physical evidence, may be limited to crimes against persons or only serious commercial armed robberies. Examinations for fingerprints or ballistics will usually be allowed in these lower-priority investigations, but there will be limitations even in

well-funded police agencies. This may change in the future when the technology becomes cheaper or more accessible.)
- Work with the victim and counsel the victim about the processes in the criminal justice system when a suspect is charged.
- Initiate the data mining as needed for the suspects, victims, and witnesses.

INVESTIGATIVE PLAN: PROPERTY CRIME

Step 1
- Interview victim and witnesses at the scene
- Conduct a crime scene examination and recover physical evidence
- Request an audit, evaluation, and/or proof of ownership of stolen property

Step 2
- Continue witness interviews and follow all leads
- Coordinate any scientific examination of physical evidence recovered
- Input stolen items in NCIC or other appropriate stolen items database
- Evaluate available intelligence

The timing of step 2 in the investigative plan is open-ended. The follow-up investigation and coordination of any scientific examinations along with careful interviews with witnesses may take days, weeks, or even months, depending on the complicated nature of the crime. The time frame can expand if the investigation is a proactive investigation targeting known individuals. Step 2 is lead-driven, and when there are no leads, the case will enter the final step. But before we discuss the characteristics of step 3, it is necessary to discuss two very important elements that are generally part of step 2.

Step 2: Intelligence

Intelligence can be from several sources. It is law enforcement–sensitive information that is confidential in nature and essential to effective law enforcement. As discussed in a couple of the previous chapters in this book, confidential sources are insiders in the criminal ecosystem in almost every community in the United States. Human intelligence can be an extremely reliable source of information that gives the name of the suspect who is responsible for the crime under investigation. It can provide important unknown details about the crime that may lead to a solution, or it may provide the location of evidence that can be used in the solution of the crime. It is also possible that human intelligence can be wrong or misleading, but that possibility is lessened by veteran investigators who maintain productive relationships with confidential sources.

Valuable and reliable sources working with skilled investigators quickly realize that their information is useful only if it is accurate. Logically, these confidential sources make every effort to ensure the truthfulness of the intelligence they provide, and if they are not sure of the value, they make sure their handlers know the limitations of the information. Referring to chapter 4 on teamwork, a veteran squad of investigators working commercial armed robberies makes sure their source base is reliable and well schooled in the kind of information that is productive. The confidential sources described above are usually career criminals whose motivations to cooperate with law enforcement are derived from the full spectrum of human motivation. A source can see an extra source of income if law enforcement is generous to its sources. A source can see a way to remove unwanted competition or simply believe that her criminal activity is insignificant in comparison to the intelligence that is provided concerning a criminal.

Personal Experience

I worked with many confidential sources in my career, but the most effective sources were those whose motivations recognized that the violence in Washington, DC, in the late 1980s and early 1990s was so bad that they had a responsibility to their community to do something about it. Sources who are motivated by personal gain usually don't last long in their efforts to help law enforcement, but the sources I worked with provided high-quality intelligence for ten years and more. They had a close personal connection with me and were determined to deliver the best information they could uncover. They knew that I would make them pay for any crime they committed while they worked with me, but they also expected that I would protect them from retaliation if they were ever compromised. The relationship was on a personal level but, at another level, very professional. It took time and effort to build that kind of relationship, but it is necessary to work at something that is as important as developing a reliable operational source.

Other forms of intelligence are *debriefings from significant career criminals* who wish to bare their souls of criminal information before they are incarcerated in hopes that some of the information will help cut time from their sentences.

Intelligence can also be obtained from *reliable members of the communities* where crime and violence are epidemic. These well-respected members of a community try to make comprehensive and accurate complaints to law enforcement about what kind of criminal activity is creating havoc in their neighborhoods. Their information is usually from an outsider's viewpoint, but it is often accurate and usually has the accuracy derived from years of observation of neighborhood troublemakers who have become serious criminals. None of their information should be ignored because it represents the people in the community who support the police.

Other intelligence sources are *analytical studies of crime data* and the *one-off intelligence reports from other investigations*, which include audio, video, and actual physical surveillance. Much of the material from other investigations is superfluous or extraneous to the instant investigation for which the surveillance was initiated, but that information may come in handy and be beneficial when viewed in the light of another case. Overall, intelligence is constantly flowing into an active criminal investigation unit. Taking advantage of that information is an ongoing, productive exercise for criminal investigators.

Probable Cause/Suspect

During step 2, discovering enough information, facts, and evidence to identify a viable suspect is a goal that is often achieved. Following all the leads, interviewing the right people, and finding out what physical evidence may yield positive scientific evidence as to who committed the crime are usually produced during this step. Marrying all the facts with a comprehensive analysis of the relevant intelligence gives the investigator what is needed to charge a suspect.

When all the testimonial, scientific, and documentary evidence come together to point out the perpetrator of the crime and you, as the lead investigator, are convinced that you have enough to charge the perpetrator and turn him into a defendant, your investigation is reaching its goal.

If you have exhausted all the investigative leads, determined that the physical evidence may offer little help in providing a name or the identity of a suspect, and exhausted all the intelligence support without gaining a helpful direction, you are reaching an unsatisfactory end. The case will have to be set aside for a pending inactive status. The case is not closed, but there is nothing left that will provide probable cause and a suspect. The final effort in step 2 is to compare the crime under investigation with all other similar crimes to determine if there is a pattern that can be detected, thereby opening a new approach or avenue of investigation. This comparison may begin early in the investigation, but it is the last resort if all the leads developed do not yield a working hypothesis or viable suspect.

Step 3

Step 3, the final step, is bifurcated based on the results of step 2. If there is a suspect to charge and the case has enough physical and testimonial evidence to move forward with a prosecution, then step 3 supports that effort. The best way to proceed is to arrest the suspect and conduct a thorough search of his residence, business, automobile, and any other constitutionally protected areas associated with him. It may have been necessary to search the suspect's residence, car, and business during step 2, but if that has not occurred, it is an essential element that should be done during the final step of the investigation.

During step 3, the lead investigator should update all the victims and witnesses to the fact that the case is moving toward a trial and make sure that any changes in their addresses or business locations are provided so that the investigator can stay in touch. The investigator should turn over all the reports, notes, records, photographs, evidence logs, scientific reports, crime scene reports, and any video or audiotapes relevant to the investigation. Any important intelligence reports, including interviews with confidential sources, should be provided within the parameters established by the law enforcement agency that protects the confidentiality of the source. After these processes are complete, the lead investigator should make himself available to the prosecutor for the investigative requirements leading up to the trial. The investigation is most likely to end with a plea bargain and final court disposition of the case. However, being prepared for trial is the appropriate goal to consider in step 3.

If step 3 is reached without a suspect and the case is put in pending inactive status, the investigator should make sure there are "bear traps" or "alarm bells" activated that will go off if a new lead is generated, a crime of a similar nature is reported, or another important fact becomes available. For example, some police agencies have serious backlogs of rape kits, and if no suspect is developed in a sexual assault case, the only chance for the biological material in the kit to be used to reopen the case is if there is a match in the FBI's Combined DNA Index System, or CODIS, which compares samples from crimes with known DNA profiles from suspects nationwide.

Another example is based on the MO discussed below. There are several serial offenders who burglarize homes, rob banks and stores, steal cars, and sexually assault and murder victims. A case that reached step 3 without developing a viable suspect may be the first in a series of crimes perpetrated by one of these career offenders. A second, third, and fourth crime may be reported that allows for a reopening of this investigation, with more leads and additional investigative theories to move forward. This is how a reactive investigation can turn into a proactive investigation.

INVESTIGATIVE PLAN: SUSPECTS

Suspect Identified
- Charge suspect; execute search warrants at home, business, and any other constitutionally protected facility or digital instrument
- Turn over all documentary material and investigative support material to the appropriate prosecuting attorney
- Prepare for trial or other court disposition of the case
- Begin witness preparation

No Suspect
- Make investigation pending inactive
- Implement "bear traps" and/or "alarm bells" in the event a new lead is developed
- Compare the modus operandi with other similar crimes
- Evaluate intelligence

THEORIES OF THE CRIME

The plan is simple and generally driven by the nature of the crime. It can be adjusted when the witnesses are few or many, by the population of suspects, and by jurisdictional or legal priorities that can affect the gathering of evidence. One thing that is universal is the need to develop a suspect. Somehow the criminal investigator can find out how, when, where, and why a crime happened, but there is no solution unless she knows *who* did it. Early in the discussion of the plan, it was explained that the lead investigator and her colleagues need to consider logical theories of the crime. These theories are usually based on the motivation of the criminal. Ultimately, the suspect needs to have a reason to commit the crime. That reason may not be logical or even realistic, but it does have to motivate the activity.

There are some starting points that a criminal investigation student can use to begin the process of building a theory. These starting points act as hints based on the conduct of hundreds of thousands of modern criminals in the United States. The theories will never replace cold hard facts and evidence, but they do give the investigator some concepts and theoretical support for how the plan should proceed. Consider the following information as a guide book that can help but does not offer answers.

Who Did It

Finding out who committed a crime is the most difficult task for the criminal investigator. It is especially difficult if the crime was not observed by any living person and the crime victim has no known association with the victim. Probably the only reliable way to identify the perpetrator in a case like that is if the perpetrator admits to the crime to a friend or associate who then turns around and tells law enforcement. If there is reliable physical evidence left at the scene, it can be compared to a universal database to yield the name of the suspect.

Where to Start

Once you can place a suspect's name with a crime and a crime victim, you can start comparing physical evidence recovered at the scene with the suspect. You can also begin to develop a timeline that places the perpetrator at the scene of the crime at the time the crime was committed. Is there a way to understand the motivation for the crime and find out how your suspect fits that motivation? The types of crimes for which this is helpful are homicides, arsons, bombings, burglaries, larcenies, embezzlements, and any other crime in which the perpetrator carefully plans the timing of the crime to coincide with the absence of witnesses.

Security Surveillance

When the timing of a criminal act is carefully planned to occur outside the presence of witnesses, it is necessary to determine if some other kind of "footprint" was left by the perpetrator. Today, in many urban environments, security and traffic surveillance cameras operate 24 hours a day and capture the activities of all sorts of people. These cameras are by their very nature hidden from open view, and even the most careful criminal may be unaware his actions are being recorded. Additionally, merely operating cellular phones and cameras in these devices can leave a discernible digital footprint. When investigators begin their effort to discover who committed the crime, they need to consider the date, time, and location of the scene as ground zero, or point zero, in their timeline and create a circle of opportunity around that point. If there is a surveillance camera in that circle, it is essential to recover that video evidence before it is routinely destroyed. Even if that surveillance video equipment is owned and operated by a private enterprise, it is essential that it be discovered and the video evidence recovered.

The recovery of this kind of video evidence is possible only if the crime occurs in an area where there is the likelihood that surveillance cameras exist. Abandoned housing projects or warehouse districts in rural areas are not likely to have this kind of video evidence available, so the investigator is back to square one in trying to independently develop a suspect.

Sources of Information

Invariably, the investigation will come back to a third-party source who happens to overhear or discover information about who did it. The only other possible way to link a person to a crime is when a pattern of serial conduct is discovered. Unfortunately, this is possible only when multiple crimes have occurred and there is something similar about the MO or signature that links the cases together. (Signature as opposed to MO is a unique feature manifest in a crime scene that does not have any logical reason for being there. It is simply the perpetrator's message that she did the crime.) An example of an MO is a series of daytime burglaries that occur during a low traffic time (midday, when all the victims are at work) in a suburban bedroom community where there is a similar pattern of items stolen, method of entry, and disturbance inside the houses. If the police see a pattern of this type develop and they can physically surveil the neighborhood where most of the burglaries occur and can observe suspicious activity, including an attempted or actual break-in, they can make an arrest, search the "lair" of the suspect (her home) and find stolen property from the other burglaries. At this point, they will likely be able to solve all or most of the unsolved burglaries in the target neighborhood.

The next step is to conduct an effective interview, which may result in an extensive confession to the crimes. Often, serial burglars and car thieves will confess to all their crimes when they are caught red-handed, to avoid facing future charges. In many jurisdictions throughout the United States, convicting a burglar or car thief of one or two counts of these property crimes will lead to the same punishment as convicting them of hundreds of counts. Career criminals are aware of this possibility, so they are very likely to want to close the books on all their criminal conduct with one "omnibus" plea agreement.

Investigators assigned to burglary and car theft should be aware that the perpetrator is likely to be a serial offender. It is simply a fact to be relied on. As a student of criminal investigations, the experience of investigating burglars and car thieves is invaluable. These two crimes are gateway crimes that more serious felons started doing in their formative years. If they serve prison time after being caught doing these crimes, they usually get postgraduate education in those crimes and perpetrate more lucrative or violent crimes, depending on their mindset.

More serious criminals, such as serial murderers, serial rapists, child molesters, and armed robbers, are less likely to provide immediate closure unless there is some important additional incentive, such as avoiding the death penalty or ensuring their safety in prison. These types of criminals also have a much more sinister mindset when it comes to law enforcement authorities, and any cooperation will usually happen only if they are totally convinced that they are indeed caught, with no way out. Additionally, many jurisdictions in the United States will have great reluctance to allow any kind of plea agreement for such a heinous criminal.

The one consistent incentive for serial criminals to consider is that there is little or no chance that any kind of effective *civil penalties* will ever be accrued against them. Most career criminals do everything they can to appear to be *indigent* and lack any ability to pay back their victims or the victims' families. Career criminals, if they accrue any wealth, will usually put that wealth into the hands of trusted friends or family to protect themselves from having any wealth that can be attached or seized pursuant to a civil court demand. Serial criminals who have mental psychosis as part of their profile are generally able to prove a lack of competence to protect themselves from civil proceedings.

As a result, the only real chance society has to stop this criminal activity is to catch the criminals and effectively prosecute them to remove the threat. Therefore, the *who* is very important. Career criminals such as the Green River Killer and the BTK Strangler avoided detection for more than twenty years. As a result, their body counts rose, and they created an atmosphere of terror in their communities. Even a serial burglar who operates for months or years makes the community believe there is no safe place, even in their homes. It is up to the criminal investigator to restore that sense of safety to the community.

THE SCIENTIFIC METHOD

- *Who:* the person or persons who committed the crime
- *Suspect:* a person who is believed to have committed a crime
- *Subject:* a person under investigation for committing a crime or series of crimes
- *Population:* the group, no matter how large, from whom that person is derived

Our investigative plan starts at the crime scene. If the suspect is not immediately known, then this process becomes an objective examination of the crime scene to determine if the investigator can make any conclusions about the suspect. For example, is there evidence that shows sloppiness or unbridled passion that makes the investigator believe that the person was not prepared to commit the crime? Is there evidence at the scene that indicates the person tried to clean up fingerprints or hide evidence after the crime happened? Are there signs of hurried actions or patient, deliberate ways the scene was left? Have points of entry and exit been thoroughly examined? Were instrumentalities (weapons, pry bars, entry tools, etc.) of the criminal act left at the scene or removed? Why were fruits (money, jewelry, documents, digital information, etc.) of the crime taken?

Create an investigative summary presented by the crime scene to see if there is any way to limit the population of possible suspects. For example, if the scene is well ordered and limited in physical evidence, could that mean the investigation should be focused on a career criminal or on an amateur who plans well? What is the motivation for the crime? Was something of value taken away, and is that item easily disposed of? A theft of unique value, such as a well-known piece of art, would indicate a high-level thief with the resources to fence the property. The murder of an otherwise average person where nothing of value was stolen indicates that the person who killed the victim had a relationship with the victim or was asked to kill the victim for money or other incentive. A bloody, sloppy murder where the victim was overkilled may mean there was personal animosity between the killer and victim or that the killer was trying to send a chilling message to the victim's family or friends.

Evaluating the crime scene is a skill that takes time to develop, but the most important part of that development is an understanding that the evaluation is only an educated guess. A professional burglar can make a scene look amateurish to frustrate investigators into believing the crime was committed by an amateur. A first-time criminal with little or no experience may act carefully and cautiously in committing a crime, and the scene might reflect that careful and cautious manner, therefore looking like the crime of a well-seasoned criminal. A criminal investigator faced with no witnesses and no real leads can proceed cautiously with educated guesses until there is something that redirects the investigation.

Examples of Crimes without Direct Witnesses When Something of Value Is Stolen

Residential Burglaries

There is a sloppy crime scene with the point of entry being a forced door or window near the ground with no street view. Items taken include electronics, jewelry, cash, guns, and prescription drugs. Consider drug abusers with substantial criminal histories for burglaries. Consider that it may be two or more persons. Conduct a thorough neighborhood check to see if anyone has noticed any vehicles or persons who appear out of place.

Commercial Burglaries

There is a sloppy crime scene with the point of entry being a roof access or forced door with no street view. Only cash is taken. Consider career criminals with substantial experience, especially if there is a large amount of cash taken or there is an indication of a quick assault, which shows inside knowledge or serious prior surveillance activity. A well-cased hit indicates the crime was committed by a seasoned criminal. The sloppy crime scene just shows a lack of concern, unless there appears to be forensic evidence left in the mess.

High-End Valuable Car Theft: Scenario 1

A stolen vehicle with no car alarm is found in a public space. The LoJack is disabled. Keyless operation is compromised by computer hacking. Consider a professional car thief with immediate access to a chop shop, a VIN reassignment operation, or even an international smuggling operation. Compare with other similar crimes. These types of thefts are rarely limited to happening once or twice.

High-End Valuable Car Theft: Scenario 2

The vehicle is eventually found abandoned in a public lot, and the car alarm and Lo-Jack are operational. Consider the suspect to be a juvenile joyrider, especially if nothing is removed. If valuable radios, tires, air bags, or electronic devices are pilfered, consider this suspect to be on his way to more serious crime.

Examples of Violent Crimes When There Is No Witness

Homicides/Crimes of Passion

Most homicides that occur in the home are perpetrated by a spouse. Love relationships turn sour over arguments about money, fidelity, abuse, and control. The investigator needs to consider the spouse or significant other in all homicides that occur in a residence. The investigator should be looking for disorderly crime scenes with indications that the perpetrator is new to violence. If the homicide is about infidelity or abuse, there may be a significant element of overkill, such as multiple stab wounds or gunshots. Proof of homicide using poison is almost always the MO of an angry female spouse with long-term emotional or physical abuse. These conclusions are best-guess scenarios, but they should give the investigator a place to start in a crime without witnesses or significant physical evidence.

Gun or Knife Assaults

These crimes should be considered like homicides. The significant difference is that the investigator will have a live witness. However, it does happen that serious assaults can cause significant brain or psychological trauma, which lessens the reliability of the live witness. In these cases, the investigator should look to the crime scene evidence and conduct a thorough background on those persons closest to the victim. Most assaults result from arguments between spouses, friends, or close acquaintances. Assaults can also be motivated by financial or witness intimidation. The investigator needs to eliminate any close relationship involving a rift that developed because of an argument or ongoing feud.

Assaults and Homicides

Blunt-force trauma or trauma from an attack in which fists are the most likely weapon should be viewed as personal and least likely to have been carefully planned unless the assailant happens to be particularly capable of inflicting serious bodily harm with his fists. The use of a weapon of opportunity, such as a heavy object that was present in the crime scene prior to the assault, indicates little malice aforethought. It also indicates an explosive situation in which the assailant acted out of immediate rage. These types of crimes are seldom the work of a person unknown to the victim unless the crime occurs in a public space. In public-space attacks, the investigator needs to determine if the victim was a volatile person prone to provoking anger and violence from random strangers.

Examples of Crimes for Which There May Be Information Identifying the Perpetrator

Bank Robbery

There are two basic kinds of bank robbery. *Note jobs* are when the robber threatens violence and gets the money from one teller, usually from the top teller drawer. Note job bank robberies yield anywhere from several hundred dollars to no more than $5,000. Small-time note job robbers may hit five to ten times per month. The investigator should be looking for a younger criminal with two to five years of criminal experience.

Counter jump robberies are carried out with multiple offenders. These robberies are usually attempts to hit multiple tellers and/or gain access to the bank's main vault. Consider career criminals with long histories of armed robbery arrests. These are violent offenders with little consideration for the safety of others. They generally require resources for weapons, getaway vehicles, and ballistic vests. They operate in gangs and are therefore vulnerable to detection from confidential sources. Counter jumpers may hit once or twice per month. Their average score yields $100,000 and up.

Since bank robbers expose themselves to witnesses, surveillance cameras, and bank alarms, they are extremely vulnerable and often get identified and caught in several ways. The investigator needs to spend time carefully analyzing all the information presented by the crime to ensure a solution.

Commercial Robberies

These types of robberies are usually from grocery and warehouse stores with high volumes of cash. The investigators should consider the same violent offenders mentioned above. The offenders score larger takes than a bank robbery and with fewer risks. Since they operate in groups and rely on others for resources, they are vulnerable to confidential sources, who help identify them and when they hit. The investigators need to consider career criminals with long histories of armed robbery. These kinds of criminals don't build up the courage to take down big enterprises overnight. They slowly build up their MO with trial and error from smaller scores.

Violent Sexual Assaults

Most violent sexual assaults, such as rape, will have a live victim witness, but the victim's identification of a suspect may not be a forgone conclusion. Serial rapists, for example, will take many steps to avoid detection. They will wear masks and clothing that obscure or frustrate the victim from observing details that may lead to an identification. The event may be so traumatic that the victim may block out certain details. It is essential for the investigator to work hard to develop a bond of trust and support with the victim so that she can help the victim overcome her reluctance and loss of control. If a female victim knows the rapist, she may be reluctant to identify him because she fears a recurrence or in some way feels responsible for the crime. It is the responsibility of the investigator to work through this reluctance to get at the truth.

The investigator needs to evaluate the crime scene and the MO of the rapist to compare the scene and the actions of the subject with any similar past crimes. This effort will provide a starting point if it appears that this rape is the work of a serial offender. Rapists aren't usually first-time offenders. They may begin their path to violent rape with seemingly unrelated crimes for which they have been arrested in the past, such as burglary, voyeurism, or minor sexual assaults, such as fondling a victim in a crowd. Rapists who are careful to avoid identification should be considered career criminals who have been arrested or convicted of rape in the past. Extreme violence, such as traumatic abuse or sadistic violence, is usually the work of serial offenders with a psychotic mental health history. Unfortunately, these kinds of offenders are very transient, and comparing the crime with other local incidents may not yield the kind of leads that produce an identification. In the case of extremely violent sexual assaults (resulting in death or near death), it is essential to get a summary of the crime out for wide distribution to other jurisdictions so that every lead can be followed. The investigator should carefully consider the facts being distributed and make sure that any unique aspects of the crime are held back so connections by MO to other cases can be corroborated. The solution of these crimes will often rely on the physical evidence left at the scene or on the body of the victim. This is still another reason the investigator needs to work carefully and compassionately with the victim to ensure the victim submits to a thorough postcrime physical examination.

SUMMARY

All these starting points provide the criminal investigator with a theoretical starting line. If the plan is followed and certain constants as described above are discovered, the theory gets stronger, and the pool of suspects gets smaller. A well-planned investigation should consider the facts and evidence and the quality of the witnesses and the value of their testimony along with the results of scientific examinations of evidence. It will also consider the most likely suspects and begin the process of weeding out the innocent from the guilty. The three-step approach to establishing an investigative plan provides a solid outline. Applying the crime motivation analysis to the suspect "pool" helps the investigator begin the process of answering that essential question, who?

Chapter Nine

Goals and Steps for an Investigation

Short-term goals and long-term conclusions.

The goal of any criminal investigation is to solve the case, uncover the truth, and de-termine who did the crime, how the crime happened, and what can be done to protect the community from the persons who are responsible for the criminal conduct. In the US criminal justice system, that means that two important stages of an investigation have to be successfully accomplished: a finding of *probable cause* against the perpe-trator and a finding of *proof beyond a reasonable doubt*, which will result in a convic-tion of the perpetrator in the trial phase. This chapter will provide a discussion of how probable cause is defined and how it can be a tool for the successful evolution of any investigation. Also, this chapter will discuss the investigator's responsibilities during the trial phase, which will lead to the final goal. Defining proof beyond a reasonable doubt is left to the triers of fact in our criminal justice system (trial judges and juries of our peers); therefore, there will be no attempt to define that goal. The goal for the investigator is simply to uncover as much evidence as possible to present to the jury or judge to meet that standard.

After the investigator has conducted all of the immediate interviews and followed the leads (logical investigative steps resulting from information or facts discovered), the next process is determining who did the crime and if there is any evidence that needs to be recovered. There should be enough information to come to a conclusion as to what happened. For example, a witness identifies another person who saw the crime who is not immediately available, a nonwitness bystander advises that a security sur-veillance camera may have recorded some part of the incident, or documents, data, or some other relevant documentary evidence is located in a place away from the initial crime scene. All of that information resulted from those interviews. The next step is to coordinate with the crime scene team, which may be a response unit separate from the investigative unit in a police department or agency. The investigator should then con-sider the impact of the physical evidence recovered and make sure that the evidence is submitted for scientific examination if needed (this process will be discussed in chap-ter 10). The investigator should conduct a review of the results of the investigation

thus far and determine the next step or steps to follow. In many cases, a good portion of this initial evaluation can be done in the immediate aftermath of the response to the crime scene examination in a reactive criminal investigation. This first review is intended as a step to begin to formulate an effective plan. As discussed in chapter 8, the step-by-step investigative plan will be implemented. In a proactive investigation, this step may involve a much more extensive review of previous crimes (via reports, interviews, intelligence summaries, and scientific analyses that have been completed with other relevant information relating to the targets) believed to be associated with the criminal targets. Once the review is complete, the investigator can begin the process of considering scenarios that fill in the gaps of the investigation, in other words, logical and fact-based theories of the crime. It is best to consider these theories with other experienced investigators, who can add reliable perspective to the case. As you consider these theories or the facts and evidence you have already obtained, you may develop or consider new leads as to where additional physical evidence of value can be located. You may also realize that you have already developed probable cause for additional evidence, which exists in some constitutionally protected residence, business, or property.

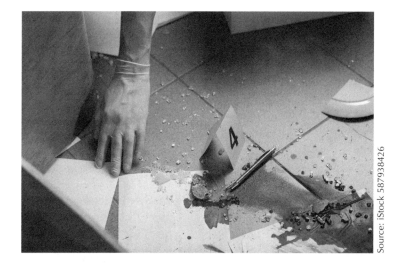

Source: iStock 587938426

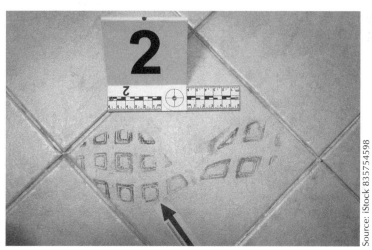

Source: iStock 835754598

PROBABLE CAUSE

Probable cause to recover physical evidence should be considered one of the most important developments in any criminal investigation. When you can begin to exercise your legal authority to act in a manner that begins the process of recovering new, pertinent evidence in your case, you are moving toward the solution to the case. An investigation requires proof, and *evidence* detailing that proof is the continuing process the investigator must follow to find the truth.

The first major goal in any criminal investigation is to establish probable cause as to who committed the crime and also to determine where evidence, especially physical evidence, of that crime can be located. This physical evidence (evidence that has physical substance, as opposed to testimonial evidence) may be stashed, stored, or present in a constitutionally protected area. That means the investigator may be confronted with the dilemma that evidence of a crime is probably located in someone's house or business or on some privately owned land. The Fourth Amendment protects these areas against unreasonable search and seizure. Following are some of the more frustrating examples of this dilemma:

1. A person has been shot inside a house. The complainant is a third party who heard the shot. The police arrive at the scene to investigate, but the owner of the house tells them that they are not allowed access to the house. It is essential that the police act "reasonably" to see if further evidence can be obtained to present facts to a judge to establish probable cause and obtain a court order to investigate and gather the evidence. This court order is, of course, a search warrant.

It should be noted that the police have the authority to act to protect and preserve life if there is a belief by the law enforcement officer that exigent circumstances exist. An officer can act and access the protected space for the purpose of determining if someone is injured and needs assistance. *Exigent circumstances* are emergency conditions that reasonably make the police concerned that life, property, and evidence need to be preserved by taking immediate action and controlling the scene of a crime until a warrant is obtained. Once police take this action, any evidence they see in plain sight can be legally recovered. Wexlaw/Cornell University Law school defines *exigent circumstances* as follows (https://www.law.cornell.edu/wex/exigent_circumstances):

> Exigent circumstances are exceptions to the general requirement of a warrant under the Fourth Amendment searches and seizures. Exigent circumstances occur when the law enforcement officer has a probable cause and no sufficient time to secure a warrant. Courts look at the time when the officer makes the warrantless search or seizure to evaluate whether at that point in time a reasonable officer at the scene would believe it is urgent to act and impractical to secure a warrant. Courts may also consider whether the facts suggested that the suspect was armed and planning to escape, whether a reasonable police officer would believe his safety or others' safety was threatened, and whether there was a serious crime involved. Exigent circumstances may also occur when the police are in hot pursuit of a suspect who is possibly involved in criminal activities and in the process of fleeing.

What should be remembered here is that exigent circumstances allow the officer or investigator to have legal access to a space, but it is not a search warrant. Evidence observed is subject to seizure, but, in most cases, the investigator will need to explain the actions that led to the seizure. On the one hand, the officers responding to the scene of a shooting can seize the weapon, ammunition, and body of the victim, but other less obvious evidence can be seized only pursuant to the additional probable cause established by the law enforcement action. Once an officer acts on exigent circumstances, the officer should immediately apply for a warrant to control the scene and meticulously gather all the appropriate evidence.

Continuing with the examples:

2. A store is robbed, and the suspect makes her escape by breaking and entering a third party's house, where it is probable that the suspect left physical evidence.

The owner of the house refuses to allow the police to enter the house to search for the evidence.

3. A confidential reliable source reports to an investigator that the drugs are being sold by a ruthless drug gang and stashed in a convenience store in the neighborhood.
4. A witness saw unknown persons stash a large barrel of explosive chemicals on a farm in a rural community.

In these examples, the investigator is provided with a significant opportunity to recover evidence that will inform an investigation. In the first example, the potential evidence will actually set the stage for initiating the process of an investigation. The question the investigator must consider is whether he has probable cause to support the issuance of a search warrant. This kind of example of probable cause is not a goal, but it is the kind of major step forward in an investigation that begins to form the tapestry of the case. Progressively, evidence is recovered that will ultimately lead to the identification of the person who is linked to that evidence, thereby leading the way to the first critical goal, identifying perpetrators.

At this point, the facts and evidence don't need to point to a suspect; they merely need to show the judge that a crime has been committed and evidence of that crime is probably located in or on the constitutionally protected property. The investigator needs to present facts, including evidence (physical and testimonial) or observations and other sensory elements that support the fact that the additional evidence in the case is present in or on the property.

The presentation of the facts needs to be in the form of an affidavit sworn to by an officer or agent whose legal responsibility is to investigate the crime. In the real world, the affidavit can be and, in most cases, is a formalized written document detailing the facts in a narrative that persuades the judge as to the probable cause. This affidavit can also be a recorded affidavit allowed by the judge or even a face-to-face conversation, which the judge acknowledges and officially records or memorializes to meet the requirements of her jurisdiction. The judge in all of these cases needs to have legally valid jurisdiction over the property to be searched. The requirement of probable cause then becomes a subjective judgment of this third-party judge or magistrate who can consider evidence and the experience and training of the officer or agent who is presenting the affidavit. The level of proof is not mere conjecture, but it is also not perfect proof. Judges and magistrates who rule on probable cause in courts throughout this country are men and women who have been elected or appointed by their communities or the executive branch representatives of their communities. Appointment to their positions can be politically dependent, and they can bring to the office certain prejudices. These persons are most often trained lawyers who have worked in the criminal justice field as prosecutors or private attorneys. For the most part, they adhere to legal precedent and training they have received to follow a coherent, logical, informed decision about what is and isn't probable cause. There is in this decision-making apparatus a range of opinion. There are judges who require extra levels of proof to sustain probable cause and judges whose standards are slightly less stringent. For the most part, when investigators begin their work in a particular jurisdiction, the standards will become apparent. All affidavits are written in consultation and/or with the approval of a state or federal prosecutor, who will be more able to judge if the standard of probable cause is met. It is for this reason that it is almost impossible to define probable cause scientifically.

The most important question for the investigator then becomes "What is probable cause?" The best way to answer that question is to use the wording in the Constitution. Probable cause is a reasonable belief that a crime has been committed and evidence of that crime is located in or on the property. Unfortunately, there is no mathematical formula; 51 percent likelihood is reasonable and is a good standard with which to start. An investigator's examination of a property for physical evidence is not likely to be anything more than an inconvenience to the property owner, unless the property owner turns out to be the perpetrator or suspect in the investigation. A search warrant for physical evidence has somewhat of a lower standard of proof than the standard needed to arrest a suspect on probable cause. It is therefore best to try to quantify the mathematical likelihood to be 51 percent or better for a search warrant. As a result of this standard of proof, hearsay evidence is allowable evidence presented in a manner most favorable to the government. Speculation of facts not supported by physical evidence or witness testimony should be avoided. The judge can consider specialized experience or training for the officer, detective, or agent that is relevant to the investigation if the specialized knowledge is properly presented or explained to the judge as part of the affidavit. Following are three examples:

- An experienced homicide investigator may have training regarding the exchange of trace evidence in a close physical confrontation crime of violence, such as a rape, violent assault, or homicide.
- An experienced narcotics investigator may have significant experience and training about drug dealers' tools of the trade, habits of keeping records of the illegal transactions and keeping records of their stash location, and propensity for keeping and maintaining readily available firearms.
- An experienced burglary detective may have significant knowledge about the propensity for burglars and fences of stolen property in keeping and maintaining property stolen from previous crimes not under investigation in the current case.

Gut reactions are commonly discussed as not being enough for probable cause, but in truth, gut reactions are usually based on unarticulated facts the investigator knows but hasn't fully formed or considered. It is best for any investigator who confronts the dilemma of how to legally obtain evidence that he believes is present in a constitutionally protected area to think about what the investigation has shown so far and what he knows from experience in dealing with similar kinds of investigations. The investigator may be surprised to discover that probable cause does exist and it only takes the work of detailing what is known and what is understood in a clear and concise presentation to persuade a judge about the proof presented. The investigator can and should add the logical basis for the "gut feeling"; in this way, the investigator's experience can be presented to the judge.

Personal Experience

As a young investigator, I was involved in an investigation of a man who was selling valuable historical manuscripts written by a famous and internationally known artist and another valuable document written and signed by President Abraham Lincoln. The suspect was selling the documents in a jurisdiction hundreds of miles from his home. I was conducting my investigation in the jurisdiction where his home was located. We had no surveillance or special information about his residence other than he was on record as residing at the home I intended to search. We also knew he had access to the stolen material as a result of his work at the Library of Congress and the National Archives. I was tasked with getting an emergency search warrant for his residence since he was in custody in this other jurisdiction. At the time, I thought that probable cause for a search warrant would require some evidence I could present to the judge that stolen property, fruits of his crimes, or instrumentalities of his crimes were in his home. I thought I needed a witness to state that to me, but in retrospect, I realize that the fact he was living in a place he would come to and go from daily while he was committing his crimes was significant probable cause. I realized that probable cause wasn't some kind of absolute certainty; it was merely a reasonable analysis of human conduct and how that conduct, if it were criminal in nature, would make the likelihood that evidence of his crime would be in his home, where he felt safe and free to consider his actions. The judge, when presented with the facts, was more than willing to issue the warrant. As a result of the investigation, I recovered hundreds of other stolen historical documents and a treasure trove of other evidence linking the suspect with the crimes of possession of stolen property, theft by stealth and trick, and other confidence schemes involving an ongoing pattern of criminal conduct. The person in that case was convicted in the other jurisdiction and in my own jurisdiction and served substantial time in prison. We were also able to recover and replace that treasure trove of historically valuable documents stolen by this person.

Later in my career, I worked on a number of investigations that involved substantial ongoing violent crime conspiracies. In these cases, since they involved conspiratorial relationships with other known criminals, evidence of the conspiracy became extremely important. Again, it was not always known if evidence of the conspiracy was present, but in a realistic analysis of human conduct, it is reasonable to consider and present to a judge that address books, photographs, letters, notes, and digital records of contacts with co-conspirators will be present in the residences of such offenders. Probable cause therefore can consist of logical argument, not just absolute certainty.

In many investigations, developing probable cause to conduct a search at the original crime scene is the first step to successfully gathering all the evidence needed to arrest the right suspect. Probable cause therefore becomes part of the investigative process of following leads or clues that eventually lead to the conclusion that you have identified the persons responsible for the crimes. To further define probable cause, it is the reasonable belief that a crime has been committed and that a specific person or group of persons is responsible for committing the crime. Probable cause for arresting or charging a suspect should be a higher standard than the above-mentioned 51 percent likelihood. In the opinion of most seasoned criminal investigators, the mathematical standard *may* be closer to 75 percent, but there is more reason to be concerned than any arbitrary mathematical calculation. A suspect should be charged only if the investigator believes that the higher standard required for a trial will be met by the time the case is ready for trial. The standard for a trial is proof beyond a reasonable doubt. In effect, you can add the genuine belief that you will be successful in proving the case at a trial to your reasonable belief that you have probable cause to arrest.

For example, an investigator may have two witnesses who positively identify a suspect as the shooter in a homicide investigation. That level of proof can usually meet the probable cause standard. If there is ballistic evidence, such as the gun used in the homicide has been recovered from the suspect's person, residence, or some other location directly tied to the suspect, the suspect has a provable motive for killing the victim. The suspect's fingerprints can be identified at the crime scene, and the suspect claims to have never been at the scene. The investigator should consider that this additional, as yet unproven, evidence will take the case over the top for a trial. The investigator can also add to the facts that a well-planned interview with the suspect may yield a confession or some usable incriminating statements by the defendant that will shore up the case even more. Then there is the very important consideration that the suspect may present a danger to the community. By arresting the defendant and removing him from the community, you may be ensuring the safety of the community. These are the kinds of factors that allow the investigator to be certain of relying on the probable cause and therefore be comfortable enough to proceed with taking the suspect's freedom and arresting him prior to obtaining all the important facts needed for trial. The reality of the criminal justice system in most jurisdictions requires the probable cause standard to be met or exceeded when a charge has been filed. That probable cause will be reviewed by a judge in a preliminary hearing and eventually by a grand jury. The trial, if needed, may not take place for months or even years in some cases. Probable cause is therefore the standard of proof that can hold a defendant in custody for long periods of time. Delays for defense strategy or court scheduling may even affect some jurisdictions that have speedy trial requirements. Usually the delay between the initial charge and the trial gives the government plenty of time to complete forensic science examinations, locate and protect recalcitrant witnesses, and follow up on additional leads that come up during the delay. These very routine delays expanding the time a defendant is held pretrial should be considered in making the investigative decision leading to an arrest. For this reason, the investigator should be convinced he has the right person charged before making an arrest.

At this point in the discussion about probable cause, it is logical to provide a chart (table 9.1) with real-life examples of probable cause. Consider the crimes under investigation and examples of early findings that in most jurisdictions would be considered probable cause. Keep in mind that statutory requirements for degrees of crimes, such as homicide, sexual assault, robbery, and burglary, will require the analysis of the state or federal prosecutors who are most likely to handle any future prosecution. The investigator has to consider the facts, present them to the prosecutor, and abide by her legal evaluation as to whether the case will proceed. The prosecutor in many jurisdictions will have his mind on the possibility of success or failure in a future trial. The investigator is probably more focused on achieving that first goal of probable cause. This dichotomy of interests can lead to conflict, but healthy skepticism and debate are necessary to prepare the investigation for the kind of legal scrutiny that reduces the possibility of charging the wrong person with a crime. Following is a chart of probable causes:

Table 9.1.   Probable Cause Chart

Crime	Jurisdiction	Facts/evidence	Forensic proof
Homicide	Local	• Two eyewitnesses with positive identification (PI) • One eyewitness and one ear witness with PI • Video recording PI • Confession or substantial admission • Confidential reliable source	• Mandatory: medical examiner's verification of homicide • Suspect's fingerprints or DNA at the scene
Rape/sexual assault	Local	• PI by victim • Two eyewitnesses with PI • One eyewitness and one ear witness with PI • Confidential reliable source • Confession or substantial admission	• Valuable: rape kit • Suspect's fingerprints or DNA at the scene or on the victim
Bank robbery	Federal	• PI by victim teller with some kind of verification with video surveillance • Confidential reliable source • Confession or substantial admission	• FDIC proof • Suspect's fingerprints or DNA at the scene • Inventory or audit

Crime	Jurisdiction	Facts/evidence	Forensic proof
Armed robbery	Local	• Two eyewitnesses with PI • One eyewitness and video surveillance with PI • Confidential reliable source • Confession or substantial admission	• Inventory or audit
Burglary	Local	• Caught in the act • Confession or substantial admission • Confidential reliable source • Eyewitness with PI	• Victim's verification of break-in and felony offense • Suspect's fingerprints or DNA at the scene
Larceny	Local/federal	• Eyewitness with PI • Video recording • Confession or substantial admission • Confidential reliable source	• Inventory or audit
Arson	Local/federal	• Eyewitness with PI • Video recording • Confession or substantial admission • Confidential reliable source	• Scientific proof eliminating accidental origin • Use of a device or accelerant
Bombing	Local/federal	• Eyewitness with PI • Video recording • Confession or substantial admission • Confidential reliable source	• Scientific proof of device used
Possession with intent to distribute illegal drugs	Local/federal	• Surveillance-eyewitness with PI • Contraband recovered from suspect or in residence • Undercover purchase by investigator	• Mandatory: presumptive chemical test indicating the presence of controlled substance

Crime	Jurisdiction	Facts/evidence	Forensic proof
		• Evaluation of the amount of contraband recovered presumed to be more than for personal use (based on experience and training)	

The chart is not meant to provide proof for each of the crimes listed in the crime column. It is simply a display of the kinds of proof that can meet the standard of probable cause in many jurisdictions. Each of the examples listed in the proofs in the facts/evidence column can stand alone as proof of probable cause. You should note that proofs of crimes where one or two eyewitnesses are the basis of probable cause are subjective and vary from jurisdiction to jurisdiction. The investigator has to objectively decide if the witnesses are solid and able to withstand withering cross-examination. Are the witnesses going to be available in the future? Are the witnesses compromised in any way, or can they be compromised? It is the responsibility of the investigator and, later, the responsibility of the prosecutor to objectively evaluate witnesses and make a determination as to their strengths and weaknesses. It is also necessary for the investigator to determine if the witnesses will be targeted by the suspect or the suspect's associates if their names are used in a charging document, such as an affidavit. Such a document is immediately made available to the defendant in a criminal case when the suspect is arrested. Danger for those persons who testify against violent criminals is an ongoing consideration in any investigation and becomes acute when a suspect becomes a defendant.

One other factor to consider is *positive identification*. No person should be charged with a crime based on probable cause unless she has been positively identified by use of mug shots or fingerprints taken from a person whose identity has been verified by an agency, a police department, or an authorized government entity. Driver's license photographs from the local department of motor vehicles and passport photographs are official government records verifying the identity of the person depicted. In cases where exigent circumstances can be articulated by the charging agency, a suspect can be arrested and charged as a John Doe if he is using false identification or his identity is unknown and his real identity can be determined from face, fingerprint, or DNA profile data. These kinds of tentative identifications will make it impossible to place that person in any universal database, such as the National Crime Information Center (NCIC) database, to notify other professional law enforcement agencies to assist in the apprehension of the person. (In serious cases posing a threat to the community, it may be necessary to make sure there is an outstanding warrant for arrest.)

The next important factor that the investigator should consider is the use of a *confidential reliable source*, as outlined on the chart in the facts/evidence column. It is possible to use a regularly employed reliable source for a charging document, such as an arrest warrant affidavit. As a result of their proven reliability and, in many cases, access to the criminal ecosystem, judges may view their identification of a suspect to a crime with serious weight. Ultimately, a source of this nature will be immediately compromised and no longer be protected by confidentiality if the source is used in an arrest affidavit or other similar charging documents. Therefore, even though a confidential source is usually considered a reliable source of probable cause, it is ill advised to use a source for the purpose of probable cause in support of an arrest. The only situation in which using a confidential reliable source should be considered for use in a charging document is when the case is so important that arresting the suspect will save lives or directly protect the community from an imminent threat of violence. Confidential reliable sources are valuable resources in a number of cases and investigations; therefore, they should be compromised only as a last resort. (There will be a discussion of further responsibilities and requirements when dealing with informants in chapter 14.)

The next important factor to consider in a review of the proofs detailed in the facts/evidence column is *ear witness*. A person is considered an ear witness if she is present and distinctly hears a suspect confess to committing a crime. This person can be a friend or criminal associate who for any number of reasons is deeply concerned about the fact that a person she knows admits to killing, raping, robbing, or committing some act of violence. This person then comes forward to the police or other law enforcement authority with her statement. There are, of course, many factors that can motivate an ear witness; therefore, the value of his statement should be carefully evaluated to consider how much weight should be given to his revelation. The investigator should consider whether the ear witness's rendering of the facts provided by an eyewitness or evaluated with facts known from the crime scene or other established facts is logical and verifiable before proceeding with the use of such testimony in a charging document.

As stated above, each enumerated proof can stand alone in providing enough probable cause to charge a person with a crime. For homicide and drug possession with intent to distribute, the proof elements in the forensic proof column are proofs that must be met for probable cause in combination with at least one of the other enumerated proofs in the facts/evidence column. These examples of proof should be viewed as parts of a whole. As stated above, the chart provides examples of proofs that can be used as probable cause. In many cases, only one of the enumerated proofs is necessary to meet the standard. However, some statutes require that two elements be satisfied; therefore, two of the enumerated proofs are required.

The actual mechanics of charging a person in a criminal case should be considered as a process with a more substantial goal. It should also be viewed as the beginning of an exposition of the investigator's case. In that respect, use only those facts that meet the standard of probable cause, and don't include unnecessary facts for that standard. For example, if the investigator has five eyewitnesses who have identified the shooter in a homicide, she only needs to use two of those eyewitnesses. By using only two eyewitnesses, the investigator is able to "husband," or hold back, the other eyewitnesses until the prosecutor is required to provide that information during the discovery process. Physical or scientific evidence that is not needed for probable cause again can be held back from the defendant until such time as it is required as part of the discovery process. All of these legal requirements are the responsibility of the prosecutor in the case, and it should be her decision as to when additional evidence is revealed to the defendant and his attorney. Any exculpatory evidence discovered in the investigation should be turned over by the prosecutor according to the rules set by the court. Evidence or facts that neither help nor hurt either side can be withheld, but such an action is fraught with problems. The prosecuting attorney's responsibility in this area should be carefully considered and discussed with the investigator and independent evaluators so the decision is correct. When in doubt, the prosecutor should turn over the evidence out of an abundance of caution. (Court standards were set in *Brady v. Maryland* [1963] and *Giglio v. United States* [1972] and a host of other rulings on precedent. Policies and procedures governing the rules of evidence and the required disclosure of evidence were put into place to ensure that the constitutional concept of due process is adhered to in a criminal case. These standards are the responsibility of the prosecutor and the defense attorney, but the investigator needs to make sure that all aspects of an investigation are known to the prosecutor so that no violations of due process occur.)

The investigator can also rely on the individual proofs detailed in the forensic proof column of the chart to sustain probable cause. Scientific proof that provides a positive, relevant basis for the positive identification of a suspect in a criminal matter is usually sufficient probable cause for an arrest. This area is where the idea of *human context*, as discussed elsewhere in this text (chapters 2 and 10 provide a more detailed discussion of forensic identifications), is necessary. All affidavits and statements of fact, including presentations to a grand jury, require a demonstration by the investigator that a crime has occurred. This is best accomplished with an introductory paragraph stating that a complainant reporting person or victim contacted law enforcement and said or reported that a crime happened and that witnesses and evidence of the crime were at a specific location at the time that the report or claim was made. As evident, if one were to use one of the proofs listed in the facts/evidence column, the paragraph often does originate from one of the witnesses or victims listed who can be relied on for proof of probable cause. There are also other elements required by the code or indicative of criminal conduct that show proof, even at the level of probable cause, that should be presented as part of probable cause, such as statements about the amount of drugs recovered and how the investigator knows that amount of drugs is not consistent with personal use. Physical injury in a sexual assault case can be offered as proof that the injuries are inconsistent with consensual sexual activity. Consciousness of guilt proof that indicates a suspect is hiding something from law enforcement may be used in many cases as an element of probable cause. A suspect's criminal history indicating the suspect has been charged in the past with similar crimes is another level of proof that is available at this stage of an investigation but is not available in most cases for the trial phase. The following textbox provides an outline that can be followed in preparing an arrest affidavit:

PROBABLE CAUSE FOR ARREST:
OUTLINE FOR PREPARING AN ARREST AFFIDAVIT

- Introduction of affiant.
- Narrative detailing facts verifying the crime.
- Facts that connect the defendants with the crime.
- Objective identification of the defendant mug shot, dl photo, passport photo, fingerprints.
- Conclusion with jurisdictional citation of crime.

- Verify jurisdictional authority.
- The narrative should contain a carefully crafted version of the facts.
- Victim/Witness description of events; video rendering of the event; or "stream of logic" connecting the defendant to the crime.
- A witness or a forensic expert should be able to positively identify the defendant from an official record.
- Limit the citation to one single charge; each defendant should be charged separately.

At this point in the discussion, probable cause should be viewed as the first goal achieved by an investigator. The investigator knows that the case will move forward only if proof beyond a reasonable doubt can be achieved. In a way similar to probable cause, proof beyond a reasonable doubt is difficult to define. A seasoned defense attorney may believe that any doubt raised by the facts presented in trial should constitute reasonable doubt and the case against his client should be dismissed. Most courts and judges have ruled that the doubt has to be reasonable. If the evidence presented as proof of guilt would require the average person to conclude guilt, then a doubt raised has to be so important as to bring into question the guilt of the defendant. In the minds of the criminal investigator, a reasonable doubt would have to deconstruct one or more of the substantial proofs of guilt discovered in the investigation. If the investigator is convinced of the guilt of a defendant and presented with a fact that shakes that confidence, reasonable doubt may have been uncovered. A number of cases don't account for every element of a crime. Murder cases have been successful without the recovery of the murder weapon. Cases have been successful without discovering the fingerprints or DNA of a defendant at a crime scene, so the absence of evidence is not necessarily reasonable doubt. Other factors that support guilt may be so compelling that the mere lack of evidence is not enough to sow the seed of reasonable doubt. It is up to the investigator and the prosecutor during the trial phase to move forward in spite of frivolous or unsubstantiated doubts. Reasonable doubt is the standard that should be adhered to at all times. There is, however, an issue to consider. In most local police departments in the United States, an arrest of the suspect is a closure of the case. The case is no longer the primary responsibility of the department, unless and until the arrest is dismissed in court and the case is referred back to the department. Since this administrative end of an investigation is a fact, the detective or investigator assigned is returned to the assignment rotation for investigations, and her time to follow up with the closed investigation is limited. Some prosecutors will have criminal investigators assigned to their office to take over following up on leads and continue the preparation for trial. These investigators will be given access to the notes, reports, and witness interviews from the police investigator. Police investigators will be subpoenaed to testify and assist in trial preparation, but some police resources will be limited at this time. Detectives or investigators who have developed significant trust relationships with witnesses and victims are essential to the case and should continue in contact with the case through the trial phase. The prosecutor's team, if available, can handle most of the other investigative areas, such as the forensic examinations, new investigative leads, data analysis, and work with expert witnesses. In federal law enforcement and many state police jurisdictions, the original investigator stays with the case until there is a final disposition in court. Thus, if the prosecutor's office has investigators employed on its cases for the trial phase, the investigative team is enhanced by these additional resources. It is the usual practice for the postarrest trial phase portion of investigations to be headed by the prosecutor assigned as the lead litigator for the trial. This change of leadership can cause conflict, but the investigator needs to resolve any conflicts to avoid problems in the process. All investigative strategy and planning toward proof beyond a reasonable doubt is at this point in the case the result that should be considered the final goal. Winning at trial, with a guilty verdict, is the primary objective of any criminal investigation.

One real-life solution to this issue is illustrated by the fact that well over 60 percent of the defendants who are charged with a crime enter into plea negotiations with the government and the case never goes to trial. Plea deals are cut for many reasons, including harsh sentences for defendants who go to trial, a lack of significant legal assistance to indigent defendants charged with a crime, and the fact that the defendant who has been charged is actually guilty and willing to face the penalty, albeit less harsh if she pleads rather than fights the case in a trial. The government's burden of proof is high, but the government has the distinct advantage of carrying substantial resources to successfully prosecute the case. Therefore, defendants are often weighing some bad options if they continue to fight the case in court. Recent studies of adult criminal cases ending in plea agreements have indicated that as many as 95 percent of all felony arrests end in a plea agreement (Bureau of Justice Statistics, https:// gb1.ojp.usdoj.gov/search?q=Plea+Agreements&site=BJS-OJP&client=bjsnew_ frontend&proxystylesheet=bjsnew_frontend&output=xml_no_dtd&proxyreload=1&f ilter=0&tlen=150&getfields=description&Go.x=14&Go.y=6).

In general, the statistics are difficult to verify. Arrest cases can be dismissed when the case is reviewed by the prosecutor's office and significant flaws are revealed. Dismissals also occur when the screening prosecutor concludes that the resources necessary to go forward with the case are not available. Arrest cases may never move beyond the original proof of probable cause, but it is still a fact that, by far, most cases end in a plea. As the case becomes more serious, such as with murder or violent rape, the likelihood of a plea is lessened. Defendants facing twenty to fifty years, even if they plead guilty, are more likely to gamble on a trial.

As a result, the final goal of any criminal investigation is to complete the work necessary to ensure the proper outcome at trial or a just resolution if the investigative findings reveal that the wrong person has been charged. The investigator at this point may continue to be the lead investigator from the agency whose jurisdiction began the case. The investigator may be a state's attorney investigator assigned to the prosecutor's office, or the case may be such that a team effort is needed to bring together both units, the original investigative agency and the prosecutor's office, to complete the task. At this point, there is a need to evaluate the case again and develop a plan to determine what needs to be done to proceed to trial.

WITNESS CONCERNS

The following list of steps are goals that need to be met by the criminal investigator to bring a case to its final conclusion.

Step 1

Step 1 is to interview witnesses, ensure consistent testimony, and evaluate the quality of witnesses already known. They may be the witnesses upon which the probable cause was met. They may also be witnesses who were developed in the initial investigation but have not yet been made part of the court record. These witnesses will generally be the core of the case. They will be able to provide the details of the crime and the specifics, such as positive identification of the suspect or proof of the elements of the crime. In other words, these witnesses put the crime event into a human context. It is within this group of witnesses that the victim of the crime is usually found. These witnesses may have provided full statements to the police or the grand jury, and as a result, they have to be briefed on these statements to ensure that what was recorded in the statement is an accurate recitation of what they know. These prior statements will be part of a discovery compilation provided to the defense attorney. Thus, if any inconsistencies exist between the statements and the witnesses' testimony at trial, the effectiveness of the witnesses' evidence may be jeopardized. Witness preparation is the responsibility of the lead prosecutor in the case, but during this preparation, the prosecutor is usually accompanied by an investigator who is familiar with the prior statements. During this preparation, minor inconsistencies can be discovered and resolved before trial. Important problems with inconsistent recollections or new facts unknown at the time of the original statements can be evaluated, and the investigator and prosecutor can prepare for any legal issues raised by these problems and make an effort to reevaluate the witnesses and determine if their testimony is still relevant and important. An example of this kind of problem would be a witness who changes his recollection of the facts in the case, refuses to acknowledge a previous positive identification of the defendant, or claims that he made up all of his previous statements. This kind of serious problem will eventually have to be made known to the defense attorney, who may then wish to make this troubled witness part of her case at trial.

Source: iStock 488240072

The obvious concern with this kind of change of heart is that there may be some kind of witness intimidation or tampering going on in the case.

Step 2: New Witnesses

As a result of the detailed analysis of the investigation conducted thus far, the investigator may also discover new witnesses who will be able to provide additional evidence that can be used in the trial phase. Thus, the same kind of care and evaluation with witness preparation needs to be implemented to make sure any new witnesses are comfortable testifying in the trial. The timing of the trial, the availability of witnesses, and the real concern that all the government's witnesses are providing truthful testimony is the focus of this part of the investigation. All efforts should be directed to ensuring that all the relevant evidence is available for the trial. Since there is no grand jury available for this investigation, it is necessary to carefully interview the witnesses to be satisfied that the testimony they provide will be relevant and effective. Reports or written statements by these new witnesses can be considered part of the prosecutor's work product and may not be discoverable. Again, this decision is the responsibility of the prosecuting attorney. In the event some protracted time issue occurs between the witness preparation and the trial, it may be necessary for the investigator to document the statements from the witnesses so that a record exists of the proposed testimony of those new witnesses.

Witness Protection

In violent crimes, investigations can occur when the suspect/defendant has the capability to harm witnesses who are courageous enough to testify in open court against him. The investigator's responsibility to protect the witnesses who come forward is an essential responsibility during the trial phase because this is usually the time when there is a need to establish a long-term safety zone for the witnesses. Resources for witness security can come from prosecutors' offices, police departments, and federal agencies. Unfortunately, these resources are very limited. Well-funded federal investigative agencies, such as the FBI and the Drug Enforcement Administration (DEA), provide substantial budgets for this purpose. However, in most federal cases (as explained in detail in chapter 6), the US Marshals Service Witness Security (WITSEC) program is the primary consideration for long-term witness care. This program extricates the witness and his immediate family from the danger zone. The witness is relocated and provided a new identity. Systems are in place to allow the witness to become employed and established in a lifestyle reasonably comparable to how he lived in the past. This program is highly sensitive and secure. A series of rules are demanded of the witness so that there is *no* contact with her previous life. Removal from the WITSEC program is the penalty for breaking the rules. The program can be very difficult for most people and so frustrating that they opt out, leaving them vulnerable to an attack. If a witness fails to follow the rules and is removed from the program, that does not lessen the responsibility of the investigator to secure the safety of the witness. In fact, that responsibility is heightened. The WITSEC program was established as a response to national and international organized crime conspiracies. The Mafia, Eastern European Bratva, and Mexican drug cartels have enormous resources and capabilities to corrupt officials in law enforcement. Therefore, following the rules of the program not only protects the individual witness but also protects the integrity of the program to ensure the security of all the witnesses being protected.

Drastic relocation and new identities are not the only answer to this serious problem. The investigator has to consider the capabilities of the defendant and adjust the witness protection plan to fit the needs of the witness. A serious predator who has contacts in the local community, who will carry out his wish to intimidate a witness, cannot be considered to be at the same threat level as a Mafia family or international cartel whose reach and influence extends nationwide or worldwide. Young, uneducated witnesses whose experience in life makes them weak candidates for identity changes and dramatic geographic relocation may need a more streamlined and individualized plan. Unfortunately, a number of witnesses who are considered for witness protection are from chaotic family backgrounds and have survived only through petty criminal activity. Reeducating these witnesses and developing their instinct for survival as a motivator to change who they are and how they live their lives can be a daunting task for the investigator who sees her role as being focused on charging and convicting bad guys. Even a witness who is a solid citizen with a solid work ethic can present significant problems. Relocating this kind of witness to another region where she has friends or family who can assist in establishing a communication network to alert local authorities that a threat has emerged may be an alternative for consideration. Solutions to providing witness protection can come from intensive debriefings about the problem with the witness so that alternatives can be considered. The most important consideration is how to make sure the witness is not harmed or attacked in the process. The goal is to have the witness available to testify while avoiding any long-term lifestyle disruption.

Such a goal is almost impossible to achieve for local police departments with limited budgets, and many local prosecutors' offices also don't have the budget for successful witness protection plans. It is more likely that the witness protection program for these agencies will be a temporary relocation in a hotel or motel. Relocation in some cases from one government housing project to another is used in some large urban areas for protection of witnesses in local gang cases. These programs are short-term solutions and may be effective in specific cases depending on the capabilities and resources of the defendant. Career criminals who are violent loners may be effectively restrained from witness intimidation and attacks by keeping them incarcerated using their bond status based on their potential or propensity for violence against the community.

To reiterate, all these levels of protection can be considered based on the needs of the investigation, but the most important aspect of this discussion is to make sure that the witness's needs are met and he does not feel so intimidated by the defendant that his testimony is affected. Truthful testimony is the goal for the witness.

The money spent by the government to protect witnesses can have a positive and a negative effect on the testimony. Some jurors will consider the money spent to relocate a witness as an effort by the state to corrupt the witness by providing a new lifestyle, free of significant jail time, and an opportunity for the witness to reset his life and remake who he is. In effect, some jurors may believe that the witness will say anything the government wants to get this benefit. On the other hand, some jurors will view the money spent as further proof that the defendant is a violent predator whose range of influence and ability to threaten the community is more of a concern than the government is allowed to present in the trial. This is the case because usually the amount of money spent is considered extraordinary. For example, six months in the WITSEC program can cost more than $50,000 dollars. If the jury is made up of average working class citizens who make no more than $30,000 per year, this amount can be overwhelming. The proper accounting for every dollar spent is the responsibility of the investigator.

Step 3: Expert Witnesses

Testimony from scientific experts can be some of the most consequential testimony provided in a trial. An expert in serological evidence can say that the defendant's DNA was extracted from the crime scene, which provides scientific proof that the defendant was at the scene. An expert in latent fingerprints can testify that the defendant's fingerprints were found at the scene. An expert in firearms ballistics can testify that a weapon used in a crime of violence is the same weapon recovered by law enforcement in the possession of the defendant. I have discussed more of the details relating to this use of forensic science in chapter 10 in this text, but for purposes of this discussion, these experts and many other experts become essential elements in the trial phase. A homicide case requires the testimony of an expert medical examiner. A rape case requires the expert testimony of a medical doctor trained and experienced in trauma cases. Computer experts may be needed to testify on some kind of sophisticated data recovery process that is relevant to the case at trial. All of these experts are called by the government to support the government's argument as to what happened, how it happened, who did it, and on and on. That is why they are generally referred to as forensic experts. The term *forensic*, according to *Merriam-Webster Dictionary*, means "belonging to, used in, or suitable to courts of judicature or to public discussion and debate." With the passage of time and common usage, the term is now considered to apply to any science used in the effort to solve crimes. The reality is that these scientists and experts provide opinion testimony. The jury can weigh the experts' opinions in the context of the other evidence provided in the trial and decide how much value or validity they will give to their opinions.

In trials, the ability of the expert witnesses to explain and describe their scientific analysis in terms that are easily understood by the average juror is absolutely necessary. These men and women are often brought in as professional witnesses, but their impact on a jury has to be weighed against what works in the investigative jurisdiction where the trial takes place. The prosecutor and the investigator have to make a judgment about the effectiveness of the experts based on how they will be perceived by jurors and how effectively they will be able to withstand the cross-examination of the defense attorney in the case. Their testimony may be challenged by a defense expert or by withering cross-examination. As much as we would like to believe that scientific certainty is unrelenting proof, it all comes down to how the expert is viewed by the jury. The investigator needs to spend time with the expert to go over the findings and to suggest the best way for the findings to be presented in the jurisdiction and to jurors who will be the triers of fact. Juries in various regions of the country will have certain prejudices and cultural differences that will color their view of the testimony provided by the expert. The expert has to be likable, approachable, and clear in his language. The use of difficult-to-understand scientific jargon will frustrate the jurors' ability to connect with the witness and may have the negative effect of untrustworthiness. Some jurors will be impressed with extensive credentials, education, and years of experience in the field, but other jurors will be moved by folksy, humorous presentations that make the jury feel comfortable with the witness. Local experts may hold more weight than those from out of town. Defense experts, whose work may not be as polished or backed by government resources, may hold sway over polished professional government experts. All of these dichotomies of effectiveness need to be considered by the investigator and the prosecutor to prevent being caught ill prepared if their main forensic expert goes over with a thud when she testifies.

To summarize, witnesses are the "straws that stir the drink" in a trial. They need to be prepared to tell the truth and to be as effective as possible in connecting with the jury. The success of the trial depends on the witnesses.

Source: iStock 91208381

Step 4: Physical Evidence

Step 4 is about preparing the physical evidence for trial. Every piece of physical evidence has to have a chain-of-custody document attached to it. The chain is a step-by-step list of every person who has had custody of the evidence, including the lead investigator, the crime scene examination team members, the forensic specialists, and any other interim law enforcement employees who maintained and handled the evidence. For photographs and documents, the first person in the chain is often called the custodian of record. The custodian of record can be a bank branch manager or security specialist who is the custodian for the bank surveillance film. The chain of custody has to be unbroken, and for the most part, the administrative clerk or officer who is in charge of the evidence control facility is the main custodian listed. The chain will be used to verify that a specific piece of evidence was subjected to a specific scientific examination. The chain will be used to prove that the evidence was found in the defendant's house or recovered from the crime scene. The investigator needs to make sure there are no surprises in the introduction of any of the pieces of physical evidence. Once the evidence is turned over to the prosecutor, she will label each item with an exhibit number for trial and will then be responsible for the physical evidence from that point forward.

SUMMARY

There are a number of other goals for investigations, such as the long-term goals of crime reduction and community safety. These goals can be achieved only after a number of successfully closed cases can be shown to have this kind of positive impact on a community. Arresting and prosecuting a group of serial offenders who commit car theft, burglary, or armed robbery may result in lower numbers of complaints and thereby be a positive long-term goal. Unfortunately, with the passage of time and as socioeconomic reasons come into play, these serial offenders will be replaced by other career criminals who consider that participating in these kinds of crime sprees are in their best interests.

So the goals of a criminal investigation are a progression of investigative elements that provide the case with the legal authority and therefore probable cause and eventually proof beyond a reasonable doubt, a search warrant, an arrest, pretrial motions, a grand jury hearing, and a trial with an appropriate sentence meted out. The recovery of a victim, the recovery of stolen property or lost valuables, and a strong possibility that a predatory criminal is removed from the community provide the gold standard of effective investigative results. At each point when evidence can be discovered and seized and at each point when a subject becomes a defendant, the investigator is meeting the interim goals that will finally answer the main goal of any investigation. The truth is learned, and the criminal justice system is brought to bear on the lawbreaker. If an investigation never achieves these goals, it is difficult to believe that the "truth" has been discovered.

Chapter Ten

Physical Evidence

Chain of custody, relevance, value, and a determination that a scientific examination can provide clear proof regarding a controversial argument or contentious fact in a legal proceeding.

Physical evidence is also called real or material evidence. It is any material object that plays some role in the matter that gave rise to litigation or was introduced as evidence in a judicial proceeding (such as a trial) to prove a fact in issue based on the object's physical characteristics. Physical evidence can be recovered at the original crime scene in a criminal case, or it can be recovered at any time throughout the course of the investigation. If that physical evidence is recovered, it also has to be authenticated by the person who recovers the evidence and the person from whom it was taken. There has to be an unbroken record that the evidence was maintained in the custody of law enforcement and representatives of the prosecutor and the defense. If the evidence is placed in the custody of a forensic expert for examination, there also has to be a log of who handled the evidence and how it was maintained to ensure the nature and physical characteristics of the evidence were not altered.

Physical evidence can fall into the general categories of evidence, including fruits of a crime, instrumentalities of a crime, or incidental evidence. Money or jewelry, for example, could be fruits of the crime of robbery, burglary, or larceny. A gun or a knife can be an instrumentality of the crime of murder, assault, or rape. A section of wallboard, a carpet with blood stains, or obvious pattern evidence can be incidental evidence in any of the above crimes and needs further examination to determine the impact of the crime, which makes the material evidence. Most physical evidence stands alone as evidence based on its connection to the crime. Some physical evidence, including fruits and instrumentalities of the crime, may need forensic examination to extract further evidentiary values from the material. For example, money and jewelry stolen in a robbery or burglary can be examined for the presence of biological material for fingerprint evidence to help in the positive identification of the suspect in a criminal case. The most used forensic examination of physical evidence is attempting to develop latent fingerprints on the evidence, verifying that the suspect handled or touched the physical evidence. Walls, doors, floors, furniture, and any other material object present when the crime occurred can be examined on the spot for latent (invisible) fingerprints. When fingerprints are located, there are methods of recovering the prints without taking the object that was handled or touched. The latent fingerprint lifts, or graphic proof, become the physical evidence recovered from the scene.

Even biological material or trace evidence can be extracted from the crime scene without recovery and removal of the object upon which it was discovered. For example, sterile cotton swabs or bulk cotton material can be used to swipe wet or moist blood, semen, and the like from a scene. As long as the process of recovery is properly documented and the wet evidence is allowed to dry in a porous container, the evidence can be successfully stored and maintained for examination by a forensic expert to determine the evidentiary value of the material. From an investigative standpoint, if there is a logical and efficient way to recover the evidence without compromising the value of the material as evidence, then it is acceptable to take appropriate samples, which can be documented and photographed by the crime scene examiner. On the other hand, if the extraction process may compromise the recovery in any way, then it is best to take the whole object for extraction and examination in a controlled lab environment. The other main example of this process is the vacuuming, lifting, or sweeping of trace evidence at a crime scene because such evidence may not be obvious or even visible. Microscopic hairs, fibers, and even fingernails or skin epithelium are likely to be invisible in a carpet or rug or even on some kind of outdoor crime scene. Methodically sweeping, raking, vacuuming, or using lifting tape can be deployed at a crime scene in an attempt to recover or extract any microscopic physical evidence that may be relevant evidence to the crime under investigation. Again, specific techniques for the recovery of such evidence is discussed in my book *Working the Scene*, but for purposes of this text, the criminal investigator should be aware of how and what physical evidence located at a crime scene can be exploited.

The decision to have physical evidence recovered in a criminal investigation examined forensically is usually made by the lead investigator and the lead crime scene technician. There are a number of forensic examinations that can be conducted on individual items of physical evidence. For example, a firearm that is suspected of being the weapon used to commit a homicide can be examined for fingerprint evidence, biological material, trace evidence remnants, and a ballistics examination. Some of these examinations need to be prioritized so one examination does not compromise, or contaminate, the next examination. A firearm that is examined for latent fingerprints using the application of cyanoacrylate or superglue fumes can destroy any chance to recover DNA evidence or even drug evidence from the weapon.

A careful and thoughtful approach to how evidence is examined and what kind of examinations should be prioritized allows for the best outcome in how physical evidence is exploited.

CHAIN OF CUSTODY

Chain of custody is a legal term that refers to the requirement that, while physical evidence is held by the government or the defense, a written log should be kept to document who obtained the evidence and provide a clear and precise accounting going forward, specifically stating the custody or control of the evidence until it is brought to court and submitted as evidence. The chain can be very simple. Evidence that is recovered at the scene and not subjected to any forensic examination may have only two persons on the chain-of-custody log. The crime scene technician who recovered the evidence submits it to the evidence control clerk for the department or agency, who then stores the item until it is needed for court. So if the crime scene technician is the witness called upon to introduce the evidence at trial, the chain will consist of just the two people who had the item in their custody. On the other hand, going back to our discussion of a firearm recovered at a crime scene, there may be a crime scene technician, a DNA recovery technician, a drug evidence recovery technician, a latent fingerprint examiner, a firearms or ballistics examiner, and an evidence control clerk. The firearm may be submitted in court by any of these experts or by the lead criminal investigator, so all of those persons may be on the chain of custody. The chain of custody is simply a log of any and all persons who had the evidence in their possession.

A *broken chain of custody* is when the evidence is lost, discovered missing, or out of the possession of law enforcement for a period of time without a custodian. This break in the chain can eliminate the evidence from use in a trial.

The other significant area of concern in the chain of custody is that the first person from whom the evidence is recovered needs to be able to *authenticate* the evidence as to its value and source. Data files, digital images, surveillance recordings, and the like need to be authenticated by a person determined by investigation to be the custodian of record. For example, someone has to be able to testify that a video surveillance recording of a bank lobby is in fact a *true and accurate representation* of the bank lobby. Business records of routine business transactions have to have a person who is responsible for those records testify that the digital records are the actual records of transactions for the company purported by the government or the defense.

For the criminal investigator, the chain of custody has to be a clear and precise log of who had the evidence in their possession and for how long. Each person in that log will have to be available to explain his effort to control and secure the evidence. The investigator is responsible for making sure there is a person, usually the first person in the log, who can testify that the evidence is what it purports to be or was recovered by the government in the official performance of the investigation. Authentication, control, security, and dates and times are properly documented for every piece of physical evidence. It is best to keep the log in direct proximity to the individual piece of evidence so the log is immediately available for review and updating.

Forensic examinations of physical evidence involve several techniques that can yield results. The side-by-side comparison of an unknown item of physical evidence recovered at a crime scene with a known item similar in nature to the unknown evidence is the first technique. It is in many ways the most often used method of forensic examination. Comparing latent fingerprints recovered at a crime scene with a known sample of fingerprints recovered from a suspect allows the latent fingerprint expert to determine if the "questioned," or unknown, prints are in fact the prints of the suspect. Pristine bullets fired into a water-filled recovery tank, the known item, can be compared with bullets recovered at a crime scene or in the body of a victim, the questioned item. These kinds of comparisons can yield a positive conclusion about the questioned items. A known person's fingerprints were found at the scene of a crime. A weapon recovered from the possession of a suspect was the weapon used to kill the victim. The side-by-side technique can also be used to provide more general characteristics. A lift of dust that resembles a shoe print found at a crime scene can be compared to a known shoe print "standards" file, and the conclusion can be that the suspect wore a particular brand of shoe. A more specific identification will be impossible until the suspect's shoes are recovered and there is specific detail in the dust print that will allow for a positive identification. This kind of forensic comparison is a pattern examination. Shoe prints, tire treads, and other items that may leave a full impression or a remnant of an impression at a crime scene provide a significant and reliable clue that can inform the investigation.

The focus of most forensic examinations is to reach a conclusion that provides some scientific certainty as to what the evidence means and how it is relevant evidence in a criminal matter. Comparing evidence with a known sample is significant, but in many cases, just making a determination about the nature of the evidence is important. So another technique is an examination that provides a qualitative and quantitative analysis of an unknown object or material on an object recovered at a crime scene. The scientific conclusion will provide a way to define the nature of the material under examination. For example, suspected illegal drugs found at a crime scene can be examined to determine if the suspicious powder or material has the appropriate chemical makeup to identify the specific drug. Stippling marks found on the clothing of a suspect can be examined to determine the chemical compound of the gunpowder used in the bullets fired into a suspect. Another kind of forensic examination is microscopic analysis. Hairs, fibers, paint chips, and other materials can reveal the source from where they were derived if they are examined under extreme magnification. Viewing suspicious or unknown substances using variations of light energy can indicate what the substance is by how it reacts to light energy. It would be almost impossible to describe every type of scientific examination that can be used to affect a criminal investigation. The purpose of this chapter is to introduce a number of the disciplines that are relied on by criminal investigators in the course of their cases.

As has been previously discussed, the presentation of the results of a forensic science examination comes from a court-approved expert whose education, training, and experience satisfy the judge that the person has sufficient expertise to be able to offer an opinion in court that meets the legal standard of proof to a "scientific certainty." Since the word "opinion" connotes a somewhat lesser standard than "certainty," it is important to discuss these experts who give their opinions. Most forensic science experts work for well-funded and approved laboratories established by federal, state, and local governments. These scientists are committed professionals who combine their academic training with significant amounts of training and experience examining real cases related to ongoing criminal investigations. They are usually "approved" to testify by the government laboratory after years of experience and vetting. When they report out their conclusions, they are routinely backed up in their results by at least one other expert. There have been very few cases where these experts have been proven to be corrupt or mistaken in their conclusions. For the most part, these professional forensic scientists are objective scientists who provide truthful and well-sourced opinions in trials throughout the United States. Criminal investigators rely heavily on these experts because they are scientifically certain when they reach their conclusions. Most government labs meet the standards for handling and examining evidence of the American Society of Crime Laboratory Directors (ASCLD). Most of these labs are certified by the appropriate crime lab accrediting body and therefore must periodically stand for inspections and reviews to continue their accreditation. Unfortunately, as discussed in chapter 6, the harsh reality of trials makes personality and performance part of the equation for whether these experts are believed. There are a number of very experienced and capable forensic experts in private or commercial laboratories who are equally qualified and, in some cases, even more qualified than the government lab experts. For the most part, there should be little discrepancy between their conclusions and the conclusions of private experts, but since these private experts are paid by defendants, there may be some level of "leaning" or "obfuscation" that frustrates or counters the government expert. Any real difference between experts should be thoroughly resolved pretrial if possible. There are also a number of private medical examiners who will testify for the defense at trials. Again, any real difference in their opinions and the opinions of the government medical examiner should be resolved by investigation. Almost every jurisdiction in the United States has a coroner or medical examiner. These persons are usually medical doctors with significant experience in pathology and experienced and are trained in performing autopsies. Coroners in some small jurisdictions are elected and, in very few cases, aren't even doctors. These non-professional coroners usually defer to a professional medical examiner from another jurisdiction when expertise is required, but it may be up to the criminal investigator or the local prosecutor to ensure an appropriate expert conducts an autopsy in a criminal case involving a homicide.

Between forensic experts from government labs and properly trained medical examiners, the criminal investigator must rely on their expertise. If for some reason they make an error in their examination, it is up to the investigator to determine how serious the error is and how much it will affect the outcome of the investigation. The investigator's concern is not the outcome of the trial; her concern is how the effort to get at the truth is altered. A scientific mistake that indicates a suspect who was presumed by the investigator to be guilty is now innocent means the investigator has to continue the investigation armed with the new facts and change whatever needs to be changed to ensure that an innocent person is not prosecuted.

Throughout the United States, criminal investigators rightly put their faith in their colleagues from government-sponsored laboratories. It is in the interest of the integrity of the expert and the investigation and in the interest of justice that the relationship between the investigator and the forensic expert be kept cordial but professional. An investigator is seeking the truth; therefore, examinations that don't verify facts or prove a connection to a favored suspect should never cause strain or disappointment between the investigator and the experts. These professionals may be government-sponsored experts, but they work to get at the truth. They don't work to convict the person the state has charged with a crime. They have to be objective and balanced in their approach. It is possible and should be acceptable that these experts testify for the defense if need be.

Private forensic scientists and private medical examiners are from a variety of backgrounds and circumstances. For the most part, they have worked for government laboratories or government medical examiners offices in the past. It is unusual for them to disagree with the findings of another scientist, but it does happen. Any corrupt reason for the disagreement is a fact of life in some very high-profile cases. In the event that this is happening, the investigator should go over the results of the government's expert and compare those results with the defense expert's. Determining the specific nature of the variance is critical. Once it is determined how and why the disagreement happened, the investigator should meet with another expert in the same discipline and determine who is right and who is wrong. This responsibility is necessary to resolve the conflict. There are "charlatans" and undereducated or undertrained persons who have falsely earned expert status in court. Once one court accepts the credentials of an expert, subsequent courts may follow suit. It is up to the prosecutor to challenge the credentials of a nonexpert expert. It may take some investigation to determine the lack of qualifications, so the investigator needs to be prepared for this eventuality.

The following sections of this chapter will be discussions of various categories of physical evidence with a summary of forensic examinations that may be conducted on the evidence. Every criminal investigator needs to become familiar with the nature of the evidence and have an understanding of what kind of scientific examinations can be done to provide helpful answers as to why the evidence is relevant to the investigation.

FINGERPRINT EVIDENCE

One of the oldest forensic sciences is fingerprint examination. In ancient Persia, fingerprints were used to identify a person in a major business transaction. This technique predated the use of signatures on contracts. So, even then, it was believed that fingerprints were unique to each person. In the later part of the nineteenth century, Henry Faulds and William James Herschel published an academic paper verifying what had been believed for centuries—that fingerprints were unique and didn't change on a person over time. An English civil servant named Sir Edward Henry, who was working in law enforcement in Bengal, India, began classifying fingerprints of persons arrested for crimes. It was his classification system, which took thirty years to perfect, that became the basis for comparison searches needed to verify past criminal behavior. In 1924, the FBI took over the first fingerprint data collection files (originally established in St. Louis, Missouri, by the International Association of Chiefs of Police) of 10 print cards documenting each arrest from law enforcement agencies nationwide. Beginning in 1905 and continuing through 1930, police agencies in England and the United States began to develop methods to recover latent, patent, and plastic fingerprints from crime scenes. Perspiration attached to the friction ridges on fingers, hands, and feet left impressions of the prints on smooth surfaces. Powders, chemicals, and other methods successfully developed or revealed the incidental prints at the scene. Once they were developed, photographed, and lifted, they became evidence, and then that evidence could be compared to known fingerprints taken from the suspect for official purposes or pursuant to a court or grand jury order.

For a criminal investigator, there is nothing more supportive in a criminal investigation than to find the fingerprints of a suspect at the scene of a crime, especially if that suspect denies being present at the scene or has no legitimate reason for being there. Fingerprints can be discovered on smooth surfaces of two kinds of material: porous and nonporous. *Porous* material is paper, cardboard, wood, and any naturally occurring material. Just as the name suggests, porous material has pores or minute holes that do not interfere with the details left by perspiration, which generates a pattern of friction ridges. It should be pointed out here that latent fingerprints on paper are the best and most effective medium for usable prints. Porous material can be subjected to fingerprint powder to develop latent prints, but it is best to have porous material protected from any further contamination and submitted to a fingerprint laboratory for examination and development using chemical processes and even laser technology to develop any prints. When a person leaves prints on porous material, there is less chance of smudging and the print is not likely to ever disappear, unless it is printed over or intentionally rubbed to obscure the print. The criminal investigator should ensure that all paper found at the scene of a crime that may have been touched or handled by the suspect should be protected for fingerprint examination. Paper that was handled hastily or unintentionally before its significance was understood should still be examined. The fingerprint examiner can eliminate any prints left on the paper or porous material innocently.

The second type of material that is an appropriate medium for fingerprints is *nonporous* material, such as steel, metal, glass, plastic, and other synthetic materials with a smooth surface. Fictional accounts of criminal investigations display investigators obtaining drinking glasses as a method to surreptitiously obtain fingerprints from a suspect. As suggested above, that is the wrong way. Handing a suspect a piece of paper and having the suspect handle the paper is actually the best method to obtain fingerprints, unless the need for the prints is more overt. Then a grand jury subpoena is usually sufficient. Nonporous materials include most weapons, such as knives and firearms and even blunt-force objects, such as candlesticks and hammers. Since the surfaces of these weapons, such as that of a firearm, are so smooth, it is a regular occurrence that any latent prints left are smudged by their simply being handled. Firearms that have a sheen of oil create still another problem for the medium. Usable or identifiable fingerprints on weapons are rare. During my career, I was convinced by a number of fingerprint experts that as soon as any metal weapon is recovered, it should be fumed in a cyanoacrylate (superglue) chamber to secure any possible prints immediately. Great care needs to be taken to use a cotton swab on waffled or imprinted surfaces that are used to manipulate the weapons action so there is at least a chance that any skin epithelium containing DNA material can be recovered prior to the fuming process. If this technique becomes a routine part of an investigation, the criminal investigator needs to coordinate the method with the fingerprint expert to whom the case will be assigned.

These pictures provide an illustration of the factors and techniques used to recover and examine fingerprint evidence.

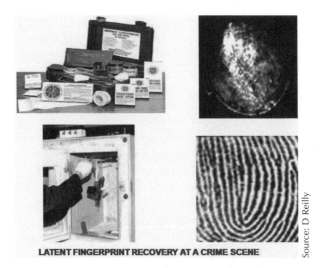

LATENT FINGERPRINT RECOVERY AT A CRIME SCENE

Source: D Reilly

A fingerprint expert usually receives his training in any bureau associated with a police agency's identification division. Learning how to compare 10 print cards to positively identify a submitted fingerprint record from a new arrest or a request for comparison with the division's records provides an extraordinary training venue for the specialist. After a few years of work as fingerprint technicians, the candidates will have the opportunity to examine thousands of records. They will become practiced at seeing thousands of examples of fingerprint details, the kinds of details needed to connect a sample from a crime scene to the one fingerprint of a known suspect. They will begin to coordinate their work with the Integrated Automated Fingerprint Identification System (IAFIS), a massive database of 10 print cards that are stock-piled in its identification files. Questioned prints from a crime scene are compared to fingerprints in the database using computer graphic technology, from which potential

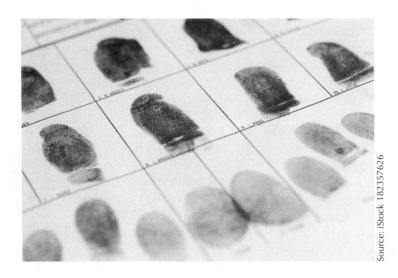

Source: iStock 182357626

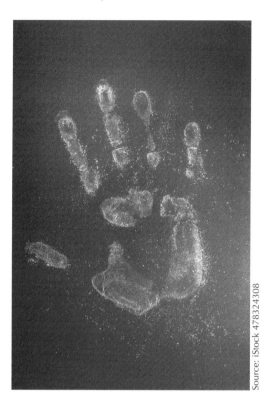

Source: iStock 47832408

positive identifications, or "hits," can be made. They will be examining these hits and making a final finding or conclusion to verify a full-blown identification. Eventually, when these technicians complete their training, they will begin to examine cases in which a particular suspect or group of suspects will have their known fingerprint cards compared with questioned samples recovered from a crime scene. They will also examine *major case fingerprint cards* (cards containing inked friction ridges on all parts of a suspect's hands, which include the palm area, the knuckle area, and the sides and blades of all ten fingers) from known suspects to ensure that their examination of a recovered partial print is not from the palm or knuckle area of a hand. Even footprints can be submitted by the investigator for comparison with the recovered questioned latent print from the crime scene. Finally, the well-trained experts will be tested and vetted to determine if they meet the standards to become expert witnesses in fingerprinting identification. From that point, the experts' positive identifications will be double-checked by at least two examiners so that if one is unavailable for trial, the other examiner will be able to testify.

SEROLOGICAL EVIDENCE:
BLOOD, SWEAT, SEMEN, AND OTHER BODILY FLUIDS

Biologists and serologists, who have academic expertise in bodily fluids, are the scientists who determine if the dried liquid evidence recovered from violent crime scenes is blood, sweat, urine, or semen. Among the ways they can test the blood are "presump-tive" examinations of human versus animal blood and then more detailed testing to determine the blood type (ABO factors) or, if the source is animal, determine what animal. If possible, the lab will need a control sample from the victim to ensure that any conclusions involve the likelihood that the victim was the donor of the unknown, or questioned, sample. Finally, the DNA extraction process, known as the polymerase chain reaction (PCR) technique, can provide a DNA profile that can be compared to the Combined DNA Index System (CODIS), which is an FBI-sponsored database that conducts computerized comparisons between crime scene DNA profiles and known DNA profiles from people arrested and charged with violent crimes and submitted under the rules of a particular jurisdiction for use in the database. Generally, for most government labs, a full examination of a blood sample for DNA can take anywhere from two to six weeks, so it is critical to provide a suspect's DNA as soon as possible for comparison with a questioned sample. Suspects' samples can be a mouth swab-bing, with particular attention to the inside upper cheek area to ensure the recovery of skin epithelium, which contains the DNA of the donor.

The future of biological evidence identification may involve the promising research in the area of human biome recovery. An "aura" of microbiotic life swirls around human beings. Nascent research indicates that this aura may be uniquely identifi-able with combinations of DNA profiling and microbiotic life forms. The aura may be the same for weeks at a time, which would allow the investigator to recover the sample from a crime scene and then compare the sample with a suspect's known hu-man biome aura if the suspect is identified shortly after the occurrence of the crime. As fantastic as this sounds, remember that in the 1970s, DNA identification was an impossible dream in all but a very few scientists' minds.

These experts will go through a process similar to their colleagues in the fingerprint lab with on-the-job training and experience. Their scientific work will be monitored. Once it is clear that they are well trained with the processes and the equipment needed for blood, sweat, urine, and semen examinations, under supervision, they will begin to handle cases. They will eventually make conclusions and be tested and vetted to reach a point where they are certified by the lab as experts in serology, DNA examination, and other biologically related disciplines.

One critical factor that the lead investigator needs to know about liquid evidence, such as bodily fluids, is that the evidence needs to be air-dried and stored in a clean, dry, and cool environment. The evidence should never be stored in plastic or metal. Paper bags, envelopes, sterile cotton swabs or balls, and blotter papers are the best recovery and storage materials for wet evidence. Samples of moist blood at a crime scene need to be recovered from multiple sites to make sure the blood is from a single source. Multiple blood stains for which it is unclear whether all the stains come from the same donor should be sampled and a careful log of the samples needs to be maintained. This kind of recovery should be the responsibility of the crime scene team, but the lead investigator should be aware of how the crime scene tech-nician handles the recovery. Again, once the samples are taken, it is best to let the blood or other moist bodily fluids dry by storing the samples in a porous container. Always remember that, for fluids, dry and cool environments avoid deterioration and contamination.

TRACE EVIDENCE: HAIRS AND FIBERS

Trace evidence is actually descriptive of a lot of microscopic material located in a crime scene. This material is not only barely visible; it is invisible. There are four ways it can be recovered at a crime scene: (1) The clothing of the victims of violent crime should be immediately recovered and secured in a large paper sack, such as a grocery sack. This way the clothing and the bag can be delivered to the lab for examination. A lab technician recovers the material by brushing or sweeping the clothing and the bag it is put in into a clear plastic container suitable for microscopic examination. (2) The material can be recovered from a scene by using a forensic vacuum cleaner. These vacuums come with a sterile filtration system, which is removed and treated as evidence until it is sterilized for reuse. It is essential that any trace evidence recovered from one crime scene never be cross-contaminated with trace evidence from another crime scene. Forensic vacuums are the best way to recover trace evidence from various locations in a crime scene because the sterile filtration apparatus can easily be used in one area and then sealed and replaced with a new filtration apparatus to be used in another venue at the scene. This makes the orderly recovery of trace evidence easy and protects from cross contamination. Again, the lead investigator will not be directly responsible for this evidence recovery method but should be familiar with the procedure so that a schematic of the recovery process can be made and the investigator will know from which areas the material came, which may be relevant to the investigation and subsequent trial. The next two methods of recovery are discussed in the order of their usefulness. (3) In the development and recovery of latent fingerprints, cellophane tape with industrial-grade glue is used to lift the fingerprint powder, which is used to turn a latent print into a visible print. This powder or dust placed on a shoe print or even a tire tread can be lifted by merely pressing the tape, glue side down, against the powder or dust. This tape comes in various sizes. It has a black-and-white backing that allows the lift to be recovered and then protected for storage by readhering the tape to the backing. This same tape can be used to recover trace evidence. It is more difficult to work with than the vacuum cleaner and adds the glue to the trace material recovered, but it is a workable solution for grabbing every bit of trace material that will adhere to the tape. It is recommended for use only if the vacuums are not available or there is a need to recover trace material separately in locations close to each other. (4) The last recovery method is a broom and a dustpan. Using this method is appropriate only if the material is easy to sweep up and the broom and the dustpan begin as sterile tools and are used only once in a single venue of a crime scene. This method is not recommended unless there is no other choice. It may require the crime scene technicians to purchase multiple brand-new brooms along with a control-sample broom to be evaluated to make sure the broom and dustpan are not contaminating the evidence.

Once the evidence is recovered, the hair and fiber technician can carefully examine the material and attempt to sort out one vacuuming and parse it into categories of material. These categories are soils, paints, hair, fur, synthetic fibers, and natural fibers. A high-powered microscope can be helpful in the initial examination, but the technician and eventually the expert examiner may use a scanning electron microscope or similar scientific instrument to thoroughly examine the items for any evidentiary value. The technicians and the expert examiners are academically trained scientists in the fields of biology, physics, chemistry, and other analytical disciplines. Again, they will conduct preliminary examinations until they can prove they can meet the standards required to be accepted as forensic experts in the field of microscopic analysis. Among the significant areas of examination are hair analysis and, if a root is available, the extraction of a DNA profile from the hair. There is an extraordinary future in this kind of forensic science. It may be that hair analysis, which is very general for making an identification, will at some point evolve into a more productive regimen for DNA recovery and extraction. A future scientific process known as *hair proteomics* suggests that analyzing genetic material and determining the protein makeup will yield a unique and identifiable profile. This would make hair analysis from a crime scene as important and suspect specific as blood or semen. Three laboratory machines currently used for forensic analysis are the centrifuge, gas chromatograph, and mass spectrometer. These very expensive tools are the workhorses of this process and many other analyses done in various disciplines in the modern forensic lab. The following pictures are of a mass spectrometer and a gas chromatograph.

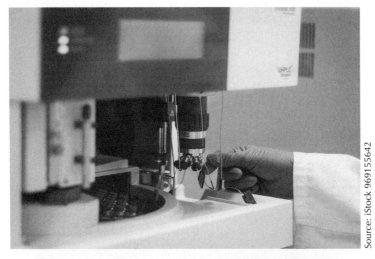

Source: iStock 969155642

Source: iStock 155368056

Scientific research on new methods for advancing the exploitation of evidence recovered from crime scenes is an ongoing and very exciting field for forensic research. Tools such as the mass spectrometer, the scanning electron microscope, and the DNA sequencer, pictured below, are the advanced machinery that forensic labs are relying on for future breakthroughs in identifying evidence.

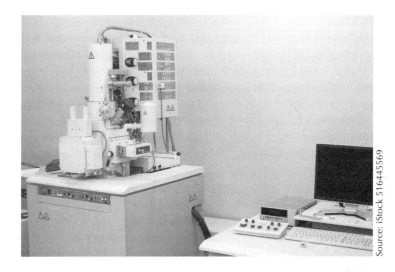

Source: iStock 51645569

Source: Urban Zone / Alamy Stock Photo B2M078

The mass spectrometer and the scanning electron microscope are able to analyze materials for qualitative and quantitative profiles. They use extreme magnification and spectral analysis to observe and document unique characteristics that can determine origin, compare with other substances, and create profiles that may provide clues of value to an investigation. The sequencer can magnify or expand the DNA sample taken from a degraded or less-than-ideal evidence sample and thus allow for the production of an accurate DNA profile.

Personal Experience

In my career in the FBI, I began my work in the FBI laboratory. I was a photographic and document analyst, but I also distributed evidence throughout the lab for analysis by various units. This work occurred in the 1970s, just before the forensic use of DNA profiles was accepted as a viable method to identify the donor of serological material. By 1985, the early method of DNA extraction was in use, but a typical DNA examination of bodily fluids could take a year to complete. The evolution of the process was extraordinary, and by the early 1990s, DNA examinations were as significant as fingerprint and ballistic examinations. I changed my career path in 1979 and became a criminal investigator instead of a lab analyst. By the time the 1990s came along, DNA examinations were routine exploitations of crime scene evidence, so it is likely that over the next twenty years, all sorts of advances in scientific research will be developed. The evolution of crime scene examination and the discovery of new and better methods to identify suspects and use those scientific examinations to solve previously unsolved cases will provide the criminal investigator with new tools to find the truth. It is therefore essential for the investigator to keep up with the advances in forensic science to ensure that all the resources available are brought to bear on an investigation.

BALLISTIC EVIDENCE: GUNS, RIFLES, BULLETS, AMMUNITION, AND TOOLMARKS

Firearms, burglary tools, and any metal tool or part that is used to commit a crime can be examined and analyzed to determine the exact weapon or tool that was used as an instrumentality of a crime. Firearms and toolmark experts are scientists, many with advanced degrees in physics and similar disciplines, who handle the ballistic examinations and tool scratching or marking examinations required on physical evidence recovered from a crime scene. The process of preparing an academically trained scientist to take on this work and develop into an expert is similar to the training paths of the previously discussed experts in a forensic lab. For the most part, these specialists rely on the side-by-side technique of examination to make their conclusions. In 1929, following the St. Valentine's Day Massacre in "gangland" Chicago, members of the Purple Gang in Detroit, Michigan, were developed as suspects. The suspects were hired by Al Capone to carry out the massacre of a rival bootleg gang that Capone wanted to destroy. Capone, of course, was never charged, but as a result of some excellent police work, the weapons used in the massacre were recovered. Calvin Goddard and Phillip Gravelle (forensic ballistic experts), for the first time, used new techniques to microscopically examine the firing pin marks on the shell casings and the striations on the bullets fired and recovered from the victims and the scene of the massacre. The tool used to make this side-by-side comparison was the newly invented comparison microscope. That tool is still a state-of-the-art device used by firearms experts. An example of the scope is depicted in the following picture.

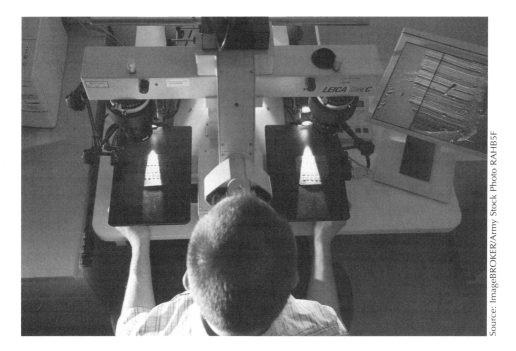

It is a relatively simple tool that has two stages with split optics so that the two pieces of evidence can be viewed simultaneously: a known sample, such as a bullet fired into a recovery tank, and a questioned sample recovered from a crime scene. The known sample, a pristine bullet fired under laboratory conditions, can be compared visually with a questioned sample, a bullet recovered from a crime scene or from the victim of a crime. The comparison microscope allows the examiner to line up the two items under examination so that marks, striations, or scratches can be compared for similarities or differences. As depicted above.

Ballistics or firearms examiners use other tools in the lab to examine the metallic composite in bullets and/or shell casings to determine the manufacturer. These examiners will also conduct chemical analyses using a scanning electron microscope to determine if the sample of material found on the hands of a suspect immediately after a shooting crime includes the elements barium and antimony along with lead residue. If these elements are present, they constitute evidence of gunshot residue, or GSR. This result is evidence that the person from whom the GSR was obtained was present and close to a firearm when it was fired. This test was mistakenly considered unreliable in the 1970s and 1980s because of factors that had little to do with its scientific basis. The gunshot test was overused and samples from suspects were sloppily gathered, which led to a number of false results. When the test is done properly under the supervision of a firearms expert, it can be helpful in an investigation.

The criminal investigator needs to understand the work of firearms experts to ensure that all of the examinations that can be done in conjunction with a crime where a firearm is used are applied to the case. Since the side-by-side comparison is effective with bullets and shell casings, it is equally effective when comparing tools that make marks on metal to determine if a particular tool was used as a burglary tool or pry bar to enter a safe or any number of other uses a criminal might find for carrying out a crime. Associate the tool with a suspect and then determine if that tool can be associated with the crime.

OTHER WEAPONS: KNIVES, BLUNT-FORCE OBJECTS, AND MISCELLANEOUS CUTTING INSTRUMENTS

Metallurgy is another scientific discipline with its own expert forensic scientists who can determine important characteristics about murder and assault weapons used in a crime. Minute metallic particles recovered from crime scenes or the bodies of victims can be examined to connect a weapon recovered from a suspect with the questioned evidence recovered from the crime. Metallurgic forensic experts undergo the same process as do the other expert scientists mentioned in the other disciplines to acquire the proper academic credentials. The tools used by the metallurgist are the scanning electron microscope, mass spectrometer, and other state-of-the-art tools that qualitatively and quantitatively analyze physical evidence.

TOXICOLOGY: DRUGS, POISONS, AND SUSPICIOUS SUBSTANCES THAT NEED TO BE QUALITATIVELY AND QUANTITATIVELY ANALYZED

Almost all well-sourced crime labs can conduct examinations for toxic substances. The material to be examined comes from a wide range of substances found during an investigation, at the crime scene, during the interview and investigative process, and during the follow-up on leads that carry the investigator to locations where physical evidence may be secreted or held for storage. When discovered, poisons, compounds used for bombs, illegal drugs, and a whole range of unknown substances, which may become relevant material in a criminal investigation, need to be analyzed. Again, the analysis of these substances can be done by chemists, physicists, and a range of scientists who are or will become forensic experts in the fields of toxicology and chemical analysis. The Drug Enforcement Administration (DEA) maintains well-resourced regional laboratories with toxicology experts, who are academically trained chemists, whose primary responsibility is the examination of drugs found during investigations. These labs are a valuable part of most law enforcement agencies' efforts to stem the tide of illegal drug distribution. The examiners are routinely called upon to testify in court about the illegal drugs recovered during the course of thousands of criminal investigations for federal, state, and local agencies. These labs can also compare the chemical makeup of illegal drugs recovered over an entire region and offer important intelligence about the source of the drugs, something that is especially helpful in heroin and methamphetamine cases. Designer drugs, such as MDMA (also called Ecstasy or Molly), and steroids and other performance-enhancing drugs (PEDs) will also have unique chemical characteristics, which can provide important investigative leads as to their source. Even cocaine and marijuana, which are natural substances, can be examined for this kind of comparison.

Most full-service crime labs will also be able to handle the toxicological work needed to provide expert testimony about substances found during the course of investigations, but the DEA lab has the extra benefit of having a huge inventory of cases from the region and the expertise from national resources to provide the broader analysis required in major drug trafficking investigations.

MEDICAL EXAMINER: PATHOLOGIST AND CORONER

As previously discussed, the medical examiner is an essential part of any homicide investigation. Medical examiners in most jurisdictions are medical doctors who specialize in pathology, which is the field of medicine that studies the causes of death and diseases. The pathologist who then focuses her studies on forensics relating to the cause of death can be certified as a medical expert when the cause of death is part of the issue that is argued. The primary examination conducted by a medical examiner is the autopsy. In order for a homicide investigation to go forward, the medical examiner must rule a cause of death that is consistent with homicide. For example, the medical examiner determines that a person died of a heart attack, which in most cases, is a natural cause of death, but he may go one step further and rule that the heart attack was caused by the stress of being robbed, assaulted, or raped, thus making the case a criminal matter. So the medical examiner's ruling is a critical and necessary element of proof required in a criminal case of homicide. There are a number of cases when the ruling is undetermined because the body is so degraded or disturbed by outside elements that the actual cause cannot be determined. It is up to the investigator to find out what happened and to ensure that the cause is developed as a result of investigative findings. This is a high bar, but having a scientific ruling of homicide clears the path for the investigation.

Since medical examiners have the authority to rule on the cause of death, they are considered to be government employees and must be approved by the jurisdiction in which they are employed. In large urban centers, the medical examiner may have a staff of assistant medical examiners and technologists who are also employed by the jurisdiction. The primary reason for the large staff is the number of deaths that have to be examined, autopsied, and ruled on. A number of jurisdictions in the United States maintain an elected official known as the coroner. In many cases, the coroner is a medical doctor but does not have to be, so a coroner can establish official proceedings when a ruling or determination as to the cause of death is made. These coroners can rely on an officially sanctioned pathologist for assistance in the ruling. Regardless of the way the system is staffed, the criminal investigator needs to have the case ruled as a homicide or as undetermined to proceed with the criminal investigation.

It is necessary for the lead investigators routinely involved in homicide investigations to have a cordial and professional relationship with the medical examiner or whoever performs autopsies on cases being worked. Usually, the lead investigator is

OFFICE OF THE ARMED FORCES MEDICAL EXAMINER

ME#:_____
Date:_____

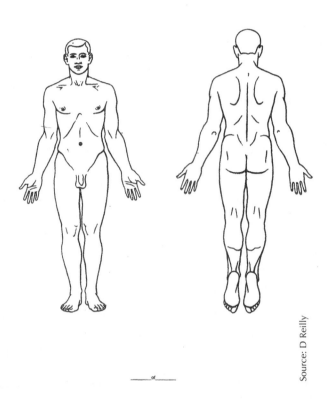

Source: D Reilly

_____of_____

required to observe the autopsy so that essential information from the examination can be passed on to the investigation. Items such as bullet size, trajectory, and closeness to the victim may be revealed. The length, width, and thickness of a knife or cutting instrument used to kill the victim may be determined. Even important information about the size, weight, and material elements or compounds of a blunt-force weapon used to kill a person may be passed on to the investigator at the autopsy. The last meal the victim ate or the premortem use of drugs, medicines, or other items of interest will be determined. It usually takes time to obtain a full toxicology report for the victim, but the positive relationship between the medical examiner and the lead investigator will facilitate the transmittal of this information in a timely fashion. It is also helpful for the lead investigator to get a full copy of the autopsy with a chart that details wounds and evidence of self-defense as an important and reliable schematic for use in future interviews. See the chart above as an example.

Medical examiners or their technicians will usually be available to respond at the scene of homicide. This can allow certain immediate preliminary findings that may be of assistance to the investigation. The amount of rigor or the lividity analysis of the victim may help in a preliminary finding of the time of death and whether the corpse was moved postmortem. The temperature of the body and the ambient temperature at the crime scene are also important indicators for determining the time of death. The preautopsy findings are just preliminary, but they may provide information that can be useful during the first step of the investigative plan (see chapter 8).

Ultimately, it is the medical examiner's responsibility to ensure the victim is positively identified via a fingerprint search, a forensic comparison with medical and dental records, or a DNA profile comparison. Contact with the victim's next of kin is usually facilitated by the lead investigator in coordination with the medical examiner for the conclusive identification by the family.

DOCUMENTARY MATERIAL: BOOKS, RECORDS, PHOTOGRAPHS, DIGITAL INFORMATION AND DATA, AND PATTERN EVIDENCE

Questioned document examinations are conducted in most full-service crime labs throughout the country. It usually takes two to three years of full-time examination of documentary, handwriting, printing, word processing, and forgery examinations for a skilled document technician to become a court-approved expert. The academic background of these experts can vary greatly. Persons with an academic background in art, photography, or computer analysis and even a standard degree in a liberal arts discipline may become qualified experts in this field. Questioned document examinations are one of the oldest fields in criminalistics or forensics. Check fraud and all manner of bank and business criminal schemes have involved phony documents, from completely made up certificates to valueless bonds and bad checks. Therefore, it is critical for an expert to examine the handwriting, printing, and paper upon which the document was made to make certain important conclusions about the origins and the manufacturing of the fraudulent materials. These schemes go back as far in history as a time when paper certificates were invented to replace or represent money. Counterfeiting of currency is its own separate discipline and is currently primarily the responsibility of the US Secret Service. As a result of its responsibility, the Secret Service maintains the most significant anticounterfeiting crime lab in the world, which also examines and analyzes an entire range of counterfeit and fraudulent documents in a variety of criminal investigations in major white collar crime cases.

The FBI's questioned document lab examines fraudulent materials from similar high-end fraud scheme cases, but it also conducts thorough examinations of questioned documents used to further kidnapping cases, extortion cases, and other violent assaults when threats against victims are transmitted to the victim on paper or by other graphic media. This kind of questioned document analysis is also carried out by many of the state, regional, and local forensic crime labs throughout the country. The extent of the analysis is usually based on the expertise and budgetary resources available to these government laboratories. Additionally, there are a number of questioned document and handwriting experts working as private contractors. Many of these experts handle both criminal and civil matters. They have even developed expertise in the commercial autograph market and the historical document verification field.

Pattern identification, or shoe print and tire tread examinations are housed in the FBI's Questioned Documents Unit. A similar placement of pattern identification into the Questioned Documents Unit occurs in other government crime labs. This happens because the analysis of print and tread patterns is very compatible with questioned document work. The lab experts come for similar educational backgrounds and are trained to detect nonrecurring anomalies that can be observed in questioned samples and finding the same anomalies on known samples. The storage and updating of reference files for shoe and tire manufacturers are also closely aligned with comparing questioned documents with reference files established for fraudulent checks and extortion notes. Systematically and process-wise, the work is similar and yields similar kinds of results. Shoe prints recovered from a crime scene can be determined to match a particular shoe manufacturer's sole pattern. Tire treads recovered in the form of solid plaster casting or an inked or photographed print can be associated with a tire manufacturer. Either of these two conclusions can be very helpful in the early stages of a criminal investigation. Eventually, a more specific examination can be conducted if specific shoes or tires are seized as evidence. Unique characteristics observable by the examiner of a questioned and known sample can lead to a positive identification of a particular pair of shoes or a tire.

The FBI's responsibility in a wide range of investigations has established its forensic role in single-image photogrammetry (determining heights and lengths of people or objects from photographs), portrait identification, facial recognition, and digital photography analysis. Comparison and analysis of photographs as to their origin, even the GPS location of where the picture was taken, and the evaluation of evidence using the broad range of forensic photography occur in this unit. Preparing high- and super-high-resolution photographic images, with infrared, infrared luminescence, and ultraviolet luminescence, takes place in the forensic photographic unit, which supports the sciences in other parts of the crime lab. So along with alternative light photography, the lab uses video spectral comparator technology to exploit physical evidence for unique and identifiable factors that verify investigative or scientific features that may be relevant to an investigation. Finally, the FBI and most document/photographic units involved in forensic examinations assist criminal investigators in determining the best methods for surveillance photography and other covert uses of photography, videography, and specialized night-capable photography.

COMPUTER ANALYSIS

Computers, including laptops, desktops, smartphones, and thousands of other computer modules that control utility plants, automobile engines, aircraft engines, bank data, identification data, and almost every kind of manufacturing and financial institution, are an ever-present reality for the criminal investigator. The internet was the natural evolution of computer interconnectivity going back to the 1950s; however, ARPANET, which was the precursor to the internet, began in the 1960s. The internet's performance as it exists today began in the early 1990s, and commercial internet service providers (ISPs) also began during that time frame. The biggest leap in computer technology occurred with the invention of the microprocessor in 1970. This invention began the miniaturization of computers and computer technology. Computer programmers and software specialists were able to incorporate a range of algorithms (the instructions and rules creating new and improved methods of communication, mechanical performance, and data storage). Eventually, all of these advances have created an industry devoted to invention and distribution of information. All of this innovation has created a digital world that is fully understood by only a few computer scientists. Hackers, programmers, and digital geniuses can take advantage of these new technologies, but for the most part, the average person has come to rely on the technology for communication and information. The average person also accepts that financial transactions, even day-to-day purchases, can be easily and safely facilitated by this technology. Some of these average persons have added skills in computer security. Encryption of personal files and protections on personal computer devices are the norm for many persons who rely on computer technology in their everyday lives.

This technology is so ubiquitous that the average person and the average criminal tend to maintain aspects of their daily lives on their computer devices. Address books, photographs, and even GPS coordinates for where someone takes pictures or makes phone calls are embedded in a person's files. Notes, Word documents, email, and text communications are obtained and stored in enormous amounts of data files protected by passwords, double access codes, and encryption. Laptops, desktops, and tablets are devices that are readily available to everyone at very low prices. Thousands of documents and images can be maintained on these devices for weeks, months, and years without filling the enormous storage capacities of the newer devices. In the past few years, cloud storage, or secure memory "facilities" physically located separate from the device in third-party data centers, is immediately accessible to the user. The user establishes an account and leases or has access to the cloud by a storage facilitator, who maintains huge data storage centers with computer servers at centralized locations away from the user and his computer devices. This means that private information that a person gathers or wants to keep away from her own devices can be kept under "lock and key" for recovery whenever needed by the user/account holder.

All of these storage operations are also available to smartphone owners. So in effect, enormous amounts of information, which can have a significant impact on a criminal investigation, is secreted away in very secure and private locations, many times out of reach of an investigator, even when the investigator has probable cause to recover and examine the material. In the predigital world, a search warrant executed at a residence or business could easily yield all the information about a suspect's financial dealings, address book, and personal correspondence and any photographs, videos, or sketches. Documentary evidence, which may be important evidence in a criminal investigation, is now stored digitally on the new user-friendly devices, not in traditional file cabinets, desks, and other similar furniture. The stored data is not the only problem for an investigator. Smartphones and computers of all sorts are used to facilitate crimes, such as murder, extortion, assault, rape, armed robbery, and larceny.

For years, criminal investigators have been able to overcome all of these issues in the so-called analog world. Heavy safes storing secret documents, money, and jewelry can be opened using brute force or sophisticated safecracking techniques.

Landline telephones can be tapped. Photographs, address books, and other documentary evidence can be removed from business locations and home addresses with a search warrant. Even cell phones can be seized and examined for some data, and the toll records and call details can be obtained by a grand jury subpoena to the phone service provider. In other words, evidence of criminal activity that is documentary or photographic in nature is accessible. If it is necessary to intercept communications by phone or letter or face-to-face, there is a way to do that in the criminal justice system. Title III affidavits for wiretaps or office bugs can be frustrated by criminals who throw away their phones every month. Smartphones containing all manner of relevant evidence, which may include a video of a crime in process, can be secured against intrusion by the police even if it is known to be stored on the phone. All of the new technology requires a "reboot" for criminal investigators so they can anticipate what is needed and seek the necessary support from IT professionals who can help solve the questions. Now, it is a "brave new world," which demands more specialized knowledge on the part of the criminal investigator. Unfortunately, this is the kind of specialized knowledge that requires an academic degree in computer science. That degree has to be enhanced by training and practice with all manner of software and computer hardware. The specialized training also involves the new world of "telephony," which is the analysis of how the smartphone systems work and what the best approach is for obtaining the account and phone usage data for personally owned smartphones, disposable phones, and sophisticated systems that redirect phone calls over several networks. On top of all that, the criminal investigator has to develop methods to ensure that the data stored on all the personal computing devices is protected against security software that immediately destroys or deletes the files if there is any effort made to recover the files by a person other than the owner. To put it bluntly, computer technology is evolving faster than laws and law enforcement. What the Fourth Amendment and the *Katz v. United States* case said about which storage facilities are constitutionally protected is in flux. The right to protection against unreasonable searches has expanded to include a "reasonable expectation of privacy." The device is separately protected from a home or business. Devices are protected in the same fashion as homes; but as a result of a commercial contract between the smartphone owner or the private computer owner and the company from which he purchased or leased the device, there is a newer form of protection for the suspect and the company's right to privacy and/or the right to protect the privacy of a customer. Law enforcement was able to enjoin the confidential assistance of phone companies, especially when the crime was a serious offense and someone's life might be in jeopardy. That level of cooperation has eroded. Even device manufacturers refuse to break faith with their customers; they will not share vital information, such as documents, images, and digital files, which may and often are evidence of a crime, even with law enforcement who have probable cause. Cell phone marketers have expanded the number of service providers; some of these providers are slow to respond to subpoenas for basic toll service records, or they limit their storage of these records so that many of the records needed in criminal investigations are deleted. Consider the example of a homicide suspect who was identified six to eight months after the killing, following a long investigation. Relevant cell phone records for calls that occurred at the time immediately prior to the killing or even at the time of the crime might have been deleted in the routine practice of certain providers.

A lack of clarity about what is available from computer and cell phone companies and can be accessed for an investigation, together with the fact that digital information of value is less available and can even be lost, create frustration. This evidence is lost or difficult to recover because the investigator doesn't stay well informed on a regular basis of advances and changes in the technology. Also, consider the courts' decisions that overrule or establish new rules of privacy that make it more difficult to access the information. Finally, add to all of that computer manufacturers' desire to please their customers and come down on the side of device privacy versus the lives and well-being of the community. In the past, if law enforcement's interest was reasonable and a third party knew how to access evidence but refused to facilitate that recovery, the company was liable for obstruction of justice. Companies should not be able to hide behind a right of privacy the Constitution never considered.

In most law enforcement agencies, computer scientists with the expertise needed to provide investigative support for cases exist as separate units involved in intelligence exploitation, but certain forensic specialists are part of separate units responsible for analyzing and exploiting digital data from the devices used in the furtherance of criminal activity. These scientists use their skills in programming and platform development to explain information from a particular device and translate the information to reveal relevant evidence. They break down programming algorithms, crack security codes, and trace locations of URLs (Uniform Resource Locaters) and websites and ISP information used by criminals in the furtherance of their criminal activity. They also work to identify the telephone networks. With the tracing of sim card identifiers, they are able to develop insight about disposable phones. Some of the security processes available for smartphone users can be defeated if necessary when the investigator develops probable cause and legally facilitates the bypassing of the encryption software that keeps the evidence hidden from the investigator.

Finally, as these computer experts are confronted with ever more sophisticated digital platforms, it will become necessary to create effective methods for downloading evidentiary material from shared internet platforms and to determine if the criminal investigator can have access to information that may assist in anticipating behavior or identifying targets related to a criminal subject. Gang and organized crime subjects will use these shared platforms as methods to communicate with each other and carry out plans, suggest future crimes, and even brag about past crimes. At this stage of development, there are computerized formulas that can exploit information from a variety of internet sources and compare the information with law enforcement–sensitive information to create a new and more substantial profile of a suspect in a proactive investigation. Legal questions will have to answered, but many of these legal issues can be overcome by internet-based covert investigation. Here are two examples of legal, albeit surreptitious, methods to recover data from a target on social platforms: (1) Develop a profile matching a gang member's friends on Facebook, and simply ask to be listed as a friend. (2) Determine if an active and reliable confidential source can fill the requirement as a friend on a social network. Newer and more challenging problems in digital technology should be anticipated. Ultimately, the newer technology will have two components: One will be user-friendly and easily understood by an average consumer, and the other will be a more "geeky," or sophisticated, aspect that can be exploited only by a trained expert. This is why the criminal investigator needs to have a productive working relationship with the computer forensics expert.

SUMMARY

New students in criminal investigations studies consider the impact of forensic sciences on the solvability of crimes as being the highest priority and the area that is most reliable and liable to provide the proof needed to find the truth. After years of working criminal investigations, most veteran investigators can point to only a few cases when forensic science "made the case." It is a fact that witnesses, victims, and everyone else involved in an investigation can be wrong, mistaken, or imprecise. It is also a fact that when physical evidence is examined by a competent scientist, the results can be right, precise, and scientifically certain. These two facts don't mean that witnesses and victims are always unreliable; nor does it mean that there will always be physical evidence that informs an investigation. As defined in chapter 1, criminal investigation is a multifaceted examination of a coalition of facts and evidence. In every investigation, it is essential to gather the physical evidence and have that evidence examined by a forensic expert, but that doesn't mean the results will satisfy or answer a question or argument at issue. In most cases, the results are neutral or predictable based on the facts presented by the witnesses. A spouse who is suspected in a homicide will logically leave DNA, fingerprints, hair, and textile fibers at the crime scene. That person lives with and has intimate contact with the victim. The scientific results will hardly be helpful or instructive in the investigation.

There always has to be a balance between the forensic science results and the facts asserted by the victim and the witnesses. One discipline in an investigation has to support another discipline, which is the dynamic that must be considered when an investigation is worked. We will be discussing interviewing witnesses in chapter 13. Part of the method to assess the veracity of a witness and a victim is to compare their statements with the physical evidence from the crime scene and the scientific results and ensure that any variation is accounted for and resolved. Scientific facts are great crutches for propping up a theory of a crime, but if the results are inadequate, the whole theory should not be dismissed. The investigator needs to find a method to prove the theory without the benefit that may derive from the physical evidence. In those cases (and there will be many) that lack physical evidence, the requirement to solve the case by finding the truth doesn't end; lack of physical evidence simply means the investigator has one less tool that he can use to make the case. The investigator is required to follow up with every piece of evidence, including the physical evidence or material associated with the crime scene even if that evidence has no real effect on the outcome of the investigation. It is therefore necessary to treat every investigation as if it had important physical evidence and any physical evidence as if it could yield important and relevant information. In this way, the handling of physical evidence and how a crime scene is examined will follow the necessary and proper procedures in every investigation. You don't quit interviewing witnesses when you think they have nothing to say, forgo working with the crime victim when you think she has nothing to add, or disregard physical evidence because it may not provide the results you want. Prioritizing all of these aspects of an investigation establishes a working protocol that eventually becomes the best method for checking off all the boxes in any given case and ensuring that there is no rush to judgment or some kind of theoretical rabbit hole that flusters a case. Finally, even negative forensic results allow the criminal investigator to narrow the field of suspects and the field of theories and helps him focus his efforts on what is needed and possible.

Chapter Eleven

Administrative Procedures

Case files, murder book, homicide jacket, and the protocol that is followed to document an investigation.

Throughout this book, we have discussed documents, reports, results, timelines, interviews, sketches, diagrams, and photographs. Each of these items will need to be compiled in an investigative folder or case jacket in a fashion that is similar to the process done each time cases are documented for a particular agency. The FBI has a certain protocol and names forms with alphanumeric designations, which allows a person who is reviewing the file to immediately understand what she is reviewing. For this text it would be counterproductive to try to cover all the administrative procedures, paperwork, and investigative reports that are compiled by the thousands of investigative agencies that conduct criminal investigations. The FBI has the FD 302; the Drug Enforcement Administration (DEA), the DEA 6; and the Washington, DC, police, the PD 123, all of which are reports of investigations, including statements by witnesses, and they are so similar the value of distinction is lost. So for this chapter, we will discuss the general categories of material that should be segmented in an investigative file.

INVESTIGATIVE FILE CATEGORIES

Section 1: Victim Interviews

All victim statements, especially the interviews that detail the crime from beginning to end, such as those documenting a rape, a robbery, or serious assault case, should take a prominent place in the case file to ensure that the best summary of the facts in the case are readily accessible for review and pretrial discovery.

Section 2: Witness Interviews

All civilian witness statements, especially those detailing the crime as it occurred, should be documented in this section of the case file. The testimonial evidence proving the crime occurred is the essential part of this section. Eventually, witnesses whose information is not necessarily testimonial evidence verifying the crime will be in this section of the case file. These are witnesses who prove motive, the recovery of contraband, the possession of or access to a weapon used, or other similar testimony proving or verifying some important relevant facts that sustain the argument proving the case. It is necessary to have immediate access to the information provided by all the persons that are expected to testify. This section of the case file will have names, contact information, and addresses for the civilian witnesses. Depending on the agency or department requirements, these statements may be in a question-and-answer format, a handwritten signed and witnessed formal document composed by the witness, or an audio or video file of the statement in the form of an interview between the witness and the investigator. It may be best to organize the witness statements as a running log with summaries to allow for appropriate access to the general contact information and an evaluation of each witness.

Section 3: Crime Scene Reports

This section of the file will contain the report from the crime scene or evidence recovery technicians as well as copies of the crime scene photographs, hand-drawn sketches, and any other graphic representations for the examination. These items would include videos and any informal photographs taken by investigators assigned to the case. The report may also contain suggestions by the technician or the team to have certain evidence examined by the appropriate experts in the crime lab. Some agencies and departments leave the transmission of evidence and lab requests for examinations to the crime scene technician, so transmittal requests may also be part of this section of the file.

Section 4: Physical Evidence, Evidence Logs, and Chains of Custody

A comprehensive list of physical evidence, including latent fingerprint lifts, pattern lifts, sterile swabbings, and vacuumings recovered at the crime scene, is part of this section of the file. Subsequent to the original crime scene examination, there may be recoveries of physical evidence by the crime scene team or the investigators. These recovery reports and a comprehensive inventory should be maintained in this section of the file.

A detailed evidence log with a copy of the chain of custody for each item may also be part of this section. The actual formal chain of custody should be kept with each piece of physical evidence. An evidence log will also be maintained by the evidence control unit or center, wherever the evidence will be stored for safekeeping until trial or disposition.

Section 5: Contraband Evidence

When valuable property or drugs are recovered in an investigation, special handling by the evidence clerk or administrator may be required. It is normal that drug evidence and valuable property are maintained in special secure vaults. Again, the chain of custody of the material will be kept with the exhibit, but a more secure process is instituted to make sure the evidence is not tampered with or pilfered.

Section 6: Firearms Evidence and Weapons Reports Recovered throughout the Investigation

Any firearms recovered during an investigation also require special handling. The handling requires making the weapon safe for storage and transport. The weapon will be placed in a secure container and may also be stored for safekeeping in a special vault or secure facility.

Section 7: Letters and Memoranda That Summarize the Investigation

Investigative summaries required by the department or agency may need to be produced at certain intervals throughout the investigation. They may also be required to have investigative or financial resources approved to support the investigation. There may even be a need to produce a summary for travel outside the jurisdiction or to obtain approval to work with an outside investigative agency. These reports and summaries should be maintained in a separate section of the investigative file.

Section 8: Timelines and Charts That Provide Investigative Summaries

In complicated investigations, there may be a need to prepare charts or graphic summaries of an investigation. These charts can be simplified representations as to when certain milestones or events happened in an investigation and contain details of when and where suspects, victims, and witnesses were present. The case summaries may be a point-by-point evolution of a crime with information about planning, coordination of the suspects or co-conspirators, coordination of instrumentalities, and an explanation as to how the fruits of a crime were converted, sold, fenced, or otherwise disposed of by the suspects. These kinds of charts are usually prepared at the end of an investigation, but there may be a need to prepare summaries and timelines before the investigation is complete to provide reliable exhibits to investigators and investigative team resource persons prior to the case being solved. Keeping these charts in a separate section of the investigative file keeps these administrative materials separate from reports and testimonial material. These kinds of charts may contain theoretical analysis and speculation based on unverified facts or suggestions.

Section 9: Interview and Investigative Notes

In most cases when an investigator conducts an interview or observes actions covertly or overtly by suspects or defendants, he will make handwritten notes. In the more recent past as a result of technology, these same kinds of recordings of investigative steps may be in the form of digital audio files or any of the newer methods of recording information using word processing. Handwritten notes and any of these digital representations of note-taking may be discoverable to the defense attorney in a trial. It is therefore practical to keep these notes in a separate part of an investigative file so they can be copied and turned over when required. In some courts, these notes will become evidence, so their chain of custody will be the investigator to the court. The investigator is creating this evidence, and it should be maintained in the custody of the investigator throughout the process of the investigation.

Section 10: Prosecutive Summaries

Some investigative agencies and criminal investigations require formal reports to the prosecutors. These reports may have copies of graphic depictions of physical evidence, surveillance photographs, and other photographic evidence depicting the crime in progress. Theses summaries will also have exhibits, such as victim, witness, and suspect interviews. Data evidence recovered as a result of grand jury subpoenas and any material that may become evidence in the trial are included to provide a potential prosecuting attorney with a complete investigative report, which establishes the proof and factual basis for charging subjects in a case and turning them into defendants. In many jurisdictions, these prosecutive reports are given in meetings with a potential prosecutor in which the investigator provides all of the above-mentioned copies of exhibits and gives a presentation of proof and the factual basis for charging a defendant. It is inappropriate at this critical juncture in an investigation to turn over actual evidence, so copies and photographs may suffice for the decision-making process that this report or face-to-face summary initiates. The formal prosecutive report or a memorandum documenting the meeting should be kept in this section of the investigative file. The prosecutor's formal response to the report or the meeting will also be maintained in this section. The prosecutor may simply authorize prosecution and suggest that the investigator create an affidavit to support an arrest warrant or authorize a grand jury investigation and name a time for the investigator to present the case to the grand jury for an indictment. The negative responses will also be detailed in this section. The prosecutor may request more investigation, with specific suggestions about facts that need to be proved, or simply state that she and her office decline prosecution. The details of this conversation between the lead investigator and the prosecutor should be carefully detailed and made a part of the investigative file.

Section 11: Mug Shots, Rap Sheets, and Criminal Histories of Victim Witnesses and Suspects

Every person who is identified over the course of a criminal investigation should be vetted with a criminal history check. Identification photographs or mug shots, a police rap sheet (list of arrests), and any other significant details from law enforcement–sensitive sources should be part of each person's packet and maintained in this section of the investigative file. If appropriate, Department of Motor Vehicle records or even ID photographs from interviews and passports can be included in this section so persons who are encountered during an investigation are positively identified and their backgrounds are known to the investigators. Suspects turn into witnesses, and witnesses turn into suspects. As such, the investigator needs to have the backgrounds on everyone encountered in a case and a logical place to maintain that information.

Section 12: Surveillance Photographs and Videos

Over the course of an investigation, the criminal investigators may have occasion to "set up on" and observe the actions of suspects in a case. These investigative surveillances should be conducted with a need to record or document what is observed in mind. Photographs taken with long-range telephoto lenses using covert techniques to observe without the suspect's knowledge provide a beneficial opportunity to "catch the suspect in the act." Of course, the act may simply be the commission of some purely innocent matter that is not relevant to the investigation, but even this surveillance should be the subject of an investigative report, which will be distributed into section 14 of the investigative file, which is where any covert actions done by the investigator are maintained.

Section 13: Audio Recordings

During the course of investigations, there may be opportunities to covertly record conversations between suspects and cooperating witnesses. There may also be the need to obtain a court-approved Title III electronic surveillance order. Any recordings obtained in the furtherance of a covert investigative step, such as using cooperating witnesses who consent to the government's recording a conversation between themselves and suspects in a criminal investigation, will be the subject of covert operations investigative reports, which will be maintained as a separate category of evidence. As a result of these recordings and/or a separate investigative strategy, the lead investigator may determine that the best method to obtain the evidence necessary in a criminal case is to target a phone, a place of business, or a residence for electronic monitoring. Title III of the 1968 Omnibus Crime Control Act and the Supreme Court decision in *Katz v. United States* allows for this possibility. There is a certain set of investigative requirements that have to be met, and the investigative support of such an investigative strategy is complicated. If the work is done to get the order and the investigation moves in that direction, the tape or digital recordings have to be maintained in the investigative file in a particular fashion with administrative controls established by the investigating agency. For the most part, these recordings are audio files, but there may be the need to capture the evidence using video surveillance. Video surveillance is also used in more routine surveillance operations, but those files will be maintained in section 12 of the investigative file.

Section 14: Covert Operations, including Surveillance Reports

Examples of overt investigative operations are gathering physical evidence at a crime scene, interviewing victims and witnesses, conducting ongoing interviews, and continuing an ongoing obvious search for material facts, data, and contraband along with the normal steps used to recover additional physical evidence. Covert operations are the less-obvious misdirections or planned insertions of operatives who are tasked with recovering evidence in a more secret or confidential manner. Specific methods of covert operations in criminal investigations will be discussed in more detail in chapter 17, such as undercover operations, long-term or extensive use of physical surveillance, the use of cooperating witnesses to conduct conversations, and transactions with suspects in a case. All major criminal enterprise investigations require other more carefully planned and resourced strategies. These covert operations may be so extensive as to require a number of new and more detailed case file categories. But for purposes of this discussion on how the average case file is broken down, section 14 will have the summaries and investigative underpinnings along with reports and results directly affecting the covert operations needed in a normal case. There will also be underlying reports and logs detailing the gathering of audio and video evidence, photographic surveillance reports, testimonial reports of covert actions taken during an investigation or potential testimonial reports summarized, and the methods used to procure the covert evidence. There is little chance that any normal covert operation in a criminal case will be subject to any extraordinary judicial review except in a case where some kind of coercion is suspected by law enforcement against the defendant or entrapment of the defendant is alleged. Methods and sources in a covert operation should be protected, and operational information about the way a covert operation is conducted should be kept confidential.

SPECIFIC INVESTIGATIVE
CONCERNS WITH ADMINISTRATIVE CONTROLS

The fourteen sections of the investigative file are most of the administrative segments that should be identified and sorted for each case. Some of these categories may never be used, especially if there is never a need for any covert operations or there is no physical evidence recovered in the investigation, but it is necessary to make the categories instructive to a person who needs to review an investigation. The segment or case subfiles may also need to be expanded to include subfiles for special investigative events. This requirement begs the question "Who needs to review my work?" Well, in truth, many people need to review the case. The management of the law enforcement agency needs to make a periodic case review to ensure that work is being completed and manpower is sufficient for the progress of the investigation. These kinds of file reviews are both helpful and demanding. If management personnel are concerned that no progress is apparent in an investigation and then they review the case file and determine that a considerable amount of blood, sweat, and tears has gone into the case, sometimes they will suggest ways they can help or offer suggestions the lead investigator may not have considered. The truth is that most of the supervisory personnel of a law enforcement agency are made up of veteran investigators who can provide some needed insight. In chapter 4 on teamwork, we discussed the productive relationship between partners and squad members and that the case file allows the members of that team to have immediate access for review of the file to provide whatever insight they may have. Beyond these two levels of review, it is not a good idea to allow easy access for anyone in the agency to review. The military and national defense concept of restricting information to those persons who have need to know protects unnecessary and sloppy distribution of law enforcement–sensitive material. Even the most innocent release of information can put victims or witnesses at risk and embolden criminals to act against or counter to an investigative strategy. Even releasing the name of the lead investigator can cause harm to an investigation. So criminal investigative files need to be kept in a controlled and secure environment. The release of the information from these files needs to be restricted to only those persons who need that information. Finally, the files need to be secured to protect vulnerable witnesses, persons associated with the case, and techniques being used in the investigation.

The next level of review and one of the most important reasons for having a well-ordered and comprehensive file is the fact that the lead investigator in any investigation may change at any time. Most criminal investigators are passionate about their cases. They consider their cases to be personal challenges and puzzles that only they can solve. In the real world of law enforcement, cases have a way of being transferred, placed in pending inactive status, or even closed, only to be reopened much later when new evidence is discovered. The new investigator needs to be able to pick up the jacket, find the categories she expects to find, and conduct a thorough review of the investigation to move the case forward with new eyes and a new resolve. Administrative oversight, reassignment, and team support are excellent reasons to create a well-ordered case file and to make that file consistent with other case files for that agency or department.

CASE FILE SECURITY

In our discussions so far, we have made references to files, reports, statements, and numerous other written documents that are on paper and seem to be the results of an analog world. That is because courts throughout the country and many investigative jurisdictions still rely on what is referred to as hard copies of these documents. The fact is that most investigative jurisdictions are transitioning to some kind of paperless digital filing system. Hard copies of case files can be secured by maintaining the file, or "jacket," in a locked file cabinet safe or some other secure facility inside the police department or investigative agency. Normally, that kind of security procedure would suffice to protect the case files from unauthorized access.

The most obvious question is, Why do case files need to be secure? To answer the question, it is necessary to realize that any release of information from an investigative file could have a negative effect on the outcome of the investigation. Suspects who become aware they are suspects may go back, literally and figuratively, to the crime event to try to change any mistakes they made or kill or intimidate any witnesses to their crime. They may threaten or attempt to bribe criminal justice employees who may become a part of the trial or criminal court proceeding. They may even attempt to threaten, bribe, or attack law enforcement involved in the investigation. Unsecure case files can be of interest to public media, which will release information prematurely and potentially cause fear and eliminate cooperation in a case where violence and the potential for more violence is possible. Witnesses who hope for anonymity will not trust the investigator to securely protect them until they are required to testify. Even confidential sources will begin to question their belief that the confidential information they provide is really protected. So the fact is that premature release of an investigative report may place people in harm's way and destroy any chance of successfully closing a pending investigation and finding the truth. It is a major concern if the suspect becomes a fugitive and is out of the jurisdiction for a time. Finally, a premature release of an investigative file may cause extreme damage to an innocent person who at first appeared to be a viable suspect but was or is about to be fully exonerated. Criminal investigations are a process, and the certainty needed by the investigator may not be immediately apparent. A person with opportunity and motive may seem to be a logical suspect until that person is eliminated as a result of more intensive investigation. Case files need to be secured until the criminal investigator has completed his investigation, presented the findings to a criminal court, and resolved all the issues that are possible to resolve. Case files may also contain methods and sources that will be used or relied on in other investigations, so even when one case is completed, it is usually best if the case file is maintained as law enforcement-sensitive until there is some compelling legal or security reason for dissemination of the file.

Original case files and copies thereof should be scrupulously protected using safe storage, carefully controlled logs that detail who has reviewed the file, and the system that protects the sensitive information in a file by dividing the file as suggested above so that, if the file review is for the purpose of an administrative review, the sections relevant to witnesses, victims' evidence, and covert operations are not routinely released for review unless required. Again, the question should be asked, "What is the reviewer's need to know?"

Digital files, emails, or any other information pertaining to a case, especially sensitive information about witnesses, victims, and covert operations, should never be transmitted over the internet. Hand carry important information directly to the prosecutor's office. Make sure the prosecutor knows about file security and maintains hard copies and digital files in a secure facility or environment.

As of 2018, the FBI maintains investigative files in digital formats on an internal network that is not accessible by the internet. This method has been effective at deterring leaks and keeping the FBI's internal network from being hacked. Investigative files may also be maintained by the FBI as hard copies. There is usually a free flow of file information to and from the federal prosecutor's office, so even in the FBI's system, there are security problems. A number of law enforcement agencies and departments have established their own digital filing capabilities within a network or on a platform mandated by their jurisdiction. Cities, counties, and states have digital networks that are used by the police, the fire department, the mayor's office, the county maintenance department, and on and on. These networks are usually developed with

significant data security, but the more elaborate and commercial the network, the more
it is likely to be compromised or hacked. Even without hacking, can a police department file be viewed by the head of the county maintenance bureau? Access is the
problem, even when significant and effective digital security is in place.

Special security precautions should be in place and made mandatory for law enforcement–sensitive files, especially investigative case files. Retired FBI Supervisory
Special Agent Robert Osgood, who is the director of George Mason University's
Computer Forensic Department, suggests the following security protocols for all investigative files.

- Encrypt all investigative files. Files, documents, and digital media stored and maintained in an investigative file should be encrypted so that the file cannot be accessed
  without permission.
- Utilize two-factor authentication. When accessing an investigative file over a secure network, the investigator and other authorized persons should have to access
  the file using two forms of authentication.
- Where cloud or hybrid services are used, require the use of a virtual private network
  (VPN). Specifically, a VPN is used to encrypt data transmitted from a private network to a public network, such as a cloud storage provider.

Ensuring that computerized files are protected is the responsibility of the criminal
investigator. Agencies and departments will have plans and resources in place, but
ultimately, the responsibility lies with the investigator to determine if those plans
and resources are up to the task. Most of the computer and internet security for a
government-wide network costs money. There are "cheap," cost-effective add-ons
available to secure investigative files. The investigator should encourage the agency
or department to adopt more secure systems or allow for an additional layer of security
to be added to the digital file storage of data. Digital and internet security has been
a problem faced by law enforcement for the past twenty years. Solutions developed
in 1995 are no longer practical. There has to be a balance between complex security
systems and user-friendly applications that will be scrupulously used by law enforcement officers and agents. Encryption software can be impenetrable, but it may be
too cumbersome for the average person to use. Sloppy handling of digital files can
compromise even the best security protocols, and internal disregard for protocols can
frustrate effective security. So the criminal investigator needs to be aware of flaws and
overcome the flaws. The investigator needs to be concerned enough about security
that he follows the protocols carefully and faithfully and needs to notify the agency's
IT security whenever there is a breach or suspected breach.

MAJOR CASE LEAD CONTROL

Major investigations with many moving parts or significant investigations with serious community interest may be aggressively investigated with all manner of graphics and investigative "icons" detailing outstanding leads; covered leads; suspects',

victims', and witnesses' photos; and images of the crime scene, physical evidence, and status of forensic examinations. Some departments and agencies place these high-priority cases on computerized presentation or an old-fashioned bulletin board as an extraordinary method for briefing a number of skilled investigators. These boards or presenters then eliminate the need to continually update the investigators on what is currently happening in an investigation. The presentations provide a glance at the current status of an investigation. Some jurisdictions do this for homicide cases and call the presentation a "murder board." Access to the murder board is again meant to be limited to a need-to-know group of investigators, but the presentation should always be kept secure for the eyes of the investigative group only. Almost every agency and department uses this method when a major all-officer or -agency investigation is conducted with an operational command post. A computerized lead board or timeline is established so that each lead developed is assigned to an investigator and the lead isn't closed until the lead is covered by a communication with the computer. This ensures that all the leads that were considered were in fact handled. This kind of major case investigative approach with up to hundreds of investigators is very effective, but the effort on each lead can be uneven and therefore may require special oversight or doubling back at a later date when time is not as sensitive. These lead-generation, commercially available computer programs are known by a number of names, but the bottom line is that they have human entry of leads that need to be covered and human entry of leads that are covered, so they are pretty straightforward, no matter what they are called. In the future, there may be programs that develop algorithms that generate leads from the brain of the computer. This kind of system may have a significant advantage, but for the most part, it is still best for the lead investigator and other supervisory or management persons to generate the leads that need to be covered. Management of any investigation should be limited to a small group of persons who can easily discuss ideas and develop solutions but is not bogged down in endless discussion. Even in these major case investigations, the development of theories and input of reliable intelligence can prompt leaps forward in the case, but the benefit of the extra investigative resources should be used to cut the time needed in an investigation, not cut or water down the investigative teamwork and process that informs and intelligently focuses the case work in the normal routine effort of the investigative unit involved.

LEAD COVERAGE

In the three steps of our investigative plan in chapter 8, we discussed the need to cover the outstanding leads. From an administrative point of view, the case cannot be complete until all the leads are covered and documented. To define a lead, again, in a slightly different manner, a lead is an investigative step or logical point when action needs to be taken by the criminal investigator to determine if a person who needs to be interviewed is interviewed or information stored or stockpiled by some third party needs to be gathered and examined to see if the information is relevant in the investigation. Leads can also involve following up with witnesses who may not have provided all the information they know. Leads can be reviewing other cases with a similar modus operandi (MO) or researching the personal backgrounds on suspects, victims, and witnesses. There are a variety of methods for documenting covered leads. If the results of the lead investigation are testimonial, it is appropriate to cover the lead with a witness statement or a report detailing the facts discovered. The statement or the testimonial report will suffice to cover the lead. There are also covered leads that yield little or nothing of value. A simple insert or typewritten note explaining the negative results is sufficient. Of course, some leads can be much more complex. Leads can be significant investigative steps, such as executing a search warrant or serving subpoenas for financial records, telephone records, and other significant and relevant records held by legitimate custodians of employment records, automobile purchase transaction records, and the like. When leads of this nature are covered, there may be a need to establish a new or customized case file section or subfile. One of the most important examples of these kinds of significant leads are search warrants and arrest warrants. Either of these investigative events requires a significant amount of documentation, and as a result, they should be afforded the administrative distinction of being maintained in a subfile under the overall case file.

SEARCH WARRANTS

Search warrants are an important example of a lead that is covered with extensive work and paperwork and they require a case file section devoted to all of the documentation generated. All the actions, from preparing for the execution of a warrant, to actually carrying out the raid, to listing the evidence recovered, to preparing an inventory to accompany the search warrant return, need to have their own subfiles. The average search warrant generates several reports and court documents. Keeping the information relating to a search warrant separate allows the investigator to secure all the material related to the search in one repository. Most criminal investigations will only average between one and three search warrants per case. Bigger cases, such as criminal enterprise cases or major drug gang investigations, may generate thirty to fifty search warrants, so in each investigation, a separate subfile will be established to document each search. In chapter 12, we will spend more time on the "how to" for search warrants and how they are handled, but for the proper administration of a case file, a subfile should be established to allow for immediate access and careful review of such an important event in an investigation.

ARRESTS

The goal of every investigation is to arrest the criminal responsible for the crime. There are generally two methods to begin the process of closing the investigation by charging the suspects, who have developed into subjects, thereby designating them as defendants: (1) Write an affidavit in support of an arrest warrant, obtain the warrant, and then arrest the subject. (2) Provide information and testimony to a grand jury; with that information, the grand jury can indict the subject or subjects. There can be slight variations of both methods. A person can be arrested immediately based on probable cause, and the affidavit turns into a statement of facts, which is then reviewed by a judge or magistrate, who approves the arrest. A person can voluntarily turn himself in once he is indicted and save himself the personal disruption caused by an arrest. From an administrative viewpoint, all of these methods should be handled the same way. There will be a charging document, an arrest warrant, or an indictment. There will be a supporting document, an affidavit, or a statement of facts, and/or there will be an indictment detailing the charges. When the arrest occurs or a subject turns herself in, there will be an administrative document, a police report, and an investigative report or the like that provides basic information about the person, such as name, date and place of birth, residence, family background, and employment background. The subject will be fingerprinted and photographed and may even be ordered to provide a DNA sample or other specific biological sample for use in the investigation. Finally, the subject will be interviewed about the investigation with the intent to hear her response to the charges. A copy or an original of an advice of rights form will be included in the arrest packet. All of these documents should be made a part of the investigative file and maintained together in a subfile for convenience and security of the case file. Each subject arrested should have a separate file section devoted to his particular arrest. Occasionally, a subject will be accompanied by his attorney to protect his rights. That is allowed in some cases when the agency and the prosecutor's office agree. In most cases, the arrest can be an adversarial confrontation and may have significant implications for the investigation going forward. If the subject refuses to be questioned or asks for an attorney, any discussion or interrogation about the case is fruitless, and any statements made by the subject will not be allowed in the "case in chief" or the government's case in a trial. Depending on the extent of the subject's involvement in the criminal ecosystem in the community, the protection of her rights does not mean that an interview about other criminal matters can't go forward. The investigator has to be careful when he proceeds with this interview. The interview should be cordial and nonconfrontational. Any rancor could be viewed by a reviewing judge as intimidation and improper conduct on the part of the investigator. Any actions that put the investigator in a bad light to a judge should be avoided.

Personal Experience

During subject interviews in the FBI, any demand for an attorney during the advice of rights part of the interview usually ends the interview. Conducting the interview with the understanding that you may not be able to use "incriminating" statements should never deter the opportunity to allow a talkative suspect a chance to "vent." It is good investigative practice to build rapport and a positive relationship with a subject whenever possible. This will be further discussed in chapter 13.

Returning to the discussion of building a proper subfile documenting an arrest, all reports, arrest forms, interview statements, and advice of rights forms should be maintained in the subfile referring to the specific arrest. Photographs and documents relating to the recovery of physical evidence like biological evidence from a subject based on a specific court order should also be maintained in the subfile referring to the specific arrest. Finally, any physical evidence recovered at the time of the arrest on the person of the subject should be documented and added to this same subfile that actual evidence, and the biological evidence recovered will be submitted to the section of the investigative file. The original advice of rights form (section 4); original interview notes (section 9); and actual physical evidence, such as a DNA, hair, or blood sample (section 4), along with the chain of custody for the evidence should be submitted to the appropriate subfile category in the above-mentioned fourteen sections.

In most police departments and agencies throughout the United States, all the sub-files, sections, or administrative separations of investigative files will have their own or similar designations. In most departments and agencies, the case file is the result of years of experience and experiment. The divisions have been the results of convenience and, in some cases, court rulings. The controls that are established usually have a screwup, a horror story, or a lost case to account for the changes and the separations. It is up to the criminal investigator to adapt to the administrative evolution of the case jacket and sort out the case and the documents, evidence, and events that make up the investigation so that the case file is organized, informative, and convenient for the users who have to rely on information reported.

Sworn officers and agents, who make up the largest number of lead criminal investigators, will have other significant administrative functions that they have to carry out. Functions such as personnel, payroll, and equipment matters are important and necessary, but they are not directly related to the functions of criminal investigation. How these administrative concerns are handled do not belong in this text.

SUMMARY

The final and most important concern relating to the administration of criminal investigations is the ability of the criminal investigator to write effectively with clarity, detail, and precision. Being able to produce understandable text explaining in detail an investigative step, composing a memorandum that effectively explains the status of an investigation, and carefully and honestly reporting the statements of witnesses or victims are all hallmarks of a proper investigation. Sophisticated and intelligent writing skill is not a requirement. What is required is solid technical skill in paying attention to spelling, grammar, and all the basic requirements of good composition. When an investigator is called upon to compose an affidavit, she should not find the task to be a major chore. The process of writing down the facts of a case, explaining the origin of each fact, and providing the necessary witness support for the facts is a very simple task. The investigator needs to be able to explain to the judge any opinion or conjecture he made based on his experience as a law enforcement officer so that the judge can read the affidavit, rely on its truthfulness, and then rely on the good judgment of the investigator. The judge also has to be able to understand the basics. A crime occurred, there is probable cause to believe evidence of that crime is in a particular location, and/or there is probable cause to believe that the person named in the document as the subject is the person who should be charged. The writing in an affidavit is one of the essential skills that a criminal investigator needs to have. Using narrative and argument simultaneously to move the judge or magistrate to accept the investigator's viewpoint is the kind of compositional text that is required. Objectively relating facts and evidence and explaining what those facts and the evidence mean provides the proper forum to present a case for judicial review, which is a very important goal in every criminal case.

Chapter Twelve

Bringing the Case to Court

Procedures for charging a suspect or suspects, court processes, grand jury processes, trial processes, the difference between closing a case and solving a case.

As discussed in chapter 9, the single most important goal in a criminal case is to charge and arrest of a suspect who has become the subject in the investigation. The arrest is the first step to bring the subject to justice. It is an event that begins the investigators' presentation of the facts to the appropriate court. It is when the person who committed a crime under investigation is identified and the judicial review process begins. That goal has several parts: determining if a suspect is the person who in fact committed the crime, ensuring that any other person who helped, "abetted," or otherwise participated in the crime is known and eventually will also be charged, and finally, determining that person is the right person to face justice for the criminal conduct. The confidence to charge the right person should not be an attitude or a well-meaning speculation; it should be an evaluation that eliminates all other suspects. It is also significant proof and, to paraphrase the proof standard for a criminal trial, proof beyond doubt, because even reasonable doubts should be dealt with and eliminated in an effective investigation. At this point, the criminal investigator is making the decision to take away the freedom of the subject and place the subject into the criminal justice system. The criminal investigator has determined that the "suspect" is no longer suspected of committing the crime, so the more appropriate designation of "subject" is applied. All of these considerations apply to co-conspirators, aiders, and abettors, who are any persons who participated in the crime or helped in the process. Eventually, a complete investigation will produce charges for everyone involved.

Even though the lead investigator has established probable cause to charge a person with a crime, the investigation is not over yet. As mentioned in chapter 9, some police jurisdictions close the case administratively at the arrest. However, this does not mean the investigation is completed. The confidence that a criminal investigator has that the person charged is the right person should continue to get stronger. It may be necessary to charge a person based merely on probable cause because the subject constitutes a threat to the community. It may be necessary to charge a person based merely on probable cause because it is essential in the investigation to hear what the subject has to say about the crime. It may be necessary to charge the person merely on probable cause because it is necessary and essential to execute a search warrant at the same time as the arrest. By executing a search warrant, the subject is put on notice that the investigation is focused on him. In that circumstance, it may be necessary to arrest the suspect to ensure that he does not have the opportunity to destroy or eliminate evidence from other locations. The arrest of one subject may lead to further arrests of co-conspirators; therefore, the arrest on probable cause is just an event on the timeline of a continuing investigation. Eventually, the court process and the actions by prosecutors and defense attorneys may elevate the proof needed in the case, or they may cause some change in the opinion of the investigator. All of these reasons allow for the criminal investigator to move forward against a suspect even if there are some outstanding facts or evidence that need to be uncovered prior to trial. The good news for a criminal investigator is that, in most jurisdictions, charging a person with a crime is a preliminary step to begin a process that can last a year or more to complete with a trial, when the subject is finally adjudicated as guilty beyond any reasonable doubt.

Also, in chapter 9, we discussed the difference between probable cause for an arrest and probable cause for a search warrant. In a case where a search warrant needs to be obtained, the criminal investigator is actually using the affidavit in support of a search warrant to initiate that same presentation of facts to the court. The main distinction in the search warrant affidavit is that the suspect or subject *may* (*may* is emphasized) not be known or is not mentioned in the facts presented. A search warrant affidavit has to present facts stating that a crime was committed and evidence of that crime is currently in a place where a search warrant is required. Presenting the additional facts revealing to the court the name of a suspect and proof that the suspect is in fact a suspect may be pertinent to the proof needed to support the belief that the evidence sought is in a particular location. If the facts prove probable cause without that nexus to a suspect and the investigator wishes to hold back that information until such time that the subject can be charged, that is a decision the investigator can make, and it is perfectly acceptable. All affidavits should be limited to the facts that are needed for probable cause; they don't need to include all the facts known to the investigator. The limitation of facts in an affidavit also applies to an arrest affidavit. Probable cause is a standard set by the Bill of Rights and is the first hurdle to overcome. But in most investigations, at the time the investigator is ready to make an arrest, there is usually more proof available to the case investigator, which should be used only as needed. It is never necessary in a court presentation to reveal all that is known about a case until it is time for trial. There will be more discussion of the facts that need to be revealed in the court process in "Discovery" later in this chapter.

If a search warrant is approved, the court expects that the warrant will be returned with an inventory of the evidence seized. Once done, the search warrant is treated by the court as a completed event. On the other hand, when an affidavit in support of arrest is approved or an indictment is returned followed by an arrest or a statement of facts that is made in the event of a probable cause arrest, the court opens a court file and begins to dictate the step-by-step process to be followed by the government. The court also ensures that the subject, now the defendant, has defense counsel and that the defendant is put on notice of the same step-by-step process. The court will also set the conditions of bail or some kind of release from custody.

Court procedures will vary in different jurisdictions; federal court processes are different from state court processes. There are also lower county magistrate's courts and district courts that handle misdemeanors and other petty offenses, including traffic offenses. For purposes of this discussion, we will consider procedures for felony offenses and capital offenses (crimes with the potential for a death penalty or term of life in prison) and major federal felony investigations. Generally, the US Constitution, specifically the Bill of Rights, mandates a trial by a jury of the defendant's peers (persons from the community who are similar to the defendant). This may mean people of the same race, but it is not required. What is generally required is that the peers are persons from the same community who can't be "dismissed from the jury based on any discriminatory practice." Race and gender can't be used by either the prosecutor or the defense attorney to dismiss a juror (Refer to the "Batson Challenge Rule" from *Bastson v. Kentucky* 476 US 79 [1986]). A grand jury indictment is required for a felony charge. So even though a criminal investigator arrests a person on a charge with probable cause, the government has to take the step of presenting the facts to an independent grand jury, which can sustain the charge, add additional charges, and bind over the defendant for trial. The grand jury may also conduct an investigation and vote not to indict, which is called a "no bill," and the charges will then be dismissed by a judge.

At the point that the subject becomes a defendant and the court process is initiated, the criminal investigator transforms into a witness. There will be testimony required at a preliminary hearing. There will be testimony required at a grand jury proceeding, and there may be testimony required at miscellaneous evidentiary hearings, bond hearings, and other events that will require testimony from the lead investigator or other investigators involved in the case.

INITIAL APPEARANCE

In most jurisdictions in this country, the defendant is brought before a judge, magistrate, or justice of the peace immediately following an arrest for an initial appearance. This is a very simple proceeding in which the document that was prepared by the criminal investigator is reviewed by the court officer; if the document is found sufficient, the release status of the defendant is established. The defendant is advised of her rights, and in most jurisdictions, there is a determination about the ability of the defendant to hire an attorney. In most jurisdictions, if the defendant is judged to be indigent, too poor to afford an attorney, the court officer will arrange for an attorney to be appointed. The appointed attorney can be a public defender or from a rotational assignment from the local bar (licensed attorneys in that jurisdiction). Since these attorneys are not expected to work without pay, or pro bono, some arrangement to pay an agreed upon hourly rate for the attorney is usually made. In most cases, the paperwork reviewed is the arrest warrant and affidavit supporting the warrant or the statement of facts supporting a probable cause arrest. The court officer will take note of the charge and determine, usually based on local statute, if bail can be made. Bail is surety, or a promise made by the defendant, that he will show up for any subsequent court appearances. The surety is usually a money amount or a substantial bond supported by real property. If the defendant fails to appear at subsequent court proceedings, the court will take the money or real estate bond and issue an arrest warrant for the defendant. The bail or release status of the defendant is subject to review at all the subsequent hearings, but if bail is set and complied with, the defendant can usually remain free throughout the court process. In many jurisdictions, for some minor offenses, a personal recognizance promise is enough for the defendant to be released from custody. This means that if the defendant promises to make all court appearances, she will be released from custody. On the other hand, in very serious offenses, such as murder, rape, and armed robbery, defendants can be held by the government without bond if two criteria are met: the defendant is a threat to the community or is a flight risk or at risk of becoming a fugitive from justice. Also, in these very serious crimes, the defendant may be given a bond, but it can be set at such a high rate that most people won't be able to make the bond and they will remain in custody throughout the duration of the trial. All of these possibilities are set during the initial appearance, but again, they are subject to change at subsequent hearings. Finally, the judge or court officer who is handling the initial appearance will then set a date for the next event in the process, a preliminary hearing.

PRELIMINARY HEARING

In almost all of these hearings and proceedings, the testimony may be what is legally referred to as "hearsay" testimony. For example, it is *not* necessary for the government to produce three or four eyewitnesses to an armed robbery for a preliminary hearing of the robber. Credible hearsay testimony is then the next best thing to ensure the reliability of the information and testimony provided. The criminal investigator who took down their statements and documented their proposed testimony can provide that evidence to the judge, who will rule on the need for the government to prove probable cause. So to further explain a preliminary hearing, it is a lower court proceeding where a judge or magistrate listens to the testimony offered by the government and can also hear testimony offered by the defense to determine if probable cause exists to hold the defendant on the charge alleged by the government. This hearing usually takes place within days of the arrest or detention of the defendant. During this hearing, the judge will usually accept hearsay testimony from the lead investigator along with testimony from other professional witnesses who have evidence that supports probable cause. The judge may also accept the facts as described in an affidavit underlying an arrest warrant and then will usually make a review of the decision about the release status or bond required by the defendant. The judge's or magistrate's ruling will also bind the defendant over for a grand jury hearing. Cases have been dismissed in preliminary hearings, but it is very rare and will happen only if the case is so flawed that the defense attorney can prove mistakes, lies, or corruption occurred during the investigation. In most jurisdictions, jeopardy does not attach to a defendant, so the case can be rehabilitated if necessary. In almost all of the cases, the government's proof of probable cause is sustained, and the case is put in the hands of a grand jury. A preliminary hearing is not mandated in most jurisdictions. If the grand jury indicts the defendant after arrest, the preliminary hearing is supplanted by an arraignment on the charge for which the defendant has been indicted. The preliminary hearing is referred to as an evidentiary hearing, meaning testimony or physical evidence is submitted to the court for verification of the facts supporting probable cause.

GRAND JURY HEARING

In almost every jurisdiction in this country, the defendant will be afforded a grand jury hearing. In some states and jurisdictions, this may be a very formal demonstration of the evidence by the criminal investigator. The lead investigator and other professional government witnesses may testify. Again, they can testify to reliable hearsay evidence. The federal or state prosecutor runs the hearing, and the information presented is usually favorable to the government's view of the investigation. Some jurisdictions allow the defendant to testify, but this is usually a strategy that most defense counsels avoid. It will give the prosecutor the right to examine the defendant under oath and could potentially lead to other charges. If the prosecutor agrees, alibi witnesses and other exculpatory evidence for the defense can be presented, but it is up to the prosecutor if this is allowed. Finally, the grand jurors themselves may have misgivings about the testimony or evidence they see and hear, and they can question the truthfulness of witnesses, investigators, and victims. Grand juries are made up of citizens from the community who may represent the full range from distrust for the government to supportive faith in the government's agents and the work of law enforcement. There are two kinds of grand juries. Standing grand juries can be a panel of citizens drawn from the same pool as petit jurors. (Petit jurors are drawn from citizens in the community to sit on "routine" trials, or the daily schedule of criminal and civil trials in every jurisdiction in the United States. They are the citizens regularly called for jury duty.) Petit jurors who then are tasked to meet regularly over a period of time. The panel may handle a review of all arrest cases to decide if the defendant should be indicted. It is unusual for this kind of panel, which may see a large number of cases per week, not to indict a case that has been reviewed by a court officer. Cases bound over by a judge or a magistrate who found probable cause are not usually controversial, and the reality is that these cases may be rubber-stamped through the process by the prosecutor, who controls what evidence the grand jury sees. Lead investigators may be the only witness the grand jury hears, and the chance that an indictment will result is highly likely. In a few of these cases, the grand jury may consider other actions by the defendant and add to charges. For example, if a defendant is charged on an arrest warrant with armed robbery of a store as the main charge mandated by the arrest warrant, there may be other offenses that the facts of the case reveal. The lead charge or count is armed robbery; however, if the robber pistol-whipped or even shot and wounded a victim or a witness, the grand jury may add assault and battery, attempted murder, illegal use of a firearm, possession of a firearm by a convicted felon, and other minor offenses verified by the facts developed in the investigation. The single charge of armed robbery was simply the most obvious charge to present to the judge to have an arrest warrant issued. On the other hand, the grand jury can consider all the other facts and potential crimes and include those additional charges in the indictment. The grand jury may also exclude an original offense charged for a specific reason and add or enhance charges the grand jury deems more appropriate. Since the grand jury is acting under the guidance of the prosecutor, the variety of charges are usually more legally specific and concise based on the statutes and the legal precedent as known by the prosecutor. Arrest warrants or even arrests on probable cause may not have been carefully considered by anyone but the lead investigator, so the charges from a grand jury need to be legally sufficient and carefully drawn based on the expertise available to the prosecutor. It is the grand jury process that makes certain the crimes charged are proper and legally sufficient.

The other type of grand jury is known as an investigative grand jury, impaneled to investigate serious long-term crime problems. They may investigate significant criminal enterprises, public corruption, and illegal drug distribution networks. An investigative grand jury may be tasked with investigating major, or serious, crimes that significantly affect a community, so a shooting by a police officer, a terrorist act, or a bombing or arson of a community gathering place may be the investigative target. These grand juries will have criminal investigators to handle the day-to-day investigative work, and again, they will be administered by the prosecutor. They can call witnesses to testify under oath. They can order compliance of the witness by way of subpoena (an order to appear), or they can order physical evidence to be turned over for examination. They can order the production of documents, data, and other material held by private or public custodians. Bank records, telephone records, property records, and even employee files or correspondence held by targets can be subpoenaed. This step is a less aggressive effort to recover documentary material than using a search warrant, but it is a powerful tool for an investigator and a much more appropriate method of getting bulk material from a legitimate source, custodian, or business enterprise. Investigative grand juries may handle several cases over the course or their impanelment. When they reach the end of their term, they can issue grand jury indictments on all or some of the cases they have considered or leave cases to be handled by subsequent panels. The main benefit of these grand juries is the subpoena power and the demand to have witnesses testify under oath as to the evidence they know. The grand jury in this case is the strong exercise of a prosecutor's authority to delve into a serious matter and reach some conclusion on the criminality involved. Criminal investigators who work reactive criminal cases don't often get involved with investigative grand juries, but criminal investigators in organized crime cases, criminal syndicates, gang cases, terrorism cases, drug investigations, and even serial crime investigations have to rely on the investigative grand jury for subpoena authority and the production of testimony under oath to lock in the testimony of a recalcitrant or difficult witness.

PRESENTMENT OR ARRAIGNMENT

An arraignment is a status hearing where the defendant is advised of his rights and told what the charge or charges against him are, and in the arraignment, the defendant will enter a plea of guilty or not guilty to the charge. It is at this point in the court process that the trial court judge is finally designated. It is normal that the trial court judge is usually one step above in a higher echelon of the court hierarchy. So a district court judge in a local jurisdiction who presided over the initial appearance and the preliminary hearing may be replaced by a circuit court judge. A federal magistrate who oversaw the initial appearance and the preliminary hearing is replaced by a US district court judge. Names and ranks of judges will vary by jurisdiction, but the process is similar in all jurisdictions. The trial court judge will take the case and make all the important decisions after the grand jury has issued an indictment. All these court processes are important to the criminal investigator because it is necessary to keep up with the process and continue to maintain a solid line of communication with the critical witnesses in the case. Open lines of communication with the victims, the eyewitnesses, or fact witnesses is an essential part of criminal investigations. The contact with all professional witnesses, the medical examiner, the forensic experts, and the patrol officers who responded to the crime scene, the crime scene technician, and any other investigators whose testimony might be relevant in the trial is necessary to successfully prosecute any criminal case. Even in cases where the department or agency has administratively closed the case, the lead investigator is usually the best point of contact between the witnesses and the prosecutor. A number of prosecutors' offices have their own investigators on the payroll to pick up the case from the police agency, but even these transitions are not ideal. The relationships established by the lead investigator may be hard or even impossible to duplicate by a new criminal investigator who takes over the case. Civilians who are unfamiliar with the court process and are not used to the length of time involved want to see and hear from a known and friendly contact with law enforcement. This transition can be hard and in some cases impossible, but a veteran prosecutor will find a way to make the transition workable. Criminal investigators in state attorneys' offices are usually veteran former detectives who are very experienced and skilled. It is also their function to conduct any new investigation that may be required with a new indictment for charges not considered by the lead police investigator. The criminal investigator for the prosecutor is usually the person who is responsible for following up on leads revealed by the defense attorney. Alibi witnesses, for example, can pop up at the last minute in the run-up to the trial. Backgrounds and vetting for defense forensic experts and the service of trial subpoenas may be the responsibility of these state investigators. It is also possible that subpoena service is handled by sheriffs' deputies or US marshalls in a federal case. The real investigative strategy for the case during the trial phase is developed by the prosecutor, who has to take control of the investigation at this point. But as was mentioned in chapter 4, teamwork and consolidation of the effort is the recipe for success.

TIMELINE OR SPEEDY TRIAL REQUIREMENTS

Federal, state, and local jurisdictions have certain time limits on felony criminal cases. An indictment may be required to occur within thirty days of an arrest. In the Bill of Rights regarding the rights of the accused, the defendant has the right enumerated in the Sixth Amendment to a speedy and public trial by an impartial jury (interpreted by precedent as a jury of peers). In the Fifth Amendment, the defendant has the right to be indicted by a grand jury, which demands that a finding of probable cause has been officially made by a jury from the defendant's community. Federal, state, and local jurisdictions have used these basic rights to establish exactly what a speedy trial is and how much time is needed by the defendant to prepare for a trial. The defendant also has the right to slow down the process if she can waive her right for a speedy trial. The government is not allowed to ask for a delay from the court schedule without the waiver from the defendant. Time constraints can end up being a burden on either side. Stretching out the timeline of a trial can also have an effect on the enthusiasm and cooperation of victims and government witnesses, and a delay may affect even professional witnesses, such as expert forensic scientists. Adhering to a strict timeline might limit the effectiveness of the defense's investigation since the government's investigation usually predates the opportunities available to the defense. It is then the responsibility of the judge to set the limits and ensure that the trial occurs in a timely fashion. The belief that justice delayed is justice denied is the concept courts try to adhere to, but each trial presents unique unexpected developments that cause delays and also support unexpectedly fast solutions. Some jurisdictions pride themselves on how quickly their dockets move along, whereas other jurisdictions accept the fact that certain presentations of evidence take as long as they take. There are no simple answers to complex problems when a person's liberty hangs in the balance.

DISCOVERY

Any premature release of facts known to the investigator can become public and may be deleterious to the case before trial. The old gambling proverb of "keep your cards close to the vest" applies to investigative security as the court process unfolds. It is the responsibility of the government prosecutor to provide discovery, which may be any additional facts and witness testimony, at the appropriate time in the trial preparation process. In consultation with the prosecutor, the investigator has to make sure this is done, and that is especially important if the investigator has uncovered information that may be helpful to the subject. There are facts or witness statements that the investigator may consider bogus, incorrect, or too inconsistent with overwhelming evidence to the contrary. The investigator can then make the decision based on logical judgment that the fact or witness statement does not need to be discussed in an affidavit or even in testimony to the grand jury or at any preliminary hearing, unless specifically asked about it. That information should be revealed to the defendant and his attorney at the appropriate time by the prosecutor. It is up to the defendant and his attorney and investigator to further investigate the so-called exculpatory information and present it in court on behalf of the defendant. As discussed in chapter 8 and elsewhere, this information is to be revealed under the *Brady v. Maryland* rule, or the *Brady* rule, which mandates the government to turn over to the defendant any information that is exculpatory. Any failure to comply with the *Brady* rule could lead to a dismissal of the case or an overturning of a conviction upon appeal. The defense is also entitled at some point in the process to obtain all the investigative information known to the government. This information is covered in general by specific rules of discovery, which are statutory and specific to each jurisdiction. Additional material may be covered as *Giglio* material from the *Giglio v. United States* Supreme Court case. This material covers a wide range of material from an investigation that is not exculpatory but may be important for the defense attorney to know. Deals cut with cooperating co-conspirators and original interview notes are subject to a *Giglio* discovery release.

In evaluating the discovery process the criminal investigator should understand that every witness and document along with every aspect of proof in a case will eventually be made available to the defendant. The concept that it is the defendant "David" going up against the full power of the government "Goliath" is the logic behind this wholesale discovery process. Going back to the discussions relating to the rights of the accused in chapter 3, the doctrine of fundamental fairness is also a key concept in understanding the logic behind discovery. It is not up to the investigator to decide what is revealed and what is held back, but it is up to the investigator to offer advice and make sure the prosecutor has all the material needed to meet this responsibility. The prosecutor's evaluation has to be sound and within the law, but if the investigator believes the prosecutor is making a bad decision that could jeopardize the case, it is up to the investigator to fully understand the prosecutor's logic and legal basis for the decision.

MISCELLANEOUS EVIDENTIARY HEARINGS

From time to time during the trial process leading up to the actual trial, the prosecutor and the defense will argue over the admissibility of certain evidence or the reliability of certain forensic scientific examinations. These arguments will usually prompt a hearing, generally referred to as an evidentiary hearing. Along with these hearings there will be regular status hearings, during which the judge listens to both sides to determine if the trial date, which is usually set early in the process, will be met. During the evidentiary hearings, there is usually some testimony, which can be reliable hearsay testimony by the lead investigator or by other witnesses in the case. The issue or concern is usually the reliability of the evidence, the relevance of the evidence, or whether the evidence is too prejudicial to the defendant. These hearings can be very controversial and counterproductive for the investigator. To present the facts discovered during the investigation, the case investigator doesn't have the prescience to determine the factors above. The investigator may discover information in the defendant's background that explains the defendant's penchant for violence and hatred of a group in which the victim was a member. This violent propensity and expressed hatred may be considered too prejudicial against the defendant and is not allowed to be presented in the trial, even though the evidence of this mindset was legally obtained and documented. At this point, the investigator may believe that the truth underlying the motive for the crime will not be presented to the jury. Truth will have to be replaced by some generic, nonspecific motive. This kind of frustrating ruling in an evidentiary hearing is not only disheartening to the investigator; it may be stressful to the victim's family who knew of the defendant's hatred from his reputation. These innocent bystanders to the justice system will not understand this kind of legal restriction. It is the kind of issue that can cause the case to be less clear and therefore lead to a not guilty verdict.

The reality for evidentiary hearings is they are not always controversial. It is usually a point of law that has to be decided, and when the judge rules, the ruling comports with the legal precedent or a specific statute providing the appropriate answer to the argument. However, if the judge makes the "wrong" decision, the ruling or the trial can be overturned upon later appeals in a court review. These hearings are frequent pretrial events that set the rules for the trial and are usually very instructive for the criminal investigator.

Status hearings are routine housekeeping events to ensure that the lawyers and the judge are proceeding forward to the trial.

Personal Experience

During my career, DNA profiles were just being accepted by courts nationwide as proof that the biological material of a suspect or victim was recoverable at a crime scene. In the early 1990s, a judge in the Superior Court of the District of Columbia had ruled DNA evidence inadmissible. I was working an investigation of one of the most prolific killers in the history of the city. We had recovered some very significant DNA evidence inside three separate vehicles where homicides by gunshot had occurred. We needed to verify the details of the murders provided by cooperating witnesses who were with the defendant when he killed his victims. The best method was showing that the victim's DNA was in the blood stains in the particular cars the witnesses identified. This provided scientific proof corroborating the testimony of the witnesses. For the federal prosecutor who was handling the case to present this evidence in trial, a Frye hearing footnote 1 (*Frye v. United States*, 293 F. 1013) was needed. This is a hearing where the government or the defense has to prove the scientific reliability of evidence to be submitted in a trial. It is an evidentiary hearing. In my case we produced the DNA expert from the FBI laboratory to testify that DNA evidence was reliable based on a mathematical certainty and a formula that explained the likelihood of an error. The federal district court judge in that case overruled the ruling of the superior court judge, and the case continued with this very important evidence legally allowed.

> Frye vs. United States was an important Supreme Court Ruling. The ruling states that any scientific technique supporting evidence in a trial is accepted as reliable in the relevant scientific community. The controversy in the case was whether the court should accept blood pressure readings as reliable scientific proof. Since Frye the rules of evidence for federal courts and State courts have been modified to establish the rules whereby scientific evidence can be considered reliable. In Daubert vs. Merrell Dow Pharmaceuticals in 1994 the standard was modified by the Supreme Court to include reliable and **probative experimental science** with the standard set that the science must be sufficiently established to have gained general acceptance in the specific field of science being considered. Most jurisdictions have some combination of Frye and Daubert, but the best way for the criminal investigator to evaluate the results of a significant forensic science result is to

make sure the expert witness can testify to his or her results as being **true to a scientific certainty**. (Arvin Maskin and Konrad Cailteux, "The Supreme Court Establishes Standard of Review for Daubert Decisions and Reaffirms District Court," March 1998)

Following is a timeline of significant events in the US criminal court system process:

- Arrest warrant based on affidavit is issued.
- Probable cause arrest is made at or near the scene of the crime with a follow-up complaint affidavit or statement of facts.
- At the initial appearance, the defendant is advised of his rights, a bail hearing is conducted, and the charges are read to the defendant.
- At the preliminary hearing/probable cause hearing, the investigator and, in some cases, the complaining witness may testify to the facts contained in the affidavit.
- A standing grand jury or an investigative grand jury hears the evidence from the government and determines if there is probable cause to charge the defendant.
- If the defendant is indicted, she is bound over for trial.
- At the presentment arraignment, formal charges are read, pleas are entered, the trial judge is assigned, and the defendant's bail status is usually reviewed.
- Trial can be preceded by a number of evidentiary hearings to determine legality and admissibility of evidence.
- Trial by judge, jury, or court martial panel in military tribunals takes place.
- At the posttrial pleadings, a judicial review of evidence and decisions made or presented at trial can be reconsidered by the trial court judge.
- Appeals in serious felony cases may involve as many as two levels of courts above the trier of fact.
- Appeals in capital cases may be reviewed all the way to the US Supreme Court.

GUILTY PLEAS, PLEA DEALS, AND DISMISSAL OF CHARGES

After a subject is arrested, all the way through the court process, the case can end with a guilty plea or a negotiated plea arrangement or deal. This precludes the need for a trial and effectively ends the investigation, unless there are other co-conspirators or a related crime or series of crimes that have been incorporated into the same investigation. This step is a voluntary decision made by the defendant, who in most cases is pleading guilty because he is guilty. This decision is usually made when the defendant, in consultation with his lawyer, determines it is in his interest to accept responsibility for the crime and avoid putting the government through the cost of a trial, during which he may receive a substantially higher penalty if he is found guilty. It is a gamble the defendant makes because he knows that there may be additional charges, disruptions to his family, and financial burdens if he endures the costs of defending himself in a trial. Even indigent defendants stand to lose a great deal if they go forward with a trial and lose. Offering alternative theories to a judge or jury in a trial that the defendant knows are not true because she is in fact guilty will make her look worse in the eyes of a sentencing judge. It is usually much better to take responsibility and work out the best deal possible with the government prosecutor, who will usually be willing to offer a reasonable deal with significant benefits. Career criminals use the opportunity to negotiate wide-ranging plea deals or agreements that dispose of numerous other potential charges they may face if a continuing investigation would yield usable evidence proving the criminal's involvement in other crimes. Career criminals who are aware of other significant crimes not committed by them are often willing to exchange information for shorter terms of incarceration, better correctional facilities, and even a chance for probation, which would allow the criminal to avoid incarceration completely. Serial criminals, murderers, rapists, and armed robbers try to arrange beneficial deals in exchange for helping the government close cases that probably would never close without their help. Criminals' offering the location of victims' remains or helping to close multiple cases in a variety of jurisdictions provides them with the chance for better conditions in their incarceration and even a time cap on the amount of incarceration they may receive. Organized crime figures, gang members, and a variety of other members of crime syndicates offer information in exchange for witness protection status and relocation of their families. All of these efforts to get the best deal and avoid further prosecution or just end the nightmare of the prosecutive process happen when the defendant chooses to plead guilty to the crimes committed. This resolution of a criminal investigation is an essential part of the criminal justice system. Cases are closed and fully resolved. Important and productive intelligence and evidence are obtained that significantly further the cause of justice. Cases that may never be closed are solved, and long strings of car thefts, burglaries, armed robberies, other larcenies, assaults, rapes, robberies, and murders are finally closed and solved without much further damage or disruption to the lives of all the victims and their families. It may be a drawback of this policy when a criminal gets such a good deal that the victims and their families are disappointed. But in most jurisdictions, plea agreements are explained to the victims and their families. Chances are they approve the agreement because they know that at least the perpetrator will be punished and there will never be a need to endure the emotional roller coaster of a trial.

Dismissals are court rulings where the judge reviews the facts and finds corrupt actions on the part of the investigator, the prosecutor, or some other significant participant on the government's side of the case. The judge considers the actions so egregious and destructive to the government's prosecution that she dismisses or cancels the trial or, in some cases, refers the matter to the management of the department or agency, the state or federal attorney's office, or for criminal prosecution. A dismissal can occur at any time during the court process and be done two ways. *Dismissal without prejudice* means the judge believes the criminal charge can be brought up again if the corrupt action is fixed or resolved. The judge in this case is usually convinced that the facts support further investigation and the investigation is potentially on the right track. *Dismissal with prejudice* is a twofold issue. It may be that the case is too far along in the process and the corrupt action is so egregious that jeopardy has already attached to the defendant and therefore a double jeopardy issue exists. This dismissal can also occur because the judge views the corrupt actions so destructive to the case that nothing the government could do would fix the case. The second kind of dismissal is usually the end of the investigation unless there is some way the investigator can rehabilitate the case and bring it in another jurisdiction. Even then, it will be extremely difficult. If the case was corrupted by the actions of the prosecutor, the criminal investigator still has significant responsibility to the victims, the witnesses, and the department or agency to find some way to close the case with a better result.

NOT GUILTY

If after the best efforts of the prosecutor and the criminal investigator the jury or a judge finds the defendant not guilty, there are a couple of things to remember. A not guilty verdict does not mean innocent. It may mean that the proof offered was insufficient in the minds of the jury to meet the standard of guilt beyond a reasonable doubt. The flaw is in the proof and the assessment of the trier of fact. This is an unsolvable problem, and the investigator can only learn from the experience. The only option for the criminal investigator is to make a careful review of the evidence and its presentation in court and decide if the investigation determined the truth and no further investigation will yield a different suspect. If the investigation resulted in the right conclusion but the presentation to the jury was ineffective, the investigation will have to be suspended with this very difficult result. It is up to the department or agency to decide if there is any need to pursue the matter further. As mentioned above, many police departments consider the case closed when an arrest is made. Primarily, this policy means that once an arrest is made, the case is no longer the responsibility of the department. It is the responsibility of the prosecutor's office, and as such, it is up to them to decide if the case needs any further investigation. The police department will not be concerned about the talent or effectiveness of the prosecutive attorneys, whose shortcoming led to such a difficult ending to the case. That may be the case, but a veteran criminal investigator who has developed a relationship with the victims, the victim's family, the deeply invested witnesses, and the other parties in the case will have a case like this disturb his peace for quite a while. His response will be a series of "what ifs?" and "whys?" The investigator will have to determine if there is any threat to the victim, victim's family, or witnesses and make sure that the security problem is handled with as many resources as are available. When the criminal investigator considers all the evidence and the witnesses that were presented in court and determines that it should have been logical for the judge and jury to find the defendant guilty, then further investigation may be nonproductive. Jurors' decisions are based on the entire range of human emotions, prejudices, opinions, and personal deliberate calculations. Jurors are asked to put those tendencies aside and deliberate about the law and the evidence, but it is impossible to shed subjective analysis. If a witness strikes a juror as unreliable and the juror can convince fellow jurors of that impression, the testimony of that witness is dismissed. If one or more jurors have prejudice against law enforcement, it is possible that testimony from all the law enforcement officers in a case could be dismissed. These are the kinds of subjective emotional responses that can lead to a not guilty verdict. There are also subtle distinctions about the definition of *reasonable doubt*. What is reasonable to some is compelling with some basis in fact, whereas other jurors think reasonable is any other possibility no matter how remote.

Any of these factors can lead to an unsatisfactory conclusion in a trial. Ultimately, the criminal investigator has to remember that an important part of the criminal justice system is discovering the truth and that acting to further justice is the goal. This may mean that an equally important part of the system is that the jury disagrees with the assessment. The criminal investigator should also consider the facts that the jury was not allowed to hear because said facts were too prejudicial or tainted in some way. Some of these facts were compelling and accurate and may have been convincing factors for the investigator, but they were not allowed to be presented in the trial—for example, factors such as the defendant's criminal history, the defendant's reputation in her community, and witnesses who were not able to testify because they were mysteriously killed before the trial. Factors like these can provide reasonable explanations for a not guilty verdict. Finally, the investigation may not have been as productive and accurate as the investigator thought. Whatever the reason, the investigator will have to move on. The system worked, the jury spoke, and the case ended.

INSANITY

Throughout the United States, criminal proceedings end with verdicts of insanity. In some jurisdictions, these verdicts are guilty by reason of insanity or not guilty by reason of insanity. The finding is interpreted in slightly different ways depending on the jurisdiction. Serious mental illness can cause people to lose touch with reality and therefore have no sense of right and wrong. Their reality might dictate that murder, rape, or any other serious crime is right, a correct action in their view of the world. These persons generally don't concern themselves with hiding their crime or acting in a manner that is consistent with avoiding detection. In pop culture, pleading temporary insanity is thought of as a loophole in the criminal justice system. It is important for the criminal investigator to determine to the extent possible if a suspect who becomes a subject has a diagnosed or undiagnosed mental illness as part of the intense background investigation of the person. A large number of mental illnesses don't rise to the point where the person is incapable of knowing the difference between right and wrong. Paranoia, schizophrenia, and other debilitating mental illnesses may cause delusions, a kind of separation from reality, but all too often, people afflicted with such illnesses are so handicapped by their disease that planning and committing a crime is difficult if not impossible. It may be necessary for the investigator to find a way to prove a defendant in a criminal case is mimicking, or faking, a mental illness.

For purposes of a trial, the defendant's attorney has to prove the defendant is or was unable to distinguish between right and wrong. It is an 1840s rule called the McNaughton rule, which has evolved from British common law to the current state of the law in most jurisdictions in the United States. Ultimately, if a person is so out of touch with reality that her actions are uncontrolled by moral norms, it is necessary to put her in a mental hospital to protect society until such time as she can be judged to be sane and capable of acting properly in the community. Insanity pleas or an insanity defense in a trial usually comes down to dueling forensic psychologists or psychiatrists. The government will usually have an experienced forensic expert to testify that the defendant was sane when he committed the crime. The burden of proving insanity falls on the defense. So the actions of the defendant will be examined for rational behavior, and any irrational behavior may be viewed as supportive of the claim of insanity. If on the other hand, the government and the defense agree that the defendant was in fact insane when the crime occurred, this is usually handled with some kind of plea agreement involving a substantial hospital care and treatment facility. This type of case should be handled investigatively with a focus on what kind of facts support sanity and what kind of facts support insanity. The more difficult aspects of this kind of pleading in a trial are newer definitions of what constitutes mental illness or "extreme stress" that "forces" criminal conduct. Is a woman who is subjected to routine spousal abuse guilty if she kills her husband when he is not putting her into immediate danger, such as poisoning his food or killing him when he is sleeping or otherwise not acting in a threatening manner? When is the crime done in self-defense, and when is it retaliation or revenge? There are all manner of unique insanity defenses that have surfaced over the past forty years, such as overindulgence in watching pornography said to cause a mentally challenged person to commit rape, and addiction to violent video games said to cause a person to commit a murder or other violence. Any of these customized insanity defenses have to be dealt with during the investigation if they become known pretrial. Are there other, more traditional motives for the crime, and can those motives be shown to be more compelling to the defendant than the impact of the aberrant pattern of behavior suggested by the defense? More sympathetic motives, such as spousal abuse, may be a matter of degree. If a woman is physically abused routinely to the point where investigation indicates that she shows symptoms of mental illness, it may be best to ensure that a reasonable and just disposition be the best result. Again, is the perpetrator just as much a victim, has the victimization led her to irrational behavior, and is that behavior proved? These are the questions the investigator should answer in the search for the truth.

DEFENSE INVESTIGATIONS, PRIVATE INVESTIGATIONS, AND OTHER NONSWORN OFFICER INVESTIGATIONS

During the trial phase is when the criminal investigator will likely come in contact with defense investigators and private investigators. These private criminal investigators should be considered under these two categories because of their roles in a case. The following discussion focuses on their responsibilities.

It should be noted here that defense lawyers who wish to maintain the position that will allow them to put their clients on the stand in a trial may never ask their clients to tell them the whole story. They may never ask their clients if they are guilty or innocent. This is legal, standard, and ethical consideration that gives the defense attorney the ability to avoid putting a witness on the stand who will perjure himself. As such the defense attorney has to be unconcerned about the community's need to solve a particular criminal offense. There may be some crimes that seem to the community to be indefensible, but defense attorneys and by extension defense investigators need to aggressively determine if, first and foremost, their clients were properly charged and are facing a trial with their rights being protected. The guilt or innocence may in fact be irrelevant to the defense.

Investigations conducted by nonsworn officers, such as defense investigators or private investigators hired by families, often don't begin until the government or state investigators have concluded the bulk of their inquiry. Occasionally, a private investigator may open a case that for some reason was not reported to any police agency. Private investigators in these cases are looking for the same result as any other criminal investigator. The main distinction is that their responsibility is to the client who hired them. This responsibility is similar to that of a defense attorney. There may be a confidential relationship between a private investigator and his client, but that confidentiality can be set aside if the private investigator is called to court or to a grand jury to testify about the findings of the investigation. Private investigators who conduct a criminal investigation and determine their clients or the clients' families are criminally culpable don't have the same confidentiality protection as a defense attorney's investigator. Any ethical private investigator who contracts with a person to investigate a crime should give her client proper notice. If on the other hand, a private investigator is hired by a lawyer, his investigative findings may be covered by attorney–client privilege.

Private Investigators

Private investigators will generally follow to the extent possible the plans, procedures, and efforts to prove the elements of a crime in the same way law enforcement investigators proceed. The main difference is that the private investigators don't have to adhere closely to observing the rights of the accused. If they do breach the rights of the accused, they may be charged with a criminal offense, assault, or burglary, trespassing, or breaking and entering if they enter a constitutionally protected space and seize evidence. If the evidence taken in the course of a criminal investigation by a private investigator is at some point presented in court to favor the government's or the defendant's case, it is likely to be excluded. Private investigators very simply don't have the authority to legally seize evidence without the support of a law enforcement officer who obtains a warrant. Private investigators are not in the position to obtain phone records, bank records, and the like by subpoena, so if they obtain these records and there is a need to present these records in court, they need to show they legally obtained the records. In general, if a private investigator is hired by the family of a murder victim or victim of a serious assault, it is best for all concerned that the investigator consult and coordinate the investigation with the lead law enforcement investigator. This coordination in the beginning of an investigation may be extremely one-sided unless and until the law enforcement investigator begins to consider the work of the private investigator to be an asset to the case and the prosecutor or agency manager approves the coordination.

It is a fact that successful private investigators are usually very experienced professionals who most likely worked in law enforcement prior to beginning their career as a private investigator. Most of the time, these investigators work for private companies who wish to stop pilferage or other security breaches at their businesses. They may have expertise in forensic accounting or digital security. Their background in law enforcement is usually beneficial in that they know what their limitations are and will always consider cooperating with law enforcement because it is beneficial to their investigative goals.

Again, if these private investigators are successful in their business, it is usually because they are skilled communicators who know the art of interviewing and are very concerned that their investigation will end up not only benefiting their client but also providing a positive result for the community. Modern fiction paints a different profile for these investigators, but the real truth is that if these investigators were as sleazy and disreputable as they are depicted, it is not likely they would last very long as a successful business. Their investigative process is very similar: they have to build their investigation by talking to witnesses, gathering physical evidence, and legally obtaining books, data, photographs, and other documentary material to support their theory of the case and, ultimately, the proof needed to find the truth.

Defense Investigators

Defense investigators are specifically employed to conduct investigations that benefit the client in a criminal case that is set to go to trial. For the most part these investigators derive from two sources. They can be skilled and professional private investigators who are very experienced and professional. They can have significant law enforcement training and experience, but their work is covered by the privilege enjoyed by defense counsel themselves. They can also be legal interns, law school students, and clerical workers in the law office. Both groups are covered by attorney–client privilege, but the second group is usually inexperienced, underpaid amateurs whose work is overseen by the defense attorney and may be suspect as to its substance. Both groups should be covered as licensed investigators, but the second group is licensed through the attorney's license. Their reports and any investigative analysis are covered as the defense attorney's work product. In the event the defense attorney plans to use a written statement from a witness interviewed by the investigator, the written statement will be made available to the government prosecutor in discovery, but the rules governing discovery by defense attorneys are less stringent.

The goal of the defense investigator is to prove the innocence of the client, but that may be impossible. The next preferred goal is to identify alternative suspects. The defense investigator can uncover persons the defense attorney can point to as viable suspects the government did not investigate or investigated shoddily. The third and most often considered goal of the defense investigator is to audit the police's or government's investigation to determine if the rights of the defendant were breached. In a case where the defense investigator is working for an innocent person, she should be able to get full cooperation from the defendant that obscures or defeats much of evidence the government intends to use. Alibi witnesses, motives for witnesses to lie about the defendant, and explanations as to why any biological material from the defendant was found at the scene of the crime are examples of relevant discoveries the defense attorney can present at trial to disprove the government's case. Unfortunately for these investigators, innocent defendants are very rare. The investigation therefore comes down to alternate suspects and improper procedures on the part of the police investigators. Analysis of police reports and a review or examination of every person who observed the police at the time of the arrest, at the time of the search warrant, and coverage of each occasion where physical evidence was recovered are examined to show improper, illegal, or corrupt practices by law enforcement. One of the areas of great significance in many investigations is when a defendant confesses to the crime. A serious target for a Fifth Amendment violation is a confession that was coerced. Evidence of torture or serious brutality to elicit a confession will have to be presented by medical records after the arrest. Photos taken immediately after the defendant was interrogated can go a long way to proving the use of violence to force the confession. This kind of violence to obtain a confession is very rare for no other reason than the police will usually have a ready explanation for any serious injuries. A bump or bruise or even extensive injuries may have been caused by a refusal by the defendant to co-operate with the arresting officers and a subsequent legal and possibly appropriate use of force by the officers. The investigator who is confronted with this kind of excuse for a beating administered by the police should ask for proof of similar injuries to the arresting officers. All of the appropriate use of force reports should also be obtained. A statement by the defendant about what happened and a catalog of injuries with photographs and a doctor's evaluation of the injuries should be obtained. Cases where the allegation of physical abuse can be proved should be "investigatively" pursued. These kinds of incidents are unusual and so controversial that the truth will usually become known. This kind of physical abuse of a suspect in a case will lead to the exclusion of any incriminating statements from the suspect and any fruits of that illegally obtained statement. The more likely defense against a confession is that law enforcement used extreme pressure or coercion to extract the statement. There are also examples of deprivation, isolation for hours and even days, where the confession is reported to be the result of extreme pressure where a defendant of limited intelligence was tricked or lied to in order to get the confession. These kinds of cases are much more common. Long video recordings of the interrogation may show solicitous behavior on the part of the law enforcement investigators, but the defense investigator will usually have a tough time proving this kind of coercion. The behavior of law enforcement and a strict timeline of an interrogation along with a record of restroom breaks and meals provide a convincing record of proper conduct. Even though a recording covers hours of interrogation, defense investigators will have difficulty proving corrupt or illegal practices. Suggestive behavior on the part of the officers can be evidence of this kind of violation, but there is a fine line between suggestive behavior and coercion. The details provided in the confession should be indicative of a person who is remembering her own actions and a person who has been provided important details. If there is a logical basis for believing the suspect is being prompted or encouraged to lie or go along, the defense investigator should pursue this theory in an effort to present the truth.

The fact is that any violation of *Miranda* is taken very seriously by most judges, and they will usually rule in favor of the defendant when the allegation of coercion or physical abuse is shown to have merit. The question then becomes how important the confession is going forward.

Claiming violations of the Fourth Amendment when a proper search warrant was obtained is a stretch under the best conditions for defense investigators. A search and seizure without a warrant is substantially easier to prove, but exigent circumstances, a vehicle exception, or a consent search will have to be defeated. For the government, the judge will rule in favor of the warrantless search if it can be proven the government acted reasonably and its motives were properly articulated.

Any other attempt on the part of the defense investigator to claim improper law enforcement conduct is impossible unless significant evidence is offered to support a claim of bad or corrupt behavior. The best defense the government can offer is well-crafted articulation of the facts known to the law enforcement investigator and the ever-recurring reasonableness and adherence to fundamental fairness.

Most of the time, defense investigators spend the bulk of their time determining if the government's results are accurate and due process was followed. Because of the late stage of their investigative effort, it is unusual for a defense investigator to spend a lot of time proving a defendant innocent. In most cases, challenging the results of the government's case can be successful if the defense investigator can prove malice, corruption, or disregard for the fundamental rights of the accused. To resolve the case in favor of the defendant, the guilt or innocence of the defendant is irrelevant. Proof beyond a reasonable doubt is a heavy burden, and if a single important factor is proven faulty, wrong, or corrupt, the defendant will walk away from the charge. This will of course leave the community with an unsolved crime. Justice may have been served, but unless and until the government continues to investigate, the crime will go unpunished.

SUMMARY

Statistically, criminal investigations that end up in a trial and not a plea are probably close to only 10 percent of the time. The criminal investigator has to act like every case is going to trial because there is no way to be certain as an investigation evolves. Additionally, the rights of the accused should always be a consideration; common-sense elements of fairness and legal rectitude should also be considered when conducting an investigation. The investigator needs to stay focused on making every fact and piece of evidence discovered available for trial. That way mistakes are lessened, and the case will proceed to a logical conclusion. Trials should be considered the final tournament, the Super Bowl, the Final Four, the national championship game. The experience will test the investigator's abilities and teach lessons that will make future investigations better. Investigators will be able to fine-tune their skills testifying and see the results of their efforts with victims, victim's families, and important witnesses. The investigator will have a chance to evaluate the importance of forensic evidence and observe how professional expert witnesses testify and again learn valuable ways to work with these experts. Constructing a criminal investigation without thinking how evidence will play to a jury is counterproductive and can lead to sloppiness and a lack of discipline. If an investigator handles witnesses, victims, and facts with care and due consideration, the cases will be successful and justice will be served.

Private investigators and defense investigators can provide the law enforcement/ sworn officer investigator with that extra motivation to meet the challenge of getting to the bottom of an investigation. Finding the truth and making sure the truth and facts are properly presented in court is the responsibility of the criminal investigator. It is therefore essential that the investigator follow the rule of law, abide by the constitutional requirements laid out in the Bill of Rights, and become the true advocate for the victim and the arbiter of the facts and evidence. Losing a case and depriving the community of a just closure of the case that results from errors in judgment or corrupt anger at the subject/defendant is a serious dereliction of duty. Unfortunately, in most cases, a bad outcome can usually be blamed on a lot of factors that had nothing to do with the effort of the investigator. As a result of this fact, it is up to the criminal investigator to do some careful assessment of his own work, effort, and commitment to the case to make sure that this kind of unsatisfactory outcome is never repeated.

Chapter Thirteen

Interviews and Interrogations

Interview techniques, subject interrogation, recalcitrant witnesses, and debriefings.

As we have progressed through this text, we have discussed definitions, criminal laws, constitutional rights, organization, teamwork, planning, forensics, investigative goals, and administrative concerns along with the court processes. The real nitty-gritty of criminal investigations and the absolute core of a criminal investigation is the basic function of communication between the investigator and persons involved in the case. In the chapters on witnesses and the criminal statutes, we discussed proof and how it needs to be obtained. The essential concern in a criminal investigation is the gathering of evidence. It is not easily understood that much of that evidence is very simply the statement provided by the witnesses and the victim that can be turned into testimonial evidence in a trial. It can also be used as evidence in an affidavit or other sworn testimony. Learning how to do interviews begins with the question "What happened?" Listening to the narrative from the witnesses and evaluating whether they are able to explain what happened and what did they see, hear, or know with their senses as compared with what they think, feel, or speculate about is the job of the investigator. Firsthand evidence versus guesses, emotional responses, or what someone else told them has to be sorted out to make sure the witnesses will testify to firsthand experience. The question becomes, Is this person a witness? Can these persons be relied on, and is the truth imbedded in their narrative so that at some point their story can become testimonial evidence? In the beginning, the investigator just needs to be able to listen and provide an administrative format for the witnesses' statements. Write a report or witness statement and interview all the witnesses available and write down their statements. At some point, the investigator will start to understand that some of the witnesses are accurate and helpful in their recollection, and some are not. As you dig into the case, you need to make sure you have some kind of accurate rendering of "what happened." Can you prove the crime you are investigating happened with the proposed testimony of the witnesses? In the case where you have interviewed the victims, you need to be able to determine their value in proving that the crime occurred. Once you have established to the extent possible that you have a crime proven by testimony, you will have accomplished an important level of proof. The ability to take the narratives you have been provided and try to move on to the next big question, "who did it," puts the investigation on the right track. As you begin the journey to finding the suspect, you will realize that some of the persons you have encountered in your search are lying and failing to remember obvious aspects of the case, and some of the persons are just acting suspiciously. ("Suspiciously" describes an action outside of the norm.) As the investigator becomes more sophisticated and experienced, lying, acting suspiciously, and failing to remember will all become indicators of the need to drill down into the stories of these difficult witnesses. It will be necessary to determine if they are holding back the truth to protect themselves and their personal lives, they are frightened, or they are trying to avoid detection because they are in fact involved somehow in the crime. The fact is that all the persons interviewed in an investigation are offering their versions of the crime or conduct before, during, and after the crime. Their version is usually self-centered and should have some objectivity and some subjectivity. Once you are satisfied that a witness is doing the best he can, it may be necessary to work more with that witness to push harder about the facts and information he provides, double-check your own assessment of each witness, and make sure you know what he knows. Even if he is unsure about a detail, make sure you know about that detail and why it was missed. Learning how to push hard or be more aggressive with a solid witness provides unique instruction on how to push hard against the witnesses you know are being evasive. A calm, professional demeanor with the probing and an incessant return to an explanation as to how he knows what he knows is a useful technique. Work hard to learn the best objective version of the truth, and then double back to the witnesses who are failing to provide what they should know but are unwilling to tell you. As you conduct interviews, you will improve your skill and begin to grasp the difference between an accurate narrative and a narrative that doesn't fit with the logic of what happened. So what technique is best to work with a witness who is holding back the truth and misdirecting an investigation?

You first have to build a solid and reasonable narrative based not only on the best witnesses' statements but also relying on the physical evidence recovered. Items of evidence such as spent shells, latent fingerprints, and disrupted furnishings can provide "blocking," or positioning, of the suspects during the crime. Items discarded by the suspect may also provide some insight into the actions of the suspects. You then have to make sure you have a complete picture and background of your difficult witness; then it is necessary to create a plan based on your evaluation of the statement she is willing to supply that is suspect. Where is the weak point? Why would one area of the narrative be more concerning than some other part of the narrative? If her whole story is a lie, what possible reason in her personal life could cause her to be reluctant to tell the truth? If it is fear, why is fear a factor? Is it some overall generalized fear of the criminal element, or is it more specific, like a personal experience or the fact that one or more of the suspects is known to the witness? In most cases, when you are dealing with some personal avoidance of being a witness, even out of fear, the truth in some fashion will surface if the witness is confronted with the lies or a failure to tell the whole truth. In a number of cases, their first statement will contradict the second rendering of the narrative because it is difficult to accurately remember a lie. As the lies and failures of truth combine, the witness will usually relent. The investigator just needs to be prepared for the second interview and be prepared to compare the details between the first version and the second version. The investigator needs to be able to use inconsistencies between more believable witnesses and weaker witnesses so it is clear the witnesses are holding back. The investigator needs to make sure he has vetted the weaker witness to determine if there is something in the witness's background that offers a hint as to why the witness is holding back. These second, or backup, interviews are part of step 2 in the overall investigative plan and should be considered essential leads to follow after the investigator has had the chance to absorb the information that was discovered during the initial investigation.

Interviewing witnesses is like many other aspects of the work in criminal investigation. Experience evolves into expertise. Being comfortable talking to people is the first level of experience. Carefully and precisely recording the narratives provided by witnesses is the next level of experience, which is enhanced by experience and even more so by court preparation of the case. The final level of experience is assessment of the persons interviewed. The assessment has a twofold concern: (1) Is the witness truthful? (2) Is the witness reliable? Assessment is a skill that, once mastered, can streamline investigations. Evaluation and then a subsequent rehabilitation of a difficult witness is one of the most productive abilities a criminal investigator can have.

There is a great deal of anecdotal information about the importance of being able to detect when a person is lying to you. Too much value is placed on being able to detect lies in a criminal investigation. Interviewers will spend time learning and looking for nonverbal clues, when in truth, there are too many reasons for people to lie. Lying happens because a person doesn't want to be involved. Lying happens because a person has a personal distrust for law enforcement. Lying happens because a person is scared of criminals. Lying happens because a person helped or aided the criminal and is trying to avoid detection. Lying also happens just because the person wants to avoid any official record that she was in the part of town or neighborhood where the crime occurred.

Since lying is so multidimensional, lying is not the primary focus. The motive for lying is more important. Eventually, detecting nonverbal clues, such as uneven eye movement and skittish or suspicious behavior, will let a veteran criminal investigator know when a person is lying, but that is only a step toward getting at the truth. The criminal investigator has to put all the witness and victim statements in context to begin the process of logically figuring out the motive for the lies, the context of the lies, and the real potential for turning the liar into a suspect if that is the motive. Again, by using appropriate analysis of the total set of known facts in an investigation and comparing the known with the witness's faulty version along with knowing the background of the witness, the criminal investigator should be able to make some headway with the recalcitrant witness and determine if the lies are personally motivated or indicative of participation in the crime. Lies that can be attributed to some unrelated personal motivation can be explained in court if necessary, but lies that are part of the criminal scheme can be dealt with only by ultimately charging the liar. Prosecutors and defense attorneys earn their pay by breaking down witnesses who lie. It is then up to the jury to rationally determine what effect the lies have on the case.

The criminal investigator needs to be able to reconcile the lies with the truth of the matter well before it comes to trial.

There are no secret formulas or tried-and-true single methods to sort out the problem witnesses; there is simply the continued evaluation and insistence on getting at the truth. In the long run, the more troubling a witness is, the less likely that witness will ever make it to the witness stand. Changing an inaccurate statements will probably force the prosecutor to leave the witness to the defense and let them try to rehabilitate a liar. The investigator needs to keep pressing the witness until a motive for lying and some reasonable version of the truth is obtained. Ultimately, it is necessary to ensure the witness who is lying is not a problem for the case.

SUBJECT INTERVIEWS OR INTERROGATIONS

At the point when a person has been determined to be the perpetrator of a crime, there is usually a need to hear from that person and evaluate her version of the facts. What may surprise students of criminal investigation is that these persons will often admit their crime and may even take full responsibility for their actions. In these cases, the statements they make are as perfunctory as any other witness interview. It can be disconcerting to a criminal investigator who carefully prepares to arrest a subject, turn them into a defendant, and finally close a difficult investigation to find out that the person who committed the crime has been bothered, feeling guilty, and even feeling great remorse about the crime and is willing to make a full confession. The objective nature of criminal investigations requires that the investigator not take a confession at face value. Evaluate and assess the statement provided by the suspect so as to follow the same standard of proof to a confession as has been applied to every step in the process of an investigation. False confessions happen, but there should be questions that can be asked and comparisons with immutable circumstances that will reveal the truthfulness of the confession. Again, motivation may be an important way to assess the confession and sort out the truth from some kind of fictional account. Is a family member trying to protect a weaker or more vulnerable yet guilty person? Is a troubled person with a mental defect confessing to a celebrated crime? Is there simply a co-conspirator trying to take the heat for a crime that her did with others? Whatever the motivation, make an objective evaluation of the confession, make sure it comports with the known facts and witness testimony, and determine if the motive for the crime is logical and consistent. The confession, if it is the truth, will contain deliberate calculation. A goal consistent with the motive for the crime is one important factor, and the details that only the perpetrator can know is the other important aspect of the admission. There should be no questions that stump the subject when she is admitting she is responsible for the crime.

A student of criminal investigation should also know that some violent criminals confess because they are proud of the crime. They confess because they believe that the victim is somehow at fault. They will confess to the rape of a child and claim the victim seduced them. They will confess to a murder and claim they had to because the victim was out to get them. They had to act first. Serial rapists and serial killers will openly confess once they are caught and act almost relieved that the police finally caught them. The investigator should recognize these bizarre claims for what they are and let the subjects fully explain and justify their actions. Let them openly berate the victim and explain about the mental and, in some cases, the physical pressure that was exerted on them. It is not the job of the investigator at this point to act as some kind of critic to the subjects' motives. It is up to the investigator to let the subjects talk and provide as much detail as possible. It is even acceptable to listen and act more like a life counselor instead of a law enforcement officer. Take the side of the subjects to encourage the whole dimension of their confession. (If the subjects try to claim some kind of mental illness or some new and unusual method of mental disease, it is essential for the investigator to get all the facts and perspective the subjects are willing to share.) A large number of career criminals, especially violent career criminals, consider themselves to be victims of their families, their communities, and society as a whole. As victims, they can justify all kinds of violent behavior. They can justify hatred, anger, and vengeance because, in their world, if anything negatively affects them, it is okay to remove the source of that effect. Knowing this kind of attitude and using some level of understanding and pathos about their victimization can produce results in getting the subjects to fully admit to their crimes. Immediate anger, disappointment, judgment, and a lack of empathy will usually cause the subjects to shut down and refuse to talk.

Returning to the lessons we learned in chapter 3 of this text, any subject interview that involves the confinement of the subject pursuant to an arrest or indictment requires the criminal investigator to advise the subject of his constitutional rights. So the question for the criminal investigator is, How much of a problem is it for procuring a full confession from a cooperative subject? Remember that to this point, we have been talking about subjects who for their own purposes are anxious to tell their story, give their side of the crime, and simply unburden themselves of guilt. They want to confess because they are in fact guilty. This pronouncement seems quite counterintuitive to lawyers and other legal practitioners in the criminal justice system, but what they don't realize is that it is difficult to lie and stick to an elaborate lie when confronted with proof of one's crime. Professional conduct is the main factor in deciding how to conduct the interview of a cooperative suspect. Carefully read the *Miranda* warning to the subjects and request that they sign a knowing waiver of the rights so they can in fact tell you their story for the record. If they choose to have a lawyer present for their interview, that is their prerogative, but it is your prerogative as the investigator to demand that the subjects be allowed to speak for themselves and answer all questions you may have. Most defense lawyers will have a problem with allowing a free-ranging interview, but if the subjects want to talk to you, they can and should be encouraged to do so.

Either with the waiver or with the defense lawyer present, encourage the subjects to give a full statement, and make sure you satisfy all the questions your investigation has raised. You can express empathy with the subjects about their perceived wrongs and personal victimization. You can act caring and concerned to get the subjects to open up and be honest without compromising your position as a law enforcement officer. This kind of sympathetic support for a confession is in no way coercive or legally suspect; it is merely the response needed to get at the facts.

Finally, cooperative subjects who are knowledgeable career criminals may wish to confess to rid themselves of any future jeopardy. They may want to begin the process of satisfying several jurisdictions to consider some kind of omnibus plea agreement. They may also want to clear the books on pending investigations that they know will eventually result in future charges against them. Serial killers and serial rapists will exchange full confessions and provide important outstanding details of their crimes in exchange for avoiding the death penalty or obtaining some kind of consideration about where they will be incarcerated. These kinds of arrangements usually involve at least one proffer interview, which consists of an overview or summary of the crimes that will be confessed to, and several debriefing interviews that cover the necessary details. Debriefing interviews for these kinds of arrangements will be covered later in this chapter. Professional car thieves, burglars, and armed robbers who are serial offenders will use significant charges resulting from a thorough investigation to roll up all their potential cases into one significant and expansive plea agreement. The first step in this process may be a full confession to at least one of the crimes being investigated. A detailed and comprehensive confession provides the federal or state prosecutor with a baseline of veracity to make the decision to allow such a plea agreement. In fact, in many jurisdictions throughout the United States, finding a defendant guilty for two or three residential burglaries will not normally result in more years of incarceration than finding a defendant guilty of twenty or more residential burglaries. Jurisdictions usually allow only one or two car theft incidents per trial, so proving that a defendant has stolen twenty to thirty cars will result in ten or more trials. All of these trial limitations tend to encourage local prosecutors to cut plea deals with career criminals whenever possible. Punishments for similar crimes are often concurrent, leaving the state and federal prosecutors in a position to close out as many cases as possible while needing to verify that the defendant is in fact responsible for a significant crime spree. Some balanced punishment reflecting the results of a large number of serious but low-priority property crime cases will, in the opinion of the prosecutor, give the community justice for this kind of career criminal along with closing a large number of felony investigations. The lead investigators in these kinds of arrangements are responsible to conduct thorough subject interviews and subsequent follow-up investigation to prove to the extent possible the truthfulness of the subject. As mentioned above, the *Miranda* warning is not usually an obstacle in these circumstances. The defendant who knows his rights and is faced with certain conviction is cooperating to the benefit of his future. For the most part, the subject will be truthful and comprehensive, but the veteran criminal investigator should be aware that the subject knows more than he is willing to share to simply dispose of his own crimes. Given this opportunity, every effort should be made to analyze the background of the subject and ask pointed questions about other criminal associates or the subject's exposure to the local criminal ecosystem. The prosecutor's arrangement should include some extra added incentive for full cooperation from a cooperative career criminal. The investigator should make the extra effort to build rapport and develop a positive relationship with this kind of subject so the opportunity is not lost.

Personal Experience

During the early years of my career in the FBI, I worked task force investigations of residential burglaries, car thefts, and armed robberies. As a result of requirements established for federal prosecution, I was unable to present certain significant theft cases for federal prosecution. Unless a single burglary resulted in the loss of $80,000 worth of stolen property or more that was transported across state lines, the proof that I developed in my investigations against somewhat lesser thefts never made the cut for federal prosecution. Government property thefts had to be significant amounts of loss, or they were not prosecuted at all. Car thefts had to be part of a car ring, such as a chop shop (stealing cars and breaking them down into individual parts to sell at close to retail auto parts prices), VIN switch operations (counterfeiting vehicle identification numbers so the car could be retitled and sold at or near market value), or international export car theft operations to take advantage of higher prices for US autos in other countries that are unable to determine they are stolen property. Any investigation lower on the criminality scale than these more commercial enterprises would not be prosecuted in federal court.

As a matter of investigative course, our cases started at lower-level cases that we were eventually able to build into major federal investigations. Occasionally, these cases required more immediate prosecution, and the subjects needed to be incarcerated to protect the community from their criminal behavior. These cases ended with the kinds of cooperation agreements mentioned above. Our squad was able to confront suspects whom we had determined were subjects, and we were able to overwhelm them with multiple cases for which they knew they were responsible, so we obtained confession after confession with very little effort. Many of these subjects eventually made arrangements for plea agreements with federal and state prosecutors. It was standard practice in Maryland, DC, and Virginia to consolidate a number of cases against career offenders for the same or similar offenses. The crooks we confronted for subject interviews knew what they were facing and usually accepted their fate and confessed to their crimes as a matter of routine. In each case, they were hoping for a quick and final plea.

UNREPENTANT SUBJECT INTERVIEWS

As satisfying as routine confessions are, the challenge of working a tough interview with a career offender is more instructive and in many cases more satisfying. Again, each interview begins with the *Miranda* warning. This is a bit of slow dance with most subjects. They are very familiar with the process and know their rights, so they will in some cases patiently wait to hear the recitation and may even ask questions about it. What they are looking for is some kind of dialogue with the investigator. They are more than willing to appear cooperative and will sign the waiver of rights because they know they won't be interviewed about the crime for which they have been charged without signing the waiver. They also know it may be days, weeks, or months before they learn exactly how law enforcement got onto them. Career criminals are often anxious to know the details of the investigation, and if they choose to wait for a law-yer, they will learn only when the prosecutor communicates with the defense attorney. They will usually have access to an indictment or an arrest affidavit, but the informa-tion in those documents may be limited and summarized. Even a search warrant af-fidavit can be kept sealed for a time leading up to a trial. Other elements of discovery, such as covert surveillance or recorded evidence, will be delayed until the appropriate time for discovery. Scientific evidence, such as fingerprints, ballistics, or biological identifications will also be held back for a time. This leaves the career offender in limbo until the prosecutor provides discovery. So career criminals who are familiar with the process will sign a waiver of their *Miranda* rights, make up an elaborate lie about their noninvolvement in the crime, and try their best to pump information from the investigator. As long as the investigator is sharing information, the subjects will continue to talk, but once the subjects determine the exercise is futile, they will assert their right to an attorney and do everything they can to end the interview.

If the investigator is willing to participate in this exercise with the defendants, there are usually a number of benefits. Lies are much harder to remember than the truth, so just letting the subjects talk and provide their alibis, alternative narratives, and even justifications for their fingerprints, bullets, or DNA at the scene of a crime can be informative. The need to keep your investigation confidential continues during this process, so choose the true facts that will be indisputable and unrevealing about witnesses to share with the defendants. They will eventually know this information, but be scrupulous in your dissemination of information. Even a lie or two by the in-vestigator can be justified during this kind of interview because you are being fed lies from the subjects; as such, it is fair to suggest that you have facts that you don't have to keep the subjects talking.

Personal Experience

During my career as a criminal investigator, I made every effort to let the subjects talk as long and with as much detail as possible. This makes it easier at the end of the interview to list all the lies the subjects have told you so that the subjects can go away from the encounter with a realization that the lies will be shown in their trials to be lies, and even if they make up a convincing story, the jury will be able to see how impossible their narrative really is. Our team, in an investigation of a violent killer in 1994, discovered the fingerprints of the subject in a house where a triple murder occurred. When we arrested the subject, the main focus of the interview was to get the subject to say if he had ever visited the house. He adamantly denied ever having been in the house. This lie was the best admission we could have ever gotten from an experienced career criminal. We also investigated another murder where the subject shot the victim in the back of the head while being a passenger in the backseat of the car. When I told him we had witnesses who had identified him, he scoffed at the idea and said, "What, did they see me hanging my head outside the back window?" In fact, that is exactly how the witnesses saw him. There were neighborhood residents who had seen him as the car passed their houses very slowly. I never mentioned anything about his being in the backseat or having shot the victim from the backseat. Even as he was trying to denigrate the facts I asserted, he used some truth to justify his disregard of what really happened. He just couldn't believe that any of the neighborhood witnesses had ever come forward. So the mantra I always abided by was, just let the subject talk. Even the most sophisticated liar will slip up and say something that may be helpful to your investigation.

CONTROLLING THE NARRATIVE

During the preparation for the subject interview, make sure you don't say anything to the subject that may jeopardize a witness, even when the subject knows a co-conspirator is turned and going to testify against her. Don't compromise the safety of that witness or any other witness. It is your responsibility to keep the witnesses safe; therefore, admit nothing that helps the subjects in their line of thinking in that case. This may be hard and in some cases silly, depending on the facts in the case, but this is a solid protocol that should always be followed. Letting the subject know that scientific evidence proves he is responsible is okay if you consult with the prosecutor beforehand. Always avoid disturbing the prosecutor's strategy for the case since the whole matter will be turned over to him. If you choose to fabricate evidence or witnesses, make sure you are not sending the subject down a path that can lead to violence against an innocent person. If you say you have three eyewitnesses to the crime you really don't have but the subject knows there were four eyewitnesses who have never been contacted or refused to cooperate in the investigation, you may have signed their death warrant. Even lies by you will have consequences. Make sure if you use that technique you will not have cause to regret it later. Generally, it is best to stick with the truth, but if you have to suggest certain fabricated facts to keep the subject talking, make the facts as vague as possible. This technique may come back to hurt you with regard to the one-on-one relationship with the subject later in the trial process when the subject chooses to plead guilty and provide cooperation. If you lied to the subject, it will be difficult for him to trust you when he needs to.

SUBJECT INTERVIEWS UNDER EXTREME CONDITIONS

In 2018, during her confirmation hearing to be CIA director, Gina Haspel testified about enhanced interrogation techniques. Haspel curiously stated that CIA agents "are not well trained and competent in conducting interviews" and, therefore, the program of enhanced interrogation following the September 11, 2001, terrorists' attacks evolved from US Army research in the area conducted by psychologists who used techniques that approached torture but "didn't go over the line." FBI agents who had to do follow-up interviews with terrorism suspects discovered these techniques were used and complained that they would taint any interviews into criminal matters. It is clear to most legal scholars that statements made by a criminal defendant that were obtained by torture or physical coercion will be disallowed in a criminal trial. For this reason alone, it is never in the interest of the criminal investigator to use torture and physical coercion to encourage a difficult subject to provide a statement. In the opinion of the writer, a confession obtained using physical coercion is automatically suspect for accuracy. A person who is subjected to torture or enhanced physical coercion will make some effort to give the interrogator what the interrogator wants to hear, and that information may not be the truth. A human being when physically harmed will do anything possible to stop the harm. The subject may believe that if she tells the truth, it may not satisfy the interrogator, leading to the decision to provide misinformation, which the subject thinks will satisfy her tormentors. This puts the results of any such interview in the category of unreliable. Taking the time and using various techniques to encourage the building of a positive relationship between the subject and the interviewer will in most cases yield positive results. Adding to that mix an awareness of details and solid facts about the subject under investigation provides the best chance at developing a truthful, or fruitful, final product. Lies about certain aspects of a crime can be just as helpful as the truth. The key is to have the subjects provide details and make an effort to justify or explain their actions. Demanding certain specific bits of information just complicates the process. Let the subjects speak and steer the interview with subtlety and purpose.

In extreme cases, such as the kidnapping of a child or any other vulnerable and innocent person, a law enforcement officer may think that a violent interrogation may be needed to save the life of the victim. There is no reliable evidence that this will work, but in frustration, it has been tried and even been successful. If it is successful and becomes part of the court record, the results may be the dismantling of an investigation in court. A substantial amount of evidence in a trial may be excluded. The subject may go free to kidnap or continue his predatory behavior. The victim may be found unharmed, and that is the balance against the bad results. Unfortunately, the victims in the few cases known to the writer have ended up being discovered dead, and other victims were lost forever.

The criminal investigator needs to understand that in these violent cases with vulnerable victims, she is dealing with perpetrators who are psychopaths and sociopaths. They lie more often than they tell the truth. They manipulate others for fun and pleasure. They consider themselves to be the victims and are so egocentric that even extreme bodily harm is worth it if having some kind of last laugh at the expense of a passionate criminal investigator can be obtained. It is understandable that a passionate law enforcement officer will occasionally let anger and hatred of the suspect overcome her professional demeanor. Just remember where the most harm can happen, and stay disciplined in your pursuit of justice.

Discipline and adherence to the rule of law make up the best path to justice. Reviewing the facts, detailing the movements of the subject, pressuring the subject in a manner that will be acceptable in court, and maintaining the integrity of the investigation is the path to recovering the victims if they are in jeopardy. Do not disregard the preparation used to identify the subjects, and use the details uncovered during the investigation to close the loop on the missing pieces of the puzzle.

INTERVIEW/INTERROGATION TECHNIQUES

Below are techniques of interrogation that are unacceptable versus acceptable. It is up to the criminal investigator to choose the right path and improve her technique with experience and the analysis of the subjects that will be interviewed.

Not Constitutionally Allowed

- *Torture* is the practice of inflicting or strongly suggesting the infliction of bodily harm to an interviewee to demand cooperation. This technique is not only likely to get the confession and any admission thrown out in court; any information used from the technique will be considered fruits of a poisonous tree and likewise be excluded. The other reality of torture is that the statements from the subject will be suspect as to their reliability.
- *Coercion* is the practice of persuading someone to give a confession or a statement by threatening to do something by using force or threats: "You will be prosecuted and your children will be taken from you." "Your family will be targeted, and you will be jailed along with members of your family or close friends." Again, this technique is likely to get the confession or statements excluded, and any evidence obtained as a result of the interview will be fruits of the poisonous tree.

Constitutionally Allowed

- *Lying or providing false information* is the practice of making the interviewee believe something that is not true. "Your co-conspirators are giving statements right now!" "Your fingerprints were discovered on the gun." "You were identified by witnesses. Your picture came up on some surveillance tape just as you ran away from the scene." If you are going to lie, it has to be about significant evidence, and it has to be plausible. This technique will often burn the bridge between the interviewer and the subject, so if a later plan to work with the subject is possible, this may not be the best approach. This technique is usually allowable and does not taint any statements or subsequent evidence, but all care should be taken to keep the falsehoods reasonable and nonexplosive, for example, "Your mother gave you up. And she is doing a written statement right now!"
- *Friendly persuasion* is the practice of claiming to be empathetic, sympathetic, and personally concerned with the interviewee. The criminal investigator has to be an accomplished actor. There is no benefit to trying this technique if the criminal investigator is not believable.
- *Anger* is the practice of using righteous anger to display disappointment with the actions of the interviewee. If the criminal investigator is rightfully angry about the crime, displaying that anger is perfectly acceptable and is a useful technique when interviewing a subject who is concerned or upset about the crime. The anger has to dissipate quickly with a return to a professional and disciplined demeanor. Consider this technique when the victim is clearly more vulnerable than the subject.

- *Demands by use of commanding presence or position* is the practice of using your authority to intimidate your interviewee. This kind of intimidation is mere bluster; it will only work on less sophisticated subjects who may think you have some kind of special power over them. In truth, the power is in the hands of the subject. He needs to decide to answer questions or not. Any demand without any real power behind the demand is hollow and will give the subject a way out. Slamming your credentials on the table and telling the subject he is in the clutches of the "baddest" detective on the planet may be good theater, but that is as far as it gets you.
- *Curiosity* is the practice of interviewing with a less passionate style motivated by simple interest and without an agenda. "You are just another in a long line of uninteresting criminals." "We are just curious as to how this particular crime went down. No rush. Take your time, and try to remember as much as you can."
- *Good cop, bad cop* is the practice of using two opposite approaches on the same interviewee to determine if either generates more useful information. This is a tried-and-true method that can take advantage of an investigative partnership with two distinct personalities. The terms *good* and *bad* are interchangeable with smart and dull, or mean and nice, or tough and mild. Just because it is openly scoffed at in modern fiction does not mean that it doesn't work. The extreme pressure on a person charged with a crime can be very disarming, so allowing subjects to choose which of two investigators they will respond to returns some semblance of control to the subjects, allowing them to try to talk their way out of trouble.
- *Fill in the gaps* is the practice of displaying your overwhelming knowledge of the facts in an investigation with the simple request that the interviewee fill in the missing pieces. "We don't really care if you confess; we just want your information to fill us in on specifics." This technique will work only if you do have extensive and detailed knowledge of the case. Again, be careful and judicious in what you give up to the subject.
- *Harsh and apparently out of control* is the practice of momentarily "stepping over the line" by displaying harsh physical or emotional treatment to "get the ball rolling," followed by recovery and more professional conduct. It is best handled by at least two and sometimes three interviewers. This technique can be a significant problem because it may seem like coercion, but if the interviewer blows up and then is immediately replaced by a more sympathetic interviewer, the technique is nothing more than theater.
- *Complete incompetence or ignorance* is the practice of displaying no knowledge of an investigation to attempt to get the interviewee to teach the investigator about the criminal event. This technique can be helpful if you have subjects who believe that they are intellectually superior to the investigator. They will make statements they don't believe you will comprehend and open the door to criminal behavior they don't think you had sense enough to note in your case. The key is the end of this kind of interview. If the subjects provide a long-winded dissertation about how innocent they are, the investigator can provide two or three insurmountable facts or evidence that prove their guilt. This should usually result in a moment of realization that frustrates the subjects and throws off their explanation. Any time mistakes are made by the subjects, there should be helpful revelations.

• *Admiration* is the practice of appealing to the ego or arrogance of the interviewee, by showing respect for the calculation, brutality, intelligence, and sophistication of his actions. Again, career criminals often consider themselves the center of the universe who have been mistreated their whole lives. Acting like a sycophant who is impressed by their expertise and ability as criminal masterminds can encourage certain criminal suspects to brag about their crimes. The simple fact is that sophisticated criminals are proud of their accomplishments, even to the point of being happy to share their experiences with law enforcement "fans."

Each of these techniques and variations on the themes are somewhat subjective and interrogator-oriented. Before the interview starts, these techniques should be discussed, and an evaluation needs to take place that provides the best method to apply to the particular suspect. Are the lead investigator and her partner the best team to do the technique, or should the interview be passed on to a different team? Once the first test of getting the subject to sign the *Miranda* waiver is passed, the game is on. Let the subjects talk, and be flexible enough to continue the interview as long as it takes to exhaust the subjects of all the outstanding questions. Other exterior protocols such as letting the subjects sit in a quiet interview room to stir for minutes or hours can be part of the process, but those protocols should be fully discussed with the prosecutor to make sure no legal impediments are anticipated by an extra-long interrogation. Make sure to provide bathroom breaks and food and water. Don't compromise an investigation by making a stupid, unforced error. If the result of the interview is full confession with plenty of investigative leads, make sure the leads are conducted immediately to avoid the subject having second thoughts and somehow getting the word out to confederates to remove evidence or scare witnesses.

If the statement is satisfactory but is a limited set of admissions, such as the subject was at the scene of the crime or the subject handled the weapon used in the shooting, make sure the statement is carefully prepared, and attempt to get the subject to sign the statement and acknowledge what was provided in the interview. Attempt to get the same kind of signed acknowledgment for the full confession. If on the other hand the statement is just a litany of lies and misinformation, make sure the subject acknowledges and owns up to the lies as well.

LOCATION AND NUMBERS

Every critical or important interview in a criminal investigation should be conducted by at least two knowledgeable participants in the case. In most cases, a third person is too many but can be acceptable if there is a special need. The interview should take place in a quiet, comfortable environment conducive to easy communication. Use video recordings, one-way mirrors allowing outside observation, and audio recordings only if they are appropriate and acceptable to the investigative agency. Replacing interviewers in the middle of an interview for dramatic reasons or for particular investigative expertise is acceptable but should be done only when necessary. Documenting the interview is usually a well-established protocol with proper administrative forms and signed statements. Each agency or department will have well-established protocols based on coordination with the judicial jurisdiction to which they most often present cases. Some interviews can take place in the homes of subjects or in the agency offices. All-important interviews need to be comprehensive enough to cover all the outstanding questions raised by the investigation. Subject interviews are usually one-time-only events. Some victims and critical witnesses may have limited availability. Consider all these extraneous factors when planning an important interview. The use of notebooks or digital devices is a preferred way to record highlights and important details. It is usually too cumbersome to record a full interview, but if that is considered necessary, it is still very beneficial to have a subject sign to acknowledge a summary of important aspects of the statement. Remember that even if the subjects are lying, their acknowledgment of the lies can be used to show they are continuing to evade responsibility for the crime when the trial happens.

DEBRIEFINGS

Subjects identified in serious felony investigations who have been a part of significant criminal conspiracies are sometimes given the opportunity to reduce the penalty they are facing by fully cooperating with the government. As mentioned above, serial killers who may be responsible for a number of murders can avoid the death penalty and may even obtain better living conditions in prison if they fully cooperate and provide details of their crimes, including the locations where they disposed of their victims' remains. Serial rapists can also be afforded benefits for closing or solving unsolved cases in the present jurisdiction and in other jurisdictions. Finally, burglars, car thieves, and robbers can close the book on their outstanding crimes by providing detailed information about their crimes. All of these interviews in the furtherance of plea agreements bring a series of special circumstances to the criminal investigator in charge of the debriefings. The following steps should be followed.

1. Preparation for the interviews should be based on a proffer interview, sometimes referred to as a "Queen for a Day" agreement with the prosecutor. These proffers usually are summaries of the nature and scope of the subject's knowledge.
2. The interview team should be investigators who have already established a relationship with the subject. The team should be fully aware of all of the potential crimes that may be discussed.
3. Expect the subject to hold back and even lie about crimes that make the subject look "extra corrupt." These lies can put the plea deal in jeopardy, so it is necessary to identify these lapses and rehabilitate the subject as the debriefing progresses.
4. There will be a need to corroborate every detail provided by the subject. Once a case is identified, it is necessary to verify details about the crime scene, the victim, and the forensics and make sure they are consistent with the information provided by the subject.

5. Determine if there is a way to identify every person who the subject knows is involved in criminal conduct. Create a photo album of those persons along with other potential suspects so the subject can positively identify all the persons he is providing information about.

6. In the event the subject is being interviewed about an ongoing criminal enterprise, a gang, a criminal syndicate, or a gambling, prostitution, or drug ring, determine the daily, weekly, and monthly money amounts generated by and for each person in the group. Explain the hierarchy, the chain of command, and the distribution of financial resources. Fully explain the nature of the violence involved in their operations. Identify every violent crime the subject knows about.

7. Debriefings of gang or organized-crime members will usually involve many interviews. It is necessary in these cases to begin to prepare the subject as a potential witness against the criminal enterprise as a whole.

Debriefing a subject about his own history of criminal conduct may involve a few co-conspirators, a fence of stolen property, a money launderer for a robbery gang, a weapons supplier, and aiders and abettors who help in the nuts and bolts of the subject's crime spree. These serious criminals, especially serial murderers, rapists, and robbers are not great candidates for transitioning into witnesses. It is essential to make sure they are providing truthful and verifiable facts and a narrative that can result in the closure of the cases committed by the subject. Gang members and organized-crime members are in some cases just as despicable, but it is usually necessary to transition these career criminals into witnesses who can be relied on to tell the truth in a trial against their former compatriots. The main impediment to this transition is the natural tendency these career criminals have to intimidate, challenge norms, and act on their own behalf with very little concern about others. The need for a witness to be humble, empathetic, and charismatic goes against every instinct these career criminals have. Part of the debriefing process for these subjects is to facilitate to the extent possible this transition. Once the investigator is convinced that the subject is being truthful and forthcoming, finding the part of the subject's character that will allow a jury to believe her testimony is the most difficult phase of the debriefing. Ultimately, the success or failure of major investigations using these cooperative subjects will depend on their ability to provide testimonial evidence as an insider and a witness to the truth.

SUMMARY

Interviews are the source of most of the testimonial evidence required in a criminal investigation. Putting a single crime or a series of crimes into a human context so the narrative that is the truth can be presented to a judge and jury or any other panel of review is the reason criminal investigators are needed. Some person or group of persons needs to be able to simplify, organize, and analyze the evidence, whether it is testimonial or physical, into a form that can be disseminated to the proper forum. Tough interviews, subject interviews, and debriefings are the biggest challenge for a criminal investigator. Meeting that challenge requires experience, preparation, and creativity.

Anyone can ask the question "What happened?" It takes an experienced investigator to continue the process and ultimately find the truth about the crime. Each part of the process has special requirements, and when the criminal investigator finally achieves the goal of charging the right person with committing the crime, the investigator has to be ready and able to be satisfied with the outcome of the case.

Chapter Fourteen

Confidential Informants

Sources, snitches, informants, stoolies, and the human relationship.

Criminal investigators and all law enforcement officials are called upon to act in accordance with ethical and moral standards. Throughout this text, we have discussed adherence to the rule of law, the protection of the rights of the accused, and the fundamental requirement to be reasonable and fair in conducting criminal investigations. Every day, people make decisions, choosing between the right and moral thing to do or the wrong and corrupt thing to do. When a law enforcement official chooses the wrong or corrupt path, it is usually a career-ending choice if it becomes known. Society expects moral rectitude on the part of police officials. In the study of ethical behavior, a blatant disregard for right and wrong is considered corrupt and should be avoided, but criminal investigators and other law enforcement professionals very often find they have to make choices for the greater good. These choices are never more apparent than the need to develop a worthwhile relationship with a criminal informant. Each criminal investigator should have or develop a disciplined and healthy moral code. Criminal investigators should choose a path through the religion they practice or a clear and faithful morality that is generally in line with some of the basic universal constants about right and wrong. For example, the Decalogue, or Ten Commandments, is a pretty consistent moral code. It is also the basis for most criminal law in Western and particularly in American and English jurisprudence. Simple commands such as "Thou shalt not kill" or "Thou shalt not steal" form the basis for a number of criminal statutes. When we begin to prioritize crimes of violence higher than crimes against property, we take that code and begin to fine-tune our reaction to the decision to choose a lesser evil over a more important and justifiable goal. If criminal investigators consider letting a burglar get a break if the burglar can help solve a homicide or a rape, are those investigators breaking their moral code or making the choice for a greater good? We also need to consider that the burglar may see the greater good and choose to tell law enforcement what he knows in spite of the fact that it may imperil him to a law enforcement official. Criminal investigators can't become so jaded as to think that morality is always missing from the minds of career criminals. Even the Italian Mafia has lines they will not cross. Killing innocent women and children is unacceptable in their morality, supposedly. For the criminal investigator, the choice comes down to what greater good is an acceptable choice. The investigator should also remember that any lasting or full pardon a criminal informant gets from telling all about a more serious crime is not his decision alone. Usually a prosecutor, the criminal investigator's supervisor, and even the commander or chief of his agency will be part of the decision.

In the case of a criminal informant who is seeking or hoping for some kind of forbearance or relief from criminal culpability, there has to be a reckoning from her that the information provided is significantly more important than her reduction of charges. In the following explanations, we will discuss the various kinds of criminal informants, confidential sources, snitches, or cooperating witnesses and how they should be handled by criminal investigators. But before we get into that discussion, it should be understood that criminal investigators will have a number of skills available to them in their pursuit of the truth. A criminal investigator should be a careful and insightful listener in conducting interviews. A criminal investigator should have absolute determination to solve every case. A criminal investigator should have knowledge and experience when evaluating the importance of witnesses and the same kind of knowledge and experience when evaluating and processing physical evidence. Attention to details, important references, and calculations should be part of the tools in an investigator's toolbox. But all those talents pale in comparison to a criminal investigator who can effectively work with and exploit confidential sources and criminal informants. Criminal investigators who can make great strides in an investigation using their skills and talents are only half as successful as they might be if they could develop their own database of criminal intelligence. It is essential to work with and develop human sources who are part of the criminal ecosystem of the jurisdictional venue where that investigator operates. When a criminal investigator has team or squad colleagues who have the same expertise and access to the human intelligence information from the same ecosystem, the chances of successfully solving cases goes up to a factor of the number of team members. There simply is no way to be successful working criminal investigations involving career criminals without confidential sources and criminal informants.

The human relationship that develops between an investigator and the criminal informant can be the most productive professional relationship an investigator can develop. Criminal informants (or human intelligence) are essential to investigative agencies because they can easily obtain the kind of inside information from the criminal underworld that is impossible for an investigator to uncover. Occasionally, when an investigator is acting in an undercover capacity, he will be privy to the kind of open discussions that occur between criminal actors in both a social and a business atmosphere. But this is rare, and the access of a criminal informant is ongoing in these venues simply because the informant is not viewed as a threat or may even be considered a well-respected co-conspirator to all manner of criminal activity.

Unfortunately, for the investigator, the only way most informants can operate and obtain reliable information is to participate in criminal conduct or appear to participate actively in criminal conduct. Sometimes the informant can merely observe the actions of his criminal associates and obtain valuable information, but for him to maintain his bona fides in the underworld or criminal ecosystem, the informant has to be feared, liked, or considered not too dangerous to be a concern about what he knows and doesn't know. Also, he may not be considered a threat because he is suspected of being involved in his own criminal behavior, which would far outweigh any desire he may have in cooperating with police. Of course, in this way, the source will have to appear to continue to operate outside the law, giving his criminal associates cause to believe that he is trustworthy and would never jeopardize his own freedom by snitching. The appearance may actually be real, so the dilemma continues. Does the criminal investigator allow a criminal informant to maintain his position in the criminal underworld? Charismatic, socially sophisticated informants with a con man streak can usually carry out the image well enough to be accepted, but these same manipulative criminals will use their skills on the law enforcement officials they inform to. Thankfully, many informants can maintain their position in the criminal underworld with a routine infusion of cash that makes them appear to be successful criminals. Most career criminals struggle to keep their finances liquid, so if a person who is a known criminal has cash at the ready, she is usually considered a successful criminal. As the nature of the criminal conduct moves into the more lucrative enterprises of drugs, prostitution, and gun running, the small infusions of cash an agency or department can make into the pocket of a working informant may not be enough to keep her running in the same circles as the targets of significant criminal enterprises. In other words, working with successful confidential criminal sources is complicated but absolutely necessary.

Positioning a criminal informant in a position where she has regular contact with important criminal targets can place the investigator in an ethical dilemma. There are ways to overcome the dilemma of maintaining a positive relationship while allowing a source to appear to be a successful criminal in her own right. Eventually, it may become known that the criminal informant is operating outside of the law, so limits to the relationship have to be set. The first way is the investigator limits his relationship with the informant to one investigation, making it clear that the investigation involves more serious offenses than the investigator believes that the source is committing. The investigator can proceed with the case with a clear conscience as long as he doesn't become personally aware of the specific criminal actions of the informant. Suspicions come with the job. Many times, we become so aware of how criminals act that we will always our suspicions. The investigator's conscience may never be totally clear, but she should act only if she knows and can prove the source is continuing his criminal ways. For example, a car thief informs on a violent car theft ring, a drug user informs on a drug gang, or a jewelry fence informs on a dangerous robbery gang that targets high-end jewelry stores. There are other benefits to this kind of short-term investigation-centric approach. One of those benefits is the informant can be used to testify if necessary. Ethically, the investigator should inform the source of this possibility before the relationship begins. No matter how the case proceeds, it is the responsibility of the investigator to protect the informant from any danger that may develop as a result of his help in the case.

As long as an informant in this kind of relationship is not burned (his relationship with the police agency becomes common knowledge), the investigator can in the fu-

ture return to using the informant if a future investigation warrants his involvement
again. It is the responsibility of the investigator to continually monitor and admonish
the informant not to be involved in any criminal conduct, even though it is likely the
informant will continue his criminal ways. Demanding that the informant set aside
his criminal activity while he works for the investigator is a reasonable demand and
should be used to let the informant know he will be called to task if he keeps up his
criminal conduct. Monitoring the informant's behavior is sometimes more difficult,
but if the investigator has troubling concerns, he may ask another investigator or even
another reliable informant to keep tabs on the informant to make sure his actions will
not compromise the investigation or the relationship with the investigator.

The second and most productive method of developing and using a criminal informant is to develop a long-term relationship with the source. The investigator has to be
very select in choosing this kind of informant. The criminal activity of the informant
needs to be superficial and minor. An informant involved in low-level property crimes
or personal drug use or even a middle man who sets up or introduces more significant
criminals to each other is less of a threat to the community than the targeted criminals
she provides intelligence about. The investigator may suspect that the informant is
participating in some kind of illegal activity, but as soon as he becomes truly aware
of the source's criminal acts, he must take action against the informant. Arresting
and charging a valuable informant may actually cement the relationship for future
productive use. As counterintuitive as that sounds, the informant will become aware
of lines that cannot be crossed, and a level of respect for the investigator may develop
in the mind of the informant. Additionally, the source's bona fides as a criminal will
actually be enhanced if she is arrested and does not openly receive any help with her
charges. The investigator should not be surprised or offended by this turn of events;
he should be relieved that the truth is out about the source and that the informant is
aware the investigator will not tolerate her being caught violating the law. Continuing
to monitor and admonish the source and all the while developing a trust relationship
will give the investigator the kind of ethical peace of mind necessary to continue a
relationship with an informant. This trust relationship is similar to a parent–child or
teacher–student dynamic where trust grows from mutual understanding and concern
for future goals, not immediate gratification. Long-term sources of this kind should
be vigorously protected from any exposure, and these kinds of sources should be protected from having to testify in court.

There are of course certain cases when a source will become a witness. If the source
personally observes a crime of violence, such as a murder or a rape, he will be exposed
as a witness for this kind of significant testimony. It is up to the trial prosecutor to
make an effort to keep the informant's relationship with the police agency protected
or limited so there is at least a future time when the source can be reacquired and
made available. The prosecutor can reveal this information to the judge in a sealed
session; the judge can then review the source's file of cases for which he has provided
information and then decide how much about the source's relationship can or should
be revealed. Most judges will reveal the whole history but may limit the ability of the
defense attorney to question the informant in open court about irrelevant prior cases. It

should be noted that a paid confidential source with a long history of payments by the government may present the trial attorney with another dilemma because by using the informant as a witness, it is usually necessary to reveal a long history of payments and other cases on which the informant has helped. This may be reducing the effectiveness of the informant's testimony. The list of payments will also connect with a series of investigations where the source provided important payment-worthy information. This will give an aggressive defense attorney a large amount of information to obfuscate the informant's truthfulness with his street colleagues and occasionally with the government if the source was ever arrested while being employed as an informant. Lies of any kind are great cross-examination fodder to call into question a witness's credibility on the stand, such as open-ended questions, "Haven't you been lying to your friends and family for all the years you worked with the police?" The net result of this kind of exposure is career-ending for a confidential source. It then becomes the responsibility of the investigator assigned to the informant to relocate and protect the source from any threats that may result from this kind of public outing.

Setting aside the ethical dilemma of working with a long-term reliable informant and setting aside problems that can develop if an informant personally observes a violent crime, this kind of informant can be extremely valuable, most importantly, because she knows what the investigator needs from her. She can sort out street rumor from actual intelligence. She can ensure the reliability of her information by inserting herself in circumstances where she will be able to observe, assess, and learn the manner and method of operation of her criminal associates. She will also be able to correctly predict the weaknesses of her criminal associates to provide the investigator with important information and the best method to attack the criminal's weaknesses. This is especially true when the source is evaluating an extensive criminal conspiracy or enterprise. But the investigator always has to come back to a standard practice— trust but verify.

Developing trust in the early part of the relationship is very taxing for both the source and the investigator. The source has to believe that the investigator will protect his identity and refrain from asking the source to do things that are too dangerous. The investigator needs to rely on the source to be smart and observant when it comes to his personal welfare. The investigator should expect that in the beginning the source will try to con her or in some other way gain the upper hand in the relationship. Again, the investigator cannot take offense to this. By working to gain the upper hand, the source is being true to his character and is making an effort to assess the intelligence or lack thereof in the investigator. Trust has to be earned on both sides of the relationship, and so a confidential source that is worthwhile will test the capabilities of the investigator to see if the investigator is worthy and able to protect the source if needed. The source is motivated in many ways to work with the investigator. Some of those reasons may be obvious, such as financial support, but having a supportive friend in law enforcement or having the ability to turn the tables on enemies in the criminal ecosystem can be just as important. (Informing on competitors in criminal enterprises allows the source to use the government agents and resources to remove his competitors.)

Personal Experience

Toward the end of my career in the FBI, I was asked to provide a series of lectures on confidential sources to assistant US attorneys from the city of Boston and elsewhere in the northeastern United States. In Boston, a highly celebrated case against an Irish American mob boss had revealed the boss to be an FBI informant. The informant had supposedly provided a moderate level of important information to the FBI agent who was his handler. That same agent eventually was charged among other crimes with complicity in a murder case. The agent was corrupted by his relationship with the boss. It was generally believed, especially by the federal prosecutor's office, that the informant had used the FBI as a shield against prosecution. An objective view of the case is that the FBI was in fact played by a charismatic con man career criminal, who was as violent if not more so than his competitors. The solution touted by the prosecutors was that all FBI informants should be vetted and approved by their office before we would be allowed to work with the informant. I disagreed with their assessment and said the relationship and the confidential nature of the relationship have to be closely guarded. I explained that in my experience, federal prosecutors' average tenure is between five and ten years, whereas a quality informant's relationship with the government can be twenty years or more. Federal prosecutors who have built a reputation as professional litigators often end up working for criminal defendants. The dilemma is, Why should an investigator reveal an important asset to a person who next year may be working for a criminal defendant? It is very disturbing that a case like the Boston mob boss could happen and the FBI's relationship was so corrupted, but the whole relationship of criminal investigators nationwide with criminal informants should not be weakened because one case of extremely bad judgment and corruption happened. I was blindsided by this controversial case, which I had not heard of before I was ready to lecture the class. After long reflection and a review of the books and news articles about the case, I still believe that confidential informants are the business of the investigative agency, unless and until they are required to testify and become witnesses instead of criminal assets.

In continuing with our discussion of why a source would be willing to cooperate with law enforcement, the motives are numerous. The source may simply be trying to build up a protective shield in the event the source becomes a target for violence by criminals he knows in his orbit who may have it in for him. Additionally, there are a number of personal needs that can be filled by associating with a reliable and, in many cases, senior mentor (a competent law enforcement officer with a quality education who evolved from the "straight world") who can offer positive advice for a future when the source leaves or ends her criminal career for good. Again, there is the possibility of a parent–child, teacher–student, or mentor–mentee relationship that the source may have never had in his life. These relationships are missing in most career offenders' biographies, and it is not foolish to believe that a person who finally meets a worthwhile and successful "friend" who values their relationship might eventually be moved to embrace that relationship. Informants will take advantage of suggestions, advice, and even lifestyle adjustments for themselves and their families.

In working or developing positive working relationships with informants, the investigator should continually assess her relationship with the source. It has to be professional and trusting. That means there will be many occasions when both the informant and the investigator will find themselves coming together in a personal friendship. This is actually a good thing. The investigator and the informant should care about each other and their human relationships. An informant's family, for example, is an important concern for the investigator. If any harm should ever come to that family, the investigator needs to ensure it has nothing to do with the informant's work. The informant may wish to know certain things about the family of the investigator. There should be a careful but candid exchange about this. Lying or holding back can sour the trust you are trying to build. The one thing that will end the relationship is if the personal connection becomes too familiar. Any kind of sexual relationship between the investigator and the informant should never be tolerated or even contemplated. Taking an informant into the home of an investigator should also be avoided. It is best if both parties think of their interaction as simple friendship with no strings attached. It is hard for most people to develop a long-standing close relationship without developing a friendly caring relationship. In the alternative, a strictly cold professional relationship without a personal connection should also be avoided. In the actual day-to-day working of a long-term informant, this kind of cold impersonal relationship will last only if there is some enormously important motive to continue the relationship. This kind of relationship will also not be as professionally productive because the informant is not likely to do more than is asked of him. The investigator should acknowledge that a confidential informant is an important colleague who should be treated well and protected.

Invariably good and productive informants will put their life in danger and be willing to go where the investigator can never go. It takes extraordinary courage to do some of the things expected of them. Certainly, basic human compassion and respect should be extended to the informant even if she has a troubled past and a less than stellar reputation. Any attempt on the part of the informant to gain the upper hand in the relationship should be looked at as understandable and dealt with by fully explaining to the informant that the relationship can and will end if she continues to try to subvert or corrupt it. The relationship is strictly voluntary, and if the informant is uncomfortable, she should withdraw; otherwise, the investigator needs to have the last word and be the decision maker.

ADMINISTRATIVE CONCERNS

Every law enforcement agency will have report writing and documentary requirements for working informants. On-the-books informants receive code names or numbers, and the investigator must follow a set of administrative guidelines for paying and supporting the informant. It is this built-in administrative system that allows the investigator to protect herself and her informants from carelessly being revealed or having some misguided internal affairs unit from starting an investigation on the investigator's close relationship with a known criminal. The informant in this context is then the responsibility of the head of the agency, and any exposure of the informant has to be formerly approved before the investigator is allowed to go forward. This fact can have a chilling effect on a judge or a defense attorney, who may wish to go on a fishing expedition to discover the identity of a productive informant. At worst, some of the disclosure/discovery efforts have ended in an en camera confidential review (legal discussion of the issue in the judge's office or chambers, which is kept confidential) of the informant's administrative file, where an evaluation of the file for *Brady* rule violations and any other memos or reports may be indicative of a witness's truthfulness. Proof or evidence of the lack of candor is discoverable to the defense if it is known to the prosecutor; therefore, if it can be anticipated that a confidential source will testify, failures to be truthful by the informant may have to be disclosed. Sources that are not subject to testimony are exempt from these kinds of disclosure efforts, unless the investigator knows there is a potential *Brady* rule issue in the informant's administrative file. Even that type of information may be disclosed if it doesn't result in the identification of the source. For example, a source may report that a person, not the defendant, is guilty of a particular crime that is set for trial. This kind of information if it is rooted in productive speculation by the informant may need to be disclosed without revealing the actual identity of the informant. Providing the name of the other person, not the defendant, to the defense attorney may be all that is required to satisfy the *Brady* requirement. The trial attorney prosecutor should control this kind of disclosure. An extensive explanation of the *Brady* rule according to Cornell University Law School is supplied below:

> The Brady Rule, named for *Brady v. Maryland*, 373 U.S. 83 (1963), requires prosecutors to disclose materially exculpatory evidence in the government's possession to the defense. "Brady material" or evidence the prosecutor is required to disclose under this rule includes any evidence favorable to the accused—evidence that goes towards negating a defendant's guilt, that would reduce a defendant's potential sentence, or evidence going to the credibility of a witness.
>
> If the prosecution does not disclose material exculpatory evidence under this rule, and prejudice has ensued, the evidence will be suppressed. The evidence will be suppressed regardless of whether the prosecutor knew the evidence was in his or her possession, or whether or not the prosecutor intentionally or inadvertently withheld the evidence from the defense. The defendant bears the burden of proving that the undisclosed evidence was material, and the defendant must show that there is a reasonable probability that there would be a difference in the outcome of the trial had the evidence been disclosed by the prosecutor.

Working any informant off the books may seem like a good idea to avoid paperwork, but if revealed, this action can make the investigator appear less than candid and therefore could have an extremely negative impact on the investigator's career. Also, an off-the-books informant is not subject to the same kinds of protections available to a code-named informant. Some informants may demand never to be known to the investigator's agency, and if this is the case and the informant's information is relevant and important, the investigator should discuss this with his supervisor and consider alternatives for taking advantage of the information offered. The fact is that unless the source is on the books, it is impossible to use the informant's information in any legal document, such as a search or arrest warrant. Also, the fact is that if the investigator's relationship with the off-the-books informant is ever revealed, there is no legal way to avoid openly disclosing information provided by the source or even the source's identity. Lying under oath in a courtroom setting will end an investigator's career. Lying under oath also carries with it the corruption of the system the investigator is sworn to protect and defend. It disrupts the very essence of what good law enforcement is all about. When we corrupt the system by perjury, we create a ripple effect that not only limits our ability to do our job; we make it difficult for other investigators to do their jobs.

A confidential source should be seen as an important resource or asset for the investigative agency and should be fully supported by that agency in spite of what the source wants or what kind of administrative headaches result from the relationship with the investigators.

INFORMANT RELIABILITY

The following cases represent important legal precedent the criminal investigator needs to know about to understand the legal guardrail for working with informants.

Criminal informants who have criminal histories are often used as reliable sources of information for search warrant affidavits. They are less likely to be used as sources of information for arrest warrant affidavits, but they can be if necessary. Courts have ruled over the years that confidential witnesses (names known by law enforcement but withheld for security reasons or specific safety concerns) who have no criminal history are reliable based on the fact that they will eventually be available as witnesses to be cross-examined and further vetted for truthfulness. Criminal informants and some confidential sources are less likely to be made available as witnesses in this fashion; therefore, courts wanted a way to determine the reliability of confidential and criminal sources who may never testify. The following landmark Supreme Court cases have provided the way to determine the reliability of a police informant.

Aguilar v. Texas
378 US 108 (1964), Aguilar v. Texas No. 548, Argued March 25–26, 1964, Decided June 15, 1964
Rule of Law—the underlying circumstances relied on by the person providing the information and some of the underlying circumstances from which the affiant concluded that the informant, whose identity was not disclosed and whose criminal history might lessen his credibility, was in fact credible or his information reliable.

Spinelli v. United States
393 US 410, 89 S.Ct. 584, 21 L.Ed. 2d 637 637 (1969)
Spinelli was running a bookmaking operation between Missouri and Illinois. The FBI surveilled Spinelli to an apartment they suggested in an affidavit was the shop for his telephonic gambling operation. In the affidavit, they included information from a

confidential source that Spinelli was running a telephone gambling bookmaking business. They did not provide any history of the informant's reliability, which made the warrant for the search insufficient.

As a result of these two landmark cases, the test for reliability was established. The sources' reliability was based on a proven track record of reliability. Along with *Spinelli v. United States* (1969), *Aguilar* established the *Aguilar–Spinelli* test, which became a judicial guideline for evaluating the validity of a search warrant based on information provided by a confidential informant. The value of the informant's reliability is in most jurisdictions based on at least two incidents of value indicating arrests made, contraband recovered, or guns and money recovered from criminal actors.

The test is simply a statement by the affiant that the informant has never provided false or unreliable information and some evidence that the source has provided information that has yielded positive law enforcement results at least twice in the past. The following is an example of a type of statement that works: A confidential source, hereinafter referred to as CW-1, is a confidential reliable source who has never knowingly provided false information to the affiant. CW-1 has provided information to law enforcement that has led to two arrests and information in a search warrant affidavit that led to the recovery of over 1,000 dollars' worth of illegal drugs and two weapons.

As a result of the *Aguilar–Spinelli* test, a source that has provided false information is no longer considered reliable and needs to be released or fired as a source. Also, it should be noted that there are simple methods for a source to reach that level of reliability. The source can act as a source of unknown reliability in an affidavit where the main weight of reliability is carried by a reliable source with a positive track record. A source can provide information about a person who has an outstanding arrest warrant, who can be arrested when seen by the investigator who is beginning the process of working with the source. A source can provide the legally accessible location of contraband to the investigator which is then recovered and seized as evidence. Any method works as long as the investigator is operating legally and the source's information is essential for the arrest or recovery of contraband. A new source can also provide extensive details meeting the requirement of the *Gates* case (see below) and then corroborated by the investigator. If the results of the search warrant are positive, the source's reliability is well on its way to being proven.

Illinois v. Gates
462 US 213, 103 S.Ct. 2317, 76 L.Ed. 2d 527 (1983)
In the *Gates* case, an anonymous tipster called in an extensive amount of information used in a search warrant. The information was so extensive and corroborated that the court considered a new rule for confidential source reliability. If the information is detailed and specific, it may be considered reliable based on the "totality of circumstances." The *Gates* case has been considered a rethinking of the *Aguilar–Spinelli* test for reliability but has not been viewed that way by most judges. In effect it is an add-on to, or enhancement of, the *Aguilar–Spinelli* test, which is still used regularly in court affidavits. As a result of *Gates*, judges may want to know more about the informant's "basis of knowledge" and be concerned that the informant has particular and specific facts bolstering his assertions in the affidavit. Phrases such as "the confi-

dential source thinks" or "the confidential source believes" are removed and replaced with words that indicate firsthand knowledge.

Based on the finding in *Gates*, the criminal investigator has to be scrupulous in composing an affidavit to maintain some distance and a looser interpretation of details to ensure the protection of the informant. Any unnecessary but too specific statement can mean the difference between obscuring the identity of an informant and identifying an informant because he is the only person who could have such firsthand knowledge.

LIABILITY OF INFORMANTS

Liuzzo v. United States
508 F. Supp. 923 (E.D. Mich. 1981), Decided February 25, 1981; Anthony Liuzzo, Jr., et al., Plaintiffs, v. United States of America, Defendant. Civ. A. No. 79-72564. United States District Court, E.D. Michigan, S.D. February 25, 1981. On May 27, 1983.
During the civil rights protests in the state of Alabama in March 1965, a civil rights worker from Michigan named Viola Liuzzo was killed by Ku Klux Klan members who followed her vehicle to a lonely stretch of rural highway and attacked her and Leroy Moton. Eventually, after a series of unsatisfactory trials in front of Alabama state jurors, the Klansmen were convicted for civil rights violations in the US district court. One of the Klansmen in the car with the assailants was a criminal informant of the FBI. Subsequent controversial speculation about the informant led Mrs. Liuzzo's family to file suit against the FBI about its failure to properly handle the informant. The suit also was directed at the source himself.

A federal judge rejected the claims in the Liuzzo family lawsuit, saying there was "no evidence the FBI was in any type of joint venture with Gary Thomas Rowe (the informant) or a conspiracy against Mrs. Liuzzo. Rowe's presence in the car was the principal reason why the crime was solved so quickly." In August 1983, the FBI was awarded $79,873 in court costs, but costs were later reduced to $3,645 after the American Civil Liberties Union appealed on behalf of the family. See Liuzzo v. US, 565 F. Supp. 640 (1983).

The ruling in the Liuzzo case generally absolves informants of criminal liability if they are acting in their capacity as government "agents." An informant can be given limited authority to participate in criminal activity as long as it serves to provide evidence of more serious criminal conduct. The criminal informant in this case was Gary Thomas Rowe, a member of the Ku Klux Klan in Alabama at the time of the civil rights struggles around Selma, Birmingham, and Montgomery, Alabama. Rowe was operating as a criminal informant for the FBI. At the time, the FBI was targeting the Klan in Alabama for acts of violence and terrorist-style operations against churches and members of the civil rights movement. On March 25, 1965, Rowe was reluctantly taken by his fellow Klansmen in their vehicle when they hunted down and murdered Mrs. Viola Liuzzo and assaulted her coworker Leroy Moton. In the 1980s, attorneys for the Liuzzo family attempted unsuccessfully to prove that Rowe was more than a reluctant participant because of the FBI's attempts to counter the bad publicity around this case when false allegations were published impugning the character of Mrs. Liuzzo. The actual guilt or innocence of Rowe and his FBI handler was and is extremely difficult to prove in the context of the allegations made in the 1980s. The fact that Rowe was immediately identified as a participant and used as a witness in at least four trials of the murderers indicates the FBI moved swiftly to solve the murder without hesitating about using a valuable source for that purpose. Rowe was also eventually identified as an FBI informant who was authorized by his agent handler to go with the three Klansmen the day they were to attack Liuzzo. As the judge said in his ruling in the civil claim by the Liuzzo family, it is unlikely that the case would ever have been solved without Rowe's testimony. Because of the nature of the Alabama public's feelings about African Americans and civil rights workers (called outside agitators) in the 1960s, at least three all-white juries and one mixed-race jury refused to convict the three Klansmen for the murder. The three Klansmen charged were William Orville Eaton, Eugene Thomas, and Collie Leroy Wilkins Jr. They were convicted of civil rights violations and unrelated gun charges in the final trial in federal court.

Based on this case and a number of other prominent cases where informants have been embroiled in controversy, it is clear that criminal informants are at once necessary and troubling. Investigators are expected to control confidential sources, but in truth, that is easier said than done. The informant Rowe initially was reluctant to go with his Klan associates, but the FBI agent handler authorized him to accompany the three, not anticipating that they would carry out a murder. So he limited the informant's authorization to act in a criminal fashion, but anticipating the behavior that actually happened was not considered. The historical fact is that the case would never have been solved if Rowe had not gone with the assailants.

WORKING INFORMANTS

It is necessary to explain at this point who the various kinds of informants are. We have discussed some of the issues relating to criminal informants. These individuals are career criminals who want to help law enforcement for a variety of reasons. They have access to important and usable intelligence because they know and have personal relationships with people who are regularly committing crimes. They may have worked in criminal conspiracies with other criminals. They may supply a service to criminals, such as fencing stolen property or laundering cash proceeds of criminal enterprises. They may be criminal competitors or lesser competitors who wish to move up and take over more lucrative enterprises. They may be car thieves, burglars, or stickup artists who supply stolen property to higher-level criminals and thereby get insider information into the higher-level operations of criminal enterprises. In the world of organized crime, they may pay tribute to the organization in exchange for protection and permission to operate in a certain neighborhood. Whatever their relationship with the other criminals, they are willing to pass on the intelligence they get to law enforcement. The quality of their intelligence is usually based on the level of respect they have in their relationships with other crooks. True competitors, for example, may have to rely on their own sources of information inside the enemy camp to obtain high-quality intelligence. Well-liked support criminals who help or abet crimes by the other criminals will hear about crimes in their planning stage and usually hear about successes and failures. In other words, their intelligence is very high quality. A burglar who supplies a street gang with stolen guns is usually in a position to know about plans to commit violence or retaliation against other rival gangs. He will be asked for weapons and may even be asked to supply particular weapons. Car thieves who provide getaway vehicles to an armed robbery gang may have unique insight into the planning and strategy for a bank robbery or a high-level commercial robbery. Whatever the basis of knowledge for the criminal intelligence, the criminal investigator needs to evaluate the source's ability and her access to determine how best to take advantage of the information. The investigator needs to understand the relationship and decide how to protect the source from being discovered by his criminal cohorts. The investigator needs to understand the source's motives so she can decide how much of what the source provides is an attempt to manipulate law enforcement against a competitor and how the targeting of a source's competition will enhance the position of the source, making him a viable future target. Investigators should always be wary of sources who are trying to remove their competition. It is likely that they will be the next big thing in the criminal ecosystem. Expect that these sources will go through extraordinary efforts to keep their own operations outside of law enforcement scrutiny while assisting the police.

Criminal informants can also be altruistic. They may be content being petty criminals and consider more violent criminals a threat to themselves, their neighbors, and their friends. These kinds of criminal informants are usually the best to work with. They are truly hoping their information will be used for the betterment of the community, and they see their own criminal conduct as minor and less destructive. There will come a time in a criminal investigator's relationship with this kind of informant when this altruism will be tested, and if the source passes the test, the source may develop into a long-term criminal asset.

Criminal informants can be in the relationship for the money the criminal investigator can pay or the protection the criminal investigator may be able to extend for minor crimes. Either of these motives will sour after a while. A source with a need for money usually becomes so demanding that there is no way to meet the need. The source will lose patience and break off the relationship, or the investigator will get tired of the demands and end the relationship. Protection against petty charges will lead to the same kind of disappointment. In that case, the source needs to be productive on serious crimes to be able to justify this kind of coverage.

The criminal informant who eventually develops a solid personal relationship rooted in trust and friendship with his handler will choose not to embarrass his law enforcement contact and will refrain from asking for money until after he has provided significant assistance. It obviously helps if this source has some personally held strong beliefs about the criminals he is helping to investigate.

The next category is a confidential source, who is usually a noncriminal citizen. This source is a person in a position to help law enforcement based on the legitimate job or career in which she is employed. A landlord in a large apartment complex where a large number of criminals choose to live can be an invaluable source of information. She is in a position where she comes into regular contact with the criminal ecosystem and hears rumors and gossip about criminal activity. It is in her interest and law enforcement's interest to keep their relationship confidential so that none of the residents in the complex become aware of the landlord's relationship with the police. These same kinds of confidential sources work for employment services, telephone companies, utility companies, banks, termite inspection companies, and any other service companies that have large numbers of customers who have to reveal their personal information to obtain the services these citizens supply. The confidential relationship has to be maintained for these persons to remain in their jobs. The benefit of having these kinds of sources is that it allows the investigator to obtain information of value in a time-sensitive investigation that keeps pace with the actions of the criminals under investigation. The criminals have these same types of employees on their payroll, and they corrupt them with bribes and drugs. But law enforcement has to rely on subpoenas that may be delayed and nonproductive. Confidential sources are an essential element of the criminal human intelligence resources.

The final category we will discuss is the cooperating witness (CW) category. These persons are criminal co-conspirators or insiders who have been caught participating in criminal activity and have decided to make a deal with the prosecutor to testify and provide assistance to one or more major criminal investigations. These cooperators are forced to assist to avoid major time in prison. The relationship that develops between a CW and the investigator can be similar to the relationship with other sources, but it is usually not a long-term relationship so the personal level of commitment and concern doesn't enter into the picture. Since a CW is a well-respected insider who has had continuing transactional relationships with the main targets of the investigation, there is usually a lesser concern about the safety of the CW when she is participating in a routine transaction that mirrors months or even years of a trusted relationship. It is the job of the investigator to understand how the CW worked with the targets in the past and to recreate to the extent possible the same protocol. The introduction of new aspects should be held back until it is just right and fully discussed with the targets. A CW operation is the tactical exploitation of the relationship in an effort to obtain evidence from the target. As might be guessed at this point, most CWs are activated insiders in drug enterprise, gun trafficking, or sex trafficking investigations. The CW is usually an experienced participant in the transactions who can make purchases, participate in money-laundering operations, and maintain social contact with the main targets to get the targets talking about operations on recorded conversations. CWs are less likely to be operational in violent crime investigations except to be there listening when the targets plan violence against a threat. They are also less likely to be needed operationally in cases other than ongoing criminal enterprises that generate large amounts of revenue.

The use of a CW is a late-stage effort in a major investigation where the targets cannot be trusted to act without suspicion even with a trusted member of their team, so any change in the CW's pattern is likely to trigger suspicion. This can be very dangerous for a CW in a violent criminal conspiracy. The investigator needs to make sure every step is carefully planned and that the CW does not become complacent or too trusting about his ongoing relationship with the targets. Constantly debrief the CW about the possibility of subtle changes in the attitudes by the targets. If they become suspicious, it is best to end the operation before the CW is confronted and possibly killed because she can't respond correctly. One other troublesome area for a CW is the introduction of an undercover officer or agent. This kind of risky operation has to be well planned, and again, if the CW has introduced new people to the criminal conspiracy, he has to follow the same script. If a CW has never introduced a new person to the conspiracy, it is best not to attempt an operation without being able to anticipate what success looks like. Placing a CW and an undercover law enforcement officer in harm's way is never a requirement for obtaining evidence in a criminal conspiracy. There will be more discussion regarding this kind of operation in chapter 17 regarding covert operations.

From an operational standpoint, CWs are a one-case-and-done relationship. If the investigation is a long-term dangerous operation, the investigator and the CW may develop a positive mutual respect, but as a result of the CW's insider status, the investigator needs to carefully monitor the off time when the CW may have second thoughts and consider sliding back into her criminal ways. "Trust but verify" as an idiom should be changed to "verify," then trust. From a human relations standpoint, as time passes and the CW begins to believe he will avoid serious jail time, he may become convinced that he can somehow hedge his bet and help friends inside the targeted group or even make some side money to hide from authorities for when he is free and clear of the jeopardy he finds himself in. It is up the criminal investigator to pay close attention and even conduct covert surveillance on the CW to make sure the case is not jeopardized by this kind of foolish behavior.

HOW TO WORK A SOURCE

The three main categories of informants can be subdivided based on their importance and the quality of their information. In the FBI, for example, high-level criminal informants who supplied important intelligence about organized-crime enterprises were labeled top echelon informants. These kinds of subdivisions are more administrative than informative. The method of handling a quality informant is the key element. The criminal investigator should have regular face-to-face meetings and, in some cases, daily contact by phone or even email. Any secure method of communication can be used, but it may be necessary to build in coded language to arrange face-to-face meetings. The reason for the personal meetings is the necessity to take the time to obtain a full report about the criminal activity the source is supplying and find out what is going on in the source's personal life to the extent the source will talk. During these meetings, the investigator should regularly explain how the intelligence provided by the source should be as accurate as possible, and the investigator should endeavor to learn the source's basis of knowledge. Meeting the requirements of the *Gates* standard is not the only reason for this need. The investigator needs to know how information was obtained so the investigator can be scrupulous about how that information is handled. What are the aspects of the information that, if used and passed on, will compromise the source? Careful source write-ups that may be used in search warrant affidavits can be carefully worded in the affidavit to ensure the source's identity is protected. Occasionally, the source will be reluctant to tell the investigator where information came from, and if there is a solid level of trust between the source and the investigator, the investigator can accept that reluctance. It is better if the information is used only for intelligence purposes and not disseminated outside of the investigation to which it is relevant. Keep in mind that confidential sources are assets that need to be protected and maintained. Be careful how a source's information is disseminated, and make sure that if the information ever becomes public, it is composed in such a way that the source's identity is kept confidential.

Every meeting and contact with a source should generate a written report. Admonishing an informant to avoid involvement in criminal activity should be regularly done during face to face meetings. Spending significant time developing a positive relationship with the source is necessary, so the source understands his valve as an asset and make sure to have regular discussions about confidentiality and security. Once a report is written, the investigator needs to decide what action is necessary. It is a fact that a quality source will have a wide range of information on a variety of criminal matters. For example, if the source provides the name and location of a fugitive, the investigator should pass that on to the person, team, or squad who is responsible for the arrest of that subject. The investigator should have confidence that the fugitive team is aware of the confidential nature of the information and should endeavor to make the subject believe the information that led to her arrest was anything but information from a law enforcement informant. The responsibility of the criminal investigator who is the source's handler is to take all the steps necessary to properly disseminate the information and then make sure the use of the information does not compromise the source.

As the relationship with the source develops, the information the source provides will be for intelligence purposes but may also be actionable. The example mentioned above about a wanted fugitive is actionable intelligence. Information that provides a psychological or mental profile of an investigative target is for intelligence purposes only but may become critical when the target is interrogated or an arrest or search warrant raid is planned. General information about the goals and anticipated actions of a criminal conspiracy is for the most part intelligence because there is little to be done until the conspirators start to act, that is, unless the plans include specific acts of violence. Actionable intelligence can be reliable information used in an affidavit, but it should be noted here that any source information from a reliable source can become testimonial if that information is used for an arrest affidavit. On the other hand, information from a reliable source used in an affidavit for a search warrant may be kept confidential all the way through the prosecution of the case. Again, remember that if a source actually sees or in some other way witnesses a violent crime, she may be required to testify in the case. The investigator in that case can't hold back that information from a prosecutor who is investigating the matter. How the prosecutor chooses to use the source is up to the prosecutor, but it is obviously a big problem if the source has provided a large amount of information to the government and can be denigrated as a "rat" or "snitch" on the stand, limiting his usefulness as a witness and eliminating his usefulness as a confidential source. Always remember that the source is an asset and requires protection from the government if she is ever revealed as a source.

Actionable intelligence can also be information that provides a basis for intense physical surveillance, the name or company that should be subpoenaed for important records, or data relevant to an investigation and any other information that informs the investigation and moves the case forward with a specific category of details that identify witnesses or the names of co-conspirators or aiders and abettors.

The next concern should evolve only once your relationship with the informant has matured to an understanding of all the factors about safety and security that have been discussed and are understood by the source. The source needs to avoid saying something or doing something that overtly compromises his safety. That concern is sending an informant into a situation to investigate and determine the answers to questions that come up in an investigation, in other words, using the source to conduct a covert investigation. Setting leads for a source is a very dangerous undertaking. If a source is gathering information in the normal course of his contact with a criminal or group of criminals, it is one thing, but if a source is asking questions and digging into a specific area of a criminal's business, he may raise suspicion and better have a reasonable and plausible explanation for being curious. Street-smart sources can often come up with plausible excuses for this kind of behavior, but the criminal investigator should exercise good judgment for the source if the investigator is not sure the source can handle any scrutiny. If a source has a reputation as a dangerous person, she can usually get away with a lot of suspicious activity by just being menacing, but most sources don't have that kind of reputation. Intelligence and being able to think fast on her feet are skills a source needs when she is asked to dig deeper than a mild curiosity about the latest criminal conduct. The reality about this concern is that a high-quality informant will become committed to assisting in an investigation and will put herself in harm's way. These kinds of courageous but foolish acts are what reminds the criminal investigator why sources should be reminded to stay safe and let the big guys make the mistakes.

Personal Experience

Information and intelligence that is actionable and informative are the criminal source's currency. The value of the currency is often determined by a source's statistical accomplishments. Over the course of years during my investigative career, sources provided me information that led to the criminal convictions of more than 200 persons. They provided information that led to seizure of millions of dollars of contraband drugs, guns, and stolen property. They provided information that led to over 300 arrests, including the arrests and convictions of some of the most violent offenders in the history of Washington, DC. As a result of the sources' information and other information provided to our task force sources, at least 3,000 lives were saved, because we were able to arrest and prosecute violent offenders who killed more than 200 persons per year before we were able to turn the violent trend back with the quality of our intelligence-driven proactive investigations. With the help of our informant base, we targeted the worst of the worst in Washington, DC, and removed them from the community, making it impossible for them to continue their reign of terror.

The value of sources cannot be overestimated. It is true that they create problems and require constant attention, but the truth is that the average law enforcement professional will never be able to see what they see, go where they go, and hear what they hear. As long as that is the case, the search for the truth has to involve working informants.

SUMMARY

In this case, it is best to understand the value and importance of productive sources. Balancing the difficulties inherent in working with criminal informants against the benefits of their quality intelligence is the motivating factor in deciding as a criminal investigator to take the time and expend the energy to commit to criminal sources. Turning insider criminals and making it possible for them earn lesser punishments is another worthwhile goal in working with informants. Making it possible for noncriminal civilians to confidentially support law enforcement efforts is another beneficial goal achieved by working with confidential sources. Ultimately, what it comes down to is whether there is a higher upside to working with confidential sources than not. The answer from most law enforcement professionals is a resounding yes. In the beginning of an investigator's career, it is very uncertain and worrisome, but it is a necessary and productive feature of investigative success. The hard work and the time spent learning how to communicate with a source and finding common ground with someone from another world of experience than you come from provides insight. Understanding that cannot be overvalued.

Chapter Fifteen

Investigative Intelligence

Crime data, big data, patrol support, community input and support, investigative files, and interjurisdictional communication.

Criminal intelligence derived from human confidential sources is not the only source of valuable information available to criminal investigators. It is important to discuss several other sources of information of value to investigations. These sources are mostly raw data or important crime-related information that has been developed from the community's response to criminal activity. The single most important aspect of this intelligence are the calls for service to the local police department. Eventually, all calls for service will be reported by the responding officers. A category will be assigned to the report, or the first responder will make a callout for investigators to further investigate the incident as a criminal violation. Therefore, the category may be a statutory violation with an eventual investigative file as a follow-up to the original call for service.

CRIME DATA

These data and their uses will vary from jurisdiction to jurisdiction. A small village or town may have very few calls for service, but there may be some identifiable pattern that can be discerned. For example, theft and larceny cases happen in the commercial neighborhood. Violent crime happens in residential neighborhoods. Drug crimes occur in low-rent commercial neighborhoods where a number of bars and honky-tonk pubs are present. In larger and more urban communities, there may be stark geographic variations based on categories of calls for service. Gang activity may be prolific around middle and high schools. Rapes may be more prevalent in residential communities when the population dwindles because most of the residents are commuting to work in the inner commercial area of the city. So along with categories, the times and specific locations of the crimes will become part of the readily available information reported in the data. The accuracy of the data is also bolstered when the number of similar calls for service is higher than a norm or baseline established by a mathematical evaluation. For example, in an urban area where crime stats routinely reach ten incidents per person in the population per category of crime and the number ten is achieved monthly in every part of the city, that would be the baseline. Spikes of incidents above the baseline are instructive as to where certain crimes are likely to occur more often.

The main reason for keeping and monitoring these stats on calls for service is simple but important. Police management needs to distribute manpower where it is most needed. The shorter the response time to an incident, the higher chance that the incident will be resolved by police intervention. More crimes will be solved by having the police respond immediately when a crime is committed. Suspects may be caught escaping the scene. All the witnesses will be available for interviews. Quicker response will be facilitated for suspect lookouts or updates on the crime reported that may match similar incidents. In general, the mere proper distribution of police resources may lead to more effective investigations.

For intelligence purposes, these fundamental analyses are helpful, but the data can be more thoroughly analyzed to provide operational investigative planning. A burglary squad can pick the time of day, the neighborhood, and even the street to covertly surveil to heighten the chance that a serial burglar will be caught in the act. Calls for service for unusual incidents in neighborhoods with high crime can be compared to see if these suspicious incidents might provide insight about the crime problem. Heightened surveillance at certain times of the day, coordination with uniform patrol officers, and intense analyses of the crime data can be major steps to solving a single crime and, in some cases, many others.

This same kind of review of data can be used for armed robberies, rapes, and drug crimes. Murder is usually so infrequent that the value of the data is less solution-friendly, but if the concern is deciding which violent street gang needs to be targeted or which two gangs are committed to a gang war, then this kind of analysis can be very helpful. Murder is a crime that is seldom if ever tied to a certain neighborhood because the neighborhood is beneficial and provides a host of different targets. It is tied to a neighborhood by convenience and individual availability of a specific target. Killing another gang member is more easily accomplished if the killer can catch the gang member in a place where he feels safe. Robbing a store or burglarizing a house is a crime of choice where the criminal can see options and make a choice from all the options.

This same kind of crime planning is used by rapists who choose neighborhoods where their profile of victims is available but anonymous. Rapists also choose to operate at bars, clubs, and after-hour clubs to catch their victims when they are vulnerable and compliant. The specific victim is chosen from a population, not a particular person, like a killer might. Understanding the data available from calls for service and determining how that data inform a certain investigation are the kinds of analyses that can be done with crime data and calls for service. It is essential that the data can somehow be geo-coded (marked by address) for a jurisdictional district, a police district, and a patrol service area. The nature of the neighborhood should be compared with the type of crimes and the unusual calls for service that should also be evaluated.

The most complete picture of the data and geographic information, along with the categories of crime, can help the investigator make logical evaluations using these kinds of very basic intelligence. In the event these kinds of data can be over laid onto the residences of criminals who have been recently released from prison (parole data), suspects can be visualized as possible perpetrators, especially if their release dates coincide with a spike in their crime of choice or even a likely evolution of their criminal preference. This, then, is how information readily available to a police department can be used to inform ongoing criminal investigations.

Most departments that function as the primary responding agency for a particular jurisdiction keep and regularly update these data primarily to properly distribute patrol resources, but their use for investigations takes a little more time and analysis by the investigative units.

BIG DATA

Big data is the compiling of digital information—crime data, calls for service data, criminal history data, and crime analysis data—provided by the computer analysis technicians working in most law enforcement agencies. The next group of digital data comes from open source internet data and social media data. Combining law enforcement–sensitive data with open source and social media data can be done as suggested in chapter 10 of this text to provide subject profiles, group profiles, and even serious attempts to anticipate personal or group behavior. These kinds of data have been used in several major cities to locate and identify persons who are likely to be victims or suspects in violent gang crimes. The police and some social agencies combine to interact with these persons to encourage them to seek help and avoid violence. These programs have been successful. But as in most similar programs, all too often the goal is unsuccessful, and the person commits a crime or is a victim.

This kind of compilation of data also has been used to judge the relative threat of a proposed demonstration or effort to protest using civil unrest. The data have been used to determine the loci of disturbances that may involve violence or property destruction. The concern of civil rights and privacy rights advocates is that this type of information is too invasive. That is difficult to prove since most of the information in social media and open source data is supplied by the protesters themselves. If violence or destruction of property can be stopped by using these data and there are no real privacy breaches, the use and evolution of the use of the compiled data should be part of the future in intelligence gathering. The critical element is what kind of sophisticated computer algorithms will be needed to develop focused and productive intelligence for criminal investigative use. Intelligence of this type has great future potential, but as in most law enforcement advances, the sources and methods will eventually be required to be vetted by the court system to ensure that the rights of the accused are not impinged.

PATROL SUPPORT

The next important source of intelligence available to criminal investigators was discussed in chapter 4, but it is important to restate it now in the context of intelligence available to criminal investigators. Patrol officers have as many as ten contacts per day with citizens in their patrol area. They also respond to crimes and have a unique perspective on the serious crimes in their neighborhoods. These officers also have contact with suspicious characters in the neighborhoods who sell drugs, case stores for robberies, and plan other crimes beforehand. Since these contacts usually lead to nothing more than a conversation, it is essential that they have a daily outlet in which to pass on what they know, even if they don't write an incident report. Criminal investigators should spend time with these overworked officers to get the information while it is fresh in their minds.

When an investigation becomes focused on a certain neighborhood, the criminal investigator should make it a point to have contact with the patrol officers who handle that neighborhood. Even if they can't offer the name of a suspect or provide some detail about a suspicious event, they may be able to provide a list of citizens with whom they have regular contact who may be of help. They may also provide the names and addresses of potential criminal informants who seem ripe for recruitment as a source. There is also a tactical benefit of having a positive working relationship with the local patrol officers. In the event of violent confrontation with suspects or other criminals, it is nice to know that the local patrol officer is readily available and will back you up if needed.

It should be apparent that some patrol officers see themselves as one day joining the ranks of criminal investigators, but even those patrol officers who have no interest in becoming a criminal investigator will be a positive source of information if they are treated with appropriate respect and deference to their professional position. Openly discussing an ongoing criminal investigation with the officers in the neighborhood and, to the extent possible, passing on the names and addresses of local suspects will engender the sense of teamwork that makes the patrol officer feel a sense of being a part of the case. If there is some need to maintain a certain amount of case security and not be all that forthcoming, then just try to provide enough information that lets the officers consider ways they can assist. Most veteran police officers understand the need for case security and won't be upset if they are not read in completely on an investigation. Providing details that may help them in their patrol duties is an important way to build the trust necessary to maximize the benefits to both sides of the law enforcement responsibilities.

COMMUNITY SUPPORT ACTIVISTS

Most communities have activists and organizers who pay attention to local crime trends, open-air drug markets, youth gang activity, prostitution, and disparate quality-of-life crimes (graffiti, vandalism, destruction of property, etc.) that denigrate their neighborhoods. These activists are anxious to provide this kind of information to the police in hopes that investigative or patrol action will take place in response. These citizens are usually long-term residents who are familiar with neighborhood career criminals and have usually known them and their families for many years. These citizens are important sources of quality information. They may not know specific details that can help inform an investigation, but they can usually provide important background information once a neighborhood thug is identified as a suspect. These citizens can usually provide significant help for drug enterprise investigations and human trafficking cases. Their support can extend to determining secure locations for covert static surveillance and identifying local merchants who can provide other kinds of support for investigations, including supplies and equipment that are not available from the department or agency conducting investigations. These citizens will usually be the first to demand action on serious threats to the neighborhood, including rapists and violent predators. Investigators should be somewhat cautious with these activists because they are often sources for the local news media and may pass on information an investigator mentions to their media contacts. Case security should always be in the mind of the criminal investigator. Finding the balance between employing and using community support must always be balanced with limiting the information provided to an uninvolved citizen.

PRIOR CASE FILE REVIEWS

Based on a recurring theme in this text, it is unlikely that a single major felony is the first time a crook carried out a crime. Criminal investigators have access to case files going back years, and if a crime is particularly stubborn, the investigator should consider reviewing crimes of a similar nature that may have happened in prior years. Suspects who have committed burglaries in the past may serve two to five years in prison and then return to the same communities. A review of the modus operandi with regard to crimes that occurred two to five years ago may yield a connection that is unmistakable. This kind of case file review would be especially important in exhausting all leads in serial rape cases or child predator investigations. First-time offenders in these cases often get limited sentences to keep the victims from having to deal with the continuing trauma of a trial. Unfortunately, these kinds of criminals are not normally rehabilitated during their periods of incarceration, and they may become more dangerous because of their experience in prison.

INTERJURISDICTIONAL COOPERATION

Criminal investigators should logically assume that career criminals in their jurisdiction will not be overly concerned about which jurisdiction they commit crimes in. It is true that some career criminals are fearful of being caught in a certain jurisdiction because the jurisdiction may have a reputation for hard judges, fast-acting juries, and no-nonsense jurisprudence. For the most part, these fears don't deter the wide assortment of career criminals from crossing state or county lines. Even a well-resourced and financed police department may not act as a deterrent. Criminal investigators from close jurisdictions should have regular meetings at least once per month where they discuss closed cases and wide-open investigations. They should pass on trends and the names of suspects and, if possible, the modus operandi of suspects and crimes that are unsolved. This kind of open communication with other jurisdictions can lead to all manner of solved cases. When the local FBI agents take part in these meetings, they can identify the kind of support they may be able to offer on crime trends, gang cases, or drug investigations that overwhelm local departments. The Drug Enforcement Administration (DEA) and the Bureau of Alcohol, Tobacco, Firearms and Explosives (ATF) can offer the same kind of support for cases in their respective purview.

SUMMARY

Criminal intelligence generally provides two main benefits. The first one is called actionable intelligence. It provides significant and very specific support for an ongoing investigation. This kind of intelligence comes from confidential sources, including detailed analysis of crime patterns that yield working theories on how to best develop a strategic plan that may yield the name of a suspect, the methods and practices of a targeted group of criminals, and/or specific anticipatory possibilities that will allow the investigator to catch the criminals in the act of a new crime.

The second benefit is called macro intelligence. It is a broader and more analytical style of intelligence. Information that anticipates trends of criminal dominance and defines differences between and among jurisdictions when it comes to addressing and prioritizing crime problems is in the macro intelligence arena. The 9/11 committee following the September 11, 2001, terrorist attacks suggested that law enforcement spend more time developing macro intelligence to anticipate and coordinate with overseas assets whose information is more general and lacks the kind of specificity needed for immediate response. As a career criminal investigator, I disagree with this trend. It is important to keep smart analysts looking at future possibilities, but it is impossible to judge the reliability of the information unless it is occasionally tested. Intelligence for intelligence's sake assigns quality to information that may be completely wrong.

In the field of interjurisdictional intelligence meetings, law enforcement is confronted with officer safety alerts. These alerts describe gang members (generically) who committed assaults on officers on the West Coast and an assurance that these same violent offenders were coming east to do the same. The problem was that the suspects were never named, the assaults on officers were never identified, and the motives for these attacks were never specific. These alerts were considered quality intelligence by the analysts who provided the information, but over the course of three years, none of these scenarios played out in real life. It is foolish to disregard immediate threats, and it is important for law enforcement to stay vigilant. False or nonspecific information does not deserve to be called intelligence. All intelligence needs to be sourced, and the analysis at the first level needs to be verified. The verification doesn't have to be exact, but to designate intelligence of high quality, there needs to be some way to install a plan to thwart the criminal activity if necessary. There must be a way to set a trip wire in operation so that the information can be considered viable and accurate. Otherwise, the information is just "sound and fury signifying nothing" (William Shakespeare and William Faulkner).

Intelligence, whether it is the report of an informant or thoughtful analyses of related data, reports, case reviews, and open discussions among professionals, should have reliability built in. Information that suggests or proposes possibilities needs to have been born of thoughtful consideration and categorized based on the quality of that consideration. Intelligence is useful only if the investigative action, the distribution of law enforcement manpower, or the results of training provides a model of success and proof of positive goals that resulted from the information.

Personal Experience

As the trends of homicides arose in the District of Columbia in 1989, my squad members and I began to understand that the homicides were for the most part related to the neighborhood drug gangs who were vying for control of the lucrative drug markets there. This understanding came from informants and crime data that geographically situated the homicides in locations where neighborhood gangs dominated the drug markets. Within two years of initiating our Safe Streets task force investigations where we targeted these gangs, we reduced the incidents of homicide by 25 percent. After five years, the homicides were down by 70 percent. That is the kind of result high-quality intelligence provides. The intelligence was a combination of actionable and macro intelligence.

Chapter Sixteen

Tactical Considerations

SWAT, hand-to-hand combat, deadly force, and search warrant raids.

In this textbook, it is impossible to provide realistic instruction to sworn and non-sworn investigators on the tactics necessary and methods required in pursuing violent criminals. These kinds of tactical operations require teamwork and safe operational drills. These drills must be done out of classrooms in environments that are similar to locations where these operations may be conducted. The drills need to simulate real conditions and establish operational rules that each team member follows. The officers, investigators, and agents involved in these drills will be armed and prepared for a worst-case scenario. The participants will simulate arrests of multiple subjects who are presumed to be armed and dangerous. Arrests may be simulated with real physical confrontations to closely match real-life experiences. Two on one, three on one, or other variations of confrontations will be tested to ensure the participants are provided with the best approach for hands-on confrontations. Eventually, arresting a subject and formally charging the subject will take away the person's freedom, which creates an angry, distressful, or violent reaction. It is then necessary to prepare for the reaction by physical training, planning, and coordinating with other investigators to carry out the arrest with a minimum chance of a physical confrontation and physical harm to the arrestee or the participants conducting the operation. Tactical training at its core is teaching of methods used for the following operations:

- Physical apprehending of a subject
- Executing a search warrant in a potentially dangerous environment
- Dealing with a physical confrontation with a criminal suspect who may react to a criminal investigator with a violent assault
- Developing heightened security for victims, witnesses, or other innocent members of the community who may be threatened by violent criminals under investigation
- Surprising and unexpected confrontations with criminals who may have no part in the investigation but may be challenged by the mere presence of law enforcement

Training for each operation listed above needs to be done as a team so that the tactical challenges that an investigative unit confronts are handled in a manner consistent with agent/officer safety and the rule of law. The result of physical training becomes an extension of best practices experienced in day-to-day law enforcement activity. In general, it is best to overwhelm or show career criminals that resistance is not in their best interests. There are some strategies that are logical preparations for law enforcement operations, which I will discuss here, although the most important training in this area should be conducted by individual agencies, departments, or units whose officers and agents will be in harm's way over the course of criminal investigations.

Resources for training vary for agencies and departments. One of the most expensive trainings for these law enforcement officers is firearms training. The use of hundreds or even thousands of rounds of live ammunition and the requirement of taking the officers and agents away from their regular duty make this training expensive but necessary. As long as there is a threat of gun violence to the community and to law enforcement, law enforcement professionals need to be trained and qualified with firearms. The FBI provides firearms training to agents six times a year. Many police departments provide firearms training only one time per year. Criminal investigators who work violent crimes investigations should have firearms training at least four times per year. The training should include standard firearms qualification with the investigator's personal firearm.

A very specific tactical firearm training that includes shotgun or long-gun training is needed to meet or exceed the threat level from well-armed career criminals. The tactical training should involve the investigators in team training with their firearms to ensure safety concerns are addressed when the investigator teams or squads are carrying out tactical operations. Concerns addressed in tactical firearms training include ensuring that there are no cross fires or bullets fired into dangerous backgrounds. These basic safety concerns should be discussed, and every attempt to control armed approaches to subjects inside buildings and on outside venues should be planned. Vehicle stops should be well planned with safety being the primary concern. Any operations in busy urban settings with innocent bystanders should be avoided. Operations inside apartments need to be planned to prevent powerful bullets blasting through the walls of one residence to do harm in another residence. When possible, approaching a subject should take place in a triangular formation, which reduces the possibility of cross fire from other team members. Ballistic shields and preoperational evacuations may be needed to avoid uncertain conditions. Since firearms training is expensive, many of the planning and control schemes or drills can be discussed in connection with dry fire exercises used to simulate real operational approaches.

Every criminal investigator should be equipped with at least Level IIA or Level II soft ballistic vests. These vests are effective against only handguns of less than 40 calibers. Since criminal investigators usually have the benefit of knowing the threat level of the criminals with whom they are dealing, soft vests may be sufficient in most instances, but more violent killers and criminals may require at least Level III ballistic protection. This kind of equipment is made available to the law enforcement professionals by their agency or department. If the appropriate level of ballistic protection is not supplied by the department or agency, criminal investigators may need the essential support of a SWAT or ERT team built into their investigative operations.

SWAT

SWAT (Special Weapons and Tactics) teams or ERTs (Emergency Response Teams) are specially trained officers or agents who conduct tactical operations full-time for the agency or department. These specialized teams are primarily concerned with tactical operations. If it is essential that the team is needed to make an arrest or secure a business or residence for a search warrant, then the team members must be fully briefed about the subjects, the nature of the criminal conduct, and any potential for the presence of physical evidence. These tactical team members are experienced law enforcement professionals and can be relied upon to participate effectively in the investigation.

Depending on the fluid nature of many investigations and the uncertainty about some operational events, the SWAT team or its equivalent may not be available. Squads or teams of investigators need to be trained and ready to handle these operations when required. It is best to act in a fashion to overwhelm the subjects with superior firepower and careful planning so that even in an operation that may not be dangerous, the steps are followed to make sure safety concerns are met. Once the persons or targeted facilities are under control, steps can be taken by the investigator to calm the tension raised by a serious law enforcement show of force. Professional and disciplined conduct, such as the operations of the SWAT or tactical teams, can be used by the investigative team as a standard of conduct for the participants in any operational confrontation.

Personal Experience

During my career in the FBI, our SWAT and Hostage Rescue teams were two well-trained tactical units available for deployment for high-risk operations. Our task force squad was called upon to conduct search warrants, arrests, and similar raids too frequently to use these teams for every operation. Because we conducted regular tactical training exercises and many members of our squad were in fact SWAT team members, our operations were conducted with appropriate planning and consistent with our training regimens. Weapons safety, room-clearing plans, and hands-on, hand-to-hand combat training skills were employed when confronted with an uncooperative subject.

Throughout the fifteen years of my assignment, we conducted hundreds of raids, arrests, and other operational events without any serious injuries or incidents. The benefits of knowing our subjects and being aware of their personal habits provided the kind of operational control that ensured that level of success. Background intelligence and details about the specific violent tendencies of our subjects gave us the upper hand as to when and where it was best to plan an arrest. Even confidential source information or information from a cooperating insider provided the background needed to properly plan an operation.

Unfortunately, most criminal investigation units don't have the resources and training exercises that a well-funded federal task force will have. As in other important aspects of criminal investigation and law enforcement, experience, confidence in your team, and careful and thoughtful planning will be the best solutions for success and safety in tactical operations. Planning for the worst case allows the investigative team the confidence needed to anticipate behavior and ensure the safety of the team and the targeted subject.

HAND-TO-HAND COMBAT

For a criminal investigator, arresting a person or even conducting an interview may devolve into a boxing or a wrestling match. Many career criminals have survived in their lives on the street and in prison by being ready to fight immediately upon being confronted by unpleasant challenges. Professional law enforcement officers and agents have significant unarmed combat training in their training academy experiences. In the past, that training may have included judo, karate, and several martial arts disciplines. Boxing has been taught so that otherwise disciplined, peaceable people know what it means to get punched in the face and to return the favor. All the martial arts skills have significant benefit, but for the most part, unarmed combat taught by the military replaced the more conventional styles. So-called street fighting skills have been taught at many training academies. Criminals are not likely to abide by any gentlemanly rules, so kicks to the groin, eye gouging, sucker punches, and any unconventional method of disabling an opponent are generally considered more effective in the kinds of ad hoc street fights that take place between law enforcement and crooks.

There is a recent rise in popularity of mixed martial arts fighting. A skilled mixed martial arts fighter is usually proficient in several areas of hand-to-hand combat. Police and law enforcement training continues to evolve in this area. Many experienced law enforcement officers consider a new hybrid, nonlethal style of ground combat to be the best training an officer can get to deal with an angry arrestee or any other person who wishes to engage in assaultive behavior. If the investigator can use one well-placed blow to incapacitate an assailant, then so be it; whatever works is the best approach. This, however, is generally not the case. Investigators and other law enforcement professionals need to engage in a combination of street fighting, judo, and wrestling. Submission holds are taught in police academies, but the day-to-day work of surviving these confrontations will usually end up in a tussle on the ground between the assailant and hopefully at least two investigators. The most important part of hand-to-hand combat is that the results should not be life-threatening, but there are obviously some cases where the skill of the criminal outclasses the skill of the investigator. Lethal force may be needed to protect the life of the investigator and should be used when necessary to defend oneself and others.

Personal Experience

In one confrontation in the early 1980s, a subject our team was trying to arrest was high on PCP. The subject was of average height and weight, but his tolerance for pain was superhuman. It took six fit and well-trained agents to wrestle the subject into submission, where he could be handcuffed and further restrained. During the confrontation, the agents began applying pressure slowly, but eventually it took serious effort to cut off his air supply using an authorized choke hold. The agents then had to hit the subject with a number of maximum blows with fists to simply reduce the effectiveness of his assaultive behavior. Each member of the team suffered injuries from this confrontation, but the arrest of the subject was finally successful. The following day in court, the subject was bruised and battered, but he did not complain to the court. The team of agents were standing by with their injuries as proof, if needed, of the subject's assault on them.

DEADLY FORCE

There is no simple solution for this kind of behavior except training and being confident enough in yourself and your partner to handle a nonlethal combat problem that is initiated by an angry subject. In all the operational and confrontational events that can face a criminal investigator, the most difficult event is a confrontation that requires the use of deadly force. Two Supreme Court cases—*Tennessee v. Garner*, 471 US 1 (1985), and *Graham v. Connor*, 490 US 386 (1989)—have established the constitutional construct that governs the use of deadly force by a law enforcement officer. In the *Tennessee v. Garner* case, the subject was running from the scene of a burglary where he had stolen $10. Two officers were giving chase, and before the subject could escape, one of the officers shot and killed him. The officers were following the state of Tennessee law authorizing the use of lethal force in such a case. In the *Graham v. Connor* case, a police officer became suspicious of a person who was suffering from diabetes and acting suspiciously because the person needed medication. The police officer forcibly stopped the person and detained him while he completed his investigation and determined the person was not actually involved in a crime. The subject suffered injuries because the officer detained him by force. The court accepted that the officer acted reasonably based on the ruling in *Terry v. Ohio*. The court recognized that the reasonableness standard for a Terry stop and probable cause can allow the officer to make an instantaneous decision to detain, arrest, or otherwise seize a person as per the Fourth Amendment. The court defined the use of lethal force as the ultimate seizure discussed in the Fourth Amendment. In the *Graham* case, the court further ruled that the seriousness of the crime must be considered when allowing this kind of seizure.

The analysis provided by these two cases combines to be instructive about what the minimal basis for using lethal force is. If an officer believes, based on a reasonable set of facts or circumstances, that her life or the lives of others are in danger, any use of force to stop the threat is reasonable. The standard of reasonableness means the officer or agent needs to be able to articulate probable cause that the threat existed at the time of his actions. In considering the standard of probable cause needed, the following examples may be helpful in the instantaneous conclusion that has to be made.

- The investigator confronts a subject who brandishes a firearm and acts in a threatening manner.
- The investigator confronts a subject who brandishes a knife and acts in a threatening manner.
- The investigator knows that the subject he is confronting has a history of violent behavior, and when the investigator approaches and identifies himself, the subject reaches aggressively for an unseen weapon near her waist or inside her jacket.
- The investigator is in a physical confrontation (fight) with a subject and comes to believe the subject is trying to get the investigator's weapon.
- The investigator and his partner are in a physical confrontation with a subject, and the subject is applying a strangulation hold on the partner. The investigator can shoot to kill the subject in defense of his partner.
- The investigator is in a physical confrontation with a subject and fears the subject will overcome and kill the investigator.
- The investigator sees the subject beating a third party who is struggling to survive.
- The investigator sees the subject point or otherwise brandish a weapon in the direction of a third party.

These examples of probable cause are simple and to the point, but they are not without controversy. State law in many jurisdictions have imposed some restrictions on the use of deadly force by law enforcement. In Los Angeles, California, the Los Angeles Police Department has established a rule for officers that states an officer must report seeing a deadly weapon in the hands of the subject prior to using deadly force. That rule does not restrict the officer's protection from criminal or civil prosecution or liability as per the US Constitution's construct mentioned above. A violation, however, will lead to dismissal from the department and civil liability for the department. Department and agency rules have some significant variations about the use of deadly force, but the bottom line for a criminal investigator is to use judgment and concern for the lives of others. Deadly force is really a last resort.

The impact on the officer/investigator of the human factors that lead to the use of lethal force is not covered by the legal analysis. The decision must be acceptable in the minds of the officer or investigator. Killing another human being by a person who has lived her whole life as a protector of life and determined to do the right thing whenever possible is the ultimate irony for an officer. Taking the life of a person, even a serious violent criminal, is not the kind of decision most criminal investigators will make easily, but in most cases of deadly force, the decision-making process must be immediate when confronted with the harsh reality of a need to defend oneself or the life of another. Dealing with criminals who have no qualms about using violence sharpens the divide between the persons who investigate crimes and the perpetrators. The Law Enforcement Memorial in Washington, DC, lists the names of the American law enforcement officers who have made the ultimate sacrifice, and some of those listed may not have been able to make the hardest of decisions to kill another human being.

SEARCH WARRANT RAIDS

As mentioned previously in this text, the criminal investigator's reliance on search warrants to recover important evidence in a criminal case is an essential tactical operation that can be carried out anytime during an investigation. Search warrants can be very perfunctory and executed with fully cooperative persons, but that is the exception and not the rule. At best, a search warrant can be executed against an empty residence or business where there are no persons who will object or express indignation at the imposition of the government's power. Most search warrants are tactical exercises that require planning and a show of serious force to the occupants of the location.

The focus of the warrant is the specific evidence to be seized pursuant to the warrant, but in many cases, other evidence, including contraband, illegal weapons, or illegal drugs, may be visibly in plain sight. A careful examination of the documentary evidence referred to in the warrant may also yield other significant evidence that was not anticipated. Also, persons in the house or business may be in possession of illegal material, wanted on outstanding charges, or simply important witnesses to the crime under investigation and are just now being located and interviewed for the first time.

A host of other positive possibilities develop during the execution of a warrant, so the criminal investigator needs to take the opportunity to execute the warrant with proper planning and flawless execution. When knocking and announcing the determination to execute a warrant, the people in the house must be notified as to what is happening so there is no misunderstanding about what is going on. A specified length of time must pass after the knock and announce before the location can be forcibly entered. The time is usually dictated by the crime under investigation. Drug search warrants where drugs can be flushed down a commode are usually the shortest time, whereas white collar crime search warrants where there is no indication the evidence can be destroyed are among the longest times. Gambling search warrants where water-soluble betting slips are used are among the shortest time, and cybercrime cases with instant delete programs are not allowed time to delete or eliminate evidence. A search for a stolen car in a garage would be an example of a knock-and-announce time that is long enough to allow the slowest respondent to answer the door. Violent crime cases, such as homicide, rape, and armed robbery, will have short knock-and-announce times to preclude the violent offenders' having time to prepare to assault the investigators. There are no-knock search warrants, but the details as to why no knock should be allowed have to be articulated in the search warrant affidavit.

While the warrant is being officially executed in the main entrance of the location, every other exit from the location should be covered by additional investigators, SWAT team members, or uniformed officers to discourage persons from escaping from the location. Some persons just may not want to be present when law enforcement officers or agents visit, but they don't have the privilege to leave until they are interviewed and their presence is recorded. The team leader of the warrant team can release any person he chooses so long as the team leader is satisfied that the person is not a threat or in any way involved in the crime under investigation. Every person present is subject to a thorough search of his person, and any weapons or contraband is subject to seizure. Probable-cause arrests can be made, and interviews can be conducted.

SEARCH WARRANT PROCEDURES

The search team will proceed with the search of the residence or business when the location is secure.

1. Photograph and sketch the location of each room and, in some cases, designate each wall with alphanumeric characters so that any evidence that is recovered is properly documented as to its specific location in the building. Details of this nature are needed for testimony about any evidence recovered and used in a court hearing.
2. Photograph all the occupants, and create a search log identifying all the persons present and all the members of the search team. As the search progresses, the team leader and a designated interviewing investigator should take a statement from each person present. When the specific items of evidence designated in the warrant are located, a log should be made of the time of their discovery and the exact location where they were discovered. Photographs should be made of any important finds. Evidence found in plain view should be likewise noted on the log, and the specific location of the evidence should be noted and photographed before it is moved. The search warrant log is the rough documentation for use in preparing a proper report created to fully explain the activities in the search warrant. Any evidence discovered that can be associated with an individual present in the house should be noted, photographed, and logged in.
3. Prepare an evidence inventory. The inventory should be a succinct description of the evidence found pursuant to the warrant. A copy of the inventory should be left with the most responsible person in the house or just posted in an obvious location if no one is present or if those present refuse to accept the inventory. All the evidence should be bagged and tagged for transport to the evidence locker or evidence control office of the agency or department. Photographs or xerographic copies of important pieces of evidence should be made for investigative purposes. A clear and precise list of all the evidence and its location should be made as a detailed list of evidence, which will be used for investigative purposes and for use by the search team as a reliable document for future reference in any testimony about the activities that occurred during the search. This list can become a part of the comprehensive report about the search warrant. All the logs, inventories, and evidence lists can be handwritten or digitally prepared.
4. Following the completion of the search, exit photographs should be taken to document the condition of the searched location. Photograph each room, and photo-

graphically document any damage that occurred pursuant to gaining access to any space in the location.
5. Execute the return of the warrant, which is the responsibility of the search team leader. It is the simple process of returning it to the judge or magistrate who issued the warrant, providing her with the date and time the warrant was executed, and providing the inventory of the evidence to the court officers.

The above procedure is tactical as well as investigative. It is a procedure that is the physical manifestation of professional law enforcement actions to follow when searching any location pursuant to a warrant. Some agencies and departments will have additional requirements and concerns. The use of force to breach a location usually requires a separate report and referral to the department's legal office for recompense for the damage, but other rules and directives should be followed as per the agency and department guidelines.

SUMMARY

Tactics are those physical requirements that are needed to carry out the important functions of law enforcement when an investigation starts to achieve the goals it has set out to achieve. Tactical operations can have significant results that enhance and improve the narrative of an investigation. Certain issues can develop during these tactical operations that can frustrate, stymie, or even end an investigation. Sometimes these issues can't be anticipated and therefore can't be avoided. For the most part, as an investigation progresses, these tactical operations will usually clarify facts. They can provide alternative theories for the investigation and give the investigator the insight necessary to successfully complete the investigation.

An arrest followed by a confession or significant admissions may give the investigator just the right amount of information to verify that the case is ready for trial. The facts and evidence already known, along with confessions and/or admissions, will provide sought-after proof beyond a reasonable doubt. Even the actions, lies, or misrepresentations provided by the subject will add to the proof for many jurors. Evidence that the subject assaulted the investigator during the arrest or presented the investigator a series of blatant and provable lies may give the jury that important impression that the defendant is very simply a bad guy who is raging or lying to avoid facing the responsibility for the crime. Innocent people don't need to lie or assault the criminal investigator! The tactical result of an arrest can provide the physical evidence that supports the overall narrative of the investigation. The subject is arrested with stolen money, a weapon used in a crime, or a smartphone with digital files detailing her efforts to case, or examine, the crime scene before the crime.

How an arrest happens and the circumstances surrounding the recovery of physical evidence that is located incident to arrest will vary a great deal. Planning and preparation are the necessary concerns of the criminal investigator. The actual physical takedown of the subject should be practiced and prepared for by the investigator's training and experience. There is no textbook that can provide the range of possible best practices, but ultimately, it is the responsibility of the investigator to ensure the safety of the law enforcement officers, the innocent bystanders, and the subjects. Once a person is taken into custody by an investigator, that person's well-being is in the hands of the arresting officer. Physical evidence found in the possession of a subject arrested and/or close to the arrestee is usually legally obtained evidence. The fact that the evidence was discovered incident to arrest must be specifically documented.

Tactical confrontations that unfold during a criminal investigation are unavoidable. The criminal investigator needs to be prepared for these incidents and maintain a tactical readiness. Bad habits such as smoking, drinking too much, overeating, and eschewing physical fitness programs are the kinds of behavior that impair tactical readiness. Staying fit and healthy provides the best chance for the criminal investigator to support investigative and law enforcement colleagues and return home each day to her family. Effective law enforcement requires physical preparedness and a steady and enthusiastic approach to training in all categories of tactical skill. Firearms training, a regular fitness regime, a healthy diet, and sufficient rest give the criminal investigator the physical confidence to take part and be effective in all manner of tactical operations. Muscle memory, strength, and stamina are the hallmarks of good training, and this allows the criminal investigator to be prepared to make instantaneous decisions and avoid dangerous and life-threatening events. The reality is that there is a time when using the flight instead of the fight response is the more appropriate decision. Discretion and choosing to fight another day are sometimes seen as cowardly, but violent criminals with the upper hand don't care about valor and honor. They only care about power and dominance. So live to fight another day unless someone's life is in danger. Machismo and a misplaced response to a tactical challenge by an aggressive criminal can get law enforcement professionals killed. It is sometimes necessary to step back and choose the best time to overwhelm the violent criminal.

Lethal force is the force necessary to stop and most likely end a threat from a subject who is attacking law enforcement or innocent bystanders. As described above, there are certain legal restrictions on the use of lethal force. Very simply the criminal investigator can use this final solution to a confrontation only when he can articulate a reasonable belief that his or some other person's life is endangered by the actions of the subject. The investigator is not shooting or using a tactical baton to kill. He is using sufficient force to end the threat.

The results of the use of lethal force can be difficult for a law enforcement professional to prepare for or to accept as a caring and law-abiding member of the community. Being prepared for this eventuality is an essential part of the work. Take the time to visualize the proper response in confrontations and train effectively to be able to carry out your responsibility in this area, and that is really the best a criminal investigator can do.

Using any level of force against a subject is regrettable, but usually there is no choice. Sometimes just showing a readiness to act will alert the subject to acquiesce to the investigator and respond with acceptance.

Finally, any operations, such as a search warrant or arrest raid, should be well planned and carried out pursuant to the training undergone by the investigator and her team. Follow the law, rules, and procedures of the department or agency. It is usually helpful to act dominating and in control. As the location where the raid occurred becomes peaceful and accepting of the legal authority, the investigator can return to a more solicitous and positive disposition to assure all persons present that the raid is merely a lawful and necessary step in the investigative process.

Chapter Seventeen

Covert Investigations

Surveillance, tactical spin, drug investigations, undercover operations, electronic surveillance, and Title III of the Omnibus Crime Control of 1968.

Criminal investigations are usually conducted in public to give the community the confidence that all appropriate steps are being taken to solve the crime and identify the perpetrator. In spite of the public effort, all witness statements and the details about the physical evidence and the suspects that are developed are kept confidential. The reason for the confidentiality is to protect the rights of innocent people along with the guilty until such time as there are enough facts to begin the public process of presenting the investigation to the court process. Revealing information from witnesses and suspects can put people at risk. Identifying a rapist before you are ready to go to court could be a death sentence for the suspect. Identifying a murderer before you are ready to present the homicide investigation to court can easily encourage the family of the victim to take action against the suspect. Law enforcement is at once a public exercise to satisfy the community and private confidential procedure that is required to protect the guilty and the innocent. Even being named a person of interest in an investigation is fraught with peril. How the community reacts can never be anticipated. In many cases, the public process of a criminal investigation lets the suspects guess about how the crime they committed is being handled and can thereby lead to the suspects hiding facts, obscuring details, and even intimidating witnesses. Serial criminals have the extra advantage of knowing all the details and can anticipate law enforcement action and thwart their ability to find that important piece of evidence that may lead to a solution. As a result of this counterbalance to an effective criminal investigation, the opportunity exists to approach a case from a completely novel and even creative direction. Even while an overt inquiry is progressing, the criminal investigator may develop a strategy that is covert, hidden from view, and possibly so new that the suspects are caught off guard. Sometimes the covert techniques are as simple as using surveillance to watch the suspects and determine their daily routine, or where the suspects go every day. The suspects' job or friends and business associates may need to be identified so all of the suspects' relationships are known and their possible relation to the crime that is under investigation can be determined.

COVERT SURVEILLANCE

Two types of surveillance can be considered: static surveillance, which entails the investigator's watching a particular location to see the comings and goings at a particular location, or mobile surveillance, which entails the investigator's carefully and surreptitiously following the suspect to wherever the suspect goes each day. For both techniques to be effective, the investigator has to be adept at keeping hidden and be close enough to see and identify with whom the suspect meets. Long-range surveillance photography is a skill the criminal investigator needs to be capable of to ensure the day-to-day activities of the suspect can be seen and graphically documented. The investigator has to keep careful and detailed notes and determine a way to follow up the surveillance investigation with a reliable method to identify every person the suspect meets with during his daily routine. The photography must be high resolution and provide graphic images that are detailed and provide sharp reproduction so the images can be compared with known identity photographs or be easily identified by witnesses who know the subject in the photograph.

The most important thing to remember about a covert surveillance operation of a career criminal is the fact that you may observe and photographically document a crime in progress. If a suspect does not have a regular job or a legitimate business that occupies her time every day, the chance that a regular surveillance investigation will capture a crime in progress is a real possibility. When this happens, the criminal investigation is simply expanded to prove the criminal activity and use that proof to leverage the suspect when it comes time to confront her in conjunction with the original investigation. In the event the crime that is observed is a violent crime or criminal conduct in the furtherance of a violent crime, the investigator will have to step up the timeline of the investigation to include the immediate requirement of thwarting a crime in progress or charging the crime that was committed in the presence of the surveilling investigator. In this event, the covert nature of the surveillance will have to be suspended in order to act on a higher-priority matter.

Photographic surveillance, as stated above, is a skill all criminal investigators should learn. From the mid-twentieth century until today, the technology of photography has improved and transformed. Film photography began with cumbersome large-format cameras that were four by five inches and larger. Huge film sheets or glass plates from the 1850s dominated high-resolution black-and-white photography with films capable of recording colors in shades of gray. Amateur photographers were able to break into the photography field with smaller-format plastic cameras invented by the film photography giant in the industry, Eastman Kodak. These cameras became so popular that professional photographers wanted to have access to smaller, more maneuverable cameras. The development of smaller high-quality cameras with high-resolution images began to provide professional and technical photographers with a crossover mix of cameras for passionate amateurs and skilled professionals along with sophisticated technical photographers. The image size of these cameras was reduced from the workhorse Speed Graphic, which was 4-by-5-inch, to a 2 1/4-by-2 1/4-inch dual lens reflex camera. The smaller size provided a handier tool for the professional and was even an important technical advancement for crime scene photography. A general category of law enforcement photography developed. The next big step in technical photography and therefore law enforcement photography was the development of the 35-millimeter single lens reflex (SLR) camera (about one-by-two-inch format). These Russian, Eastern European, and Japanese cameras were high quality with extraordinary lenses that were solidly constructed and capable of providing high-resolution images in spite of their small format size. These cameras were introduced over time from 1934 to 1951. A whole telephoto lens production developed around these cameras, making them ideal for long-range surveillance.

Along with these camera advancements, film production advanced to the point where high-speed, high-resolution films with color capability became another technical advancement that improved law enforcement photography. Telephoto lenses were capable of producing images from extraordinary distances, but the lenses were usually so long that the intensity of the light was reduced, which required the film to make up for the loss of detail. High-speed film suffered a loss of detail because the resolution of the film was limited. Photographic surveillance by law enforcement was a technical challenge, and the equipment and film could fall short in the lower ambient light in the evenings and at nighttime, times that need to be covered in covert surveillance. Specialized night vision optics were used to overcome the loss of light, but the best resolution was obtained by returning to black-and-white film. All these developments improved over time, but in 1994, digital photography was developed by the combined efforts of a photographic company, Kodak, and a computer company, Hewlett-Packard. Digital photography was developed in much the same way the Kodak Brownie amateur camera was developed. It was for the amateur world of photography and was eventually improved to the point that the resolution replaced film photography. All that is needed to produce an image is a computer and a printer. There is no longer a need for an expensive and technically challenging darkroom. Since the late 1990s, law enforcement photography has embraced the use of digital photography, so it is fair to speculate that all law enforcement professionals will need to become skilled at taking advantage of this new photographic advancement. Expensive digital cameras in the hands of skilled technicians can produce high-resolution images similar to the best images available with film photography. Low-light photography is improving with the image receptors on large-format photo sensors, which can record the light transmitted via the high-quality lenses provided on the newer model SLR cameras. The light sensors can be as large as 2 1/4-inch square reusable plates in the back focal plane of the camera, but even a light sensor similar in size to a 35-millimeter plate can provide an image of extraordinary clarity. All these advancements appear to be continuing so that by the time law enforcement students reach the professional stage of their careers, law enforcement photography will most likely be all digital. Advancements can even be seen in the small amateurish imagery provided by smartphone technology.

This short dissertation about the history of law enforcement photography was provided as a prelude to some basics for the criminal investigation student about the best way to evaluate photographic equipment for covert surveillance.

In the United States, the average roadway is 36 to 40 feet wide, which gives the surveillance team members a rule of thumb for choosing the appropriate telephoto lens. A high-quality image can be obtained using one millimeter per yard, subtracting the standard focal length of the camera 50 to 55 milliliters for a 35-milliliter size SLR or DSLR (digital single lens reflex) as the maximum allowable distance from camera to subject. This formula may seem complicated, but, in more simple terms, you consider the estimated distance from your surveillance location to the likely position where the surveillance subject will be standing. Then you multiply the number of yards by one millimeter of "focal length" for the telephoto lens, and add 55 millimeters to the figure. Then you have a best estimate of the focal length of the lens needed so that when a subject is 60 yards, or 180 feet, from your surveillance spot, you need a 125-millimeter telephoto lens for optimum results, which should provide enough distance so you can avoid detection. In reality, there are very few 125-millimeter lenses, so your next best option is a 135-millimeter lens, which is a routine size lens available for police surveillance work. This generally means that if you are located across the street from a subject, you need 135 millimeters of focal length on the camera lens to take identifiable pictures (pictures that can be viewed and compared with mug shots, driver's license ID photos, or passport photos). Taking into account the 20-yard distance across a standard roadway and adding some extra yardage to avoid detection, the overall distance across an average street will fall well into this range for a 135-millimeter telephoto lens. Finally, you always want to err on the side of a higher focal length if available. You need to consider that most law enforcement surveillance cameras are equipped with a standard package of lenses, usually including a 50-, 135-, and 250-millimeter zoom lens and 300-, 400-, 800-, and 1500-millimeter focal length telephoto lenses. Telescopes or Celestron folded optic lenses have extreme telephoto capability, but the quality of the images is substandard due to a need to provide extreme stability and significant ambient light for them to be effective in routine surveillance applications. As the distance increases, the mathematical formula mentioned above becomes even more accurate. In the day-to-day operations of surveillance photography, a good, stable surveillance location, or nest, coupled with a distance to the subject inside the 200-yard range, 300- to 400-millimeter lenses produce the best results while providing a secure distance from the subject so the investigator can avoid detection.

Since you always have to be concerned about surveillance-conscious criminals, ensure that you make a good judgment about the optimum distance for covert activity. A focal length of 300 to 400 millimeters gives the best comfort zone of 200 to 800 feet for setting up your static or mobile surveillance location needed for photography.

Using a well-equipped surveillance van or some kind of permanent surveillance nest provides maximum comfort and photographic stability for the investigator who is tasked with being the "eyeball" (surveilling investigator), but it is essential to constantly conduct countersurveillance to ensure the safety and security of the eyeball.

Positioning of the static surveillance location has to be well considered based on the camera equipment available, the duration of the surveillance, and access to and from the nest. The eyeball should be in a comfortable location and have bathroom facilities available. The eyeball should be prepared to defend his position. The eyeball needs to have a partner or replacement who can take over the surveillance if needed and on

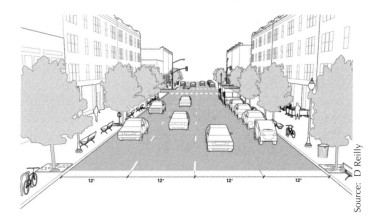

Source: D Reilly

a reasonable rotating basis. Visual obstructions should be kept to a minimum, and radio communications and any other internal noise should be restricted or lessened. Noisy or whirring camera equipment, droning air-conditioning, and open radio talk can easily compromise the nest. Exposure by the criminals or even by a neighborhood passerby can kill the surveillance and compromise the whole investigation.

For mobile surveillance, the same concerns have to be addressed, but since the eyeball has to be in a position to settle into a secure location at the right safe distance away from the locations where the subject lands, the eyeball has to effectively adjust for all subsequent moves and relocations. In mobile surveillance, there is always a need for four or five vehicles, which can change the look of a mobile surveillance and maintain contact without giving the subject too many repeat looks at the same vehicle. Mobile surveillance conducted with an airplane, helicopter, or drone can provide the critical ability to maintain eye contact with the subject without compromising any ground unit. A skilled pilot can stand off and orbit in an urban or suburban area and cover many square miles without ever being detected. The pilot can then call in the other mobile units to position themselves around a location the subject is visiting and be prepared to continue the mobile surveillance as soon as the subject moves. Air support has its drawbacks: the duration of the surveillance may be limited and certain cities and most airports and military bases will restrict air access.

Covert surveillance is an important tool in law enforcement. It can be an ad hoc exercise that takes advantage of some special information from a source or a witness that calls for immediate action, but it should be used when a solid plan, with appropriate resources, can be deployed. Covert surveillance requires a significant expenditure of resources, so choosing the best time to deploy the resources should be an important consideration.

The quick and fast ad hoc surveillance should be undertaken by only experienced and well-equipped investigators who carry surveillance photographic equipment with them at all times and are properly schooled in the skill. Most important, the surveillant needs to have training in driving skills that won't compromise the investigation and should always back off and break off the surveillance if she is detected. Feeding into the paranoia of a criminal suspect is not usually a bad thing, but making a suspect too surveillance conscious usually eliminates the benefits that can be derived from the use of this covert tool.

Covert surveillance is a necessary tool for the criminal investigator. It should be used as often as possible, but there needs to be training, planning, and resources available to the investigator and his team. It can be dangerous when the criminals know or believe you are out there. Law enforcement professionals are not exempt from making tactical mistakes that put them in dangerous positions. A group of investigators involved in a mobile surveillance or even a static surveillance are usually operating in one-person vehicles and can become spread out over dangerous and unpredictable neighborhoods. Radio contact may not be enough to thwart an attack or an ambush. Constant situational awareness and countersurveillance techniques need to be employed to lessen the danger involved.

Personal Experience

Special Agent William "Billy" Christian of the FBI's Washington Field Office was an agent assigned in May 1995 to participate in the mobile surveillance of a meeting between a suspected cop killer Ralph McLean and his girlfriend in Landover, Maryland. Billy was my friend and colleague. What the surveillance team didn't know was that McLean had come to the conclusion as a result of a media report that his girlfriend was cooperating with the police. McLean was lying in wait in the neighborhood where the meeting was to take place and just looked around the neighborhood in hopes of catching the police surveillance. He spotted Billy sitting alone in his vehicle, slipped up behind him, and shot him dead while Billy was waiting for the surveillance to begin. McLean was subsequently shot by the remaining agents who were on the surveillance detail, but that didn't stop Billy from being the fourth service martyr I personally knew in my career. Training, planning, and resources may not always be enough to keep you safe on a surveillance, so maintain situational awareness and maybe just an extra bit of paranoia to ensure you survive dangerous covert surveillance of violent criminals.

TACTICAL SPIN

From time to time during an investigation, situations will arise that require some creative thinking. For example, locating a phone number that is somehow related to an investigation, but the subscriber to the number is not immediately available may require a surreptitious phone call to try and identify whose number it is. The investigator can use a made-up story that flummoxes the person who answers the phone and may prompt information of interest to the investigation. It is also possible that it just provides a number to a local pizza delivery business or some other public business of no importance to the case. Either way, the questions about the phone number may be solved. Using bogus or cover information to resolve a lead in an investigation without revealing the law enforcement interest is an investigative technique that expedites the gathering of information that hopefully doesn't arouse suspicion from the suspect or their compatriots. Rather than label this technique undercover work, it is best to refer to it as tactical spin. It is a method used to bypass time-consuming searches or subpoenas for basic information that may be of value. The best approach to this technique is to develop believable stories with a logical premise to generate conversation and an explanation from a knowledgeable person about unknown telephone numbers, unknown storefronts, and unknown persons. The results may not fully satisfy the need for information, but they may provide details unavailable without direct contact. It requires the investigator to be genuine in her presentation and flexible in the process so the person on the phone or in the business or the suspicious person readily talks and explains his situation. The primary result is to make sure that no suspicion is raised by the inquiry. When posing as a phone or a utility company employee or a maintenance employee, make sure you operate in a fashion consistent with the manner in which these persons operate. Rely on your own experience or even anticipate the need to use this kind of scam and perfect it with a legitimate but cooperative person who fills that job description. You are trying to catch a person off guard with questions that seem simple and nonthreatening. If the recipient of your tactical spin, or ruse, operation is a legitimate person, this technique will be easier to employ than when the person is a suspicious criminal, but even a suspicious criminal can be caught off guard by innocuous questions that appear to be legitimate and an appropriate inquiry.

This technique can be very helpful in resolving those recurring unknown telephone numbers, street addresses, and persons whose involvement in an investigation can be better determined with a little background information. Obviously, by posing as a non-threatening service person, you are vulnerable to lies and misdirection, but you should always follow up with the inquiry in a more substantive manner that will resolve the questions once and for all. Grand jury and administrative subpoenas may take time, but the information provided in response is usually accurate and officially more evidentiary if that is needed. Suspicious persons who are encountered in an investigation may not be identified by a subpoena, but eventually you will be able to describe or show a candid photograph of the suspect to witnesses and confidential sources who can either identify the suspect or provide valuable information leading to an identification. Using this technique does potentially expose you to the chance that the target is immediately suspicious of your inquiry and shuts you down. If the person then follows up on the suspicion and proves you are not who you said you were, the next logical conclusion for the person to make is that you are the police or a bad guy. Either way the mere suspicion may cause a change that frustrates any attempt at fully identifying what the connection to the investigation was. In most cases, there is little chance of anything more than suspicion. If you are unsuccessful with a ruse, just move on to plan B, which is finding out what you need through official channels or further investigation.

DRUG INVESTIGATIONS

Since the beginning of the much-touted war on drugs during the Ronald Reagan era in the United States, the trafficking of illegal drugs has been a priority criminal investigation effort. Drugs are not only dangerous because the harder drugs, such as heroin, cocaine, methamphetamine, fentanyl, and prescription drugs, are addictive and harmful to human health; the trafficking of these substances generates enormous revenue for serious and violent organized-crime syndicates. Every major criminal syndicate, from the Italian Mafia to the Eastern European Bratvas, all the way down to homegrown street gangs, uses drug trafficking revenues to purchase weapons, pay bribes to public officials, and create huge levels of wealth for the bosses and the second- and third-tier members of their organizations.

Street-level drug businesses, which will be referred to as retail sales–level traffickers, are the point of the spear for this insidious activity. Relatively small amounts of heroin, for example, yield 200 or more user transactions per ounce at a retail cost of $4,000. At the end of the day, when the retail distributors are caught in possession of one or two ounces of product, they are viewed as small-time offenders whose penalties should be limited, but as we have discussed in our consideration of other criminal conduct, catching a career criminal for one burglary is only the tip of the iceberg. A single retail drug dealer who has a normal distribution routine and sells two ounces of heroin per night is selling to more than 350 buyers every night. That kind of impact on the community is a substantial blight on the average neighborhood. Heroin users are a substantial part of the criminal population. They need the drug to keep current with their addiction, so they steal, rob, and burglarize to feed their habits. The same can be said for other large segments of the criminal population, and the habitual use of drugs of all kinds contributes to the overall crime rate. Even violent predators use illegal drugs to self-medicate in reaction to their mental anguish and a perpetual reaction to their own sense of victimhood. For all these reasons, targeting and investigating retail drug sales are productive investigations. The most significant reason to aggressively investigate this level of drug distribution is to obtain primary actionable intelligence on major drug suppliers who operate a wholesale level of distribution. The purpose of this section in the chapter is to explain some of the approaches to follow to conduct a drug investigation.

Source: iStock 178133760

As discussed in chapter 3, the drug statutes are fairly simple. Mere possession of any of the most dangerous drugs is a felony charge. So stopping and searching a person who you have probable cause to believe is possessing heroin, cocaine, methamphetamine, PCP, LSD, or fentanyl can lead to a felony arrest if you find an amount of any of these dangerous drugs in her possession. You then have probable cause to search the residence or business of the person who was arrested with a distribution level of drugs. Any of the drugs mentioned above and other more exotic substances are usually listed under the Controlled Substances Act (CSA) and divided into the five narcotics and dangerous drug schedules. An updated and complete list of the schedules is published annually in Title 21 Code of Federal Regulations (CFR) §§ 1308.11 through 1308.15. Substances are placed in their respective schedules based on whether they have a currently accepted medical use in treatment in the United States, their relative abuse potential, and the likelihood of their causing dependence when abused. Schedules I and II contain most of the dangerous drugs that are regularly sold or trafficked illegally in this country. The person in whose house the substances are found can usually be charged with "constructive" (which means the property owner or proprietor has knowledge of the drugs in his house, residence, vehicle, or business) possession of the drugs. All illegal drugs are listed on the federal schedule, and it is updated periodically to include the many new and very dangerous designer drugs manufactured to disrupt this system of identifying dangerous substances. For purposes of this discussion, the drugs listed above are generally considered the most prevalent drugs sold on the street, including marijuana, which is a hallucinogen and listed on schedule I, and would probably account for more than 90 percent of all the illegal substances distributed in this country. Marijuana distribution is legal in a number of states and considered a misdemeanor crime in most other states. It is believed to have significant medicinal purposes, but as of 2019 it is still considered a crime in the federal system. Federal prosecution of a marijuana case would probably involve an extremely violent distribution network and hundreds of pounds of marijuana.

The next criminal charge that is possible for investigation is possession with intent to distribute. Again, you have to prove possession or constructive possession. Proving the intent to distribute can be accomplished a number of ways. You can conduct covert surveillance of a public distribution location and arrest and gain cooperation from buyers who leave the location with drugs and are willing to tell you who they bought the drugs from. A reasonable number of these kinds of witnesses would probably be needed to sustain a case through trial. At least five to ten persons willing to identify the seller would probably be needed in most jurisdictions. Keep in mind that an addict would probably be a very unreliable witness; however, a couple of addicts who agree to cooperate are likely to help provide probable cause along with intense surveillance and a confidential reliable source for a search warrant and/or an arrest. How the case progresses from there would depend on what kind of evidence you can obtain in the search warrant and/or the arrest and the search incident to the arrest. Sending a confidential reliable source or a cooperating witness into the location to make a purchase can also get you to the level of probable cause for an arrest, but using a confidential source for this kind of low-level charge is counterproductive. Other options available to you are dependent on the location where the drugs are sold.

Drug dealing as a crime has a couple of serious drawbacks. To meet the demand and encourage the large number of customers needed, drug dealers can't be too discreet. They have to sell the product in open-air public locations that allow for a steady flow of traffic. They can't be too particular about their customers because that can cut down a steady flow of revenue. Drug dealers sell in big-city clubs, bars, restaurants, and after-hours spots. They sell in alleys or on street corners or in front of liquor stores. If they sell in an apartment or a house, they have to make sure the word is passed among an unreliable and potentially bigmouthed group of people whom they shouldn't trust. Because of this drawback, major or successful retailers use unreliable runners, with more reliable lieutenants to distribute their drugs. They usually exercise dominion over the sales and, in some cases, give a nod of assent for each sale. There is really no way of telling how the individual systems work until you are able to evaluate the operation with the help of a confidential source or from substantial covert surveillance. In the event the drug enterprise is a significant business with a stream of big revenue, it is worth the time and energy to develop several sources of information about how it works. One important aspect of the intelligence needed to make the best case possible is to clock (determine when) the recovery of money is made from the location and when the re-up of the drugs occurs. Several days of static surveillance may be needed for this purpose, so a secure and accessible surveillance nest is required. If the operation is transparent, with each transaction approved by the main dealer through the lieutenants who then pass on the approval to the runners, the case can and should be made when the most money and drugs are present. It is absolutely essential to follow up the close down (arrest of the main dealer and lieutenants) of the overt retail drug operation with search warrants at the residences of the main dealer and the lieutenants. Runners who are caught with drugs in their possession have an opportunity to testify and save time in incarceration, but they are not essential if you have the surveillance documented with photographic evidence and you have recovered a significant amount of drugs and money. Ancillary physical evidence and contraband, such as guns and stolen property, add frosting to the cake. High-dollar cars and any indicia of wealth, such as high-end entertainment centers, expensive clothing, and proof the dealer traveled extensively for resort vacations or gambling junkets, provide additional proof of a high-revenue business, especially if the subject is not employed.

More opaque business models for these street-level retail drug enterprises may require more surveillance and details supplied by insiders. Arresting drug users and

Source: iStock 521667623

debriefing them about the place they buy their drugs in exchange for lesser charges or even giving them a free ride on a possession charge is like shooting fish in a barrel. Most users will give up information about a retail drug dealer as quickly as you ask for it if you have arrested them immediately after they have been caught with drugs they just purchased from the dealer. It is true that some dealers are scary and intimidating. But addicts are mostly concerned about where their next fix is coming from, and they will do anything to get a break so they can return to the streets. Unfortunately, these same insiders will fold when confronted with the likelihood of testifying in a trial about the same situation. Additionally, their memory will become really suspect if they continue to use drugs while a case is pending. If an addict is cooperative and wants to be put into rehab, then it is your responsibility to do what you can to help, but there are very few success stories.

One important forensic examination should be mentioned before continuing with the discussion of drug investigations. For most of the serious drugs, such as heroin, cocaine, and methamphetamine, there is a preliminary test kit used to provide a presumption that you have in fact recovered a controlled substance. These kits are manufactured by pharmaceutical firms for the purpose of providing a reliable, fast, and accurate method to make sure the questioned substance is what it appears to be. Drug dealers have scammed their customers with all sorts of look-alike substances, so a criminal investigator who reaches an important point in an investigation needs to have a reliable and user-friendly way to make sure the substance is in fact an illegal drug. Eventually, the substance will have to be subjected to a more accurate qualitative and quantitative scientific analysis, but that examination is only required at trial. The controlled substance test kits are required for probable cause and should be performed immediately on any suspected substances.

Personal Experience

In the early 1990s, I executed a search warrant at the home of a drug dealer. I discovered a large plastic bag containing three pounds of fine white powder. I conducted several preliminary tests on the substance to see if it was a controlled substance or some kind of cutting agent. Heroin is often cut with a powdered milk–like substance, such as mannitol, which is used to expand the amount of powdered drugs while reducing potency to a point where the drug is not immediately a life-threatening poison. If a person uses 100 percent quality heroin, she would immediately suffer an overdose and probably die. None of my tests for the powder I found were positive for a controlled substance. I sent the powder in for examination by the FBI laboratory because even if I were able to prove the powder was some kind of cutting agent, it would still be evidence that I could present of the ongoing nature of the drug conspiracy. Two weeks later to my surprise, the powder was identified as 98 percent–pure heroin, commonly referred to as "China White" heroin. It was the most potent heroin found in Washington, DC, in many years. Either my procedure in conducting the preliminary test or the test kit I used was faulty. Whatever the case, I have always suggested that any substance found hidden or in any way appearing suspicious in a drug dealer's house or business should be fully examined by a toxicologist just in case a mistake is made.

Returning to considerations in conducting a drug investigation, it should be apparent at this point that proving a drug case is really dependent on proving some kind of possession of the actual drugs and then, in some way, verifying or proving distribution of the substance. Possession proof is discovering the drugs on the person of the suspect. Constructive possession can be proven by the substance discovered in a location where the suspect has dominion and control, such as her residence or business. Additional proof may come in the form of testimony from cooperative insiders who, when faced with their own criminal culpability, testify that the drugs recovered from a particular location are in fact owned or in the possession of the defendant. All in all, proof of possession should be very straightforward and easy. There are examples of drug cases that are referred to as dry conspiracies. Testimony from witnesses who can attest that a defendant has been involved in a substantial drug distribution enterprise is the type of evidence that is required. This kind of testimonial evidence needs to be overwhelming, and additional evidence, such as indicia of wealth with unexplained revenue, can support this kind of dry conspiracy case. Unfortunately, juries will find it hard to be swayed in these kinds of cases unless the proof is very compelling. Having a drug case without drugs as evidence may be considered a result of corrupt and vindictive associates criminalizing an otherwise innocent person. There may even be a belief on the part of the jury that the defendant may be guilty, but without the drugs, there is simply a reasonable doubt.

So at this point, what do we have to sustain a drug investigation? (1) Can we observe the actions of the drug distribution operation? (2) Can we be certain the substance that is being distributed is a controlled substance? (3) Is there an opportunity to recover the controlled substance from the targeted suspect? (4) Can a case be made for proving distribution? If the answer to any of these questions is no, what investigative step can be taken to turn that around?

Pertaining to question 1, the drug distribution occurs in a closed, less-than-public venue, such as a nightclub or bar. The investigator needs to develop persons on the inside who can explain how the enterprise operates. These persons can be uninvolved bartenders, DJs, or wait staff. They can also be users who frequent the establishment and can sit and observe without arousing suspicion. They can be nonusers who are in the same category of being able to sit and observe. They can be confidential reliable informants who blend into the venue and report back to the investigator. Finally, they can be undercover police officers or agents who fit the profile of the customers who can sit and observe without arousing suspicion. The main drawback of this kind of surveillance is that documenting the activity with photographic or videographic evidence may be impossible. If users are the observers, the same concerns about using addicts as witnesses may frustrate the investigation. Uninvolved staff people may lose their livelihood if it is ever revealed that they assisted the police. Most bar and club owners would not tolerate a drug distribution operation in their business if they were not getting a piece of the action. This then leads us to what is possible with any of these observation sources. This kind of information should be reliable based on the sheer volume of reporting, especially if the sources are citizens without arrest records, confidential reliable sources, and/or undercover police officers acting as legitimate customers.

If the investigator has developed information via the testimonial reporting of these sources that shows the target is carrying out a drug distribution enterprise, the investigator should be able to prepare an affidavit in support of a search warrant for the residence of the target and any other conspirators identified by the observations. Adjusting the timing of a search warrant to coincide with a logical timeline of the drug operation may provide the best time of day to execute the warrant when the target is present in the residence, possibly immediately prior to when he would leave to carry out his business at the club. Then the likelihood is that question 3 will be answered positively.

Question 2 can, of course, be answered positively when the substance is given the preliminary test and followed up by the more significant toxicology examination. Catching the suspect in possession of a significant amount of drugs indicates distribution and not personal use. For the trial, the observations of the persons inside the venue will become less important than the evidence found pursuant to the warrant.

One method of proving possession with intent to distribute is by using court-approved experts in street drug sales. These experts will explain to a jury the relevance of a person having a certain amount of drugs in her possession. With their expertise, they can offer an opinion that possession of ounces of heroin or cocaine is most likely an amount consistent with distribution and not personal use. They are usually able to take an ounce or two of powder and break it down into normal street-level dosage units so the jury can judge why a distribution charge should be sustained. As mentioned earlier in our discussion, just two ounces of heroin can be broken down to represent more than 350 individual sales of heroin, making even this relatively small amount of product indicative of a large-scale drug operation with implications for a significant impact on the community. The implication of this kind of testimony is simple. If the weight of controlled substance found is indicative of distribution, then question 4 can be answered in the affirmative.

Obviously, if the investigator can produce witnesses who are buyers of the dealer's product and can testify effectively to the distribution operation, question 4 becomes a slam dunk for proof. As a result of these kinds of findings from a search warrant, if the testimony of a confidential source or even information provided by troubled addicts was used to sustain probable cause for a search warrant and their evidence is not used at the trial, the confidentiality of those witnesses can be maintained. Defense attorneys may demand to know the identities of the underlying witnesses, but most judges will not support that demand unless the defense attorney offers some evidence of corruption or lies from those witnesses. Their truthfulness is generally sustained by the evidence recovered from the person of the defendant and the evidence found in the residence or business searched pursuant to the search warrant.

This provides a general outline on how an investigation can proceed against a retail drug business: stick to a productive surveillance operation, incorporate some insider witness testimony, and rely heavily on a search warrant or arrest to bolster the possession aspect of proof. Remember that a drug investigation on the surface is not very complicated and if a retail drug operation is to ever be successful, it has to rely on high numbers of customers and a steady flow of customer traffic. These customers are not the kind of persons a criminal can believe will be loyal and closemouth about their operation. If there is a need for using undercover officers in this kind of investigation, it should be well controlled and limited. The officers should follow the tried-and-true routine observed or explained by insiders so everything that can be done to maintain officer safety is done. Cooperating witnesses who will make controlled purchases for the investigator should be handled in the same way as undercover officers. All steps necessary to protect the witness should be taken. Retail drug dealers have turned from drug entrepreneurs to armed robbers at the drop of a hat; this metamorphosis should be expected as a possibility. This makes any drug transaction a potentially dangerous exchange. Cooperating witnesses and undercover officers should be blanketed with coverage so the team backing up the operation can immediately respond to a call for help from the drug buyer. Unfortunately, a lot of bad and unpredictable things happen in the drug world. Criminal investigators have to consider worst-case scenarios and try to have a plan that covers their covert transaction.

WHOLESALE DRUG DEALERS

Open-air markets for drugs are the logical point at which drugs are distributed to the highest numbers of customers. These retail markets on street corners and in nightclubs and alleys provide the main fuel that makes the drug business thrive. Young, aggressive entrepreneurs who wish to establish themselves in the criminal ecosystem can spend time learning the drug business from the ground up. They may even get caught a few times by the police; then they start to develop strategies for avoiding jail and moving up the chain in the drug world so they can eventually achieve the lifestyle that drug-fueled wealth can bring. Eventually, they realize that the retail market is the most lucrative, but if they can be the wholesale supplier to several retail operations, they can make lots of money and avoid the pitfalls of the retail operations. They can pick and choose their criminal associates in the hope that since these dealers are vulnerable to the same penalties as they are, they will most likely stay firm in not cooperating with the police or law enforcement. If they can develop a "connect" who provides significant amounts of product at a reasonable price, they can then turn the product into a profit when they sell lesser amounts off to a small cadre of retail dealers. It is age-old capitalism at its best—buy low and sell high. In the cocaine business, for example, a kilo of cocaine could be purchased in the early 1990s for $18,000 and broken down into 16- to 62-gram packets for sale to a retail dealer for more than $30,000, generating a profit of $12,000 per kilo. If the wholesale dealer has a solid connect, moving 10 to 20 kilos per month is not unheard of. A profit of $100,000 to $200,000 per month is possible. This kind of profit predisposes no interruptions and no loss of product as a result of law enforcement interdiction. It also predisposes the reliability of the retail buyers along with some financial discipline on the part of the wholesale dealer. When the wholesale dealer gets the $30,000 from the sale of the cocaine packets, he needs to keep the $18,000 secure for when a new delivery is expected. He doesn't want to get caught short when the next delivery is ready. The other unexpected reality is the

price may go up the next time around. The dealer needs to decide whether he can easily pass on the raise to his customers or take the hit himself just to keep his customers
happy. All those possibilities are real-life scenarios that wholesale drug dealers find
themselves in constantly. The most important disruption is the simple fact that on
both sides of the business, the dealers are working with violent career criminals who
become angry at any minor offense and constantly try to "get over" on each other.
Being a reliable business partner is important in the straight world of business, but
being reliable and having integrity in the drug business can make you seem weak and
vulnerable. Drug dealers at this level expect to be robbed and taken advantage of when
the business starts to be disrupted. They will even accept big losses as long as they
can see a time when they can get back at the offender. It is an extraordinary business
that almost never delivers the wealth and independence it suggests when things are
going well. There are huge amounts of money involved in the business. There are
also times when the money is just out of reach and not available. Suppliers begin to
front product to their customers who don't have ready cash, and paybacks are slow in
coming. Prices constantly fluctuate to meet demands and account for loss of product
in the pipeline. Heroin and cocaine originate in the Middle East, Southeast Asia, and
South America, but in the past fifteen years, Mexican cartels have forced the pipelines
through their distribution networks. Even street-quality fentanyl, which is manufactured in China and used as a cheaper adulterant to heroin, comes through the cartels.
The Mexican cartels have established themselves as the most reliable conduits for
international drug trafficking to the biggest international market—the United States.
International crime syndicates, such as Eastern European gangs, control European
and some Asian markets. The bottom line is that these current pipelines will change
and establish new transit locations for international drugs. Meanwhile, America's
own product, methamphetamine, can be locally manufactured but also has import
pipelines from Mexican cartels and Canadian manufacturers. What seems to affect
these sources is the amount needed by the end users. Small midwestern communities are satisfied by local cooks, but large urban demand centers usually require large
volumes of product from the international manufacturers. Outlaw motorcycle gangs
are dominant in this business throughout the United States, but local drug syndicates
can also thrive if they are willing to keep the product flowing and use a high level
of violence to secure their operations. All of these main suppliers rely on wholesale
distributors to control and organize the retail dealers to keep the petty disagreements
to a minimum. In the event sanctions are needed or law enforcement intervention is
suspected, these main suppliers are more than capable of delivering punishment and
death where it is needed.

   The ultimate goal of any wholesale drug investigation is to get at and disrupt that
pipeline and change the flow of drugs to more than one community. This is an extraordinarily ambitious goal and is accomplished only when law enforcement at all levels
along with international law enforcement join together to disrupt and dismantle the
pipeline from the community level to the top of the pyramid. Cases against Pablo Escobar, Joaquin Guzman, and Rafael Quintera (Latin American cartel bosses) required
enormous cooperation and the combining of the results from numerous wholesale
dealer investigations. The centerpiece of all of these cases was the financial investiga-

tions that proved how the enormous amounts of money spent were generated from a huge international distribution network. Even the case made in New York against Frank Lucas (one of the most successful heroin dealers in the history of New York City), who went personally to Southeast Asia and set up his own connection directly from the jungle to the streets of New York, took years of investigation and some important lucky breaks just to get him in the first round of the investigation. Lucas was the closest law enforcement has ever seen to having an almost perfectly insulated operation that relied heavily on trusted family members. Most wholesale drug operations rely heavily on unreliable career criminals who owe their loyalty to themselves and their greed. All criminal organizations sell hatred for snitches and preach a heavy reliance on an old Mafia term *omertà*, but keeping quiet in the face of serious jail time or death is not a choice that most career criminals are willing to make. Once an insider has been shown how replaceable she is to an organization, it is only a matter of time and good timing by a veteran investigator with many of the right answers to break the code of *omertà* and begin the compromise campaign. When a top-level manager in a Mafia family, such as Sammy "the Bull" Gravano (number two boss in the Gambino crime family who became a government witness in the successful prosecution of John Gotti), can break and roll, it is not likely that anyone in the business can expect sheer loyalty. This then is the first approach to dismantling a wholesale drug operation. Conducting an investigation or a series of investigations against retail dealers will yield cooperating witnesses who will provide the inside information necessary to build a case against the local wholesale supplier. Making that case stick is essential, but building in flexibility so the target can be stung from two or more levels provides the unbreakable case that offers only two alternatives: life in prison or cooperation for a lesser penalty. In the event the wholesale dealer has used violence to enforce his will and secure his operations, he will still face significant jail time, but he will have a light at the end of the tunnel and may be able to provide safe harbor for his friends and family.

Conducting a successful investigation of a major wholesale drug dealer is similar to an investigation of any criminal enterprise ensconced in a criminal syndicate, such as a gang, Mafia family, or cartel. The investigator has to start with identifying insiders who are in need of help, such as insiders who have made the boss angry and lost favor. They may even be pending a significant punishment. Identifying these unfortunate souls can be accomplished through knowledgeable confidential sources or competitors who are willing to talk to law enforcement. The investigator may even consider targeting the at-risk insider in order to have legal leverage to hang over her head to further encourage cooperation. Once the focus of the investigation is initiated, the investigator should continue to monitor the actions of the dealer to develop even more potential targets. Eventually, it will be necessary to target trusted associates who have more current information. In this kind of case, the wholesale supply transactions that occur are usually done in private, and money transfers may even be done with electronic digital exchanges, which reduces the possibility of obtaining physical evidence of the drug transactions except for the drugs themselves. Wholesale dealers who take possession of large caches of drugs are developing more sophisticated methods of taking custody of the product, so the investigator will find it more difficult to interdict the controlled substance and prove the possession requirement. Large quantities of drugs are left in the trunks of rental cars, and the car keys are given at the exchange. Other "one-off" security measures are used to avoid transactions that resemble the traditional satchel of cash for a suitcase of drugs. For the investigator to be prepared to interdict the transaction, it is necessary to learn the procedures the wholesale dealer uses to take possession and make sure that when possession happens, there will be a method to prove that fact. A witting insider is the single source who can provide this information. After a transaction, the investigator needs to be able to identify the warehouse storage, weigh station, or transfer location where the bulk kilos are broken down for the retail dealers. In a major organization, these retail supply transactions may be done by employees who will take the heat if law enforcement interrupts the transaction, but these employees can be pressured to cooperate and are vulnerable especially if they have individual weaknesses. The drug laws throughout the United States provide some of the toughest penalties possible, so negotiation for lesser punishments is always a possibility. The day-to-day reality of investigative steps like this brings us back to the basics. The investigator needs to be a capable interviewer/interrogator who uses the full range of skills to develop an open line of communication between the target employees and law enforcement. In some cases, threats can be effective, but it is likely that pointing out the isolation from support will be the most effective approach to gain cooperation. Drug gangs or enterprises always promise legal support but rarely come through for low-level mules. Eventually, these employees, who may have only limited knowledge of the overall operation, can provide significant testimony about the transition of the wholesale quantities to the retail distribution, but they may not have any face-to-face interaction with the boss of the enterprise and therefore their testimony will come up short.

As a result of these difficulties in observation of the whole operation, the investigator will find the evidence may be missing important details. One way to fill these gaps is to trace or follow the money. When the retail purchaser makes a transaction with the wholesaler, dirty old cash will be the payment medium. The retailer cannot be dealing with ATM machines and credit card transactions. Large, bulky street money, such as 20-, 10-, and 5-dollar bills, will be counted and put into large containers to pay the wholesaler. The wholesaler will then have to find a way to deposit this cash into a bank or other financial business. The money will have to be laundered through some kind of legitimate enterprise so it can be turned into actual wealth for use in buying cars, houses, and businesses. This kind of money laundering usually requires a corrupt money manager who can take the bags, boxes, and containers of street money and transform it into useable business revenue. Because of this essential requirement, the wholesaler is vulnerable to forensic auditing. The investigator needs a team of skilled certified public accountant with professional business experience who can review any financial records that can be subpoenaed through legitimate channels and discover the method the wholesaler uses to transform the street money. Cash business fronts, such as beauty salons, delis, fast food restaurants, and car washes, are the types of front companies the wholesaler may use, but the accountant for the business will have to know the truth of the matter to make sure the books look normal. An average fast food business may take in $50,000 per month. How can an income of $200,000 be explained? The drug retailer can avoid this kind of vulnerability by purchasing cars or paying rent for relatives and employees. Developing a method to buy resort vacations and spend lavishly at bars, restaurants, and other entertainment venues can be a cover for using the significant wealth. But the wholesale dealer is involved in much larger amounts of money, so the money has to be accounted for in some legal way. Small businesses are the most likely remedy for this kind of money laundering. The tax audits, bank records, and business licensing reports are open and available sources of financial records that have to be "cooked" to make up for the dirty street money. Front-business operators may not even know the nature of their backer's business and are just happy to have the financial support for their neighborhood business. A service business can be a front to cover the large transactions between the wholesaler and the main drug supplier. A legitimate-looking service invoice with claims of consulting work product turned into another company allows huge transactions to be accounted for in a transparent manner, but the street money will always require more finesse from the wholesaler's business manager. There may even be corrupt bankers, lawyers, and CPAs involved in a major wholesaler's money-laundering operations. This is an important vulnerability for a wholesale drug distribution enterprise.

When drug distribution enterprises reach or establish a network criminal activity that becomes a major business with extraordinary wealth, the routine criminal statutes don't carry penalties significant enough to deter the activity. Additionally, the drug business is so lucrative that the US Congress and state legislatures have established forfeiture laws that allow for the recovery of major assets, cash, vehicles, and homes. Federal and local statutes advance the possession with intent to distribute statutes to include conspiracy and the so-called kingpin statute, which expands the proof from a mere conspiracy to a specific hierarchy with middle management–level drug conspiracy lieutenants and lower-tiered soldiers. For the federal statute, the magic number of six or more members (including the boss) of the organization raises the crime to the drug kingpin level. The statute is titled Continuing Criminal Enterprise (CCE). These more serious statutes still have the possession with intent to distribute character. The added legal element of using employees and the vulnerability of their major assets allows the investigator to potentially punish the target and his associates with periods of life imprisonment. If the members of the enterprise are successfully prosecuted any assets derived from the proceeds of the drug business are turned into assets available for enhancing the investigative budget of the law enforcement agency. The other significant aspect of the CCE statute is that if the enterprise uses violence in the furtherance of its business, each count of murder in the furtherance of CCE carries the federal death penalty.

Drug enterprise cases where the organization is a street gang or violent criminal syndicate can also include a federal charge of RICO (Racketeer Influenced and Corrupt Organizations Act, which was discussed in chapter 3). The RICO statute also has built-in forfeiture penalties and enhanced punishments for the use of any violence in the furtherance of the RICO conspiracy. The main distinction between RICO crimes of violence and CCE violence is in the interpretation of "in the furtherance." The RICO statute recognizes the need to consider the motive for the violence in a much more open-ended manner. The violence can result from the need of the member of the conspiracy to maintain her position in the gang or group. The CCE violence has to be directly related to a drug transaction. This distinction becomes more important when you consider that violent street gangs need to use violence to control territory, whereas a nongeocentric wholesale drug enterprise may never need to exercise violence except when a transaction is compromised.

Finally, as has been mentioned in several chapters of this book, using the information obtained from informant insiders and the examination of financial records, search warrants should be considered whenever possible. Interdicting drug shipments, especially large ones, can throw off a smooth-running business operation. Locating the real books of a wholesale drug business and finding personal diaries, business plans, notes, letters, photographs, and other documents can provide inside information that can be used to plan investigative approaches. Search warrants can uncover vulnerabilities unknown to an investigation, which can be exploited as the case proceeds.

The two most-used strategies for a drug investigation at this level are (1) electronic surveillance, such as telephone wire tap, bug inside a specific location, and any other court-ordered and authorized interception of audio, video, and digital communication among and between targets and (2) an undercover operation. Both of these strategies are very productive and usually successful, but they have drawbacks and should never be considered unless the investigative agency has the manpower and resources to carry out these strategies. The evidence obtained can be some of the best evidence possible. The investigators get to hear directly from the target how the operation works and what is expected of the other persons with whom the target is involved.

UNDERCOVER OPERATIONS

One of the most dangerous investigative strategies in law enforcement is introducing an undercover officer or agent into a criminal enterprise. The first step in this process is to establish a rock-solid backstory for the undercover and ensure that the story will hold up under any scrutiny. In this digital age, being off the grid is almost impossible, so any person who doesn't have a digital persona is more suspicious than a person who is openly on Facebook, Twitter, and all manner of other social media. An undercover officer, or UCO, is also usually required to have a criminal history, which comports with the UCO's proposed cover personality. So a UCO who is pretending to be a drug dealer should have a criminal history of a drug dealer. The further back the backstory goes, the better. An old arrest for dealing drugs in a faraway jurisdiction will be difficult if not impossible to double-check. Social media footprints can also be ancient, such as still available profiles that satisfy the curious but do not provide any way to verify recent interests. Driver's license, passport, and bank accounts all need to be up to date but not too new, and able to provide some real backstopping if questioned. Even a recent employment history or an indication of a bad breakup in a UCO's personal life may be needed. In other words, the UCO's profile has to be as real as possible with a few solid ways to verify information if possible. Depending on the dangerousness of the operation, the UCO may need to be a very dangerous person so her persona is not taken lightly by violent targets. The support for the UCO when he is meeting with the bad guys has to be a priority. If the UCO is meeting with violent drug dealers for the first time or for a money transaction, security for the UCO has to be priority one. Much of the backstopping is overkill if the UCO is conducting a one-time meet for a single transaction. The transaction's bona fides must simply be any person who has enough money to make the buy. Even this kind of UCO should at least have a driver's license that can pass a demand made at gunpoint. These single-meet undercover meetings are used in retail street-level drug buys, purchases of stolen property, or even meet and greets with a cooperating witness who needs extra security. The UCO may simply be a serious and intimidating figure meant to portray a bodyguard or security feature. Any serious confrontation should be met with a serious lack of cooperation and a fast ending to the meet. This kind of UCO should be tactically sound and ready to take action in self-defense. If need be, two UCOs can be utilized, but again, the most important aspect of this kind of undercover operation is that the bodyguards seem more than capable of defending the cooperating witness and dealing with any unnecessary attack. The more imposing the UCO is, the more likely the meet will end peacefully.

So a UCO may be required in many roles. Anything that would involve more than one meeting should be covered with a well-put-together backstory. The greater chance the UCO will need to impress, justify, or develop trust, the more substantial the need for a well-planned and supported backstory. If the UCO is simply window dressing, such as a bodyguard, support employee, or boyfriend, the less fine-tuned and substantial the backstory has to be, but the basics need to be covered, such as ID, work history, financial background, and some social media presence. A well-developed social interaction between the UCO and any cooperating witness is also an essential element. If the UCO is present as muscle or backup to the cooperating witness, there needs to be an easy and well-established banter between them so the target does not suspect they just met. An outward display of trust and familiarity should be the picture presented by any undercover team, no matter the makeup.

It should be noted that the primary need in an undercover operation is to have a professional law enforcement officer as a witness to a criminal conversation, transaction, or crime. The UCO, a cooperating witness, or both may be wired for audio recording. New digital technology makes the equipment needed for a recording small and easy to hide, but advanced criminals will resort to a number of methods to frustrate or deter recordings of their conversations. Electronic devices that sweep for transmitters sending the conversation to outside units can easily compromise an operation. The UCO should be ready for this kind of compromise and be prepared for an easy and fast exit. Digital recorders that maintain a local voice recording may not be detected by this kind of device, but undercover teams have been forced to strip down so the target can examine them for hidden recording devices. Smartphones and all kinds of innocent devices can be altered or set up to record without seeming to be operating in this fashion. Sophisticated recording devices should be available to a UCO to frustrate any kind of detection, but the most certain way of avoiding detection is to not use a recorder for a first meeting unless there is some way to know beforehand that the target is not concerned about being recorded. One other method by the UCO is for her to demand to protect against recorded conversations. This demand can be made first by the UCO and the team, throwing the suspicion onto the target and away from themselves. Some aggressive behavior in the furtherance of acting in a criminal manner can deflect suspicion. Whatever approach that is agreed on—not to record, putting the shoe on the other foot, or believing in the high-grade technology supplied to the UCO—should be planned in advance so the team follows the protocol and makes the best effort to document the meeting via digital recording or a follow-up report. Even if a recording is made, the UCO needs to prepare a full report detailing the specifics in the meeting so the UCO can provide effective testimony about the meeting. There may be missed nonverbal communication or whispered unintelligible words that are important communications the UCO heard or saw that may be important for documenting the details of the meeting.

Undercover work is stressful and requires confidence and flexibility. The UCO has to maintain his cover identity and backstory even when it seems to be falling apart. A criminal can always find escape in saying, "So what if you think I am lying? What do you expect from a criminal?" UCOs need to receive extra training in tactical areas, such as firearms and hand-to-hand combat, and be prepared to act aggressively to protect themselves. The investigators need to be able to respond immediately to situations that are becoming dangerous. Code words that ask for help from the outside should be agreed on by the surveillance team, and extraction plans should be discussed. UCOs who are acting in an open-air drug market or other outside venue and are vulnerable to patrol interference should be very familiar with the color of the day or other universal codes to let uninvolved officers know they are dealing with a UCO. This is especially important if the UCO has had to exercise self-defense and lethal force in an undercover situation gone bad.

Undercover operations have significant benefits, but no matter how important an investigation seems, it is never worth the life of an officer or agent. Prosecuting attorneys consider undercover operations a very useful tool, but they don't understand the level of danger involved. When a violent criminal realizes he has been duped by a UCO, the reaction can be immediate and life-threatening. These criminals don't have to have some kind of objective assurance the person they suspect is a UCO; they only have to have a gut feeling or suspicion. They can act on that suspicion with no remorse or internal concern. The investigator has to make an evaluation that the target is not the type who will act based on such little provocation. The investigator has to believe that the target will refuse to have contact with a person she doesn't trust. The investigator has to believe that the target will graciously if angrily accept the fact that she was duped but will hold back from any violent response to that anger. The criminal investigator has to raise concerns about the target's tendency toward violence with every source and witness, so there is good reason to believe that introducing a UCO will produce positive results. Otherwise, considering an undercover operation is foolish.

There are inherent dangers using a UCO in a drug, murder, violent gang, or criminal syndicate investigation. These dangers need to be carefully assessed, and the decision to use UCOs should be limited and well planned. The single most important part of the planning should be to mirror, to the extent possible, prior normal conduct. If a UCO is going to buy drugs, make sure to follow the protocol used in the past by the person who is introducing the UCO to the transaction. If the UCO is being offered for his expertise and special skills, make sure the target has expressed the way those special skills will be and have been used in the past. The investigator should make the best effort at reflecting past performance and procedures. Don't give the target any reason to suspect or challenge the way a meeting is happening, a transaction is occurring, or how money or contraband is exchanged. Let the target be comfortable with the UCO so that each contact is routine and not something extraordinary.

One very subjective drawback to an undercover investigation is the entrapment defense. Investigations involving the use of deception, which automatically includes undercover investigations, tend to be considered on the borderline of corrupt practices. A target with a long history of dealing drugs, fencing stolen property, laundering money, or employing violent services, such as hiring a hit man, will have trouble making a judge believe that she was not predisposed to commit the offense. But a woman whose husband is violently abusive and who is apparently at wit's end may be susceptible to hiring an undercover hitman, though any second-guessing on her part may be cause to end the operation. If she is determined to carry on with the plan, the evidence of that determination should be absolute and on a recorded conversation so the judge and the jury are convinced that she is committed to the plan. The critical judgment is that word "predisposed," meaning the target of the operation knows what she is asking of the UCO. When the government takes the step to encourage the committing of a crime, there has to be an easy way out. The problem may be that the UCO is not the last person the target may talk to about committing the crime. If a real alternative drug dealer, hit man, fence, or money launderer is contacted, the investigator and the UCO may never know the crime continued. If the UCO's persona is threatening, a reasonable "out" of the operation is something to consider; otherwise, the target may claim she wanted out but was scared of the UCO. Even major drug deals with neophyte wannabe players should be carefully monitored to make sure the target is totally agreeable to the crime. Finally, it should be remembered that entrapment is a defense and not a certainty. The UCO and lead agent should consider all the aspects of the scenario and make sure the target can opt out if it is obvious that the target's heart is not into the crime. It is a real challenge to insert a UCO into the position where the target appears to be conspiring to commit a crime, so the investigator should make sure the operation is fully planned and executed so the results are positive.

Any UCO needs to be charismatic and easy to like or to fear, depending on the undercover scenario. In some cases, the UCO needs to be invisible, but in other cases, the UCO needs to be a dominant force. Whichever personality makes sense for the scenario is acceptable, but either way, the source is on stage, and even low-level employees need to be convinced. A shy and retiring UCO to the target may need to be much more open and transparent to employees in a criminal organization who can express suspicion as an insider. With that being said, the UCO may need to have a chameleon-like personality to satisfy everyone he comes in contact with that the UCO is not a threat to the organization, unless that is the role that is being played.

TITLE III ELECTRONIC SURVEILLANCE

In the early part of the twentieth century, electronic devices known as recorders were invented. Eventually, they were improved and "miniaturized" to two- by three-foot tape recorders that could capture hours of conversations on a single reel of tape (acetate, filmlike material), which would turn sound into magnetic "scratches" that could then be immediately played back and filed away for future use. These magnetic tapes could be turned into vinyl disks and replayed thousands of times as music and other entertainment. As usual with all forms of technology, law enforcement developed its own uses for the equipment. Telephones sent audio conversations over telephone company lines, and often, these lines found their way to switching stations, which could be tapped and the conversations overheard and recorded. The actual words, plans, and actions described in words by criminals could be memorialized by these recordings and become direct evidence of crimes and criminal conduct. These conversations could also be picked up on small, secretly installed microphones inside a variety of locations in a residence or business, not only capturing telephone conversations, but also capturing face-to-face meetings inside houses, businesses, and social clubs. As microphones developed to have the capacity to send out radio signals containing the conversations, they also could be attached to phones and other wire sources to send the audio out of the original structure to remote listening posts with reel-to-reel recorders. Eventually, all this technology was referred to by law enforcement and the intelligence community (spies and counterspies) as electronic surveillance. In the first half of the twentieth century, this technology was used sparingly because ongoing criminal activity that could generate a lot of this kind of evidence was involved in gambling and bootlegging investigations. Initiating a wiretap or a bug required significant manpower; the support of the phone company, and in some cases, a court order to enter a residence or business to plant or install a bug or a microphone. There was also the need to monitor the electronic surveillance, which also required manpower. Agencies such as the FBI and the DEA and big-city departments used the technique, but most smaller investigative agencies and departments refrained. Even in the early days of its use, electronic surveillance seemed to libertarians a serious breach of privacy. It was almost viewed as unfair intrusion, but there were no rights that were being violated, at least on the surface, especially if the telephone wire where the tap was placed was outside of the parameters of the target's residence. The Fourth Amendment did not seem to apply. At least one distinguished jurist said in a later discussion of this kind of investigation that the founding fathers knew about eavesdropping and were perfectly fine with it. If a criminal were foolish enough to speak about her criminal conduct loud enough to be overheard, she was certainly foolish enough to speak about it over a telephone wire. As discussed in chapter 3, three cases are relevant to a modern-day discussion of electronic surveillance: *Olmstead v. United States*, 277 US 438 (1927); *Katz v. United States*, 389 US 347 (1967); and *United States v. Jones*, 132 S. Ct. 945 (2012).

These three Supreme Court cases have set the parameters as to what is allowed as evidence from conversations, texts, emails, and other forms of communication carried by telephones, computers and smartphones, and face-to-face conversations. The net result of the constitutional evaluation established in these cases and others is that if the subject has "a reasonable expectation of privacy," then the seizure of the conversation is protected by the Fourth Amendment and can be accessed only by law enforcement if a court order based on an affidavit demonstrating probable cause is obtained. After the *Katz* case and pursuant to belief held by a large number of legislators at the time, the court order had to meet certain statutory requirements set by the Omnibus Crime Control Act of 1968 Title III. So the court orders are nicknamed Title III court orders. The affidavit not only has to lay out the probable cause required but it has to include other investigative steps that have been tried without success or could be tried. This affidavit has to be specially approved by the US Department of Justice before it can be presented to a federal judge. At last count, forty-six of the fifty US states can also apply for a Title III court order if they follow a similar set of rules in their state legal system. In other words, this kind of overhear is not to be considered unless there is a very compelling reason and substantial benefit to be had from recovering this evidence. To summarize the three cases mentioned above, *Olmstead* allowed wiretapping and did not consider it a violation of the Fourth Amendment. That was the law of the land until *Katz* in 1967, when the court reversed its opinion and determined that the Fourth Amendment protected people and not things, so that if the conversation was made with the belief that it was a private conversation and there was a reasonable expectation of privacy, it was protected by the Fourth Amendment as an unlawful seizure. *Jones*, a much more recent ruling, bolstered the ruling in *Katz* and included a variety of digital data collections as protected communications. Right now, the files and images on a smartphone are protected material and require a court order to access. There is no reason to think this kind of material will be available if a Title III affidavit is submitted to a judge, but it is likely that all of the digital data will be the subject of legal wrangling in the courts for a long time.

Referring back to our discussion about drug investigations, the single most considered investigative strategy for a major drug investigation is to get a wiretap: a smartphone court-ordered overhear, a bug in a particular room or residence, or an interception of digital communications, such as emails and messages on instant messaging platforms. Any covert method requiring a court order that can lead to the seizure of direct communications detailing import, distribution, sale, and financial benefits of the drug enterprise is an essential part of a major drug investigation. Without this direct communication from the mouths or minds of the subjects, it is very difficult to prove the facts needed to show a major narcotics distribution operation. The electronic surveillance orders usually require Title III affidavits. The process is very cumbersome and has several difficult angles to overcome to make the strategy successful. In the first place, the investigator has to know and identify the method the target uses to set up, arrange, and carry out transactions. If this is not known, the focus of the investigation has to make this determination, so again, an insider has to be turned and his cooperation needs to be extensive. Once a phone line is determined to be "hot," meaning used for criminal activity, the investigator needs to begin to analyze pen register data. For cellular phones, this data is called airtime data. Either designation provides all of the outgoing and incoming phone calls with their numbers and the duration of calls and times the calls happened. This information, nicknamed metadata, provides a profile of the subject's telephone or cell phone activity over the course of months. Analysis of this basic information will include the identification of numbers called and who the subscribers are to those numbers. The analysis will also determine the regularity of calls and begin to establish any patterns regarding the length, times, and dates that coincide with events that should have generated conversations. Pursuant to this analysis, the investigator, with the help of a telephone analyst, begins the difficult process of obtaining the subscriber's information and comparing that information with any previous investigative targets or suspects. This analysis will also attempt to compare the phone numbers and subscribers with other investigations so that access to previous intelligence about all the numbers can be located. After all of this analysis is complete and turned into an ongoing project, the investigator should begin the preparation of the pen register or airtime report for use in the Title III affidavit. A full and up-to-date report will be an important part of the final affidavit when it is presented, but the conclusions need to be investigated for accuracy. For example, if a number is preliminarily determined to be a major drug supplier in another city or town and the target has regular contact with that person, regular surveillance on the subject needs to be arranged. If the other town has an interested investigative unit that wishes to pursue an investigation of that person, then a coordinated investigation should be initiated. In this fashion, the pen register or airtime phase can provide enormously important leads to be followed over the remainder of the case. Since this is so important and time consuming, the earlier in the case the pen register or airtime evaluation is set up, the better. Even during the initial stage of a drug investigation, you may have one or two numbers associated with the target to subpoena for records. With those phone records, it is then necessary to ask the prosecuting attorney's office for the pen register order or a continuing order for airtime records for any known cell phone. As the investigation proceeds, the investigator may become aware that a crime business phone is being utilized. This then would be the most likely target phone for the electronic surveillance. Make sure that as the airtime data and pen register data are obtained, there is no crossover. It may be that the target uses all of his phones for crime business, and the earlier you determine that the better. Realizing there is a cell phone for business creates still another problem. Over the past ten years, throwaway, or prepaid, cell phones have been used by major drug dealers to frustrate Title III investigations. A dealer will use a phone for two to three months and then discard the phone, leaving the investigator with all the facts in the affidavit relating to a number that is no longer in service. In most Title III investigations, the affidavit may take as long as two to three months to get approved. Administrative and approval adjustments have been made for this problem, but it is essential that the investigator keep up with the target's rotating schedule and prepare several ways to immediately identify the new phone when it is activated. Specialized software and algorithms can provide an analysis using all the numbers called and documented by the pen register or airtime records that can successfully identify the new phone. The most effective method is to maintain solid coverage on the target by the cooperating witnesses and any confidential sources who can report any changes in the phone number immediately. These human sources will also provide another required benefit. As the time to approve the Title III extends, the Department of Justice or approving state prosecutor may ask for the investigator to "freshen up" the probable cause. The simplest way to do this is to have a cooperating witness or source make a controlled drug buy using the new phone and ensuring the target is using the phone for "dirty" business. This buy needs to be consistent with the normal operation and, as mentioned in the section on undercover operations, a routine transaction that will in no way make the target suspicious. At this point, being so close to approval of a Title III, extensive manpower and tactical operational planning should be in place and scheduled. Raising suspicion at this point can be disastrous for the investigation. If all the investigative eggs are in one basket, then the Title III must go forward.

This brings us to the next main drawback for a Title III investigation. There is an enormous manpower requirement. Electronic overhears may require 24/7 monitoring by prosecutor-approved officers, agents, technicians, and analysts. There will also be a need for an administrator for the wire, who will make sure all the shifts are covered and the monitoring agents are following the rules of monitoring. In the case of multiple lines, or bugs, the administrator and the lead investigator may need reviewing officers or agents who are very familiar with the overall investigation to provide briefings and instruction to the monitoring agents regarding new targets that may come up and be identified. They may also have to update the monitors about additions to the rules governing minimization.

Minimization requirements for any Title III monitoring begin very liberally. It is, after all, logical that it will take a few days of listening to conversations for the monitors to sort out the innocent conversations from the criminal conversations. Based on the Fourth Amendment admonition that the evidence to be recovered be specific, the monitors must make an effort to decide if a conversation is of evidentiary value. In the early days of monitoring, the overhears will include all sorts of mundane conversations, such as ordering a pizza, making plans for a social event, or arguing politics, religion, or sports. To begin to pare down these mundane conversations, the monitors need to listen to a portion of the conversation, make a determination whether it is relevant, and if it is not, turn off the listening and recording capability simultaneously. The monitors can then wait a specific time (for example, one minute) and then return to the conversation. If it is still ongoing, then the monitors can record for another 10-second interval to determine if the topic has changed and decide if the persons being overheard have begun to speak about criminal matters covered by the Title III affidavit. This is the pattern of minimization that has to be followed to be in accordance with the limitations of the Fourth Amendment. Title IIIs cannot be fishing expeditions; they must be focused on the criminal conversations that are expected based on the probable cause in the affidavit. If the target is a drug dealer, drug transactions, money laundering, and conspiracy with other members of the drug organization are fair game for monitoring, but discussions about baseball games and movies should be minimized.

Violations of the minimization requirements are the single most significant actions that can lead to the audio recordings being excluded as evidence. There simply is no remedy if the monitoring agents violate the rules in this regard. The Title III investigation then becomes a waste of much effort and resources.

The plain view doctrine applies to a Title III. As an example, if a Title III investigation is initiated for a drug or stolen property case or other so-called nonviolent criminal matter and the monitors overhear plans, schemes, or discussions about other serious crimes, the judge can be immediately notified, and the court order can be expanded to include the new crimes. If evidence of a crime not included in the search warrant is seen in plain view, then the investigator is able to seize that evidence because she was legally present when the evidence manifested itself.

Personal Experience

In the early 1980s, I was assigned to a Title III wiretap of a small syndicate of criminals who were involved in credit card, bank, and wire fraud and identity theft. They used a religious cult as a front for their criminal activity. The prosecutor who oversaw the Title III conducted a minimization lecture to make sure that all the monitors were notified that the case involved nonviolent criminal activity and the monitors would not have to be concerned about listening for any other criminal activity except for the theft and fraud crimes. I had a monitoring shift the first night of the thirty-day duration of the wiretap. My first phone call was between a female member of the group and the person who sounded like her boyfriend. She began to ask him if the false identification she had made for him worked. He said that, yes, it worked great. He had been stopped by the police on his way out of town, and he had just showed the false ID and was immediately released. He told her he would hide out in Cleveland until the heat cooled down on the triple homicide in Chicago. This nonviolent white collar crime enterprise supplied false identification and hideouts for violent gang members in Chicago. The next day, based on my overhear and report, the murder fugitives were apprehended in Cleveland at a safe house that the small syndicate used as their operational headquarters in Ohio. The court order was immediately expanded to include the relationship the group had with violent street gangs, and significant additional evidence of criminal activity was obtained.

This experience brings up another point that should be clarified for all criminal investigators. Drug investigations are by far the most used cases where Title III operations are instituted, but most categories of serious crimes can be the underlying offenses where electronic surveillance is used. Homicides, terrorism, and substantial larceny-related investigations, such as car theft rings, major stolen property fences, and armed robbery rings, can be the targeted activity for a Title III. Generally, these kinds of cases take more substantive investigation to get the overhear order approved unless there is a very compelling belief that a life-and-death emergency can be thwarted by an emergency overhear. The affidavit will have to contain that exigent circumstance. To avoid any harm coming to a potential victim, the overhear wire may have to be compromised. The government can't just listen in when a person's life is in danger. Even if that person is himself a violent criminal. So Title III investigations on gang cases and organized-crime syndicates may be compromised if the monitors overhear plans to kill or maim a person. The investigating agency must take action, and by doing so, the fact that the evidence was obtained by a wiretap or bug may be immediately discoverable.

One final drawback (or not) for Title III investigations is the fact that the lead investigator on the case is no longer the detective, agent, or other law enforcement officer assigned to the investigation. The lead investigator becomes the prosecutor overseeing the overhears. Investigative steps, such as recovering drugs, interviewing witnesses or subjects who have been identified on the wire, or even conducting surveillance, should be approved by the prosecutor. The prosecutor is the decision maker; any steps outside of her approval are not defensible as simple investigative leads. Any operation that may invoke a response on the wire needs to be considered carefully by the person who will have to defend the actions of the investigations in court to the approving judge and eventually in any trials or court hearings related to the investigation. Title III overhears are controversial and have an enormous body of prior case disputes where very specific avenues of investigation are or are not sanctioned, so the legality of every operation needs the scrutiny of a competent lawyer.

Since Title III investigations provide a unique inside look into an ongoing criminal conspiracy, the takedown of the investigation should be meticulously planned to provide maximum evidence recovery when arrests and searches are done. Targets need to be "bedded down" (the investigators need to know specifically where all of the targets are). The operation should coincide with an important operational action of the targets so they are caught off guard with something important occupying their thoughts. Descriptions and floor plans of all businesses and residences should be detailed. The propensity for violence should be well documented, and if there is a need for a SWAT or other tactical operations squad, the plan needs to include that. Forensic computer support is necessary, and any mobile surveillance needed is planned and arranged. Any major takedown of multiple targets with a number of arrests and searches requires a detailed operational plan. Title III operations have the additional benefit of providing real-time updates on the targets, so surprises can be kept to a minimum.

SUMMARY

Under the general heading of covert investigations, certain techniques are considered for their potential. When the suspect or the target is unaware of the investigative efforts of the investigators, it is more likely that law enforcement will be able to take advantage of mistakes, sloppiness, or arrogance on the part of the target. It is essential to keep these techniques hidden from view and confidential. The use of confidential sources and cooperating witnesses, as discussed in chapter 14, provides some basic lessons in case security. Investigative intelligence and secure case administration provide other levels of security, but in these covert techniques, law enforcement lives are at stake, and developing strict rules of informational dissemination makes security a priority. As the case develops and these techniques are utilized and, in many cases, combined, the investigator should be sure that the targets are kept in the dark. In this way, even if the target knows the police are onto him, he should never be sure from what direction the attack is coming. Surveillance investigations and tactical spin are reasonably secure operations. Even if the surveillance is compromised, the investigator is usually able to withdraw and let time pass to try again. Drug investigations may require covert surveillance, cooperating insider operations, and even undercover transactions. These transactions call for face-to-face meetings usually with violent career criminals. Security needs to be stepped up for a drug investigation, and attention needs to be paid to the planning and scheme being considered when you arrive at the need for an undercover operation in a drug or a stolen property case or some kind of violent crime investigation, such as posing as a hitman, infiltrating a terrorist cell, or working as a service person for an armed robbery gang. The UCO needs to be as protected as possible. Part of that protection is very simply being smart and alert to attitude and overt levels of suspicion. The operation has to be well backstopped, and the UCO needs to be provided a handling agent or officer who is a trustworthy colleague to accompany the UCO on meetings, write detailed reports about meets, and handle the UCO's investigative paperwork. This kind of support is needed only for undercover operations that extend over weeks, months, or even years. The UCO in a long-term assignment may even need periodic counseling from a clinical psychologist or psychiatrist. Mental health becomes an issue when the UCO no longer works in the law enforcement office and takes on the persona of a career criminal. There is just no way to evaluate the effect on the officer or agent without a professional evaluation. UCOs who keep their assignments short-term and continue to work in a law enforcement office need to avoid any public exposure and steer clear of any news briefings or overt operations that may draw media attention. The UCO should also avoid social outings with other law enforcement personnel unless the venue is a closed or private gathering.

Finally, wiretaps and electronic surveillance are very productive investigative techniques, but unless and until the criminal investigator has significant experience with them, they should be avoided. Work as a monitor or wire administrator provides much of the experience needed, but there are overall responsibilities that may balance that experience by working on a squad where the technique is a regular part of the investigative process. Working on an active drug or a gang/organized-crime squad usually provides an environment for the investigator to eventually run her own wire case.

Epilogue

Being a criminal investigator for more than thirty years was the best job and career I could have ever imagined. The intensity of the work and the passion and dedication that it brought out in me was as close as I could be to having a spiritual vocation. In my years after high school, when I went into the US Army and was sent to fight for my country in Vietnam, I recognized that I felt that service to my country was what I was cut out to do. I just wasn't sure at that point what work would be best for me. I had failed to meet important academic standards in high school, but my wartime experience taught me what real work required. I left the army with a work ethic that drove me beyond the halfhearted approach to improving myself when I was in school. Eventually, I went back to school and began to realize that schoolwork was playtime compared to real work. When I graduated from college with much better grades than I ever would have imagined, I realized that I was prepared to make a real contribution to my community, so I had the combination of wanting to serve my country and make a real contribution. Luckily, I was able to secure a job with the FBI right out of college, but I was still not sure I would ever be a criminal investigator. It was while I worked in the FBI Laboratory as an analyst that I began to understand that the complicated matrix of a criminal investigation was just the kind of puzzle I was cut out for. I did not consider myself an expert in any particular area of law enforcement, but I did have a way of communicating that engendered trust. I was a student of many subjects, and several fields of art and science prompted my curiosity. I believed that all of this passion for learning and, to be honest, having a really nosey attitude, told me repeatedly that I could do this work. The strict scientific discipline of the lab was not as satisfying as working the whole puzzle.

In the late 1970s and early 1980s, I began devoting myself to federal investigations, and I discovered I had an affinity for the uniqueness of each case. I savored the reconstruction of the timeline and the careful attention to every interview. My talent with developing trust and careful consideration not only made my work with witnesses easy but I also discovered I could work with and challenge confidential sources to provide the clearest picture possible of the criminal ecosystem. Ultimately, I realized that many of the persons I arrested were willing to talk to me and, in many cases, confess their transgressions. All of this just pushed my work ethic and inflamed my passion to help others. The service I gave to my country was real and valuable. Over time, I just wanted to get better and more capable. I wanted to make bigger and better cases. I wanted to show the community in Washington, DC, that we not only cared but we were also willing to pay the necessary price to save lives and make the city safer. My only regret is the loss of eight friends and colleagues. I would like to dedicate this book to them: Kevin Welch, Martha Dixon Martinez, Hank Daly, Mike Miller, Billy Christian, Bob Roth, Melissa Morrow, and Dave LeValley. I carry the pain of their loss with me every day, but the challenge of service to our country compels me forward. Being a criminal investigator was the high plane to which I aspired as a young man, and now, I am happy to say that I made that happen.

Glossary

Actionable Intelligence   Information from data collection, data mining, confidential sources, and other reliable law enforcement sources that can be verified by investigative actions.

Affidavit   A document describing the evidence and facts discovered in an investigation that proves an investigator's assertion of probable cause.

Agents/Special Agents   Terms designating state and federal investigators which verifies their authority. The designation of "special" refers to the fact that their authority is limited to the collection and investigation of criminal matters.

Aggravated   A term describing a crime as more serious based on extra violence or crimes against special victims who are more vulnerable in our society.

Analog Photography   Photography using film and chemical or "wet" laboratory image processing.

Arraignment   Court appearance following a grand jury indictment where the charges are provided to the defendant and the trial judge makes an appearance.

Assistant Commonwealth Attorney (ACA)   Local prosecutor in a state that identifies itself as a commonwealth.

Assistant District Attorney (ADA)   Local prosecutor in many jurisdictions who handles criminal cases for the district attorney.

Assistant State Attorney (ASA)   Local criminal prosecutor as designated in many local jurisdictions. Some local criminal prosecutors are called state attorneys general, but most local jurisdictions refer to their main criminal prosecutors as ASAs.

Assistant United States Attorney (AUSA)   Criminal prosecutor for federal jurisdictions, who are assigned to federal districts throughout the United States. They serve under the US Attorney in those districts in the same way the ASA and ACA serve under the state attorney and commonwealth attorney in local jurisdictions.

Ballistic Evidence   Physical evidence that is related to firearms: guns, bullets, shell casings, gun powder residue, gun barrel striations, and the like.

Brady Rule   Exculpatory evidence which has to be provided to the defendant and their attorney in preparation for a trial. This evidence is in the possession of the government and is an essential element in trial discovery.

Capital Crime   A criminal offense that carries a punishment including execution.
Capital Offense   A criminal offense that carries a punishment including execution.
Case   A compilation of information in a criminal investigation.
Combined DNA Index System (CODIS)   An FBI-sponsored national database of DNA profiles from crimes and criminal offenders. The database is used to assist in developing suspects in criminal investigations where the suspect left DNA evidence at the crime scene or when the suspect was arrested for a serious criminal offense. Most of the states participate as contributors to the database.
Commonwealth Attorney   Lead prosecutor in states that use the designation of commonwealth instead of state.
Confidential Source   A person who provides information to law enforcement and requests their identity to be withheld. This person can be a career criminal who is familiar with the criminal ecosystem in their community. This person can also be a private citizen without a criminal record whose job, profession, or position in the community allows access to information of value to law enforcement.
Confidential Witness   A person who will have to testify in a criminal case and be exposed publicly at trial time but is willing to provide ongoing support to law enforcement over the course of an investigation and in support of that investigation. This person may be an insider in criminal conspiracy or noncriminal citizen who is inextricably tied into the criminal actions of others.
Consent   A knowing and voluntary waiver of constitutional rights.
Constables   Small town or community local law enforcement officials. These officers are "holdovers" from early twentieth-century town marshals or magistrates.
Controlled substances   Drugs, hallucinogens, and other mind-altering substances listed as controlled substances in the 1970 Controlled Substances Act administered by the FDA and enforced by the DEA. These drugs have been determined to be dangerous unless they are properly administered or prescribed by a physician or appropriate medical professionals.
Cooperating Witness   A civilian, non-law-enforcement witness in a case, who can provide testimony of value to the investigation.
Criminal Code   A compilation of the criminal laws.
Criminal Informant   A person who is a confidential source of information and is familiar with the criminal ecosystem in the community.

Deadly Force   Physical force which when applied to person is likely to cause death. It should only be used by professional law enforcement in defense of the life of the officer, detective, agent or, any bystander in a confrontation.
Digital   Computerized data.
Digital Photography   Using a computer to produce imagery to record observations made in the furtherance of a criminal investigation. Obviously, it is also used for many other purposes, but in this context, it is crime scene photography, surveillance

photography, identification photography, and any other appropriate use to record imagery either still or video with digital cameras.

Discovery   The responsibility of the government prosecutor and the defense attorney to turn over evidence, reports, notes, interview reports, and any other documents and evidence in a criminal trial. Discovery also has civil court requirements, but it is rare for those issues to be raised in a criminal investigation.

District Attorney   A state or local "chief" prosecutor.

Drug Schedules   A list of drugs, hallucinogens, and other substances found on the 1970 Controlled Substances Act. It is five separate schedules or list of drugs based on dangerousness that are incorporated in Title 21 of the United States Code.

Due Process   The single phrase that incorporates the US Constitution's mandate that the government, local, state, and federal have to abide by the rights detailed in the Bill of Rights (first ten amendments) and other relevant legal precedent when prosecuting a citizen for criminal violations. The term is also used in civil litigation but is not relevant in this text.

Electronic Surveillance (ELSUR)   Phone taps, email monitoring, computer interception, cell phone interception, and "bugs" or overhear microphones installed in residences, businesses, and other constitutionally protected spaces.

Evidence   As defined in *Black's Law Dictionary*. "Any species of proof, or probative matter, legally presented at the trial of an issue, by the act of the parties and through the medium of witnesses, records, documents, exhibits, concrete objects, etc. for the purpose of inducing belief in the minds of the court or jury as to their contention."

Exclusionary Rule   The court-ordered removal or barring of evidence obtained because of a violation of due process. This removal or barring of evidence also involves any evidence that is "tainted." The term "fruits of a poisonous tree" applies.

Exigent Circumstances   An emergency condition that requires law enforcement action to save lives, property, and evidence when a real and articulable threat is identified.

Fence   A person who knowingly purchases stolen property.

First Responder   The first officer or emergency person on the scene of any incident, but for purposes of this text, the first officer called to the scene of crime who is responsible to take control of the scene.

Force, Use of   Any physical effort to force, promote, or ensure compliance from a person who is or may be resisting the appropriate and legal exercise of law enforcement authority.

Forensic Laboratory   A scientific facility involved in the examination of material and evidence of value in a criminal investigation. Alternate terms are crime lab or police lab.

Giglio Material   Documentary, digital, or written material reflecting the testimony or potential testimony of a witness in a trial. Examples of this material are interview notes from investigators, statements provided by witnesses, and any documentation from persons who the government may call as witnesses. The distribution of this material to the defense is the responsibility of the government prosecutor and is more succinctly defined by each jurisdiction.

Grand Jury   A panel of ordinary citizens called together by the local, state, or federal jurisdiction to oversee the actions of law enforcement and provide the constitutional authority to indict or formerly charge a criminal defendant. There are two kinds of grand jury panels, "investigative," and "indicting." Facts and evidence from investigations are presented and, if the panel finds probable cause a crime has been committed, they can issue a formal indictment.

Ground Combat   Tactical training for law enforcement officers to use wrestling and ju-jitsu holds to assume control of an assaultive and uncooperative person who is interfering with the lawful exercise of police authority.

Hand-to-Hand Combat   Tactical training for law enforcement officers to use boxing and fighting skills to defend against assaultive and uncooperative persons who are interfering with the lawful exercise of police authority.

Informant   A confidential source of information to law enforcement.

Integrated Automated Fingerprint Identification System (IAFIS)   An FBI sponsored database where known fingerprints of criminal suspects from all contributing police and law enforcement agencies are maintained so that latent and other recovered fingerprints from crime scenes can be graphically compared in order to provide an investigation with a list of suspects who could potentially be responsible for the crime.

Jurisdiction   A geographic location with legal authority established by a ruling or responsible government as authorized by the people who established the government. Local, state, or federal jurisdiction can be concurrent and is usually well defined by mutual agreement among the governments affected.

Jury of Peers   A group of citizens called together by a local, state, or federal jurisdiction that represents a cross section of the community from which the defendant in a criminal trial is drawn. The panel of citizens should match to the extent possible and feasible with the economic, racial, and cultural profile of the defendant. An effort should be made to avoid discriminatory dismissal of jurors from the community for any of these reasons, especially racial.

Macro Intelligence   Information that is developed and provided for the purpose of developing community planning and policy development for law enforcement purposes. It is information that is deemed reliable and productive when considering law enforcement manpower distribution, policy changes, and economic resource distribution for law enforcement agencies.

Marshal   A Deputy US Marshal, an employee of the United States Marshals Service, who acts as a primary federal law enforcement officer in US courts and in investigations of interstate flight of fugitives.

Miranda Warning   Statement provided to a criminal subject who is in a "custodial" interview to ensure that the subject is made aware of their right against self-incrimination and their right to have an attorney present during an interview or interrogation. This warning was established as a Supreme Court ruling in the landmark case *Miranda v. Arizona* that commanded police throughout the United States provide this warning to inform a criminal defendant prior to giving any statement to the police.

Mobile Surveillance   A covert observation of a suspect in a criminal investigation that follows and discreetly observes the actions of the suspect in habitual activities. This kind of surveillance is usually facilitated by the use of a vehicle so when the suspect travels to different locations the investigator will be able to keep a log of the routine.

Mug Shot Photo   An official record photograph of a person who is arrested and charged by a law enforcement agency. When a person is arrested, they are usually photographed and fingerprinted to ensure to the extent possible that the person can be positively identified at a later date. The photograph is usually a head and shoulders front and profile image, but it can also be a full body, front and side view. It is an official record and can be used to sustain a positive identification of the suspect in a criminal case.

National Crime Information Center (NCIC)   FBI-sponsored database designed to provide immediate access to warrant, criminal history data, and intelligence data on gang membership and terrorism-related intelligence. The database is searchable by law enforcement officers for official use only and requires the name and date of birth of the subject to be searched. Other non-recurring identifiers, like the FBI number and some police department ID numbers, can also be used for searches.

NCIC Stolen Article File   A section of the NCIC. Any personal property that is reported to law enforcement as stolen and has a non-recurring numerical serial number can be entered into the database so if it is ever located, it can be easily traced back to the original criminal investigation.

NCIC Stolen Motor Vehicle File   A section of the NCIC that contains information about automobiles that have been stolen from jurisdictions throughout the United States. The vehicles can be searched by state tag number and VIN (Vehicle Identification Number) with the make and model of the vehicle.

Night Vision Device   A telephoto lens with a capacity to enhance nighttime imagery to provide photographic surveillance capability to the criminal investigator. The equipment utilizes UV- and IR-range light energy to provide the enhancement needed.

Pattern Evidence   Physical evidence like shoe prints and tire treads detected at a crime scene that exhibits characteristics of identifiable patterns which can lead to the identification of the make and model of a shoe, or the make and model of vehicle tire. The pattern identification is verified by comparing the questioned print from a crime scene to shoe or tire reference files provided by the manufacturer.

People   The community, society, and/or population of the citizenry, which is the source of law enforcement authority in this country. "We the People . . . in order to ensure domestic tranquility . . . do hereby ordain and establish this Constitution."

Petit Jury   A panel of citizens from the community who become the triers of fact in most criminal trials. A defendant can ask to have their case decided by a judge, but most cases are decided by a jury of the defendant's peers.

Photo Surveillance   A physical observation of a suspect in a criminal matter, which is documented by the use of a camera or video recorder and the gathering of photographic images depicting the actions of the suspect.

Preliminary Hearing   A court hearing immediately following an arrest of a suspect who is then redesignated as a "defendant." The judge or magistrate must reach a finding of probable cause as to the charge levied against the defendant based on a limited amount of testimonial evidence and an affidavit or statement of facts detailing the probable-cause proof. If the finding is sustained, the defendant is bound over for grand jury action. The defendant can offer significant evidence proving innocence, but it is not a necessary requirement. There may also be discussion in the hearing about continuing the defendant's "bond status" if the defendant is in custody. The testimonial evidence offered by the government can be hearsay evidence.

Prima Facie   Accepted as fact until proven otherwise.

Proactive   An investigation based on information suggesting that a particular person or group of persons are regularly committing crimes. Also, it is information that generates an investigation about a pattern of crimes that are believed to be committed by the same person or persons.

Probable Cause   A constitutional standard of proof based on facts and evidence that is used by a judge or magistrate to reach a conclusion that it is reasonable to believe that crime has occurred, and at least two possibilities exist: (1) particular evidence of that crime is stashed, stored, or simply present in a home, business, or private property or in an otherwise constitutionally protected space; (2) that the facts and evidence prove to a reasonable judge or magistrate that a particular person or group of persons probably committed that crime. Their judgment must be based on the reasonableness of the facts and evidence presented.

Prosecution   Legal process of proving the government's contention that a person or group of persons who are charged with the commission of a crime are guilty by a standard of "proof beyond a reasonable doubt." It occurs in a trial with a finding from a jury or a judge.

Reactive   An investigation initiated by a particular crime reported to the police authority and determined to require investigation of the conduct reported and related criminal acts.

Recidivism   The return of a formerly imprisoned person for another prison stint, a repeat offender being sent back to prison.

Serial Sexual Predator   A criminal offender who compulsively sexually assaults victims to satisfy a need to dominate and overpower a victim.

Sex Trafficking   Commercial exploitation of sex workers and/or potential sex workers, male and female, adult and juvenile, for the purpose of facilitating a criminal enterprise involving prostitution, pimping, and child sexual abuse.

Sheriff   The most senior law enforcement official in a county or parish in the United States. The sheriff, is usually established by each state constitution as the main and in some cases the only law enforcement officer holding that constitutional position. In several US counties, the sheriff has become the primary official responsible for the security of the local court system, the responsible officer for judicial service, and the local jailer for persons held in custody awaiting trial. In these counties the sheriff's criminal investigative authority and patrol responsibilities have been curtailed or reassigned to a county police agency. However, sheriffs continue these responsibilities in most of the other counties throughout this country.

Squad   A law enforcement unit or group that handles a particular range of investigations inside a police or federal agency. Squads are usually no larger than twenty sworn officers or agents with a supervisor and a small cadre of civilian support staff.

Stare Decisis   The legal adherence to prior decisions made in courts, courts of appeals, and supreme courts as the law of the land. Legal precedence establishes the best way forward in answering sticky and in some cases controversial legal arguments.

State's Attorney   A lead prosecutor whose "client" is the people of whichever state jurisdiction has named the prosecutor as such; the chief prosecutor in the geographic region.

Static Surveillance   Observation of the actions of a suspect or business, a residence, or other permanent location for the purpose of obtaining evidence of criminal conduct at the target location.

Statute   Law, including one that refers to a crime, as defined by the local, state, or federal jurisdiction.

Surveillance Nest   A vehicle or permanent location used to make ongoing observations and collect detailed notes of actions observed and provide a safe place to photograph or video ongoing actions under observation.

Surveillance Van   A specialized vehicle with surveillance equipment and a nondescript outside profile that provides a mobile secure facility for conducting surveillance over long periods of time in extreme conditions.

Tact Squad   A tactical unit in a police agency designed for an intense covert crime prevention mission to flood a crime-ridden neighborhood to thwart and decrease an ongoing criminal threat from rapes, armed robberies, burglaries, and other serious felonies.

Tactical Training   Law enforcement readiness training in firearms, unarmed combat, raid and arrest tactics, and tactical planning and coordination among units, squads, and agencies.

Task Force   A joining of police agencies to combat a serious criminal threat to a community. Major drug trafficking task forces, gang task forces, fugitive task forces, stolen property task forces bring together local state and federal agencies in an effort to exploit the strengths of the agencies and fill in the weaknesses by adding manpower, jurisdiction, and financial or technical expertise together so the serious threat is dealt with effectively.

Telephoto Lens A long focal length lens used to allow high-quality photographic images from distant secure-surveillance locations. These lenses should be at least 135 to 400 mm in focal length and should have high-quality light-gathering capabilities to ensure the best-quality imagery under difficult ambient light circumstances.

UCO Undercover operation.

Victimology A thorough work, social, business, and family profile of the victim of a crime. This will be an effort to establish a timeline and a clear understanding of the victim's actions and venues before a crime and afterward if necessary. The victim's friends, enemies, and relatives need to be interviewed in order to complete a detailed profile of the victim to determine if any actions or personal attributes of the victim might be instructive as to why the victim was picked for violence or as a victim of theft, a con scheme, or other crime.

References

Adelson, L. *The Pathology of Homicide*. Springfield, IL: Charles C. Thomas, 1974.

Barnes, "Leroy" Nicky, and Tom Folsom. *Mr. Untouchable*. New York: Rugged Land, 2007.

Barnum, Clive A., and Darrell R. Klasey. "Factors Affecting the Recovery of Latent Prints on Firearms." *Journal of Forensic Identification* 47, no. 2 (1997): 141–49.

Berg, Erik. "Digital Enhancement and Transmission of Latent Prints." *Journal of Forensic Identification* 46 (1996): 573.

Berg, Erik. "The Evolution of the Crime Scene Diagram." *Journal of Forensic Identification* 45 (1995): 25.

Bettencourt, Delores. "A Compilation of Techniques for Processing Deceased Human Skin for Latent Fingerprints." *Journal of Forensic Identification* 41, no. 2 (1991): 111.

Bing, Leon. *Do or Die*. New York: HarperCollins, 1991.

Bobev, K. "Fingerprints and Factors Affecting Their Condition." *Journal of Forensic Identification* 40 (1995): 28.

Bodziak, William J. "Manufacturing Processes for Athletic Shoe Outsoles and Their Significance in the Examination of Footwear Impression Evidence." *Journal of Forensic Sciences* 31, no. 1 (1986): 153–76.

Bomb Investigations, National Bomb Data Center, Picatinny Arsenal, Dover, New Jersey. *Estimating Blast Pressures Resulting from the Detonation of Explosives Commonly Used in Improvised Explosive Devices (IEDs)*. General Information Bulletin 73-2, dated April 6, 1974.

Booth, Martin. *The Dragon Syndicates: The Global Phenomenon of the Triads*. London: Transworld, 1999.

Boudreau, John F. *Arson and Arson Investigation Survey and Assessment*. Washington, DC: National Institute of Law Enforcement and Criminal Justice, Law Enforcement Assistance Administration, U.S. Department of Justice, US Government Printing Office, 1977.

Bradford, Lowell W., and Alfred A. Biasotti. "Teamwork in the Forensic Sciences: Report of a Case." *Journal of Forensic Sciences* 18, no. 1 (1973): 31.

"Building Material Evidence in Burglary Cases." *FBI Law Enforcement Bulletin*, 1973.

Cassidy, Michael J. *Footwear Identification*. Ontario, Canada: Royal Canadian Mounted Police, 1980.

Chable, J., C. Roux, and C. Lennard. "Collection of Fiber Evidence Using Water-Soluble Cellophane Tape." *Journal of Forensic Sciences* 39, no. 6 (1994): 1520–27.

"Classifying Sexual Homicide Crime Scenes: Inter-Rater Reliability." *FBI Law Enforcement Bulletin*, 1985.

Contreras, Steven J., and Ann R. Bumbak. *The Evolution of Policing in America.* Nokesville, VA: Dynamic Police Training, 2017.

Cooley, Charles Horton. *Human Nature and the Social Order.* Los Angeles: HardPress, 2012.

Copeland, A. R. "Multiple Homicides." *American Journal of Forensic Medicine and Pathology.* 10 (1989): 10.

"Crime Scene and Profile Characteristics of Organized and Disorganized Murderers." *FBI Law Enforcement Bulletin*, 1985.

Culliford, B. J. *The Examination and Typing of Blood Stains in the Crime Laboratory.* Washington, DC: US Government Printing Office, 1971.

Dalrymple, B. E. "Case Analysis of Fingerprint Detection by Laser." *Journal of Forensic Sciences* 24 (1979): 586.

Dalrymple, B. E., J. M. Duff, and E. R. Menzel. "Inherent Fingerprint Luminescence Detection by Laser." *Journal of Forensic Sciences* 22 (1977): 106.

Davis, J. E. *An Introduction to Toolmarks, Firearms, and Striagraph.* Springfield, IL: Charles C Thomas, 1958.

Debbaudt, Dennis. *Autism, Advocates, and Law Enforcement Professionals: Recognizing and Reducing Risk Situations for People with Autism Spectrum Disorders.* London: Jessica Kingsley, 2002.

Dhole, V. R., M. P. Kurhekar, and K. A. Ambade. "Detection of Petroleum Accelerant Residues on Partly Burnt Objects in Burning/Arson Offenses." *Science & Justice* 35 (1995): 217.

"Don't Miss a Hair." *FBI Law Enforcement Bulletin*, 1976.

Dutelle, Aric W. *Introduction to Crime Scene Investigation.* 3rd ed. Burlington, MA: Jones & Bartlett Learning, 2017.

Early, Pete. *The Hot House: Life inside Leavenworth Prison.* New York: Bantam, 1993.

English, T. J. *Born to Kill: The Rise and Fall of America's Bloodiest Asian Gang.* New York: HarperCollins, 1995.

English, T. J. *Paddy Whacked: The Untold Story of the Irish American Gangster.* New York: HarperCollins, 2005.

English T. J. *The Westies: Inside New York's Irish Mob.* New York: St. Martin's Press, 2006.

Enos, W. F., J. C. Deyer, and G. T. Mann. "The Medical Examination of Cases of Rape." *Journal of Forensic Sciences* 17 (1972): 50.

Epps, Charles R. *Pulled Over: How Police Stops Define Race and Citizenship.* Chicago: University of Chicago Press, 2014.

Escobar, Edward J. *Race, Police, and the Making of a Political Identity: Mexican Americans and the Los Angeles Police Department, 1900–1945.* Berkeley: University of California Press, 1999.

Federal Bureau of Investigation. *El Rukns.* Washington, DC: BiblioGov, 2013.

Ferguson, Andrew Guthrie. *The Rise of Big Data Policing: Surveillance, Race, and the Future of Law Enforcement.* New York: New York University Press, 2017.

Fisher, Barry A. J. *Techniques of Crime Scene Investigation.* 6th ed. Boca Platon, FL: CRC Press, 2000.

Fortier, Zach, and Derrard Barton. *I Am Raymond Washington.* Canon City, CO: SteeleShark Press, 2015.

Fremon, Celeste. *G-Dog and the Homeboys: Father Greg Boyle and the Gangs of East Los Angeles.* Albuquerque: New Mexico University Press, 2008.

Garner, Bryan A., ed. *Black's Law Dictionary.* 7th ed. Eagan, MN: West, 1999.

Garner, Daniel D., Mary Lou Fultz, and Elliott B. Byall. "The ATF Approach to Post-Blast Explosives Detection and Identification." *Journal of Energetic Materials* 4, no. 1-4 (2006): 133–48.

Garrison, D. H. Jr. "Reconstructing Drive-By Shootings from Ejected Cartridge Case Location." *Journal of Forensic Identification* 45, no. 4 (1995): 427–33.

Gianelli, P. "Evidentiary and Procedural Rules Governing Expert Testimony." *Journal of Forensic Sciences* 34, no. 3 (1989): 730–48.

Golden, G. S. "Use of Alternative Light Source Illumination in Bite Mark Photography." *Journal of Forensic Sciences* 39, no. 3 (1994): 815–23.

Goldstein, Arnold P., and C. Ronald Huff, eds. *The Gang Intervention Handbook.* Champaign, IL: Research Press, 1993.

Grispino, Robert R. J. "The Effect of Luminol on the Serological Analysis of Dried Human Bloodstains." *Crime Laboratory Digest* 17, no. 1 (1990): 13–23.

Grubb, A. "Legal Aspects of DNA Profiling." *Journal of the Forensic Science Society* 33, no. 4 (1993): 228–33.

Havard, John D. J. "Expert Scientific Evidence Under the Adversarial System: A Travesty of Justice?" *Journal of the Forensic Science Society* 32, no. 3 (1992): 225–35.

Hazelwood, Robert R., and Janet Warren. "The Serial Rapist: His Characteristics and Victims." Part I and Conclusion. *FBI Law Enforcement Bulletin* 58, no. 10 (1989): 14.

Henderson, R. W. "Fire Investigations from the Consultant's Point of View." *Fire & Arson Investigator*, 39 (1988): 23.

Herod, D. W., and Menzel, E. R. "Laser Detection of Latent Fingerprints: Ninhydrin Followed by Zinc Chloride." *Journal of Forensic Sciences* 27, no. 3 (1982): 513–18.

Hildebrand, D. "Using Manufacturing Companies to Assist in Footwear Cases." *Journal of Forensic Identification* 44 (1994): 130.

Hueske, E. E. "Photographing and Casting Footwear/Tiretrack Impressions." *Journal of Forensic Identification* 41 (1991): 92.

Huston, Peter. *Tongs, Gangs, and Triads: Chinese Crime Groups in North America.* Lincoln, NE: Authors Choice Press, 2001.

James, R. D. "Hazards of Clandestine Drug Laboratories." *FBI Law Enforcement Bulletin* 58, no. 16 (1989).

Jones, B. R. "Putting the Fire Scene in Perspective." *Fire & Arson Investigator* 38 (1988): 59.

Kaplan, David E., and Alec Yakuza Dubro. *Japan's Criminal Underworld.* Berkeley: University of California Press, 2003.

Kavieff, Paul R. *The Purple Gang: Organized Crime in Detroit, 1910-1946.* Fort Lee, NY: Barricade Books, 2000.

———. *The Violent Years: Prohibition and the Detroit Mobs.* Fort Lee, NJ: Barricade Books, 2001.

Keefe, Patrick Radden. *The Snakehead: An Epic Tale of the Chinatown Underworld and the American Dream.* New York: Doubleday, 2009.

Kelling, George L., and Catherine M. Coles. *Fixing Broken Windows: Restoring Order and Reducing Crime in Our Communities.* New York: Touchstone, 1996.

Keppel, R. D. "Signature Murderers: A Report of Several Related Cases." *Journal of Forensic Sciences* 40 (1995): 670.

Kinnear, Karen L. *Gangs: A Reference Book.* 2nd ed. Santa Barbara, CA: ABC-CLIO, 2009.

Klein, Malcolm W. *The American Street Gang: Its Nature, Prevalence, and Control.* New York: Oxford University Press, 1995.

Knox, George W. *An Introduction to Gangs.* 3rd rev. ed. Levering, MI: Wyndham Hall Press, 1994.

Kodak. *Basic Police Photography.* 2nd ed. Rochester, NY: Eastman Kodak Co., 1968.

Le, S. D., R. W. Taylor, D. Vidal, J. J. Lovas, and E. Ting. "Occupational Exposure to Cocaine Involving Crime Lab Personnel." *Journal of Forensic Sciences*, 37 (1992): 959.

Leap, Jorja. *Jumped In: What Gangs Taught Me about Violence, Drugs, Love, and Redemption.* Boston: Beacon Press, 2012.

Lee, H. C., R. E. Gaensslen, E. M. Pagliaro, M. B. Buman, K. M. Berka, T. P. Keith, and P. Phipps. "The Effect of Presumptive Test, Latent Fingerprint and Some Other Reagents and Materials on Subsequent Serological Identification, Genetic Marker and DNA Testing in Bloodstains." *Journal of Forensic Identification* 39, no. 6 (1989): 339–58.

Leovy, Jill. *Ghettoside: A True Story of Murder in America.* New York: Spiegel & Grau, 2015.

Lucas, Frank, and Aliya S. King. *Original Gangster: The Real Life Story of One of America's Most Notorious Drug Lords.* New York: St. Martin's Griffin, 2011.

MacDonell, Herbert L. "Bloodstain Pattern Interpretation." In *Wiley Encyclopedia of Forensic Science,* edited by Allen Jamieson and Andre Moenssens. Hoboken, NJ: Wiley-Blackwell, 2009.

Mack, H. Jr. "Identification of Victims: The Beginning of a Homicide Investigation." *Journal of Forensic Identification,* 45, no. 5 (1995): 510.

Mankevich, A. "The Determination of Shoe Size in Out-of-Scale Photographs." *Journal of Forensic Identification* 40 (1990): 1–9.

Meng, H., and B. Caddy. "Gunshot Residue Analysis: A Review." *Journal of Forensic Sciences* 42, no. 4 (1997): 553–70.

Menzel, E. Roland. "Detection of Latent Fingerprints by Laser-Excited Luminescence." *Analytical Chemistry,* 61, no. 8 (1989): 557A–61A.

Menzel, E. R., and K. E. Fox. "Laser Detection of Latent Fingerprints: Preparation of Fluorescent Dusting Powders and the Feasibility of a Portable System." *Journal of Forensic Sciences* 25, no. 1 (1980): 150–53.

Miller, Walter B. *The Growth of Youth Gang Problems in the United States: 1970–98.* National Criminal Justice References Service, April 2001. https://www.ncjrs.gov/pdffiles1/ojjdp/181868-1.pdf.

National Fire Protection Association. *Fire Protection Guide to Hazardous Materials.* Clifton Park, NY: Delmar Cengage Learning, 2010.

Nichols, R. G. "Firearm and Toolmark Identification Criteria: A Review of the Literature." *Journal of Forensic Sciences* 42, no. 3 (1997): 466–74.

Nown, Graham. *Arkansas Godfather: The Story of Owney Madden and How He Hijacked Middle America.* Little Rock: Butler Center Books, 2013.

O'Connor, D. I. "Developing a Standard Operating Procedure for Crime Scene and Identification Processing of Illicit Methamphetamine Labs." *Journal of Forensic Identification* 38, no. 6 (1988): 299–302.

Patraco, N. "A Simple Trace Evidence Trap for the Collection of Vacuum Sweepings." *Journal of Forensic Sciences* 32, no. 5 (1987): 1422–25.

Patraco, N. "Trace Evidence: The Invisible Witness." *Journal of Forensic Sciences* 31, no. 1 (1986): 321–28.

Pizzola, P. A., S. Roth, and P. R. DeForest. "Blood Droplet Dynamics I." *Journal of Forensic Sciences* 31, no. 1 (1986): 36–49.

Pizzola, P. A., S. Roth, and P. R. DeForest. "Blood Droplet Dynamics—II." *Journal of Forensic Sciences* 31, no. 1 (1986): 50–64.

Posey, E. P. "Outline for Fire Scene Documentation." *Fire & Arson Investigator* 38 (1988): 55.

Reilly, Dan. *Working the Scene.* Mobile, AL: SB Glove Security Inc., 2008.

Roux, C., J. Chable, and P. Margot. "Fibre Transfer Experiments onto Car Seats." *Science & Justice* 36, no. 3 (1996): 143–51.

Sampson, W. "Latent Fingerprint Evidence on Human Skin." *Journal of Forensic Identification* 46, no. 2 (1996): 188–95.

Sanchez, Reymundo. *My Bloody Life: The Making of a Latin King.* Chicago: Chicago Review Press, 2000.

Sanchez, Reymundo, and Sonia Rodriguez. *Lady Q: The Rise and Fall of a Latin Queen.* Chicago: Chicago Review Press, 2008.

Schiro, George. "Collection and Preservation of Blood Evidence from Crime Scenes." *Journal of Forensic Identification* 47 (1997): 557.

Shalhoup, Mara. *BMF: The Rise and Fall of Big Meech the Black Mafia Family.* New York: St. Martin's Press, 2010.

Sikes, Gini. *8 Ball Chicks: A Year in the Violent World of Girl Gangs.* New York: Anchor Books, 1998.

Simpson, Colton, and Ann Pearlman. *Inside the Crips: Life Inside L.A.'s Most Notorious Gang.* New York: St. Martin's Griffin, 2005.

Spitz, Werner U., and Russell S. Fisher. *Spitz and Fisher's Medicolegal Investigation of Death.* 2nd ed. Springfield, IL: Charles C Thomas, 1980.

Stewart, G. D. "Sexual Assault Evidence Collection Procedures." *Journal of Forensic Identification* 40 (1990): 69.

Stoffel, J. F. *Explosives and Homemade Bombs.* Springfield, IL: Charles C Thomas, 1962.

Taupin, J. M. "Hair and Fiber Transfer in an Abduction Case: Evidence from Different Levels of Trace Evidence Transfer." *Journal of Forensic Sciences* 41, no. 4 (1996): 697–99.

Tsaroom, S. "Investigation of a Murder Case Involving Arson." *Journal of Forensic Sciences* 41, no. 6 (1996): 1064–67.

US Department of Justice. *Forcible Rape: A Manual for Sex Crime Investigators, Police Volume III.* Washington, DC: US Government Printing Office, 1978.

US Drug Enforcement Agency. *D.E.A. Narcotics Investigator's Manual.* Boulder, CO: Paladin Press, 1988.

US Federal Bureau of Investigation. *The Science of Fingerprints: Classification and Use.* Washington, DC: US Government Printing Office, 1973.

Usher, Alan. "The Role of the Pathologist at the Scene of the Crime." *Journal of the Forensic Science Society* 10, no. 4 (1970): 213–18.

Warlen, S. "Crime Scene Photography: The Silent Witness." *Journal of Forensic Identification* 45 (1995): 261.

Waugh, Daniel. *Off Color: The Violent History of Detroit's Notorious Purple Gang.* Holland, MI: In-Depth Editions, 2014.

Weeks, Kevin, and Phyllis Karas. *Brutal: The Untold Story of My Life inside Whitey Bulger's Irish Mob.* New York: HarperCollins, 2006.

Wilkinson, D., and J. Watkin. "A Comparison of Forensic Light Sources: Polilight, Luma-Lite, and Spectrum 9000." *Journal of Forensic Identification* 44 (1994): 632–51.

Wilkinson, D., J. Watkin, and A. Misner. "A Comparison of Techniques for the Visualization of Fingerprints on Human Skin including the Application of Iodine and x-Naphthoflavone." *Journal of Forensic Identification* 46, no. 4 (1996): 432.

Williams, Stanley Tookie. *Blue Rage, Black Redemption.* New York: Touchstone, 2004.

Williams, Stanley Tookie. *Life in Prison.* San Francisco: Chronicle Books, 2001.

Index

abduction. *See* kidnapping/abduction

actionable intelligence, 186, 322–23, 330

administrative procedures and organization: for confidential sources/informants, 310–11, 313–15; FBI and DEA, 257; for forensic laboratories, 11, 14, 235–36; for investigative files, 257–70; of squads, 97, 102–3

advice of rights form, 94, 268

affiant, definition of, 72

affidavits. *See* arrest warrant affidavits; search warrant affidavits; Title III Court Orders

AFOSI. *See* Air Force Office of Special Investigations, US

aggravated qualification, 24–25, 35–36, 44

Aguilar–Spinelli test, 316–17

Aguilar v. Texas (1964), 315, 316

Air Force Office of Special Investigations, US (AFOSI), 16, 130

American Society of Crime Laboratory Directors (ASCLD), 235

Arkansas v. Sanders (1979), 77

armed robbery, 50; aggravated, 44; crimes connected with, 45; Hobbes Act cases and, 130; probable cause for, *218*; proof of, 44, *57*; "rush to judgment" example in, 193, 194; serial/career burglars in, 43, 173–74; specialized units for, 127–28; weapon considerations in, 44–45. *See also* bank robbery

Army Criminal Investigation Command, US (CID), 16, 129, 130

arraignment hearings, 275, 276–77

arrests, 23; approach to, 200, 268; investigative file coverage of, 267–68; police department role after, 222–23, 271; positive identification prior to, 219; probable cause for, 216, 219–20, 221, *222*, 271–72; tactical training for, 333, 341–42

arrest warrant affidavits, 89, 221, *222*, 272–73

arson: accidental fire compared to, 47; elements of, 46; expert proof for, 46–48, *58*; motivations in, 47, 48; probable cause for, *218*

ASCLD. *See* American Society of Crime Laboratory Directors

assault: armed robbery relation to, 45; battery, 34, 35–36, *57*; extortion relation to, 35; between family and friends, 136, 204; with intent to kill, 34–35, 36, *57*; investigative plan for serious, 189, 197, 206; on mental health of person, 34; proof of, 35, 36, *57*; serious gun, 36, 189, 206; simple, 34; stranger, 206; types of, 34; on victim witnesses, 36

ATF. *See* Bureau of Alcohol, Tobacco, Firearms and Explosives

Atlanta Child Murders (1979 to 1981), 177

Attorney's Office, US, 129, 152

"aura" evidence, 240

autopsies, 187, 247

background records, 116–17, 178

bail, 65, 272–74, 281

ballistic evidence: fingerprinting with, 232, 233–34, 237; in gun assaults, 189; investigative file section for, 259; in organized and gang crime, 178, 244–46; for positive identification, 26–27, 216; recovery and handling of, 233–34, 245–46; training and education on, 10, 244–46; types of, 244
bank robbery, 44–45, 173, 207, *217*
banks, larceny on, 51–52
battery, 34–36, *57*
B&E. *See* breaking and entering
bicycle patrol units, 115
big data, 196, 327
Bill of Rights, *62*, 121; as due process framework, 61–64; establishment of, 61–62; *Miranda* rights relation to, 92, 94; on probable cause, 214, 272; rights of accused in, 61–95, 273, 289. *See also specific amendments*
Black, Hugo, 70
blood. *See* serological evidence
Blood stains, 231, 240, 280
blunt-force object evidence, 246
bodily fluids. *See* serological evidence
bombings: first responder at, 154; jurisdiction for, 48–49; malice aforethought in, 48; probable cause for, *218*
bomb techs, 48
Brady rule, 71, 278, 314
Brady v. Maryland (1963), 96, 221, 278–79, 314
breaking and entering (B&E), 4, 18, 49–50. *See also* burglary
Brewer v. Williams (1977), 74
Brown v. the Board of Education, 63
bullet evidence. *See* ballistic evidence
Bureau of Alcohol, Tobacco, Firearms and Explosives (ATF), 13, 330; bombings jurisdiction of, 48–49; financial crime priority of, 129–30; role and responsibilities of, 16
burglary: case example of, 28–29; crime scene analysis discussion exercise for, 163–66; crime scene units for, 99; definition of, 4, 49; disruption/order assessments and conclusions in, 165, 166, 167, *167*, *171*; drug crime

relation to, 113, 133, 167, 173, 203; elements of, 50; evidence in, 50–51, *218*; as gateway crime, 18, 50, 51, 162; homicide intent with, 50; intelligence from crime data, 326; locks and security alarms in assessment of, 166, 167, 168, *168–70*; MO analysis in, 51, 164, 174; NCIC stolen article database and, 28; prioritizing investigations and, 123, 127–28, 297; probable cause for, *218*; proof of, 50; psychosexual motivations for, 163; serial/career criminals of, 43, 50–51, 163–66, 173–74, 203; specialized units for, 127–28; tact squads responsibilities and, 114; victim witnesses of, 148
burglary, commercial: crime scene analysis for, 172–74, 190; perpetrator identification for, 207; scenario without witnesses, 205; smash-and-grab technique in, 173; target and location choices for, *172*, 172–73. *See also* armed robbery; bank robbery
burglary, residential: beginner compared to career burglars in, 163–66; crime scene analysis for, 163–66, 190; disruption/ orderliness assessment in, 165, 166, 167, *167*, *171*; dogs as factor in, 166; entry, locks, and alarms assessment for, 166, 167, 168, *168–70*; "rush to judgment" example in, 193, 194; scenario without witnesses, 205; target and location choices for, 166–67, 170, *170–71*

calls for service, data from, 325–26
capital crimes/offenses: criminal codes distinctions on, 24–25; defining, 4, 273
Capone, Al, 244
Carroll Doctrine, 77–78, 79
Carroll v. the United States, 77
cartels, drug, 134–35, 360–61
car theft. *See* motor vehicle theft
case, definition of, 7
case file. *See* investigative file
CCE. *See* Continuing Criminal Enterprise
chain of custody (for evidence), 110, 229, 232–36, 258–59, 268–69
children: battery of, 35–36; kidnapping of, 126; murder of, 177, 181; parental consent for search and seizure with, 82;

prioritizing crime against, 126, 132, 136; sex trafficking of, 132, 136; sexual assault of, 40–41, *57*, 180–81

CID. *See* criminal investigation division

CID (Army). *See* Army Criminal Investigation Command, US

citizen informants, noncriminal, 319–20, 324, 328–29

civil rights: big data usage and, 327; due process in protection of, 61–64; US Constitution mission in protecting, 61–62

Coast Guard Investigative Service, US, 16, 130

cocaine, 128, 133–34, 173, *353*, 358, 359

CODIS. *See* Combined DNA Index System

coercive behavior: confessions gotten with, 89–90, 288, 289, 299–300, 301; in consent searches, avoiding, 77, 84; *Miranda* rights and, 89–90, 289

Combined DNA Index System (CODIS), 14, 26, 201

commercial crime scenes: arson in residential compared with, 46, *56*; crime scene analysis of, 172–74, 190; forensic evidence at, 173–74; investigative plan steps for, 189–94, 197–98; locations for, *172*, 172–73. *See also* armed robbery; burglary, commercial

common law, history of, 4–5

commonwealths. *See* states/commonwealths

communication technologies: electronic surveillance and evolution of, 87, 253–54, 369; stalking crimes and, 34. *See also* electronic surveillance/wiretaps; phone records

community impact: in investigator career, 375–76; in prioritizing investigations, 123–24, 130, 136

community relations: bicycle patrol units and, 115; intelligence sources from, 199, 328–29; with police department, 122–23

computer analysis: evolution of technology and, 251; expert witnesses on, 155; for leads, 266; partnership talents balance of forensic knowledge and, 106. *See also* digital devices and data

computer squads: digital device and data analysis of, 118–19, 195–96, 250–54; electronic surveillance and, 119; in

homicide investigations, 195–96; NCIC used by, 116; public data sources used by, 117–18; role and responsibilities of, 116–18; training and education for, 252, 255

confessions: coercion in, 89–90, 288, 289, 299–300, 301; evidence without, 128; formal signing of, 303; plea bargains with, 282, 296, 297; reasons behind, 203, 294–96; from serial/career criminals, 203, 296–97, 302–3; of vehicle theft, obtaining, 297

confidential sources/informants: actionable intelligence from, 322–23; administrative concerns with, 310–11, 313–15; altruism of, 319; *Brady* rule and, 314; citizen, noncriminal, 319–20, 324, 328–29; CW category for, 93, 320–21; in drug investigations, 354, 357–58, 364; examples of and approach to, 102–3, 307–13; FBI, 312, 317–18, 321; *Gates* standard for, 316–17, 321; investigator relationship with, 199, 307, 308–11, 315, 321, 324, 373; levels of, 321; liability of, 317–18; moral conflicts in using, 307–8, 311; motivations of, 199, 311, 313, 319; in motor vehicle theft investigations, 192; in organized crime and criminal syndicates, 308–9, 312; payments to, 311; in positive identification, 28; in proactive investigations, 22; profiles of, 318–21; protection of, 310, 320–21, 322, 323; reporting of meetings with, 322; squad use of, 102; Supreme Court cases on, 315–18; trustworthiness of, 198–99, 219–20, 311, 312–13, 315–17, 321–22; value of, 323–24; as witnesses, 310–11, 315, 320–21; working with and handling of, 310–11, 321–24

consent: battery definition and, 35; behavior in obtaining, 77, 84–85; objective reasonableness standard for, 82–83, 84, 86; search and seizure (warrantless) with, 77, 81–86, 96; standing to object in, determining, 86; in vehicle search and seizure, 82

conspiracy, criminal: armed robbery relation to, 45; to commit violence, 54–55; in complex crimes, 46; in drug distribution operation, 55; insider witnesses of, 45, 55; jurisdiction for, 126; kidnapping relation to, 42–43; proactive investigations of, 22; proof of, 55; statutes, 54, 55

Constitution, US, *61, 62*; branches of government established under, 2; digital devices and data under, 252–53; due process under, 2–3, 63, 96; on federal powers, 61–62; Fourteenth Amendment added to, 63, 65; on grand jury hearings, 63, 65; history of, 1–2, 61–64; on interrogations and interviews, 299–300, 301; investigator responsibility to follow, 10, 63–64, 76, 95–96, 290; mission and beliefs behind, 1–2, 61–62; on probable cause, 214, 272; states rights, 61–62, 65–66; on trial requirements, 63, 65, 273, 277–78. *See also* Bill of Rights; *specific amendments*

Continuing Criminal Enterprise (CCE), 363–64

contraband evidence, 258–59, 355, *355*

Controlled Substances Act (CSA), 353

cooperating witness (CW), 93, 316, 320–21, 359, 364

coroner. *See* medical examiner/examination

corruption: in criminal justice system, 136, 178; dismissals of cases because of, 282–83; investigative grand jury for, 276; RICO statute and, 52–53, 54, 363

counterfeiting. *See* fraudulent materials

counterintelligence/counterespionage, 13, 14, 17

counterterrorism squads, 124

court cases. *See* Supreme Court cases; trial requirements; trials and court process

court team: crime scene examiner in, 109–10; forensic scientists in, 109; lead investigator role in, 108–9, 117, 223, 275; teamwork of, 107–11, 119. *See also* trials and court process

covert operations: CWs in, 320–21; on drug use and distribution crime, 351–71; FBI, 350; investigative report on, 262; tactical spin in, 350–51, 373. *See also* electronic surveillance/wiretaps; surveillance; undercover officer

crime: defining, 4–5, 23; proof and related, matrix, 55–56, *56–58*, 58–59; statutes and categories of, 25; white collar, 12, 14, 19, 52, 249

crime databases, overview of, 116–17

crimes against persons: defining, 186; investigative plan for, 186–89, 194–97, 206. *See also specific crimes*

crime scene analysis: for burglary, commercial, 172–74, 190; for burglary, residential, 163–66, 190; discussion exercise and examples for, 163–72; disruption/orderliness of scene in, 165, 166, 167, *167, 171*, 174–75, 176; documentation approaches for, 160–61; for homicide, 174–77; logical conclusions upon, examples of, 159–60; MO considerations in, 164, 167, 174, 177, 178, 207–8; for motor vehicle theft, 163, *167*, 191; with organized and gang crime, 177–79; physical evidence in, conclusions on, 160, 208; in proactive investigations, 181; questions considered for, 159–60; in reactive investigations, 159–62; for sexual assault, 179–81; training and education for, 161–62

crime scene examiners/examinations: chain of custody beginning with, 233; in court team, 109–10; crimes requiring, 98, *99*; evidence handling for, 99; FBI, 110, 160; first responders role as/in, 19–21, 161–62; initial protocol for, 98–100, 160; in investigative plan first step, 189, 190–91, 198, 204–5; lead investigator relationship with, 109–10; for motor vehicle theft, 191; questions addressed in, 204–5; specialized units for, 98–100, 110, 160

crime scene reports, 258

crime scene search unit, 98–100, 160

criminal code, 23–25, 29, 121. *See also* statutes

criminal informants. *See* confidential sources/informants

criminal investigation division (CID), 98, 100, 124–25

criminal investigators: deaths in line of duty, 338–39, 376; defense attorneys relationship with, 67, 70–71; federal, types of, 12–17; "gut feelings" of, 76, 214; municipal/county, types of, 7–11; passion in work of, 375–76; private and defense, 18, 285–90; state, types of, 11–12; veteran and young, relationship between, 103, 106; as victim advocates, 144–45, 147, 196–97. *See also* teamwork, investigative; *specific investigators and topics*

CSA. *See* Controlled Substances Act

curiosity, with interrogations and interviews, 302

custodial circumstances, 93

CW. *See* cooperating witness

DEA. *See* Drug Enforcement Agency

deadly force, 337–39, 342

death penalty, 24

debriefing interviews, 296, 304–5

defense and private investigators, 18, 285–90

defense attorneys: court-appointed, 67–68; criminal investigator relationship with, 67, 70–71; expert witnesses working for, 155; funding of public, 68; insanity plea proof responsibility of, 285; in interrogations, presence of, 71; investigators working for, 18, 285–90; role and responsibilities of, 108; witnesses treatment by, preparing for, 149, 156–57

Department of Defense (DOD), 16–17, 130

Department of Homeland Security, 16, 47, 49

Department of Motor Vehicles (DMV) records, 116–17, 178, 192, 261

detectives: municipal/county, 8–11; state police, 11–12

digital devices and data: authentication of, 233; computer squad analysis of, 118–19, 195–96, 250–54; for crime scene analysis documentation, 160–61; daily logs using, 153; intelligence from, 116–19, 195–96, 327; investigative plan addressing, 195–96, 198; for motor vehicle theft investigations, 192; search and seizure of, 251–53; security in case file, 264–65; suspect information in, 251–52; US Constitution on, 252–53

digital photography, 33, 151, 346–48

discovery process, trial, 298; prosecutor responsibility for, 220–21, 278, 279; rules on, 71, 220–21, 278–79; witnesses in, 220, 225, 278

dismissals, 273, 282–83

DMV records. *See* Department of Motor Vehicles records

DNA extraction, 240, 244

DNA profiling: CODIS for, 14, 26, 201, 240; comparison, 249; evidentiary hearing example on, 280–81; evolution of, 244, 280–81; positive identification with, 26; with serological evidence, 240; with trace evidence, 240, 241

documentary evidence: FBI handling of, 251; subpoenas for, 252, 286, 362, 369–70; training and laboratories for, 251–52. *See also* digital devices and data; fraudulent materials; pattern evidence; photographs/photography

DOD. *See* Department of Defense

domestic violence, 136, 206

drive-by shootings, 36, 178

Drug Enforcement Agency (DEA), 13, 330; administrative protocols of, 257; role and responsibilities of, 15–16, 134; task forces, 134–35; toxicology experts under, 247; witness protection under, 225–26

drugs: DEA control of legal and illegal, 15, 134; schedules (categories) for, 353; toxicology evidence of, 246–47

drug use and distribution crime: addict witnesses in, 354, 356; burglary relation to, 113, 133, 167, 173, 205; cartels role in, 134–35, 360–61; CCE statute for, 363–64; cocaine, 128, 133–34, 173, *353*, 358, 359; confidential sources/informants for, 354, 357–58, 364; conspiracy in, 55; covert operations on, 351–71; crime databases of, 117; drug type relation to seriousness of, 133–34; electronic surveillance/wiretaps for, 364, 370, 371, 374; forensic tests in investigations of, 234, 246, 356–57; gang crime relation to, 53–54, 360; as gateway crime, 113; heroin, 133–34, 352, 356–57, 358; intelligence from crime data, 325; locations for, 354–55; marijuana, 135, 353–54, *354*; money laundering and, 362–63; murder related with, 113, 128, 331; organized crime relation to, 134,

135–36, 361; other crimes connected to, 113, 128, 131–33; prioritizing investigations on, 126, 133–36; proactive investigations of, 22; probable cause for, *218–19*; profits in, 359–60, 363; proof requirements for, 356–57; prostitution connection with, 131, 132; public data sources in prosecution of, 118; resources for, investigative, 134; RICO charge in, 363; search warrant affidavits and raids for, 339, 354, 355, 356, 358; short- and long-term investigations for, 113; small-time offenders of, 352; statutes on, 353, 363; surveillance types for, 364; task forces for, 134–35; UCO in, 364–67; vice units for, 113–14, 115; wholesale dealers in, 359–64; witnesses in investigations of, 354, 356, 358–69, 362, 364

due process: *Powell v. Alabama* violation of, 63, 68–69; rights included in, 61–64; under US Constitution, 2–3, 63, 96

Eastman Kodak, 346

education. *See* training and education

Eighth Amendment, 65

electronic surveillance/wiretaps: affidavits and proper procedure for, 88–89, 119, 369–70; authentication of, 233; communication technologies evolution and, 87, 253–54, 369; computer squad role in, 119; for drug investigations, 364, 370, 371, 374; evolution of, 367–68; manpower required for, 371; of organized crime and criminal syndicates, 372–73, 374; plain view doctrine with, 371; probable cause for, 88–89; search warrant affidavits for, 88–89, 369–70; Supreme Court cases on, 87–89, 368–69; sweeping devices for, 365; Title III, 88–89, 119, 252, 261, 367–73; UCO use of, 365–66; violations of rules on, 371

embezzlement, 51

Emergency Response Teams (ERTs), 335

evidence: "aura," 240; in bombings, 48, *218*; in burglaries, 50–51, *218*; confessions lacking in, 128; contraband, 258–59, 355, *355*; crime and related, matrix, 55–56, *56–58*, 58–59; crime scene examination handling of, 99; crime-specific probable

cause, *217–19*; defense investigators search for, 287–89; definition of, 24; due process rules on gathering of, 63; as element of proof, 23–24; evidentiary hearings on debates over, 279–81; exclusionary rule with search and seizure, 73–74; from fact witnesses, types of, 149; first responders handling of, 20–21; "fruits of the poisonous tree" doctrine for, 73–74, 301; in grand jury hearings, 23, 150–51, 273–74; from homicide victim witnesses, 142–44; human context of, 141; murder, types of, 26; pattern, examples of, 10, 26, 250; positive identification, overview of, 25–28; search warrant raids procedure for, 340–41; serological, 10, 26, 239–40; toxicological, 179, 234, 246–47; trace, 10, 26, 241–43; types overview, 4. *See also* physical evidence; *specific evidence types*

evidence response teams (FBI), 110

evidentiary hearings, 279–81

exclusionary rule, 63; cases involving, 73–74; in "stop and frisk" procedures, 81

exigent circumstances, 20, 212–13

expert witnesses, 109, 154–56, 227–28, 235–36, 280–81

extortion, 35, 45

family and friends: assault between, 136, 206; consent to search from, example of, 85–86; of homicide victim, notification of, 189, 196; murder investigation and interviews of, 176, 186–87; in search and seizures, treatment of, 85; victim advocacy with, 144–45; victimology beginning with, 143

FBI, 244; with investigative files, digital format, 264

Federal Bureau of Investigation (FBI), 11, 330, 375; administrative procedures protocols of, 257; bombings jurisdiction of, 48–49; confidential informants for, 312, 317–18, 321; covert surveillance by, 350; crime scene examiners in, 110, 160; DEA task force aid from, 134; DNA database of, 14, 26, 201, 240; evidence response teams for, 110; fingerprint

database of, 14, 236, *238*, 238–39; history
of, 14; Hobbes Act cases jurisdiction of,
130; jurisdiction, 14, 15, 48–49, 129, 130;
in kidnapping cases, 43; motor vehicle
theft and, 14; pattern evidence database
of, 250; photography analysis of, 250;
prioritizing investigations for, 129, 130;
role and responsibilities of, 14–15, 250;
specialized units/squads examples of,
100, 250, 333; training and education for,
15, 334; witness protection under, 152–
53, 225–26; in WMD crimes, 49. *See also*
National Crime Information Center
federal government: branches of, 2;
Fourteenth Amendment on rebellions
against, 66; medical examiner employed
by, 235; plea bargains for cooperation
with, 282, 302–3; "police" power of,
121–22, *122*; state trials compared with,
273; US Constitution on powers of state
compared to, 61–62
federal investigators: bombings jurisdiction
of, 48–49; defense/private investigators
finding errors by, 18; DOD special agents
as, 16–17, 130; ICE special agents as, 13,
16; IRS inspectors as, 15, 16; military
background for, 13, 15, 16; overview and
types of, 12–17, 100; prioritizing criminal
investigations for, 125–26, 129–30;
training and education for, 12–15; USPS
inspectors as, 13, 15, 16, 129. *See also*
specific federal agencies
fence, 28, 50, 167, 173
Ferguson, Andrew Guthrie, 196
Fernandez v. California (2014), 84
Fifth Amendment, 65, 92, 94, 278
fill in the gaps, 302
financial crimes: challenges in prosecuting,
128–29; money laundering, 15, 136, 320,
362–63, 367, 371; in prioritizing criminal
investigations, 127–31
fingerprint evidence: ballistics and, 232,
233–34, 237; FBI database for, 14, 236,
238, 238–39; history behind use of,
236–37; for positive identification, 26,
216, 219, 231, 234, 239; recovering and
handling of, 10, 231–34, 236–39, *238*;
surfaces appropriate for, 237; training on,
238–39; whole hand, 239, *239*

fingerprints evidence, forensics and, 86
firearm evidence. *See* ballistic evidence
firearm training, 334–35
first responders: "call out" protocol of, 100;
crime scene examination role of, 19–21,
161–62; investigative plan including
information from, 185; patrol officers as,
7–8, 19–20, 98; role and responsibilities
of, 7–8, 19–21, 98–100; witness and
victim handling of, 20, 139–40; as
witnesses, 141, 153, 154
force, use of: in armed robbery proof, 44, *57*;
in kidnapping crimes, 43–44; in sexual
assault proof, 38–39, *56*. *See also* deadly
force
forensic evidence: of arson, 47; of bombings,
48, *218*; in child psychosexual murder,
181; at commercial crime scenes, 173–74;
crime-specific probable cause, *217–19*;
in drug investigations, 234, 246, 356–57;
fingerprints and, 86; with homicide, 142–
43, 181, 187–88, 196; human context for,
25, 141; investigative plan addressing,
195, 197; partnership talents balanced in
computer and, 106; recovery and handling
of, 231–32, 233, 254–55; toxicological,
179, 234, 246–47; trace, 10, 26, 241–43;
victimology with, 144; witnesses and
victims testimony compared with,
55–56, *56–58*, 58–59, 143, 189–90, 191,
254–55. *See also* ballistic evidence; DNA
profiling; fingerprint evidence
forensic laboratories, administration of, 11,
14, 235–36
forensic scientists, *112*; as court team
members, 109; private, 236; testimony
of, 109, 152–53, 227–28, 235–36;
trustworthiness of, 234–35
founding fathers, 61
Fourteenth Amendment, 63, 65–66
Fourth Amendment (search and seizure):
Carroll Doctrine applied to, 77–78,
79; details of, 64–65, 71–72, 337;
digital devices and, 252–53; electronic
surveillance and, 87–89, 368–69;
Supreme Court landmark cases impacting,
72–74, 76–84, 87–90, 252; violations of,
289
fraudulent materials, 249–50

"fruits of the poisonous tree" doctrine, 73–74, 301
fugitives, 13, 72, 264, 322

gambling crime, 132–33, 136, 339
gang crime: ballistic evidence for, 178, 244–46; crime scene analysis of, 177–79; databases of, 117, 178; debriefing interviews for, 305; drug distribution operations and, 53–54, 360; homicide in, 144, 176–77; intelligence from crime data, 325, 326; investigative resources for, 116, 124, 125–26, 137; membership factors in, 53; MO for, 178; organized crime connection with, 53; prioritizing investigations on, 126, 137; proactive investigations for, 22; social media resources for investigating, 118, 253–54; specialized units for, 116, 117, 124, 125–26, 135, 137, 331; statutes covering, 54; task forces, 117, 126, 135, 137, 331; witness protection in investigations of, 152–53, 178–79, 225–26; by youth, 54
Gates standard, 316–17, 321
gateway crimes: burglary as, 18, 50, 51, 162; drug crime as, 113; motor vehicle theft as, 162; prioritizing, 137
Georgia v. Randolph (2006), 83–84
Gideon v. Wainwright, 63, 70–71, 94
Giglio material, 71, 96, 221, 279
Giglio v. United States (1972), 96, 221, 279
goals, investigative: long-term, 229; overview of, 209–10, 229; probable cause as primary in, 200, 209, 222; trial outcomes as, 222–24, 271, 289–90
Goddard, Calvin, 244
GPS tracking, 192
Graham v. Connor (1989), 337
grand jury hearings: case dismissals by, 273; evidence in, 23, 150–51, 273–74; investigative, 276; lead investigator role in, 150–51; probable cause reviewed in, 216; procedure, 273; standing, 275–76; US Constitution on, 63, 65; witness testimony in, 150–51, 275, 276
Gravano, Sammy "the Bull," 361
Gravelle, Phillip, 244
guilty plea: investigations resulting in, 23; plea bargains in place of, 281–82

gun assaults, serious, 36, 189, 206
gun evidence. *See* ballistic evidence

hair. *See* trace evidence
Haspel, Gina, 299
heroin, 133–34, 352, 356–57, 358
High Intensity Drug Trafficking Area (HIDTA), 135
highway patrol, 11–12
Hobbes Act cases, 130
homicide: autopsies for, 187; body in, visual analysis of, 174, 187, 196; burglary with intent of, 50; categories of, 29–31; crime scene analysis for, 174–77; data mining for suspects of, 195–96; domestic arguments relation with, 136; drug use and distribution relation to, 113, 128, 331; family notification in cases of, 189, 196; forensic evidence with, 142–43, 181, 187–88, 196; in gang and organized crime, 144, 176–77; investigative plan for, 31–32, 176, 187–89, 193, 196, 206; manslaughter, 32–33; medical examiner/ examination role in, 24, 30, 187, 188, 195, 196, 247–49; motivations behind, 143–44; positive identification in, 189, 249; in prioritizing investigations, 124, 136–37; probable cause for, *217*; "rush to judgment" example in, 193, 194; in self-defense, 32–33, 174–75, 178, 248, 285; specialized squads for, 124–25; stranger, types and challenges with, 143, 175–76; vehicular, 33–34; victimology, 31–32, 143–44, 176, 195, 196, 197; victims of, evidence from, 142–44; witnesses, 31–32, 142–44, 176, 187–88, 195, 196. *See also* murder
Hostage Rescue teams, 335

IAFIS. *See* Integrated Automated Fingerprint Identification System
ICE. *See* Immigration and Customs Enforcement
Illinois v. Rodriguez (1990), 83
Illinois v. Gates (1983), 316–17
Immigration and Customs Enforcement (ICE), 13, 16
impartial jury (jury of peers), 63, 65, 273, 277–78

imprisonment (as crime), 41–42

incarceration, historical view of, 5

indigent defendants, 70–71, 204, 281

informants. *See* confidential sources/ informants

insanity plea, 284–85

insider witnesses, 45, 55, 320, 358, 364

Integrated Automated Fingerprint Identification System (IAFIS), 14, *238*, 238–39

intelligence, investigative: actionable, 186, 322–23, 330; benefits of, 330, 331; big data in, 196, 327; calls for service role in, 325–26; from citizens, noncriminal, 319–20, 324, 328–29; community relations and, 199, 328–29; coordination of, 36, 327–28; crime data in, 325–27; digital data as, 116–19, 195–96, 327; geographical information as, 325–26; interjurisdictional cooperation role in, 329–30; in investigative plan, 195–96, 198–99; macro intelligence in, 330, 331; patrol support as, 327–28; prior case file reviews for, 199, 329; from social media, 118, 195–96, 253–54; sources of, 198–99, 203–4; surveillance aided by, 326, 329; tactical training aided by, 335; types of, 325; veteran investigator base of, 103. *See also* confidential sources/informants

Internal Revenue Service (IRS) inspectors, 15, 16

internet security, 264–65

interrogations and interviews, *140*; coercive behavior in, 89–90, 288, 289, 299–300, 301; comfort compromised as technique in, 303; curiosity with, 302; debriefing, 296, 304–5; defense attorney presence in, 71; ego-stroking in, 303; extreme conditions for, 299–300; fill in the gaps with, 302; "good cop, bad cop" technique in, 302; intimidation tactics for, 90–91, 95, 288, 292, 301–2; investigative file sections for, 257–60, 262, 268; investigators present for, 303; on kidnapping/abduction, 300; locations for, 139, 303–4; lying in, detection of, 292–94, 298–99, 305; lying in, investigator use of, 301; *Miranda* rights delivered in, considerations for, 91–92, 295, 297–98;

Miranda v. Arizona decision impact for, 90–95; *Miranda v. Arizona* details on, 89–90; narrative control in, 299; physical abuse by officer during, 288, 289, 299–300, 301; physical evidence compared with information from, 254–55; of suspect/defendant, approach to, 71, 104, 105, *105*, 203, 268, 294–306; teamwork in, 104–5, 302; techniques for, 301–3; torture in, 299–300, 301; un-constitutional practices in, 299–300, 301; unrepentant suspect, handling, 297–99; of victims, 257, 262; of witnesses, approach to, 31–32, 104–5, 176, 185, 187–89, 195–98–294, 305–6; witness protection considerations in, 299

interstate crime, 42–43, 130

interviews. *See* interrogations and interviews

investigations: defining, 3–4; key aspects of, 23; overview and history of, 1–7; pending inactive status for, 200, 201; types of, 19–22. *See also specific topics*

investigative (case) file: advice of rights form in, 94, 268; arrests in, 267–68; case-specific considerations for, 262–63, 269–70; chain of custody in, 258–59; on covert operations, 262; criminal histories in, 260–61; intelligence from reviews of prior, 329; interviews and interrogations in, 257–60, 262, 268; lead coverage in, 266–67; notetaking, 259–60; photographic evidence in, 260–61, 262; physical and contraband evidence in, 258–59, 268–69; prosecutive reports in, 260; search warrant affidavits in, 267; security of, 263–65, 329; summary of investigation in, 259; surveillance evidence in, 261–62; teamwork on and reviews of, 262–63; timelines and charts, 259; writing skills benefit in, 269–70

investigative plan: approach to, overview of, 102, 184–86; "catch up" with suspects in, 186; commercial crime scene, steps for, 189–94, 197–98; crime and proof matrix use for, 55–56, *56–58*, 58–59; for crimes against persons, 186–89, 194–97, 206; without crime scene, 185; crime scene examination as first step in, 189, 190–91, 198, 204–5; criminal statutes as guide for, 55; definition of, 31; digital devices and data addressed in, 195–96, 198; first responder information in, 185; flexibility in, 185; for homicides, 31–32, 176, 187–89, 195, 196, 206; investigative intelligence in, 195–96, 198–99; lead investigator responsibility for, 102, 187; leads outlined and followed in, 185, 194, 197, 198; medical care as first step in, 189, 190, 197; for motor vehicle theft, 191–92, 297; physical evidence recovery and treatment in, 187–88, 189, 195, 196, 197, 198, 200; for proactive investigations, overview of, 186; probable cause/suspect identified in, 200–201, 209, 222; for property crimes, 189–94, 197–98, 205–6, 207; prosecution as final step of, 200–201; questions addressed in, 184; for reactive investigations, overview of, 185–86; "rushing to judgment" scenarios in, 192–94; scientific method approach in, 204–8; for serious assault, 189, 197, 206; for sexual assault/rape, 189, 197, 207–8; steps of, outline and discussion, 186–201, 210; theories for finding suspect, 201–4, 210; timing factors in, 198; trial and court process preparation in, 198, 200–201; victimology in, 31–32, 143–44, 176, 195, 196, 197; victims outlined in, 185; witnesses in, approach to, 31–32, 176, 185, 187–89, 195, 196, 197, 198, 201

IRS. *See* Internal Revenue Service inspectors

ISP information, 253

jewelry theft, 173

Johnson v. Zerbst, 69–70

joyriding, 162

judges: designations in arraignment hearings, 277; on "gut feelings" of investigator, 76, 214; improper behavior by, 64; on *Miranda* rights violations, 89–90, 289

jurisdictions: for bombing cases, 48–49; cooperation between, 329–30; for criminal conspiracies, 126; for DOD special agents, 17; FBI, 14, 15, 48–49, 129, 130; federal agencies limitations in, 12; fugitives and, 13, 264; reactive crime investigation and, 20–21; for task forces, 126

jury of peers. *See* impartial jury

juvenile offenders, 50, 54, 162

Katz v. United States (1967), 87, 252, 368–69

kidnapping/abduction: of children, 126; imprisonment definition relation to, 41; interrogations about, 300; prioritizing of, 126; proof in cases of, 41–43; ransom and interstate aspects with, 42–43

knives, evidence about, 246

Ku Klux Klan, 317–18

larceny: armed robbery relation to, 45; definition of, 4, 51; as gateway crime, 18; probable cause for, *218*; proof of, *58*; as theft by embezzlement, 51; value-related priorities with, 51–52

law enforcement officers: deaths in line of duty, 338–39, 376; detectives as mentors for new, 9; due process responsibility of, 63–64; memory skills for, 153, 154; principles of, historical models for, 121–22; roles and responsibilities of, 2–3, 183; statutes understanding of, 5–6; US Constitution on state control of, 62; as witnesses, 141, 153, 154

lead investigator: court team role and responsibilities of, 108–9, 117, 223, 275; crime scene examiner relationship with, 109–10; family of homicide victim notification responsibility of, 189, 196; in grand jury hearings, role of, 150–51; investigative plan responsibility of, 102, 187

leads: "bear traps" for new, 201; computer program for, 266; day-to-day, responsibility for, 101–2; disclosure to prosecuting attorney, 108–9; investigative file coverage of, 266–67; investigative plan addressing, 185, 194, 197, 198; major case control, 265–66; MO comparisons to generate, 201, 203; with murder board presentation, 266

legal representation: advice of rights form and, 94, 268; court-appointed, 67–68, 70; prosecutor responsibility for right to, 67; Sixth Amendment on right to, 63, 65–66; Supreme Court landmark cases on rights of, 63, 68–71

lineup, police. *See* police lineup
Liuzzo v. United States (1981), 317–18
loan sharks, 133, 136

manslaughter, 32–33
Mapp v. Ohio (1961), 72–73
marijuana, 135, 353–54, *354*
Marshals Service, US: role and
    responsibilities of, 13, 277; witness
    protection under, 151–52, 226
material evidence. *See* physical evidence
McLean, Ralph, 350
medical care: as investigative plan first step,
    189, 190, 197; for victims and witnesses,
    101, 140
medical examiner/examination: government-
    sponsored, 235; homicide investigations,
    role of, 24, 30, 187, 188, 195, 196, 247–
    49; private, 236; in sexual assault cases,
    39; staff for, 247–48; testimony from,
    155, 235–36, 248; types of, 247
mental health: assault on person's, 34; in
    murder proof, 29–30
mental health professionals: insanity verdict
    testimony by, 284–85; for sexual assault
    cases, 38, *57*, 146–47; UCO need for,
    374; for victim witnesses, 38, *57*, 146–47;
    for witnesses, 140
mentally disabled adults, sexual assault of,
    40–41
metallurgical evidence, 246
method of operation. *See* modus operandi
microscopes, 232, 241–43, *242–43*, 245–46
military background, 13, 15, 16, 375
Miranda rights, 82; form acknowledging
    delivery of, 94–95; in interrogations,
    delivering, 91–92, 295, 297–98;
    violations of, judges on, 89–90, 289;
    waiver, defendant reasons for, 92, 297–
    98; waiver, formal signing of, 93–94
Miranda v. Arizona (1965), 89–95
modus operandi (method of operation)
    (MO): for burglary, analysis of, 51, 164,
    174; comparisons for leads, 201, 203;
    crime scene analysis of, 164, 167, 174,
    177, 178, 207–8; for motor vehicle theft,
    192; for murder, 177; for organized and
    gang crime, 178; in sexual assault/rape
    cases, 39, 207–8

money laundering, 15, 136, 320, 362–63,
    367, 371
morals crimes. *See* vice crimes
morals units. *See* vice units
motor vehicle theft: confessions to, obtaining,
    297; confidential sources in, 192; crime
    scene analysis for, 163, *167*, 191; FBI
    jurisdiction and, 14; frequency of, 191;
    as gateway crime, 162; investigative plan
    for, 191–92, 297; MOs for, 192; scenarios
    without witnesses, 205–6; search warrant
    affidavit for case of, 75; serial/career
    criminals of, 192, 203; US Attorney's
    Office guidelines for, 129
muggings, 100
mug shots, 26, 260–61
murder: categories and degrees of, 29;
    of children, 177, 181; confessions to,
    considerations with, 294–95, 296; crime
    scene analysis for, 174–77; criminal
    code on, 25; definition of, 29; deliberate
    design in proof of, 31–32, *56*; disruption/
    order assessments and conclusions in,
    174–75; drug crime relation to, 113, 128,
    331; elements of, 29–31; evidence types
    in, 26; family and friends interviews in
    cases of, 176, 186–87; investigative plan
    in cases of, 31–32, 165, 176, 187–89,
    196; malice aforethought in, 29, 30–31,
    56; manslaughter compared with, 32;
    MO assessment for, 177; motives for,
    assessing, 175; by professional assassins,
    175–76; proof in, 24, 26, 29–31, *56*;
    psychosexual motivations in, 176–77,
    181; serial, 176–77; sexual assault
    relation with, 177, 181; sound mind proof
    in, 29–30; stranger, types and challenges
    with, 143, 175–76; struggle signs at scene
    of, 174–75; victims, identification of,
    189; weapon choice for, 175; witnesses,
    secondary, 31–32; witnesses of, on-the-
    scene, 31, 187–88
murder board presentation, 266

narcotics investigation squads. *See* vice units
National Crime Information Center (NCIC),
    14, 28, 116, 192, 198
National Integrated Ballistic Information
    Network (NIBIN), 14

Naval Criminal Investigative Service
(NCIS), 16, 129
NCIC. *See* National Crime Information
Center
NCIS. *See* Naval Criminal Investigative
Service
NIBIN. *See* National Integrated Ballistic
Information Network
9/11 terrorist attacks, 299, 330
Nix v. Williams (1977), 74
notetaking, investigative file, 259–60

objective reasonableness standard, 82–83,
84, 86
OCDETF. *See* Organized Crime Drug
Enforcement Task Force
Olmstead v. United States (1928), 87,
368–69
Omnibus Crime Control Act (1968), 88–89,
119, 368–69
organized crime and criminal syndicates:
ballistic evidence for, 178, 244–46;
bombings as part of, 49; confidential
sources in, 308–9, 312; counterattacks
to criminal investigation by, 53; covert
operations for, 262; crime databases of,
117; crime scene analysis with, 177–79;
debriefing interviews for, 304, 305; drug
investigations and, 134, 135–36, 361;
electronic surveillance of, 372–73, 374;
gambling operations associated with, 133;
gang crime relation to, 53; government
cooperation from, 282, 304; homicide,
144, 176–77; investigative grand jury
for, 276; investigative resources for,
116, 124, 125–26; jewelry theft by,
173; membership to, 52; MO for, 178;
prioritizing investigations on, 125;
proactive investigations for, 22; RICO
statute covering, 52–53; social media
resources for investigating, 118, 253–54;
specialized units for, 116, 124, 125–26;
witness protection in response to, 151, 226
Organized Crime Drug Enforcement Task
Force (OCDETF), 135
Osgood, Robert, 265

partners, investigative, 104–7
pathologist. *See* medical examiner/
examination

patrol officers, uniformed: bicycle, 115;
career paths for, 8, 328; highway,
11–12; intelligence from, 327–28; role
and responsibilities of, 7–8, 19–20, 98;
vehicular homicide cases aided by, 33
pattern evidence, examples of, 10, 26, 250
perjury, 315
perpetrators: crimes with information
identifying, 207–8; victims as, 19; victims
blamed by violent, 294–95; victims of
sexual assault relationship with, 145–46,
179–81. *See also* serial/career criminals;
suspect/defendant
petit jurors, definition of, 275
phone records, 252, 286, 369–70
photographs/photography, *6*; in armed
robbery proof, 44; in crime scene
analysis, 160–61; digital, 33, 151,
346–48; evolution of, 87; FBI handling
of, evidence, 250; in investigative file,
260–61, 262; positive identification using,
26–29; in search warrant raids, 340–41;
surveillance, 261, 346–48
physical abuse (by officer), 288, 289, 299–
300, 301
physical evidence, *211*; chain of custody for,
109, 229, 232–36, 258–59, 268–69; in
crime scene analysis, conclusions about,
160, 208; digital data, authentication of,
233; environmental considerations with,
99; expert witnesses for, 109, 154–56,
227–28, 235–36, 280–81; fingerprints
on, 86, 231–32, 238; for homicide,
142–43, 187–88, 196; human context of,
25, 141; interrogations and interviews
compared with, 254–55; investigative file
sections for, 258–59, 268–69; recovery
and treatment of, 105–6, 189–90, 191,
195–98, 200, 231–34, 252–53; in sexual
assault/rape investigations, 39, *56*,
146, 177, 189, 208; for trial, preparing,
229; types and categories of, 155,
231–32; witnesses and victims testimony
compared with, 55–56, *56–58*, 58–59,
143, 189–90, 191, 254–55. *See also*
forensic evidence; *specific evidence types*
Pink Panthers, 173
plain view doctrine, 78–79, 371
plea bargains: confessions relation to, 282,
296, 297; debriefing interviews for, 296,

304–5; government cooperation as, 282, 304–5; process of, 281–82, 289, 296; for serial/career criminals, 23, 203–4, 282; statistics on, 194–95, 223, 289; for violent crimes, 203–4

police department: after arrests, role of, 222–23, 271; community relationship with, 122–23; divisions within, 8, 97–98; hierarchy of, 98; historical model for, 121–22; interjurisdictional cooperation with, 329–30

police lineup, 27–29, 149

"police" power, governmental, 121–23, *122*

positive identification: ballistic evidence for, 26, 216; case example of proper, 28–29; evidence, overview of, 25–28; fingerprint evidence for, 26, 216, 219, 231, 234, 239; in homicides, 189, 249; mistakes/caution with, 28–29; photographs for, 26–29; police lineup for, 27–29; prior to arrest, 219; probable cause and, 149, 216, 219, 221; trace and serological evidence for, 26; witnesses for, 25–28, 149

Powell v. Alabama (1932), 63, 68–69

preliminary hearings, 150, 216, 274–75

presidential protection, 14

prima facie, definition of, 26

prioritizing criminal investigations: burglary and, 123, 127–28, 297; children and, 126, 132, 136; community impact and role in, 123–24, 130, 136; Congress role in, 130; on drug use and distribution, 126, 133–36; for federal investigators, 125–26, 129–30; of gambling, 132–33, 136; on gang crime, 126, 137; of gateway crimes, 137; historical view into, 122–23; homicide in, 124, 136–37; key factors in considering, 123; kidnapping in, 126; political agents in, 127–28; on property and financial crimes, 127–31; of serial/career criminals, 128; of sexual assault, 124, 126; specialized units resources and, 124, 125; of terrorism, 137; US Secret Service and, 129; on vice (morals) crimes, 131–36; violence in, 123–26

private and defense investigators, 18, 285–90

proactive investigations: actionable intelligence initiating, 186; confidential and surveillance sources in, 22; crime scene analysis in, 181; examples of,

21–22; investigative plan steps overview for, 186; reactive investigations becoming, 22, 201; search and seizure consent example in, 85–86; steps required for, 22, 183–84, 186

probable cause: for arrest, 216, 219–20, 221, *222*, 271–72; Bill of Rights on, 214, 272; chart outlining crime-specific, 216–17, *217–19*, 219; confidential sources in developing, 219–20; courts review of, 216; for deadly force, 337–38; defining, 211–12, 215–16; developing, 24–25, 209–14; for electronic surveillance/wiretaps, 88–89; evidence sources and types for, 217, *217–19*, 219–21; "gut feeling" of investigator and, 76, 214; investigative plan goal of, 200–201, 209, 222; logical argument for, 215; positive identification and, 149, 216, 219, 221; search and seizure with, 77, 79, 84, 209–14, 272; for search warrant affidavits, 211–15, 272–73; witnesses as sources of, 220–21

proof: of armed robbery, 44, *57*; of arson, 46–48, *58*; of assault, 35, 36, *57*; of assault with intent to kill, 34–35, *57*; of battery, 35–36, *57*; beyond a reasonable doubt, 24–25, 209, 222–23; of burglary, 50; of conspiracy, 55; crime and related, matrix, 55–56, *56–58*, 58–59; crime-specific probable cause, 216–17, *217–19*, 219; in criminal code, 23–25; in drug investigations, 356–57; elements involved in, 23–24; human context of, 25, 55–56; for insanity plea, 284–85; in kidnapping/abduction cases, 41–43; of larceny, *58*; of manslaughter, 32–33; in murder cases, 24, 26, 27–29, *56*; for positive identification, 25–28; in RICO cases, 52–53; of robbery, *57–58*; in sexual assault/rape cases, 38–40, *56–57*, 145–47; for stalking crimes, 35; steps in finding, 24–25; of vehicular homicide, 33–34; witnesses and victims primacy in, 23–24, 55–56, *56–58*, 58–59, 183, 254

property crimes: challenges in prosecuting, 128–29; investigative plan for, 189–94, 197–98, 205–6, 207; prioritizing investigations and, 127–31; types of, 189; without witnesses, 205–6. *See also specific crimes*

prosecutor (prosecuting attorney): discovery responsibility of, 220–21, 278, 279; investigative file report to, 260; investigators working for, 109, 200, 277; leads disclosed to, 108–9; role and responsibilities of, 67, 107–8, 119, 223, 225; search warrant affidavit resistance from, 75
prostitution, 131–32, 136
psychosexual motivations: in arson, 47, 48; for burglary, 163; in murder, 176–77, 181
public defenders, funding of, 68
Puerto Rico, 24

"Queen for a Day" agreement, 304
Questioned Documents Unit (FBI), 250

racial injustice/profiling: in *Powell v. Alabama*, 63, 68–69; *Terry v. Ohio* impact for, 79–81
racketeering in corrupt organizations (RICO), 52–53, 54, 363
ransom, 42–43
rape. *See* sexual assault and rape
reactive investigations, 102; crime scene analysis in, 159–62; crimes often beginning with, 98–100, *99*, 183; defining, 19, 98; first responders role and responsibilities in, 19–21, 98–100; investigative plan steps overview for, 185–86; jurisdiction for, 20–21; proactive investigations as next step for, 22, 201
reasonable suspicion, 80
recidivism, 5
resources, investigative: distribution of, 97, 102; for drug trafficking, 134; for gang units, 116, 124, 125–26, 137; for organized crime units, 116, 124, 125–26; prioritizing, for specialized units, 124, 125; for sex crime units, 124; for tactical training, 334, 336; for terrorism, 137; for training, significance of, 137; for witness protection, 152–53, 225–27. *See also* prioritizing criminal investigations
RICO. *See* racketeering in corrupt organizations
right to counsel. *See* legal representation; Sixth Amendment

The Rise of Big Data Policing (Ferguson), 196
robbery: bank, 44–45, 173, 207, *217*; distinctions of, 43–44; proof of, *57–58*; street (muggings), 100. *See also* armed robbery; burglary
Rowe, Gary Thomas, 317–18
"rushing to judgment" scenarios, 192–94

Safe Streets task force, 135, 331
Schneckloth v. Bustamonte (1973), 82
scientific evidence. *See* forensic evidence; *specific evidence types*
scientific method approach, 204–8
search and seizure: behavior during, 79–81, 84–85; breach procedure in, 339, 341; consent for warrantless, 77, 81–86, 96; consent of multiple occupants in, 83–84; of digital devices and data, 251–53; evidence from, 73–74, 340; exclusionary rule with, 73–74; exigent circumstances for, 20, 212–13; Fourth Amendment details on, 64–65, 71–72, 337; objective reasonableness for warrantless, 82–83, 84, 86; plain view doctrine in, 78–79, 371; probable cause in, 77, 79, 84, 209–14, 272; racial profiling in, Supreme Court cases on, 79–81; reasonable suspicion for, 80–81; standing to object in, determining, 86; Supreme Court landmark cases impacting, 72–74, 76–84, 87–90, 252; tactical training and procedure for, 339–41, 343; for UCO, 83; vehicle, rules governing, 75, 77–79, 82; warrantless, 76–86, 96, 212–13, 289; warrantless, probable cause in, 77, 79, 84, 212–13; warrantless, stopping for legal warrant in, 84; wiretaps and electronic surveillance relation to, 87–89, 368–69
search warrant affidavits: composition and parts of, 64, 71–72, 272; decision for, in warrantless searches, 84; for drug investigations, 339, 354, 355, 356, 358; for electronic surveillance, 88–89, 369–70; exigent circumstances and, 20, 212; Fourth Amendment on, 64, 71–72; "get feeling" in obtaining, 76; importance of, 75–76, 96; investigative file coverage of, 267; in motor vehicle theft cases, 75;

persistence and time factors in obtaining, 75; probable cause requirement for, 211–15, 272–73; raids with, 339–41, 343; in trials and court process, 272–73; for vehicles legally impounded, 79

Secret Service, US: fraudulent material lab of, 249; prioritizing investigations for, 129; role and responsibilities of, 13–14, 249

self-defense, 95; deadly force in, 338; homicide in, 32–33, 174–75, 178, 248, 285

semen. *See* serological evidence

serial/career criminals: of armed robbery, 45, 173–74; of arson, 48; of burglary, 43, 50–51, 163–66, 173–74, 203; confessions from, 203, 296–97, 304–5; detection challenges of, 204; development of, 19; lone-wolf, 46; *Miranda* rights waiver by, 92, 297–98; of motor vehicle theft, 192, 203; of murder, 176–77; plea bargains for, 23, 203–4, 282; prioritizing investigations of, 128; proactive investigations for, 22; of sexual assault, 37, 39–40, 177, 179, 207, 208. *See also* confidential sources/informants

serological evidence, 10, 26, 239–40

sex crimes unit, 124

sex trafficking, 131–32, 136

sexual assault and rape, 36–37; of children, 40–41, *57*, 180–81; crime scene analysis for, 179–81; date, 179–80; drug crime relation to, 113; false claims of, 40; force proof in, use of, 38–39, *56*; intelligence from crime data, 325; investigative plan for, 189, 197, 207–8; locations for, 179–80; male victims challenges in cases of, 38; medical examiner/examination with, 39; mental health professionals for cases of, 38, *57*, 146–47; of mentally disabled adults, 40–41; MO in, 39, 207–8; motivations for, assessment of, 180; murder relation with, 177, 181; physical evidence of, 39, *56*, 146, 179, 189, 208; in *Powell v. Alabama*, 63, 68–69; predator profile, 39, 126, 207–8; prioritizing cases of, 124, 126; probable cause in cases of, *217*; proof types for, *56*; provocation consideration in, 37; rape

definition and, 36–37; reporting of, 37, 145–46; as serial crime, 37, 39–40, 177, 179, 205, 208; specialized units for, 124; statutory, *57*; stranger, 179–80; victim relationship with perpetrators of, 145–46, 179–81; victim witnesses in proof of, 38–40, *56–57*, 145–47; victim witnesses relationship with investigators, 38–40, 146–47, 148, 196, 197

sheriffs: grand jury security by deputy, 151; history of, 121; subpoena service handled by, 277

shoplifting, 162

Sixth Amendment: *Miranda* rights relation to, 92, 94; Supreme Court cases on, 63, 68–71; on trial requirements, 63, 65, 67–68, 277–78

social media, 34; homicide investigations using, 195–96; investigative intelligence from, 118, 195–96, 253–54

sociopaths, 126

sources. *See* confidential sources/informants

Souter, David, 84

special agents. *See* federal investigators

specialized units/squads: bicycle patrol units as, 115; for burglary/armed robbery, 127–28; for crime scene examinations, 100–102, 110, 160; FBI, 100, 250, 335; for gang crime, 116, 117, 124, 125–26, 135, 137, 331; for homicide, 124–25; Hostage Rescue, 335; for organized crime, 116, 124, 125–26; resources for, prioritizing, 124, 125; role and importance of, 111–12; surveillance squads, 115; tact squads as, 114–15; for terrorism, 124; types of, overview, 100, 111–12; vice units as, 113–14, 115. *See also* computer squads; task forces

Special Weapons and Tactics (SWAT) teams, 335–36, 339

Speed Graphic, 346

Spinelli v. United States (1969), 315–16

squads: administration of, 97, 102–3; criminal investigator role in, 58; role and responsibilities of, 100–104. *See also* computer squads; specialized units/squads

stalking crimes, 34–35

states/commonwealths: branches of government established under, 2; crime

databases sponsored by, 116–17; criminal
code for each, 24; criminal investigators,
types of, 11–12; federal trials compared
with, 273; US Constitution on rights of,
63–64; as victims, 6
statutes: conspiracy, 54, 55; crime categories
and, 25; on drug use and distribution
crime, 353, 363; gang crime, 54;
investigative plan guided by, 55; law
enforcement officers understanding of,
5–6; location-specific, understanding, 4,
5–6; on organized criminal enterprises,
52–53; RICO, 52–53, 54, 363
"stop and frisk" procedures, 79–81, 96
strike force teams. *See* tactical squads
subpoenas: bypassing, methods for, 351;
definition of, 276; for financial records,
362; investigative grand jury, 276; for
investigator testimony, 223; for phone
records, 252, 286, 369–70; reliance on,
320, 351; responsibility for generating,
277
suicide, 193, 194
Supreme Court cases, 64; on confidential
sources/informants, 315–18; on deadly
force, 337–38; on discovery process,
278–79; Fourteenth Amendment and,
63; on indigent defendants rights, 70–71;
racial profiling "stop and frisk" impacted
by, 79–81; reviews of, understanding,
64; on search and seizure, 72–74, 76–84,
87–90, 252; on trial requirements/legal
representation, 63, 68–71; on warrantless
search and seizures, 76–84; on wiretaps
and electronic surveillance, 87–89,
368–69
surveillance: comfort considerations in, 348–
49; crime in progress during, 346; in drug
operations, types of, 364; as intelligence
for other investigations, 199; intelligence
sources aiding in, 326, 329; investigative
file section on, 261–62; mobile, 114,
346, 348–50; nest, 348–49, 355; in overt
operations, 345; photography, 261, 346–
48; proactive investigations reliance on,
21; security, recovery of, 202–3; squads,
role and responsibilities of, 115; static,
329, 346, 348, 350, 355; van, 348–49. *See
also* electronic surveillance/wiretaps

suspect/defendant: charging, procedures and
considerations in, 271–73; cooperation
from, 203–4, 268; digital data on, 251–52;
indigent, 70–71, 204, 281; interrogations
of, approach to, 71, 104, 105, *105*,
203, 268, 294–306; investigative plan
goal of identifying, 200–201, 209, 222;
investigator relationship with, 268, 296;
Miranda rights waiver for, 92, 297–98;
theoretical approach to finding, 202–4,
210; unrepentant, handling, 297–99. *See
also* arrests; confessions
SWAT teams. *See* Special Weapons and
Tactics teams
syndicates. *See* organized crime

tactical considerations: deadly force in,
337–39, 342; physical fitness in, 342;
teamwork in, 333
tactical spin (in covert operations), 350–51,
373
tactical squads (tact squads), 114–15
tactical training: for arrests, 333, 341–42;
for detectives, 10–11; firearm, 334–35;
funding for, 334, 336; ground combat in,
336; hand-to-hand combat, 10, 336–37;
intelligence aiding in, 335; operations for,
333–34; for search warrant raids, 339–41,
343; for surveillance squads, 115; SWAT,
335–36, 339
task forces: case-centered, 126; databases
shared and used by, 117; DEA, 134–35;
drug crime, 134–35; gang crime, 117,
126, 135, 137, 331; multijurisdictional,
126
teamwork, investigative: assignment
protocols in, 100–101, 183;
communication and support within, 101–
2, 117; competitive spirit in, 102; court
team in, 107–11, 119; first responders
role in, 98–100; in interrogations and
interviews, 104–5, 302; on investigative
file, 262–63; lead investigator role in, 102,
119; partners relationship in, 104–7; squad
role and responsibilities in, 97, 100–103;
tactical considerations and, 333; veteran
and young investigator relationship in,
103, 106; in victim advocacy, 147. *See
also* specialized units/squads

Tennessee v. Garner (1985), 337

terrorism: 9/11, 299, 330; 1980s case of, 154; proactive investigations of, 21; resources for fighting, 137; specialized units for, 124

Terry stops, 79–81, 96, 337

Terry v. Ohio (1968), 79–81, 337

testimony: assuring consistent and honest, 151; emotionality of, problems with, 151; expert, handling, 109, 152–53, 227–28, 235–36; of fact witnesses, 149–51; forensic evidence compared with witness, 55–56, *56–58*, 58–59, 143, 189–90, 191, 254–55; of forensic scientist, 109, 152–53, 227–28, 235–36; in grand jury hearings, 150–51, 275, 276; hearsay, 274; from medical examiner, 155, 235–36, 248; by mental health professionals, 284–85; in preliminary hearings, 274; in sexual assault cases, 38–39; victim, preparation for, 108–9, 198; witness, preparation for, 108–9, 147–49, 156–57, 198, 222–26, 275, 276

Texas v. Brown, 78–79

theft. *See* armed robbery; burglary; larceny; motor vehicle theft

Title III Court Orders, 88–89, 119, 252, 261, 367–73

toolmarks. *See* ballistic evidence

toxicological evidence, 179, 234, 246–47

trace evidence, 10, 26, 241–43

training and education: for arson investigative expert, 47, *58*; assignment protocol based on, 100–101; for ATF special agents, 16; on ballistics, 10, 244–46; for computer squads, 252, 253; for crime scene analysis, 161–62; for DEA special agents, 15–16, 247; for detectives, municipal/county, 9–10; for detectives, state police, 11–12; on documentary evidence, 251–52; for DOD special agents, 17; for FBI, 15, 334; for federal agents, 12–15; of fingerprint recovery and handling, 238–39; for first responders, 20; on fraudulent materials evidence, 249; for investigative file composition, 269–70; for private and defense investigators, 18, 286–87; resources for, importance of, 137; on toxicology, 246–47; for US

Marshals, 13; for US Secret Service, 13–14. *See also* tactical training

trial requirements: impartial jury in, 63, 65, 273, 277–78; Sixth Amendment on, 63, 65, 67–68, 277–78; speedy, 216, 277–78; Supreme Court landmark cases on, 63, 68–71; US Constitution on, 63, 65, 273, 277–78

trials and court process, *3*, 108–9; arraignment in, 275, 276–77; arrest and search warrant affidavits in, 272–73; bail in, 65, 271–72; cases ending in, percentage of, 194–95; confidential informants in, 310–11, 315, 320–21; discovery process in, 71, 220–21, 225, 278–79, 298; dismissals in, 273, 282–83; evidentiary hearings in, 279–81; federal compared with state, 273; guilty pleas in, 23; initial appearance in, 273–74; insanity ruling in, 284–85; investigative goals including, 222–24, 271, 289–90; investigative plan preparation for, 198, 200–201; investigators role in, 223; *Miranda* rights violations in, 89–90, 289; not guilty ruling in, 283–84; perjury in, 315; physical evidence preparation for, 229; preliminary hearings in, 150, 216, 274–75; private and defense investigators during, 18, 285–90; probable cause reviewed in, 216; proof beyond reasonable doubt in, 209; significant events in, 281; status hearings in, 280; teamwork and positions in, 107–11, *110*, 119; tilting of, 2, 25, 107; timelines for, 216, 277–78, 281; witness death before, 284; witness discovery during, 220, 225, 278; witness preparation for, 108–9, 149, 156–57, 198, 222–26; witness protection in, 151, 225–26. *See also* grand jury hearings; judges; plea bargains; Supreme Court cases; testimony

UCMJ. *See* Uniform Code of Military Justice

undercover officer (UCO): CWs placed with, 321; dangers in using, 366–67; in drug investigations, 364–67; mental health help for, 374; protection of, 364, 373–74; requirements and characteristics for, 264, 364, 367; warrantless search and seizures for, 83; wires/recording devices on, 365–66

Uniform Code of Military Justice (UCMJ), 130

United States. *See* Bill of Rights; Constitution, US; federal government

United States v. Rich (1993), 82

United States v. Ross, 77

United States v. Jones (2012), 368, 369

US Postal Service (USPS) inspectors, 13, 15, 16, 129

vehicle identification number (VIN), 192

vehicles: consent for warrantless search of, 82; impounded, 78; plain view doctrine in warrantless search of, 78–79; search and seizures with, 75, 77–79, 82. *See also* motor vehicle theft

vehicular homicide, 33–34

vice (morals) crimes, prioritization of, 131–36

vice units, 113–14, 115

victim advocate, 144–45, 147, 196–97

victimology: defining, 143; family and friends help in, 143; forensic evidence in tandem with, 144; in homicide investigative plan, 31–32, 143–44, 176, 195, 196, 197; victim advocacy in, 144

victims: assault proof from, 35, 36; burglary proof from, 50; determination and considerations of, 6–7; first responders handling of, 20, 139–40; forensic/physical evidence compared with testimony of, 55–56, *56–58*, 58–59, 143, 189–90, 191, 254–55; interviews in investigative file, 257, 262; investigative plan outlining, 185; medical care for, 101, 140; murder, identifying, 189; not guilty ruling impact on, 283; as perpetrators, 19; perpetrators blame of, 294–95; as proof element, primacy of, 23–24, 55–56, *56–58*, 58–59, 183, 254; of prostitution, 131; of sexual assault and rape relationship with perpetrator, 145–46, 179–81; state as, 6; testimony preparations for, 108–9, 198; of white collar crime, 19

victim witnesses: of abduction, investigator relationship with, 42; of armed robbery, 44; assaults on, 36; of burglary, 148; as

eyewitnesses, 149; homicide, evidence gathered from, 142–44; investigator relationship with, 38–40, 42, 146–48; mental health professionals for, 38, *57*, 146–47; programs for helping, 148; of serious violence, 147–48; of sexual assault, investigator relationship with, 38–40, 146–47, 148, 196, 197; of sexual assault fear of reporting, 37; in sexual assault/rape proof, 38–40, *56–57*, 145–47

VIN. *See* vehicle identification number

violent crimes: conspiracy to commit, 54–55; crime scene analysis for, 174–77, 179–81; with gambling crime, 133; investigative plan for, 186–89, 194–97, 206; plea bargains for, 203–4; prioritizing criminal investigations and, 123–26; with sex trafficking, 131; types of, 29–45; victim witnesses of serious, 147–48; without witnesses, 206. *See also specific crimes*

virtual private network (VPN), 265

voting rights, 63, 66

VPN. *See* virtual private network

warrants. *See* arrest warrant affidavits; search warrant affidavits

Warren, Earl, 80–81, 89–90, 91

weapons of mass destruction (WMDs), 49

white collar crime, 12, 14, 19, 52, 249

Williams, Wayne, 177

witnesses, *140*; of bank robberies, 207; burglary scenario without, 205; as confidential sources/informants, 310–11, 315, 320–21; cooperating, 93, 320–21, 359, 364; death of, before trial, 284; defense attorney treatment of, 149, 156–57; defining role of, 4, 140–41; in discovery, 220, 225, 278; drug addicts as, 354, 356; in drug investigations, 354, 356, 358–69, 362, 364; ear, 220; expert, 109, 154–56, 227–28, 235–36, 280–81; eyewitness, 27–29, 149, 220–21; fact, testimony from, 149–51; first responders as, 141, 153, 154, first responders handling of, 20, 139–40; forensic/physical evidence compared with testimony of, 55–56, *56–58*, 58–59, 143, 189–90, 191, 254–55; of gang crime, 152–53, 178–79, 225–26; in grand jury hearings, 150–51,

275, 276; homicide, 31–32, 142–44, 176, 187–88, 195, 196; human context for, 25, 141, 155, 183; insider, 45, 55, 320, 358, 364; interviews of, approach to, 31–32, 104–5, 176, 185, 187–89, 195–98–294, 258, 305–6; investigative file security in protection of, 264; investigative plan approach to, 31–32, 176, 185, 187–89, 195, 196, 197, 198, 201; investigator relationship with, 38–40, 42, 139, 146–48, 151, 152, 156–57, 375; law enforcement officers as, 141, 153–54; lies of, detection of, 292–94; medical care for, 101, 140; murder, on-the-scene, 31, 187–88; murder, secondary, 31–32;

positive identification from, 27–30, 149; in probable cause development, 220–21; as proof element, primacy of, 23–24, 55–56, *56–58*, 58–59, 183, 254; property crimes without, 205–6; protection, in subject interviews, 299; protection and relocation for, 152–53, 225–27; reliability of, 45, 141, 291–92; testimony and trial preparations for, 108–9, 147–49, 156–57, 198, 224–28, 275, 276; violent crimes without, 206. *See also* victim witnesses

Witness Security Program (WITSEC), 151–52, 226, 227

WMDs. *See* weapons of mass destruction

Wong Sun v. United States (1963), 73–74